ElDoradu Affair

A

True Story of Pioneers

In

Rural Guyana, South America

by Jane Joseph

Published by Sapodilla Press

First edition 2015

i

Published by Sapodilla Press, England.

e-mail: janejoseph967@btinternet.com

© Jane Joseph

ISBN 978-0-9932409-0-4

A catalogue record of this book is available from the British Library

Printed and bound in England by

Garnsons Ltd
2 Icknield Way
Letchworth Garden City
Hertfordshire SG6 4GY

Jane Joseph studied History as graduate and postgraduate at the London School of Economics under the tutelage of Dr David Starkey, Dr John Gillingham and Dr Antony Bridbury in the late 1970s. She then qualified as a teacher and taught history, geography and humanities in secondary schools in the United Kingdom and Dubai until 1991 when she migrated with her Guyanese husband Edwin to Guyana, South America. Together, they set up their own home and eco-tourism ranch in Hopetown West Coast Berbice, Edwin's birth village. It failed as a business but evolved into a private charity school for the children of poor villagers. They named it Sapodilla Learning Centre. Wherever Jane has taught, her dedication and passion for local and social history and the natural environment has driven her work and motivated her to set up school and local museums and to use art, music and drama to keep children in touch with the history of their ancestors.

Jane and Edwin's life in Guyana began in an era of political change and turmoil when the country was emerging from a dark era of political oppression following the death of its dictator President Forbes Burnham. Although they were widely travelled in Europe, Africa, the Middle and Far East, the couple were not prepared for the culture shock of living permanently in such an undeveloped economy as they found in Guyana and the years of planning and preparation they had both made proved inadequate due to factors they could never have foreseen. Finding a way of surviving in the rural economy of their village and trying to help it to develop in a positive way became their life's work for eighteen years. Following the life threatening medical condition Edwin developed, they were forced to return to England in 2009 and sadly, for want of suitable successors to continue it, to close down the charity school. Since her return she has written and published magazine articles and books. She is currently working on her first historical novel set in early colonial Guyana.

OTHER PUBLICATIONS

"Fit for a Queen: The recipe Book of Ada Parsons, Head Cook to the XIV Earl of Strathmore"
Published by Cranfield Press at Cranfield University ISBN 978-1-907413-12-4
email: c.u.press@cranfield.ac.uk
http://store.cranfield.ac.uk/browse/product.asp?catid=99&modid=1&compid=1

Acknowledgements

I would like to thank my brother Guy for his loyal help and professional expertise in preparing this digital copy for the printing press and for his help in achieving the effect of the cover design.

I also thank Edwin for his unstinting support at all times both throughout our eighteen years in Guyana and in the work I have undertaken with my books, especially this one. He has listened to my repeated readings of the drafts and I have consulted him on the accuracy of some of the details of events that concerned him more than me.

CONTENTS

Into the Fire

Chapter 1

NO TURNING BACK

Although I had flown over rainforest coasts in antiquated planes countless times, it had even now not lost its magic for me. I gazed down over vast swathes of green broccoli landscape, picking out the distinctive blue ribbons of the mighty Essequibo and Demerara estuaries. As the plane banked eastwards aligning itself with the Pomeroon coast, the tangled roots of red mangrove, fringing an unpeopled expanse of silver sand, grinned at the Atlantic surf like gigantic teeth. Now we headed southwards along the Demerara valley and began our descent, finally swinging a full hundred and eighty degrees into the approach to the Timehri runway. It seemed as if we would crash into the canopy any minute when suddenly tarmac appeared and I could let out that bated breath with relief. We exchanged excited glances, to the castanet clicking of seatbelts, knowing this was the point of no return. Our new uncharted life together had begun. In optimistic trepidation, we disembarked into the monstrous bosom of South America.

The journey by private hire minibus to Hopetown was a little more comfortable than our previous ones because Bryan had followed Edwin's instructions not to come to the airport with a whole load of people. That way we had a bit of space to stretch out our legs and still find room for the four large suitcases we had travelled with. Much of the conversation between Edwin and Bryan concerned plans for the running of the snackette Edwin had placed Bryan in charge of. I could not hear too well owing to the noise of the engine and the fact that I was not in the front seat. Instead I took in the scenery of East Coast Demerara and West Coast Berbice. It was quite familiar by now but I was in a better position to appreciate the detail of the villages we were passing through. The recent yet rundown architecture of the outskirts of Georgetown was drab and uninspiring. We passed the non-descript flat-roofed modern concrete Bata Shoe Factory building. An Indian style cinema frontage here and a cricket ground there were interspersed with numerous little gabled wooden houses. Many had shop frontages cramming the road sides, all competing to sell the same plastic buckets, mattresses and aluminium cooking pots. Then, on the right, there was the tall red-brick disused chimney smoke stack, the only surviving remnant of the original Chateau Margot sugar plantation.

Once we left the suburbs and entered the countryside, a picturesque string of villages with a unique style of wooden architecture emerged. Most of them had not had a coat of paint for decades and had rotting steps or shutters hanging by one hinge, yet they were beautiful. The massive ancient mango and breadfruit trees that launched out of their tiny yards, waving their leaves at the occasional passing traffic seemed to speak to me. "We hold the spirits of the dead," they called out. Stretches of the road passed through acres of coconut plantation flanked by shallow canals. A flat-bottomed wooden boat was moored in one of these trenches but there was no sign of its human occupant apart from a woven basket and an item of clothing draped over its plank seat. Nestled among these coconut trees was a large unpainted wooden house adorned with beautifully symmetrical mouldings. Locals called it "House of a Thousand Windows". Further on, the trees gave way to vast open pastures filled with hundreds of grazing cattle. Beyond them, a reef of swaying coconuts formed the skyline, screening the view of the sea. The solitary coast road bored its way through forests of wild Sand-coka trees and thick tangled undergrowth. Then it opened out into flooded rice fields and more village settlements with their roadside stores and steep gabled roofs. Despite the poverty within them, their shingle-clad wooden huts with "cow-mouth" kitchens were very much a centre of family life. Occupants sat on their steps or busied themselves about their yards. The oldest houses still had their original Demerara windows of slanting fretwork sides fronted with slatted wooden louvers directed towards the coast so as to make the most of the prevailing cool sea breezes. Rags performing the function of long rotted doors or windows served a similar purpose in humbler dwellings.

The potholed tarmac gaped mockingly at the minibus as the vehicle veered and lurched to avoid large chasms. Red brick-dust littered the crumbling road shoulders. Along the verges fronting many of these linear villages were scattered the rusting skeletons of long dead coaches, tractors and combine harvesters. Papaya trees popped out of the spaces where their windows once had been and vines scrambled through their framework. Emaciated humpbacked zebu cattle grazed around them and occasionally wandered aimlessly across the sun-baked, dusty road, forcing us to slow down or swerve. They seemed not to belong to anyone but of course everyone living nearby knew exactly whose beast each one was by its physical characteristics. The cattle, not the occasional motor vehicle, owned the road. They looked up as we passed, munching their cud and spattering their dung as they moved. In a clearing on one side of the

4

route, a huge mound of red laterite was piled up in readiness for road repair that never took place. Another mound of this 'burnt dirt' was still smouldering as testimony to someone's means of livelihood.

At a bridging point on the Mahaica River, the road passed through the mammoth structure of a colonial Meccano bridge which was the bustling focal point of a market. Tiny boys surrounded the bus excitedly pushing bunches of ginips at us through the open windows. These green skinned acidic fruit with flesh similar to lychee were more refreshing and healthy to suck than any commercial sweet. The boys were devouring far more themselves than they sold to passers-by. Hands of bananas, pineapples, star-fruit, star apples, red cashews, mangoes and papaya piled high on the roadside stalls, had all been brought to this thriving centre of local commerce by boat up the Mahaica River from the hinterland riverine settlements. This bottleneck for converging traffic and pedestrians forced our pace to a crawl over the massive timber beams that spanned the water. Small boats could pass out to sea under the bridge and were moored among the mangroves that skirted the deep black water on both sides. Amerindian faces were preponderant in the boats and around the water but the market stalls were manned by East Indian or Afro-Caribbean women. From the dark shadowy doorways of nearby rum shops emanated the raucous shouts of drunken men slapping down dominoes. Mahaica was by far the liveliest of the settlements along the coast road to Hopetown. Two more rivers had to be crossed at Mahaicony and the Abary River respectively, but the latter was dead and uninhabited. At Mahaicony, after passing over the Meccano Bridge, there was a large Amerindian hostel on the coastal side of the road. Indigenous women and their chattering children hung out of the large dilapidated windows. Behind them, hammocks bulging with reclining occupants swung in the breeze. This large communal shelter was an overnight stopping place for those who plied the river with their fruit, vegetables and craftwork to sell to the coastal villagers at the Mahaicony market. It was a hub full of life, noise and colour.

The final stretch of our journey once more quietened down into verdant scenery and isolated shacks. At every juncture, nature had the upper hand and was reclaiming control of the environment from its brief abuse by man. Vestiges of abandoned agricultural projects now almost smothered by bush would have escaped my notice if they had not been pointed out to me by Edwin. He shook his head and sucked his teeth in disappointment at the lack of effort by those privileged with access to the funds and their abject failure to develop a country so rich in natural resources. Excitement mounted as we reached the turn off the main road where the "snackette" had been built next to the Catholic Church in "number 22" Belair village. Bryan had certainly wasted no time in getting the snack bar completed and up and running after we had returned to England the summer before. We were impressed. The delight faded into disappointment when we turned off the main road onto the mud track and drove past what we expected would be our completed home.

"It doesn't look as if anything more has been done to it since the photos were taken in January!" I said in dismay.

The huge wooden structure, fronted by an imposing cast concrete staircase, looked a bit like a fancy shed for livestock. This image was reinforced by the fact that a herd of goats were sitting on the treads and standing on the veranda looking over at us. The openings for the door and windows had been blocked off with recycled rusting galvanised corrugated iron panels, but the goats had broken it down and taken up their living quarters inside. Edwin was silent. I knew he was fuming.

Chapter 2

The House That Pappa Dan Built

We had been back for a few days, acclimatising to the conditions and the shock of discovering we had nowhere to live for the time being. Edwin had brought a large amount of cash in pounds as he wanted to exchange it at the cambio for the best exchange rates. He had planned this in order to settle the final expenses for windows, guttering, electrics and painting to complete the building. Now it appeared that we would need to do more than that. The tour we had taken around the inside of the house revealed to our horror that the builders had not been able to read the plans. We knew in advance that the dimensions shown on the plan had been too big for the house to fit on the width of the plot we had. Having given the telephoned instruction from England to adjust it to fit the land, we naturally assumed that the builder would scale it all down slightly. The problem was that our Canadian style hexagonal wood cabin presented too much of a challenge to the less than basic mathematical skills of the village labourers employed for us by Edwin's mother. They had sited the hexagonal lounge in such a way that two of its sides were parallel with the boundary of the plot. Because they did not see the need to change which side of the hexagon the annexes would have to project from in order to fit on the plot, they had to squash the rectangular extensions containing the bedrooms and bathrooms into diamond shaped wings. To our disbelief they had further subdivided one wing into a honeycomb of diamond shaped cells not big enough to contain a bed or a bath. How on earth could we salvage this disaster? The whole lot would have to be gutted and the corners squared off somehow. The cash we had between us was enough to cover the estimates we had been sent for the final fix plus a contingency fund but this would all be eaten up by the cost of demolishing and rebuilding half of the edifice. Where would we get the extra funds from now that neither of us was working?

For a while we focused our attention on what had been done well. The staircase was very solidly built with an aesthetically pleasing curve. The main structure of the house was of massive greenheart beams. This hardwood stands the test of time and lasts for hundreds of years. There was no doubt that the basic frame was sturdy and sound. The hexagonal ceiling was beautiful. It had been closed off with tongued and grooved hardwood boards radiating from the centre and where they joined, mouldings of a lighter coloured timber had been cut to cover them decoratively, creating a pattern reminiscent of a kaleidoscope. The upper floor of the building was of wood supported on concrete pillars with more pillars supporting the concrete veranda wall. Underneath, the hexagonal lounge was cased in by hand made concrete block walls. Young boys had made individual blocks by pouring cement into the wooden mould they had been taught to make by Pappa Dan, the contractor. We kept coming back to the fact that before any more work was put into the building, the diamond shaped extensions had to be squared off before they could be usable. How could we break it to the dear old octogenarian master builder that he would have to undo some of his work and rebuild it? It needed a diplomatic approach. I realised that they had no idea what a bathroom should be like since no local house had one inside it. The normal village home had a tin-roofed shed in which you threw buckets of water over yourself. The toilet was a separate earth pit. No baths were available for sale in the capital. That is why we had imported ours. How could we expect them to know what size or shape a bathroom had to be?

Papa Dan proudly showed us around his project. He stood barely five feet high with a bald head, twinkling eyes and a beaming smile. I could not help but like him. He had a very charming disposition and kept trying to impress me with his knowledge of Shakespeare and Julius Caesar. We praised him for the excellent work he had done with the lounge ceiling and marvelled at how he and his team of boys had managed to do such excellent work with only the few hand tools that they had. Electric tools would have been no use anyway, since there was hardly ever any electricity supply in the village. However, we apologetically explained that there was a problem with the diamond shaped rooms and that they would have to be changed. The problem this presented became apparent to him when we went out onto the concrete walled veranda on the southern extremity of the house. It also followed a diamond shape to match the room it surrounded. It seemed unthinkable that the concrete casting would have to be demolished in order to correct the mistake. In the end we decided that the concrete veranda could stay as it was, as long as the wooden wall was squared off within it. This would also mean that the roof would have to be reshaped to make it square also. As for the northern end, the partition walls would have to be taken out and the end squared off. We would have to work out a better way to divide up the rooms and tell him what we wanted in a day or two. The old man accepted the news in good heart. He would start the changes at the southern end first.

The more we thought about the gulf between what we had and what we had expected to have, the more we realised that we were going to have to find some more money from somewhere. We realised that the size of the existing building would have to be extended in order to have the four self-contained guest bedrooms. The only way we could subdivide the northern wing into rooms of an adequate size would be to have no internal access corridor. They would all have to be separate and accessed from the veranda by their own patio doors. Edwin decided that we would have to make a big extension at the end of this to accommodate our own bedroom and instead of having the kitchen integrated in an open plan lounge we would have to put it into the northern wing which had originally been meant to be our bedroom and bathroom. This seemed to be the best idea, but we would have to get plans drawn up for that, and passed, and see if we could borrow some extra money from a local bank to pay for the materials and extra labour costs it would entail.

Weeks dragged by during which very little happened. It was a new experience for me as I was accustomed to being very productive and efficient in my life thus far. I prefer getting on with things to sitting around in idle gossip and chatter from dawn to dusk. In this environment, that was the only occupation of most people. Sunny and warm as it was, the only thing to stimulate my intellect was to soak up the natural world around me and observe every little plant jostling for its place or creature making its home in the mud.

Watching the builders at work was an education itself in Guyanese culture. Day after day there was no progress on the building. No one seemed to be able to explain why. Edwin's mother when asked would say, "Dem boy gone out" or some equally vague excuse which left us feeling powerless. Edwin having been used to managing a workforce with military efficiency was getting increasingly frustrated. When workers eventually did turn up, the building seemed to be swarming with people who were not actually doing anything but standing around "gaffing" (gossiping) in groups in different parts of the site. One boy was making blocks. As he unmoulded one he put it to dry in the sun and refilled the mould. Every now and then as he tipped out a block, it fell apart. For every three successful blocks, one was wasted in this way and the cement crumbled into dust. Edwin was trying to keep a tight rein on the purse-strings as the cash we had carried in with us was all we had in the world to complete the house. Young boys left unsupervised to saw pieces of timber panelling or door and window frames, cut without measuring and when the piece did not fit, cut

9

another piece, discarding the first. Small children would come after them collecting up perfectly good offcuts that could have been used elsewhere in the build and carried them off for firewood. Seeing this, and alarmed that funds would run out prematurely if it continued, Edwin tried to make the boys understand how to avoid waste, but it fell on deaf ears.

With so much left to do, the prospect of being able to move into a home fit for receiving paying overseas guests seemed to be diminishing in front of our eyes. Edwin's patience was getting tested severely. This was not helped when workers approached us in the village asking for backdated wages for several months before our arrival in the country and claiming that they had not been paid by Pappa Dan the contractor. They told a tale so convincing and compelling about their desperation to feed their large starving families that we immediately took pity and believed them. All the same we found it hard to believe that sweet old Pappa Dan could have neglected to pay his workers in this way when Edwin's mother had been sent all the money in advance from England. Edwin questioned her. She said she had personally paid the workers. There was no evidence of receipts or wages books signed to prove this. Requests to produce any were met by repeated procrastination or politely ignored and forgotten about for days. Meanwhile Bryan, who had so efficiently built the snackette in our absence, began to sow in our minds seeds of distrust in Pappa Dan and family friend Dickie, who had acted as Power of Attorney for Edwin on the original land purchase and building. According to Bryan, "Everybody know Dickie tieff an Pappa Dan lie". Not wishing workers to suffer hardship caused by people acting in his name, Edwin paid the workers again and determined that in future he would pay any wages directly himself and get workers to sign for it in our own receipt book. He told his mother to send for Dickie, asking him to bring all the receipts and paperwork relating to our business. Several days later there was still no sign or mention of him. It was one of those frustrating aspects of Edwin's modus operandi that mystified me in these early weeks. Why didn't we just go to Dickie's house, find him and ask him to explain?

The day came for confrontation. Dickie arrived, greeted Taa, Edwin and myself in turn and perched on the veranda rails, holding in the gap between his knees, the trilby Edwin had brought him as a present from England. Edwin and I were seated on the only two wooden stools that could fit on the tiny front veranda landing. Taa kept out of the way downstairs. After about half an hour of polite small talk to prepare the ground, Edwin finally asked Dickie,

"Can I see all the accounts and receipts for what you've done so far?" Dickie reached into his trouser pocket and pulled out a folded dog-eared piece of school exercise book which he handed over. Edwin flattened it out and studied it carefully for a long while. At length he handed it over to me and said,

"What do you think of that?" It did not really mean much to me, but I noticed that although the total at the bottom was over 800,000 Guyana dollars, the itemised costs detailed in the account above it did not add up to half that amount. I said so, adding,

"I'm not so good at mental arithmetic but it looks like a mistake here". Edwin got out his pocket calculator for me to check the figures again. I duly did so but confirmed that there was nothing wrong with my mental computation so he checked it twice himself with the same result. After that Dickie was asked to do the calculations again himself. This only further confirmed the error. He sat stunned, mystified and speechless. He had absolutely no explanation. It seemed to be a complete shock to him that anyone would check the arithmetic and call him to account. This never happened to him before. People he gave his accounts to usually just looked at the bottom line and accepted it. Embarrassment filled the air between us but did not show on his face. Edwin delivered a long monologue about not being able to afford such losses as he was now retired without an income and he had no house to live in unless it could be finished. He had already been forced to use the funds he brought with him to remodel the mess made by the builders through not understanding the plans. He could not afford to give money away for nothing and he wanted Dickie to produce the missing four hundred thousand dollars we had given him that he had not accounted for. That was the last we saw of Dickie for a very long while. Needless to say, the missing money never materialised.

Edwin had various missions to complete with the Education and Sports ministries in Georgetown. He was on the road early in the morning. Bryan, his escort for the purpose, was meeting him there to catch a minibus. When he finally got home after dark, very tired and irritable, I could easily see why. He threw his shoulder bag down in disgust and slumped down on the stool at the top of the veranda. Sensing his anger, his mother Taa said,

"Wha' happen' Edwin?"

"Brian and I were waiting for a bus to come along this morning, when an Indian man jumped out of another bus going the other way and threw an envelope at me. When I opened it I could see it was a writ served against me by Eddie Lall's son, for not paying $962,000 dollars for materials. I can't believe it. I've already paid him over a million dollars last July through his father and sister in England. I don't know what he's playing at."

I just stared at him in disbelief. Taa looked scared.

"What did you do?" I asked.

"There was nothing I could do there and then. He drove off in the bus and left us standing there. I'll have to go to a lawyer in New Amsterdam to show all our evidence. Thank God I kept every single document and receipt and I've got it all organised in a folder that's easy to hand. While we're at it, I'll ask the lawyer to get to the bottom of the missing money we tackled Dickie over. I'll have to go across on the ferry to New Amsterdam tomorrow with Bryan and Dickie to see a lawyer they know."

Mr Rupert Trim agreed to take the case for $50,000 and countersue for non-delivery of materials paid for. Edwin would have to search out and bring all information about it to him the following week. We spent time searching out all the receipts, check stubs and letters he had recording Edwin's dealings with the Lall family in England and Guyana from the start in 1990. As if we did not have enough problems with money, now an unsolicited legal case was going to add to the expenses.

More days and weeks came and went but nothing happened. We knew we would have to get a loan from somewhere to get more materials soon. 'Brother' Pat, the Congregational Church Minister from New Amsterdam, paid us a visit while we were contemplating this. He suggested going to the only bank in Guyana who would lend the kind of sums we would need to borrow. It was the bank used by the church as well as his own personal bank and the manager was a member of the same Georgetown 'Lodge' as Brother Pat. This is where I first learned about lodges and the important role they play in Guyanese society. They were a local version of the "who you know club" similar to freemasons, that all middleclass locals use to socialise and network through and also obtain patronage. Brother Pat said he would be happy to recommend us to the bank but they would only consider lending to customers who had two references from respected and upstanding citizens who already held accounts there. Apart from

Brother Pat, we knew no one else in Guyana who fitted that description. Pat therefore sent us to meet Maurice Watson, Pat's insurer and lodge brother, so we could get him to supply our second reference. This meant a trip to the distant capital again to meet Mr Watson. It was bad enough travelling to town to get to meet the man, but worse still with no telephones in Berbice, to have to travel all that way just on the off-chance of a meeting, only to be told we would have to make an appointment to go back another day. That is how difficult life was for those living far out of Georgetown. That is exactly what happened.

Hours of hot dusty futile journeys in packed minibuses, waiting around at their numerous passenger stops took their toll on my health. A four hour ride in ninety per cent relative humidity, when the sun was at its hottest, with no stops for refreshment on the way and no drink from home to travel with, left me with a dehydration migraine by the time we reached the city. No bottled water was available anywhere, only sickly sweet bottled fizzy drinks which made me feel thirsty the moment I drank them. Edwin's military background and "don't stop for a break till you've done what you came to do" attitude led him to plough from one point of call to the next without considering his own body let alone mine. Repeated requests from me to find a drink were ignored until he had done what needed to be done. He did not need to be hindered by a wimpy 'civvy'. Despite finally getting a curry lunch in a halal restaurant by the bus park, and taking several bottles of horrible fizzy drink there, a two-hour wait in "Nello's" claustrophobic bus for a full complement of passengers in the post meridian heat of the afternoon, followed by a four hour snail's paced journey home to Berbice nearly finished me off. The tell-tale symptoms of cystitis set in during the night and woke me up in the small hours. I had to spend my night dividing my time between the donkey pen, on the primitive wooden toilet 'seat', being attacked by mosquitos and cockroaches and on a wooden seat inside Taa's sitting room window, waiting for the building burning sensation in my bladder to reach a level where I would have to empty it again to relieve the symptoms.

Next morning I faced Edwin with the news that this problem would not go away without getting medication from a doctor. I could not travel outside the house as I needed to sit on the loo for the best part of the day. I also explained to him that I needed to drink lots of boiled water or weak tea to try and flush out the infection while waiting for medication to arrive and to take effect. He told me that there was no doctor and that was impossible. The pain reduced me to tears. I knew what this would lead to, as it was serious and debilitating and I had suffered it before. He sought advice from his mother and came to the conclusion that he would travel alone to a pharmacist in New Amsterdam to get the antibiotics and bicarbonate of soda I needed. Meanwhile his mother, cold and politely distant, made a pot of weak tea for me and another flask for me to keep in the bedroom and drink. I spent the day, when not frequenting the empty donkey-pen latrine, lying on the bed haplessly staring up at the zinc roof, counting the agonising hours until Edwin got back again.

Although New Amsterdam was only ten miles away, the ferry crossing over the Berbice River and back took the whole day from 6 am to about five pm so it was not much quicker than going to Georgetown. At last he returned with my salvation. I had asked for the antibiotic Septrin which had been prescribed to me by English doctors for this ailment in the past. He had found a Chinese lady pharmacist who reluctantly agreed to sell him some without seeing me. She had insisted that I should be taken to a doctor first for diagnosis and prescription but he had explained that it was an emergency and I could not travel to see a doctor while experiencing these symptoms. I slowly recovered full health after about a week but lived in fear from then on in case there was a recurrence. Knowing that there is no doctor focuses one's attention on the ways to prevent getting ill in the first place. I would have to boil my own water to keep myself constantly rehydrated. It is not entirely true that there was no doctor at all locally. There was a doctor at the Fort Wellington Cottage Hospital but knowing the poor state of local education, we had no faith in the ability of any local doctor. It seemed especially futile going to him since he could not do his own tests. He would send patients to New Amsterdam to get them done at a private test laboratory and a couple of days would pass before results could be got. I could not face such insecurity, so like most poor villagers, resolved to be my own doctor. Most of the population we lived among could not afford doctors, tests or drugs. How must they feel when incapacitated by ailments, knowing that there was no cure except the relief that bush medicines could bring. Slow and lingering death could easily be the result of a minor complaint that in the developed world is quickly and cheaply cured. We weren't prepared to accept this state of affairs. We would have to work to improve the state of education in the country. Only that way would there be adequate health provision for all in the future.

Two weeks later on a second trip to the capital, we finally got to meet Mr Watson. He was a jolly, bald headed character whose heavy black rimmed spectacles dominated his face. Judging by his size, he enjoyed his food. He welcomed us in and immediately asked me,

"How you like Guyana Jane?"

"It's a beautiful country," I replied, honestly, "but I'm accustomed to people being more hospitable towards strangers."

"What do you mean?" he asked, shocked.

"No one offers you a drink when you visit them. This I find strange, since in English culture, we offer tea before a visitor can sit down and in all my travels in the Middle and Far East, even shopkeepers offer you a drink when you're looking around their shops." I explained, feeling it best to keep to a simple side of the coin rather than open up the conversation into the general hostility we had so far been subjected to. He recoiled in horror.

"We must put that right straight away," he said and turning to his rear, swung open the door of a mini-fridge behind his desk which was overflowing with cold drinks and snacks. "What cold drink would you like? We Guyanese is renowned fo' awe hospitality ya know!" I could now see why he was well-fleshed out. He certainly did not go without himself. After gratefully gulping down his lemonade, we got down to business. Edwin told him the long story of why we had ended up short of cash to finish the house. Maurice seemed sympathetic and knowingly imparted a few tips based on "local knowledge".

"People wid local knowledge realise when a contractor in Guyana build a house, a good part of ordered material "drop in de yard" before dey reach de building site, especially when de contractor work out in de village for a power of attorney to an absentee landowner. Ya don't have local knowledge, so people take advantage." Maurice had already won our confidence and trust by his warmth and hospitality, so he obviously was not about to shaft us like everyone else had done so far. He would willingly recommend us to the GNCB Trust Bank especially since we would become insurance customers of his to insure the house. He would have liked to sell us life insurance but was disappointed to learn we had already substantial policies taken out in England. However, he would have to charge us a fee for his recommendation because it would involve paperwork and time and there was a vague suggestion that people might have to be persuaded (through bribes). The fee was $20,000. We paid up and thanked him for his help. His secretary typed up the letter of recommendation and he handed it to us. Then he made a phone call to Mr Nelson to fix up an appointment to see us in a short while. He achieved this, conferring with us while we were waiting. He would take us along to the bank to see Mr Nelson the manager now. His little Morris Minor was parked outside the office. I couldn't help but smile as he squeezed his huge body into the tiny front seat. He chattered all the way to the bank, a few blocks away, where he dropped us off. What a nice man. I would refer to him affectionately as "Morris Major" from now on.

The bank interior was grand and impressive by Guyanese standards. A cool atmosphere and imposing interior design greeted us. The seventies style modern architecture was dominated by massive dark wooden beams, adorned with African wood carvings. Massive tropical vines scrambled up and along them. We presented our letter at the reception and were asked to sit in a waiting area. Some time went by before a young girl appeared and escorted us up two flights of stairs to "Mr Hewley's" Office. She told us where to sit and then disappeared. We sat expectantly staring at his closed office door for a good twenty five minutes waiting for it to open. In the open plan office area outside it, various employees lounged at their desks, occasionally getting up to walk to the stairwell. One girl with tightly plaited corn rows sat filing her finger nails. A man in the corner appeared to be reading a local paper. An untidy heap of files towered on one side of his workspace. There seemed to be no urgency to deal with any business. Was anyone behind that heavy hardwood door? At length, a tall woman with a tight skirt and high heels breezed past us carrying a cardboard file. She opened the door and went inside. More waiting followed. Finally she came out and held the door open for us. "Mr Nelson will see you now" she indicated. We soon came to realise that in Guyana, waiting times were a tool of power employed to humiliate the customer. To be shown directly into a manager's office would give the impression that the customer had the upper hand and the manager was a servant of the public. After a long wait, by contrast, the customer would be so grateful to be fitted into the manager's busy schedule and intimidated by his god-like presence that they would allow him to impose the harshest of terms on any deal he was grudgingly prepared to participate in. So it was with Hewley Nelson.

The meeting went in a very different direction from what either of us had anticipated. Hewley was a sharp dresser with all the high powered patter of a Mercedes car salesman. After hearing Edwin's humble and somewhat embarrassed explanation of why we now needed a substantial loan from his bank, he quickly deduced that he had a couple of easily duped idiots in front of him whom he could blind with financial science and humiliate even further. The first thing he asked for was the papers proving we owned the land we were building on. Edwin got out the wad of documents including the lawyer's bill of Sale and the Power of Attorney instructions showing that Dickie had acted on our behalf in the purchase back in 1984. This was when the bombshell was dropped on us. These papers did not prove Edwin owned the land. They only proved he had paid the money for it to the vendor. Until he had a document known as "transport" for it, then it still belonged to the vendor. Our first task would be to go to the lawyer to get the registrar to obtain the transport as soon as possible or the bank could lend us nothing. For the first time, the horrifying reality that he had spent thousands of pounds on plans, wages and materials on building a massive house on a piece of land he did not own, began to sink in.

"So you mean that if we can't get the transport, then our house belongs to someone else?" I asked, wishing to clear up any possible misunderstanding.

"Yes," said Hewley, "you could of course knock it down and take the materials away and build on another piece of land that you do own". I think Edwin was more embarrassed by the fact that I was learning all this in front of him than he would have been had he been there on his own. I could almost feel the anger rising in his blood at this revelation.

"OK, well I will get that done," he said, "but what about getting a loan once I have the transport document?"

"Well I would need proof that you have a source of income to guarantee repayment of the loan," Hewley replied.

"I have come here to set up an international eco-tourism resort with my wife," said Edwin, with a hand gesture towards me. "We intend to make an income once we are up and running but we have to complete the building before we can do that. Meanwhile we're depending on the income I get from my early retirement pension from England."

"Oh well, that's no problem then, which bank does your pension come into?"

"It's paid into my bank account in the United kingdom."

"Ah, then you would have to set up a standing order with them to send your pension directly to your Guyana bank account every month because we need documentation to prove that you have a regular income within Guyana. If you supply me with all the details of your pension income we can put in a loan application for you." That was not at all in our plan, since Edwin had been warned by Brother Pat to leave his pension in England and pay tax there rather than allow it to be directly paid into a Guyanese bank that at any time could be nationalised by the government or go bankrupt so that we would lose all we had. Very few expats returning to Guyana since the dictatorship of Burnham in the 1970's when Barclays had been driven out of the country, had kept their savings or stored all their overseas income in Guyanese banks. They all knew that it was a huge risk to do so.

"I'd rather not do that," said Edwin. "I have expenses and commitments in England which have to be paid out of it and I am already paying tax on it in England. I don't want to send regular sums to Guyana to be liable for tax on it there as well. I'll be using income earned in Guyana to repay the bank's loan. I have a snackette in West Berbice which is already earning an income here and can use that to repay any loan I take out here."

"Well of course, in that case you will need to produce a feasibility study showing us the projected income for the future and proof of income you are already getting from your land assets," advised Hewley. My mind was racing as the conversation proceeded. How could we prove income from a place we had not built yet and had no hope of finishing until we got the loan? It was a catch 22 situation, but Edwin had already told him we had a snackette on the Berbice road which was earning us a small steady income from its trade. I heard him quoting figures at Hewley for the amount of income it was currently producing. These figures seemed to be plucked out of the air. They were far more than anything I had witnessed. They seemed to satisfy Mr Nelson as long as we could bring him the documentation and proof along with the transport document. He could recommend a good accountant for us to set out the feasibility study in a way acceptable to the bank. We shook hands and got his secretary to find us the address of Mr Atterley the accountant. We took a taxi to Atterley's premises in Brickdam before going back to Berbice. A brief meeting with him to find out whether he would do the document for the bank for us, what information we needed to provide for him and how much was his fee, ended with us making an appointment to see him the following week. We headed home racked with doubts, confusion and insecurity yet we both summoned up a steely determination not to be beaten by all this.

Chapter 3

The Containers

At the docks in Water Street, a striking blue and scarlet macaw clung to the rusting wire mesh, sharpening its wicked looking beak on the links. Porters and officials jostled past each other through the litter of the unwelcoming entrance, trying to make their voices heard above the deafening engines of cranes, forklifts, and the shouts of dockyard workers. Bryan seemed to know where to go. We had come down to the docks in Georgetown in his mother's minibus in order to release our forty foot container from England from the port. He shouted something in Creolese at a passing man who took the lading bill from Bryan and kept walking into the dingy building. All three of us followed on his heels. He disappeared with our paperwork and we waited behind Bryan for an interminable time. The man eventually brought out a wad of new documents and Edwin was asked for details so the clerk could complete them. We then waited for over an hour until he reappeared with them and waved us over to another section.

We were shepherded round the quayside to a stack of containers where Edwin used his key to open one of them. This had to be done in the presence of the officials who proceeded to poke around inside the boxes nearest the door. It was a bit like watching children pulling parcels out of their sacks on Christmas morning. They inquisitively broke open the cardboard boxes and began rummaging around under the packing material to bring forth a present out of the 'lucky dip'. Having retrieved a prize, one of them held it up. It was a book.

"They are donations for my local school in Berbice" Edwin explained helpfully. A few more boxes were investigated and then they decided they had seen enough. I let out an imperceptible sigh of relief as they got down and locked back the container. Thank God we were not going to be accused of bringing in illegal goods or having them confiscate something they liked the look of. The man explained we would now have to go back to customs house for payment of the duty before we could take the container away.

"But we've been told that we have no duty to pay because I am repatriating," Edwin insisted. Mumblings were exchanged between the man and Bryan, who explained to us in turn that if that were the case we would have to get a certificate of exemption from the Office of the President and bring it back to Customs House for them to authorize release of the container. We also had to go to see the manager of the shipping Office Laparkan.

He was a sullen, fat Indo-Guyanese man whose mouth seemed larger than his face. He was very rude to us and most unhelpful. As far as he was concerned, they would not deliver the container to where we lived so we would have to pay for the carriage from port to door. He also informed us that storage fees of ten US dollars per day would be payable. Edwin was angry about this, having believed he had paid door to door for it in England. The need for us to get the container out as quickly as possible was urgent as the storage charges would soon mount up. We would have to go to the Office of the President to get our customs papers sorted out. After a few hours, we were getting weary of bureaucracy and inefficiency and being sent from pillar to post but were still believing that we would be getting the container released the same day. At the gates of the Office of the President, we explained the purpose of our mission and were told we must see one Rose Ragnauth. She was on leave that day so we would have to go back the next day at 9.30 a.m. This was a daunting thought. Another four hour minibus journey back to Berbice in darkness was to be followed by a repeat of the whole performance the next day.

Rose Ragnauth turned out to be a young Indo- Guyanese woman. She seemed very personable and educated. She explained that we needed to show her our lists of items that were in the container and she would prepare papers for us to take to the Ministry of Finance who would then give approval for us to collect our possessions free of the 5% tax. This was because Edwin was repatriating and so would be exempt. Edwin got out the wad of pages we had painstakingly itemised when we packed the previous summer. As Rose perused the list we soon realised that her educated façade concealed a somewhat limited intellect.

"What is this?" she asked, pointing at the words 'Pole vault trough' on the list.

"It's a special piece of equipment that athletes use to plant their pole vaults in before they can lift themselves up over the bar", Edwin explained and she looked none the wiser. "I'm coming home to help develop the country by building a sports tourism resort and have brought specialist sports equipment to enable local athletes to improve in track and field events that I will be coaching them for." She nodded, but seemed more interested in the amount of items we had listed than in the nature of our intentions. We were beginning to feel that she was assessing the size of our bank account on the basis of our list. We were on the defensive since much of the container was filled with second hand objects donated by schools and sports clubs Edwin had canvassed support from. Their value bore no relationship to the size of our income, which for the foreseeable future was Edwin's very small early retirement pension.

At the end of our meeting with Rose, we returned to Laparkan Shipping Offices to get a delivery date from them. Although this time we spoke to a more polite senior manager and attempted to convince him through Edwin's personal friendship with the Laparkan boss in England that we had already paid in full, our documents did not state this. Edwin reluctantly accepted that he would have to pay extra delivery from port to door. No delivery date could be given until we had dealt with all the customs procedures. Dejectedly we returned to Berbice realising we would have to go back again the next day to further this procedure. We could not afford to stay in Georgetown hotels overnight. At least when we got back to Belair that evening, Eddie Lall's lorry had delivered the materials we had been waiting for. The letter from lawyer Trim must have made Lall act even though he still had a court action pending for alleged non-payment. Now perhaps we would see some progress on the building.

Next morning we braved a ride in a 'sick' minibus crammed with long-suffering placid passengers and after frequent breakdowns finally transferred to another healthier bus to reach the city. Before we could collect our papers from Rose Ragnauth, we had to sit with a clerk not long out of school while he searched a massive book of Biblical proportions listing all conceivable goods and their taxable values. Painful hours passed as he fumbled his way through the alphabetical directory in his vain attempt to match descriptions to items on our twelve page document. His reading age was surprisingly low for someone in such a responsible post. He seemed to need an explanation of nearly every item listed. Having found the coffee table section, he asked which of the coffee tables listed was equivalent to my "glass-topped" one. I saw a long list of different coffee tables, none of which was glass topped, and next to each one, a customs tax value of thousands of Guyana dollars. I panicked at the thought of how much the total tax calculation would come to if every item in our container had thousands of dollars tax to pay as listed in this massive tome. I could see nothing that matched ours but quickly stabbed my finger at the one listed with the lowest value and declared "that's the one". He seemed satisfied and proceeded with his interminable task. After hours of waiting, it seemed we would have to go away and come back later as it could take him days to get through it all. We would go and see Orin Thompson at the Ministry of Finance, as he was from Hopetown and a friend of Dickie. Our long meeting with Orin achieved nothing more than making it clear that he had no authority to waver this tax for us. He advised us to write a letter to the Minister of Finance explaining our project. Edwin should mention his meeting last year at the Guyanese High Commission in London with Prime Minister Hamilton-Green and Mr Pilgrim, the Guyanese High Commissioner where he had been promised tax free exemption if he repatriated to Guyana to set up this project. Orin promised to try to contact the Prime Minister later that day or before Congress ended to sort out the matter. He would let us know when to come back. Uncertainty was likely to prevail for the foreseeable future.

Back in Berbice for the weekend, we distracted ourselves with making plans for the farm and the reconfiguration of the house, interrupted by a never-ending stream of visitors who all seemed preoccupied with the fact that you could not get a tin of sardines any more. The workers had come in to enclose the space under the living room which would eventually become our Gym. It had to be got ready for the container's imminent arrival so we could store our possessions securely in it while the rest of the house was being completed. Monday, a national holiday, was the fourth night of village dances; part of the annual emancipation celebrations. It was a small miracle that anyone had come in to work at all when such festivities were going on as no one usually worked on a Sunday. The novel prospect of having extra pay to spend at the dances had drawn them in to do overtime. Monday, therefore, no work was done on the house. Instead we had to entertain more visitors keen to remind Edwin that they had been in his class at primary school or were a distant cousin on his mother's side. Bryan would be going to town to get stock for the snackette the next day. He would call in with our papers to see about the container for us while we walked up to Fort Wellington to introduce ourselves to the Regional Chairman. That evening the fish Tita cooked for us was even more unappetising than usual, since it was cold and covered in burnt sugar sauce. I had already eaten part of this when I discovered it was raw in the middle. I left the rest and just finished the rice. We sat on the veranda in pitch darkness, watching candle flies flare up and disappear over the pasture, dancing in the air to the distant musical racket from the school hall. Bed in this house was not a pleasant place to be, so we tried to put off going into it until we were absolutely dropping.

It was blistering heat at 9.30 a.m. and we had over a mile to walk in it. We had to say "Hello" to every villager as we passed them on the road carrying their shopping baskets on their heads, waiting for a minibus, or pushing improvised go-carts laden with buckets of water from the street stand pipes. It was considered good manners to greet people you passed on the street. When we got to Fort Wellington,, the Chairman was away for the day in Ithaca so we had to make an appointment to go back. The craft centre was closed because of The President's intended visit next day and the post Office was closed due to audit. Edwin met someone called Barry and spent at least an hour chatting about the local sports club and how to get some sand to fill up the low areas on our building plot. Everyone we had spoken to thus far seemed to blame each other for things that were wrong about the country. We parted company from him and found the Post Office had opened. We approached the rickety wooden steps leading up to the open door just as my salivary glands warned me that I was about to vomit. It just took over. I stood helplessly watching the contents of my stomach gush out all over the side of the steps by the letter box. I was an object of curiosity to the staff of the offices. Edwin looked embarrassed and went inside to get some stamps while I tried to regain some composure.

"Are you OK now?" he asked as he came out.

"I think it was that undercooked fish I ate last night".

I don't know how I managed to walk all the way back to the village but was relieved at last to reach the snackette where we sat in the shade and had a couple of beers to recover. Bryan returned from Georgetown with the news that Orin had not managed to see the Prime Minister yet, but would do so the next day. We went back to Taa's house feeling wasted and fed up. It was a rough night for me in the donkey pen toilet, staring at big white larvae clinging to the sides of the earth-pit latrine as wave after wave of bilious liquid ejected itself from my mouth onto the accumulated pile of human excrement. I felt a bit better when dawn came and Edwin suggested we tidy the room and wash the sheets to freshen up our surroundings. He got the broom to sweep out while I took the clothes and sheets downstairs. I had to wash them under the house in Taa's large wooden washtub. I took water from the tank to do this. Diamond, a three year old child from another villager's family, who for some reason was resident in Taa's house at the time, reprimanded me.

"Ya cyan' wash close in good drinkin' water" she objected, with a look of disdain that said it all. I felt foolish but had not wanted to draw muddy trench water which would make my clothes dirtier than before they were washed. The realities of being a guest in such an environment were starting to hit home. Compared to anyone in England or Dubai that I knew, I had been coping well and unlike Edwin, had been taking great pains to try to empathise with and understand the local living conditions, but I had still managed to be manifestly insensitive.

Although work on the septic tank was due to begin that day, Lyo and the other workers did not show. No news came from Orin about getting the duty free concession. No one seemed to be authorised to make a decision. There was a good deal of talk but nothing seemed to get done and no one apart from us seemed to care. We were both getting worn down by this fact. Bryan already had the store-room at the snackette completed and Edwin had only told him to get it done two weeks ago and yet our house had not moved on one centimetre.

"Maybe we should get an Indian to do the work for us," Edwin said to Bryan as he learned the reason for his efficiency compared to ours. "I just want to give the black workers in Hopetown a chance because they say they don't have work and now I'm giving them some they're messing me about. Don't they realise that if they aren't efficient and reliable then they'll never get work off anyone?"

"Black people does be disgusting" consoled Bryan. "If ya does want tings done, ya gatta get Indian workers ta do it". He gave Edwin the prices of sand and truck hire from an Indian in Bushlot and we left.

Days passed and no more progress was made. I was languishing with what seemed like food poisoning without realising I probably had a mild case of typhoid which was rife in the hot season in Bushlot. Edwin did not have much sympathy and told me I had to pull myself together. I managed to muster up the strength to walk across to the half-finished house with him. I could hardly walk when so much of my strength had been sapped. When we got to the top of the steps and chased away the neighbour's herd of goats, we found the lounge floor covered in goat droppings and piles of slimy mucus. The sight of it made me retch. There was nothing for it but to get a couple of pointer brooms and sweep up the distasteful mess. This took a couple of hours. To keep the goats from getting back in, we wedged some old corrugated roof panels across the entrance doorway and jammed some concrete blocks in front of them. That evening we got a visit from Shirley, the wife of a local headmaster Edwin had met back in 1984 but who was now on his deathbed. She had heard I was sick and had brought some rehydration salts for me to mix with water and some oranges which were a very welcome present. It was a very nice gesture and took away some of the sting of all that was going wrong up to now.

Edwin went to Georgetown without me next day as I was too ill to travel. When he got home after dark, he had changed nearly two thousand pounds into Guyana dollars to pay for the materials which had been delivered at last. He handed over most of this money to the supplier who arrived as Edwin had barely got in the door.

"I saw Orin today, and got a letter from him," he told me. "He's coming to Hopetown on Sunday so we'll be seeing him then. Then I had to go to Rose Ragnauth again to get the papers stamped, Next stop was Laparkan to get 'em signed, then took 'em to the wharf but they sent me back again to Laparkan to get another paper signed. I'm well and truly pissed off with all this crap. After all that, customs cleared five pieces of kit, but said the container will take too long to do, so I'll have to go back the day after tomorrow to do it."

Another sleepless night for me and another day of inspecting the progress of work in the house passed before Edwin went back to town with Bryan and got the container opened and cleared. They were told to come back for the papers at two o'clock but when they returned customs had still not finished laboriously writing out lists of articles by hand. They finally got the paper by late afternoon, and went on to Laparkan to arrange transport. "They gave me a lot of crap so I left the papers with them. I'll have to go back and collect them next week". Edwin said angrily when he got 'home' at last. I was still very ill and this news did not speed my recovery. I just felt hopeless. At least Edwin had brought back some antibiotics for me, so if I had a bacterial infection, I had some chance to rid myself of it if I took them. Aided by these, I began to make a slow recovery.

We busied ourselves with long walks down the back-dam into the rice fields or along the beach watching the 'four-eye' fish leaping up from the sands into the waves of an incoming tide. Some wood was delivered and had to be unloaded one day, a load of sand the next. I was still weak and ill. If I ate food, I was sick soon afterwards. Over the weekend, Edwin had a visit from Huette, a female athlete who was going to Japan to represent Guyana at the World Championships. He gave her lots of advice and some Athletics magazines he had brought with us. On Sunday we went to the snackette to meet Orin from the Ministry of Finance who was in Hopetown for the day to see his family. Orin told Edwin how good the government felt about his project. This cheered Edwin and next day, although he was beginning to wonder what to do with me as I was still very ill, he got the boys organised to fill in the ruts in the mud street leading to our 'house' in preparation for the container lorry to come down it soon. Two more days of boredom followed with nothing for me to do apart from redrawing plans of the newly arranged kitchen for the electrician to be able to quote us a price for the work.

My illness was now compounded with constipation due to dehydration caused by the fever and vomiting. Edwin was beginning to have doubts about whether I could cope with the living conditions in Guyana. I was upset that he thought this. Just because I had got some sort of infection that he did not have, he seemed to think I was not capable of living in the tropics. This attitude was being nurtured by his mother and the fact that as yet I could not shake it off. I knew it would go away eventually but I wanted access to copious amounts of boiled drinking water or tea which was too much trouble to obtain because of the scarcity of firewood for boiling the water. It seemed crazy to me that we could not just buy a gas bottle for the unused calor gas stove that Taa had under her house. We had the money. If it was up and working I could boil my own water at our own expense without causing anyone else any problem, but I was told the bottle had to be fetched from New Amsterdam and that was too far to go to bring a heavy gas bottle. They sold gas bottles in the village but apparently they were for the wrong type of connector. The choice in bottled drinks was between sickly sweet fizzy drinks and beer. I could drink neither of these in the amounts I needed to rehydrate. I resorted to drinking the cold un-boiled water from the rainwater tank with a squeezed lime added. This seemed to work the trick by the end of the week and I gradually began to feel better. Another week of sleeping during the day to catch up on lost sleep at night, helped by flasks of wholesome soups sent down to me by Cousin Irene and I was getting a lot stronger.

The following Thursday when Edwin returned dispirited after a fruitless trip to Georgetown to clear the container at Laparkan, he was pleased to find me helping at the snackette. Bryan went back next day to move things on and returned with news that he would get it next week. He had also found the pink folder with important papers that Edwin had been looking for all day and realised he must have left in one of the offices in Georgetown the day before. The following Monday, Bryan did the journey again and said things had gone well but he would have to return the following day to finalise it all. This he did. It entailed paying Laparkan a further $99,000 Guyana dollars for storage before they released the container. It would be delivered the next day. We spent that whole day at the snackette waiting for the appearance of a container lorry. At 6.15 pm, when dark fell as usual, it was obviously not going to arrive after all, so we went back down to Taa's house before it got too dark to see where we were walking. There was the usual electricity blackout. We sat in the pitch dark on the veranda discussing the day's visitors and mail when at 7.30 pm, suddenly all hell broke loose. It was the container. Eon from the snackette and a couple of other boys were running excitedly down the street to us with the news.

"I don't bloody believe it! Why on earth couldn't they have left town earlier so they would arrive here in daylight?" grumbled Edwin. The driver was parked at the end of the road and had walked down to test the condition of the street before he would drive down it. It took a bit of bribery to persuade him to do it but at length it rumbled down towards us with its headlights the only illumination of the street and our delivery point. It was now September 11th. This whole process had taken six weeks. Suddenly, every boy in the neighbourhood appeared like ants ready and willing to help unload the container. We had to borrow Taa's hurricane lamp and use our little hand torches to supervise the movement of packing cases from the container into the store room we had prepared under the house and to stack it all in an organised way. It took two and a half hours to do this. At the end of it all, after the driver reversed back out onto the main road, we locked up the door and took all the helpers up to the snackette to reward them with a drink each. Later, on Taa's advice, Edwin appointed two of the boys who were working on the house to be night watchmen in the store room with the container load. It would not have been safe to leave all that stuff in an empty building at night with the whole community knowing it was there. If Lindy and Ogden slept in with it, then it would be safe. No one would break in knowing someone was inside.

Sunshine streamed in through the opened door in the morning, so we were able to inspect the contents that had arrived. Edwin was disgusted that quite a lot of his things were broken. They had not been packed properly because it had been done by neighbours and friends he had drafted in to help him in England. Bryan and Taa both came to survey the contents and put in their requests for what they wanted. Quite a few boxes of stuff had been shipped with the snackette in mind. A second-hand microwave, two old but working chest freezers, a drinks cooler-dispenser machine, boxes of polystyrene cups, food trays, plastic cutlery, food-handler's hats, disposable paper hats, numerous snack-bar crockery and catering utensils were there specifically for the snackette. Above all, there was a small but robust generator which would supply power during the evening blackouts so that they could keep the food and drinks cold and sell ice. Bryan was quick to notice Edwin's personal stacking music centre.

"If we have dat in de snackette it'll bring in plenty customer," he said. Edwin allowed him to take it up there later in the day. Taa was beside herself with pride at the sight of all the boxes of items her son had brought in. Her eyes twinkled with expectant delight as they darted back and forth over the sea of boxes. The two boys had new found power in their role as keepers of the store. It did not seem to worry them that they were sleeping in a dungeon full of boxes. They fixed up makeshift beds amongst it all and seemed very happy with the arrangements.

On the 18th September, the postman brought a letter from Georgetown to me. It was the lading bill for my own thirty foot container from Dubai having arrived in the port. At last we were getting somewhere. Edwin and Bryan were making yet another Georgetown trip the next day. They would visit Laparkan to present the lading bill, go to customs house and back to Laparkan to get papers for customs to process. This done, on Thursday 26th September, now I was fully recovered, we both went to town but had too many appointments with finance and lawyers to tackle customs, so that had to wait till the following Monday when we also failed to fit it in. Another week later, on 7th October, our main mission was to clear my container. This time we had to visit a different wharf. I had used Pickfords in Dubai to ship my belongings and they had set it up with the GNCB wharf which was the government wharf. Everything seemed to go much more efficiently and smoothly at this wharf than at the John Fernandes wharf we had visited last time. The officials seemed very friendly and helpful. We got our paperwork from them, and watched them open and check the container without any fuss. The customs clearance had been done by lunchtime. A nice chap called Dexter was handling it for us.

The 8th October was a memorable occasion not just for me but also for the rude sullen assistant manager of Laparkan. In sorting out the transport of my container to Berbice, he once again insisted that carriage must be paid from port to door.

"My documents clearly show I have already paid Pickfords for door to door delivery." I insisted, presenting them to him. He was having none of that and brushed them aside without a glance.

"We do not do prepaid delivery from the port here," he said.

"But you must have already had the money for it from Pickfords as this is my receipt for the extra charge they took from me for the port to door carriage and I do not intend paying twice."

"It means nothing to me," he scoffed. " If you don't pay, we will not deliver it." "This is an outrage," I said beginning to feel my blood rise in anger and thinking at last I could stand my ground as this was my container and I personally had dealt with the entire transaction. Whatever Edwin had agreed to do with the other container was his affair and I could not interfere, even though I felt he had been robbed. In my case, I knew what I had paid for and was not going to let myself be swindled.

"I refuse to leave this office until you telephone Pickfords on the number on this receipt so they can verify to you that your company have already been paid for this service by them."

"Kindly leave, as I have an important meeting in here now," he said, getting flustered.

"I'm not going anywhere," I said and sat down and made myself comfortable on a ledge opposite his desk.

"I will call security to have you removed."

"You can do what you like but I'm not moving until you agree to deliver my container as you're supposed to". He looked frustrated as I continued to sit there. Then he picked up his phone and made the motions of a call to security. No one came and he looked increasingly embarrassed. Then he walked out of the office and left me there on my own. Edwin said to me,

"Come on Jane, let's go"

"I'm not going anywhere until I get them to agree to deliver my container". He left me and went outside to wait in a corridor. I sat and twiddled my thumbs and settled myself into a comfortable position for what was obviously going to be an all-day sit-in as far as I was concerned. After about ten minutes the fat man got fed up with waiting outside his office and came back in.

"Kindly leave my office as I have a meeting in here now."

"You'll have to hold your meeting somewhere else as I'm going nowhere."

"I do not have authority to make overseas calls."

"Then get someone who does."

He went back out again very flustered. Eventually he came in and said I could speak to the manager who was outside the office. I thought it was a trick to get me out of the office so I refused. Eventually Edwin came in and said the manager was outside and I could speak to him there. I tentatively followed him out of the office into an open plan area, still feeling I was being tricked but complying. A very softly spoken and altogether more civil man in a dapper suit was waiting to speak to me. He listened attentively to my complaint and eventually made a phone call to his head office to verify that the payment had been made in Dubai and I would not have to pay again. He had a pleasant chat with Edwin about the impressive cricket ground we usually passed. Apparently he was a club member. What a nice, helpful man. Why couldn't we have dealt with him from the start?

The horrid man was not in evidence when we returned on 21ˢᵗ October, after another visit to Rose Ragnauth for the request of the "ST" letter required by customs, to complete the arrangements for the container to be transported. Then, on 4ᵗʰ November, it was to Georgetown again, taking the "ST" letter and customs papers to one Joy Joseph (of no relationship to Edwin). When she came through with our papers I was told I would have to pay duty amounting to the equivalent of £6,000. We both went ballistic. This was more money than either of us had in the world.

"What was the point of me making all those lists if they are going to charge me duty anyway? If I have to find that sort of money I would rather pay to ship it back to England than let some corrupt official here get it." I told Edwin. He agreed, but said he would have a chat with Joy to explain the situation, that although the container was coming in separately from his, it was still part of his repatriation consignment as I was his wife and thus it was part of our joint possessions for our new home together. He would get her to sort things out. They went into her office, leaving me to wait in the reception. After he came out, we went to Laparkan to collect the papers to bring back to Joy at Customs House. This time, she altered the papers so we did not have to pay duty. Dexter processed all the papers. Then we went back to Laparkan, paid the $1000 storage fees and were told the container would be coming on Thursday. In spite of us doubting every bit of this pledge, it arrived safe and sound on Thursday 7th Nov. Things could only improve from now on.

Chapter 4

The Organic Farm

"Why is it that we never get any greens to eat in our meals?" I asked Edwin. "For weeks we've been living here in Taa's house and yet every day, I see the two boys she's got working for you picking heaps of them from your garden. You are paying their wages, your mum is selling their harvests, you keep telling me she is making hundreds of dollars a day from the sales and yet we get none of it to eat ourselves."

"I don't know," he said, "I'll ask her." but nothing changed. We had numerous three way conversations with Taa about whether you could grow the same vegetables in Guyana that you could grow in England. I had done a lot of reading and research on the subject prior to coming to live there. I had learned that tropical heat, rainfall and soil combined with the type of pests and restricted daylight hours prevented most European vegetables from growing successfully there, although of course I kept this knowledge to myself out of respect for her seniority. Taa had asked us to bring vegetable seeds with us as there was a shortage in the country. We had complied at great cost but they were all English varieties. I wanted to see whether the seeds would grow. I had noticed that the boys doing the gardening seemed to be spending a lot of time playing and sitting around and that the vegetables were fighting to survive amid the weeds. I was not going to criticise them but I was sure I could do better and the best way to improve results was to lead by example instead of lecture. I loved gardening and longed to be able to get back into doing something. I had not been allowed to do anything since I had arrived and it was driving me mad. I began to wander off into the farm every day and pull out any weeds I could see, once I had learned from Spear and Ronerick how to identify them.

When our containers finally arrived and we had been able to unpack the seeds as well as some of the garden tools and plastic flowerpots we had brought. I used the opportunity to escape the mindless round of gossip and chitchat between Edwin and his mother, by going out into the farm every day and cultivating some of the seeds we had brought in the way I knew would work.

This was how I was going to get some fresh vegetables to eat and start having a healthy enjoyable diet again. At last I had something worthwhile to do. I could be digging, hoeing, weeding and watering. Every day I went out into the farm exploring some new marvel of the beautiful natural environment. Every day I could learn more about the ecosystem of which I was now a part and would have to fit into. The savoy cabbages grew large like footballs. The leaf beet and spinach grew healthy and strong and the abundant tomatoes began to swell and ripen. I also learned how the local beans (bora), sweet potatoes, cassava and groundnuts were cultivated. My efforts were an astounding success which drew comments from many villagers,

"Jane, ya get powaful garden". I was an object of curiosity for doing physical work on the land. Apart from those deemed by some locals as 'poor' women, no other females in the village would be seen doing physical work, much less so a white woman (of which there was no memory in the village since at least the 1960s.) Then the pressure came via Edwin from his mother, who told him he should not let me be working out in the hot sun like that as it would "Bun up she skin".

As my lovingly tended crops began to mature, I harvested them and brought them up to the snackette to cook or make salads for our lunch. My first lettuces, cucumbers and tomatoes were the treat I had been craving for. Before going to Guyana my diet had consisted of mainly salads and crunchy fresh Mediterranean vegetables. Now I was condemned to a diet of rice, fat with a tiny amount of meat or fish, and any vegetable present in the dish could barely be detected with a magnifying glass. Whatever the poor plant had begun as, it was cooked to an unrecognisable pulp or chopped into tiny shards and mixed into a huge quantity of heavily seasoned noodles or rice. I had dreamed for months of crunching into refreshing bowls of my produce for a rush of vitamins, minerals and fibre to restore my feeling of wellbeing. Now at last I would be able to do so. I washed the lettuce leaves with great care to collect and reuse rather than waste the rain water. After cleaning and preparing them along with shallots, tomato and cucumber, I took a large red pepper and carefully deseeded it adding fine slices to the mix. Cousin Irene had prepared appetising gingered pork with noodles for us that day, so I took my mixed salad to the table so we could share it. Suddenly I felt my right nostril was on fire. I could not understand what was causing the sensation. Had I been stung? Was I going down with the symptoms of some deadly tropical disease? I panicked. The fire was spreading to other parts of my face. It was excruciating. The ladies in the kitchen watched helplessly wondering what was ailing me and unable to suggest any course of action. The fire began to spread all over my fingers like a kind of hot-ache. It lasted several minutes and then began to subside. We sat down to eat and soon realised what had caused the problem. As soon as we started to eat the salad, the lovely cool red pepper slices turned out to be angry "Ball of fire" hot peppers which I had mistaken for sweet peppers since they were a similar shape and size. After this I paid much more attention to the individual characteristics of every plant I came across.

As we worked together in the garden, I got to know Spear quite well. He was in his late teens, a strong and good looking boy with a cheeky sense of humour. Ronerick, on the other hand was not good looking at all. He was rather timid and shy and quite a lot younger than Spear, so Spear was the more experienced and the leader of the two. Spear lived with his mother and siblings in a simple one roomed wooden house right opposite our building. No father was resident in the house but there were eleven smaller brothers and sisters. Spear, being the eldest of them, was the main breadwinner. His sister Trudi worked as the post girl for our area. She had already extended the family with a baby of her own. What I liked best about Spear was that he listened and was willing to learn. He and Ronerick liked to teach me what they knew about local crops and wild plants and the insects and other wild animals or garden pests. Spear would willingly try the new tools we brought and follow what I showed him about the best way to sow the small foreign vegetable seeds in pots and why. When we had first arrived, Edwin had been annoyed that he was paying boys to stand around in a garden full of weeds all day "gaffing" and when his requests and incentives had failed to change their ways, he had sacked them. Spear and Ronerick were hard workers who turned up for work more regularly, but they too wasted a lot of time when unsupervised. It made a lot of difference once I was working on the farm because they could not get away with standing around idle if I was there being busy and setting an example. They respected that and responded. Besides, if I saw something that needed doing and they seemed not to be doing anything, I would just ask either of them if they would help me out and we would do it together.

One day there was a lot of hooting and screaming coming from the lime trees at the back near the pond. I looked up to see what was going on and saw Ronerick up a coconut tree and Spear chasing wildly through the cassava plants. He let out a Yahoo as he grabbed something I could not see. He slashed at it with his cutlass then held it up by its tail.

"What is it?" I asked.

"Yarawee" he said, dangling the poor hairy grey possum by its tail as blood dripped from its slashed mouth.

"Why did you have to kill it?"

"It eat people chicken" explained Ronerick. "It get sharp teeth an' bite bad," he added apologetically, pointing at its nasty looking dentures.

"Yarawee meat sweet!" said Spear and called over Diddi from the house building. I watched as they broke off from work, built a small campfire in the clearing between the cassava and the sweet potatoes and dangled the dead creature by its tail in the flames to singe off its fur. The smell took me back thirty years, remembering my mother singeing the feather shafts off plucked pheasants before roasting them. Diddi began to disembowel the creature with deft strokes of his cutlass. Then he threaded it onto a pared stick and set up a spit roast over the burning coconut husks. When he was satisfied that it was cooked, he cut off a small piece of flesh for me to taste. I found it pleasantly reminiscent of smoked bacon, not at all what I had expected. They shared out the meat between the three of them chattering and laughing about their hunting exploit and how they outwitted their prey. Moments like these seemed to typify their carefree simple lives and they were worth savouring.

Chapter 5

Bottomless Pit Economics

Back in September, Edwin had decided that the massive amounts of money he had up to now been handing over to his mother for the weekly shopping did not seem to be translating into appropriate amounts of food on the table. We were ravenously hungry most of the time. The through traffic of neighbours to and from the house leaving the downstairs kitchen with covered bowls and bulging bags seemed never ending. Before long, he had concluded that he was supporting half the village. This would not have been so bad had we been eating our fill ourselves, but now we had almost exhausted the cash we had brought with us in August. It was clear that if he continued subsidising the rest of the village community, we would not be able to pay for any shopping to sustain ourselves. Since Taa was at church most of the time doing what seventy year old village women do at churches, was she aware that all and sundry were taking away food cooked by her niece in her kitchen during her absence? Taa responded to her son's suspicions with sharp words. They were cousins and aunties. It was the Christian thing to do to share what you have. Edwin said that was all very well but how did they manage before he came back to Guyana? They must have bought their own food then. It would have to stop. If she wanted to support them all, she could do so but not with his money as he had a house to finish building. From now on we would eat at the snackette and not in her house, so he would not be contributing to her food bill any more.

The following days of taking our meals at the snackette began to give us both an insight into how things were operating there. We had to take a close interest in the business practices now because we had to demonstrate to the bank that we could run a profitable business that could repay the loan we were asking for. It did not take long for Edwin to start seeing how better to manage the operation and this came as a shock to Bryan who until then had been running Edwin's business as if it were his own. The food Cousin Irene prepared for our private meals was more palatable and satisfying than what we had been eating up to now. I found myself helping her to prepare vegetables and watch how she cooked them. I learned from her and the other ladies we employed, the way to cook unfamiliar ingredients and recipes such as green plantain chips, cassava balls, egg balls, patties, home-made ice-cream custard, pine tarts, sugar cake, "solara", "shingles" and other products which local customers demanded. The products for sale were prepared in advance during the day and surplus ones placed in the freezer. When they were needed in the evening after the cooks had gone home, they were reheated in the microwave we had brought with us. Our generator could just about power this and the lights, so it gave us the edge over other local snack bars when there was a blackout. During the evenings I would take turns at selling at the counter or cashing up the till while Edwin and Bryan were chatting out front with the customers, encouraging them to stay and spend their money.

The first problem Edwin noticed was that there was no record of sales or costs apart from a few receipts from the suppliers stored in an old wooden drawer. There was no cash register because it would have been pointless with intermittent electricity. It was all very well having a generator to supply current but it only made economic sense to run it at nights because the cost of the petrol to run it would outweigh any profits on drink or food if the generator were on in the daytime too. At nights it would give customers a reason for coming out and staying out on the premises for entertainment. In the daytime, we would only put it on if power cuts were long enough to endanger the safety of frozen food or render cold drinks warm. We had to devise a record sheet which all sales staff must use to record every sale and manually total up with a calculator at closing time. Without a duplicator, this had to be hand written with hand drawn columns. I had to prepare a number of these in advance so they could be ready to use in the busy times. It was a discipline which none of the staff took kindly to because they had for nearly a year been working without being accountable in any way. To them this seemed like unnecessary work. Never the less Edwin said they must learn good business practice if they were to be able to make good profits and grow the business. Black people in Guyana, he reminded them, were notorious for being poor at running business and he wanted to teach them how to become better so they could earn enough to eventually set up their own businesses and run them successfully.

Another change was in hygiene and safety. Bryan had disregarded Edwin's plans in the building of the snackette and used the rooms at the back of the single story shop to accommodate his wife and three children. They were not supposed to be living there but they had taken the liberty of moving in. When Edwin pointed out that these rooms were meant for storage of stock and for a kitchen and food preparation area, so should not be full of children's school bags, numerous pairs of dirty shoes and garments, family laundry and broken furniture, Bryan protested and begged to be allowed to stay because he had been evicted from his mother's house. Besides, he said, if he did not live on the premises, people would break in during the night and steal everything. Edwin gave in and allowed him to stay on condition that all family possessions and laundry were kept out of the kitchen and either in the parent's room or the children's room.

Most days from now on, we not only ate our lunch in the snackette, but also spent the evenings there until the wee hours, when we had to cash up, tally up the takings with the stock sold and remaining stock and calculate what our profits were. It did not take long to realise that some items were making a loss. The drinks were not a problem but the food was. We asked Bryan and Lorraine to show us a breakdown of ingredient costs and show us the mark-up on each item. Blank stares suggested they had not even done this before they started selling. They just bought a bulk package of ingredients and decided on an arbitrary price in line with what other locals sold the same item for. They could not even tell us how many cakes, egg balls or ice creams were produced from each particular recipe. I would have to sit down and calculate all this to show them how it was worked out. Vagueness was a local speciality and it was not long before we realised that there was a vested interest involved in their "not knowing" how much an individual cake cost to make. Once we did know, and also knew how much each was sold for, we could start matching the amounts of ingredients to the amounts of products and ultimately to the amount of profit made over the expenditure. We explained that gas, wages and other overheads also had to be taken into account in the item costs. After a couple of weeks of nightmarishly complicated calculations and cross-checking, all with the aid of nothing more than a calculator, it became clear that ingredients were somehow disappearing out of the products and no one could explain where they had gone. In truth, they had never expected that by mathematical calculations one could detect the disappearance of flour, fat, eggs, sugar, cheese or meat. When confronted with this proof and questioning, they were left speechless and mystified much as a three year old would when questioned about a missing chocolate bar, unaware of the tell-tale chocolate smears on their face. As the weeks went by the mystery of the missing ingredients shifted from cake to ice cream and back to cake or over to patties. There was always a new mystery to solve and my brain was fully exercised in trying to keep on top of this deliberate confusion. Edwin, not known for patience, bent over backwards to make allowances for them but in spite of my attempts to justify their ignorance with an understanding of the poor education system, he became increasingly suspicious that wholesale theft was occurring.

There was always a crowd of people at the open door of the kitchen and a steady stream of Bryan and Lorraine's family visitors. The two cooks and their families also seemed to be always in and out at the back. Edwin would have liked to keep the back door shut but this was impossible, since the heat from the oven would make it far too hot inside without the extra ventilation. He told Bryan the visitations would have to stop because too many people in food preparation areas increased the risk of food contamination by germs. People thereafter stopped coming when we were present, but we were well aware that as soon as we walked away from the premises, the distant hidden eyes constantly trained on us would alert those awaiting our departure so they could go and collect their food at the back door without us seeing. Bryan tried to impress us with his managerial skills by sacking one of the sales girls summarily one evening.

"Where is Maylene, tonight?" asked Edwin, thinking she was off sick.

"Me sack she," Bryan announced. "She bin teefing." There was no arguing with that. We believed, as we were meant to, that she had been responsible for all the mystery disappearing ingredients up to this point. It was years later that we learned Bryan had kicked her out after a row when his wife Lorraine had discovered he was having an affair with the girl.

The kitchen was swarming with flies and maribuntas (local hornets). Unlike other tropical places we had previously lived in, there was as yet no locally available mosquito mesh to screen insects out of open windows and doors. The health and hygiene standards we wished to attain were on a different planet from what our staff were accustomed to or could understand. Clearly our financial situation prevented us from putting necessary building improvements in place. The simple cost-free changes in behaviour that our staff would need to make were outside their comprehension. They simply ignored Edwin's instructions however tactfully he explained them, so he had to lower his expectations. He had allowed Bryan to purchase an ice-cream machine before our arrival. Daily sterilising of this and the fruit juice cooler-dispenser we had brought with us, added to the growing list of jobs we had to insist on being done. Staff wanted to be paid a daily wage for standing around gossiping and wearing a smart uniform. We required them to be gainfully occupied in providing a healthy environment for customers to eat food that would not hospitalise them. The staff sucked their teeth resentfully when they thought we were out of earshot, so some did not bother to do the cleaning when we were not present. It meant that if we were going to ensure things were done properly and honestly, we would have to be constantly present, watching and managing the place and leading by example. It depressed me. Was this what I had spent seven years at university doing a degree, doctoral research and a teaching qualification for? I hoped we would have our house finished so I could build up the tourism business I had expected to be running by now, but as a means to that end, I would have to do this so we could get our loan from the bank.

After three weeks of personal supervision in the running of the snackette, guiding and teaching Bryan and his staff in how to do it properly, we compiled a feasibility study for the bank and took it to the accountant. Incorporated in this study was the combined income projected from the snackette based on the three weeks we had records for and the projected earnings from our as yet non-existent eco-tourism resort. Mr Atterley took two weeks to prepare a document for us and when we finally collected it to take to the bank, it seemed that he had merely got his secretary to type out my figures neatly on his headed paper, signed it and put his official stamp on it. Several tens of thousands of dollars lighter in the wallet as we headed for Mr Nelson's office, we concluded that it had been a very expensive typist and signature! This time our meeting with Mr Nelson was from a position of strength and he was happy to announce that we could be given the loan of three million Guyana dollars needed to complete the project. However, there was a catch. Before we could collect the loan we would have to bring not only the original transport document for our land, passed and stamped by the central housing and planning department but also the sum of sixty six thousand dollars fee for the bank. Where would we get that money from? We would have to sell the sheep that presently were residing in the pen next to the watch hut at the back of our unfinished house. The interest rate on the 15 year mortgage we would be given was an eye-watering 43 per cent. This, we were told, was because it was a commercial premises we were building. Assuming we had been given a standard repayment mortgage, Edwin resolved to pay the mortgage off as quickly as we possibly could, so as to minimise the amount of interest we would have to pay.

Coming up to Christmas, we spent every available moment in the snackette. It was vital that we maximised our income, so Bryan was made aware that the profits had to pay the huge mortgage to finish our home, since we had run out of money. We had used money intended for building our home to finance the snackette in the first place and it now needed to be paid back. He seemed to understand and be cooperative. He even suggested a big fun-day event to bring in extra customers, as well as planning for a great New Years' Eve Party. As the days and weeks went by, Edwin made never ending alternate trips to New Amsterdam and Georgetown in the vain quest for our transport document while I sat at the counter of the snackette serving local customers with their drinks, pastries, cakes and ice creams. Each time he returned he seemed more frustrated than the last. The Georgetown Office always told him our application was in New Amsterdam yet when he got to New Amsterdam they told him the papers were in Georgetown. Finally he had to stoop to bribery by taking a young lady in the registrars' office in Georgetown out to lunch so that she would seek out the documents and speed up the process. My decision to stay away from all this was deliberate since I was by now convinced that a white woman's presence would prevent any cooperation whatsoever in the process. I have no doubt that the reason Edwin finally got the treasured documents was because he allowed the young lady to think she was in with a chance of becoming the mistress of this big new property he was building or at the very least getting access to his perceived massive bank balance!

I hated being trapped in the snackette and hated being a snack bar assistant all day, but at least it took my mind off watching a half-finished building with no work in progress. Watching sand grow is a kind of imprisonment when you have no way of influencing outcomes. It was during my time at the snackette that I began to get a real insight into the way local minds worked. By now my ear was becoming more attuned to the local creolese dialect, so I could understand more of what was being said. I overheard many conversations between the staff which they did not think I understood. It was here that I learned that there was a lot of rivalry among black people in the village. They resented one of their own becoming successful. Bryan was envied since he was making a lot of money as manager of Edwin's snackette. Edwin's mother, Taa, resented Bryan as she had wanted to be allowed to sell stuff for herself in the shop. She believed by virtue of being Edwin's mother, she had a right to do this over Bryan. She had been feeding stories to Edwin about Bryan "tekkin' he eye pass Edwin" but Edwin ignored this because he was aware of his mother's bias.

He wanted to retain control over the income from his investment which would have been impossible with his mother involved. Black villagers resented anyone coming back from overseas and running a successful business in their midst. To this extent they were prepared to boycott the businesses by walking a mile further up the road to the next village to buy their goods at the shop of an Indo-Guyanese and pay higher prices for it rather than shop nearer in a "white" black person's shop and get the goods cheaper. This kind of resentment explained why most of our customers at the snackette were of East Indian origin from other villages, rather than the black Afro-Guyanese locals living in the village itself. How could you run a successful business in this kind of environment which defied normal economics?

Rumour, nevertheless, is usually founded in fact and we soon became aware of stories of Bryan's children having three or four hundred dollars to spend at school. This was not only causing some of the jealous remarks from the local have-nots but also suggestive that some misuse of snackette profits was going on and people in the know were trying to warn us about it. It prompted Edwin to look more carefully at the accounts Bryan had presented to us. He spotted repetitions and inconsistencies which made no sense. There was also the continual cash-flow problem which Bryan seemed to have. He never had enough money for raw materials or stock replenishment and kept coming down to ask Edwin for some cash to buy chicken, groceries or crates of drink.

"You should be saving the takings money to buy that stock and it should be covering it and still making a profit. If you cannot do that you are running the business at a loss," Edwin said, flatly refusing to give him any more of our fast disappearing cash. We had a meeting with him and Lorraine about it. They had no answers and clearly did not expect to have their accounts scrutinised so closely. We allowed them the dignity of pleading ignorance of proper record keeping methods. It might have been their employees that had made the arithmetical mistakes. Edwin suggested that I not only teach them what to do, but check their records against the takings and receipts daily, so that we could nip any mistakes in the bud and have steady improvement. From that day on I became a mental slave of record books, calculators and receipt checking. Every day there was a discrepancy and a problem that needed getting to the bottom of. Every day I spent hours puzzling over the records to spot where the missing money for that day must have gone. Every day, I had to sit down with Lorraine and confront her with the findings and suggest a remedy to prevent a recurrence.

"Why me?" I thought. "I hate doing this sort of work," but I knew our survival depended on making the money we had invested grow some returns instead of shrinking and disappearing. Edwin was clearly not going to bother to check. His solution was to get angry and sack everyone in turn until he found someone who could do it properly. That might work in other places but I could see that it would not work in Guyana because we would run out of resources before we found anyone who could or would do it properly. I believed that all this teaching would be taken on board so we could expect them to follow our example and instructions without such interference in future.

Chapter 6

The Vultures

The pastures surrounding the village were common grazing for a variety of stock animals kept by local villagers as a way of banking their savings. There were no commercial banks apart from one or two in Georgetown and New Amsterdam and most villagers could not afford to travel to these places. Unless they had overseas relatives sending back regular amounts, or they were one of the few lucky adults in employment, they spent their entire lives within their own village or moving between the nearest two or three villages either side of their own. There was no need to travel. They did not demand much out of life so their needs were basic and could be met by their immediate environment. If they came into a sum of money somehow, they would buy a sheep or a goat or a few chickens which would roam freely in their unfenced yards and out into the neighbours' and to the pasture beyond in search of grazing during the day. These would return to be penned up under their house at dusk. Small boys in the family would have the job of rounding them up and searching for any strays. Inevitably there would be squabbles between neighbours when one accused the other of stealing one of their "stocks" because it had gone missing.

I was recovering from my previous day's ordeal at customs, sitting at the top of the steps in the late afternoon, looking out on this pastoral scene. The grass was scrubby and uneven with thick tussocks of longer coarse blades standing out above the shorter scrubby bits. Here and there were the clumpy shrubs of 'carrion crow bush' with their distinctive yellow candle-head flowers. Cows were scattered all over the pasture munching away the afternoon, some of them wading deep into the drainage channels that fringed the road in order to graze the sedges that locals called 'bisi-bisi' grass. Ronnie was standing at the side of a nearby trench throwing a large cast-net into the water. He did this every afternoon to catch his evening meal. Moments like these were calming ones that I loved. What did it matter if the officials in Georgetown were incompetent and inefficient haters of white people? I could avoid them by staying here in this haven of tranquillity among my husbands' people who would now be my people also. It was rough and basic but that did not seem to matter in moments like these. One day, when we had finished the house, we would have living conditions that were more comfortable and would be able to provide employment for those around us who wanted it. We could inspire them to want to work if they saw what one of their own "sons of the soil" had achieved. He had come back to his home village to help develop it. They too would want to follow his example but do it in their own country.

I looked up into the sky above the distant animals and saw some large brownish-black birds circling overhead. One of them swooped down and alighted on a brown lump in the grass. I realised it must be a flock of vultures who had just found a dead sheep or calf to peck at. The birds landed one by one and joined in the feast. They picked and picked at the flesh of the tiny carcass until it was completely bare and the white bones caught the light of the setting sun. What they may have left, I thought would not be there by morning, as the thousands of ants swarming in the anthills around it would waste no time in stripping them as clean as the lizard bones at my feet.

It was always at dusk that visitors came to call at Taa's house. This afternoon was no exception. An elderly blind man led by a young girl slowly passed through the gate and made their way up the steps to where I was sitting. Taa had already called Edwin to come out to see the visitors.

"Ya know is who?" she asked Edwin when the two reached the top of the stairs and settled on the extra stools she brought out. Edwin looked quizzically at them but could offer no identification. "Is Crystal Lowe and she father, Jamesie".

"Crystal!" Edwin said in genuine delight. Then turning to me, "Jane, Crystal was my class mate at Hopetown Primary School when I was 8 or 9 years old. She and I used to dance square-dance together and everyone said she was my girlfriend!" I laughed at the thought and exchanged greetings with them. Then I sat and listened as Edwin acquainted himself with their doings in Guyana over the previous forty five years since he left, and how blindness had come upon Jamesie due to his diabetes. He was now totally dependent on Crystal. After an hour of this catching up, it became clear that they had come to ask us for some financial help, because "Tings very rough here in Guyana" and Jamesie needed medicine which he could not afford to buy. Edwin took pity as he always did on cases of hardship. Before they left, he found the twenty thousand dollars they had asked for and they went away very grateful for his generosity.

46

It was barely a week later when Crystal returned to ask for a second instalment the same size as the first. Edwin again obliged and thought that was the last of it until he got a third visit and request not long after. He had to refuse this time explaining that he could not afford to keep giving help now. We had to pay the builders and for materials.

November had come and gone. My container with all our new furniture had been delivered as promised but we had no house yet so it had to be stored in the same place as our other container load. The loan still had not materialised from the bank. We had had to use up more of our shrinking pool of cash to cover the enormous expense of paying for a private hire car to bring a Mr Carter, surveyor for the bank, on a return journey from his home in Georgetown only for him to tell us that the builders had not put enough pillars to support the weight of the building and that they would have to double the number before he would agree to recommend the bank lend us the money. This of course meant not only twice the planned expense on concrete, but also double the expense on Mr Carter, as he would have to make a second visit to check that we had complied. Word came back from our lumber supplier in Bushlot that no Purple-heart wood was available anywhere at present, so there was a further hold-up. All in all it was a depressing picture as Christmas loomed and we began writing our Christmas cards to post overseas.

The snackette staff was very excited about Christmas and began dropping hints about a grand New Year Function which sounded like a good business idea to bring in revenue, so Edwin agreed. More immediately, the idea of a grand fun-day was mooted. Advertising on the radio to bring in customers from distant villages all seemed the right way to maximise the returns. Bryan would organise that. Edwin had brought from England many items such as tea sets and large toys that could serve as attractive raffle prizes. He planned out games and fun-sport competitions that would keep a crowd on the premises so they would want to buy the food, ice-creams and drinks. Then news came from Bryan that the ice cream machine had broken down. He would get his friend Patrick from Georgetown to bring two technicians down to Berbice to fix it because there was no one local who had the expertise. They did not waste time in doing so, but it was at a cost of twenty two thousand Guyana dollars which was more than two months turnover at the snackette never mind profit. The machine had better not break down again as it was completely uneconomic to repair. The pressure was on to make the money back from the forth-coming fun-day and think of imaginative ways to increase the profits. Meanwhile, the money had to be got from our personal reserves as did the extra stocks that would be needed for the fun day. The electricity supply had been off more than on since we arrived in the country and Bryan told us that we really needed a generator at the snackette so that drinks could be kept cold and we could sell ice. His reasoning was that when everyone else was in darkness, the sound of a generator going at the snackette would draw everyone from the neighbourhood to the place that had lights and music and so they would spend their money on drinks and food all evening. This also seemed to make sense and appeared to be borne out in practice when we gave him one of the generators we had brought from England that really had been intended for our house. The snackette had priority as it was our income, so while we sat at Taa's house in the darkness, Bryan and his family had light, music and a fridge.

Being very ambitious, Bryan was easily dissatisfied with his status quo. Within a short while of operating with our new generator, he began to complain about its shortcomings. It had broken down. He had a friend, Benjie, who had a Lister generator for sale. This was a much bigger and more powerful one than the little one we had supplied. Lister was a very good British make. It was arranged that he would bring it that evening to the snackette for us to see. We went up from Taa's house at about five thirty, so there was about an hour of daylight left. The forecourt was full of people sitting at the painted blue wooden tables drinking and eating. Benjie was already there, next to a massive cast iron relic resembling Stephenson's rocket. It looked about a hundred years old. He had at least made the effort to paint it in bright green gloss paint.

"Can you start it up so we can see that it works?" said Edwin.

"If ya get gasoline to put in den we can",

"How much do you want for it?"

"Tree hundred and sixty tousand dollar"

"You're a bit of a comedian aren't you?" Edwin laughed out loud. "I think the best place for that thing is in a museum. Sorry to disappoint you mate, but I'm not paying that sort of money for a piece of scrap metal that I can't even see working. Look at it! The exhaust is off. There's oil leaking out all over the concrete here. It's made a mess so I've got to clean it all up so my customers don't get it all over their shoes."

"But it cost me plenty to get it here. Bryan tell me ya want it," said Benjie, clearly disgruntled.

"Well you better get it out of here with all these other bits of junk as quick as you can" snapped Edwin in a tone menacing enough to produce quick results. "Don't bring anyone else like that to me, Bryan. I want all this mess cleaned up by the time I come back in the morning or there'll be trouble." With that we left and walked back to Taa's in the dark. We sat in the porch and sang together for a couple of hours. As we lay in bed that night, a rat scuttled round the top of the wall under the eaves. It was so bold as to be unperturbed when I shone a torch in its face. It defiantly looked down its pointed snout at us as we lay there in bed as if to say, "What you strange creatures doing in my house?"

The next day, Bryan came down to tell us that he had got our generator fixed, adding that Benjie had sent his machine to the antiques fair in Trinidad. I swallowed this at the time but in retrospect realise that it must have been the start of a long tradition of bullshit. Having come from a sheltered, educational world where truth and straight talking was all I knew, this fantasy world in Guyana was alien to me and at first I was a victim of it. After a time I came to see that Edwin was as good at dishing the bullshit out as receiving it. My first experience of this was a day or two later when we went on a visit to the local office of the Ministry of Agriculture. Edwin had intended to see a Mr Charles but predictably, he was out when we arrived so we were entertained by a group of Indo-Guyanese gentlemen. The mission had been to establish how he could get the promised compensation (in the form of alternative land) from the government for a piece of Edwin's land that they had confiscated in the late eighties in order to put in a drainage canal for neighbouring farmers' rice fields. In the course of the conversation it became apparent that they would be more favourable to him if he was going to use it to grow rice. I soon found myself aggrandised by Edwin as an agricultural expert based on what he had observed of my personal efforts on our farm. The men immediately directed their technical cross-questioning towards me.

"I have a lot of experience growing vegetables in England as I come from a farming family," I explained, "but I know nothing about rice growing so would like to learn so we can do it properly."

"We can take care of that" they said in the distinctive Indo-Guyanese twang that I was not used to hearing thus far. "You can go with a party of local rice farmers to region 3 next week. There is a lecture about rice cultivation methods you can attend." It was agreed. The following Thursday, we were picked up on the road at 6.50 a.m. by a lonely jeep. The three hour drive took us over the Demerara Harbour Bridge, the longest floating bridge in the world (at that time). The agriculture ministry field-worker who met us on arrival at a rice mill took us on an informative guided tour of the mill as well as a number of farmers' rice fields nearby. Passing through the bustling free port of Parika, we learned that contraband goods from Venezuela and Brazil were sold there, but the visible trade we witnessed was an abundance of locally grown tropical fruit such as pineapples, melons and ginger. I bought some ginger tubers to try and grow on our farm even though advised that they would not grow well in Berbice. They needed the pegasse soil only found around Parika.

Dr Gopal Singh gave a clear and practical lecture about rice cultivation methods with techniques aimed at the eradication of "rogue red rice" which seemed to be a major problem for commercial growers. I scribbled furiously into my notebook and felt for an hour as if I was back at university. I even asked a few intelligent questions at the end which took the Doctor by surprise as all the other farmers who accompanied us remained silent. Clearly he was not used to having a thinking audience. I felt I had learned a lot and thanked him for that. Rice growing depended on having a tractor, however. We did not have one but Edwin said he intended to get one when we had finished our house. Before the long journey home we sat for a couple of hours in a local rum shop with the East-Coast farmers who had attended the lecture. There we were treated to an insight into the genial but inebriated rum-shop culture of local Indo-Guyanese men. These farmers and our companion travellers were all sizing us up with a good deal of cynicism. What black man ever came back from overseas and actually grew rice? Indo-Guyanese believed it to be their preserve. Black landowners in recent decades rented their rice lands out to Indian neighbours to do the farming because black people did not have tractors. They did not expect any rice growing to materialise on our farm, and time would eventually prove them to be right.

With December, came Norma the fisherwoman from the waterside. It was quite a surprise visit as we had almost forgotten about her with all the recent house and snackette problems. Perhaps we would have been reminded sooner had the promised fish supply materialised when we moved permanently into the village, but there had not been so much as a sprat. We had inquired on a beach walk back in August and been told that she had left the village and although disappointed not to see the flourishing fishing boat that Edwin had given her the money for last year, we were sure her boys were out at sea in it so would catch up with them later. Norma was overjoyed to see us. Her broad smile dissecting her face like a cutlass slash in a watermelon, she opened her arms to embrace Edwin just as if he were a long lost relative.

"I so glad ta see you and de mistress come back to Hopetown. Jane, gal, ya lookin' good. When ya goin' back?"

"We're not going back this time," I stated. "We now live in Guyana for good. This is our home."

"Ya does like Guyana den?" she said.

"Oh yes. It's very beautiful and not at all cold like England. I don't like the cold."

She chattered away for a while, filling Edwin in with the details of where she had been in the last few months, looking after a sick relative in East Coast Demerara.

"We came to find you a few months ago because we wanted to see how you were getting along with the fishing boat," he said.

"Oh!" she cried, "Dem Indian boy in Bushlot did tief out de seine, so me can't fish na more, da's why me come ta see ya, If y'all can gi' me a brace to get a new seine." By now I could understand enough Creolese to realise that "tief" meant "steal", and that a seine was a fishing net, so her net had been stolen from the boat and she wanted money (a brace) from us to replace it.
"You mean that Indians from Bushlot come all the way up the beach to Hopetown to steal your nets off the boats? Why? Didn't you chase them off when you saw them?" I asked.

"De boat leff at Bushlot beach na Hopetown," she explained. "De bridge at Hopetown waterside gone. Dem people fetch out de wood fo' burn. Ya can get to de sea by Bushlot bridge alone." I wondered what had happened to the Hopetown bridge we used when we visited last year. It had been very rickety but you could still get across. Now it appeared that certain residents of the village had decided to take the wood for their cooking fires rather than go further afield to search for fuel. Going down to the beach was of little importance to them, but they had no thought for those who wanted to fish in the sea.

Edwin said he was sorry but he could not spare any more money at the moment because we had to pay for materials to finish the house but he hoped she could get the boat working soon as he wanted to use her services when we were up and running to give boat ride experiences for tourists visiting us. We would also want plenty of fish to eat ourselves and for our guests so his investment in her fishing boat would hopefully grow into a thriving business with regular custom from us. Norma seemed to like the idea but was clearly disappointed to be walking away empty handed.

Work was progressing slowly on the house and we did what we could to speed it along. As well as working in the garden and doing regular stints at the snackette including their weekly accounts, I helped Edwin to do what labouring we could on the building site. It raised a few eyebrows among the workers when we cleared up a lot of the materials they had scattered in a disorganised mess. They did not like seeing us do physical work that they were supposed to do. It was a surprise for them to see that we were not helpless wimps but able to lift heavy steel rods and dense planks of hardwood for several hours until the job was done. I think also it seemed to them an unnecessary waste of energy to tidy materials such as these. Edwin's motivation, however, was to cut down the waste that was going on. He got very angry at watching this "lack of common sense and waste," as he called it. On being told yet again that work could not continue because the nails had run out, he complained to Pappa Dan.

"I'm not going to keep spending thousands of dollars on nails when they just drop them on the ground and leave them there. Look at the floor! There are hundreds of good nails all over the place!"

Pappa Dan in turn echoed the complaint to the workers. "It waste, sheer waste," he repeated, sucking his teeth and shaking his head in his usual genial tone of voice, as he shuffled off back to his part in the process, shaping and deciding on the angle of a balustrade spindle to support the veranda roof. The old man was a craftsman trained during the colonial period. The boys he employed were not being supervised or taught in any particular way. They were just given instructions and left to get on with it while the old man did the tricky bits.

It was by working alongside them doing little jobs like tidying up or picking up the hundreds of nails they dropped and left on the ground that I began to notice how it was happening. Youngsters did not have to pay for materials themselves. It was nothing for them to cut up a large piece of wood to get a small piece, and to cut it out of the middle of a plank without using a ruler or a tape measure. I watched them guessing at the size they wanted. They would saw it or cut it with a sharp cutlass, and then when they found it was too long, cut it down a bit until it fitted. On more than one occasion, I saw them doing this and cutting too much off, leaving the piece too short, so they would go and get another piece to start the process again. The scraps were littered around and none of them thought to search among the scraps for a suitable sized piece in the first place. Later in the day, Taa would send over one of the small children that always hung around her back door, to pick up all the scraps of wood, put them in an old rice bag and carry them back for her to burn on her mud-oven fireplace. When Edwin realised this was happening he was really cross.

"That's good wood that the carpenters can use for the fine work on the house instead of cutting up a great big new plank," he yelled. "If you want firewood, there are plenty of old branches that have dropped off the trees or coconut branches and husks you can use for cooking. Or come to that we can buy a gas bottle so you can use that cooker that's standing there," he told his mother when she came across in person to scavenge. Taa gave him one of her old-fashioned looks and said defiantly, "Is notin' but scrap wood!"

"What I saw going in that bag was big enough for a window frame. When you pay for it then you can use it on the fire but as long as *I'm* paying for it, it stays over there until I bring over the real scraps that no one can use," he argued. From this time onwards, he and Taa were always at loggerheads and he was not going to give in to her on any point.

Watching 14 year-old Carwyn making a mess of yet another piece of wood, I asked him,

"Why don't you measure it before you cut it? You all have tape measures Uncle Edwin brought for you to do the work?" In a gesture of compliance, he went and picked up the measure from the tool tray. As I watched him, I could see he did not know what to do with it. " You need to hold it here where you want the piece to fit," I showed him "and then take the same mark and put it on the piece you want to cut, like that." I said, marking the board with a pencil from the tool tray. "Then you cut along that pencil line." He seemed grateful for the guidance and set about cutting the plank along the mark. Then he tried it out in place. He was happy to see it fit perfectly. After nailing it in position, he tried the next one for himself. This time it did not fit and was too short. He looked disappointedly at it. I asked him to show me how he measured it. It was during this process that I realised he could not read the markings on the tape measure. They meant nothing to him. He could read the numbers and know the units of measure, but he had no idea of the concept of counting the divisions in between them. I tried several times to get this through to him but in the end realised it wasn't getting anywhere. It was something he should have learned in school but had not and it was too late now. Lindy got round the problem by making a mark on a long stick and using that as his own measure so he made fewer mistakes. I discussed it all with Edwin that evening and he resolved to get Carwyn put onto general labouring, not carpentry. However this led us onto an evening of enquiry about the sad and sorry state of the local education system.

"Teacher Caro" paid us a visit that very night. Taa introduced her to us as the music and maths teacher at Fort Wellington Community High School. We greeted her warmly, and Edwin said "Jane's a teacher, she does music too." On hearing this, she gave me a withering look. It was obvious he had put her back up.

"My main subject is history though," I reassured her. "I'm not qualified to teach music, it's just a hobby of mine." She purred with relief. I was no longer such a threat. Our conversation turned to the poor standard of education we had observed in Taa's household and among our workers. Edwin wanted to know why the education system in Guyana was so bad when in the 1950s it had been the best in the Caribbean. He blamed it on Independence and the dictatorship of the late President Burnham when all the colonial books were burnt and new books promoting the cult of Burnham distributed in the schools along the lines of the cult of Mao. This seemed to go over Caro's head a bit but she nodded and then added that the headmaster Mr Maloney was a terrible man who was never at school because he was always out running his own car as a taxi.

"De school don't get no book an' when it rain de roof leak and all de student get wet" she complained. "We na get de result in de exam. De children need book"

"We have lots of boxes of books that were donated by schools in England and from my school in Dubai. Some of them are complete class sets of English books" I said.

"Ya get any matematic book?" asked Caro with obvious self-interest.

"No I'm afraid not, but I have lots of maths worksheets. You can have them for your school if you think they would be suitable but they are mainly meant for primary children. I'll show them to you when we have found the box they are in." She nodded, pleased at the thought of a possible teaching aid.

"Jane wants to help teach when we're settled in" said Edwin.

"Well she can gi' English lesson to me children" Caro told him, looking straight at me.

"Of course," I said, willingly. "How old are they?"

"De twins be eight year old an' Alicia be six next burday. Me send dem to ya Sunday afternoon?"

"No problem," I said and so it was agreed. Meanwhile, the subject of the primary school concert came up and it was arranged for us to go to it.

The house was quiet on Sunday, Edwin had gone up to the snackette to meet with the West Berbice Football Association about a tournament he was organising for them. Taa was at church with her Sunday school. It was a good opportunity for me to go across to the building site and have a look for some of those school books. The last few weeks had been very wet with torrential rain falling every night and even though it was sunny and hot during the day, it was also very humid and oppressive. There was mud everywhere. I struggled to pick a dry path on tufts of grass to get out of Taa's gateway onto the dam, as the street was called. The cows in particular had churned up the mud as they herded in and out of the gate morning and night. Their great weight pushed their hooves deep into the soft alluvium tearing up the turf and burying it in a squelching mess of a pool. I made giant strides from one higher dry patch to another. It was good exercise but one which left my calves and thighs coated with mud. It got worse when I reached the street corner where the dam dipped lower and became wider as there was a sea of hoof-pits and dung splats to cross. This was a major livestock highway to the pastures at the back-dam and it was level with the gate of our new sheep pen where Edwin's prize ram now resided along with its harem of ewes. I stood on my tiny island studying the terrain before I committed myself to a route. I could almost feel an audience of tiny eyes peering at me from hidden crevices in the neighbours' houses, waiting to witness the amusing sight of the white lady slipping headlong into the mire.

Today they would be disappointed. At last I made it to the makeshift coconut branch fence surrounding our site and unlocked the padlock.

The wooden door sealing off the ground floor of our main building had a sturdy English mortise lock. I unlocked it and entered the gloom. The boxes we had unloaded months ago were all underneath the ones from Dubai that had arrived in November. I searched around in the dim dappled light from the airbricks that topped the walls and the streak of sun streaming through the doorway to see if I could locate a box of primary school readers that I could use to help Caro's girls. Here was one that looked promising. I shifted the crates from on top of it so I could open it. No, it was a set of secondary geography books. I was horrified to notice black stains and mildew growing on the pages of the book I had pulled out from the side of the cardboard box. How did that happen? As I tried to lift the box nearer to the doorway to see, the whole soaking bottom of the box dropped out. Further inspection revealed that all the boxes resting on the concrete floor were sucking up water through the foundations which clearly had no damp course. I would have a nasty surprise for Edwin when he came down from his meeting. We would have to get all these boxes off the floor for now to prevent further damage. Then we would have to find out why there was no damp course to the building. For the moment, I managed to find a box with appropriate books for my reading lesson and selected a couple with nice bright pictures and simple words.

"Inside," called out a little voice from somewhere outside. This was the local way of asking "Is anyone at home?" I went to the doorway and looked across to the gate to see three little girls and a couple more tiny tots huddled around the gate.

"Hello" I said, smiling at them, "You must be Roberta and Reanna," I said to the twins, who nodded shyly, "and you are Alecia," I said to the smaller girl, "but who is this?" A tiny boy with a very large head looked up at me in wonder.

"Booker-T" giggled Alecia. She seemed full of beans and not at all shy. I locked the door shut behind me and opened the gate to let them into the yard. Then we climbed up the stairs onto the half completed veranda and I sat them down on the floor beside me and chatted to them for a while about themselves and school. Then we got down to business. I tried each one of them in turn with one of the books. Their reading skills were severely limited. The elder twins could read only the basic words. They had no phonic skills with which to tackle new words. Pictures were not always helpful clues as their vocabulary was different. It was no use pointing at the picture of a roof to help them understand that word in the story, because the local Creolese word for roof was "zinc", since a roof was just zinc sheets. They did not understand the word "wind" because they used "breeze". Even a simple nursery rhyme story like "three little pigs" was full of such problems. The definite article "the", locally pronounced as "ze", illustrates the scale of problems encountered on a single page. Phonics would not be a straightforward solution. In one of the simplest stories I could find we soon came up against the word "autumn" which of course is a season that does not exist in Guyana, so the concept was alien to them before any decoding could begin. I found myself telling them in the simplest terms about the four seasons in cooler climates and realising that they could hardly begin to understand what I was talking about. We were not going to make much reading progress with these books. I would have to just talk to them and answer their questions about the pictures we were looking at. I asked them to tell me about things I pointed to in the pictures so I could learn from them what was in their vocabularies. In fact this was more of a lesson for me than for them.

The afternoon flew by. Suddenly Edwin called up to us as he passed by on his way down from the main road. I said goodbye to the children and sent them home so I could show Edwin the damp damaged boxes. Together we sorted out some spare blocks and boards to raise all the boxes that had been on the floor and rearranged all the damaged crates to a point near the door where we could see what could be rescued and what would have to be destroyed. Thank God all the new furniture and clothes arrived last and were on top of all the other boxes. We put the wooden and chipboard pack-flat kitchen on top of the baths and toilet suites, which would not be harmed by the damp. The other boxes and crates of furniture and household equipment were carefully arranged off the ground in the centre of the room and the sports equipment at the back. "We better get in touch with the schools to come and take these books off our hands." said Edwin, "Shit! Why on earth haven't they put a damp course in this floor?"

The fun day at the snackette was a roaring success. The forecourt was heaving with people that had come from other villages, miles away. They were spilling out onto the wide verges outside the gates of the premises where Edwin and Bryan had roped off an area for quoits, various potted sports and darts. The dartboard was a novelty, as no one had ever seen one before and this was something adults not keen to exert themselves could participate in. The afternoon's activities continued into the evening. Bryan sold completely out of drinks and ice cream and had to fetch more drinks from a nearby supplier. The last customers went away at around midnight and we helped the cashing up and calculation of total takings. Edwin was pleased. There was a business potential here after all, provided there were interesting activities and it was well advertised and organised. He was not so happy when it was calculated that the cost of the radio adverts swallowed up most of the profits. No more radio adverts was his edict to Bryan. We would advertise by word of mouth and posters in future. Bryan's preoccupation with celebrity among his peers coloured his judgement about what made business sense. He was playing the business tycoon without any idea of a realistic budget and that was easy to do when it was someone else's money.

Over the next few days we had further initiation into the local mind set and the difficulties of improving educational opportunities with a view to sustainable development. First of all there was the local 'youth club'. Wilfrid Barry was the prime mover in this. He had apparently tried to get permission from the local council to let them have the pasture behind Taa's house as a recreation ground for sport. Unfortunately this was historically designated as a burial ground so Wilfrid's own father-in-law had protested and blocked the move. Edwin soon became entangled in the street politics of the youth club. We visited 'Sister Derrice' the elderly retired teacher, to let her know about the books we wanted to give to her school. She warned Edwin that Mr Barry was "a very wicked man" who wanted to stop the youth club which she said she set up. It was not long before we realised that certain villagers were blacklisted by the community owing to their past record of political allegiance. Mr Barry, like Mr Maloney the headmaster of the Fort Wellington Community High School, was demonised because he was a "PPP supporter" (People's Progressive Party) and had opposed both the Burnham government and its successor, under Hoyte, which was PNC (People's National Congress). PPP supporters tended to be regarded as "Indian lovers" either because they were in a mixed marriage, as with Maloney, whose wife was Amerindian, or Franklin Bowman, whose wife was an Indian from Bushlot or because they worked with Indians and were not born in the village, as in the case of Wilfrid. The PPP purported to be in favour of democracy as opposed to Burnham's dictatorship. I began to see how tribal the people were. Black people from Hopetown were PNC. They expected Edwin to be PNC too, but the PPP supporters tried their best to win Edwin over into their camp. He, sensibly, resisted all their attempts, now and later, to get him to join any political party, saying that he was just there to help his country and that he wasn't interested in politics. This pleased no one, yet prevented anyone from being able to use his politics as a stick to beat him with. No one could understand this stance because the local way of life necessitated that you joined a political party to gain advantage in your career or business. You could not survive without it. If you tried to, as we did, you were in for a rough ride. The only reason we could survive was because we already "owned" our land and our source of income was not from, or dependent on, the government.

A special youth club meeting was arranged for our benefit. The last one had been over a year ago. A handful of local youth and adults assembled in the empty downstairs room of Edwin's brother's house which had been made available for the purpose. Sister Derrice, Wilfrid Barry and members of their families filed in. They set great store by electing officers to the youth club before anything could be discussed. Wilfrid and Derrice, Teacher Caro, Mr Bruce her father and a few others were clearly interested in holding official titles as chairman, president, secretary and treasurer. It seemed from their discussions that they expected funds to be coming into their hands through this club. (Their official position would give them access to such funds, perhaps for their own purposes). Edwin and I were introduced to the group and asked to give a talk to the youth gathered there. Edwin gave his much anticipated proposals to start a sports club with lots of activities such as football, athletics, basketball, volleyball, cricket, tug-of-war and so on and that we had brought the equipment needed to do these things. He had the expertise to coach and organise these sports for them and show them how to do it properly as he had worked at the highest level in the UK. They received this news with enthusiasm. Edwin said he wanted action not words, so he didn't want to sit around in meetings making plans for things that never happened. He would make a start by organising an obstacle race the next day for those interested. They wanted to know what an obstacle race was, and when they found out, seemed especially keen to try out this new aspect of sport. He fixed a time they said they would be able to attend.

Then it was my turn to speak. I briefly explained how I had trained to teach in England and spent a decade teaching big children in English secondary schools before I was lucky enough to get a post teaching in Dubai where I had been for the previous three and a half years. I explained why I had liked living and working there and that I had only left because of marrying Edwin and moving to Guyana. The adults and older ones were extremely interested in that. When I threw it open to questions, they had quite a few to ask. They found it particularly strange to know that the schoolgirls in Dubai were not allowed to mix with boys at school or in recreation. They also wanted to know why the books had to be censored before they could be used in the school there. A tall, softly spoken girl wanted to know if I could give her English lessons and some of the others wanted to be included. I said I would hold a class for them in our unfinished building and we agreed on a day and time when they could come. The meeting closed. It was then that Wilfrid Barry introduced the tall girl to me as his daughter, Tracy.

The following morning, we went over to check on the building in progress. While there, I opened up the store room and pulled the damaged boxes outside into the sun and began to spread out the books in the hope that they would dry out. Some of them were too far gone. The pages were welded together and tore as I tried to peel them open to dry. It was heart breaking knowing that these had been brand new books in beautiful condition when they were packed a few months ago. Now they were stained with mildew or the printed colours had bled into each other. It seemed to diminish the gift if they were in this state. I tossed the completely unusable ones into one of the empty rotted boxes for burning and leafed through those that could be rescued. With a damp cloth I wiped off the worst of the stains, setting them out all over the steps and bannisters in the hot sun and breeze. They soon began to dry out. There were also many that had escaped damage altogether so I sorted them into sets and put them into some new dry boxes I had got that morning from the snackette. Edwin had been at the snackette with the youth club athletes since lunchtime but had just got back when Sister Derrice arrived about four in the afternoon to look at them. She was most impressed with the number and quality but implored me not to give them to the schools.

"Ze children does use dem fo' toilet paper" she explained in lowered tones, her eyes looking down at her feet. "Why y'all don't keep de book an' set up a library fo' de village. We does need a library."

"Oh we are going to do that," I said, "but there are so many books of the same sort here. There are class sets that a teacher could use to teach lessons from so that every child in the class can have a copy of the same book that the teacher has. We need to give those sets of books to the schools and just keep the books we have only one or two copies of for our library." I could see that she did not really understand what I meant because she said that the school would share the books with other schools in the region. At length she said she would tell the headmaster of Bushlot School about them and arrange for someone to collect them.

"All we ask for is a letter of thanks from the school to let us know they received them safely," said Edwin. He confided in me afterwards that this was to make sure they reached the school and did not get sold off by the person conveying them.

Edwin was frowning after Derrice left. "What's the problem?" I asked, "You seem a bit annoyed about something",

"I'm pissed off about the youth club obstacle race. Only five of the athletes that said they would be in the team turned up, of which Ogden was one! I specifically asked them what time they would be able to do it so that it suited everybody and they still don't turn up or even send a message. They're all a waste of space. I just had a load of little kids there, so I got out the high jump kit and they all had a little competition. Ogden won it, obviously. He's bigger and older. There's no point in presenting medals for anything like that. They can't get recognised for just turning up for what was more or less a high jump practice. In any case where's the glory in winning when you're up against someone half your age? They don't deserve my expertise. I didn't come here to be a babysitter for a load of little kids." I tried to reason away his anger and frustration. He was not in the mood to listen.
"I'm gonna complain to the Sports people in Georgetown." His cockney accent was always stronger when he was annoyed.

"What good will that do?" I asked.

"The A.A.A in Georgetown is supposed to know if one of their registered clubs is functioning properly and as far as I can see it, this one is not," he grumbled. Until he said that, I had forgotten that the "Officials" elected at the youth club meeting we had attended had, in their long rambling speeches, indicated that the club was supposed to be the local branch of the Amateur Athletics Association if it was looking to compete at a national level in sports competitions. Edwin, having been a member of the National Sports Council in England and the National Decathlon Coach for the United Kingdom before moving to Guyana, had expected to be able to be able to train athletes from his own village to reach an international standard under his coaching. He had hoped to be able to do it through this youth club. Hopes of this were now dashed as far as he was concerned.

"The problem is," I said, "that from what I've seen, their educational level is so low that they don't understand the importance of reliability. Look at the workers! It's not surprising that they don't know how to measure or read and write if they don't turn up at school, and when they do, the teachers aren't there because they're doing their chores at home. The headmaster doesn't even know his teachers are missing let alone his pupils, because he's off driving his taxi."

"It's hopeless" said Edwin.

"Things can change," I said, "if they're taught properly and by teachers who set a better example. Perhaps I can do that when we get settled in."

"This place will never change!"

"Don't be such a pessimist" I told him but I was soon put to the test myself. When Monday came I got everything ready for my class for the youth club, sat on the steps of the house with it all at the agreed time and waited and waited and waited. Not a soul appeared. After an hour I packed up and went back over to Edwin at Taa's house.

"I knew it," he said, "That's it. They're all hopeless every one of them, but at least you did try." I was not ready to write off everyone as hopeless like him, but I could not understand why not a single person had showed up, especially since they had asked me to do this. I was annoyed that I had wasted my time getting resources and a plan ready and then had been stood up.

We voiced our feelings to Bryan up at the snackette over supper. Perhaps by way of explanation Bryan told us that Taa had been inventing bad things about me and spreading them around in the village. Edwin was upset.

"It's all lies. Jane's a lovely person. She couldn't harm a fly" he said. "She's my wife. My mother resents her presence because it means I'm not like her other sons, under her control."

"Before ya come back, Taa tellin' everyone dat she movin' into de big house an' she mekkin' de kitchen dis way and dat way," said Bryan.

"So that's why she was so insistent that we had the kitchen downstairs on the ground floor, underneath the rest of the house," I said. "The idea that the zinc roof should be sealed off from view with a wooden ceiling made her lose her temper one night, when we first came back, telling me that I don't know Guyana and we don't do things that way in Guyana. She kept insisting that the bats in the roof would make the boards rot like they did in the church roof. I know it's true that the bats will go in to the zinc at night, but they do that in her house anyway and because she doesn't have any ceiling, they fly straight in and out while you sit there, and when we're asleep and all the lights are off, they hang from the roof and their dung drops all over the chair seats and tables. I don't want my furniture to be covered in droppings every morning like hers is, especially if we're going to have overseas tourists staying with us." I added.

"Well it's our house not hers and we'll have it the way we want it" said Edwin.

Bryan seemed to understand our point of view. "Dey does get dis special sponge ya can put on de edge of de zinc to keep de bat out," he advised, "I seen it in dem house in Linden."

"That sounds like a good idea" said Edwin, "I'll ask Pappa Dan if we can get some."

As we made our way back down the dam to Taa's house in pitch darkness, Edwin kept chewing over what we had been told. He kept asking me,

"Why doesn't my mother like you?" I could find no answer for him. I had done nothing to deserve her dislike as far as I could see. I had been very polite and respectful to her, I had gone out of my way to offer help but this had always been declined. I could only suspect that it was because I was "The other woman", not Edwin's first wife whom she had once met.

"No, that doesn't make sense because if she was so concerned about that why would she keep trying to set me up dates with girls from her church in the village?"

"Does she?" I asked, somewhat shocked. "Well I suppose that it's because I'm white. She wants you to have a black girl for a wife." He did not seem completely convinced as he kept going over the same questions until I stopped listening and started concentrating on where my feet were slithering in the slimy mud that we could not see. The lights in the few houses that fronted onto this street were all out due to the nightly power cut so it was impossible to see a dry foothold. The journey down this dam was especially treacherous in such conditions as there was a very deep drainage canal full of reeds and refuse on one side and the thought of accidentally sliding into it terrified me. Although we had a torch, the beam only lit up one step ahead. I had to depend on Edwin picking the path and me keeping up with his fast pace which I could not do. I had to keep asking him to slow down because the torch he held only illuminated his next step and not mine. Suddenly my foot slid deep into the soft warm slip half way up my calf. I gave up trying to avoid the puddles and just resigned myself to having to wash all the mud off my legs and feet when we finally reached the trench by the bridge into Taa's yard.

That night, as we lay in our rickety cot listening to the ducks scratching around on the zinc sheets over our heads, I felt more wretched than I can ever remember feeling. I could see no escape from this situation. I had a mother-in-law who hated me and was plotting ways of driving me off. I was perpetually filthy even after I washed and my legs were covered in angry red sores from the mosquito bites. All romance and sex had gone out of our marriage. Even if I had wanted to leave Edwin, which I did not, neither of us had the fare to get to Georgetown. There was no employment in the country for me, a white woman. My house in England had not yet sold owing to the recession and its market value was steadily dropping. Any equity from the sale would be swallowed up by mortgage arrears I had no income to prevent. All my worldly possessions were by now rotting away in a damp concrete cellar under a half built wooden house that there was no prospect of finishing because we did not have the money to do so. We could not borrow from the local banks because we did not yet own the land the house was standing on. The reason we were in this hole was because the builders did not have adequate building skills so if we did finish the house the finished product would be far from what I had originally envisaged. Why had I left that lovely school in Dubai with all the comforts of life I could wish for? Tears of desperation and unhappiness began to roll down my cheeks. Edwin's back was all I could see as I listened to the deep rhythmic breaths of his troubled sleep. We were imprisoned in a spartan cell in a community of unparalleled ignorance surrounded by vultures that only wanted to peck our eyes out and then strip our carcasses bare before leaving our bones white and bleached in the sun.

Chapter 7

The Prize Ram

As the rising sun shed rays of light on to Taa's front yard, Collis shooed Edwin's sheep over the bridge and onto the dam. We sat overlooking the procession. Among the flock strutted a splendid looking ram with the most enormous gonads. I marvelled at how it could walk with them dangling between its rear legs. It was the envy of the neighbourhood.

"That beast cost me twenty two thousand dollars," Edwin announced with a certain pride. "Dickie got it for me last year from someone at Lovely Lass village. It should produce a good crop of lambs this year and we'll eventually get the money back from selling its offspring." It sounded a reasonable assumption. Every day, Collis herded the animals out to the pasture at "the back-dam" and every afternoon at about four o'clock, he brought them back and penned them up in the thatched shelter next to our building plot. He was thirteen years old and had recently been withdrawn from school by his grandmother, Taa. In reality, he had been expelled. He had admitted to us that he had refused to sweep the school yard and for his insolence to Mr Maloney, his education had terminated. Edwin thought Taa had been wrong not to smooth things over with the headmaster, but she found it convenient to have Collis at home looking after the stocks and doing errands in the same way that every local family sacrificed the education of one of their younger children for this purpose. At night, we paid Hence, a watchman, to come and spend the night in the pen to guard the animals against theft. This was standard local practice for any kind of property that was distant from an inhabited dwelling. Most people kept their stocks under their own houses and thus guarded them without needing to pay out such wages, but there was not enough room in Taa's back yard for her cows, our cows, our donkeys and the sheep as well.

This was the sixth week that there had been no electricity supply at all. The rumour yesterday was that the Indians in Bushlot had sabotaged the main generator for the district and there was no spare part available so it had to be imported and that would take weeks. Today the explanation offered was that two Indians in Bushlot had been electrocuted trying to remove cable from the overhead wires that ran along the old railway line at the back-dam. I wondered what explanation would be offered tomorrow. The lack of current did not really bother anyone since they were without it so often. They organised their lives as their forefathers had done before such modern technology. Light at night was provided by a hurricane lamp or a flambeau (a small glass bottle of kerosene with a wick pulled out of the neck). They cooked on an open hearth made of mud or used a small kerosene burner. When the radios fell silent, entertainment reverted to sharing 'jumbie stories' in the darkness. You did not keep food in a fridge that was off more than on as it would waste. Food was cooked fresh and consumed the same day. No electrical home appliances were of any use.

Edwin had abandoned trying to charge up his electric razor and gone back to his old Gillette hand one. He sat next to me on the veranda with a calabash of hot water in his lap and a shaving mirror balanced on the sill in front of him.

"You deserve to be out of this situation as soon as possible," he said to me as he drew the blade across his soap lathered cheek. "I don't understand why my mother doesn't like you."

"No reason," I said but soon found myself being drawn into his persistent search for answers. It was wearing me down. He just could not accept irrational resentment or racism as an explanation.

"My place is with you and what is mine is yours," he concluded, "God, what can I do about all this?"

"Nothing," I said, "It's not your fault, just ignorance. It's not nice to be a victim of it, but I will just have to try and ignore it." Our conversation was interrupted by a clattering sound from the kitchen. I ran down to see what it was as Taa had gone out to church and no one else was at home. Lurking in the shadows, an opportunist cat dashed between my legs and fled into the yard. It had managed to open the door of the antiquated food safe and the remains of what had been someone's cooked 'breakfast' of rice flavoured with an orange coloured sauce was scattered all over the disintegrating linoleum floor. I did my best to clear up the mess and then went up to tell Edwin what had happened.

"Someone's going to be pretty angry when they come back and find they have no food to eat," I said. "It disturbs me to see that those children never get any fish or vegetables with their rice. No wonder they look so malnourished. It's not as if they don't have those things in abundance. The garden is full of beans and callaloo and there are plenty of fish for free in the trenches."

"It never used to be like that when I was a child," he complained. "I always had my fish or shrimps. My father made sure I helped to catch them with a gilgira right here in the pasture and he always made sure we had squash, ochro or callaloo. He used to grow a thing called nenwah like a long cucumber that we'd chip up and cook in with the shrimps."

I could understand why meat was a luxury. If anyone had chickens in the yard, they kept them for eggs not meat. Sheep, goats and cows, like poultry, were not eaten except for a special occasion. Goats and cows were milked but the supply was erratic as calves or kids were not separated from their mothers, so often drank it all before they could be milked, especially in the dry season. Fish, on the other hand, was plentiful and easy to catch, yet reserved for the adults in the house. Not much difference in attitude, I thought, from my mother's own childhood in the 1930s when she being the youngest was always served up with the parson's nose as her father was given the best of the Sunday roast chicken and the rest of the family got the remainder. They had no electricity, a well for their water and a bucket toilet in the back yard. Guyana in the 1990s was a bit like going back in time to pre-war England. I wondered how mum was, what she was doing, and whether my dad's multiple schlerosis had worsened. There were no telephones except in Georgetown and you had to wait in a long queue for several hours to book a call for very high charges that we could not afford. Most Guyanese reversed the charges when they called relatives in England but I could not inflict that burden on my parents who were both pensioners. I had written lots of long letters home but the replies were very few and far between and contained very little information. It was strange feeling so cut off from everyone and everything of my former life. This present existence in this unfamiliar culture was surreal but I would have to get used to it. I would have to make a future here that was better than the present. I strongly believed that Edwin and I had what it took to make a difference to this community and that is what kept me going.

The school concert was in the afternoon at two o'clock. I wanted to know why it was so early and during what ought to be lesson time. I discovered that only women went to the school concerts usually, so it was convenient for them to attend during the daytime since most of them did not work. Also, they feared going out at night when it was blackout and others could break into their homes unseen and steal their possessions. Grandmothers came in place of the few mothers who did have jobs. When we arrived, there was complete pandemonium. The assembled crowd had come there to catch up on the latest news. Edwin was the only grown man present in the barn-like hall. Wooden benches for the audience had been arranged like pews in a church facing a small stage at one end of the room. The deafening noise of chattering children echoed around the high pitched roof and the women supposed to be teachers had absolutely no control over the children or the public. The only reason we knew the show had started was the sight of a portly woman getting up at one side of the stage and ringing a little bell which no one seemed to take any notice of. A row of little children stood up on the stage each holding a page from an exercise book with a large letter drawn on it. As in turn they held up their page to the audience, each child recited a sentence beginning with their letter: "S is for study to get a good mark" "U is for uniform clean pressed and smart" and so on. Together they appeared to be spelling the word "S-U-C-C-E-S-S". We could hardly hear any of it above the chatter and felt very sorry for the poor children trying to perform. It reminded me of once trying to perform a fundraising cabaret in a noisy Milton Keynes pub. A choir of teachers sang a local folk song in beautiful harmony and then a small girl stood alone reciting a poem. As she did so there seemed to be a clattering of stones on the glass panes of the side windows and a hooting and hollering from outside the hall. Inside, some of the older women at the back set up a commotion and started railing at an unseen enemy. The poor child on the stage was completely drowned out. There followed a long pause between acts as if no one knew who was on next. Then a group of teachers came on and performed a short skit in Creolese which raised raucous laughter from the back of the crowd. We shuffled restlessly on our wooden bench. Neither of us was used to this kind of parental ignorance and we were both getting very impatient and disgusted with it all. Edwin snapped before I did. "Come on let's get out of here," he said to me. "I can't stand any more of this."

We made our way out of the school yard with Edwin's Aunt Agnes who lived in a tiny house opposite the school. "What was all that commotion just before we left?" he asked her.

"It's dem big boy from de village, dey does run aroun de buildin' hittin'de windows wid stick an mekkin all kind o' noise," she said.

"Why do they do it?"

"Dem jus' want to friken everyone. It disgustin'."

"Why doesn't anyone stop them?"

"Dem teacher na get experience. Dem mostly children jus leff school."

"Don't they have to get trained at a college first?"

"College? Dem en't get no qualification at all. Some leff Bushlot school las' year, en't even get no CXC." She sucked her teeth in disapproval. "Dem en't get no men teacher no more. When men teacher deh, zey get discipline." I was beginning to understand more of the local dialect now: *en't* was their version of 'ain't' and deh meant 'there'.

"It is possible for women teachers to have good discipline, Auntie Agnes," I argued. "I certainly never have any discipline problems when I teach. It's all down to how you go about it, and learning how to get children to behave in an orderly way is a skill you have to learn by working with experienced teachers who already have good discipline. It looks like there are none of those in Hopetown Primary School so there's no good example to follow."

"Burnham chase off all dem good ol' time teacher from colonial time," she sadly acknowledged. "If dem na leff de country fo' go overseas, Burnham punish dem by send dem in de interior." So the former president had punished any remaining colonially trained teacher who might have objected to his education "reforms" such as book burnings, by sending them to remote schools deep in the Amerindian jungle of the country. This would have meant being cut off from their family and friends for decades and living rough. It was a fate dreaded by anyone who had grown up in these tightly knit, lively and interconnected coastal village communities. They felt they were living in modern civilisation with roads, motor vehicles and electricity (albeit intermittent). The 'interior' or 'hinterland' of Guyana was definitely beyond the pale of civilisation to them.

"Burnham's got a lot to answer for," Edwin railed, "He was happy enough to take what the colonial masters had to offer him in the way of education. I remember him when the Munroe's opened their doors and took him in as a guest when he was a no-body, a law student in London. I had to share a room with him. Butter wouldn't melt in his mouth then. What ever happened to turn him into the monster dictator that destroyed this country that I remember was so beautiful when I grew up as a small boy here?"

"Me wish de British come back an' tek over de country again," sighed Agnes. "We get clean pipe water an' never get blackout in dem day, an' de railway come dong from Georgetong right till at Blairmont."

"What happened to the piped water that you used to have in colonial times, Aunt Agnes?" I inquired.

"Well, after Independance in 1966, de local people dem na do good maintenance wok, so de pipe all destroy an' de pump all brek dong, so de water na run na more," she answered.

"What about the railway?" I probed, "It doesn't make sense to remove such an expensive piece of infrastructure."

"Dem say Burnham sell it out to Indira Ghandi in India after Independance," she replied.

"Typical corrupt black leader, just looking to fill his pockets at the expense of the country," grumbled Edwin.

"Me glad he dead," she snapped. "He ban flour an' onion from de country an get he people fo' shoot dead anyone who try an' import it from Surinam. Dem Indian in Bushlot smuggle it by boat fo' sell on de Black Market an' you cousin Julius de policeman help de black people get it in secret. Dem all meet up in Annie Jordan rum shop fo' get it. Burnham people come an' tek away all de farmer rice fo' feed he soldier. It brek yo' father Lewis heart, so he stop farming. Burnham give de people of Hopetown street-light, an' then he tek it away from dem." There was real hatred in her tone of voice when she said this. She was not the first elderly negro villager whom I had heard decrying the Burnham regime. I was building up a picture of collapse following British withdrawal that was universally blamed by the village elders on the policies of its post-independence leaders, especially Forbes Burnham. You did not hear the same condemnation from those who grew up and went to school after Independence. They tended to defend 'the Bocassa', as they called him, by saying that he banned imported western goods to try to get the people to produce their own food and make the country self- sufficient. Their explanation for the disappearance of the street lights was the leap in fuel price rises in the seventies' international oil crisis, meaning there were insufficient exports to pay for imported oil. I kept an open mind because I had not been present, but Edwin was very opinionated and felt he had the right to be so.

We said goodbye to Auntie Agnes and made our way back through the centre of Hopetown. Edwin wanted to pursue the theme we had been discussing.

"Thank goodness Hoyte lifted the ban on flour and other imports since he took over from Burnham," he said. "I wasn't going to come back here if it stayed the way it was when I came here in '84 for my father's funeral. I couldn't get any food for the wake because there wasn't any in the shops. There were no shops at all. Can you believe that? The whole of Georgetown had no shops. They were all empty and boarded up. The markets were deserted and there were no vendors. Nello took me and my sister, Olive, to Georgetown in his car... it was the only car in Hopetown at the time... and it got a puncture. We were stuck in the middle of nowhere for about four hours while he had to walk to an Indian friend he knew miles up the road to get a spare tyre. When he eventually got back it didn't fit so he had to make it fit. I wanted to know why the car swayed every time he braked. He had to compensate with the steering and drive like a snail. He told me he couldn't get new brake pads, so he had to build them out of a piece of wood with a scrap of rubber stuck to it." I had heard the story several times before but by now I was getting used to repetition. It was of course a very bad place that Guyana had been in for twenty years and was now beginning to find a way out of. We both needed to remember that when judging the conditions we were now in. They had improved considerably since Burnham's death in 1988.

Clouds had been building up while we were inside and now it was starting to rain heavily. We got soaked to the skin before we could reach the snackette where we sheltered, shivering, until it eased off. Collis was there. Edwin spoke to him about not attending the sheep and cows. He had not taken them to the back-dam because it was raining so he let them all loose in the pasture around the houses. The snackette staff had all disappeared: Aylene was late, Lorraine had gone to Linden to visit her mother, Cousin Irene's cousin was ill and Lindy's grandmother had had a problem. Bryan was the only one there. How could you run a business when staff just disappear and leave you high and dry with no forewarning? We only discovered the reason for their absence when we sent to ask for them. Edwin let them know his feelings about their behaviour and what he expected of them. It would be an uphill task getting them to change their work ethic. Having started by being amiable and reasonable with them, Edwin was now beginning to harden.

"They're all in for a shock when the money comes through from the bank," he confided in me.

The next two days were hectic and full of problems. We both had to go to Georgetown because we had to clear a crate of donated items sent to us by an English acquaintance of Edwin. The usual trail of wharf, customs house, Ministry of Finance and back and forth again to get sizes of crate, took up most of the day. It was most annoying to be sent back for details that the previous official might have thought to warn us we would need to take with us. Edwin went to the Deeds registry to see if he could pick up our Transport documents but they seemed to know nothing about it nor have any records of it. They tried to telephone New Amsterdam but their line was continually engaged so we arranged to go back again later in the afternoon. By 4 o'clock there was still no joy so Edwin would have to go to New Amsterdam to find out what had happened to it. We got back tired, dehydrated, hungry and totally pissed off at seven. The next day, at New Amsterdam, Edwin found that our papers were still there and not until he went to the Supreme Court did he discover from the registrar that another plan was required before it could proceed. This would mean more delays as we would have to chase up Sonny Jaundoo, the vendor, to do this.

"Right now, I just want to chew balls, bite off heads and eat these wankers' ears!" Edwin snarled after explaining his wasted day to me. "When I went to check on what work had been done in the house while we were in town yesterday, Pappa Dan was late, supposedly because he has a fever, but I got told he's working on someone else's house. Hardly anything had been done. People were all standing around. I told them what to do and sent Ogden to order some cement for tomorrow. The whole thing's a mess, everyone's lying and I'm being pissed about. If it wasn't for you calming me down, I'd set fire to what we've built so far and leave this hopeless place!"

That night, the 19th of December, it was blackout. Torrential rain fell all night long. We felt quite cold and shivery in bed now we were used to the blistering daytime heat. When we woke up late next morning, everywhere was flooded. We had to go and dig a channel to let out the floodwater from the garden into the trench. Then Ogden arrived to tell us that seven of the sheep were missing including the prize ram. They found the skins of the slaughtered sheep had been left in the garden at the back of our half-built house. We immediately went up to the police station at Fort Wellington to report the incident. They arrested Hence the night watchman, brought him to the station and charged him with the theft. He naturally said he knew nothing about it because he fell asleep due to the heavy rain. Edwin wanted to know why he did not report the theft to us when he woke up at daylight. He said nothing, as if he did not have the intelligence to work out that it would have been the obvious thing to do if he was innocent. Edwin wanted his sheep back but since that was not possible, he wanted their value back. Hence threw himself onto his knees pleading innocence and begged to be let go as he was a poor man with no money. Edwin had run out of sympathy by now and wanted Hence punished for not doing the job he was paid to do, namely stay awake at night to prevent theft. The officer put Hence in the cells and told him he would have to stay there until his bail money was paid. Then he took Edwin outside the station building and told him that he did not believe Hence was innocent, as watchmen were notorious for stealing the very things they were paid to protect. However, he could not bring a criminal prosecution against him because there was not enough evidence to stand up in court. Edwin was livid and made his views known in no uncertain terms. He wanted the money for his sheep, but all Paddy the police officer could do was shrug his shoulders.

"Mr Joseph," he said. "You are a rich man... and dis man is very poor. Even if you pay a lawyer to tek him to court, he can't pay you because he na even get a job now. Why you don't rest yourself and let it drop."

"I'm not a rich man," protested Edwin, "I haven't got a job either. I'm a pensioner and I haven't got two cents to my name at the moment!" Paddy did not look at all convinced. I supposed that this was because in his eyes, Edwin must have a limitless pot of money because he had a white wife and had come to Guyana from England. He did not know or care that we had no title yet to the land our house was built on and no money to finish the building unless we could borrow it from a local bank. Even if we did finish it, the bank would own it for years until we could repay the mortgage.

When we got back to the house, we had to collect the sheep skins, all showing Edwin's brand marks, and dry them out so they could be kept for evidence. Edwin was still seething about the impossibility of getting justice when the police were in sympathy with the culprit and not the victim. He got more determined than ever to get his gun licence, which he was entitled to as was any farmer needing to defend his property.

"I'll go and get it on Monday," he said to me. Meanwhile the theft was being talked about all round the village as we soon found out from the fact that everyone we bumped into confronted us with the news. We found a quiet spot away from them all and mulled over what to do next.

"There's no point wasting money on a lawyer to take him to court," I said, "when there's the likelihood that they'll dismiss the case for the same reason Paddy did. In any case, we haven't got any money at the moment. It seems to me that the most sensible thing we can do is to sell all the other sheep right now before they go the same way as the seven we just lost." I never had understood why Edwin had thought it was a good idea to buy a flock of sheep when we had not even got a house to live in. He had been led into it by Taa before we came to live in the country because she had encouraged all her other sons to buy animals even though they all lived in New York. She liked the local status it had accorded her to have this flock with its prize ram in her yard. She could act as if they were her own, and when she wanted some cash, she would sell one of them and they would never even notice as long as they multiplied enough to mask the loss. They probably would not have minded anyway, as it was easier than sending her cash. Edwin looked at me, thought about it and agreed that I was right.

"I'll get them sold at once to someone in Bushlot who'll give me the best offer," he said, "Then there'll be no need to waste any more money on paying for a watchman who lets thieves in."

"Yes," I said, "and we can use the money to pay the bank the deposit they're asking for so we can get the mortgage."

That night, we went to bed at ten thirty but soon got woken up by Lindy and Ogden who had come to get Edwin to go out in the back-dam searching for three men who were presumed to be the thieves. Predictably, they did not find anyone who was so foolish as to go back to the scene of the crime the following night in order to get caught. However, it may have sent out a message to light fingered neighbours that even though there were sheep without a watchman now, security had been stepped up so it would be difficult to get away with a repetition just yet. A couple of days later, we heard that Hence was now a free man. His relative had taken the bail money up to the station.

It was Christmas Eve and we had to go to New Amsterdam to collect the Transport document from our Lawyer, Mr Trim, It did not seem at all like

Christmas in this tropical heat and without the commercial build-up to the festive season that we are subjected to in 'western culture'. The last thing on our minds was Christmas, especially with all the worries and problems we were experiencing. The only clue that a festival was nearing was the fact that none of our garden or building workers were prepared to work on Christmas Eve so had not turned up. "No work , no pay," Edwin had said, trying to disguise his annoyance at more delays. This ought to have forewarned us that our voyage would be a futile one but preoccupation with all our recent bad luck blinded us to that possibility. Bad luck was going to be the order of the day, as when we arrived at the ferry terminal at Rosignol, we had just missed the ferry and had to wait over an hour for the next one. When we finally made it to Mr Trim's office, which was a very long, hot, dry and dusty walk from the ferry stelling, it was clear that there was a party going on and the staff members were all tipsy. Mr Budhoo told us that something was wrong with the transport as it needed a stamp and that he had sent Edwin a telegram. We had not received any such message. From there we walked another long distance to the Registry only to find that the Registrar was not there. Edwin spoke to the ladies who were sitting around outside. They were quite helpful in the end and checked through our papers. They also gave us a few home truths about Trim, Budhoo and the Registrar. From this, Edwin concluded that they were all liars and useless at their jobs.

We collected the Transport document in order to take it personally to the Registrar at Georgetown the following Friday. I was getting really confused by all these different Registrars. Apparently, it dates back to the times when the country was three different colonies ruled by different colonial powers: Berbice was Dutch, with New Amsterdam as its capital, Demerara was French with its capital Stabroek (now Georgetown) and Essequibo was also French with its capital Parika. When the British had taken over all three colonies at the invitation of the Dutch during the Napoleonic wars, these territories were merged into one British Guiana, but their provincial administration remained distinct and stayed that way even after independence. Since our land was in West Berbice, we had first to register it in Berbice, at New Amsterdam, and then take it to the central Registrar in Georgetown for a final stamp of approval and publication. I learned this from The Reverend Pat Munroe, Edwin's 'brother' who resided at the Congregational Mission Chapel in New Amsterdam. While we were in the town, we had paid him a visit and had lunch with him in the Manse. Pat was a welcome sight here, because he was the only person in the country we felt we could trust by now. Edwin had grown up with him in the village since he was three and had travelled to England with him in 1950. Pat had gone to university in London, obtained his doctorate there, and worked in London's top hospitals before getting a job in the World Health Organisation based in Jamaica. He had been the Guyana Minister of Health under Burnham after Independence and had the sad job of dealing with the aftermath of the Jim Jones mass suicide scandal in Jonestown. He had started to get nervous about Burnham's dictatorship and the way the country was going, so he had studied for the Congregational Ministry and taken up as Pastor in order to obtain God's help to put the country right after this trauma. Pat understood what we were going through and could give us trusted advice. It helped Edwin calm down and certainly cheered us both up as he gave us a lift back to the Ferry terminal.

It was our first Christmas Day in Guyana and probably the worst Christmas either of us had ever had. In Taa's house, which I supposed of be typical of Guyanese village homes, there were no stockings at the end of the bed for the children, no Christmas decorations of any kind up and no family gathering around the breakfast table. For that matter there were never family gatherings around the table at any mealtime on any day of the year. Mealtimes were as and when you could get them, seated on the back steps of the house you happened to be in. No presents were given out by the locals or Edwin's family, and in fact I had not thought of a Christmas present for Edwin or anyone else as I had no money to buy one with. Edwin was morose. He had received a letter from his twenty-three year-old son a couple of days before Christmas asking for financial help as he was training as a full time decathlete in Germany and had run out of funds. It had been playing on Edwin's mind because he lacked money to help him with. We needed help ourselves. He also missed his other, older children and being together with them as a family. He assumed I missed mine too and was feeling the same way as him. He was wrong really because I had not spent Christmas with my family for years. I had been divorced for over ten years. Before that I had always celebrated Christmas with my former husband as a couple, so although I worried about mum and dad and felt funny not being in telephone contact with them or my siblings, I did not miss spending Christmas with them. I was just wondering why I had given up my well paid job and luxury lifestyle in Dubai to come to this.

Taa had made a pepper-pot for breakfast. It was a special traditional dish normally eaten on Sundays for breakfast, so also on Christmas Day. It was a dark, almost black, beef stew cooked in a special sauce called casareep, the residue from squeezing grated cassava, boiled down and flavoured with burnt sugar and hot pepper sauce. We ate it with home baked bread to dip in and mop up the sauce. I liked the unusual flavour with a hint of cloves and orange peel. Taa headed off to spend the day in church as usual. We had decided to spend the day on our own in the snackette since Bryan and his family had vacated it for the day to visit their extended family in the village. My first thought was to go and pick some of the tomatoes and a cabbage that I had grown in the garden so I could cook a more familiar kind of dinner for us. We had ordered a ready plucked chicken from Uncle Arnold who reared them and who for quite a while had been supplying the snackette with his meat birds every seven weeks. I would be able to use the calor-gas oven in the snackette kitchen for once, because today, the shop was closed.

At last we were on our own, with the gate locked and no interruptions from anyone. It was bliss having a bit of privacy. In this community the word privacy did not exist. I hated it. For five months now, I had had no space where I could enjoy peace and quiet, free from other people's noise. Private conversations were not possible till now because where ever we were, someone could overhear what we were saying. The first thing we tried to do was to make the little kitchen clean so we could feel happy about preparing food for ourselves and eating in it. It was filthy. The food inspectors back in England would have closed the place down immediately. Edwin picked up three pairs of assorted muddy trainers and an abandoned school bag from one corner and opened the door of the room that was supposed to be a store room but which Bryan and Lorraine used as their bedroom, put the shoes and bag inside and shut the door. He then went outside, found a broom and started sweeping the floor. I tried to clear the work tops of pots, pans and other equipment so I could wipe the surfaces down. The cupboards were full of mice droppings and dead cockroaches, so had to be emptied and cleaned out with disinfectant before the stuff could be neatly stored. As there was no piped water or tap in the kitchen, I had to fetch water from a rain tank at the back and wash up the items in a bowl on a wooden table out in the yard. This did not help me to get enthusiastic about Christmas, but I was certainly looking forward to the food I would prepare. At last I put the chicken in to roast, and began preparing the vegetables outside while Edwin tried to set up the rickety table and chairs inside with a table cloth and cutlery. Just when we were about to put the longed for food out on the plates, a voice called out,

"Uncle Edwin". It was a young boy looking over the next door's fence. "Taa send zis food for you." Edwin went out, collected the bag and brought it in.

"I told him to tell Ogden and all the other boys who work for us to come here at four o'clock for a little celebratory meal with us," he said, adding, "We can share this food mother sent between them."

It was a good time to be frank and honest with each other now at last we could not be overheard. As our music centre and cassettes were already in the next room, we were able to put some nice carols on as background music.

"How do you feel about all this shit?" he asked me.

"It's not what I was expecting," I said, "It seems like there's no one you can trust, not even your own family. I suppose it's just because of the poverty."

"Rubbish!" he snapped. "We were a lot poorer here when I was growing up as a kid and people didn't steal and cheat you then like they do now."

"Are you sure you aren't just looking back on it all through rose tinted spectacles?" I asked, "After all, you weren't even ten years old when you were living here. You wouldn't have seen the kind of things we're experiencing now even if it was happening. As a child you wouldn't have been involved in transactions that adults enter into involving relatively large sums of money. Maybe the elders back then sometimes stole off each other or from the British."

"They didn't dare because they'd have been locked up and sent to the prison in Georgetown. They wouldn't have been let off like Hence for a couple of thousand dollars bail, which'll soon find its way into the policeman's pocket." He did not seem convinced by my argument that the people must have been the same in the past, so I dropped it.

"I suppose you've got a point," I said, "The colonial police would have done their job properly because they weren't part of the thieves' family. This is such a small community that everyone's related to each other in some way and so every thief is a cousin of some sort to someone at the station. The police will find a way to let them off or they'll be seen as betraying their own family. I've noticed that the tribe sticks together to protect their own when accused by outsiders, even if they're guilty. When you live in a society like this, then you know you'll get away with crime so you can carry on being a criminal with impunity. The only time they carry out justice is if the culprit is an Indian and that's racism, so it's justice only for some." The sound of Bing Crosby crooning out 'White Christmas,' seemed a little incongruous at this point, so I went and changed the tape.

"I'm not as affected by the dishonesty as you are because I kind of expect it," I went on, "but I'm really fed up with being permanently filthy and looking like shit all the time."

"You don't look like shit," he reassured me kindly, "because if you did I wouldn't be sitting here with you now."

"Thanks for trying to make me feel better," I said, "but I have to face facts. Look at my legs, they're just one mass of suppurating sores with all these mosquito bites, and my hair is like rats tails because I can't stop sweating. It must be full of dust and sand because of having to wash it in muddy trench water, and it's all tangled up with the breeze blowing all the time. I used to be able to keep myself looking nice all the time before we came here, but now we can't live like a normal married couple. We don't touch each other or even kiss because there's no-where private and I'm sure the way I look must put you off the idea of having sex with me." I was getting choked up. Tears were welling up in my eyes despite a superhuman effort to try and hide them.

"It's not that," he said, putting his arms around me and looking straight into my eyes at close quarters, "I just can't think about sex with all this going on and living in these conditions. I just want to set fire to the lot of it and piss off back to England."

"How can we do that?" I said, "We've got no-where to go to and every possession we have is now here, locked up in that concrete room. We haven't got thousands of pounds to pay for the containers to be shipped back to England and in any case after all the trouble we had getting them brought down from Georgetown, I can't see any likelihood of getting them to agree to come down here, deliver and collect a container to take back to port. We would probably never see them again. Neither of us has got a job in England, nor anywhere to live there. The sale of my house has just gone through. I don't know if there'll be any money left after the mortgage and all the arrears I ran up since being here is paid off. I'm not entitled to any unemployment benefit because I haven't been paying any contributions since we've been here. We've got no choice but to stick it out and get the house finished as best we can. I've no intention of leaving all my worldly goods that I've worked for over the past twenty years to be a free gift to whoever wants them. I'm sure it'll get better once we have our own house to live in." He hugged me tightly. I could feel intense emotion in his grip.

"I'm a very lucky man," he said. "You're good for me, a balancing force." We kissed. I felt months of frustration drain out of my body and began to sob freely. It was so much better to feel a bit of tenderness return to our relationship. We were both burning with desire for each other but although it might have been the time, it was certainly not the place for it, so we resisted.

Having cleared the air, I began clearing the table and we did the washing up together.

"I'm going to close off the gap in the fence around the building, and the pen and garden and padlock them all with separate padlocks so people can't walk across my land on a path I've provided. It makes it easier for them to break in without being seen. They'll have to walk all the way round it," he said. "If they think I'm a soft target and they can come and walk away with stuff off the site, then they'll have a shock."

"How much did you get for the sheep?" I asked.

"Thirty thousand Guyana dollars," he said. "I'll have to get Samo to come and take my cow away to the savannahs to keep with his. He suggested the other day, when he heard about the sheep theft, that I could do that. There's no point having it in the pen here for someone to come and steal. At least when they're with him, he won't leave them unattended or with a thieving watchman, because he lives all the time in the savannah and he's got a gun licence, so the fact that he has a gun keeps thieves away."

"What happens to the cows when he comes out of the savannahs?" I asked.

"Oh, Kenneth lives out there with him all the time, so they take turns in coming out to the village. When Samo comes out, he knows that Kenneth will be there all the time and when Samo goes back then Kenneth can come out."

"Sounds like a good arrangement. Let's do it," I said.

It was four o'clock and the boys arrived so we gave them soft drinks each and shared out the food for them. While they sat out around one of the snackette forecourt tables eating it, Edwin gave them one of his talks. At about five thirty, Shirley Robertson sent a messenger to tell us to hurry up as she was waiting for us at her house on the road. When we got there, she was clearly narked.

"It's all been ready and waiting for you since two o'clock!" she said, ushering us in to a massive spread of local festive dishes on her dining room table. We were astonished and embarrassed.

"I'm so sorry. We had no idea you were expecting us to come up for Christmas dinner at lunchtime," I apologised. "When you invited us, we thought you just meant come in the evening like we've done before." Although we were both completely stuffed with the huge meal we had not long eaten, we made a brave effort to politely partake of her hospitality. We spent the whole evening with her till late. Edwin was regurgitating all the trials and tribulations we had gone through since arriving in Guyana, and soul searching as to why his own people were punishing him so. Shirley offered commiserations and diplomatic explanations based on her knowledge of the local characters involved. I just sat and listened for the most part, since I had heard it all many times before and only chipped in with an extra piece of information where understanding of the full situation warranted it.

Shirley seemed kind and intelligent to me. I put her in the same mould as teachers I worked with in England and the UAE. When Edwin had finished decrying the standard of education of the entire community and how disgusted he had been with the school concert, she attempted to bring me more into the conversation.

"Why don't you teach in one of our schools, Jane, since it was your job before coming here, and as Edwin says, you are so well qualified?" she asked. I squirmed a bit, because I knew one of his less helpful traits was to keep 'bigging me up' to people. He had made sure to tell her on more than one occasion that he thought it disgusting that the Minister of Education had personally told him that I was too qualified to teach in a school in Guyana and the best place for me was the University of Guyana in Georgetown.

"Oh, I would like to help, but I don't want to take a job away from a local person who really needs it, and in any case, I need to learn a lot more about the local culture and the education system before I do any such thing," I explained, in an attempt to show that I was far more humble than Edwin's picture of me would suggest. "The last thing I would want to do is to offend people because I don't understand their culture. Especially if other staff would think I was trying to change everything and that what they were doing was wrong. I would want them to see me as a colleague who did things the way they did them. At the moment, though, I couldn't work in a situation where there's such a lack of discipline. It would annoy me and I would want to make the children behave in a more disciplined way so there's an environment where effective learning can take place."

"All the more reason for you to get involved, then," she said earnestly.

"Well before I can even think of it, I need to see what the curriculum is like so I can get an idea of what information and skills they're supposed to learn in school. When I was in England, I wrote and asked the Minister of Education to send me the current syllabuses for primary schools so that I could bring some appropriate books with me when we moved here, but I never got a reply."

"Oh, I should be able to sort some out for you," she said.

"It would be great if you would," I added, "We've brought some books to donate to the local schools and we're also going to set up a library when we're settled in to the house. I may be able to get more books in the future and it'd be better if they're tailored to the syllabus so they help the children with their school work."

The rest of the evening's conversation drifted towards the village Christmas Dance which all our workers were going to that night. We had hired out our generator to them for the evening for the princely sum of $2000 (equivalent to £10). As we walked home late in the pitch black of a power cut, the main street looked quite magical with the pin points of light from numerous vendors' flambeau lamps lining both sides of the road. It could have been a candle-lit mass if they had all been singing carols, but instead the silence was broken by the distant whir of the generator, the sound of taped reggae music, the cackling of female vendors sharing a joke and the drunken shouts of domino players in the rum-shop. Mingling with the dank smell of mud, fresh cow manure, and the warm fumes of a kero-stove, was the aroma of fish frying in coconut oil and rice bubbling away in coconut milk. Yes, Edwin was right: Christmas in Guyana was all about dances, drinking and eating and not about family. I could have reminded him that for many people in Europe, especially in England, the same could be said. It depended on how important your own family members were to you, and whether you were a real Christian at heart, not just one for lip service. I could have reminded him, but I didn't.

The day after Boxing Day was a Friday. We went into Georgetown early so we could hand in at the central deeds registry, the Transport papers we had collected in New Amsterdam on Christmas Eve. Luckily the office was one of the few business places open that day, so a girl named Simone took them and agreed to see through the process. I had told Edwin to go there alone while I waited in the cafeteria of Guyana Stores, as I realised my presence just caused unnecessary delays. The moment any Guyanese saw me next to Edwin, they became un-cooperative. I was white and English. I must therefore be a money tree. The fact that I was in a mixed race marriage led females to resent me for taking a man they considered as one of their own that they could target. I knew that without me there, Edwin would be able to work his charm on them and they would put themselves out for him on a hint of an imagined promise. It worked like a dream.

When he returned with the news, we went on to the Ministry of Sport, where Edwin was able to see the Minister, Ivor O'Brien, introduce himself and explain why he had repatriated in order to help develop the sport in the country through the sports and eco-tourist resort he was building in Hopetown. He showed Mr O'Brien a thick folder containing his C.V. and a mammoth dossier of newspaper cuttings, letters and programmes of sports events he had organised in England and other parts of the world. Mr Obrien seemed impressed as he glanced at it. Putting it on one side while Edwin asked him for the addresses of all the sporting bodies in the country, he got up and leafed through a huge mass of untidy paperwork dumped in one corner of his very higgledy-piggledy office until he found a small directory. He opened it on one page and showed it to Edwin, who scribbled down the details he wanted in his desk diary. We got up to thank him and go when Ivor astonished both of us. He asked us for a loan of two hundred thousand Guyana dollars. He said he needed it to go overseas for an operation to correct a sports injury problem with his leg.

"I'm very sorry," said Edwin, "but we're a bit short of cash at the moment as we've run into some building problems and all our cash has been taken up by that. I wish I could help. Good luck in getting your leg sorted, though!"

On the way back to Berbice, the enormity of what we had just witnessed began to sink in. "A Government Minister, stooping to that level!" I said. "They're all lowlifes," scoffed Edwin. "It would have been bad enough for him to beg like that if he had a serious problem like gangrene. Then you might have felt some sympathy even if you still couldn't help, but there was nothing wrong with him! Does he think I'm stupid or what?"

"What kind of a government is it when people at the top behave like common beggars on the street?" I said. "There's no wonder that the poor people in the villages are like it when that's the example they have to follow."

Preparations and excitement were mounting among the staff for the New Years' Eve Party. Brian had ordered sand, cement and stones for extending the seating space and some beautiful large fan palms to enhance the appearance of the forecourt. There was some discussion about the price of the tickets being too high. Edwin had said it was a profit making exercise, so they would have to limit the kind of food they were laying on to fit within a budget that would give at least 50 per cent profit margins on each ticket. Cousin Irene had in mind to try out fancy vol-au-vent recipes that her daughter in Georgetown gave her. They were normally laid on at government receptions. The weather worsened as the day approached and still Bryan had sold hardly any tickets for the event. Word was circulating in the village that people thought the tickets were too expensive. There were a number of rival dances and parties going on at other venues. Edwin and I did not share the enthusiasm of the locals for celebrating anything at present, least of all New Year's Eve. We were worried about the house being burgled as everyone else would be out celebrating, including all the boys that normally slept in the storeroom as guards. We said we would not be at the party because we would keep watch over at the house while the boys went out and enjoyed themselves.

On the morning of the 31st of December, we went up to the snackette early to help get things ready for them. A decision had to be made as to how many people to cater for based on the few tickets we had sold and the expected numbers who would come and pay on the door. We were entirely dependent on Bryan for these figures as we had never been in Guyana over a Christmas period and had no real idea of the earning and spending patterns of an impoverished rural community many of whom, whether employed or unemployed, had overseas relatives sending regular remittances of US dollars to them. I offered to help as a skivvy in the kitchen following the orders of Cousin Irene. It soon became clear that her ideas of catering on a grand scale were not backed up by experience. She was panicking as she got bogged down in fiddly jobs that took far too long. We were running out of time. It was a food safety nightmare. Only a handful of tickets had been sold in advance. The whole thing looked like being a spectacular flop. While we were in the midst of all this, Edwin got a message that some visitors had come to see him at Taa's house, so we left to find out who it was.

We soon discovered that the mystery visitors were a couple of sisters called Violet and Cheryl Embrack. They were in their forties and the younger sisters of Evadne who had been a primary school friend of Edwin. I found it quaint that people from one's distant past should come from the far corners of the country to reacquaint themselves, as I could not imagine anyone of my own primary school contemporaries having more than the slightest interest in my returning to visit my mum in my own home village. However, the difference in this context was that they were unattached women; he was an alpha male and one of their own, come back after having made it good overseas. He would be a catch if he were unattached. Clearly my presence did not present any deterrent to the goal they had in mind. They were both scantily clad and decorated with copious amounts of lipstick, nail varnish, dangly bauble earrings and other bling. Cheryl had face like a carthorse. Her hair was woven into elaborate corn-rows piled up on top of her head. Vio's by contrast, was straightened and styled with an inward curl at jaw-length. It was clear they had no interest in any conversation with me, so I left them on the veranda with Edwin while I went inside to read a book. I could overhear the two women asking pointed questions to which his answers were all "no". Then he came in and told me that he was going to take them across to show them over the house. When he came back, he was without them. "Why do women here think I'm looking for a screw?" he said to me. I didn't have an answer.

It was now dark and the power was off as usual. Heavy rain had been falling since late afternoon and now a strong cold breeze was blowing northeast wards from the interior toward the coast, directly opposite to the usual prevailing winds from the sea inland. We made our way over to the empty building with our torches and tried to find a spot on the veranda that was sheltered but even inside the rooms we were exposed as the wind drove the rain in through the unglazed window holes. I had nothing more than a thin cotton shirt on, so was soon shivering wet. The hours dragged by as we tried to distract each other from the boredom by discussing village characters, local gossip, plans we would carry out as soon as normality returned after the two week workers' holiday and ways of putting the ills of the country right. Then at five minutes to midnight, as there was a break in the rain, we walked up to the snackette to wish Bryan and Lorraine a Happy New Year. It looked like the evening had been a wash-out. Music was blaring as the generator was on, but the place was dead with just a couple of customers and the staff. It seemed as if they had just put on a party for themselves to enjoy a feast and drink-up. We had a few drinks with the boys and then went back down to the house taking two bottles of rum with us. Not long after sitting down on the veranda, uninvited guests arrived to join us. The voices of Cheryl and Vio called up from below, so Edwin went down and let them in. For what seemed like hours, I had to endure their mindless tittle-tattle as Edwin kept plying their paper cups and ours with rum. It looked like they would soon all be mindless and the women were getting looser and looser. I wanted to get rid of them but they were clearly not going to go until the drink was all gone, so to speed up their departure, I surreptitiously emptied out most of the second bottle over the edge of the veranda, unnoticed by Edwin or them. It worked, they went and I rejoiced inwardly. It was as if by their departure, I had seen off the bad spirits that had up to now blighted our lives so we could enter a new year with a positive turn in our fortunes.

Chapter 8

The Day of the Donkey

The winter rainy season in Guyana is a shorter and cooler one than the summer rainy season that falls between May and July. It was the first wet weather we had experienced since coming to live there. Rain fell relentlessly every night and also on some days, with a cold breeze blowing towards the coast from deep in the interior. Between late November and January, the sun is most concentrated over the Tropic of Capricorn much further south in the continent. The moisture in the winds must have been picked up on their way across the thousands of transpiring hectares of Amazonian rainforest, the northern boundary of which was only ten kilometres south of our village. Technically, the rainforest in Guyana is not part of the Amazon Basin, because it is separated from the latter by the Pakaraima Mountains of the Central Guiana Shield, but it might as well be regarded as part of the Amazon Rainforest, since it is one vast uninhabited wilderness. The equatorial rain falls very heavily, and since the water table is near the surface on the coast, the pastures around us were flooded because the water had no-where to go.

The main public road through the village that runs parallel to the coast was at that time a poor quality metalled surface on a raised foundation of laterite ('burnt dirt' to the locals). During colonial times, the red brick laterite had been put down, but after Independence, Burnham's government had surfaced the road with tarmac to make it more weather proof and capable of withstanding the modern motor traffic expected to ply it. Road transport had been seen as the way forward for goods and people rather than maintaining the national railway system inherited from the British. The problem, however, was that any system of infrastructure needs maintenance, so the road had fallen into disrepair like everything else. Equatorial heat and torrential rains combined with the daily passage of minibuses and trucks had undermined the surface and left it pitted with treacherous potholes. These were occasionally patched up with sand in the dry season only for the rainy season to wash it all back out again. Nevertheless, it was high, dry and warm compared to the flooded mud flats either side of the road. As a consequence, all the stray animals from miles around congregated in herds on the road, presenting a further traffic hazard. Cows were not so much of a problem, as they were more valuable, so even if they sometimes strayed, their owners usually sent them with a cowherd to the coastal savannahs during the day time and penned them up at night. Donkeys, however, roamed for miles along the public road searching for a mate and often decided to lie down in their group right in the middle of the highway.

The minibus we were travelling in to Georgetown screeched to a halt just in time, and Nello, the driver, let forth a stream of swear words at the beasts he had nearly hit when we rounded a sharp bend in the road.

"Dam people! Why dem leff de dankey loose fo' go on de road?"

"Someone should put them in the pound at the station and the police fine the owners when they come and collect them!" said Edwin, brushing from his trouser legs the globules of Pepsi-cola that had just shot out of his bottle when we had braked. We were heading to the capital once again, this time to pay the deposit we had raised from selling the sheep, to the bank giving us the mortgage. We had a sense of mission about us. We could now finish off the house with the money from the mortgage and move on with our plans to start a business that would transform Hopetown and bring prosperity to Edwin's people. We would lead them out of the dark ages into the modern world! There must be lots of other Guyanese expats like him who would soon be doing the same thing now that Burnham had died and his successor had opened up the country to foreign investment with the promise of the first properly democratic elections for twenty years on the horizon. The Carter Centre were sending people to monitor them, so there would not be the usual corruption that had maintained the dark days of Burnham's dictatorship and led to the assassination of his political opponents, such as the famous Walter Rodney. We were on the cusp of a new age of reform. We felt like pioneers of the Wild West, except in a public minibus instead of a hooped horse-drawn wagon.

The two weeks of Christmas holidays were at last over and we could look forward to work on the house resuming at a pace with Edwin in the driving seat. The workers had not shown up after the two weeks of extended public holidays. Edwin had learned from his mother that they were staying away until he paid them a Christmas bonus.

"I'll get someone else to do the work!" he had threatened, but the threat had been ignored. "My mother thinks I'm just saying it," he told me as we jolted over the potholes, "but they'll all get a shock when we come back with this money because the first thing I'm going to do is to pay Bobby for all the materials he has let us have so far on credit, and give him a down payment for the next set. Then I'm going to get another builder from Lovely Lass village to come and finish off the work. The others can all go to hell if they think I'm paying them a bonus. They don't deserve one because they turn up when they feel like it and disappear without even a word of explanation. Most of the time when they're supposed to be working, they're just standing about gaffing."

"How do you know that this other man can do any better?" I asked.

"Because he's just finished building that new house next to Aunt Winnie's vegetable booth we passed on the road."

"Oh, you mean that lovely little house with the gabled roof?"

"Yes, I went round it with him and Bryan when I came up to Onverwagt about the football league last week. He's agreed to come and start work tomorrow."

"Great stuff," I said. Little did we know that neither that day nor for many more trips to Georgetown and New Amsterdam, would we get the Transport document or the money. Meanwhile, we continued to get materials on credit from Bobby 'Slow Daddy' in Bushlot, and had to depend for our food and travel on my efforts in the garden and the increasingly meagre takings from the snackette.

During January, the business at the snackette came to a standstill. Some days there were hardly any customers and even some of those were children asking for a free glass of water on their way home from school. We always obliged. At least their presence made it look like we had customers, so potential real customers in vehicles on their way to the ferry or to Georgetown, would not pass by thinking we were closed. It helped us to understand that when wages had been spent at Christmas in this economy, there was literally no more to come until wage earners got paid at the end of the month. Something would have to be done to get business from elsewhere in order to pay the staff or they would have to be laid off. Bryan was allowed to keep all the takings for replacing stock so we had to manage without receiving any cash from him to buy materials or pay the building workers. He suggested that with Mashramanie, a festival in February, overseas based Guyanese would come back to Guyana for the holiday, so there was hope on the horizon for a better month of trade to follow. February came and the only thing that had improved was the weather, which was now very hot and dry. Bryan came to ask us for an injection of cash to buy beer. Where did he think we could get money from? Wasn't he supposed to be making a profit on the stock he sold and to use some of that to buy stock in order to build on the profit? We flatly refused and found ourselves giving him an impromptu lesson in economics.

A few months back, in the nearby village of Litchfield, Edwin had started up a friendship with a Rastafarian woodcarver with a passionate interest in football. Arthur Tudor, whom everyone called "Dred" on account of his shoulder-length plaited locks, lived in a tiny, aged wooden hut along the main road in that village. He had overheard Edwin's English accent as he was coming out of the Anglican Church that day. Dred had asked Edwin why he was visiting Guyana and as soon as he found out, had persuaded him to get involved with the football club "Roots" of which Dred was a keen member. Dred told him that he had been a merchant seaman and travelled widely overseas himself. He wanted to see a better standard of football in the country if only Edwin with his FIFA qualifications could help. He had taken Edwin back to see Roots' football pitch and then into his little house for a drink. Edwin had been amazed at the beautifully carved wooden ornaments that adorned the interior of the little hut and the way Dred's little daughters were lovingly polishing them with brown wax polish. He had commissioned Dred to make a special carving for me for Christmas and told him that when we had our tourism resort up and running we could get our guests to buy them as souvenirs. It was through this friendship that Edwin began to go and watch all the local teams play football on their cow-pasture pitches. It was also through this friendship that he was introduced to Albert Straker, a Litchfield intellectual with a passion for sport and education.

Albert had been a supporter of Walter Rodney during Burnham's reign of terror and had been forced out of his job as Minister of Education for political reasons after Rodney's assassination. Now he was supported by overseas family and academics while he found it safe to be back in Guyana to care for his elderly mother. Over the previous couple of months, we had seen a lot of Albert, as he was helping Edwin to orchestrate a West Berbice Football League, which Edwin thought was the best way to improve the standard of local football. Albert knew all the right people to contact in Georgetown. We liked him because he was intelligent and we trusted him because he was in close contact with a member of the Munroe family who had taken Edwin to England in the fifties. He understood some of the problems we had encountered in settling in and had given us some good advice on how to deal with them. He also warned Edwin about the terrible corruption in the various national sporting bodies as well as in the government. For his part, he was very interested to know about Edwin's sporting career and background, especially his experience as a professional footballer in Germany while serving with the British Army there in the seventies, and his role as youth developer helping Dave Pleat at Luton Town Football Club when it was in the first division in the eighties. Albert had set up meetings between Edwin and the manager of a local agricultural development co-operative known as the MMA. The Dutch Company that had engineered this massive drainage and irrigation project locally in the late seventies had handed over to the country the extensive sports and accommodation facilities it had built for its staff. Albert also introduced Edwin to the Guyana Football Association, in the hope that Edwin could soon become a candidate for a change in leadership to reform football in the country. It was clear to Edwin that one of the reasons that village level football was such a low standard in Guyana was because the referees did not conduct themselves properly. Albert confirmed that none of them were properly qualified.

Edwin, a FIFA-qualified referee, with Albert's help, organised an official referee course for locals to get properly qualified before the planned league could begin. He put on the first such course ever held outside Georgetown and he put it on in the empty shell of our incomplete house just after the New Year holiday finished. With the help of the two farm boys, we carried down all the available spare stools from the snackette and arranged them in auditorium style in the middle of our large hexagonal lounge-dining room. We borrowed a blackboard and easel from a local who gave private lessons under their house. Lots of men full of self-importance came down from Georgetown for the opening. The fact that there were as yet no glazed windows in the house was an advantage, since the breeze, passing right through, kept all the participants cool. It was a rent free space for the fledgling West Berbice Football organisation to start in. With its English-trained FIFA coach doing the teaching free of charge and the blessing of the Georgetown top FIFA referees, no one was going to complain about the conditions.

"I'm going to make a start at putting us on the map," he told me. I kept out of the way for the duration of the course because by now I had borrowed some tattered copies of local history books and had started to research and make notes on what I had learned from reading them. Albert had given me some helpful advice about certain topics and gave me a better book to read, so I had something to exercise my brain with at last. Guyana had a fascinating history and I wanted to fully understand it so that I could be an informative tour guide to our visitors when they came, especially if they were on educational visits from overseas.

Some of my research had been into all the edible plants native to the coastal region of Guyana as we wanted to include specimens of every such plant in our organic farm. It was a fascinating new world for me, an amateur botanist and lover of gardening since childhood. Albert, knowing that I was interested, would occasionally bring me plant curiosities, such as "stinky toe" or "awara" seeds. He lent me a university of Guyana research project which was a directory of local edible plants and their properties. At the same time I was designing some promotional copy and taking photographs that we could use to start marketing our resort to the wider world. I would have to sketch it out and send the draft by post to a friend of Edwin's back in England who had a small leaflet-printing business. He would do the professional job not available in Guyana in the early nineties, charge us at 'mate's rates' and then post the leaflets to us. We had to think of a brand name for our resort that would be unique and memorable with tropical associations. 'Sapodilla' came to me when I was doing my botanical research. I had never heard of a sapodilla before and was sure not many other people would have either. We had a beautiful little sapodilla tree right in the middle of our farm that was laden with hard skinned fruit looking a bit like spherical kiwi-fruit but which when soft and ripe, tasted like a mouth full of caramel soufflé. It had an exotic tropical-sounding name and represented all that was sunny and warm. I thought it had a memorable ring about it and Edwin agreed. From now on, we would be 'Sapodilla Farm', an organic, health and fitness resort on the West Coast of Berbice, Guyana, South America.

The referee course was a resounding success for Edwin. Albert visited us frequently about the West Berbice Football Federation of which he had been elected President. It was always pleasant having him around, since he always treated me with respect, as an intellectual equal, unlike most other local men, who tended to assume I was born without brains as that was a characteristic of being female. Albert would always greet me warmly and share a snippet of information he knew I would be interested in. I enjoyed the discussions we would have about local and international politics, the education system, the local environment, culture, history and literature. The Football League was getting underway and they were planning a Phagwah Day Football tournament which involved meetings with officials from the MMA grounds to organise the preparation of the pitch, stands and clean, hygienic public flushing toilets for the spectators. Edwin was keen to set high standards to show the participants how it should be done properly, since such facilities were unheard of at the time. Albert warned of the pitfalls of such arrangements but Edwin's insistence on them always led him to find ways of overcoming the perceived problems, such as paying toilet attendants to maintain cleanliness and prevent vandalism, so Albert acquiesced.

By the middle of February, Albert had arranged for Edwin to meet Colin Klass, the president of the Guyana Football Association in Georgetown. World Cup preliminaries were coming up and Guyana would be playing matches against Barbados and Surinam in order to qualify for the next round. Edwin was keen to see his home country succeed in getting through to a higher level than it had before. He had a lot of expertise to offer and wanted to help, so was quite flattered when Colin Klass offered him the job of National Coach. However, he politely declined saying that he would help out the team when he could. He had just watched the Barbados versus Guyana match which Barbados won 1-0 and felt it was poor and that the Guyana team had a lot to learn. Within four days, Edwin found himself being interviewed by Quentin Taylor of the Guyana Chronicle, about a report he had prepared for Albert on the standard of play at the Barbados game. Albert had decided that he wanted to make trouble for the GFA using Edwin's critique. He also took it to the Sports correspondent at the Stabroek News offices in Robb Street where press photos were taken of him and Edwin. The GFA officials were supposed to meet him and Albert but they did not turn up. This was a foretaste of what was to come over the next couple of months.

The February morning sun was oppressively hot, but we braved a walk to Bushlot because we wanted to speak personally to Mr Phagoo, who ran the first shop you came to in the village. It was not far to walk but in the heat of that morning, the cool shade inside his cluttered entrance was a welcome relief. A few customers preceded us and I took the opportunity to scan the wares he had on sale. The tiny room at street level under his house was stuffed from floor to ceiling with everything a local could possibly want, from plastic bowls and buckets, chained to the counter to stop them walking out of the shop unpaid for, to shelves with bottles of oil and tinned foods like corned beef, sardines and ghee. There were buckets of margarine, large boxes of processed cheese, dried pulses, sugar, flour and rice, potatoes, garlic and onions. At the back from floor to ceiling, were boxes of nails, tins of various shades of paint, varnish and economy-quality ceramic tiles, huge rolls of linoleum, wire mosquito mesh and net curtain fabric, not to mention rolls of cheap plain and patterned poly-cotton dress cloth.

Mr Phagoo was pleased to make our acquaintance in person once it was our turn to be served. By now there was no one else in the shop but us, so he was free to chat about his longstanding relationship with Edwin's family. They were valued customers and he was glad that Edwin now paid off his mother's large bill at the shop.

"How you like Guyana, Mistress?" he asked me, and seemed happy to know that I was settling in to my new adopted home country. Edwin took the opportunity of the privacy of an empty shop to say,

"Mr Phagoo, thank you very much for all you have done for me and my family in the past, but from now on I would be grateful if you would NOT supply goods to anyone asking for things in my name unless you first receive a note asking for it in writing personally signed by me or my wife, Jane, here."

"Oh yes of course Mr Joseph," he said obligingly. The knowing look on his face said that there was no real need to explain why. "I hear ya does have some problems with de builders," he commiserated, shaking his head sympathetically. "Some people does do very shoddy wok."

"Yes," said Edwin, "I'm afraid that it's cost me a lot of money with all the waste and I was only trying to help by providing employment for local people rather than getting builders from Georgetown."

"Is good to see you come back to live and help develop de neighbourhood fo' tourism. Is lang time we na see overseas people in de country, since de Dutch people make de resort in Onverwagt. Is real shameful how de government destroy de place since de Dutch pull out. It was a beautiful place, ya know, but de MMA workers move in an' dem na get no maintenance, so de place gone right dong." It was a strange accent, I thought, 'dong' and 'tong' for 'down' and 'town', but I was getting much more attuned to it and now more able to follow conversations among locals.

Some minutes later we were rounding the corner to Onverwagt. It was the first time I had been into the compound there and Edwin wanted to have another look at the facilities, since he had a plan in mind. The wooden estate houses that flanked the main road were shabby and in dire need of a coat of paint. It was quite a long walk up the red brick access road to the entrance gate of the compound. Apparently there were a lot more houses within there that could not be seen from the road. We squeezed through a rusting, metal-framed chain-link gate in a ten-foot high fence that had been overtaken by rambling wild vines. On the other side of the fence, the space opened out into a large expanse of waist-high grass with a scruffy looking pavilion barely visible at one side of it.

"That's the sports ground and spectator stand," Edwin told me, "No one keeps the grass cut, but Albert says we can get a slasher to come and cut it when we are ready to hold the football tournament. I reckon it would be an ideal place to use for an athletics track and develop it for local and international competitions." I nodded, because I knew what experience Edwin had of all this sort of thing. It was well within his capabilities to make it work once the owner of it came to some realistic business arrangement.

We decided to explore other parts of the compound and came to a paved area with a concrete swimming pool sunk into it. The water was thick with green algae and blackened windblown leaves.

"God knows what other wild-life are in there!" I said, "Fancy a swim?" Edwin gave me a withering look. A kind of club-house was on one side of the pool. Peering through the grime-coated window panes, I could just make out the shape of a wall-mounted blackboard, a bar thick with dust, with seating and tables stacked up on one side and a somewhat damaged poole-table in the centre. It gave me an eerie feeling, like a ghost town.

"Look at this!" said Edwin, disgusted. I came round the other side of the clubhouse and saw two speedboat carcasses leaning against the wall with great holes in the hulls and eight foot high saplings growing through the middle of them. "It's a criminal waste!" he grumbled. "With a bit of care these things need never have got like this. Just imagine what you could do with a place like this!"

"Yes," I said, but did not really share his enthusiasm. I was beginning to panic a bit, thinking, 'Why start dreaming of expanding to such projects when we haven't got a finished house to live in and not even enough money to do that?' We wandered on past some derelict tennis courts which had started out as hard courts but now were well on their way to becoming grass ones. The chain-link fences around them were now host to wild semitoo vines and triffid-like creepers.

"We can come here and play tennis if we help clear all these weeds away."

"I thought we were going to build our own tennis court at the house," I reminded him.

"Yes, but we can come here in the mean-time," he added. It all looked too far gone to be viable to me, but as we wandered back to the road I could see his mind was working overtime with grand designs that I did not have the vision for, given our economic circumstances.

Albert arrived at the snackette a few days later, with a young lady he wished to introduce us to. Desiree Wintz, a reporter from Stabroek News, who used to be a pupil in his English lessons when he was a teacher. She was there to interview us about our tourist resort plans, Edwin's reasons for repatriation and his new role with the Guyana Football Association. He had agreed for the period leading up to the World Cup, to be technical director of the team without a salary, because he was not able to be committed full time to the job. However, he was given the promise of a car to get him to Georgetown. It was over a lunch that we provided for Desiree at the snackette, that I discovered Edwin's plan was to get the national football team to come down to train in camp in Berbice under his direction, provide them with accommodation at the MMA compound in Onverwagt, and arrange for their meals to be cooked at the snackette by our staff. It seemed a good business idea, and Albert was to take Edwin to meet with various corporate sponsors who would support the costs of the players in this, by donations to the GFA.

We took Desiree on a tour round our building site and explained what we were hoping to achieve. I showed her the books we had brought to donate to local schools and how we hoped our resort would help the education of and provide employment for local youth. She was a bright and lively young girl who asked lots of intelligent questions, so we gave her plenty of information. She scribbled it down in her note book. When the article came out on March 1st, Edwin was very pleased with how he was presented in it.

"We've now put Sapodilla Farm and eco-tourist resort on the map," he said. I was startled to see that some of the private comments I had made to Desiree in confidence after the interview, had found their way into the article. No harm was done in this instance, but it gave me a lesson about being on guard when entertaining journalists in future.

It was so hot, as we walked down the dam from the road, that Edwin fanned himself with the folded newspaper. Suddenly, a swarm of flying insects appeared from nowhere and we were right in the middle of them. He started flapping furiously at them as someone called out,

"Follow Me! Uncle Edwin, Follow Me!" I looked to see where the voice was coming from, and thought Edwin was being invited into someone's house to escape them. I did not know what to do except avoid the swarm by moving as fast as I could away from them. Edwin's mistaken instinct was to keep swatting at them moving this way and that, but wherever he went the swarm followed him. It was only later that I discovered that 'Follow-Me' was the local name for these hornets because that is what they do when they get attacked. The swarm sustained their pursuit of Edwin for some seconds before he managed to escape. By that time he had been badly stung all over including his face and throat. I could see signs of panic as he realised that his tongue was swelling up inside his mouth and he would choke.

"Get Ice quick, I need ice to suck!" he cried in anguish to Taa as we managed to get up the steps into the house. "I'm allergic to bee stings and if you don't get ice quickly, I'll choke to death," he started gasping for breath. Getting ice was not a simple task in a place where daily power cuts prevented any freezer from working. Taa sent one of the boys sprinting off up to the snackette to get ice. Meanwhile, I rummaged through my suitcase for my first aid kit where I knew I had a pack of Hismanal tablets for people who were allergic to antihistamine. I gave the dose to Edwin with a glass of cold water from the rain barrel and told him what they were, so if he quickly swallowed them, they would start acting before the swelling obstructed his windpipe. This calmed him down a bit and when Ogden came back with the ice, the swelling had already slowed down.

This trauma put Edwin out of action for the day, but the Mashramanie celebrations had meant no work would be done on the house for another week after it finished. It was something of a mystery to us why this should be, until we realised that the presence of New-York based Guyanese expats in the village for a two week period every Mashramanie, meant that locals all spent the entire time hanging around them in the hope of free drinks, food and even a few U.S.

dollars guilt-money. Many of the girls were happy to have sex with such male visitors, deliberately getting themselves pregnant in the hope of regular US remittances being sent to them for the upkeep of the child. It was not only a source of income for them but also a way of securing a future for themselves in the USA when the male sent for the child, as eventually the child would send for the mother. This strategy worked for some but it also failed for many, who were stranded in beggary with too many mouths to feed. Their only recourse was to get pregnant by another expat in the hope that his remittances would cater for his own child as well as all the others and the mother too. The visiting men were happy to do it also, since they gained macho prowess by having sired the most children in the neighbourhood. It was a kind of status symbol among them. Edwin abhorred this behaviour. It was irresponsible in his view.

The National Football Team arrived at The Snackette on the 20th March. With another twenty two new male faces on the village scene, there was plenty of attraction for female customers at the snackette, but most of them would be expecting to be entertained free of charge by the footballers who were not paid any professional wage. In fact some of them were in jobs like police and immigration officers, while others had overseas relatives sending back a regular stipend. Some supplemented their income by moving cocaine and weed around the local economy. Bringing them into the village in a group like this therefore gave rise to general excitement for a number of reasons. Getting the GFA to agree had been a bit of a problem for Edwin, because it was unheard of for the national team to leave Georgetown unless to travel overseas to a match. Their main objection was that the men would never agree to do it because they would not want to be away from the 'scene' they usually 'pumped' nightly in the capital city. There was something about Edwin, however, that won the players over once he had taken a couple of training sessions with them at their home training ground. He had a charismatic magic that made them believe in him and the training he gave them certainly produced results. Up to the last minute, no official word was given to Edwin of the GFA decision, but they announced in the papers on 18th March that he was coaching the team, and came down to an event Edwin organised at the MMA the following day. There they officially announced that he was the National Football Coach. They had not formally agreed to any of his terms, however. Their promise of a car for him, the payment of fifteen thousand Guyana dollars per week and to supply all food for the team to be fed at the snackette, remained purely verbal between Edwin and Colin Klass. So they were here at last, billeted free of charge at the MMA compound in Onverwagt, courtesy of the local manager who had these empty government properties at his disposal. Edwin's torrid affair with Guyana Football had begun.

The players' first shock was that after their meal at the snackette, they would have to run back the two and a half miles to Onverwagt to do their training. They would have to make the same run back to get their breakfast, lunch and evening meal, so an army style fitness regime was built into their survival for the next few weeks. All meals were provided at our expense while awaiting the promised money and food from the GFA. It soon became apparent that neither the food nor funding was going to come quickly and there was no sign of the promised car. Rather than have this turn into a grand fiasco by sending a bunch of hungry men back to town, Edwin urged Albert to get food from somewhere and quickly. Albert approached a generous sponsor in Georgetown, George Humphries, who donated daily bread from his bakery and a sum of twenty thousand Guyana dollars towards the cost of meat, fruit, vegetables, groceries and rice. Another sponsor, Demerara Distillery Limited, gave some crates of drinks for them as did other local businesses and farmers, so it was all done at no cost to the GFA.

Locals turned out in their hundreds to watch the national team training on the local beaches. None of them had seen anything like it and the talk of the moment was seeing them do harness resistance work, pulling old car tyres roped to their bodies and training with Edwin's weighted jacket on. The jacket soon became a motivational tool as the novelty factor had all of them wanting to try it out in training. Once they had experienced how much harder the jacket made the training exercises, then they were not so keen. Its motivational effect then came from the fact that it was used as a punishment for being the "donkey of the day" as Edwin capitalised on the players' own expression of mockery. Every day there was a new set of exercises, every day a new set piece to practice and every day some new tactics taught. The greatest difficulty was that many of the players were completely illiterate so could not take notes of any important information to refer to later.

One evening, after the team had eaten and left to go back to their cabins at Onverwagt, Edwin and I arrived at the snackette to find some of the young local men behaving very strangely at one of the tables in the forecourt. They were extremely drunk, I thought at first and yet their hilarity was so raucous, I began to wonder. Bryan was on his own behind the bar performing to the crowd through the security grill that separated the staff from customers. He liked to be the centre of attention and to banter with customers he knew well. I watched him giving out small packets of white powder with the beer to some of these boys. They were all opening the packets and pouring the contents into their beer before drinking it. As they did so, the beer effervesced and frothed up, spilling over the top of the beer mug onto the tables and so the uproar increased. I was horrified at what seemed obvious to me.

"Bryan, what were you doing giving that stuff to those boys?" I demanded sternly.

"Oh it nuttin'." he smiled, "It just bicarbonate of soda."

"It didn't look like it to me. It looked more like cocaine," I said cynically. "Bicarbonate of soda in beer doesn't make people behave like that. Don't take me for stupid, because I'm not." He continued to grin, but I did not reciprocate. I went straight over to Edwin and told him what I had seen.

"Don't worry," he said, "I'll have a word with him. This is supposed to be a family cafeteria. I'm not having that sort of thing going on in here and he better make sure he takes note." With that he went over, took Bryan to one side and the expression on Bryan's face immediately changed. I never saw packets of 'bicarbonate' in the snackette again.

The end of April drew closer and still we had no transport document for the land, no loan for completing the house and no gun licence for Edwin. It was out of our hands anyway, so the fact that Edwin's life had been taken over by the National Football Team was not the reason for the delay. At least it gave him a distraction from the frustrations caused by local bureaucracy. I divided my time between tending the garden alongside the boys we employed there, doing my local history and wildlife research, and going to the snackette to help out around mealtimes when I had to go there to eat anyway. While preparing vegetables for them or making custard for their local ice-cream, I was taking in their conversations and getting to understand more of the local dialect and the kind of views and attitudes they had to what was going on around them. I could also learn a lot about what mattered to them. I found out what problems Edwin was having with the footballers when we were alone together after they had gone to the MMA at the end of their day's training. The excitement was mounting as the 26th April loomed, since that was the day of their first World Cup Qualifying match with Edwin as technical director. Guyana was playing Surinam at the famous Bourda Cricket ground. Although I am not a football enthusiast, I was invited to go along to support Edwin and so was happy to do so.

The team needed a lot of work. Edwin was shocked to discover that none of the players knew any of the seventeen laws of the game so he had to spend one and a half hours teaching them that alone. They were poor on both fitness and skills but they worked hard and Edwin had them eating out of his hands. He organised games for them against local teams so as to put into practise the newly learned tactics. The first weekend in April, the players had been allowed to go back to Georgetown to see their families or girlfriends. This had created more problems, since they did not return for training as agreed at 10 am on the following Monday. Edwin was stunned to learn by late afternoon that without telling him, they had all signed a letter of complaint which they had taken to the press and they were now all packed up and ready to leave. Next morning, they presented Edwin with a claim to give to the GFA for their weekend travel expenses and announced they were leaving his training camp the next day if they did not get it. He told them the GFA had neither paid him for his work nor for any of their food. He was on their side, but persuaded them to wait for the GFA to come down and talk it over with them. The three officials did not arrive for the meeting with the players until 7 pm, keeping them from their evening meal. They spent three hours thrashing out the important things, but by the time they called in the players, it was 9.30 and they were tired, hungry and very angry. Their conduct at the meeting was rude but their main complaint was that they wanted expenses paying.

"They seem to have missed the point. They're supposed to be in camp to focus on training away from the distractions of home and to stay here for the duration. If they want to go back to town in their free time, then it's at their own expense. They didn't know the GFA haven't paid me a cent for their food or anything else," he told me that night.

"What did they say when you told them?" I asked.

"They were shocked. They had no idea, and then they got even more worked up against the GFA, but I calmed them down and reminded them that they're doing this for their country. It's the World Cup!"

The plan had been for the team to stay in Georgetown for the Easter weekend and following week leading up to the match against Surinam. Edwin, who had by this time given up hope of getting any car off the slippery Colin Klass, had spent all morning on the Tuesday trying to find the team, who were not where he had been told they would be. He eventually found them by accident, all in one room with no food. They said they preferred being in camp at Onverwagt. After training, he left the team in Georgetown with their coach, Gordon Braithwaite in charge, and did not return till Thursday when he had been told he would get accommodation to stay in Georgetown. Quentin Taylor of "The Chronicle" was pestering him for the names of those selected for the World Cup game on Sunday but Edwin said he would not announce the team until the day of the match. This had really annoyed the veteran press sports guru, who began his series of character-assassination reports on Edwin from that day. Lunch for the team arrived late and when Edwin asked Carl, the GFA Secretary, about his accommodation, he was told to stay in the one room with the team. Edwin came home to Berbice that night much to my surprise.

"I felt like kicking his fucking head in," he said to me, after telling me about Carl and the accommodation. He was getting more and more exasperated about the GFA's modus operandi and treatment of the team and himself. He did not go back to town again until the Sunday of the match when we travelled together.

The streets surrounding the stadium were heavily choked with traffic on the day of the much publicised game. It was just as well that, in the absence of the promised car, we had to use public transport to get there, as parking would have been impossible. We had arrived several hours in advance. Already, long queues had formed at the turnstiles. When we finally took up our seats, we watched the stands fill up to capacity. Legs dangled from the branches of the trees in the street outside the ground, as people unable to get inside, or unable to afford a ticket, had climbed up into them to get a free balcony view of the match in play. The atmosphere was electric. All the papers had been full of anticipation of a great result with the new technical director from England (Edwin) orchestrating play. Quite a while before the start, Edwin had to go to the team dressing room, so I was on my own in the stand, soon watching my husband on the manager's bench down by the pitch, shouting instructions to the players as the game got underway. I never thought of myself as a 'wag' but I suppose for a while I was one. I took notice of the game as I never had before, with the interest of a loyal wife in the projects of her husband. The crowd roared every time the ball went near the Surinam end, but it never quite made it into the net. Then due to goal keeping errors in the Guyana team, Surinam scored the two goals in the first half that won them the match. After half time, Guyana came onto the pitch with renewed fervour and delighted the crowd by scoring a goal. They played much better than ever before, according to onlookers who had never known their national side come back from behind in a match. Even I noticed the vast improvement in them since I had seen them totally destroyed by Mexico on 27th February when they lost 4-0. Edwin was pleased with their performance but thought they should have won the game. However, they lost 2-1 to Surinam and so everything now hinged on the return game that would be held in Surinam.

Just before it was time to leave, Edwin brought two young white men across to introduce to me.

"You'll never guess what, Jane! I've just bumped into a couple of blokes from Blighty!" He turned towards the milky-skinned companions behind him, one very tall, with wild, wiry ginger hair protruding from a pork-pie hat and the other rather shorter and better-looking with neatly styled short brown hair. "They're here as VSO's. This is Trevor Ward, doing journalism and helping Guyana Radio broadcasts, and this is Mitch Mason, a printer, here to help The Stabroek News update to modern methods of printing."

"Hello," I said, "You must be the first white faces I've seen for the past nine months! How long have you been here?"

"We've been here a few months now. Today, we've come along to do an outside broadcast for this match. It was the last thing we were expecting to hear..... a cockney accent coming from a black face up in the press box," laughed Mitch in his broad Essex accent. He made up for his looks with a very warm, outgoing personality and a great sense of humour.

"What made you decide to do VSO?" I asked.

"I've just come out of a bad relationship and decided to chuck in me job and 'ave a change of scenery. I thought I'd be able to get me leg over some of the female talent doing VSO, but he's the good lookin' bastard," he said gesturing towards Trevor, "who pulled all the birds when we did the weekend selection camps before coming here. No such luck for me! Whereabouts do you two live in Georgetown, then?"

"Oh, we don't live in Georgetown, we're building an eco-tourist resort in West Coast Berbice," I said. "It's about two and a half hours' minibus ride away in the countryside." Edwin, who had just been discussing his views on the football with Trevor, but had overheard what I was saying to Mitch, said,

"Why don't you and Trevor come out and visit us for the day while you're here. We can't offer you anywhere to sleep yet, because we're still trying to finish building the house and in the meanwhile we are staying at my mother's tiny little place nearby, but we can give you lunch at our snack-bar on the road, show you around the village and some of the local wildlife, can't we Jane?"

"Of course," I said, so before hurrying back to Berbice, we invited them to come to Hopetown on the forthcoming May Day Bank Holiday weekend, when they would not have to be at work.

The historic day when we were finally issued with the Transport document at New Amsterdam Registry was Thursday 30th April 1992, for the piece of land Edwin bought in 1984. It had taken him eight years to get it. We now owned the title for the land which we had already built our house on and could take this document to the bank so that they would lend us the three million Guyana dollars we had been told would be needed to complete the building according to the plans. Everything was now happening at once. We owed our supplier about half a million dollars and he was starting to make excuses as to why he could not send down any materials at present. The guttering contractor had begun work and had started finding fault with the roof which had not been built level, making his job impossible. Pappa Dan had gone off in a huff at having his workmanship criticised and we were left with the consequences. The Easter holidays had further interrupted the working calendar. Our house was at a standstill with no visible way forward until we could go to the bank in Georgetown. Our ability to do this was now hampered by Edwin's world cup football commitment.

He was supposed to be taking the national football team to Surinam but was repeatedly being told conflicting information or no information at all about the arrangements. The day after the Bourda game, he had to go back to the Police HQ at Eve Leary in the capital, to meet up with English FIFA officials who had come to give a football administration course there. He met the referee Alex and the coach Carey.

"Hello Joe, what the hell are you doing in a place like this?" Carey asked him.

"Bloody Hell, I could say the same thing to you," Edwin laughed, on recognising the two from his time with Luton Town. He was so happy at last to be speaking to some like minds from the real football world. They were also angry with the way they had been messed about by the GFA administration. According to their experience doing such courses, Guyana was far behind other Third World countries in its football administration. At a Press Conference at the GCC grounds, which Klass had called Edwin to attend Edwin used the platform to give a thirty minute speech about the future of Guyana's football, in which he set out how the administration would have to change. Apart from two day-trips to New Amsterdam to collect our transport document from the court and to be told he would not be granted a gun licence, Edwin had travelled to Georgetown every day to supervise the football team training. He soon discovered that the players had demanded 2000 guilders each a day for out-of-pocket expenses when in Surinam, but had been told by the GFA that they could only have 500 guilders (equivalent to $2.87 U.S.). This incensed him because he knew that the FIFA ruling at the time was a minimum of $25 U.S. a day per player and that the GFA would have been given more than enough by FIFA to cover this. He felt the time had come for them to be exposed.

"They're a bunch of crooks! Their administration is crap, finance even worse" he snarled as he packed his case ready for the Surinam trip that as yet he knew no details for. "The two boys from the media are coming down tomorrow. I'll tell them what's going on!"

We were sitting at the snackette just after midday awaiting lunch and looking over their accounts, when I heard a minibus pull up and its door slide open with a thump.

"Who's been a naughty boy, then?" announced the unmistakable, cheerfully teasing voice of Mitch Mason as he strode up to Edwin and held his hand out to him. "Who's been upsetting Quentin Taylor, then? We noticed he didn't agree with your team selection, didn't we Trevor?"

"He did give me a bit of a roasting, in the papers, didn't he?" Edwin laughed, "But you know what? I couldn't give a shit! What does he know about football? What world class professional team has he played in or worked for?" We welcomed the two of them to sit down and have a drink and then we ate lunch together while Edwin unloaded his grievances on them.

"They haven't told me which hotel we'll be staying at in Paramaribo, they've given me no flight details for myself or the players. I tried to speak to Klass over the last few days and I got told he's gone to Trinidad to buy some football boots. What kind of bullshit is that? I wanted to know details of the travel insurance for myself and the players and I'm still waiting to hear. I've given them an ultimatum that if they don't insure the team and make arrangements for us all to travel together, then I will not be going. They're disorganised, uncaring bastards and I can't work with people like that." They looked on in disbelief, as he went back over the events of the whole affair of the last few months. "When I went to town last week they were having problems with the team members travelling. One of the players has no passport at all and another has passport problems with the police." Trevor was making mental notes of it all. In the course of the conversation, he told us that his dad was a journalist with the Sunday Times. He asked Edwin if he could do a taped interview with him for a Guyana Broadcasting Company radio programme to be aired next day. Edwin agreed and invited them to go down to the house for that, where it would be quiet and we would be undisturbed.

We made our way down to the building site and there I was able to share our vision of what the 'eco resort' would be like when it was completed and what kind of business trade we were expecting to get. I still believed, in spite of our uphill struggle with the finance and legal ownership documents, that we would be able to achieve a finished product that was as up-market as any I had stayed in during my travels around Malaysia, Indonesia, Thailand or the Middle East. We had two container loads of top class furnishings and fittings we had shipped from Dubai, and once we had a business turnover, we would reinvest to improve what we had to offer. "We hope that people looking for exotic adventure experiences, who still want to sleep in comfort in a home from home, will want to stay with us. They'll be able to eat local food without spending their entire holiday in a pit latrine toilet hawking up the contents of their stomachs," I said. "In the process of doing this, we'll be employing local craftsmen and tradesmen. To start with, I'll be doing all the catering, service, laundry, and maid work for the small number of guests we'll be able to accommodate. We're growing all our own fruit and vegetables organically here on the farm, and I'm expecting to be able to act as a tour guide for visitors interested in the wildlife, culture, geography and history of the place. As we expand in the future, we'll train up local people to be able to do some of these jobs to the standard we expect to set ourselves." I explained. "The Sapodilla philosophy is all about giving hope to the youth of the country and helping to develop them."

"So, Edwin Joseph," Trevor said after he switched on his portable cassette recorder, "On the eve of the Guyana-Surinam world cup football preliminary, what are you doing to prepare the team for the big match?" "Well, the team are now in Georgetown doing light training with their coach, Gordon Braithwaite, while I'm here in the quiet relaxing atmosphere of Berbice, because we've had a very busy time over the last month. The team have been training very hard and I've had to go backwards and forwards to Georgetown every day for the last ten days, so today we are resting and tomorrow we have a day of hard training before setting off for Surinam."

"In the context of the current social and political climate of Guyana, what difference does a mere football match make?" asked Trevor.

"Well, I don't see it as a mere football match," explained Edwin. "You look at other third world countries such as Costa Rica and Tunisia and how their success in world cup football has helped them in recent years, by giving young people something to be proud of their country for, bringing their country to the attention of the world and giving them hope. I think if we can lift the standard of football in Guyana, then we can do the same for young people in Guyana."

"Finally, what do you think the future holds for Guyana in football?"

"There is potential if it's managed in the right way. It's great that FIFA courses have been going on here in the last week in coaching, sports injury, which is neglected here, and administration. There are so many things we need to get right, but the administration here is very poor. The team still have difficulty in keeping concentration for the duration of the game and that's what cost us the home match against Surinam last week, which we should have won, and a lot of work needs to be done to improve that concentration. We've improved a great deal over the last month, however, and I'm looking for a win 2-0 against Surinam in the next match." With that, Trevor stopped his tape.

"What kind of wildlife is there in this area?" he asked me.

"We've got plenty of birds," I said, "and things like armadillos, possums, anaconda snakes and alligators"

"Alligators!" he exclaimed. "What, here?"

"Yes! We've seen them on our land at the back," I said, "If we walk down there now, it might be possible for you to see one or two as its getting cooler now it's late afternoon."

Behind the coconut reefs where the houses were, lay old rice fields, uncultivated for at least a decade. Drainage canals flanked by raised causeways sliced through them perpendicular to the coast. All four of us walked along the causeway forming the long boundary of our eleven acre estate as the setting sun provided a scarlet backdrop to the distant coconut reef. I led the way with a running commentary for our guests, pointing out the 'spurwing' or southern lapwings in the marshy fields either side of us, the nests of the 'cotton strainers' (pied water tyrants) in the bisi-bisi sedges of the choked up canals, the snowy and cattle egrets and green backed heron that frequented this wetland habitat. I was not aware at the time, that Trevor was taping it all to edit for his broadcast.

"We're going to clean this up so that it's a nature reserve for our visitors," Edwin said as we reached the remains of the old railway line.

"Well," I contradicted, "I don't think we would want to clean it up if it's going to be a nature reserve, because the reason so many birds and creatures want to live here is because it's so wild and overgrown, and all the insects and creatures they feed on can thrive in this sort of natural habitat."

"This is the part of the trench where we usually see the alligators," Edwin pointed out. "It's quite difficult to spot them, because they hide under the water." We stood still for a few minutes staring at the reflections on the surface of the water at a point where the trench was wider and floating weeds were missing. Suddenly he spotted something looking like a stick floating on the water. "It moved. Yes, it was the nostrils, there, look! Yes! Over there, Trevor, Mitch," I whispered, "It's a big one! From its nostrils to the back of its head is about a foot long... Now you can see more of it: its back and the end of its tail... It's about six feet long!" They were very excited and Mitch snapped some photographs of it.

"Is it a very aggressive creature?" asked Trevor, slightly apprehensive.

"Well I wouldn't like to get in a fight with one!" I laughed. "It's like most wild animals, if you go near its babies or start throwing things at it, it'll probably attack you, but for most of the time, they don't really like humans so they'll move away or hide if they hear you coming." We enjoyed the moment, with the residual warmth from the heat of the day radiating up from the baked soil beneath us.

"I can't get my head round this," said Trevor," In the last two weeks, we've been within a few feet of wild macaws and howler monkeys in the rainforest, and now alligators in their natural habitat." With that he shut off his tape recorder and put it in his bag and we made our way back to the road to see them off.

The very next day, Edwin was due to go to Surinam with the football team. He set off by minibus with his small bag of personal belongings at seven in the morning. I was not expecting to see him for ten days or so. I felt fed up knowing that without him around, there would be a cold reception for me in Taa's house because they did not want me there. Taa always ignored me or disappeared when Edwin was not around and conversation with the teenagers in the house was always an effort on my part which was made worse by knowing that their replies to my questions were wild fabrications. "They must think I'm stupid" I thought to myself. It wasn't difficult to sense that someone had poisoned them against me just because of my skin colour. It was enough of a sin to be white, but to be white and married to one of their black family was a far worse crime. Fortunately, I am not reliant on the company of others. I enjoy my own company and have many interests. In this situation, I had a few books to research and plenty I could do in the garden. I wondered what sort of goings on there would be at the snackette and on the building site without Edwin being there to "kick arse," as he would say. It would be no good my trying to do this, as the workers already resented my presence. If I were to try to exert any kind of authority over matters that were regarded as Edwin's business, then I would be demonised as a white slave-mistress. At lunchtime I went to the snackette as usual. The ladies in the kitchen commented on the radio broadcast with Edwin earlier in the day.

"We listen' to Uncle Edwin talkin' about ze football …..an' Auntie Jane *buttin'* in," they giggled. I felt a little hurt at their suggestion that by answering questions put to me I was butting in on Edwin's patch. Women in Guyana were not supposed to have an opinion or a voice. I helped them as usual and then went down to water and tend the plants on the farm. The day was drawing to a close, so I ate my evening meal at the snackette and made my way down to bathe in Taa's shed and change for bed before dark. I decided to go into our little bed-room early and read before the electric light got cut off. It had been dark for a couple of hours when I heard Edwin's voice announcing his arrival from downstairs.

"Hello, I'm back!" I sprang out of bed, put on my bathrobe and rushed out to see him.

"What happened?" I asked, "Why aren't you with the team?"

"The GFA are a bunch of jokers!" he said in disgust. "They didn't get me the flights or any insurance for us. I couldn't find anyone from the committee. I got told that the team would be travelling to Surinam in a minibus and I would have to travel with them. They would send the details of the insurance on to me when I got there! They didn't budge on the 500 guilders a day for the players' expenses and no one had any idea which hotel we're going to stay at till we get there. I had a long meeting with the team after their training finished at ten a.m. and explained to them that I wouldn't be going to Surinam. I can't go on an international journey with all its possible dangers without knowing where I'll be staying and without any insurance to cover me while I'm away. I'd insisted that the players should all be insured as well or I wouldn't go. If there's an accident and any of us are injured or killed while we're out of the country, insurance would pay the medical bills and could help support wives and children who depend on any one of us."

"So what did they do?"

"They said they weren't going either, but I said I didn't want them to back out just because I wasn't going. They knew what they had to do and 'Braff' (Gordon Braithwaite) would be able to take charge in my absence just as he had done before I came to help them. I wanted them to go and play for their country but to understand why I wouldn't be going with them. I felt bad but I can't take this kind of treatment anymore! The GFA can find another mug to trick. So here I am!" He held out his arms to me and gave me a big bear-hug. Although I was sad for the team and that it ended up this way, I felt enormous relief inside, as we could now move on with getting a home to live in.

Two days later we were able to go to Georgetown together to take our Transport document to the bank and sign up for the mortgage. Edwin made sure that he got a receipt from the bank for the document. I suppose this was wise, since the officials we had so far had dealings with in the country did not have an honest track record and we had been caught out too many times to let it happen again.

110

He did not want to let any bank claim that he did not give them the document that he had waited so long for and paid so much in cash and sweat to get. Two days later, in town again, we were able to collect a cheque from the bank for $779,000 to pay Bobby for our materials and another $200,000 for us to pay for the gutter-fitting and other workers' wages. The rest of the loan would have to wait until after Mr Carter's next inspection.

While we were in town, I went to the main library to read some local books in the reference section. Edwin met up with Mr Charles from the MMA and went to see the football sponsors DDL. He discovered that the sponsors had given the GFA $64,000 dollars to cover transport costs of the flights for him and the team, and were shocked to discover that Edwin had not been given any air tickets but they had sent the team overland by minibus. He was fuming when he found me in the library later in the afternoon.

"The GFA officials are crooks!" he said. "I hope they all get jailed! I bet Klass pocketed that money to fund his personal trip to Trinidad. I definitely won't go back to help out any more when they're back in camp in Georgetown. I feel sorry for the players, but if they don't like it they should walk out as well. Otherwise, they get what they deserve."

Sadly, the news of a 4-0 win by Surinam came out over the radio next day. The Guyana team redeemed themselves a bit by winning their next match against Aruba 3-0. It was no surprise that the press report about the Surinam match tore into Edwin for being absent from Surinam. However, what infuriated us was the accusation in the report that Edwin had cheated them and the nation by walking out on the team at the last minute. They said he had been accommodated at the best hotel in the country and paid a massive salary in U.S., costing the GFA millions of Guyana dollars. Nothing could have been further from the truth. He had not received a cent from them. Quite the contrary, in fact he had paid out of his own pocket to support the team of 22 men in food and drink for over a month to supplement what donations had been given by the sponsors. Even the sponsors had been found by Albert and himself with no help from the GFA. He had worked for nothing and even paid for his own numerous return trips to Georgetown to meet with the GFA and to train the team, in spite of being promised a car that never materialised. In short, he had been a mug and they had seen him coming from a mile away. Luckily he had walked out in time and had not been tricked into paying his own airfare and hotel bill in Surinam expecting reimbursement, as he certainly would not have got the money back from them.

The footballers did not seem upset with Edwin at all for his actions. They knew what had happened and expected nothing better. They understood what it was like in Guyana, grumbled and protested at times and walked off in disgust when it suited them, but had an inbuilt ability to cope with it because they had never experienced anything different. When their minibus passed through Hopetown on its way home from Surinam, they stopped off for lunch, shouting out cheerful greetings to Edwin when they saw him in the snackette forecourt. He was happy to see them and talk over what had gone on in the matches and why they thought they lost. They did not blame him and understood fully. He wished them well as they left and gave them good advice for the next leg of the tournament.

Ironically, just as we were about to get major works going on the building, now finance was in place, the main rainy season announced its arrival with three consecutive days of torrential rain. The deliveries of materials were now hampered by the weather. Trevor dropped in at the snackette on his way to the ferry at Blairmont. He was doing a report on a project of a major aid agency in the country known as "SIMAP". He had a chat with Edwin about the recent football developments and Edwin had promised to look him and Mitch up when we were next in town. After his vehicle left, some greenheart panel-boarding for the interior facing of the rooms was delivered. 'Slowdaddy,' the lorry owned by Bobby Sugrim's family, could not attempt the mud street leading down from the main road to our site owing to the softness of the mud with all the rain, so he dropped off the lumber at the corner of the street. Edwin and I started to carry the boards one by one for the three hundred yards to our site. It wasn't easy. The eight or ten foot long dense hardwood planks were very heavy for me. We picked our way along the grassy high spots of the dam so as not to lose our shoes in the puddles of slimy mud between them. We were only a few days into the rains and it would be a week or two before the real floods came. Seeing us at work, the boys came out of their hiding places and started helping to shift the pile. Soon it was all packed up inside the house to protect it from the wet. The workers would now be able to get on with something inside, so they would have no excuse to stall the building because of bad weather.

A truck load of sand was dropped off at the roadside the next day. It was important that it be moved before nightfall as unguarded sand would disappear by morning into unknown yards. We were set to travel to town that day to order the double-glazed windows and sliding glass doors and to pay Maurice Watson

$80,000 for an insurance policy to cover the building. Edwin got out two of the four wheelbarrows he had brought with us from England and instructed two of the boys before doing any other work to use the barrows to move the sand from the road down to the house so it could be heaped under the building before it could be flattened by goats, rain and people. We went off in a minibus and spent a useful but exhausting day in Georgetown ordering the windows and paint in bulk to get discount. This done, we set back for Berbice in order to reach Hopetown before dark. The pile of sand we had left on the roadside that morning was white and shining and in exactly the same place when we pulled up in the minibus at four thirty.

"It's been dry all day today, so they can't tell me the rain stopped them from moving it," he said, preparing what action he was going to take when he confronted them.

We passed the site, now silent after the workers had all packed up and gone home. They had padlocked the gate. As we entered Taa's house, Edwin saw Ogden, one of those supposed to have helped move the sand. He was not a family member, but he lived in Taa's house rent free and ate all his meals there.

"Why didn't you shift that sand like I asked you to do today?" The tone of Edwin's voice was sharp, loud and angry.

"Taa send us fo' look donkey" he said, sheepishly.

"Donkey?" repeated Edwin, mystified, "Why the hell were you looking for the donkey? You had important work I set you to do and when I pay your wages it's my work you do for it." Taa leapt to Ogden's defence, saying,

"Dem borrow Franklin donkey cart fo' mek de wok more easy, but somebody leff de gate open an' de donkey go up de road so dem boys spend de whole day lookin' for it."

"They had no need to use the donkey cart. I gave them two brand new wheel barrows and shovels and if they expect to get their pay for today, they should have done the work! They prefer to sit around doing nothing all day and get paid for it. The same thing happens every time we go to town or New Amsterdam. No work gets done. They're all useless and you encourage it!" Taa began to raise her voice in combat against Edwin,

"Na talk to people so, ya need 'em to help you. If dem all walk off de job den you'll regret it," she warned.

"Ha! Regret it? They're not the only workers in the country you know! If they can't do what I want them to do to get the job done efficiently and properly, then I'll sack the lot of 'em and get someone else to do it," shouted Edwin.

"Yes, Edwin's right," I joined in, foolishly thinking that I could freely express my opinion. "They should be grateful that he's given them a job, otherwise they wouldn't have any work at all!" Taa turned all her venom openly on me now, forgetting the careful act she normally put on in front of Edwin.

"You shut you mout' Jane, I'll trow water on you!" Edwin understood the full implication of this, but unaware that this is the worst local insult anyone can give a person, it went right over the top of my head.

"Right, that's it!" Edwin shouted in his most assertively loud voice. "Come on Jane, pack your bags, we're moving out! We're not staying in this house a minute longer! I'm not having my wife insulted!"

Chapter 9

Hunting Big Game.

A day had gone by since the day of the donkey. We had moved all our belongings out of Edwin's mother's home and carried our double mattress, still covered in the polythene that it left the Dubai furniture warehouse wrapped in, up into our bedroom from the storeroom under our house. The rough, wooden floors, panelled walls and ceiling were not as yet sanded smooth or varnished. The splinters and dirt would have ruined anything new, so I left the wrapping on the mattress and we spread out my old sleeping bag on top of it. The room temperature was so warm we didn't need even a sheet to cover us. I suspended my double mosquito net from a hook screwed into the ceiling and tucked the bottom under the mattress. There was no glass in the holes where the windows and patio door were going to be and no basin, bath or toilet in the bathroom. We had cobbled together a temporary three-sided roofless shower cubicle in the yard, by stacking concrete blocks like Lego bricks in a dry-stone bond. The side facing the house was the open doorway, so people in the street could not see us naked as we used a calabash shell and a bucket of water to 'shower' off the soap lather and day's grime. The workers' pit latrine toilet was at the far end of our farm. It was a long walk from the house but it was better that way! We could keep a bucket in the designated en-suite for emergency use in the middle of the night until the plumbing had been completed. It was rough and ready but it was all 'clean' and it was ours. We did not have to share it with anyone…. except the bats.

That first night in our own home, we did not get much sleep. It was Bat-Central Station. They flew in and out from dusk to dawn and we watched them swoop and circle from under the safety of our mosquito net. Now and again one would land on the outside of the net and cling there for an hour or two's rest, continuously squeaking to the others from its roost. Edwin was restless anyway. Every little noise had him sitting bolt upright, thinking he had heard intruders. He had taken a sharp cutlass upstairs and had it lying beside him on the floor next to the mattress. In the early hours of the morning, a hooting sound emanated from the pitch blackness out in the pasture. It was a human imitating an owl as a signal to an accomplice. Edwin sprang up, slid out from under the net and grasped the cutlass. He tiptoed over to the window hole overlooking the pasture.

"Can you see anything?" I whispered.

"No," he whispered back. "I'm going for a look around the veranda," he continued, slipping on his flip-flops so as not to get splinters in his feet. I waited as I saw his shadow pass the window hole on my side of the room. It seemed a long while before he came back and when he did, he was no longer creeping.

"False alarm?" I inquired as he re-entered the room.

"Yes, it was only Lindy going to the trench at the back to bathe," he answered.

"People get up so early here don't they?" I said, hearing the clattering of pots in a nearby kitchen, "What time is it? Half past three." I had never really noticed all this activity when we were at Taa's house because we were usually asleep at that time of night. "We might as well try and get a bit more sleep as its Sunday and there'll be no workers coming today," I said and waited for him to climb back in under the net so I could tuck it in at the edges again.

We must have dropped off into a sound sleep for a few hours because the next thing I remember was opening my eyes in broad daylight to see a cheeky little face staring down at me from the window opening. It was Kelta, Taa's seven year old neighbour. She was leaning right into our bedroom as if it were a climbing frame in a public playground.

"Good mornin', Auntie Jane," she said, once she could see I was conscious. I sat up with a jerk, grabbing the sleeping bag from under me to act as a screen for my nearly nude body. Feeling as if I had been stripped naked in the middle of the street, I said as softly and kindly as I could,

"What are you doing here, Kelta?"

"Me come ta find Uncle Edwin," she said innocently.

"Well I'm sorry, but you better go home and come back later," I said, "we have to bathe first because we've only just woken up. What time is it?" She looked blank.

"Meanno" she answered. I was reminded by this Creolese "I don't know" phrase, that time was an irrelevance here, especially to children whose only clock was sunrise, sunset and the pangs of hunger. I looked at my watch.

"God, it's only half past six!" but by this time Edwin, having slept in boxer shorts, was decent enough to get out of the bedroom and usher her along the veranda, down the steps and out of the yard.

"Doesn't anyone here have any consideration for other people's privacy?" I said to him when he returned. I was exasperated. "We'll have to do something to keep people out now we're living here." I was not sure quite how we would do this as there was no way to secure the building which still had no windows or doors.

"I'll tell the boys there's no need for them to sleep in the storeroom any more now we're here so we won't need to leave the front gate unlocked for them to come and go. We'll padlock the front gate from the inside at night," he said. It was an uneasy security, knowing that a three foot high rustic picket fence could be scaled by anyone apart from an arthritic geriatric and the building within was open house to all living creatures. However, in the daytime, any fence with a locked gate made a statement of 'no entry unless invited' to all creatures of the human kind, so it was a help.

I put on some clothes and together we sorted out a few broken concrete blocks and made up a hearth for cooking in a sheltered site under the house. I collected a few sticks and got a fire going so I could boil some water for tea. The previous day, we had sorted out a box of camping equipment, some old pans and a kettle that could be sacrificed to use on an open fire. We now hunted around the site for scraps of wood to burn and as I chopped them into smaller pieces to keep the fire going, Edwin began singing,

"Ro- Ro-Robinson...."

"Ha! Ha! Very funny," I said, trying to sound annoyed, but ending in a giggle. Somehow, seeing the humorous side of our predicament made it less of a chore. Later on, we got some groceries from Phagoo's shop. To keep it from cats, rats, ants and other insects, our rice, dried shrimps and other dry food was stored in sealed plastic buckets hanging from nails we had driven into the joists underneath the upper floor of the house. We were a bit of a curiosity to the neighbourhood now, as numerous villagers that never needed to walk down our street, now made a special detour past us in order to view the unique new tourist attraction in 22 Belair: a "white lady cooking on a bush fire in she yard".

Over the next few months (in fact the next ten years), I could also be seen trampling our laundry in a big plastic tub of water and spreading it out to dry on the fence and the bushes in the garden, but to stop it blowing away or snagging on the twigs, we soon bought a washing line and fixed it up so I could use my clothes pegs. However, we were in the middle of the main rainy season of the year, so this soon became a drudge of repeatedly picking the collapsed line up out of the mud to rewash it all. The washing never seemed to get dry and by its second day in the ninety percent relative humidity, began to stink and need washing again. Fortunately, before the rains had started, the gutters had all been connected to a massive concrete water tank at the kitchen end of the house. The roof was so big that thousands of gallons of rain falling in a short time could not travel the full length of the gutters without overflowing and flooding the foundations, so we had reluctantly followed the plumber's advice to build a second reservoir in the middle of the house to take the pressure off the gutters. It was an eyesore that ruined the appearance of the front elevation, but there was no alternative. An underground tank would be below sea level and would have been asking for trouble. It appeared with our two gigantic tanks that we would have copious supplies of water for everyone. When the first rain had fallen, a couple of weeks before, the tanks had filled up very quickly and locals had all been bringing their buckets to help themselves from our tap. We hadn't really taken much notice but Taa had said to Edwin that he should stop them from doing so because they "Tek dey eye pass you", meaning they were taking advantage of him. Now we were dependent on our own water supply, it became more obvious why we needed to preserve it for our own use and not give it away. The locked front gate helped in that respect. After all, public standpipes were along the main road and piped water was free to all at them. Those who wanted to take our water just wanted to save themselves a few hundred yards of walking.

The imperative to get our house finished was greater than ever, but it also became easier once we were living in it. We were now present on site at the time workers were supposed to arrive in the morning, so Edwin could see exactly who arrived and at what time. He started to keep a personal record of their attendance and timekeeping instead of just relying on Pappa Dan to do so. He took over paying them personally (instead of handing over the entire wage bill for Pappa Dan to disburse) so he could now dock the pay of absentees to encourage them to turn up. The positive side of this from the workers' point of view was that they would actually receive their pay and receive it on time, which was a novel experience for them. Edwin could also now personally monitor deliveries of materials, supervise safety on the worksite and scrutinise wastage.

Just as World Cup Football involvement had allowed workers on the house to take advantage of his absence, the staff at the snackette had also been "getting away with murder" in Edwin's eyes. The same eyes were now fully turned on to their handling of his business. They too were about to suffer the consequences. He had more than enough reason to scrutinise their activities. He had run up a £22,500 overdraft with his account at Barclays Bank in England because of waiting for a VAT refund on all the goods we had purchased in England to export to Guyana over a year ago. The overdraft had been costing us £351 per month in interest which was most of Edwin's monthly early retirement pension. I had been given the task of completing all the paperwork for this once we had received the container shipment documentation. It had taken until now for the Inland Revenue to process it and send us the cheque for £13,000. We still had £9,500 to pay off, but it was a huge relief to have a greatly reduced interest bill. The fact that Edwin was still helping to support Rafer, his adult decathlete son, through the Barcelona Olympics took up the rest of his retirement pension. Any progress on our having a home to live in had to come from income earned in Guyana, and at present, that would have to be at the snackette. Unfortunately, up to now, the majority of any income the snackette earned had gone on paying the staff and on raw materials for their products. The bottom line showed such small profits that as it stood it was not a sustainable business.

Earlier in the year, I had helped out with keeping track of sales and takings by drawing up a duplicable daily sales record sheet that the staff would have to fill in as they sold items. This was the only way we could know the amount of different products sold since we had no cash register. Even if we had the funds to import one, there was no constant electricity supply to operate it. We assumed from the start that the people we employed were as honest as we were and that any discrepancy in the accounts was due to mistakes in their arithmetic. We bought calculators for them to add up bills, sales and takings, but even with this technology to help them it was a huge challenge getting total sales minus expenses to equate to the takings they should have realised at the end of each week. Every day there was an inexplicable shortfall which I could only solve by conducting a forensic detective exercise. It seemed that as soon as we had cracked it, Bryan decided to change the product range without asking first, so the sheets did not have columns for some of the new products that were sold. Was he really too dim to think of changing column headings and prices with a pen to substitute new stock for discontinued items? Or did he know exactly what he was doing? Was he deliberately trying to confuse and wear me down so I would give up trying to keep on top of it all? I gave him the benefit of the doubt by assuming he had not thought of it because it was all new to him.

In the last week of the football while Edwin was away a lot, $5000 was missing and unaccounted for. This was over half the expected minimum weekly profit. Edwin erupted in an outburst of anger at Bryan and Lorraine (whom he was convinced was a thief) and I did my best to mediate, giving them wriggle room by showing them how it was possible for us to see where the money had gone missing by going through the accounts in detail with them. They both looked stunned and at a loss to know where the money had gone. It was very convincing. However, Edwin was not at all convinced.

"The party's over!" he kept saying to me.

"I really don't think they expected anyone to do the arithmetic to connect the quantities they buy with the quantities they produce for sale," I said to him. I had just checked the latest receipts for raw materials because the purchase of ingredients for our meals seemed to be in quantities that would feed another ten people besides the two of us. "Maybe now they know we are checking these things daily, they will start being more careful." We had a meeting with them. Edwin told Bryan that he must spend more time at the snackette and not be plying the road, leaving all the work to Lorraine and the ladies in the kitchen. He was supposed to be a manager and that meant being there most of the time to manage it. From now on, we would not eat at the snackette. This would prevent them from being able to hide their "losses" in the excuse of cooking our meals. From now on, I would do all our cooking on the campfire under our house and Bryan would have to feed his family out of the wages we paid him and Lorraine. The other staff would also have to pay for their own food since they were all receiving better wages than they could get elsewhere locally.

A few days later, Bryan came down early one morning to see Edwin.

"I been tinkin'," he said. "I need to learn how to do accounts and business management, so I want to enrol in a business course in town so I can learn to do ze job properly. If ya can sponsor me to do ze course zen I can do a better job of runnin' ze snackette," he proposed.

"Well Bryan," said Edwin, "That's all very admirable, but I'm afraid I don't have the kind of money to send you on a course. When I gave you the job you had me believe that you already knew how to run a business like this. I was expecting to employ a manager who knew how to manage, not someone whom I would need to train for the job while I pay them a salary for doing it. If you want training then you'll have to pay for it yourself out of your wages and you'll have to do it in your own time, not when you're supposed to be running my business." Bryan looked frustrated that he had been foiled in his attempt to wriggle free of the tightening constraints he was now facing. I broke the silence by offering to teach them both myself, free of charge. It did not need Richard Branson to teach them what they needed to know, since it was basic arithmetic, profit and loss, reasoning and common sense. So my daily agony continued as I became a human cash register and financial Agatha Christie to prevent us from being outwitted.

Meanwhile we were making progress with the house, albeit at snail's pace. The sliding windows were fitted to our bedroom first, then the rest of the house. The beautiful purple-heart channel-board was delivered to panel the lounge walls and when that had been completed we were ready for the house to be sanded, plumbed and wired. Vernon, the electrician, was a new experience for us. He came on good recommendation since he was the man who did all the electrics for the church. He had worked in the past for the English in Mackenzie (now Linden), and more recently for the Dutch at Onverwagt. He was a jolly man, always sending his canvas bag of tools a day or two ahead of his own appearances as if to reassure us of his intention to show up. Eventually he would arrive on his bicycle, wearing knee length shorts and leather boots. His short-sleeved shirt was always unbuttoned to the waist, revealing his large, hairy, black pot belly. Vernon could gaff and when he and Edwin got together, a lot of gaffing went on, so the work progressed very slowly. He had an amusing repertoire of stories and gossip which kept us entertained. Sex was always a favourite topic among locals and with Vernon, there was no exception.

"How me can get son?" he asked rhetorically, "when me woman get face like she get? Me put paper bag over she head!" he chortled and we both split our sides at the thought of it. After all, ugly as she might have been, Vernon had no room to talk. He had a round black face to match his belly and his bloodshot eyes, protruding either side of his flat snub nose with its flaring nostrils, made him resemble a bloodhound wearing a short curly black wig. Maybe a bag over her head would do her a favour.

"Ya wanna know why me do it at all wi' she? It because me na want people call me anti-man." This would lead Edwin and him into a long discussion about how local females behaved because it all astonished Edwin. He did not question Vernon's aversion to being thought of as 'anti-man' (gay). He just could not understand how the care of children procreated by casual sex seemed to matter so little in local culture because masculinity, custom and economic gain were more important. These early friendships with villagers we employed were the gems in our new social life in Guyana as well as the fakes. Many who had originally seemed genuine revealed themselves to be shams as the glitter wore off, whereas Vernon was one of the gems that would stay true.

Although he had a son whom he idolised, Vernon had never married nor wanted to. Delon, his son, lived with his mother and grandmother in the maternal home, Vernon lived in his paternal home with his aged and ailing father who now depended on him as a carer since all Vernon's siblings had migrated to New York decades ago. This meant that he picked and chose what work he did to fit around his father's needs so his very erratic working hours did not suit most contractors. They could not be bothered with Vernon as he took too long to do the work. It may seem strange therefore, given our need for urgency, that Edwin should have favoured him to do the work on our house. After our experiences with the sharks who wired the snackette using American voltage and cheap unsafe Chinese fittings that kept breaking, Edwin was determined that we would only have English BEAB approved fittings. Also, we needed a 240 volt system to suit all our imported appliances. Vernon was universally acknowledged to be the only local electrician who was familiar with English electrical fittings and indeed he refused to work with anything else. He also had a reputation for being honest and to charge reasonable prices. There was no question about it. He would be the only electrician to work at Sapodilla.

While Vernon was dropping wires and putting in fuse-boxes and distribution boards, the carpenters were completing the facings around the windows and doors and masons were plastering the blocked in downstairs rooms. One of the masons, Duff, had relatives who were getting married. He had to ask us for time

122

off work to help his family strengthen the floor of their house for it and so he invited us to the wedding and prenuptial 'Que-que.' I had no idea what to expect of a que-que but was intrigued as to why they would need to strengthen the house floor for it. I had been told that it was always held at the bride's house the night before the wedding and that the groom's family had to come into the bride's house to search for the bride and buy her from her kin with a bottle of rum.

When we arrived at Duff's tiny wooden house on stilts, there was a long queue for the wooden steps leading up into it. The guests in front of us kept squeezing in through the door at the top of the steps, so I was sure we would never manage to get inside the tiny hut. When we eventually arrived in the packed room, which cannot have been much more than fifteen feet square completely cleared of furniture, the stomping started. All the guests grabbed the waist of the one in front, forming a conger line that wound round in two or three concentric circles. The leader, Samo, started singing,

"Come to my que-que, Come to my que-que, Come to my que-que oh! Come to my que-que," I joined the conger line as we all stamped in slow rhythmic time round and round the room like a circling snake, singing loudly in unison with the leader. In an instant, I was part of an African slave plantation wedding two hundred years ago. It was a thrilling moment connecting me to Edwin's tribal roots. He must have felt the same as he had never been to a que-que before either. After singing many verses of a number of traditional afro-guyanese que-que songs, it was midnight and the bride was carried in on an uplifted stool, her head and shoulders hidden by a white veil. The groom entered, singing,

"Oh where me bride deh?" and we visitors all sang back to him,

"Search 'am go find 'am." After three repeats of this refrain, the singing switched to, "Nation awe' dem nation, nation awe dem deh, nation awe' dem nation, nation awe' dem deh" as the groom reached the veiled stool and uncovered his bride. He passed the rum he had brought over to her kinsfolk and carried away his bride to his own family house while the bride's family shared out the rum and traditional food and the guests partied on into the night. Now I could understand why the house floor had needed strengthening, to take the weight of so many well-wishers stomping around on it.

I cannot explain why I felt included by these tribal traditions, but I did. I embraced them as if a part of my own DNA connected me to them, not just my own marriage into the tribe. Maybe my Dutch great grandmother had African blood, since her father had been a tea merchant. Maybe all the stomping and chanting had awakened the spirits of their dead who had reached up and touched me. I wholeheartedly wanted to adopt this country as my own now I had come there to make a life with my new husband. I wanted to find out all I could about the past and culture of my husband's tribe and help them to prosperity within their own environment. I wanted us all to live together in a harmonious future, in which the community could obtain the education they sought for their children and improve their wealth and health and living standards while keeping their unique ancient traditions like this alive. It was a dream that I strove to realise from these moments and which carried me through the many nightmares that were yet to come.

Black people on Guyana's coastal plain saw themselves as stockmen primarily. While there is a long tradition of cattle farming in African history anyway, the conditions favouring cattle rearing on Guyana's coastal plain date back to colonial times when cotton plantations became uneconomic to run after slavery ended. Plantation owners, absentee or resident, lacking sufficient labour for arable farming, turned over the outlying areas of their estates to cattle grazing. They employed the few newly emancipated black villagers still willing to do wage work for them, as stockmen, grazing and tending their herds of cattle and horses. Some notable local ancestors, such as Cudjoe Macpherson who had founded Litchfield village a few miles up the coast from Hopetown and made a fortune for himself from breeding and selling horses and cattle, built up large herds of their own which they grazed on the common pastures and crown lands miles inland from the villages themselves. It was a proud tradition among the old men. Edwin's father and grandfather before him had reared cattle which they had kept out at Crown Dam while they farmed rice in the fields nearer to Hopetown and Belair village. The cattle were used as draught animals to plough the rice fields as well as to thresh the rice at harvest time. As a child of seven or eight, Edwin could remember 'bull mashing' for his father. While sitting atop a post in a threshing circle, he used a stick to drive a small bull tied to the post to run around in circles trampling the grain and separating it from the rice straw. Samo's father had inherited his own father's cattle, and when he died, Samo inherited the accumulated herd which had grown to over two hundred heads by the time we arrived on the scene. Samo had given up his taxi and moved into the savannah near Blairmont to look after his inheritance full time.

Samo was Edwin's younger cousin on his mother's side. He was very tall, thin and strong with greying hair and a warm outgoing personality. After his performance at the que-que, we sat and ate with him under the wedding house and chatted about local traditions such as these which he seemed to enjoy and wished to preserve as much as we did. Since the sheep theft, he had taken our cows into the intermediate savannah by the Guysuco sugar estate at Blairmont where he lived most of the time. He was part of a co-operative of several Negro cattle-rearers who leased a large section of the savannah from the government. It was part of the inherited rights to pasture that their ancestors claimed after slavery ended. They called themselves The Domino Cattle Rearers Association. In order to keep our cattle there, Samo wanted Edwin to become a member of this co-op so he would contribute to the cost of developing it. Edwin's aim was to help bring overseas tourism and thus income into the savannah by offering visitors the chance to sample a cowboy's life and work and venture into the adjacent rainforest to see wildlife and do bird-watching. Samo, as a member himself, had introduced Edwin to the other committee members and requested for him to join. They had welcomed him in as a new member, so attendance of their monthly meetings became another feature of Edwin's busy timetable.

A few days after the que-que, Samo called round to discuss the co-op with Edwin and they were reminiscing about all this in front of me.

"I want to show our tourists all these local crafts and traditions," I said, "Like Norma knitting her own fishing nets down by the sea."

"Me can knit seine net ya know," said Samo, "Me learn from me father an' me does knit me own cast net fo' fish in ze savannah. Me bring it an' show ya," Sure enough within a couple of days he had brought his twine and shuttle and did a demonstration of how to knit a 'cast-net' for us while I took photos of him at work which I was aiming to display at a later date. It was his birthday in July and he invited us to his house in the village to celebrate. Iguana curry was on the menu with its eggs being regarded a delicacy. They were enclosed like all reptilian eggs, in a pliable spherical membrane instead of a shell. The repugnant smell of these eggs cooking in the curry sauce put me off trying any of them. The curried meat however, was palatable since it was a bit like chicken or rabbit neck. I dare say there were meatier cuts that would not have been a mouthful of

125

vertebrae bones but as one of dozens of guests, I had to accept what came out of the pot. Bones are a delicacy to all Guyanese whose molars grind them into powder with great relish. I have never been fussy with food. I eat almost anything as long as it is well cooked and the ingredients are fresh. Living in Guyana was always a culinary adventure for me and certainly pushed even my boundaries ever outwards. There was one wild meat, however, that I never got to sample because I got there too late, and that adventure came at the start of September.

By the middle of August, the main rains of the wet season begin to die down into intermittent deluges punctuated by more prolonged hot dry periods. It is at these times that the higher ground begins to dry out and the streets become less boggy. The pastures around our plot suddenly drew crowds of small boys wading into the rapidly shrinking mud-pools where a few weeks earlier they would have been up to their armpits in water. Now September was close, they were calf-deep and bending down to scoop up handfuls of tiny fish and throw them into their quakes or plastic buckets.

"I used to catch shrimps with a gilgira here when I was a kid," Edwin told me, showing me how the circular sieve-like gilgira net that Samo had made for us was used to scoop through the water. "They'll take all of them home, season them and cook them and those they can't eat, they'll salt down and dry in the sun on their roof, and store for another day." One of the boys, called Shaun, who lived nearby passed us. He was naked except for shorts and his bare skin was almost completely white with a coating of dried mud. Even his face was streaked with it.

"Come na," Edwin called to him, using an intonation more familiar to the boy than Edwin's usual cockney accent. Shaun approached with his quake and Edwin peeked inside it. Large crabs were teeming under the lid of the basket.

"Crab-a-march" said Shaun.

"Ya get 'em by waterside?" asked Edwin. Shaun nodded. "I could eat some o' them right now" laughed Edwin and let the boy go on his way home with the promise that he would bring us some crabs the next day. I was becoming quite an expert at one-pot cooking on a campfire using whatever ingredients were available in the community and the season.

Edwin had put pressure on the workers to finish the house by 25th August. He told them his mother had received a message that President Hoyte would be visiting us when he came to Hopetown in August to open the Sports Pavilion in the village. It was true, but of course was an impossible deadline. It did increase the urgency of them all. Unfortunately, Pappa Dan had to go to hospital "for a groin x-ray", so Edwin, desperate to meet his target, took on an extra carpenter, Mr London, to finish all the woodwork. The eighty year-old man was nearly blind, so the work he did was remarkable. When Pappa Dan was fit for work again, Mr London remained part of the team. Archie Garrat, an Indo-Guyanese man from Bushlot who owned an electric sanding machine, came in to sand the floors and walls as soon as the supply of current was connected to the house. The progress of this work was erratic as the current was cut off for several days at a time and he was standing around doing nothing, waiting for it to come on.

Carlton, the plumber, now started fitting the water and sewage pipes and in order for him to do that, Edwin and I had to carry up the baths, hand basins and toilets to position them in the en-suite bathrooms. It was a bit of a disaster assuming they would fit the bathroom suites in the way we expected. Left to their own devices, they improvised seals for the sewage pipes using thick black sticky adhesive that ruined the peach coloured bowls. They fitted the white plastic pipes straight to the taps on the hand-basins without any u-bends, so they were not concealed inside their pedestals and looked unsightly in stark contrast to the dark natural wood panelling behind them. They admitted they had never fitted a bath before and asked for help, so I had to assemble all four of them according to the written instructions which they could not follow, and secure them to the floor before the pipes could be connected. After this happened, Edwin decided he was not going to entrust the assembly of our kitchen units to the carpenters. We knew none of the boys could read properly and if they were to guess how to put them together with hammer and nails instead of the fittings supplied, it would be ruined. I ended up doing it all myself with help from Edwin to move, level and fit them in place once I had assembled them.

The boys were astonished to see me use my electric drill. Few had ever seen one in use but none had seen a woman do that kind of work before. Fortunately, they were busy in a different part of the house during the day, but always came to see what we were doing before they packed up to leave. When they saw what I could do, they respected me more. I knew what I was talking about because I could do it myself. I could show them how to do things they expected

127

to learn from men. They also watched how Edwin respected my opinion, did not talk down to me or command me and indeed even took direction from me when it came to the kitchen-building. He set a good example for them which cut across local norms and customs. Perhaps this would have had no impact on them had he been a weak and timid person. The fact that he was a strapping, muscular man with a loud domineering personality made him someone to take notice of.

We had to work as a team to fit the work top onto the base units and hang the wall units securely. Edwin also helped me to cut the hole for the sink in the work top so we could inset the sink and fit the taps. Then Carlton the plumber could connect up the water pipes in the kitchen and to the water tank. It was another major operation installing the water pump to the tank so rainwater collected in the lower tank could be pumped up to an overhead plastic tank at the top of the trestle to supply the house taps with water. A team of men recommended by Samo came in to paint the exterior woodwork of the house with white oil paint while our other labourers on the roof slapped bright red on to the corrugated metal sheets. The inside walls were treated with kerosene and linseed oil to kill insects and preserve the hardwood without masking its naturally beautiful colours.

The house was nearing completion and it was very early morning on the first Friday in September. Edwin was up sweeping dust from the veranda outside our room when a car horn tooted on the dam outside. Bandar, Samo's Indo-Guyanese friend, called up with an urgent message for Edwin,

"Samo shoot jaguar in de savanna last night. It attack de cow dem." He had come to collect us to take us into the savannah to see the beast. One of us had to stay behind to manage the workers at this critical stage so Edwin decided to go with his video camera to film the scene of the drama and I would stay behind, because I would be able to see it in the video when he returned. I would go there another day when there were no workers at the house. He set off with Bandar in his battered old car.

At sundown, the car rolled up outside our gate and Samo, Kenneth and Bandar all jumped out making a commotion. When I looked up, they were huddled round the open boot calling out "Jane, Jane!" as they dragged a large animal skin with its head attached, out of the boot and across to the house. Kenneth was proudly displaying the jaguar's dismembered muzzle as if it were a pair of false dentures.

"My God, look at the size of those teeth!" I began, but then noticing a bedraggled Edwin coated in thick mud up to his armpits, "What the hell happened to you?"

"It's a long story," he said, "Just get me a towel and a bucket of water so I can get out of this stuff, will you, please?"

"Of course," I said. I rushed to the secondary water tank in front of the house with a large bucket and began to fill it from the tap. While he was standing there in his underpants, washing off his legs using handfuls of water from the bucket, I collected up his mud-impregnated tracksuit pants and put them in the plastic wash tub for later.

"Here's a towel."

"I think I'd better go in the bath shed and strip off completely and wash it all off before I use that. I'm covered from head to foot. I fell into the swamp and nearly got swallowed up in it. My boots are still in it. If it hadn't been for Samo here, you'd have lost me." I let him disappear and turned my attention back to Samo, Kenneth and the jaguar skin. Samo, rifle under his arm, was clearly basking in the machismo of having single-handedly slain this most feared and majestic of local fauna.

"How did you catch it?" I asked, trying to seem enthusiastic and full of admiration, but feeling privately sad that such a beautiful creature had met its death and was now a trophy. I understood, however, that cows were Samo's livelihood and to him the jaguar was as much a thief as any burglar who steals one's hard-earned TV set. Out in the savannah, a peasant farmer has no other way to protect his own life and that of his herd than to kill the predator. There on the fringe of vast tracts of uninhabited rainforest, jaguars which can live and feed unmolested by humans in the deep interior, find it easier to take their meals from the plentiful supply ready-made for them by their neighbour, man. There would at the same time be a need to educate the young in Guyana to value the wilderness and protect the natural animal kingdom from man's gratuitous slaughter. For now, I would help Samo to feel proud of his moment of heroism. He too was a rare breed in danger of extinction.

"Me go out riding Saddam, me horse, yesterday and me see one-one calf lyin' dead in ze far savannah, so me tink is tiger at wok. Me see where ze calf get eat by sometin' so me say well lemme watch out in ze night, see if he come back fo' more. Anyway me get me ladder an' me walk back near ze dead calf an' go up inside a big tree an' wait till dark come, an' me watch long, long time. Moonlight last night, so after a time, me see ze tiger come an' kill a next calf an' drag ze calf a far, far way back to eat. Me wait till me can get a good shot at him, then blam! me tek a shot an' he done dead."

"I'm sorry I couldn't come along as well," I said, "I could have taken some photographs"

"Ya can tek out me photo! Wid ze skin!" he said, getting very animated and instructing the timid Kenneth to stretch out one end of the pelt in front of our fence while he held the other end and affected a dramatic pose with his gun. Kenneth, not wishing to miss out on the glory, then posed the savage jaws with their menacing canines. By now a small crowd had gathered to hear the story and a clean dry Edwin wearing some fresh shorts had reappeared on the scene.

"I think this video camera has had it," he said. "I dropped it in the swamp when I fell in." The rather clumsy piece of equipment was in a plastic carrier bag. I certainly did not hold out much hope for being able to clean it and have it working again. We left the hunters with the crowd they had attracted and walked towards the house to put the camera away.

"So how did you fall in?"

"Well it was miles we had to walk and the grass was very uneven, a good place to break a leg! I was taking pictures of the carcass and the tree with the ladder where Samo shot it from and I walked backwards not realising the mud was still so soft in that part. I lost my balance and went in with both feet up to my thighs but the mud was so sticky that I couldn't pull my feet out to take a step towards the firmer ground. Then I felt myself sinking further down so I called to them for help and they were all panicking and going hysterical. I had to shout at them to throw me a rope so they did that and I tied it round my waist but they didn't have the strength to pull me out. By this time I had sunk right down to my armpits and I was getting a bit worried that I was a gonner, so I had to tell them to tie the other end of the rope to the horse and get the horse to pull me out otherwise they wouldn't have thought to do it. Thank God they took notice. If it hadn't been for Samo and his horse, I wouldn't be here talking to you now."

"Did it take them all day to get you out?" I asked, incredulously.

"Not far off, and if it was down to me I'd have come straight home, but they dragged the body back to Samo's hut. They had to use the horse because the jaguar must have weighed about 300 pounds or more. It was a beauty. They wanted to skin it and cut up the meat. Samo salted some of it to dry for later and they made a curry out of it so they could all share it out."

In the morning Samo came across with a small plastic container full of "curry tiger" for us. That was one meal I decided to pass on. However, I couldn't wait to be able to go into the savannah to see for myself what it was like, so it was arranged and a couple of weeks later, we all set off for a Guyana style safari with Samo. It was quite complicated to arrange, as special passes to allow us through the Guysuco Estate had to be obtained first. The public road leading to the ferry ended at Blairmont and thereafter it became an un-surfaced track much like the side streets in the villages, but it was deserted and wound through lush green cane-fields which were sectioned off in blocks by deep canals. These were where the punts, flat elongated floating pans like enormous herring tins, were loaded up with the harvested cane and floated off to the sugar factory near the road. We had to walk the very long winding road for three miles in the hot sun, but we were both fit. I had my plastic flask of rain water slung over one shoulder and my precious camera on the other.

"Wow! Do you know what that massive bird is, Samo?" I asked, as a huge white stork with a wingspan of six or seven feet wheeled over the nearby cane stems. It had a chocolate brown head and neck and a beak something like a pelican. At the base of its neck between the brown and white plumage was a scarf-like ring of scarlet.

"Nigger Cap" he answered, knowledgeably, "Some does call 'em Jabiru Stork."

"So that's what they look like," I mused, remembering being intrigued at hearing Taa mention the name 'Nigger Cup' and wondering what on earth it could look like as that name was not listed in my Book of South American Birds. I had been told it was a big bird like an ostrich so had got a completely wrong picture of it in my head.

It was energising being confronted with this vast expanse of natural grassland as we reached the edge of the cane fields. On the horizon, the canopy of the distant rainforest loomed under a feint mist. The swamps had dried out considerably since the jaguar had been shot, so it was not quite so dangerous walking over the lumpy grass but Samo was still careful to take us along a trail that was on a higher level and led right up to the nearest patch of jungle. He had his gun at his side for protection, I thought. The trees were bordered by dense thickets of undergrowth which we had not come intending to slash a path through. We just wanted to take a peek in from the margins to see what kind of plants and wildlife were visible to the outsider. Plenty of birds could be heard and seen. There were strange shaped nests as well. Then I spotted a very large brown nest high up in one tree, curled around its trunk. On a second look I could see it was furry looking. "What's that thing up there looking like a nest?" I asked Samo.

"Where?" I pointed to the tree and looked at it, expecting to be told another local name. Instead I heard a loud explosion behind me and saw the leg of the poor thing swing violently downwards, a signal of sudden death.

"Oh you killed it!" I said, horrified. "I only wanted to know what it was!"

"It Barim!" he said calmly. Then he leapt in among the vines and creepers and scaled up the tree to retrieve its limp body. "Anteater good wild meat ya know! We does eat barim out here in savannah. Mek nice cook-up!" He smiled proudly and slung the beast over his shoulder as he picked his way back to us. We walked on. I was in shock and made up my mind not to draw his attention to anything else I noticed while he was carrying that gun. I did not want any other poor innocent sleeping creature's death on my conscience. Never-the-less, this wasn't the plastic tourism I had experienced in South-East Asia and the Far and Middle East. It was real. It was life how people lived it. It was something to savour.

Samo took us back to his little wooden ranch-hut while he was skinning and salting down the ex-anteater. He had a little garden next to the hut, fenced off with a palisade of stripped coconut fronds. A deep duck-pond to the front of that was where he fished with his cast net to supplement his diet. He shared the fish with local wild duck, heron and other predators. His flock of creole hens, which had complete freedom to range the sunny grasslands, preferred to stay close to the hut where they could find an abundance of insects and worms and a safe shelter to run under when marauding savannah hawks circled greedily overhead. I noticed his calabash shell hanging on one of the fence posts next to the pond and imagined him scooping up the pond water to bathe at the end of the day. All his simple needs were provided for while he was out here. This was how Edwin's father and grandfather had lived, out in the savannahs, away from their womenfolk and their village churches, away from the children, except when they walked the separating miles to bring cooked lunches in stacking carriers to their fathers as a treat at weekends. Then the men would be making a kill and they could carry back some beef for a Sunday breakfast of pepperpot and sell the rest in the village to buy a few groceries they could not produce themselves. Time had not moved on at all out here in the savannah. It was a place to be closer to God than any man made place of worship. Here God was all around you, showing you his artistry and testing you by throwing you up against it in the battle for survival.

Up the stairs inside the hut was a tiny room where a simple bunk, a table and chair provided some comfort and rest at nights. A wooden partition with a door in it led into a second room containing Kenneth's bunk, chair and possessions. The hurricane lamp was hanging from the beam and a newspaper and a couple of elderly books were on the table, next to a box of dominoes. Samo and Kenneth would entertain each other in fierce competitions to while away their downtime. They would knit cast nets, sew rice bags, repair their torn clothing and socks, and talk for endless hours, knowing that they would face days on end with no company when one of them had to go back to Hopetown on family business. Life here was without electricity, but since supply of that was so erratic in the village, nothing much was missed.

Under the house, Samo was cooking over an open fire of dry coconut husks. He had cut an old oil-drum in half and rested the semi-cylinder on a sturdy wooden trestle. Inside, the coals glowed red and his fire-blackened cauldron was bubbling away over it, suspended by its metal handle from a hook on the beam above. It smelled good.

"Me does grow me own black-eye peas an' shell 'em out when me get nuttin' else fo' do" he said. The coconut grater he had used to make his coconut milk was an old piece of flattened tin that had spiteful nail-holes knocked through it in numerous parallel rows. I could see no sign of the anteater meat. He had seasoned some of it and it was now in the pot with the rice and peas.

"Me put ze balance of ze meat in salt fo' me an' Kenneth later," he explained. I took up one end of the bench at his rough wooden table and Edwin settled down at the other end. Hanging against the wall behind him was his cast net, loosely knotted in the centre, its rim weighted down by tubular pieces of lead secured at intervals around its perimeter. His sharp cutlass rested against another oil drum full of rainwater. Apart from these few simple possessions, and his gun, which he had stowed on the wall over his bed, he had nothing, and yet he craved nothing. It was a simple life and a hard one, but he knew no other. The cook-up was ready to eat, so Samo scooped some of it into empty calabash shells and handed them over to us keeping one for himself. I was not sure whether to start eating it with my fingers when he handed us a couple of forks he kept in a tin cup. It was a hearty and welcome feast.

"You're a good cook," I complimented.

"This anteater, tastes a bit like fatty bacon. I like it," added Edwin after finishing his mouthful.

It was Kenneth's turn to be away, so we could sleep in his bed in the room at the back for a day or two. We decided we would decline this 'luxury' and prove ourselves equal to this outdoor life. I unpacked our two hammocks from Edwin's backpack and Edwin fixed them up downstairs at the other end of the kitchen by the window. The sun was dropping down into the treetops against a crimson wash of sky. Samo and Edwin started discussing what developments could be done to the ranch if tourism brought income there in the future but the exertions and heat of the day had knocked me out so I climbed into my hammock and fell asleep. I was awakened after a while by the persistent buzz of mosquitos around my face and the cries of Samo as he rounded up the calves and other selected cattle into his coral behind the hut for the night. It was dusk and swarms of mosquitos were suddenly active because of the presence of the herd. Edwin and Samo repaired up to his small porch to take a shot or two of rum and carry on their earlier conversation. I hadn't brought a mosquito net with me so I wrapped the hammock around me like a cocoon, gripping the edges together under my chin. The only way I could keep the mosquitos from besieging my face was to cover it with a spare tee shirt that I could breathe through. I lay there for a while listening to the jostling of the cattle against the corral fence and straining the smell of fresh cow manure through my shirt as I inhaled. Eventually the gentle rhythmic swinging of the hammock rocked me back to sleep.

Next morning, after a cup of warm milk for breakfast, Samo said he was going to brand Edwin's two calves that had recently been born to the two pregnant cows he had sold us in May. We helped him stack up a pile of sticks and coconut husks over the two branding irons he had arranged criss-cross on the dirt inside the paddock. He lit the fire and got it blazing. Most of the cattle were let out into the savannah before breakfast, but the calves were still penned up. Now he would have to rope them and that needed an extra pair of hands. Samo looked the part in his straw cowboy hat as he looped the rope and tossed it over one of the calves' neck. It leapt and bucked to try and free itself, but he strained against it and brought it down on its side. Yelling instructions to Edwin to hold its hind leg while he tied a rope around it, Samo drew its other legs in and tied them all together. The little steer stopped struggling as it was now powerless to escape. Leaving it there, with terror in its eyes, he took up the lassoo from its neck and got ready to rope the other calf. It was trussed up in the same manner a few feet away. Then Samo collected one of the brands from the red hot embers, carried it over to the animal and plunged the lettered end onto the fleshy part of its rump. Smoke obscured my view of the moment of impact but nothing masked the hissing sizzle and burning smell of hair and skin. The iron went back into the embers for a while and the traumatised creature was released from its bonds. It leapt to its feet and raced out of the paddock with a burst of adrenalin. The process repeated, I could not help but feel the irony of a situation where humans unfeelingly inflict on living creatures treatment we have condemned others for inflicting on our own ancestors.

Sapodilla and the Quest for ElDorado

Chapter 10

How Green We Were

It was probably Desiree Wintz's article about us in the Stabroek News and Trevor Ward's radio broadcast that attracted attention to the existence of Sapodilla Farm because we had quite a few chance visitors from Georgetown over the next few months. The first ones were Harry Lovell and a group of four Americans called Charisma Travel Tours. I gave them an extensive tour of the house which was still in a fairly unfinished state, but we outlined what we would be offering and they seemed to enjoy their day out. A few weeks later, a Guyanese expat called Zena, who was setting up an eco-tourist resort on her recently inherited family land in Essequibo dropped in on us out of the blue. She had really come to size up the competition and see what we were offering. Her aim was completely different from ours, since she would be offering thatch-and-pole 'benab' accommodation for adventurous tourists to sleep in hammocks in a remote location in the interior. We wanted to offer something more comfortable than that, especially since we were permanently living in it, whereas Zena was leaving a local to manage the place while she retreated to 'civilisation' in the USA and just visited every now and again. It had always been Edwin's aim to live in the community he came from and really put it on the map. He wanted to help develop it properly, in line with the modern world and see locals obtain permanent employment that would give them self-respect, enabling them to live in conditions which would uplift their lives. Neither of us wanted the kind of absentee exploitation of locals that the tourism industry is often accused of.

Tony Thorne, an Australian student-turned-tour operator, whose partner was a local Georgetown girl, turned up a week or so later. The Thornes were organising tours from Georgetown into various destinations in the interior. It was useful to have links with people like them and Zena because we would be able to put business their way from any visitors who stayed with us and wanted a trip to the spectacular waterfall locations or other publicised natural marvels of the country. Tony said he was trying to get all the tourist businesses to form a co-operative group that could get a stand for Guyana's Tourism industry at a World Trade Fair. The government would have to be behind this for it to get anywhere, so we made an introductory visit to the Ministry of Tourism with our details and brochure. After a long period of silence, we were paid a surprise visit one day by the Minister of Tourism, a Mr Sawh. He was a tiny man, very pleasant and friendly but he did not seem to have the first idea about tourism or anything much else. He had no answers to any of our questions about any kind of help we would get from the Ministry to set up our resort, such as obtaining a telephone line. He seemed to have no policy or guidelines for us to follow, but was obsessed with the idea that we would have to provide two staircases into the house rather than the single one we had, because of health and safety regulations. Otherwise, he was encouraging and wished us luck. That was about the only thing the Guyanese government ever had to offer us: luck.

Later in the week, a surprise note delivered by a passing minibus from Georgetown contained advance notice that when we were up and running, Maurice Watson and his Insurance company employees would all like to come down for a workers' week-end 'camp' and have a 'picnic.'

"What kind of a place do they think we are?" Edwin said in disgust. "They can go and have their picnic somewhere else! Would they tell the same thing to the Tower Hotel or the Pegasus?"

We soon realised that we were becoming a free day trip destination for people staying elsewhere to come and have a nose around, get a free meal and drinks. To begin with, we did not mind as we had no accommodation to offer. The house was still under construction. Edwin maintained that to get business to come eventually, people would remember our goodwill shown on these early visits and thus advertise us by word of mouth. He always gave them his business card and a copy of the brochure we had had produced in England. However, we would have to be careful that when we were ready to open, we got in pre-booked paying customers who were prepared to pay a fair price for the standard of comfort and service we would be offering. For security reasons, we could not operate like a bed and breakfast taking in unknowns who arrived on the off-chance. Much work had been done by both of us in writing to our friends back in England and other countries, enticing them to make a visit. The first of these had already booked up their flights to arrive in November, so it became something of an emergency to get the place finished and guest-ready by then.

Clifford Jaundoo, an Indo-Guyanese son of the man who sold us the land we were building on, came to weld a wrought iron cage around the front entrance steps as a security measure. He would also make bars for the bathroom windows. They were the wrong size for any available prefabricated window frames, so could not be glazed and only had metal mosquito mesh fitted over them. We resisted putting iron security bars at all the glazed windows and doors as well. Neither of us wanted to live in a prison and felt such an appearance would be off-putting to guests even if all local advice was to have them fitted like every other house. It was only a couple of years ago that 'Kick down Door Boys' used to terrorise the country by doing what their name implied, attacking residents in their own homes and taking away their valuables. Thankfully the new President Hoyte had re-introduced the death penalty and six culprits had gone to the gallows as an example. This immediately stopped the kick down door threat but still people feared break-ins and robberies so iron grills at all the windows was a standard design feature in homes up and down the country.

I had placed an advertisement in 'The Green Magazine' in May, spending £50 that I could ill afford for one small box with no illustrations, in just one monthly issue. We had a lot to learn about advertising a product such as ours in a distant overseas market. Months went by without a single response. I don't really know what in my naivety I had expected, but clearly in order to get customers we would have to keep putting regular adverts in numerous holiday magazines before one might get any take-up at all and we did not have that kind of money. Apart from that, we had no telephone, so who would want to book a holiday at a place they could not make a telephone call to? We knew that fact before we started building, but did not realise that it would take ten years before we would be able to get telephone lines to the place we were living. Some six months later, we received a mystery letter from Lithuania, which intrigued the local post master because he had never seen that kind of stamp before. Inside the home made envelope was a handwritten letter in barely comprehensible broken English. The potential holiday maker was a Lithuanian student who said he wanted to know what it was like in the rainforest of South America as he was very interested in conservation and would love to come and stay at our resort which he had seen advertised in the Green Magazine. Unfortunately he had no money but in return for his board and lodging he would do the washing up for us! Needless to say we did not take him up on his offer as we could do our own washing up without needing to have an extra mouth to cook for.

Work on Sapodilla was progressing on many different fronts. We could not leave the builders working on the house while both of us went out for the day together. Edwin went out alone and I had to stay behind because there were valuable items on site that could 'walk' if one of us was not there. I could also ensure the work was done in the way we wanted it, so began my long-term incarceration as prisoner of circumstances. Mitch Mason had met up with Edwin on one of his solo trips to Georgetown. He was due to end his stint as a VSO in June and arranged to have a few beers with Edwin at the Tower Hotel before his departure. Mitch told Edwin that Trevor Ward had been ordered to leave early, as he had been conducting his own private investigation into corruption by the local administrators of the international aid organisation known as SIMAP (Social Impact Mitigation and Amelioration Programme) but the official he had tried to expose had friends in powerful places. It was a salutary lesson to me that anyone attempting to prevent corruption in any part of government would not succeed. Even aid organisations are not controlled by their donor countries. They have to leave the aid money in the hands of local officials who have achieved these posts through nepotistic connections with members of the local establishment. Aid organisations do not want their volunteers to cause trouble that would prevent them from being able to operate within a country, so they have a vested interest in being deaf to such revelations. Trevor had been given 24 hours to get out of the country, so was unable to say goodbye to us. However he had asked Mitch to pass on to us the tape he had made for his broadcast about us. Mitch promised to keep in touch with us once he was back in England. We had no idea that in keeping his promise, he was to become a lifeline for us as Sapodilla developed.

We got our first letter from him around the end of September as we were getting ready to unpack our furniture and books in the completed upstairs rooms. Moving them upstairs made it possible for the gym to be completed in the room under our hexagonal wooden lounge.

"Mitch wouldn't recognise the place if he were to see it now," I said to Edwin as we unpacked the personal books we had accumulated between us over the years and set them out on the bookshelves that had been varnished the week before. The smell of freshly dried varnish mingled with linseed oil pervaded the room. Warm orange tones of Kabakalli glowed through the glossy polyurethane, reflecting the titles of the tomes as I arranged them. Edwin nodded.

"Mr London made a beautiful job of that purple-heart door," he said. "It's amazing that he's still able to do carpentry to such a high standard when he can hardly see," It truly was remarkable. With three coats of linseed oil on it, the deep maroon red of this unique hardwood stood in sharp contrast to the white simarupa beading around the door panels. The artistry of Mother Nature had been enhanced by that of man. Through the frame of the doorway, the panelled walls of purple-heart from floor to ceiling looked stunning. Glossy varnished floorboards in a medley of deep tans, sienna and umber were balanced by the subdued sheen of the oiled purple walls.

"It would be a terrible shame to varnish the whole room," I said, "It's necessary on the shelves to make dusting them easier, but it would make the walls look oppressive and harsh if they were glossy. We should keep the natural look by leaving them matt like they are now." Edwin agreed, so it was decided. The unpacking of books took more than a day to complete. Then I had to remove the packaging from the suite of tables and chairs for the lounge and dining room and assemble the desks for the study. The first night we had enough electric current to power the electric cooker, I rejoiced at being able to abandon the campfire to cook our evening meal. This was not complete liberation from our Robinson Crusoe lifestyle, however, as most evenings were blacked out, so I still had to cook on the campfire. Even when Vernon, with the help of his friend Philip, had connected up the generator on the veranda outside the kitchen with permanent changeover switches, we realised we would still have to camp cook for a good while to come. He told us the cooker pulled too much current for our generator to cope with, so we would not be able to use the electric cooker during power cuts. At least we had all the lights and the fridge working.

Carlton's plumbing, guttering and sewage connections were now all finished, the water pump had been fixed up and primed and the overhead tank filled. We now celebrated having our first use of a proper, clean, flushing toilet since entering the country over a year ago, and a shower in the sparkling clean bath tub in our en-suite. There were many teething problems as the plumbing was a bit 'Heath Robinson.' We had very weak water pressure especially in our bedroom, which was at the end of the house furthest away from the tank. We had to depend on gravity to convey the water to the rooms and since the water tank could not be raised any higher than the upstairs rooms, there was not enough height for the water to drop down with sufficient force. The fact that the water had to travel 150 feet from the tank end to the other end of the house did not help either. It was all falling far short of the standard we had set out to achieve as a tourism resort but it was sheer luxury to us compared to the way we had been living thus far. Tourism at Sapodilla Farm would have to be eco-tourism because we did not have the facilities for any other kind. It was about to be put to the test with our first real guests: two acquaintances from England, who had written to us after receiving our Christmas card, telling us that they had booked their flights to arrive at the beginning of November.

Dorothy and Jim were not typically adventurous people. I personally would never have recommended them to come for a holiday in a country like Guyana but I did not want to put them off. We needed customers. I knew Dorothy. She had led a very sheltered life since her childhood in suburban Tunbridge Wells in the sixties and seventies. Mildly neurotic and dependent on her mother, she had married her school-friend, Jim, on leaving school at sixteen to work in a factory warehouse. When their factory had expanded into the new city of Milton Keynes in the late seventies, they had been given generous removal incentives including the chance to buy a newly built first home. There they had stayed ever since and were now in their mid thirties. As far as I knew, they had never been anywhere except the Lake District and Germany. Dorothy did not like children so they had a dog instead. They liked wildlife programmes on the television and had told me in advance that they would like to see the giant otters I had told them about in the Rupununi region down by the border with Brazil. Since I knew how unreliable everything in Guyana was, several weeks before they arrived, to make sure of a booking during the period of their stay, I paid $30 U.S. to book that tour for them with a family company in Georgetown that organised flights into the interior.

A few weeks before their arrival, Edwin's sister, Olive, who lived in London, paid her first visit to Taa since our arrival in the country. We were not quite ready for guests so she stayed with Taa. I got on with unpacking crates, assembling the beds, fitting bathroom accessories such as towel rails and soap holders in the guest rooms and setting out the table lamps, while Edwin took Olive out to visit local markets, beaches and elderly relatives. In an attempt to smooth things over with his mother since we had our bust up, he had agreed to produce a Christmas Nativity show with Taa's Sunday School Youth Club. Some of the time, he was out at rehearsals with them in the Congregational Church and other times he was involved with Albert and The West Berbice Football League, putting on another referees course at a nearby primary school, helping The Amateur Athletics Association and the Guyana Badminton Association which Albert had recently drawn him in to help.

I had plenty to do at home, unpacking my shoes, handbags and clothes from the boxes packed up in Dubai. They were now coated in mildew from the damp room the boxes had been stored in so I had to clean and polish or wash and iron them all before I could store them away. I un-wrapped the ruins of what had been packed away brand new eighteen months before. I had no idea this was going to happen. Edwin for his part had lost thousands of pounds in wasted materials, and stolen resources, so I could hardly complain about my losses which by comparison paled into insignificance. I had been wearing and washing the same few tops and shorts and slopping around in flip-flops over the last year. Now I could exercise some choice in apparel, I realised that the majority of what I had was too smart. It would be un-wearable in this environment because the climate was too hot for it. Besides, it was too dressy for any occasion I could ever envisage in the country. It would now just have to hang there as a daily private reminder of the life I left behind.

Olive and the others returned to England and it was now time for things at the snackette to come to a head. While Edwin was out and about in the village, 'Sister' Derrice had whispered in his ear that Bryan's children were flashing hundreds of dollars around every day in Bushlot school 'canteen' (snack shop). She thought children should not have that sort of money to carry around in their pockets when other children normally had very small amounts to spend on snacks. It was hinted at that Bryan's children were stealing from Edwin's business. Takings at the snackette were high but profits were negligible, as wages for the staff and receipts for raw materials and stock gobbled most of it up and missing products were now being categorised on the cash-flow sheet as 'damaged or spoiled'. One day, Edwin had noticed that a good half of thirty pounds of chicken bought that week had been put down on the sheet as 'spoiled.' Bryan could not provide any satisfactory excuse for such wastage. Suspicious that this meant free food for someone, Edwin had forbidden him to sell any more chicken at the snackette, because wastage was eating up any chance of a profit. The bank was telling Edwin that he would have to increase turnover or get rid of staff. Only the previous month, Bryan had asked Edwin if Marzine, a Guyanese resident in the USA, could park her minibus in the snackette forecourt for safekeeping. Edwin had almost allowed it but then refused because he suspected Bryan might have agreed to run the bus for her.

"If you want to run the bus for her, you'll have to move out of the snackette. You can't do two jobs at once. You're struggling to do one job properly as it is," he told Bryan firmly. "The accommodation goes with running the snackette, not someone else's bus".

"No Edwin, I'll tell Marzine to find somewhere else to put she bus. She get someone else to look after drivin' it, na me," Bryan assured him.

Things had now got worse, as minibus drivers at the park in Georgetown complained to Edwin that Bryan was driving a bus in competition with them. He was running someone else's bus when he was supposed to be running the snackette. Not sure who to believe, Edwin went up to the road after midnight that night to check for himself. The bus was parked inside the locked snackette compound. That was it. The next morning he went straight up to the road early while the bus was still there and hammered on the gates until Bryan came and opened them.

"You ignored my instructions about this bus. Get it off my premises right now. You've got until the end of the day to move out your family and all your stuff. I'll be up here by the end of the day to get the key off you and you can go and run Marzine's bus from somewhere else. I'm taking over the running of this place now, until I find a replacement manager that I can trust."

It was no use pleading for mercy. Edwin had run out of that. Did he not remember that Edwin had never given him permission to live on site? Had he forgotten that the room he had moved himself and his wife into and put up a dividing wall in for his children to sleep in was supposed to have been a store room? The available mercy had been used up when Edwin had allowed himself to be persuaded to let them all stay in the building when he first found out they were squatting there. Bryan had lied to him repeatedly and repaid that kindness by defrauding him of profits as well as doing another job in his first employer's time. Bryan had no leg to stand on under the employment legislation of the country at that time. He would be lucky if Edwin did not take him to court for theft. Edwin had plenty of written evidence.

I felt bad at witnessing this scene of instant dismissal and eviction.

"Don't you think you're being harsh turning a family onto the street with no-where to go?" I asked Edwin. I felt by association, partly responsible for making them homeless, but as we walked back to the work we had to do at our house, he explained to me what he already knew and I did not: They could go back to live at Bryan's mother's house which was where they all had lived before he moved into the snackette and where he was supposed to be living anyway.

A red faced Bryan, disgraced among the local community, collected his belongings and family and began walking the first of several journeys up the road to his mother's home. She lived in New York and he had charge of the key anyway, so he could go straight back with no difficulty. Edwin went back and stayed to watch them move out and make sure that they did not take any snackette property with them. Then he sent for one of the boys to come up and change the locks while he explained to the rest of the staff what had happened. A replacement manager was soon found in the person of Philip, Vernon's friend, who had been chatting with us a few nights before about how he envied Bryan's position. He was unmarried with no children and was allowed to live in the room vacated by Bryan, so his role was security as well as full time manager. Edwin felt a measure of relief at this, but I knew it meant a whole load more work for me as I would now have to explain all our sales sheet systems to him from scratch. Still, he had been a teacher at New Amsterdam Technical Institute, so he should grasp everything straight away and then it would be plain sailing.

There was a lot of tension in the first week of October as the first elections for 25 years were to be held. The workers stayed away from work for fear of attack because we were in between a Negro village and an East Indian one. I did not really understand why they should be afraid until it was explained to me that in the elections of the 1960s, after Independence, there had been a lot of racial violence in the country between the two races. Under British colonial rule, they had been kept apart to some extent but neither race had a political advantage. Edwin was never aware of any overt racism in the country when he was a child. Negroes and Indians did live in separate communities in rural areas, since lands which were given to the East Indian indentured workers to settle on were usually near the sugar plantations or on virgin government land. Negro ex-slaves had already made their own free villages on land they bought from planters after slavery ended. There had been some inter-marriage and mixing of race during the late Victorian period and early twentieth century. However, after the British handed over the government to locals in 1966, politics increasingly polarised the two main races vying for government. The indigenous Amerindians were completely ignored in all of this because they mostly lived scattered in remote village locations in the interior, not in Georgetown or along the coast. The largest segments of the population were the descendants of African slaves on the one hand and the descendants of East Indian indentured labourers on the other hand. It was these two main groups who became bitter rivals for political power and who ended up separating into their segregated villages along the coast from where they terrorised each other at election times. Bitter memories were harboured in these respective communities about the atrocities visited upon their families by the other race. I was married into the Afro-Guyanese tribe and as such only got to hear one side of the problem at first. I heard stories of how a black woman canvassing in Bushlot in elections in the late sixties was murdered by the Indians there. I also heard how Janet Jagan, the American born white wife of Cheddi Jagan, leader of the PPP, had been in communist uniform rallying racial hatred against Afro Guyanese in Indian villages like Bath calling for "Apanjat", which apparently meant "stand alone" and favoured segregation of communities.

Edwin went to the polling station for the first time he had ever voted in Guyana. I had no local passport, so was not enfranchised, but at the time I felt I had no knowledge of who to vote for or why, so had no right to participate. The tension continued for two days after the election when the results declared that the PPP had won with 55% of the vote but the turn out had been very low. Only 25,000 of the 800,000 population had voted. The election had been monitored by The Carter Centre so it was declared fair and free. President Hoyte had signed a promise before the election that he would accept the result whatever it was, so he spoke to the nation on the radio appealing for peace and by the end of the week, Cheddi was called to be sworn in as President of Guyana. Although I had not voted, and Edwin had voted for Hoyte, having been pleased to see the improvements he had introduced since Burnham's death, we were all hopeful that the new government would herald an era of openness to the world, of development and of progress. Above all, our expectations of improvement in the electricity supply were high. We had understood it was the corruption of the black politicians and their cronies, the black state-run industry bosses, who had caused the supply in our region to be so bad hitherto. If it wasn't their corruption, syphoning off money that should have been spent on maintenance and fuel, it was because 'Indians from Bushlot' sabotaged the supply by cutting out metal cables distant from inhabited areas in order to discredit the then ruling PNC government. Two Bushlot residents had recently fried on the wires in the act of cutting into them. Either way, we hoped it would all end now the PPP was in power as both of those alleged causes would be removed.

The first of our water supply problems became apparent eight days after we began using the flushing toilet, taps and shower in our bathroom. The tank ran dry and so did all the taps. One black tank of water had lasted two people eight days. We had learned to be very sparing in our use over the last year or so. What would happen when we had guests staying in the rooms? We would have to ask them to be sparing also, but would they take any notice? Would they even really understand what sparing meant in a place like this? It was a terrible nuisance if the water ran out before we pumped up and refilled the tank. We had to send for Carlton to come and bleed air out of the pipes at the end near our bedroom. The way he had constructed the pipework meant that he had to stand on a stool outside the back wall of our bedroom and get soaked while I ran along opening all the taps in every bedroom till water ran out of them and I could shut them off. I then had to shout to him to shut off the valve he had opened so as to avoid wasting any more water. Edwin would have to learn how to do this in case it happened again in the middle of the night when we had guests. We began to realise that the limited water supply we had would not sustain a permanently full set of guest rooms even if we were able to get that many bookings. Edwin kept asking why the piped water that had recently been supplied to the main road in the village could not reach down to the street where we were. He was told by the local official at Guywa (the state-run water authority) that the pressure from the well at Fort Wellington was not enough to get it to our house which was at the extremity of the village. Local people kept breaking into the line and fixing up their own water pumps to divert it illegally into their own premises and this further reduced the pressure. We were stuck for the foreseeable future and dependent on the heavens in more than one way.

We all worked flat out for the month of October, with no letting up. Everything had to be ready as far as it could be for Jim and Dorothy to arrive. On November 1st, Edwin hired Nello's minibus to go to the airport to collect them. I was still working through the night to put the finishing touches right in the rooms before they got back. Finally, I turned down the sheets and pulled the mosquito nets over the two single beds, set out mosquito coils and matches on a metal plate, put a torch next to the bed and towels in the en-suite. I boiled water, cooled it in the fridge, then put it in a flask and neatly set it out on a tray with some plastic cups. They arrived at Sapodilla at 4 a.m. completely whacked and jet lagged. We had not slept either and appreciated the chance to get some sleep while they did. Before they retired, I had to show them around their room and explain that it had been impossible to install a water heating system as yet because no one in the country knew how to install the solar kit we had purchased in England and shipped out with us. All water coming out of their shower and taps would be cold. I also had to explain why they needed to be very sparing of water.

"Don't be surprised if tiny green frogs jump around in the hand basin or toilet bowl," I warned Dorothy, "They come up the waste pipes and live in the overflow outlets, so there's nothing you can do to keep them out, but they are harmless and quite sweet really. Like the little gecko lizards you'll find in the room, they help to eat up the mosquitos, and if you hear scratching on the zinc roof in the night, don't be alarmed, it's just the owl we have nesting in the roof somewhere, feeding off all the bats!" Dorothy giggled nervously, trying to conceal her shock with a display of false bravado.

I got my head down for a couple of hours but then had to be up and ready early before they might want breakfast. I was glad I had done this, because the heat of the morning sun beating down on our zinc roof had woken Dorothy up. May be the thought of sharing her room with so much wildlife had prevented her from going to sleep in the first place, but she never let on. Thus the relentless cycle of taking care of a visitor's needs began. They were staying with us for four weeks. After breakfast and a long chat with Edwin and me about their flight and the problems we had encountered so far, trying to get the building finished, Jim paid Edwin for their four week stay. We had charged them £50 per week each for full board and lodgings since they were friends and we did not have a perfect set-up as yet. At least it would cover their food costs, but paid me no wages for the chef, waitress or maid work I had to do. There would be no employment within the house for locals for the foreseeable future since we had no regular trade, were too small an outfit to need such staff and would have to charge a lot more than £50 per week if we were going to make any profit as it was, let alone pay any staff.

Edwin took our guests for a walk down to the beach during that first day, and left me to get on with planning the menu for the next week based on the crops we could reap from the garden and the meat we had managed to obtain locally. I would be cooking local cuisine but knowing them as I did, I realised I would have to serve up dishes that would seem familiar to them, modify them and introduce new items gradually, in an anglicised way, so they would be willing to try them. Since it was a very hot day when they returned from the beach, Edwin took them to the snackette to get some drinks at the same time as checking whether Philip had got everything under control. He had been in charge there for over a week now and still had not prepared even a daily sales sheet for me to check over. Edwin was rightly concerned that he would still have no accounts for me to scrutinise. Edwin, polite in front of the guests, made a determined attempt to get Philip to see that he must comply by the next day, or it would cause serious problems. Behind the scenes in the kitchen, the staff, who did not like Philip, raised complaints about him. Edwin was also haunted by a letter from his trusted friend Constance warning him that Philip had been sacked from his teaching job at New Amsterdam for stealing money. Leaving all this turmoil in his wake, Edwin took our visitors in a hire car to the stelling at Rosignol to visit a carpenter's workshop where we were having some bedside chests of drawers hand-crafted out of crab-wood. Here they could see a local cottage industry at work with one of the country's main natural resources: tropical hardwood. The electricity supply held out long enough for me to cook our first guest meal that night and when black-out came, after we had eaten, we sat up on the veranda in the darkness with all the ears of the neighbourhood listening to our conversations, until power came back on again and it was bed-time.

There was a big problem as soon as we finished washing up the dishes a couple of hours after they had gone to bed. The water tank had run dry and we would have to pump up more water in the dark.

"Twenty four hours and we've used up an entire tank of water that normally lasts us over a week!" I said in horror, "It's a good job the power's come back on or we'd have no water to shower ourselves before bed."

"How come they've used so much?" puzzled Edwin as he went down and connected up the water pump flex to the extension lead I threw down to him.

"When you ask people from the developed world to be careful with water, they don't really know what that means. They never face the problem of the taps running dry in England or the USA. I think we should pump up water every morning and afternoon, so we prevent there from being a problem," I suggested.

"Good idea," he agreed and so it became a routine whenever we had guests.

The following day I did my maid and scullery work while Edwin took Dorothy and Jim on a nature walk through the rice fields to the old railway line so they could take some wildlife and scenic snapshots. After lunch we all went to see Aunt Lucy, the herbal medicine woman of the village, at her little house on the corner. There, prompted by our questions, she showed us forty different local herbs and explained their medicinal use to local people. I took some notes of it all because I wanted to add this information to the research I had been doing on edible plants. I aimed to make up a display of it for visitors in the future.

That evening I got half way through cooking the meal when the power cut off, so I had to take it down and light a campfire to finish cooking it on. It all seemed like a bit of fun for them to see me transfer the food from the blackened pot back into the clean one from upstairs, take it up into the kitchen and transfer it to serving dishes for the table. They made corny quips at my expense about the 'five-star camping' they were experiencing, while Edwin retold the story of the jaguar and his near disappearance into the quick-sands. At least we had the generator to light up the dining table and rooms, so the rest of the meal was as normal as it could be with the generator pounding away like a pneumatic drill outside the open windows and a tinge of exhaust fumes mingling with the appetising savour of fried chicken and green plantain chips.

In the nineties, the only banks in Guyana were the Bank of Baroda in the capital, Georgetown and the co-op in New Amsterdam. Village peasants, whose income was sporadic because they were subsistence farmers, lived from hand to mouth with any cash they had. Some even operated by barter. There was no regular paid employment unless you worked in a shop or on a minibus for a small investor. A few locals were employed by the state as teachers, in the regional offices or in the state-run sugar estate at Blairmont. They often did not get paid for months on end so had to supplement their income by subsistence farming or taxi driving. No one was really self-employed because the capital to buy a bus or to stock out a shop came from overseas relatives who invested it, leaving it in the hands of a family member who remained in the country to look after an elderly parent or grandparent. These kinds of investments had started to spring up in the country since Burnham's death. Overseas Guyanese periodically sent barrels full of cheap American products to their relatives, which they then sold to other villagers 'under the bottom house' (within the space under their own house) to get cash. They stored the money in hidey holes in their homes because the travel expenses to Georgetown were usually more than the value of the cash they had. It was a fact of life but it meant that our guests would have to bring banknotes in sterling or U.S. dollars, not traveller's cheques, as the Bank of Baroda did not accept them. For now it meant that Edwin would have to take them into Georgetown the next day so they could change money legally at the Bank or licenced cambio.

When they all returned by seven o'clock that evening, it was dark and I had already started cooking their evening meal expecting them to be hungry and not wanting to eat late.

"I don't want anything," said Edwin, "we ate a huge meal in Guyana Stores in Georgetown at lunchtime and I'm still full."

"So am I," said Jim.

"Oh," I said, deflated, "What am I going to do with all this food I've cooked?"

"I'll eat with you," Dorothy blurted, peering over her old-fashioned spectacle frames, "I didn't fancy eating in that place we went in."

"That's about the best place to eat in Georgetown, so it's a good job he didn't take you anywhere else," I laughed. We all sat around the table making small talk while Dorothy and I ate and then they decided to go to bed early.

"It's so hot," Dorothy complained.

"I don't like a lot of heat. It makes me uncomf'table," was Jim's parting shot in his slow Kentish drawl. They said good night and disappeared around the veranda en route to their room.

Edwin waited till they were out of earshot and said, "They've been complaining about the heat all day. What do they fucking expect, snow? We're on the Equator."

"Did you have a bad day?" I teased, knowing what kind of things he must have endured.

"They nearly drove me mad. I had to go everywhere with them. They didn't want to do anything by themselves. Whatever I suggested they could do, they wanted me to take them there and go round with them. I think they were scared."

"Well I suppose they felt a bit threatened, being the only white people in sight and not really being able to follow what people might be saying. They've never been anywhere hot for a holiday before. Every year they go up to the Lake District for a week or two. You'll have to get used to them trailing round with you, as we've got another three and a half weeks of it!"

By the tenth day of their stay, Edwin was climbing up the walls at having to babysit our two English guests who did not want to go anywhere or do anything on their own. He had at least persuaded them to walk alone up to the post office at Fort Wellington to post their cards and had got Speer, one of our garden helpers to take them around the garden, explaining what the different plants were. That gave him an hour of freedom to sort out a few problems such as the leaking sewage pipe at the back of the house. He did not have much peace, however, as they were soon back and following him around, waiting for him to entertain them. As yet we had no outside areas completed and suitable for sunbathing and swimming, for them to lounge around. But they could have walked back to the beach for that. The truth was that neither of them liked sunbathing or swimming. Perhaps they had assumed, since they knew us, that we would be jumping into a car with them and driving them the length and breadth of the country to 'show them the sights'. That wasn't something you could do in a car in Guyana. You had to charter an internal flight or a special boat and cover vast distances. We did not have a car of our own in the country. I had sold mine in order to raise the shipping costs for my container. I knew it would be ruined on Guyana's rough roads. Edwin had given his to his son in England before he left, telling him to put it together with his own as a trade-in for a new car. We had to get by in Guyana without a vehicle and go by the only available public transport, which was minibus. Perhaps Dorothy had assumed I would be living in luxury and comfort since she knew that was how I had been living in Dubai. She knew I had stayed in high class hotels in my previous travels. Perhaps she assumed I could not cope with roughing it and so the idea that I might have done so did not enter her head because she had never had to do that herself. If that is what she assumed, she was quite wrong.

The savannah story which Edwin had told our guests had not deterred them from asking if they could do a safari there. I suppose Dorothy thought: if Jane can do it, then I can. It had all been organised for them to go in with Edwin and be left with Samo and Kenneth next day. Edwin set off early in the morning, with them and their overnight bags. He would take them in and leave them there because we had things to do. After a couple of nights he would come back and collect them. That afternoon, he did not return alone as expected. He had left Jim in the savannah, but Dorothy had come back with him. She had a migraine. I put her to bed straight away with plenty of water to drink. The migraine suddenly disappeared within fifteen minutes of her being back at Sapodilla, however, so I suspected she could not bring herself to camp out overnight even though Samo had gone to a great deal of trouble making up comfortable beds for them in his little wooden house.

"This is what you're going to get when you run a tourism business," I told Edwin when we were getting into bed that evening, "Unless you make it clear to people before they book that such adventures are not for the fainthearted, you will get people coming out to us that are totally unsuited to being here. Even when they do get told, people in developed countries don't realise what a sheltered life they lead and think they're not one of the fainthearted ones. They see David Attenborough hacking through the undergrowth on TV from the comfort of their living room and have no idea what his senses are experiencing all around him, so they see themselves in his position."

"You mean they're only armchair naturalists?"

"Yes, exactly,"

We had an exhausting day as usual next day, since we both had to get on with work we had planned. Materials were being delivered for Edwin to see to and help unload at his brother's house and I had the snackette books to go through, laundry, cleaning, menu planning, reaping vegetables, making bread, pasteurising milk and other essential food preparation. I did not want to have Dorothy looking over my shoulder distracting my attention while I was trying to get things done efficiently, so she had to spend her day reading in her room or on the veranda without any company until mealtimes. When Edwin collected Jim from the savannah next morning, Dorothy did not want to go with him. I began to panic about the giant otter trip I had booked for them. It surely would not be something they could cope with. Jim's face was a picture of happiness when he and Edwin got back. He had a miserable looking expression at the best of times but it was worse than usual. They spent most of their day recovering in their room, only emerging for extra soft drinks and water or teas on the veranda.

That evening, we managed to get the video player working, so before we put on a film of their choice, we could show them some short tapes we had made of our first months in Guyana. It was funny looking back at the shell we first lived in compared to its current luxurious state. It seemed a good time to remind them about their proposed other excursions.

"We have to know which of the wildlife tours you want to go on so we can confirm the bookings for you before you go back," I said, "Do you want to go to the Kaieteur Falls as well as the Rupununi Giant Otter trip, or just leave it at the one?"

"Will you be going?" Dorothy blurted out without answering.

"Well, no."

"What about Edwin?"

"No. We can't afford that. Its hundreds of US dollars and we haven't got any income for pleasure trips while we're still trying to get this house up and running," I reminded her.

"Then we don't want to go," she said, flatly.

"But you'll be perfectly all right without us," Edwin reasoned, "You'll be safe with the tour operators in Georgetown, and Nello will take you to the airport and wait for you and bring you back, so you won't be going with strangers on public transport."

"We don't mind going to Georgetown again to buy some souvenirs in that place you took us. We don't think we've got enough spare money for the trips," said Jim, sheepishly, "We've got to pay for that carving we ordered from the Rasta bloke you took us to the other day, and Shirley wants to get something made in gold like you said we could."

"Okay, I'll get that sorted for you, but I won't be going to town again until I take you back to the airport, so you'll have to go alone with Nello. It's all right, Nello will take you everywhere you want to go and show you what to do," Edwin reassured, realising why the sudden look of panic flashed across Jim's eyes as his brain slowly processed this information.

By the end of two weeks, we pumped up water to the black tank for the last time. The concrete rain reservoir had run dry. Edwin made enquiries about how we would get the water tank lorry to come from Bushlot so we could buy some extra water to replenish the reservoir if it did not rain by the next day. We had not had rain for five months and everywhere was bone dry. The November rains were expected any day, so we did not want to waste money buying in water just when we would get a free supply from above. I thought about doing a rain dance, but it wasn't necessary. The heavens opened before morning and filled up the massive reservoir within hours, saving our skin in the nick of time. The rest of their stay dragged on, punctuated only by their day shopping in Georgetown, a visit to the goldsmith's shack in Bushlot, one to the church nativity rehearsals and another to Hopetown Primary school with Edwin. When asked to introduce herself to the children at the school, Dorothy, who had taken some elementary piano exams at school, told them she gave children piano lessons in her own home. The teachers asked if she could teach the children how to read music while she was there.

Edwin announced at dinner that night that he had fixed up for her to give a music lesson to a group of primary school children from Hopetown while she was with us, using the little toy electric organ we had down in our storeroom. Their class teacher would be bringing them to Sapodilla for this after school finished in two days' time. Dorothy seemed alarmed and insisted that she could only do one-to-one piano lessons and not a group music class. To take the pressure off her, I offered to do the introductory class for a group of interested children, while she took one or two separately on their own with the keyboard. Over the next day or two, I prepared a really simple short lesson to introduce the idea of reading music and went through it with her beforehand. I made some simple teaching aids from scraps that cost nothing. They could be copied by the school teachers so they could move on with what they learned when they got back to school. It was to please Edwin and show willing really, because I knew that it was futile giving a musical instrument lesson on just one day when it would not be followed up by many more lessons and practice. He was trying to push the teachers into teaching the children to play the recorders we had given them at the primary school. He did not know that the teachers themselves could not read music so could not teach it. I discussed this revelation with Dorothy as we evaluated the session afterwards. They both must have been shocked by the appalling state of education in the country even though neither of them had as much as an "O" level. This prompted them to leave a donation of about twenty pounds in Guyana dollars to use "educational-wise" before they left for England. They proudly informed us that the holiday hadn't cost them as much as they thought and for the first time they were going back from a holiday with money to spare. They were taking back £750 with them.

After seeing them disappear in the distance at three a.m. on their day of departure, I couldn't help thinking that they would have had more than enough to pay for their trips to Kaieteur Falls and the Rupununi. The real reason for cancellation must have been fear of the unknown. Edwin returned from the airport late in the day. Their flight had been delayed four and a half hours before take-off so he had stayed there with them until the embarkation call because Jim was a bag of nerves. It was a relief that Edwin had managed to get a refund for me on the deposit I had paid for the cancelled trip. He had told the tour operators a concocted story that our visitors had been sick on the date we had provisionally booked and had to return suddenly to England.

"They were very nice about it," he said, "They managed to get some Georgetown people to fill the places when we didn't pay the balance in full within three days of their trip date." It was all a useful trial run. We both knew we had a long way to go before we could say we were ready for proper commercial operations, but we still believed it was a realistic goal and worked tirelessly towards achieving it over the next year or so. We had shown the local community that our vision could happen and have an impact on their lives and we did not want to let them down.

As soon as we had the opportunity to go into Georgetown again, we went on a mission to buy a local gas cooker. It might not be the quality we would have liked but it would be essential for the future knowing now that our electric cooker could not be powered by the generator when there was a power cut. It was ludicrous that during the month of our first guests, I had spent at least half of the nights cooking on a campfire when it was time for the main meal of the day and a sparkling new first world cooker was lying idle, almost mocking me for having bought it and shipped it out there. We had to order the gas cooker on our first trip and go back to collect it just before Christmas. Another feature we tried to rectify was our lack of hot water. Albert recommended someone who worked at the University of Guyana who was the only expert in solar powered energy in the country, so we asked him to contact us. The young man in question turned up with a friend one day and inspected our solar panels. He explained to us that he had never fitted any solar water tank but had been on a course in England where he had worked on the very same kit we had. He could not give us a quote for the work yet and suggested that we would have to get all the copper pipework fitted before he would come down and mount the tank and connect it. He was also unsure how we would mount it on the galvanised roof as the weight might be too much to be supported without extra strengthening. If not on the roof, it would have to be mounted on some sort of trestle next to the roof.

As the rains of the season became heavier, the condition of the roof was far from satisfactory. There were still many leaks everywhere. The boys who had hammered in the flat headed nails to secure the sheets in the first place had not been methodical in applying Acotite sealant over them so water trickled through onto the rafters. It became a frenzied game for us every time heavy rain fell, to guess where the water would start dripping so we could move the furniture out of the way before it got stained from the natural dye in the wood as the water passed through it. No matter how many times we sent someone up on the roof with Acotite, there was always a new leak when it next rained. The thought of having more interference with the roof by people whose ability and pedigree was uncertain and who might be very expensive crooks for all we knew, influenced Edwin's decision not to go ahead with installing the solar kit. I was upset because I felt it was another nail in the coffin of our commercial tourism prospects. People who pay hotel prices want to be able to bathe or shower in warm water. I also wanted the prospect of returning before too long to the living conditions I had been accustomed to in the past. For now I would have to boil up water in a huge maslin pan on the gas stove and cart it down to the other end of the house every night to pour in our own bath. Carlton plumbed in my brand new imported washing machine, but it would not work because the water pressure was insufficient to make the drum rotate, so it too lay idle while I continued to trample my laundry in a large plastic tub under the house.

Norma's son, Sean reappeared on the scene before Christmas. He had been away 'in the gold bush' trying to make his fortune but had found none and had now come back with a medical problem which he needed help for. A white patch of skin scarred the part of his face near his nose. Edwin had given him the money to go to the doctor for tests. Now the results had come back and he needed help to get "special antibiotics" to treat what he had been told was Hansen's disease. I looked this up in our medical encyclopaedia and discovered it was another name for leprosy. I could not help feeling that the "doctor's" prescription for gentian violet solution would not have been an adequate treatment for Hansen's disease although it might help with a fungal infection. However, I was not a doctor and perhaps I was completely wrong. Edwin gave him the money he needed and asked him if his mother had caught any fish lately. He said they had not been out fishing for six days. Sean had a new smile on his face. One of his front teeth had been capped with gold since we last saw him. Sean had no thought of using his gold to pay for his own doctor's bill instead of using it to decorate his tooth. What an irony it was that the desire for fashionable gold teeth drew people like him to live in even more squalid overcrowded conditions than they did in their home villages, to stand all day in muddy water up to their shoulders, in hot humid forested areas where the biodiversity of microbes, like any other living thing, is greater than anywhere on the planet. It was little wonder that they came back with serious health problems.

Now I had time to myself, I drew up a design plan for the front garden and Edwin and I pegged out some string to mark out the boundaries of grass and borders before we could plant some ornamental trees and shrubs. There were no garden centres or horticultural nurseries in the country at that time. The local market sometimes had a stall with a few paint cans of rooted bougainvillea cuttings for sale. Taa had given us parlour palms and a piece of her rubber tree. Various aunts had supplied succulents, cannas, cacti, and crotons of different shapes and sizes. Edwin canvassed anyone and everyone he knew to get flower plants for the gardens and they responded, glad to play a part in building this showpiece in their village. Sometimes they raised an eyebrow at his requests:

"Bamboo? Nobody does put bamboo in garden! Dem big ting does tek over de whole place!"

"Well I want one and I'll cut it back if it gets too big!"

Before the week was out he had managed to get someone to dig up a root from beyond the railway line and I planted it where my plan had envisaged it.

"Buck cotton?" Taa sneered, "Dem is slave plant. No garden should have slave plant inside."

"I want at least one example of every local plant in the garden," Edwin had said many times.

This idea appealed to me. I saw how it could create a point of interest for visitors if there were labels on the trees and garden plants with a little information on the origin and role of the plant in the country's economy or history and this could be part of a little discovery trail throughout the grounds. Aunt Lucy had given us a local wild bush with attractive copper coloured leaves and an interesting fruit with seeds looking like coffee beans. It was called 'Physic nut' because of its historic use in herbal medicine. I discovered in my research that the fruit was highly poisonous and that a domestic slave had served it up to his hated master in coffee on one plantation. The master only discovered the plot because he always used to let the cook's three year old child drink the last bit of coffee in his cup but the child innocently announced on that day that he wouldn't be drinking the coffee. When asked why, he revealed that his papa had put physic in it, so the cook was made to drink all the coffee and from the effects of that, he soon died. It was by using such evidence that I wished to bring alive the hidden history of the place for our visitors and for the local people too.

We planted the physic nut in our herbaceous border, much to Taa's disgust. Along with the more controversial plants, we included local food plants and flowers. A clump of sugar cane, some bananas, ethotas and plantain suckers, a flamboyant tree and caladium with pink and green heart shaped leaves, some heliconia tubers dug up from the savannah, soursop, Malacca cashew trees, mangoes, papaya, castor oil plants and fan palms took their places in the informally curving sweep of the borders. They were still tiny specimens looking lost dotted around in the huge overall space, but I could imagine them fully grown. For now, we needed some man-made structures to add interest, so we needed someone to build us a rustic archway for the bougainvillea to scramble over and a little round benab as a seat to shelter from the sun and admire the scenery. Edwin asked a young man from the waterside who lived in a mud hut himself, if he would build us the benab and the arch using traditional skills and so it was done.

This gave me a new idea. Couldn't we build a replica of the thatched mud hut Edwin was born in: Aunt Betsy's house? It could be part of the trail and its interior could be set out just as it was when Edwin lived there as a small boy. It could be a little museum of village life. We could dedicate it to Parson Munroe whom Edwin spoke so fondly of. Edwin fell in love with the idea and as soon as Georgie finished building the benab and arch, he got a quote for building us a mud hut in the farm area at the back. This provoked scorn from Edwin's mother who really thought he had taken leave of his senses. In her eyes you did not shout about your lowly origins when you had made it in life. It was something you should hide from people so they thought you had always been well to do. She refused to help him find artefacts for me to display in the museum, but Edwin would not allow her to thwart our aims, so he just found other relatives and elders in the village who willingly gave old jars and farm tools to the museum. Others responded to a poster I displayed at the snackette offering to buy such items. The boys in the garden even dug up some old ink-pots that had been used as flambeau lamps and then discarded. Our environmentally green dream and educational vision were growing and merging at the same time.

The last part of the garden plan to be constructed was the pond. I needed a deep hole to be dug which could be big enough for the lotus lilies which so beautifully filled the roadside trenches at Bath. Local Indo-Guyanese villagers had used lotus leaves in the past to serve and wrap food as natural disposable plates. Much more environmentally friendly, I thought, than the paper or polystyrene "sanitary" plates and boxes, which now littered the roadsides near snack-bars. Edwin and I started to dig out the pond ourselves. Edwin wanted to prove to the silently watching eyes that he was not afraid of hard work and could dig a trench as well as the next man. He was powerfully built after years of army training and international competition in every sport you could name. He had chosen to pay others to do such work up to now because he had wanted to provide employment of the kind local people had the skills to do. Sadly, because of this, he had been taken as someone who only knew about football and running races. They had wrongly assumed that he did not have the strength or stamina to dig a trench or do physical work in the hot sun. Now we had to save every dollar we had, so there was no money left to pay for labour costs on the garden. We hacked and dug, throwing the soil into a heap at one side where I was going to construct a rockery among which to plant my cacti and succulents. After a couple of hours we had made good progress. I climbed out to take a breather on the edge of the crater we had made in what had formerly been open rough pasture. Edwin, in his tough lace-up army boots, was still digging down in the centre. I confess it was not really sensible for me to be doing this kind of work in flip-flops but it was hot dry weather and I disliked feeling my feet enclosed in such conditions. I was laughing and joking with him when I felt something like a fly tickle my bare toes as it ran over them. I looked down and saw a massive brown hairy tarantula sunning itself right next to my foot.

"Oh my God, Edwin, look at what just ran over my foot!" I said, frozen to the spot.

"Blimey. Have you got you camera with you?"

"No! Stay still and watch it while I run and fetch it. I bet by the time I get back, it'll have gone back into its burrow," I said, lifting my foot slowly and deliberately away from the creature which was clearly depending on its colour for camouflage against the baked clay background. Once I was far enough away, I sprinted upstairs to get the camera and crept back up to find the spider had not moved a millimetre. It's defiance of me seemed to say,

"Don't expect me to move. I was here before you came and dug up my home."

The snapshot I took was a trophy to include in my growing collection of local fauna. We left it in peace while we went to have some drinks in the shade of the house. When we returned, there was no sign of our furry- legged friend, but I put on some proper footwear and was far more careful about how I excavated the rest of the pond, especially when it came to moving large rocks and stones for the rockery. A full year had passed since the theft of the prize ram. We had faced enormous setbacks but battled against them and overcome many of them. We had made great progress. Our house was finished enough to live in relatively comfortably. Going into the New Year of 1993 with a new government in power, our plans for the future could be as optimistic as ever. Our green dream was becoming greener by the day and the greenest thing about it was me.

Chapter 11

Philanthropy on a Shoestring.

As I washed up the dishes in our new "dream" kitchen, I had a good view down over the back garden, farm and coconut reef. I could see Georgie arriving with courida poles on his bare shoulders. He let them drop in a heap by the old sheep pen which had been dismantled since we sold the sheep last year. The area that had previously been a night time corral for a flock of sheep and several cows now had a thick layer of humus on it so would make rich crop land. I had asked the farm helpers to dig it over during the long dry season when we first moved out of Taa's house. Apart from the sugar cane rattoons we had set in a clump along the fence, we had not had time to plant a crop on it after the main rains started. As I looked out over it, I remembered how one morning, after a couple of days and nights of heavy deluge, I had raced across the back lawn and what I had thought was dry, firm, ridge and furrow soil in order to go to the pit latrine, our only toilet at the time, at the far end of the farm. I had leapt onto the ridge in my flip-flops and sunk into liquid mud right up to my knees. I had been completely fooled by the thin dry crust on the surface. My flip-flops must still be buried under all the dirt, as I had only been able to extricate my bare feet. Now the rains had eased off, it had dried out enough to plant. I would make a start on a suitable vegetable crop. The back of that area, where the sheep shed and watch hut had been was a bit higher than the rest of the pen so it was a good site to locate the replica mud hut that Georgie had offered to build for us. He had set the fee and Edwin had agreed to pay it.

Georgie had cut the courida, or white mangrove poles from the waterside miles away and carried them all that way on foot in the blistering heat. He had started at dawn and we had to get up early to let him in. His lean black back was coated in beads of sweat. He must be hot and thirsty, I thought, so I filled a plastic milk-jug with cold water from the tap and took it down to him with a beaker.

"Here's something to drink, Georgie, you must be ready for it,"

"Thank you mistress," he said. I didn't like it when the locals called me that. It made me feel like the planter's wife and there I was standing in shorts, vest and flip-flops ready to do some weeding, planting and reaping. I couldn't stop them, however, because they used it as a form of politeness. While Georgie would sometimes call me Jane as requested, he often forgot and relapsed. It was one way I always knew that I was never really accepted. I was an outsider, somehow up on a pedestal. It was a legacy from colonial times that I would always be associated with the evils and excesses of both the slave ownership and colonial rule of the past. I was more acutely aware of it than ever now, yet in Dubai, I had experienced no such feeling. The U.A.E. was a cosmopolitan hub. The local Bedouin in whose country I had been a guest worker had been my employers and I felt very much the subservient one. Here I would have to work hard against the ingrained respect of some and resentment of others because of the actions of ethnic ancestors my white skin made me feel the need to apologise for.

"Georgie, do you mind if I take some pictures of you while you're doing the work?" I asked, "Only once you've finished building it, the visitors who stay with us won't really understand how you built it, so I'd like to be able to put up the photos on a display board so they can see the different stages in your work."

"Is OK mistress Jane," he said cheerfully. He seemed quite proud of the idea of such recognition of his skills. His friend had just arrived with another bundle of poles, so I ran up to get a second beaker and refill the jug. With only a sharp, thin cutlass as his tool, Georgie stripped the bark off the poles and arranged them in groups according to diameter. His helper borrowed one of our local post-hole shovels and began to dig a deep hole to plant a corner post. Georgie rammed the post down hard into the base of the hole and threw some stones down around the bottom of it before ramming it and shovelling in soil to firm around the post. When they had the four corners securely in place, they began to tie in the cross beams and roof ridge pole with some of the stripped bark before they nailed it. I supposed that lashing with home-made rope would have been the only method for the poor hut dwellers of the past, who could not even afford nails, but it was easier and quicker for him to nail our replica and it may have been stronger too.

"Why do you use courida wood?" I asked him as he was using the cutlass to sharpen the tips of the poles that would be roof rafters. His blade was slicing through them as easily as if he were sharpening a pencil with a pen-knife.

"Insects stay away from courida, Miss Jane, and ze courida bush grow all along ze waterside so ya could find it right zere near where ya buildin'. An' it grow-a plenty."

"Really, insects don't eat the wood? Why is that?"

"Well zey say ze wood does taste bitter to zem."

"I suppose it doesn't rot easily either, if it grows right near the water."

He nodded, happy to answer my questions as he worked.

"It could be a problem if everyone goes and cuts it, though, because there'll be none left," I said. I was a bit worried about wholesale deforestation causing coastal erosion. I didn't want to be contributing to that.

"Most people does buy board fo' build now. Is more better fo build board house if ya does get money."

I took a few more snaps from different angles. Then I let them get on with the build as I had to fetch some barrow-loads of rotted cow manure from the heap at the back of the farm and use it to fill up the raised beds Spear had made for me earlier in the week. This part of the farm, behind the mud hut, was a low spot so I thought raised beds boxed off by wood divided by firm paths reinforced with a paving of coconut husks, would be a way to reach the vegetables in wet spells without sinking knee deep in soft mud.

It took a day for the two men to build the mud-hut frame and another for them to weave wattle panels for the four walls and gables. The cutlass was the only tool they used apart from our shovel and hammer. When they had fixed all the wattle wall panels in place, a third day was used to prepare the coconut branches for the thatch. It was a painstaking process of plaiting the leaves over to one side of the stiff midribs. Although both men had each brought a large bundle of coconut branches from somewhere in the village, Georgie asked if he could take the rest from our trees on the farm. This and the plaiting took up another full day, so the following day was spent lashing the plaited branches horizontally at intervals to the rafters, starting from the base of the eaves and overlapping them closely until the top one met the ridge. Once both sides of the roof had been thatched from the inside, with one of them standing on an upturned barrel to tie them in with nylon fishing twine, while the other passed up the branches and held them in place, they reached up from the outside to secure and reinforce the join at the ridge.

Georgie came alone the following day to prepare the daub and begin coating the walls. I went up as usual with my camera to watch this process more closely. It was a mixture of cow-dung, wet mud from the trench and chopped rice straw that he was mixing and churning on a flat area of hardened ground he had cleared. He dolloped it all back in the plastic margarine bucket that he had used to fetch the mud from the nearby drainage trench, and began to slap it thickly onto the wattle with his bare hands. It took two more days to complete this process because he could only work in the cool of the afternoon or the midday sun would dry the daub too quickly and it would crack. On the final day of the process, he used more coconut branches to weave the gable ends, door and window shutters on to frames of thin courida offcuts. He did this last bit to please me because the original mud huts had a piece of jute sacking hanging at the door and windows, like a curtain. We did not have enough such sacks to hand. Local rice sacks were now made of woven recycled plastic and would have looked ugly and anachronistic. I had taken plenty of photos of every stage in the process and was especially pleased that he made a little courida wood table to set inside the parlour of the two- roomed hut and a low bed frame topped with a jute-sack mattress and pillow stuffed with soursop leaves, just like the one little Edwin had slept on as a small boy. He said that soursop leaves were used to keep away bedbugs. Georgie even made a little mud oven and fireplace outside the hut just like Taa's. He lived in an identical hut that he had built for himself down by the beach. It must have seemed odd to him to be building a life sized replica of it just for show, but he was pleased with the money Edwin paid him. It was more than he had asked for.

I was delighted with this little reconstruction of villagers' past life when it was completed. Over the next few days, I set out on the table some of the old jars and bottles and other artefacts I had been given or bought and hung the gilgira and the cast net Samo had made for me from the rafters. A rice mortar and pestle on the mud floor just inside the door completed the setting. It was the implementation of an idea which I intended to build on in the future, but my first development of it was to create some quality postcards unique to Sapodilla to promote our resort and to sell to our visitors. I selected the best of my wildlife photos with Spear, holding an armadillo he had caught rooting through the vegetation on the farm. There was also a close up of an iguana Boyo had caught and brought to us, a view of the rainforest where Samo had shot the anteater, the finished museum hut set against the coconut reef and a flattering view of our finished house. The post cards on sale in Georgetown were all dull and very poor quality. I was sure I could do better than that. I had tried to find a local printer but the government run press had never answered my letter requesting a price quote, so I decided to send off my selected photos to an address I found for a company in England that I had seen advertised in a magazine. I would have to order a minimum run of 2,500 cards and pay the postage costs from England but I invested the money and sent off an order, calculating that I could sell the cards at eighty pence each and make a bit of profit if I sold them all. Perhaps I could sell some to the shops in Georgetown so they had a better choice on offer.

The educational problems of the village, indeed the country, filled both of our minds all the time. My experience of giving free English lessons to the youth club teens and neighbours' tots in my spare time had shown me the dire problems of widespread illiteracy and poor teaching. Why was it so bad? We kept puzzling. The dictatorship of Burnham and the driving out of anyone perceived to be influenced by colonial ideas in the nineteen seventies, had led to a black hole in the education system and in all areas of employment. Such migration had been effectively a brain drain. Those who were left behind were mostly the educationally unsuccessful, so the poor skills they possessed were all that could be passed on to the children in school and work. Albert told us that part of Burnham's policy was deliberately to prevent village children from getting a good education, because he wanted them to remain on the land and farm it so that the country could be self-sufficient in food. Burnham had rightly, in my opinion, wanted to reduce the demand for imported food from the USA which was a drain on the economy, but it was totally the wrong way to achieve his aim.

"You can educate children to a high standard so they understand the need to farm effectively and enjoy doing so," I had said to Albert. "Farmers in other countries are educated to a high standard and farm scientifically. They're richer than many people who don't farm in my experience, provided they've a good business head and enough land. There's no shortage of land in Guyana, but most of it lies idle."

"You don't understand the hatred black people have of agricultural work after being made to do it as slaves," he had told me.

167

"True. All the same, it's inexcusable to deliberately keep the population uneducated," I argued.

"When you want to keep political power over them, it's best if they're kept stupid, because you can brainwash them to keep voting for you," he said. That said it all.

"If the British had thought like that, Burnham would never have gone to England," said Edwin, "and he would never have been in power in the first place." Albert ignored this remark and shifted the conversation around to politics.

"Burnham wanted to humiliate all those black people who held the top posts under British rule as well as their spoilt children that looked down on poorer people. They acted superior and opposed a lot of his policies. He thought if he could work on the young people, he would get his support from them, so he used to send buses down to the country villages every weekend to fetch young people, women mostly, for his rallies, where they would get free food and drink and he would get his pick of them."

"You mean the Guyana National Service?" asked Edwin.

"Yes. He could get to know who he could rely on to run the party in the various villages and promote them to positions of power in the local area."

"Sounds a bit like The Hitler Youth Movement," I said.

"They called him The Bocassa. He used to come into a village and ride around on a white horse like a planter and check on the forced labour works he'd decreed that the young sons and daughters of the Georgetown middle class elite had to do."

"The idea being to humiliate them and make them realise what it was like doing the hard work the majority of the population did."

"Exactly."

"I can see the reason for doing so, but it can't have been the right way to go about it."

"No, because it just drove most of them out of the country and there was nobody to educate the ones who were left."

168

"But why aren't there any books in the schools?" I asked.

"Well Burnham made the teachers have to burn all the old colonial books because he said they were indoctrinating children in the colonial mentality."

"Well maybe the books did need a different approach to make them more relevant," I said, "but wouldn't it have been better to keep on using them until he had others to replace them with?"

"When I visited Hopetown Primary School in 1984, when I came back for my father's funeral," Edwin cut in, "I found a pile of books in the storeroom which shows Burnham was worse at indoctrination than any colonial books I ever read at school. They had pictures of Burnham in them and under the pictures it read things like 'Burnham is our Saviour' and 'In Burnham we see no wrong'. I said to Shirley, the headmistress, 'What's this shit? He's making a God out of himself', and she was embarrassed and said, 'Oh, we don't use them now, that's why they're in here'. I was disgusted. I promised that when I got back to England I would send some proper books out to them."

"It sounds like the Cult of Mao," I said.

"It was," agreed Albert, "Burnham was close with all those third world leaders in the seventies in the Non-Aligned Movement: People like Indira Ghandi, Nkrumah and Castro at the time when they were making a stand against western imperialism. Maoism was popular and many African leaders as well as Burnham here, copied Mao's example."

"Well, that was why we brought with us all those books that were donated by schools and friends in England, and by the school I worked for in Dubai. Although we've already given the class sets to the appropriate local secondary schools like Bushlot and Hopetown Community High, Hopetown Primary School and even Queens College in Georgetown, I kept back all the primary school books that we had only one copy of, so we could set up a lending library here for the village children. All the children around here tell us they're not allowed to take home books from their school library. They have to buy books to use at school, so if the parents don't have money, the children don't have books to use in class."

"Good idea. If you like, I can get you some help in setting up the library from someone I know in Georgetown," Albert offered.

"OK," I said, "Thanks very much."

I left Albert and Edwin alone as they started discussing the West Berbice Football League they had been running, but I was still thinking back to the question of all those books we had given away to the schools. I wondered whether they were going to be used at all. Taa had told us that the teachers kept the books locked up in the school library and children weren't allowed to borrow them. She had said that the children went in to school in the daytime but the teachers were hardly there because they were out of school doing their own business. The same teachers gave extra lessons under their own houses to cover the work they should have taught during the day, but they charged the children money for this. When it came time for exams, they would only enter the children who went to these extra classes. If children were too poor to afford to go to them, they never got put in for the exams, so they could not get jobs. The teachers kept any donated books for their own children and so they were the ones that passed the exams and got the jobs needing qualifications. I did not really want to believe this as so many distortions of the truth had come to our ears from Taa, but the more I saw of the schools, the teachers and the children, the more these things seemed to be true. It was appalling.

We had been invited to the primary school teacher's Christmas Party at the end of term because Edwin had donated food, cakes and drinks from the snackette for it. We had both attended, sat down at the long table, ate together and mixed in with them just as we always had when invited to various people's thanksgivings or birthday parties over the past year. Then Edwin had invited all eight of them to come for dinner at our house on Christmas Eve. It had been a bit embarrassing because although I had gone to a great deal of trouble cooking something Caribbean, not English, it was different from what they usually served up, so most of them did not eat it. They had all come expecting to find a set of men for them to party and dance with and said they were disappointed to find that Edwin was the only man and there was no music and dancing, only serious conversation about teaching and books and why the children's education was so poor. Edwin was soon to get himself a reputation for being obsessed with education. He didn't mind that at all because he was obsessed with it and he wanted everybody to know it. His approach was to shame them into action and, by relentless pursuit of that goal he intended to achieve change.

Since he had tried to help train some of the teenage athletes in the youth club, and found them to be unreliable and lacking in self-discipline, he had decided to do things differently when we had settled into the house and our visitors had gone. Now the upstairs of the house was as complete as it could be, given the circumstances, he was getting the downstairs sorted out. The hexagonal room under our lounge was to become a gymnasium. We had cleared out all the storage boxes and either unpacked them upstairs or moved them into the new store room under our bedroom. Geoffrey had laid a concrete floor in the gym. He had made a beautiful hardwood inclined bench, three long gym benches and some wall bars to fix between the window shutters. Edwin's plan was to start training his athletes in the gym and set up a free membership system. The carrot was that they would want to use the equipment but would not be able to unless they became club members and attended training every weekday. He would forget about the Youth Club people since they all had bad habits that could not be changed. It would be better to work with younger ones and mould them into something successful with the right kind of regular training. He had spoken with Caro and some of the other teachers who organised the school sports and they were all keen to get their best athletes to come and join his sports club. He had also announced it in Church when working on the Nativity Play with the Sunday School. Things would be done differently in the New Year and it would all happen at Sapodilla.

I had suggested that we put our small lending library in the large room under the extension that we eventually expected to use as a 'conference' room. If we lined the long wall with some bookshelves, we could put all the children's books in there and I could easily run it for a couple of hours on a Saturday morning. It had easy public access as the door was near the front gate and Edwin said he was prepared to man the gate while I was inside the room checking books in and out. He would make sure no one strayed away to other parts of the building. I would make up a simple set of rules and membership cards and children would be able to borrow books for a couple of weeks free of charge. Edwin, putting the donation from Dorothy and Jim towards the cost, had paid Geoffrey to make the shelves and a wall mounted blackboard. Now they were ready, I could set out the books and start organising them so I could quickly find what I was looking for. It didn't need much to sort it out. The books were mainly small paperback children's stories, children's classics and old Ladybird books both fact and fiction. I sorted them into categories according to type and age range because it made more sense to do it that way. There were a few adventure stories for older students and even a few adult thrillers, so I put these on the highest shelves and the beginner books down at the bottom. We had five rickety old painted wooden tables and half a dozen damaged stools spare in the snackette store room, so Edwin told Spear to strengthen them and bring them down to the library for me. The biggest table would be a librarian's desk with my stationery, an old office date stamp and ink pad and a clip-file ready to take names addresses and membership numbers of those who joined. I drew up a format for the library membership card and typed it using the old typewriter Edwin had brought with us. I had to type the format several times over to fill an A4 sheet, making extra copies with carbon paper. In the same way I duplicated a letter of agreement for parents to sign and some basic library rules. I made up an official looking Sapodilla Stamp out of an old 'John Bull' toy printing set I still had. It was all common sense to me. I was not a trained librarian, but it was good enough for its intended purpose.

I had also decided that I would use the afternoon on Saturdays to teach a class in the library for all the students wanting to have English lessons with me. So many had been asking for help but I was not going to spend all my time giving one to one private tuition for them, which as far as I could see was what many of them wanted. Some of the parents had been complaining to Edwin about having to pay the local teachers for 'Common Entrance' lessons that would secure them a pass to get into the best secondary schools at the age of eleven. They had heard I was giving free lessons so wanted me to do common entrance classes. Edwin had borrowed the syllabus from the primary school for me, so I had seen it. It was about thirty years behind the times. How could I live in this community, knowing I had the necessary education and teaching skills, without trying to address the black hole I had observed in the education system? I had to give the lessons free of any labour charge because the children I wanted to help most were those who had the ability and desire to learn but whose parents had nothing.

I would be happy to teach in the way I had been trained and in subject areas I was qualified in, but the demand was only for English grammar lessons and common entrance cramming. I had no intention of becoming a reincarnation of some Dickensian schoolmarm teaching dry as dust verbs, nouns and adjectives. I could teach these things, but in an incidental way, through the medium of interesting subjects and activities that would be fun. The children would remember what they learned because they enjoyed it and if in the process, I corrected some of their grammar, then that would be how they would learn it permanently. When sorting out the boxes of books to donate to the various local schools the year before, I had kept back a few class sets for this purpose. One of them was a brand new set of colourful primary humanities books I had been given in Dubai. I would design a syllabus around the topics in this book and use them with a class of children to practise their reading, writing and comprehension. Being sensitive to their feelings, I was afraid of potentially alienating local teachers. I did not want to set up as a rival to them, cutting off one of their income streams, so I made it clear my lessons would not be a replacement for their classes but an extra to them, a supplement to help the school get even better results than it already did. Edwin had taken a notice about the classes, the library and enrolment times on the forthcoming Saturday to the primary school that week. We also displayed one at the snackette. Everything was set up and ready, waiting to see how the locals would respond.

Quite a lot of people were waiting at the gate by ten o'clock on Saturday January 9th 1993. About twenty children had come, each with a parent, grandparent or adult guardian as advised by my notice. I had them seated under the house on benches which we had carried out of the gym earlier, while I explained the rules of the library to them as a group. The use of the library was free as long as they followed the rules. The parent would have to sign agreeing to pay any fines if the book were not returned or renewed on time and the cost of replacing the book if it were lost or damaged. They would have to pay a small joining fee of twenty Guyana dollars. This would cover the cost of the plastic film that covered their card once I stamped it and they signed it. This they must keep in a safe place and bring it along to the library every time they came. I had to make it seem official and worth joining. Sister Derrice had told me that if I did not, they would not value the books but would use them for toilet paper and they would all soon disappear. I explained that I would call them into the library one by one to take their details down for my records and get them to sign their membership cards. They would be allowed to choose a book which they must get me to sign out. Then they could take it home to read. Edwin stayed outside chatting with those waiting, partly to get to know them and answer any questions, and partly because he wanted to keep an eye on the gate. He did not want people coming in and wandering upstairs into the house without being seen.

I met a few faces I already knew that morning, but the majority I had never seen before. Hopetown was a small village but there were hundreds of inhabitants and hundreds more children. One boy was taller than all the rest and older. He was Indian-looking. I remembered him as having come the previous September to ask me if he could buy one of the 'cabbage-callalloo' plants (savoy cabbage) he had seen growing in my garden. It was a crop unfamiliar to the country. He lived in the house at the corner of the road opposite the snackette. His father worked at the regional offices. Having checked out his library book, he asked me if I would give him lessons in English. I told him I was doing some classes but I would be having simple tests later in the week in order to see what standard students had reached before I would take them on. He said he would like to do the test. The children were mostly shy and full of supressed excitement at the prospect of choosing a book for themselves. They seemed entranced by the bright photographs and colourful illustrations which most of the books had. Little eyes roamed the walls where I had hung posters of spectacular scenery from different environments, old calendars and framed pictures. My collection of costume dolls from different countries was arranged on the shelves of an old welsh dresser in one corner along with an array of soft toy animals, roller skates and board games. Everywhere they looked was a new stimulus. Dealing with the queue was slow and laborious but it was the only way I could do it. More children kept arriving as we went on. It took two hours to enrol them all and sign out their books. Then we could close the gate.

The following Saturday, even more children turned up to join the library along with some of those from the week before. I now had over fifty library members. Edwin was kept very busy on the gate, managing things outside the library. To keep waiting children occupied, I put a different board game at each of the tables and sent them to sit in groups around the tables to play the game until I called up their group to return, choose and sign out their books. They were allowed to carry on playing the board games until I closed the library for lunch at midday. A fair number turned up that afternoon for assessment in order to join my classes. As I marked their written tests over the course of that week, I could see that I would have a major problem helping them to read and write. Some of their stories were unintelligible to me. They had written in Creolese because that is what they spoke, not English. Creolese is a corruption of English, so its similarity to the parent language made for confusion. What they heard at home, at school and in the community was Creolese. Learning English would be like learning a foreign language for one hour a week, only much more difficult to remember than a completely foreign tongue, since the differences between Creolese and English were so slight.

I realised that I would have to split up the children into two broad ability groups: the younger primary age group and the early secondary age group. The latter were about the right ability to use the primary humanities books I had. The former did not read well enough for that, so for them, I would have to use my ingenuity to devise topic based lessons without books at first. Perhaps I could get them talking about some of the slides I had, then transfer what we talked about into some simple writing. I could cover subject areas that were needed for their common entrance exam using the humanities books and other library reference books I had. If I made a small charge for the classes, I could use it to pay for pictorial sheets I could prepare with captions in suitably simplified language and "cloze" sentences for them to copy and fill in the blanks. I could get these photocopied in Georgetown when we did the snackette sales sheets. If I filed them, I could keep them to use again in the future. After the library closed on Saturday lunchtimes, the classes for these two age-groups would be held consecutively on Saturday afternoons while Edwin's sports club was in session. There was an older group who had already been doing English with me using the few English text books I still had, but they would have to come on a Sunday morning from now on.

Albert turned up one weekday with a lady from Georgetown he wanted to introduce us to. Her name was Cecilia and she had come to visit relatives in Hopetown where she had been born. She now worked for the Finance department for the Ministry of Home Affairs but previously had worked for the 'Futures Fund' a Canadian Aid Agency. In that capacity, she had helped the Hopetown Congregational Church sewing group with funding in the past, so Albert had brought her to advise us on how to set up the library. He was surprised to find that I already had it up and running.

"Oh, I see you have a very nice place here," Cecilia said, swinging around for a full panoramic view of the room. The home-made blackboard on the wall at the end of the room was flanked by a wall map of South America and a large world map I had stuck up with 'Blu-tack'. The wall surfaces not covered by shelving were crammed full of brightly coloured posters and old calendar pictures of places all over the world with different activities going on. The four rickety wooden tables stood on the mud floor of the room with the home-made wooden stools. The larger table now had my library membership folders and an assortment of old tins filled with pens, pencils and scissors on it. Apart from that, there was little furniture in the room other than the bookshelves crammed with well-used books and a number of old car tyres stacked under some of the tables.

"As you can see, we've improvised with what we could find. The children use the tyres as seats when all the stools are occupied," I explained with a smile.

"How have you organised the books," she asked me. "Have you done it by author or is it the Dewey system?"

"Oh, I haven't done it by either, I don't even think I would know how to do the Dewey system," I said apologetically. "I only have a fairly small number of books of each category, so it seemed to make more sense to organise them according to the reading age of the children. I have all the fiction in this section, with Ladybird books and very simple primary books on the bottom shelves where the smaller children can reach them, and harder books for older children on the upper shelves. The non-fiction books are on these shelves over here. This is the reference section with books like encyclopaedias and books that we need to keep here for people to use in library only."

"Oh, but you must have a proper system. You can't have a library without organising the books in a proper system."
"Well, it works like this for me, because I don't have much space when all the children come in and want to find something. If it's organised any other way, they won't know where to go to find a book easily and I won't be able to show them where they are. As it is, I know where everything is and can easily direct them to the shelf suited to their needs so they can choose something appropriate."

"Well you have a catalogue for that," she said patronisingly, as if she now thought I was an unqualified idiot who needed talking down to. She did not seem very impressed with my little lending library. I wanted to tell her that when children are having a job reading a simple sentence off a page, a catalogue, however simple, is not something they can easily use, It also may not inspire them to want to read a book if so many hurdles are put up to make it difficult for them to do so. What was wrong with just letting them pick out and browse through pictures until they felt there was something they liked the look of and could understand most of? I thought the better of it and bit my lip.

Cecilia was a mature, rather haughty educated Guyanese, typical, as I was later to discover, of many of those women whose education had elevated them to posts in government and funding agencies in Georgetown. She had attended Hopetown Primary School as a child, but had passed exams to go to one of the leading secondary schools in Georgetown. From there she had made use of the opportunities of social and party connections to progress her employment and promotion under Burnham. Having made up her mind by now that I was not a grovelling kind of person who would take everything she said without question, she decided to try to humiliate me further.

"Who is the librarian for the library?" she asked.

"It's me," I said.

"Oh, but why don't you train one of the local people to do it for you?"

"Well maybe in the future I will do but as I'm not a librarian, I wouldn't be able to train them as proper librarians. In any case, none of the children who come here are capable of doing such training because they can barely read,"

"Plenty of people in the local community here are capable of being a librarian," she scoffed.

"Well maybe they are but they'll expect to be paid and we have no money to pay them, so I'm doing it for free. The experience we've had since we've lived here so far is that if we leave things to local people to do, they don't do it properly, so very soon all the resources disappear without trace."

"If you want to stop that happening, you have to involve them in the process so they see it as part of their community and then they won't want to steal it because they won't want to steal from themselves," she said. I wondered why she was deluding herself with this idea. During our first year in the village we had watched how children stole items from their own grandmother right under our noses in Taa's house and how every family in the village was plagued by the same problem. Why did Taa lock up her fridge and her own bedroom to stop her possessions from disappearing? Why did the schools have no books? Why was there no library outside Georgetown that poor people could use to take books home from until we came and set up ours for free?

"You should make a small charge for membership. People will appreciate things more if they have to pay for them. There are ways that we can arrange for funding for sending a local person on a librarian course at the Public Library in Georgetown. They can be paid for doing the job when they finish the course. Of course we will have to send a team down from Georgetown to assess what best to do with the room and how to change the layout and shelving," she said snootily.

"Since it's all happening in our house, we want to keep control of what is going on in here," I said. "Can I be given the training as the librarian myself?"

"Oh no, it would have to be a local person, and you will only get help to improve the library if you do it all properly." I let her finish putting me down in front of Albert and Edwin and thanked her for her advice. She seemed to be missing the point. We had no money to pay someone to be a librarian in a free service we were setting up for the children in the village. What was wrong with me doing it the way I was doing it? The children had no library at all until we opened up our house to them. I was doing what I was doing voluntarily. I did not want strangers from Georgetown coming into my home and taking over what was going on in it. Did she think that no library could rightfully exist unless it was a miniature version of the National Library in the capital? What was the point of organising a couple of hundred books under the Dewey system? She switched her attention back to Edwin and was clearly more interested in getting to know him better than continuing her conversation with me. His ideas for the development of sport in the country were just what the country needed. After she left us, she was going to visit his mother, to see how the church sewing group were getting on with their sewing project. Futures Fund had helped them with six new sewing machines a few years back. She was going to get a shock then, because Edwin had already told me Taa had been complaining that all the sewing machines had disappeared and she did not know where any of them were.

At that point, we were interrupted by the arrival of a girl in her late teens who worked at the regional offices. She had recently joined the library and then asked me if I could teach her a foreign language. I said I could teach her French if she wanted, as that was the language I knew best after English. She seemed happy enough with that, so I had started her off the previous week and found her to be quite bright and able. Now she was here for her second lesson. I let Edwin take Cecilia and Albert off to the gym, relieved to be able to get down to a more worthwhile interaction: that of passing on a skill to a willing student.

The Library and my lessons were going from strength to strength. Noticing the children's interest in my costume dolls on display when they came to enrol, I photocopied a colouring book of national costumes and at the first of my classes, gave each child a different picture. There was a simple sentence under each one naming the country the costume represented. I had a huge pack of assorted old colouring pencils which I shared out to them. After they had coloured the picture, which process they enjoyed immensely, I collected in the crayons so I could use them again another time. Then I asked them each to read aloud the sentence under their picture. I corrected them if necessary. Then I put them to work in pairs with the other child in the class who had the same picture. They had to talk to their partner about what they could see in their picture, and write down some sentences about it in the exercise books that they had brought with them. They could work at their own level, some writing more than others: an ideal mixed ability task. I marked and corrected their work as they were doing it. Then I gave a mark out of ten for the colouring of the picture, and another mark out of ten for their sentences. I passed around some flour and water paste I had made and put into a few of the disposable cups we had from the snackette. When they had finished, they pasted the pictures into their exercise books. At the end of the lesson, I set homework for them to copy the corrected sentences and write something more about it in their exercise books. They would have to write words that they knew, so they would be able to read it back to the rest of the class next time. It was just a standard teaching method which in English schools we would do for any children with limited literacy but it had been fun for these Guyanese children, unlike anything they had done in their normal village school. It gave them something they could take home to show their parents after I had marked and corrected it. I was getting positive feedback via Edwin from parents in the village. They were telling him that I was the only teacher that corrected their child's work so they could learn from their mistakes. They were also helping their children to practice their reading at home using the simple library books they were borrowing from my library.

The next time I saw them, I called each child in turn to the front of the class and asked them to read their sentences out loud to me. This gave me the opportunity to see what they were trying to say if their writing was illegible or unintelligible. I corrected their spelling as they spoke and marked it before they sat down. This process took up most of our time so I needed something to occupy the others while it was going on. In order to explore the ability of each child, I had in advance sorted out a simple library picture-book on each of the countries I had distributed pictures of. In the same pairs as before, they had to use the library book to find out some information and write about it in their exercise book. Next time, I would get them to read out their sentences to the class, so their homework was to practice reading what they had written during the lesson, This process enabled me to see which of the children were blindly copying things they could not read and did not understand, and which ones were literate enough to cope with more demanding tasks. It stretched the weak without exposing them to ridicule by others, and it stretched the able ones so they did not feel they were wasting their time in my classes. As the weeks went by, each child had a complete set of pictures and countries in their books. When we had exhausted the topic, I had a better idea of their general ability. It had worked well, so I followed it up by getting them to choose one of the countries that they had in their exercise books to do a special project about. I paired them up again with the library books to share and gave out some old travel magazines and postcards we had of the relevant countries for them to cut out pictures from and paste onto blank pages I gave them. Then they could write about what they could see in their pictures about life in that country. The natural conclusion to all this work was to get them to be able to recognise the location of the different countries on the map of the world. That would be my next challenge.

It was March. Albert called in with Mr Mitchell the Regional Education Officer. It was about the Region Five teachers' Physical Education course Edwin had agreed to put on free of charge in our library room under the house. They arranged for Edwin to meet with the Minister of Education about it. Mitchell was a stocky, smartly dressed and very polite man on first impression. Since Edwin always involved me in any educational matters that took place on our premises, I found myself having a long conversation with Mr Mitchell on the teaching of reading and phonics.

"You have a very nice library here Mrs Joseph. Thank you for the help you are giving to our local children. How are you finding their reading ability? Are you having any problems with this?" he asked. It was as if he had read my thoughts. Maybe he was expecting me to fail like the local teachers did.

"I've noticed that none of the children I've been teaching seem to have been taught to read by phonics, so they're held back by having no tools to decode unfamiliar words with. They have to rely on word recognition by memory and only know to recite the alphabet by letter names which give them no clue as to the sounds the letters make. I've been helping them to learn the phonic sounds as I've been hearing them read, so they're making faster progress now." Mr Mitchell was keen to impress me with his knowledge on the subject.

"Oh yes, phonics is very important," he said in his best academic tone of voice. "When I did my degree in English at the University of Guyana we had to study phonics. In fact phonics is part of standard teacher training that all teachers have to do before they can become qualified teachers in Guyana." Although I said nothing, I found this rather surprising, since the teachers who had come to us on Christmas Eve had revealed that none of them had any teacher training at all. They had learned on the job by working with the older untrained teachers in their schools.

"Jane will be giving an input on food and nutrition to the teachers on the P.E. Course because she has more expertise on the subject than I do and she is a highly qualified teacher," said Edwin. It was one reason why he had suggested to Mr Mitchell that he could organise a teacher training course for them in Physical Education at no cost to the government. Mr Mitchell had jumped at it, presumably seeing the promotion points he could chalk up by telling the new Minister of Education that it was his own idea to do this in his region.

"It could be a pilot study for extending to the whole country," he told Edwin enthusiastically. As he left, I also offered to help the region in any way I could with teacher training. However, from the icy stare he gave me as he said goodbye to us, I could not help sensing his hostility towards me for some reason.

Two days later, twenty one teachers turned up for the course. Edwin took down their names and asked each one in turn to say a bit about themselves and why they were there. This was enlightening as some of them freely admitted it was a way to get out of school for the day. He spent a long time talking to them to find out what they thought about sport and PE and why it was important for education. They were all happy to discuss these things with him but it soon became clear that their general agenda was to excuse themselves for not doing things because the schools did "not have the gears" (meaning equipment) to do P.E. and they did "not have a proper track" to put on competitions.

"You don't need gears or a track to do good sport," he explained, aware that he was being seen as some sort of aid agency, "You just need to teach it the right way. You can make equipment from the stuff you find around you. When I was a kid we used to play football in the pasture with a cow bladder we blew up and tied a knot in like a balloon. There's no need to go back to that now, but if you have no money at all you can improvise, recycle, just like I see people doing all around me in their daily lives. Anyway what happens to all the money they make at the school sports every year? Why can't you use some of that to buy a bit of equipment and gradually build it up over the years?"

"People thief it," they all chorused. Edwin and I both had the same thought: Why should anyone donate expensive imported equipment if they openly admit it will be stolen? Instead he said,

"Why can't you stop people stealing it? Don't the schools have watchmen at night?"

"Watchmen thief it," cried one.

"Who gonna pay watchmen?" shouted another amid murmurs of agreement from the others. The memory of our prize ram flashed through my head as I observed from the back of the room.

"Well if you want sport to happen, you've got to find a way of safeguarding your equipment yourselves. Not only that, you have to take the control of the school sports and stop the thieves from running it."

"We can't do that," said a softly spoken mature Indian female teacher named Bibi, "It's always done by the Guyana Teachers' Union."

Edwin looked deflated, having hit a brick wall.

"Well who puts the people in charge of the union?" he asked.

"Members vote in elections every year," said Caro who was there representing her school, "I am GTU representative for Hopetown Community High School."

"So what's to stop all you teachers here on this course going to your next GTU election, voting out the thief who stole the takings last time and voting in someone else who is honest?" Edwin's suggestion was simple and seemed all too reasonable but met a wall of silence.

"We've sat here and talked enough, let's go out and do some practical work," he said, "I must say though, that some of you haven't come dressed properly, in spite of the fact that the letter I gave Mr Mitchell to duplicate and give out to all the schools clearly said you needed to come in sports kit. How do you think we can do practical work if you're wearing high heeled shoes and skirts, or hard pants and button up shirts?" A few glances were exchanged in shock and horror.

Clearly some had come thinking it was going to be purely a classroom exercise of note-taking.

"Let's get this straight. You can't teach P.E. unless you can do it yourself. I have to see what you can do before I can show you what you need to know. That means every week you'll have to spend some of the time doing practical work, although I'll take it slowly. I realise from what I've learned from you this morning that some of you haven't done any sport since you were at school yourself and so you're a bit out of condition." Edwin was being kind and diplomatic. From the shapes and sizes of some of them, they had never done sport at all. He pointed out Caro as an example and said, "Look at Caro over there! She's wearing suitable stuff: trainers and tee shirt with stretchy track pants so she can move easily.

"Sir, we can't travel in minibus in such gears," said one girl.

"Well if that's the case, then bring sports gear to change into when you get here and you can use our changing room over there," he said, pointing towards the gym, "Anyway, today you'll have to do it dressed as you are. Those of you with hard shoes will have to take them off and go barefoot like the children do when you teach them."

They followed him out of the library and round to the front of the house where the grass of our lawn was nice and soft, flat and short. He began a simple warm-up for them and I watched from the side-lines. It was a pitiful sight. They had only been doing a couple of minutes of gentle jogging and some of them were out of breath already. A few gentle stretches and working through the body exercises and I could see the frustration in his eyes as he said he would warm them down and end the practical. He would do a bit more next time when they were all properly dressed. The rest of the session was devoted to discussing why warm up was necessary before sport and what topics he intended to cover in the coming weeks. He was interrupted by the arrival of a van from the education office carrying a carton full of savoury smelling cardboard food boxes and a crate of drinks. Refreshments having been consumed, one or two of the teachers asked to leave, offering various excuses. Albert and Mr Mitchell turned up towards the end of the afternoon. I had set up the TV and video in the classroom enabling Edwin to show them one of his sports videos which he followed up with a discussion about it. The session finished at three o'clock. Bibi Zulaika Ishak lingered behind the others, clearly wanting to buttonhole Edwin for a private conversation. She had a very obsequious manner. One of the black female teachers glared daggers at her but was noticed by no-one except me. I saw them all out of the gate and chatted to a few who asked me some questions. Edwin had gone into the gym with Bibi, so I went upstairs and got on with a few jobs until I heard the clanking of the chain and padlock on the gate at the bottom of the house steps, followed by Edwin's footsteps thumping around the veranda to the kitchen.

"You deserve a medal for patience and tolerance for what you do with those kids," he said when he thrust open the kitchen door and entered. "I can't work with these people. I was completely shocked today to see the poor standard of everything they do. It's far worse than I thought. They haven't got a clue about anything. Your input was great. Thanks for that because it helped a lot."

"That's OK," I said. "It's all part of teaching, it's just that you don't expect teachers to need the kind of handling you would give to kids, because they've normally gone through all the academic exams and four or more years of higher education including supervised teaching practices before you've had to deal with them in the past. You could make certain assumptions about what they could do and understand. Here you can't make any assumptions. They don't seem to have had a proper basic education themselves let alone any higher education or professional training. You'll just have to take that into account and change your strategy."

"That Bibi doesn't have any interest in PE at all. She's the deputy head of Cotton Tree Primary and she just signed up to get herself a day out of school, so now she's trying get herself special treatment so she doesn't have to do the physical stuff. What the hell's the point of trying to teach sport to schools when the people they select to do the course have got no ability whatsoever in the subject? They should select someone who's young, fit and interested in sport to represent their school on the course. It's hopeless. Far worse than I thought." His dejection was exacerbated by our financial situation. The power blackouts had been so long and frequent in the previous few weeks that the cost of all the extra gasoline for the generator at the snackette had been eating into the profits so there was a shortfall again to pay the bank.

"I've completely lost interest in sport since coming here. There's nothing here for me. I feel like pissing off back to England." When Edwin was in these moods of despair, the emotion he transmitted in what he said and threatened to do in frustration, put me on a knife edge, as if any moment he would disappear and leave me there on my own with all the problems. I was powerless. All I could do to alleviate my own sense of insecurity was to try and calm him down by persuading him that things would get better.

The following week there was no teacher's P.E. course as Edwin had to go with Mr Mitchell to Bygeval School at Mahaica to meet with the Minister of Education, Dale Bisnauth. Apparently it was to obtain the minister's approval for the teachers to be doing this course at Sapodilla. He would have to give them permission to be absent from their schools on the one day a week for the next six months and to be given travelling expenses to get there by the Ministry of Education, otherwise they would not have attended the course. The Ministry of Education would issue participants with a certificate of attendance for this physical education course, which, Dr Bisnauth was surprised to find out from Edwin, he was teaching free of charge. Mr Mitchell must have led him to believe that he would be paying Edwin a fee for his services.

Edwin soon found renewed enthusiasm for his course. He assembled all the equipment the day before and set out a circuit in the gym for their practical work. On the day, only thirteen of the original twenty one turned up. Some schools had sent a different teacher this time from the one who came to the first session. He planned to show them the athletics implements that they should use for field events and how they could improvise with local materials to practice the events until they had built up the funds to purchase the proper ones. He showed them a couple of International educational supply catalogues that I had in the library to counter their complaint that there were no sports supply shops in the country. They could order anything the school needed and provided they paid with the order, we would send for it for them by post. His philosophy was always to encourage them to be self-reliant but almost certainly these suggestions were as real to them as castles in the sky. The recent history of post-colonial Guyana was that the government was supposed to provide everything and if it didn't, international aid agencies would. Self-reliance was about helping yourself to community funds if you couldn't get remittances from overseas relatives. The economic potential of running a business in the local rural economy was too small. Unless you got a kick start to set it up by a hefty investment from overseas, then you couldn't even get it off the ground. From Edwin's perspective, when this happened, as with Bryan and more recently with Philip at the snackette, the investment became a never ending donation. The local 'business partner' or manager found it easier to spend someone else's money than they would if it had been their own. They were also less concerned if there were poor returns. There was a perception that a 'foreign' investor such as Edwin was perceived to be, was a latter-day Midas with access to a private goldmine.

Now his expectations had been adjusted to a more realistic level, Edwin was determined to make a difference. Attendance reverted to twenty one again now he was sending a register each week to Mr Mitchell the R.Ed.O. The Easter break at the beginning of April was an interruption, but by working closely with Mitchell and others at the Regional Education Office in the days between each session, Edwin managed to find out a lot more about how they worked and how he needed to handle them. I learned too, but by osmosis. He was my eyes and ears on the ground in the local community, since I did not go out and about myself, at least not alone. I had no need to. Now the house was complete and we had a home with all our belongings unpacked, I had a thousand things to do in the way of teaching work, marking and resource preparation, housework, research and hobbies.

The community was apparently concerned about not seeing me. At first, I was touched by their interest, but the pressure that they tried to exert on me through Edwin to go out of the house, became obsessive. It seemed that these enquiries all came from young girls and women in the church. These were females that had never even spoken to me. I began to realise that it was very frustrating for them to know that I never left the building unless Edwin was with me. There was nothing they would have liked better than to see me passing on the road without him, as they would immediately conclude that he was at home alone so they could make a quick dash down to the house to catch him on his own and try to take advantage of such an opportunity. Their apparent kindness no longer seemed genuine. I trusted Edwin, and had absolutely no doubts about his fidelity, but I was not going to go out alone just to give them the satisfaction of trying their luck.

It was a disappointment to some to discover that I did not want any maids or cooks to work in my house. When Shirley from the Education Office, who herself employed a housekeeper and cook, enquired as to why I did not have one, I told her that I was perfectly capable of cooking my own food, scrubbing my own floors and washing my own laundry.

"I don't want anyone else doing my dirty work. I didn't have a maid or a cook in England or in Dubai, so why should I have any in Guyana?

"Oh but it provides employment for women in the community," she had said.

"Well that's not the sort of employment I want to be helping people to get because it just keeps them in poverty. For a start, we can't afford to pay a maid's wages until we have a continuous flow of tourists staying here. If we could afford it, they would just earn a small amount. I would much rather give them my time free of charge to educate them so that they can get the qualifications to go out and get a better job than maid. There are electrical devices that do such demeaning jobs these days. Women can use their brains to earn money from more fulfilling forms of employment rather than being paid domestic 'slaves'. I haven't come back here as a white 'slave' owner reincarnated in twentieth century format. I want to help things to improve." I had hit the right raw note, so she made no further mention of the subject.

Just before Easter, Edwin and I both went to Georgetown to meet the Minister of Education about the PE course. We arrived at the Minister's office at 8.30 a.m. and found he was not there because he had gone to watch the West Indies play Pakistan at Bourda Cricket Ground. We were both disgusted to know that the Minister was at a social activity on a workday when a reasonable person might expect to find him doing the job he was paid for. Such futile trips were a normal occurrence as there was no way to confirm anyone's presence by telephone if you lived outside Georgetown. Edwin left our details and card with his secretary. He was determined not to waste our journey, so he decided to go instead to see if we could make an appointment to see the British High Commissioner. Initially we met a lady called Sandra Seenan who worked there. She was an English expat married to an Indo-Guyanese lawyer. She had lived in Guyana for decades. Sandra was a very warm, friendly person who had a broad Yorkshire accent and a northern sense of humour to go with it. Edwin's idea was to invite the British High Commissioner, David Johnson, to come to a prize giving at Hopetown Primary School which Edwin would be organising. His scheme, he had confided in me, was to shame the primary school teachers into upping their game in anticipation of a visit from such an important person. On several occasions where we had been invited to school functions, the dignitaries from Georgetown who had promised to attend and make presentations never turned up, so the school was kept waiting, often for hours, expecting the VIP to arrive. In the end, the show went on without them but the occasion was ruined and the morale of those who had put in effort was steadily eroded. Edwin would make this occasion different because he knew the British High Commissioner would not let them down.

We also needed to get help ourselves. We had already sent a letter and brochure with all our details to the High Commission in the hope that diplomats or English visitors who went into the High Commission would see our advert on the noticeboard and want to book a weekend to stay with us for a short break. We had not as yet had any response to that. We needed to introduce ourselves to the High Commissioner and let him know what educational charity work we were doing in our area. I also hoped we might be able to buy a second-hand photocopier off the High Commission if they were going to upgrade theirs. Perhaps one of the diplomats leaving the country might have a British system television we could buy off them as ours was already being damaged by the voltage fluctuations in Berbice. Luckily, High Commissioner David Johnson was able to see us that afternoon. He was a delightful man, tall, slim and balding, with silver-haired temples and kind, twinkly eyes. He sat and listened patiently as both of us gave him a rundown of ourselves and why we were there. He did not think he would be able to help us with the photocopier, but would keep us in mind if he did replace it. He was concerned, however, that it might be a problem if it kept breaking down and needed maintenance out where we were. He also wondered how we would obtain supplies for it such as ink. As for the television, there was no one leaving in the near future but we could put up a request card on the noticeboard to see if we got a response. I had not realised quite how naïve I was about how diplomatic missions worked until I asked him how they got the TV's for their staff. Would it be possible when they next brought some in to get an extra one which we could buy off them?

"Good Lord no! I couldn't possibly do that! I wouldn't be allowed to!" he exclaimed. Then he started laughing as I felt myself going bright red and he realised that I just had not thought of the diplomatic implications of my request. Edwin, also shocked at my suggestion, which he had no idea I was going to make, echoed "No, Jane". He was much more experienced and knowledgeable about diplomatic protocol than me. I apologised immediately. I had not meant to ask Mr Johnson to do something illegal. Edwin quickly shifted the conversation to the subject of the primary school prize giving. We would like to invite the High Commissioner to visit Sapodilla with his family at the same time. I hardly listened to what was said after that, since I was burning with self-reproach.

What must he think of me? I must seem very stupid or ignorant! I must be an embarrassment to Edwin! By the time I had recovered my composure our invitation had been accepted, with the proviso that the school's headmistress sent him an official letter of invitation, and Mr Johnson found time to engage us in personal conversation which he seemed genuinely interested in. I left the High Commissioner's Office that day a good deal wiser and more politically aware than I had entered. I was now thirty eight and my own education had hardly begun.

Beverley, the Headmistress of Hopetown Primary School and another teacher visited us the following day unaware of the surprise Edwin had in store for her. He broke the news about the end of year prize-giving that we would be donating the prizes for, which she was delighted about. Then he added that the High Commissioner would be coming, which she was not so thrilled to hear. She went into a panic about it. Edwin tried to calm her down by suggesting that nothing special was required of her, just to get lots of the children's artwork up on the walls to make the school bright and colourful. He was sure if the High Commissioner saw that they had made an effort with what little resources they had, more help would probably come their way. She was terrified at his idea of children's art work, because she knew that they never did any. Even though it was on the curriculum and was supposedly being done, it was all pretence.

"We haven't got any art materials," she blurted, expecting to hear that we would be donating some for her to use.

"You don't need any," I suggested. "I'm sure that the High Commissioner would rather see art work done by the children using the natural materials you have all around you for free. What about some of the children scratching patterns on calabash shells? Or plaiting rice straw to make corn dollies? There's plenty of clay in the trenches for them to make little clay models. You can make things out of paper mache,"

"But we need paste," she said searching desperately for an excuse to avoid action unless she got further financial input from us.

"You don't need to buy paste," I reminded her, "There are plenty of paste berries growing on trees in the back dam and even if you can't find any, you just make your own paste from flour and boiling water." I showed her the children's work on countries of the world from my classes which I had put on display in the library. The children had cut out letters and pictures from scrap magazines and stuck them on the unprinted reverse of old calendar pages using the flour and water paste I had showed them how to make. Their written work was on and around the pictures. I had got the smaller children to make masks out of paper plates with cut-out eyes, nose and mouth and decorated them with feathers we found out in the street, berries and coloured seeds and bits of old torn-up coloured rags. The two of them inspected the children's work on the library wall and seemed suitably impressed, but as they wandered off I could hear Beverley grumbling about Edwin making a lot of extra work for her. I knew that he was trying to force them into changing the way they taught but without saying so directly. He hoped they would follow my example.

During the May Day Bank holiday week, Edwin decided to capitalise on the school holidays to intensify his PE course. They would attend a full week of teacher training at Sapodilla, sponsored by the Ministry of Education Allied Arts Department. Two ladies from the department based at Queen's College Campus in the capital had visited Sapodilla and been happy with what they had seen. Desiree was a Dance specialist and Avril was in charge of Physical Education. They wanted Edwin to include on his course some other teachers from region five who were involved with Physical Education for the annual Mashramanie carnival. 'Mash' was a Guyanese festival in February which, in addition to the carnival style dancing costume parades, involved P.E. in 'mass games' such as human pyramids and other group formations. Twenty seven teachers were participating in all. By the end of the week the course had been a great success. However, both our video recorders had broken down from the usage they had been subjected to in the course because, unknown to us, the tapes we were using all now had a fine coating of mildew on them from the humid conditions, so had clogged up the tape heads. We had to take them into Georgetown to find a repair shop. I decided to use some of my savings invested in an offshore account in Jersey, equity from the sale of my house in England, to send for a spare new video player and an overhead projector from the educational supply catalogue I had. I saw it as an investment that could eventually be recovered from proceeds we would charge for conference room use to business customers.

Our first commercial guest was expected in a weeks' time, since an overseas monitor from the Caribbean Agricultural Research Development Institute was coming to assess the progress of a sheep rearing project in Region Five. The Ministry of Agriculture had needed to find somewhere decent to accommodate him without having to put him in a hotel in New Amsterdam over the other side of the Berbice River. They had approached Edwin and booked him in with us. It had taken us nearly two years to get to this point but at last things were looking up. I spent a lot of time preparing professional looking menus and suitable drinks and cocktail lists for him to choose from that I would be able to produce from fresh organic ingredients in my kitchen. I wanted to impress him with a standard of service equal to any international hotel I had stayed in. If I succeeded, he would recommend us to his organisation for future occasions when they needed it. "Who knows what other customers we might get as a consequence of such word of mouth recommendations?" we thought when we discussed the arrangements for his arrival. Harold came from Trinidad. He was an appreciative guest and very easy to please. His delight at having such high quality accommodation, food and customer care compared to the conditions he had had to endure on previous visits, was no secret. We were getting enthusiastic feedback from many quarters and soon had confirmation of a follow up booking for two vets from Georgetown who would be taking advantage of our special low rates for local customers. It all augured well for our tourism business to grow in the future, especially if we could get a telephone connection. However, despite repeated attempts to press for one at the Georgetown and New Amsterdam Head Quarters of the Guyana Telephone and Telegraph Company, our rural location would prove to be an insuperable obstacle.

I had started the library and classes in January. The students had completed their national costumes projects, so after Easter I had selected a suitable textbook for reading and comprehension which had a different passage with questions on each page. I only had one copy but I could photocopy class sets of each page to use as worksheets. These I used to develop reading and English skills in the summer term. Since I had set up the video and TV for Edwin's course on Fridays, I did the same for my classes some-times. It would be useful if I wanted to start a new topic with a short video clip to arouse interest or to show things outside their experience and comprehension so they could understand them properly. Nobody in the village had television in their homes in those days and only a few rum-shops in the country showed pay-as –you-enter video films for adults. The children were transfixed by the short clips, which I explained carefully, linking them to whichever passage we were reading. Attendance of individuals was erratic from week to week but there was always a full house. More children were coming to join the classes which filled the void of others who were absent, perhaps because of illness or chores to do at home or perhaps because of not having the few dollars to pay for the lesson contribution that week. As numbers grew, the classes spread into weekday afternoons after three o'clock and Sunday afternoons as well. I did not want to turn anyone away. Edwin was getting annoyed at this. He felt that I should review my timetable when September came so we also had time for ourselves. Irregular attendance was making it impossible for me to build any progress into the children's development. I could not devise a sensible curriculum to give them foundation skills in geography or history if they did not attend every week. In order to improve this, I decided to make parents commit to paying the total sum of the term's small contribution per lesson as an upfront fee at the start of term. If they knew before the summer holiday that this would happen, it would give them time to save up the money before term started and once they paid for the whole term they would make sure their children attended regularly. This would ensure the few children I had room for in my class were serious in their attendance habits and would be able to make progress. At the end of the term, I tested all the children and wrote detailed but simple reports on their progress and marks. Along with these, I sent home letters to the parents calling a meeting to explain the new system for enrolment that would start in September. They seemed to understand and were willing to cooperate. I had meanwhile set up a committee of a few of the parents and local teachers so that we could apply for official registration as a charity in some way. All 'bottom house schools' in the country were private money-making schemes run by retired or practising local teachers. I wanted to be able to show that by contrast, that was not what we did, since any money being paid to me went entirely on providing resources for the children and none of it benefited me personally.

I soon regretted ordering the audio-visual equipment. Edwin received an unexpected notice from John Fernandes Shipping Company of a donation of goods for Hopetown Primary School for which Roland, an acquaintance we had met in England shortly before migrating, had given Edwin's name as the contact person. Edwin had to pay ten thousand dollars for it to be released. Within a few days this had risen to $16,000. Unable to get any reimbursement from the Education Department even though the items were a jumble sale of used books and equipment for the government schools and not us, Edwin reluctantly paid, but quickly realised this was an imposition that could grow into a big financial problem for us. We were now regarded as a 'private school' so would be liable for commercial tax rates just as if we were an exclusive fee-paying school for the rich elite: a business, not a charity. We sent an urgent letter to Roland telling him not to send any more donations for the local school, as it was a financial burden on us if he used Edwin's name. I was dreading the thought of what I would have to pay for the video and overhead projector when they finally arrived.

Some of my older students, who were doing public exams that term, came to show me their CXC questions for history. They were delighted with the paper, since the topics I had spent time helping them with all came up and they felt they had done well. I also had a big turn-out for an after-school humanities project on Amerindian life which I had organised for the younger students. That weekend, my classes were in full swing when Desiree Wintz, the Stabroek News reporter who had published the first article on Sapodilla as a tourist resort, came to visit us for the day with a friend of hers. They stayed until five o'clock, observing my humanities class before Edwin gave them a tour round the finished house upstairs until my classes ended and I could join them. Desiree could not believe how the place had transformed. It had been a building site when she last visited and she had never imagined that it would become what it now was. It was a surprise for her to find the extent of the educational work we were both doing. It had grown out of a need we had discovered but had not originally envisaged. It had filled the void while we had been forced to wait for our tourism business to take off. How would we reconcile the two when guests started arriving in greater numbers, she wondered? It was a question that Edwin and I had spent a lot of time debating recently. We had come to the conclusion that we would maintain the two side by side, devoting future profits we made from tourism to our educational work for the local rural community. We had learned that it would not work if we simply handed over funds to the locals to manage for themselves. It would just disappear into the economy producing no educational improvement. The only way our donations for education would have a lasting positive effect would be if we provided high quality education ourselves at Sapodilla Farm, We would rebrand it as 'Sapodilla Learning Centre' to suggest our genuine altruistic educational aims: to promote healthy minds in healthy bodies.

Chapter 12

Balls of Fire

It was one of those nights between full moon and new moon when there was no moon at all in the night sky. The power had cut off some time around six thirty, just after dark fell. It was completely pitch black outside. The chirruping of frogs in the pasture seemed amplified by the darkness. We were sitting in the lounge on the sofas where we had been since the lights went out. We had made a conscious decision not to move, as one of us would invariably trip over the coffee table on the way to the kitchen, to throw the mains switch off and start up the generator. We didn't really need to burn gasoline for light tonight as we were just sitting talking. The owl made a scuffle with some bats in the corner of the roof and there was a great clattering on the zinc sheets as it pounced on its prey. These were nightly contests we had grown accustomed to. We called the owl 'Hoodwink' after a story book I had used with the children in my classes. Without the electricity to power the fan, the temperature was stifling inside, but the open windows allowed a little cooling sea breeze to funnel through the house. I was looking towards the back of the farm through the window mesh, towards the barely visible black silhouettes of the coconut trees on the reef. Edwin was facing the same way. Suddenly, a ball of fire shot up into the sky from behind one of them. It made a flaming arc as it travelled through the air across the back of our farm from one side to the other. Then it extinguished as suddenly as it had appeared somewhere near ground level behind the old tamarind tree.

"Christ what was that? Did you see that?" I started and sat bolt upright, staring at the blackness with the image still seared onto my eyeballs. Edwin had stood up and moved towards it, but it had gone. "Somebody's trying to scare us!" I said, "Do you think it's Ramsammy?"

"He better not be on my land or he'll have me to contend with," Edwin growled aggressively.

"How do you think they did it? It looked like something had been lit and thrown up in the air and it landed and went out,"

"Probably put kerosene on some old rags and set light to it and then threw it." Edwin said. He had picked up the solar torch from the glass topped table next to him and switched it on, pointing its beam out towards the back to see if he could see anyone. Then he moved towards the back door and shone it out over the garden like a searchlight. We could see nothing but the moths and mosquitos that honed in on the beam. We waited for a while but there was no repetition. I stayed up on the veranda while he went down, unlocked the gate at the bottom of the stairs and walked down towards the back of the farm carrying a cutlass and another torch. He came back after a while and locked up.

"See anything?" I asked. He shook his head. We went back inside again.

"I hope they don't start throwing stuff like that near the house and set fire to us," I said. "They must think we're as easy to frighten as all the locals seem to be but they don't realise we aren't scared by all this sort of stuff. Remember how Shirley Robertson was last Christmas time when she thought she heard noises at her back door? She was really terrified by it. I suppose when you've lived through the era of the kick-down-door boys you might be a bit more jumpy out of experience, but if they think I'm going to be spooked by the thought of evil spirits they don't know what kind of a person I am."

As we were speaking, the current came on again and white security lights flooded the grounds at the back and front of the house.

"Ramsammy was on my land at the back with Brakes and another man a few weeks back, waving and pointing," said Edwin. "I got my javelin and threw it at the tree next to where they were. It embedded into the bark of the trunk and made them jump out of their skin. They don't like it since we put up this fence because they used to walk across this bit of land before we put up our fence and started farming. Now they can't do that so they've got to walk the long way round it. That's why Ramsammy keeps pulling up your pineapple plants that you put at the back there."

"We don't expect him to take down the fence he has round his pig farm so we can walk across it, so why does he expect to be given a pathway through ours?" I asked.

"That's what these people are like. That's why Berta at the village office came down a while back, asking to be allowed to come in with some Indian man from the region to survey the land. I told her he can survey it from the outside if he wants, but no one's coming inside my property unless I've invited them here. Apparently Ramsammy had gone and complained at the village office about me fencing off my land. Because the Indians are now in power, they think that they can scare off black people from developing the place, by bringing in government officials to intimidate them."

"I suppose they're trying to get revenge for all the years they've been intimidated by their black neighbours and officials," I reasoned, "It's just our hard luck that we've come here at the very time when they've the chance to do this, and so we're now an easy target for them."

"Ramsammy's just an idiot. That's why the locals call him 'idiot'. He's the local PPP activist according to my mother, so everything we do, they go and gripe about in their party meetings."

"Well the best thing to do is to ignore it then. Obviously these kinds of tricks would normally scare people away because they think it's a sign from evil spirits. They'll find out that we don't believe in jumbies and spirits and so we won't be scared into doing what they want."

Local society was steeped in superstition. I could understand why this was. With educational standards so low and the historical tribal influences so strong, village peasants had little incentive to question what they heard from elders on their back steps at nights. Children grew up with no entertainment at nights in the darkness other than to listen to the 'jumbie stories' told by their grandmothers or grandfathers. I had seen this myself when we lived with Taa. Children are easily scared by the dark in any case. It was no wonder that they did not venture out at nights without an adult. They must be scared out of their wits by these stories which were always set in the darkness of night. One favourite was telling tales of 'the ol' higue' that would come in the night to 'suck' children. I had found out a lot more about this strange creature from talking to the children about their stories I was reading in my classes, where this figure kept cropping up. I wanted to understand what it was. From their explanations I discovered that it was some kind of female vampire that liked to kill children. I imagined that it had grown out of the reality of vampire bats existing in this environment and having free access to the interior of houses at nights just like all the other harmless bats. It may also have been a way of explaining sudden child deaths. Perhaps adults also used it as a way of improving their childrens' behaviour. At any rate the belief in the old higue was very real and I was not going to try to dispel this by ridicule in class. I would just hope that as education improved, and childrens' sense of reason was strengthened, they would grow out of the superstitions for themselves eventually.

A few weeks later during July when my Overhead projector had arrived and I was using it to make a new teaching aid for the classes I would restart in September, a voice called out "Edwin" from the gate and I went out to see who it was. A slightly built Afro-Guyanese lady was standing there. When I approached her, she behaved very secretively, as if she didn't want anyone to overhear what she said. She asked for Edwin, saying she had a message from his friend Constance, who lived at Number 8 village on the way to Rosignol. She was the retired headmistress, who now ran the Regional Teachers' Resources Centre that I had donated books to not so long ago. The woman at the gate seemed really creepy but I called upstairs for Edwin to come down to her. When he answered and came down, she pressed a note into his palm and whispered something to him as I left them to it and went back to the library to finish my task.

When rummaging through the store room to find the slide projector screen he had brought from England, I had found an old plain beige roller blind. This would make an ideal base for a world map that I could fix over the top of the black-board and pull it down whenever I needed to show them the shape and location of the seven continents and oceans, I thought. The children were supposed to know these for Common Entrance and yet I had discovered that they only memorised a list at their normal school because none of them had any idea what or where they actually were. The exam just required them to select a multiple choice answer. Getting it right was a matter of parrot fashion learning and lucky guesswork of words that seemed to have no meaning or relevance to their lives. My only world map on the library wall was a free poster from some magazine that was an extremely complicated political atlas map. It did not show the continental shapes clearly. I planned to make my own display-size map of continents by drawing the outlines onto an overhead transparency, projecting it onto the library wall at the right size for the roller blind and tracing the outlines onto some white paper that I could make patterns from to cut out shapes from dress material scraps I had in my sewing box. If I cut out the seven continents in seven different colours of plain fabric, I could stick the shapes onto the blind with some cow-gum and have a bright colourful wall-map of the world's continents that would easily roll up over the blackboard when not needed. I did this and made some large removable name cards for the continents and oceans. These I could use to get the children to come up to the front and hold in front of the right shape to identify them all visually.

I was just feeling proud of the result of my work when Edwin came in having let the visitor out of the gate. He was impressed when he saw the map. Then I asked who the strange lady was.

"That was Patsy," he said, "She looks after Constance's house when she goes away to visit her son in America. Apparently, someone set fire to her house at number eight village while she was away and some damage was done but it's been sorted."

"Why would someone set fire to her house?"

"Jealousy. She has overseas relatives in England. Her sister sends her lots of stuff and she goes to California quite often. Her son's got a job there. Also, her ex-husband used to work for the government and there's an on-going dispute over his farmlands. It could be any one of those things. Poor woman! Her house has been broken into a few times since 1984 and stuff stolen."

"She's such a kind person," I said, "I can't believe that anyone would do that to her. She doesn't deserve it. She's always so nice to me and genuinely interested in what I'm trying to do."

As I was speaking, I noticed the grisly looking decapitated head of a white doll impaled on a picket of Auntie Lucy's fence. It sent a shiver down my spine at the thought of what diabolical message it seemed to symbolise. Edwin had told me that it was there to prevent 'bad-eye' which, he had explained to me was to stop evil coming to you from the covetous eyes of neighbours on your property. Samo had given Edwin a small test-tube half full of mercury sealed with a cork when we were living at Taa's and were trying to finish off our house. He said Edwin needed it to keep 'bad-eye' off him because of the big house he was building and told him to keep it in his trouser pocket. I remembered being horrified at the thought of such a poisonous substance being carried around in such a dangerous fashion and did not even want it kept on the shelf in the same room we were sleeping in. Edwin didn't know what to do with it, so in the end he threw the sealed tube into Taa's pit latrine in the relatively safe knowledge that it would soon be deeply buried in a place that no one would ever dig around in to accidentally break or discover. Perhaps I should look for an old doll's head to put on our fence picket, I thought, half-seriously.

'Bad-eye' was one of many superstitious beliefs that underpinned daily life in Guyana. Obeah was the local name for a type of Voo-doo religion that prevailed in the rural community particularly the Afro-Guyanese. Obeah was frowned on by the church but practised by many who were church-goers. Shirley Robertson's estranged husband had been suffering from a long and lingering illness that no one could publicly name. We had suspected it was probably AIDS which at that time was denied to exist in Guyana. However, Shirley had described what medicine the local 'obeah man' had given to her husband. It consisted of putting a pile of assorted herbs on a plate on the floor of the room and burning it while chanting incantations as the smoke rose into the air around the patient. Sad to say that it cannot have been very effective medicine, as a few months later, Mr Robertson finally passed away. This man had been a revered Headmaster of a local secondary school and the Minister of Hopetown Congregational Church. His wife, a member of the local Catholic Church, worked in the Regional Education Office and had been a primary Head Teacher herself. It was to us an unexpected fact that educated people with such status in the local community should still adhere to these beliefs in 1993.

Samo, who was disgruntled for personal reasons, came complaining to Edwin one day that his wife Caro and several other teachers from the primary school were participating in obeah orgies at a place called Ithaca by the Berbice River. Ithaca was notorious for its 'strange' black people. The Uncle of one of Edwin's PE course student-teachers was the Obeah High Priest of Ithaca. Samo was upset because this obeah-man was exerting influence over all these black female teachers, so they were attending night time rituals of a sexual nature alone with him. Man to man, Samo wanted advice. He wanted Edwin to talk to Caro to dissuade her from going. There was always one rule for men and another for women in this society. Samo himself attended all-male obeah sessions with this same man and had earlier tried to get Edwin to go along to one of them. That was when he had given Edwin the tube of mercury. He had described how the high priest dressed up in special clothes with cow horns to perform a fertility rite of some sort. Edwin had refused, saying he did not believe in all that sort of nonsense. Now that Samo, a mature man in his late fifties, was probably feeling sexually challenged by his younger wife, he felt the need to call in some moral support from a non-believer like Edwin. Edwin had declined getting involved in such a delicate manner, saying it was Samo's problem and it was best he deal with it himself.

I was interested in the origins of the kumfa drumming we could hear nightly in the village as July was coming to a close. We were invited to what they called 'swaree' on the eve of Emancipation Day which was August 1st, to commemorate when slavery had officially ended in the British West Indies. I supposed 'swaree' to be a corruption of the French word 'soiree'. That night, the air was alive with the tribal beat which carried for miles across the silence of the neighbourhood. It had an exciting power. When we went down to the school hall nearing midnight, the tempo was approaching fever pitch. There were hundreds of people lining the roadsides with stalls, their flambeau lamps flickering. The Community High School was where the local army band would be playing. They had borrowed Edwin's drum set for the occasion and invited Edwin to do some drumming for them during the evening. As we neared the Congregational Church, we passed many of the village women dressed in beautiful African print floor length robes and turbans of various styles. The elder men wore pillbox or boat-shaped caps and embroidered kaftans of similar materials. They were all going to the Society Hall for their celebratory feast. We had not been invited to that one and I was disappointed. The young people were all teeming around outside the school hall to listen to the band's music for free. Inside, working people or those with money who had come from far and wide had to pay to go in. This was to raise funds to donate to the Community High School for its repair and refurbishment we were told. It also covered the cost of the traditional food which was shared out after midnight. None of the participants inside the school hall had on any African costume. To please Edwin, and satisfy his sense of nostalgia, a group from a distant village who still knew how to do square dances, had been invited and paid to perform, but it was not as exciting for me as it would have been if they had been dressed like the older women up the road. When we asked why they did not do this, the younger people laughed at the idea. They wanted modern and foreign things and did not seem to value their grand-parents' traditions.

I thought this was a shame. I wanted to help to keep these traditions alive as I had heard that Hopetown was one of the last villages to keep up the practice of Swaree and que-que. I had asked the children in my classes if they knew how to do African dances and they said they did not. I suggested that they could learn to dance to the Kumfa drums if we could get the drummers to come to Sapodilla to teach them. Georgie knew who they were. He would send for them a few days after emancipation celebrations died down. When Kevon and his two friends came to see me, I suggested that if they taught us the dances we could get some colourful tie-dye costumes made for them so they could play for us when overseas visitors stayed at Sapodilla in the future. They seemed to like the idea and agreed to do it. We arranged a time for a practice and the first one went quite well. Reliability soon became a problem, presumably because they wanted paying for practising and that we could not offer. However, we persevered and even though I rehearsed the group alone most of the time after the first couple of lessons, I still entertained the idea that the village drummers would come to perform at tourist performances when we would be able to pay them.

Cousin Elfrieda in the village was one of the elders everyone respected. She was the expert in African tie-die techniques in the church craft and sewing group. She had made some beautifully dyed cotton cloth which Edwin had bought for me. I asked him if we could get the drummers and our dancers measured up for costumes to be made by Elfrieda and Taa's sewing group. Edwin agreed, but since the expense was so high, his condition was that we would keep all the costumes at Sapodilla and the dancers and drummers would only put them on when they performed. We would launder them and keep them safe till the next time they were needed. Now the African dance group became part of the living history display of the Parson Munroe Museum of Village life which was based at Sapodilla Learning Centre and would be a tourist attraction for the area in the future.

I bought an emancipation magazine in Georgetown and found out about the Kumfa religion from it. It had originated in Africa with the slaves and, like voodoo in other parts of the Caribbean, ritual sacrifices were held on important occasions, such as a death, or Emancipation day, when a chicken would be ceremonially sacrificed by a high priest. The drumming would be a part of the occasion because it was a form of communication with the spirits of the ancestors. An important part of the beliefs were to do with wealth and money. There was a hierarchy among the races as seen in Guyana and economic prosperity was to be obtained by getting close to people of a race that was higher in the pecking order. The order described had Amerindian at the bottom, then Indian, African next, then Chinese, then various shades of mulatto through quadroon up to octoroon and white or Dutch at the top. This part of the religion seemed contrary to my own philosophy of life: that prosperity came through one's own efforts to make the best use of the skills and talents one had developed in life and that race should not be the basis on which one made judgements about people. I had grown up in a Christian society that believed in racial equality. The idea of a racial hierarchy that was accepted and embraced by those at the bottom of it seemed distasteful. I could only put it down to the history of the country, that the voluntary and forced migrations which had brought this mix of six races to one geographical location had given rise to such a coping strategy. I was interested to know about these beliefs because I knew they underpinned the lives of many of the children I taught and their families too. I would have to take this into account in teaching them. It could be dangerous, however sensitive I was.

We had been invited to many functions in the village since our arrival. I had never been to any without Edwin. He felt the need to protect me from possible harassment or harm. I suppose if I had grown up there it would have been different. Although on the surface, the villages were sleepy, peaceful farming communities, there was a distinct absence of law and order and an undercurrent of violence from the recent political past. This was evident from the lack of response by the police to the recent theft of our sheep. It was also a fact that every now and then, news like the arson attack on Constance's house, or a late night gunpoint robbery at Zando's rum shop would come to our ears. There had been a spate of burglaries in the village attributed to notorious bandits with nicknames such as "Pickaloo" and "Pumpkin". Edwin wanted to have a gun licence so that he could keep a weapon at home for our personal self-defence should it come to the worst, but his attempts to get one had been fruitless. He had come to the conclusion that he had been denied one because of his military background in England and the fear that he might lead a group of young black men in revolt against the government. This of course was ludicrous to us as he had no such intention. Not only that but there were numerous illegal weapons among youths and others in the neighbourhood, so if he had wanted to do that, he could have just asked one of them to get him an illegal weapon too. It seemed more likely that by keeping him unarmed, the local police could intimidate him if they wanted to.

I was getting to know Edwin better than ever, now I had been married to him and living with him for two years, but I had known him for nearly ten years and one thing that no one could do to him was intimidate him. In fact his chief method of dealing with difficult people was to use their own methods on them before they could use them on him. If anyone looked like they would try to intimidate him, he would soon show he was more forceful and could unleash far more devastation with the power of his body and brain than they could. It always worked. The mere suggestion of it was usually all that was necessary. Thereafter, they backed down and showed him a healthy respect, even if they did mutter under their breath and see him as a bully. Edwin never bullied anyone, nor bothered them, unless they tried to put him down or threatened him first.

The local police were notoriously ineffective because many of them were barely literate. Most of them came from the same village where they operated, so would not take action against members of their own extended family even if one of them had committed a crime. They also expected and took bribes even though it was against the laws of Guyana to do so. How can there be law and order when the officials of the law disregard it and only apply it selectively, we thought. Once again, the solution was to be education, but that would take time. These were widely accepted principles that were much talked about in the community but no one local applied it in practice because no one else did. It was a cultural norm. No official had the courage to stand up against censure by their neighbours. It was difficult to live near people who ganged up on you and lashed you with their tongues when all you had tried to do was to enforce the law on them. Only a very strong person who had not grown up in this culture could make significant changes. Edwin soon became the one who they all looked to in order to sort out their disputes. An innate leader, he unwittingly stepped into the shoes of the British Colonial Rulers who had fulfilled this role in the past. It was ironic how this situation began to develop, however.

One night the previous year, when Bryan was still manager of our snackette, the local branch of the Special Forces drugs unit who operated in our area, had all come to the snackette to get some food and beers. Edwin was there in person that night chatting with customers and serving them. After the other customers had all now left, the boss of the unit had called him over while they were waiting for their chicken and plantain chips to be cooked.

"Bailey was already a bit tiddly when he called me over," Edwin had told me later, when he came home. We both liked Bailey, who was on a plane higher than the average local police officer and also had a good sense of humour. "He said, 'Hey Mr Joseph, You bin big soldier man in Hengaland. Ya ever seen a weapon like zis one?' and he waved his piece in the air at me. I sat down at their table and said, 'Blimey I haven't seen one o' them for years, let's have a closer look' and held my hand out for it. He passed it to me and said 'Is loaded. Careful how ya tek it,' I inspected it in my two hands saying 'This is a museum piece, it's amazing', and they were so busy laughing and joking that they didn't notice me slipping the bullets out of it into my left hand and putting them in my pocket. I joined in the jokes because the others were now trying to ridicule me a bit, suggesting that I was only a sportsman not a real soldier. Then I cocked the gun ready to shoot and they all panicked and ducked in case the gun went off accidentally. As they calmed down a bit, I slowly put the gun to my head and looking Bailey straight in the eyes, pulled the trigger. They all yelled and dived under the table in sheer terror, thinking I'd blown my brains out at the table. I waited until they realised that I had shot a blank. Then I spun the barrel and offered it up to them. 'Who wants to take the next turn?' I asked. Not one of the cowards volunteered, so I got my own back. I said 'Only a sportsman, eh? It seems I've got more balls than any of you lot.' I don't think they'll be mocking my capabilities as a soldier in future."

"What did you do with the bullets?" I had asked him, a bit shocked and wondering whether he still had them.

"I waited till they were all going home at the end of the evening and I called Bailey back as they were going out of the gate. He came up to me and I said in a low voice so the others couldn't hear, 'I think you've forgotten something.' Then I quietly slipped the bullets from my closed hands into his and he put them in his pocket and thanked me as he went out of the gate." It did not take long for Bryan to spread his version of what had happened and what he thought he had witnessed to the patrons of the snackette over the next few weeks. It was exactly what Edwin had wanted. His reputation for being a tough madman from England who had played Russian roulette in real life in front of Bailey and his men was to become a local legend.

More recently, Edwin had found himself at Zando's bar one night on his way home from a co-op meeting and had faced similar ridicule from the men drinking there. He had been outside in the yard listening to stories about a spate of local break-ins and burglaries and had grown impatient with the helpless acceptance of it. He had asked them why they didn't do something about it since they knew who it was committing the crimes. They had complained as usual about the police not acting to arrest the culprit because he always went and hid far away from the area and couldn't be found. Edwin had said, "Well if it was me who got broken into, I'd find out where his house was in the village and throw a Molotoff cocktail through his window! That'd give him the message not to break in to my house." After that, there had been much laughter and mockery of Edwin as a 'Big tough soldier man' by people who thought he was just saying it and would be just as helpless as everyone else. It had ignited Edwin's uncontrollable urge to prove them wrong and shut them up. He had told me all this much later, when the fuss had died down. He said that he had allowed the drunken rabble to carry on ridiculing him, while he called over Auntie Molly, Zando's mother, to ask if she could bring him some kerosene and an old rag. He had got up and taken these items with his empty beer bottle to the darkness at the back of the yard, where he assembled the cocktail before bringing it back to his table. Then he had told Zando and his fellow drinkers to look over towards a rickety old pig-pen at the far side of the yard. When they were all looking in the direction he pointed to, he had lobbed the Molotoff cocktail into the pig-pen and on impact, it had burst into flames, sending them all into pandemonium, running and fetching buckets of water from the trench to put out the fire. He had got up and walked out, leaving them to reflect on whether he was a man to be mocked, whether he was a man who would utter idle talk or whether he was a man who did what he said he would do. I was horrified to hear of this calculated vandalism but it could not be undone. He had regretted doing it also, because it had upset Auntie Molly. These two incidents had left an indelible mark on the folk memory of his people, however unpleasant at the time. He had gone down as someone not to be messed with and we were certainly going to need that kind of help in the coming months and years.

Chapter 13

The Green Shoots of Ecotourism

It was on the basis of equal opportunity to all races that Sapodilla Learning Centre would operate. I would dedicate my life to it. So would Edwin, although he believed he could hand over to younger people to carry on where he left off as soon as he had taught them. We were a self-funding Charity that would get its income from the Eco-tourism we would host at our centre. Recognising as we did the local corruption that had a stranglehold on the purse-strings of international charities, we knew we would never be able to get any help from funding agencies. There was also a certain sense of national pride in Edwin that a country should make an effort to help itself rather than go around with a begging bowl. What was applicable to a country was applicable to its citizens. He was of the generation who strived and so was I. Old age was something in the remote future that we did not concern ourselves with at that time. We thought nothing of what position we would be putting ourselves into by pursuing this aim. We both believed that development could and would happen and that we were at the forefront of it. I knew it would take time, maybe a decade or two, but it would happen, like it had in Dubai, now the politics of dictatorship had ended. Edwin was impatient. He wanted it to happen yesterday, like everything he undertook, and he worked tirelessly to achieve it, dragging all around him along by the scruff of their necks.

We had a lot of business at the snackette for C.A.R.D.I. lunches in June and July because their local expert Dr MacPherson had made friends with Edwin since Zando had introduced them to one another. Mac had become a regular visitor, like Albert, so I had got to know him quite well too. He had studied for his PhD at Glasgow University and had my sympathy for that. I did not envy anyone who had to do veterinary field work on hill sheep farms in a Scottish winter. It was Mac who managed the CARDI sheep project in our area and so he was living in one of the government houses at the MMA in Onverwagt. This enabled him to come down most mornings for a free training session with Edwin in our gym. Since Harold Patterson had stayed and then the two vets from Georgetown, we had not had any more of the locals staying at Sapodilla.

According to Mac, there had been some questions raised at CARDI headquarters in Trinidad as to the amount we were charging. Mac had tried to get Edwin to reduce our prices as we were in a rural location. Edwin stood by our tariff as it was less than Georgetown prices and yet far better quality, plus the fee was inclusive of all meals. In order to reach a compromise, Edwin arranged for meals to be cooked for the CARDI team by Cousin Irene at the snackette. They would not be staying overnight at Sapodilla. Since Philip had left by mutual agreement with Edwin, Spear was now sleeping at the snackette. He would be the night security for which he was happy to accept free accommodation instead of extra wages. It was a step up in the world for him to have his own comfortable room, and a home to himself instead of sharing a two roomed hut with his mother, seven brothers and sisters and several of their children. The rest of the staff was just left to do what they always did but without a manager apart from Edwin who checked the goings on every day.

I was no longer doing their books because I now had more important work managing any tourists and their food at Sapodilla. Any spare time I had between guests was now fully taken up with the library, my increasing number of classes, and preparation and marking of students' work. Edwin was doing the snackette books himself now and with a lot less scrutiny than I had done. He just checked their receipts, approved their shopping order, did a weekly stocktake, glanced over their sales sheet and counted the daily takings Spear brought down for him when the sales girls closed up at nights. There was usually a bit of profit after the wages and expenses had been paid and if it looked as if it was less than Edwin calculated it ought to be, he just gave the girls a talking to and then it all carried on as before. It was a happy equilibrium and I was glad to have it out of my hair. Since we had finished the house and received the mortgage from the bank, we no longer had to supply official accounts to them to show our income. There was still a need for us to make money from the snackette, but by now, Edwin's pension had paid down his debt in England from twenty two and a half thousand to around five thousand pounds so there was less pressure on us to extract every last cent of profit from the snackette. Nevertheless, we still kept accounts of it all for our own records and Edwin dealt directly with all the tax, electricity bills, repair bills and National Insurance Scheme payments for the workers' sickness and unemployment protection.

The ongoing P.E. course for teachers of the region culminated in a primary schools athletics quadrathlon which Edwin organised in July. Seventeen teams turned up. It attracted interest from the Ministry of Education in Georgetown, who then tried to copy the idea in the capital. Although the June rains had flooded out the library floor for a time, the waters had receded and I had cleaned up the mess in time for a visit to Sapodilla Learning Centre by the new Regional Education Officer from Georgetown, who had recently replaced Mr Mitchell. By a strange coincidence his name was also Mr Joseph. He was far more intelligent than Mr Mitchell and eager to embrace change and see improvements. He was very impressed with Edwin's work with the PE teachers and what he saw of our Learning Centre facilities. Following the conversation I had with him, he was happy to give his teachers permission to bring parties of school children on educational visits to Sapodilla for what I called lead-lessons using resources I had which were not available in the schools themselves. It was my way of showing them different teaching methods which they might take on board themselves back in their own schools and it could lead to improvements in educational standards all across the region.

I had done one of these lead lessons for a class from Hopetown Primary School before term ended. It involved a dramatic role play in a Treasure Hunt around the Sapodilla grounds as part of an introduction to simple map work. I used the zooming satellite images of the earth from the start of our E.T. video, my globe, my overhead projector and my new applique wall map of the continents to follow this up in the classroom. The children had to do some colouring in of outline maps of the seven continents and five oceans I had duplicated for them in advance, and could look for guidance at the colourful roller blind hanging in front of the blackboard. My aim was to help the children to better understand the concepts of continents they were being asked to memorise and to show the teachers that this would help their classes remember more effectively and so get better results on those kinds of questions in their Common Entrance Exams. The day seemed to go well and Yvonne went away happy that her class had enjoyed their day visit. Hopefully more of these would follow.

In the lead up to Emancipation, we had received a letter asking us for a booking from someone at the British High Commission who wanted to stay over for a weekend with us in August. This was great news and we pulled out all the stops for her. It was a pleasant experience for us to have Elaine, an educated female not too much younger than me, as new company for us both in the house. She was very interested to know what we were doing, why we had come there and how we were managing. She was also very interested in travel, the local environment and what we had discovered about the nature of the local community by living in it as we did. We told her everything we knew that we had time to cover during her short stay. We had no reason to hide any of the truth, including what we had observed about the racism, the corruption, the dishonesty we had been a victim of and the lamentable state of the education system. We even revealed the problem that drug usage was causing among working age men and what we had observed and put an end to at our snackette. In some ways Elaine seemed a little green about the realities of life, but she was living in Georgetown in the protected shelter of a diplomatic residence and had far less experience in life than either of us. Elaine liked to use her time off to travel around and see all parts of whichever country she was working in, so it was useful to us to know what she thought of the other eco-tourist resorts in Guyana that we had not visited ourselves through lack of funds and inability to escape from Sapodilla for an overnight stay anywhere. She complimented us in saying we had a better standard of accommodation, service and catering than any of them. This was a great boost to us. We hoped it would lead to a stream of other similar business from overseas. Although I did not realise it at the time, she must have also been checking us out on behalf of the High Commissioner, whom we had invited to visit us and the local school. It was only a few weeks since Edwin had got the Headmistress, Beverley, to write a formal invitation to the British High Commissioner. I had already bought new books as prizes for the top exam students in all the academic subjects for him to present on November 4th.

I wanted to build up the Parson Munroe Museum of Village Life not only for the Tourists at Sapodilla to see, but also for something to use as an educational resource for the school children. It had saddened me at Swaree that young people had so little interest in the history of their country and culture. They seemed more interested in Yankee fashions and music. It was what their relatives sent back for them in barrels and was a kind of status symbol among them. I discovered that little or no history was taught in school and few children took the CXC history exam at secondary level. It was a shame I thought, and found out that children took other subjects that were easier to pass because nobody passed history. It was too difficult. I felt sure it was because it was taught badly and also because it was all based on memory. There seemed to be hardly any visual evidence of history present in the country. Unlike the neighbouring South American Countries with great temples of the Maya or the Inca civilisations, there was little remaining physical evidence of any ancient Amerindian civilisation. Only the rumours of El Dorado from the time when Walter Raleigh had sailed the Guiana coast in search of it in Elizabethan times. El Dorado, the Golden One, if he had lived in gold-rich Guiana, did not leave any great pyramids in the rainforest or visible ruins yet known about. There were a few beautiful old nineteenth and early twentieth century colonial buildings of wood still standing in Georgetown, but the clock was ticking for when they too would crumble and be replaced by concrete modern ones. It would be very difficult to make the rich history that was undoubtedly there visible to children. If they were taught about something they could see and relate to, then they might value it and have more of a sense of belonging to the place than a desire to escape it. I wanted to tie their understanding of their history to the local physical environment it happened in.

If only I could track down some photos that had been taken of things in the period of Edwin's childhood that he remembered with such affection! Mac had taken us to Georgetown one day in August, to the University of Guyana. It was useful to me because I was able to visit their library and read a few books. I learned there from the librarian, that a Mr Raymond Smith from England had done his PhD on Hopetown in the 1950s and had written a definitive book on his research. I spent some time reading the book and making notes from it. Surely he must have taken some photos when he lived there, I thought. Once back in Hopetown, Edwin had discovered from Taa that Dr Raymond Smith had married Flora, sister of our newspaper vendor Brenda whom he had fallen in love with during his period of study in Hopetown. I wrote to him explaining who I was and what we were doing at Sapodilla and asking if he could let me have the details of the publisher of his book as I would like to obtain it for our library. I also wondered if he could supply me with copies of any photos of daily life in the village in the 1950s if he still had any. My idea was to display them in our small museum as an educational resource. Brenda kindly agreed to post my letter to him. I soon had a reply enclosing a complimentary copy of his book and a letter in which he promised to search out the negatives of his photos when he could find time.

At the end of the summer, we got a surprise visit from Flora and her son. They brought me a package from Raymond with some wonderful photos of bull-mashing, the Hopetown street market, the blacksmith and coffin makers at work, and various other activities. It was a wonderful start to my displays and I lost no time at all in getting them copied, mounted and laminated. Spear helped me to make a six foot high framework for a folding screen using some spare hardwood battens we had in the storeroom. I covered the frames with old rice-bags stretched and stapled onto to them like an artist's canvas. The same rice bag fabric served to hinge the screens together so they would open and close concertina-fashion. Then I painted over them with grey gloss paint on both sides. These would be the display boards for my first museum photos.

I had visited the National Museum in Georgetown and the Walter Roth Anthropological collection, which had Amerindian archaeological finds and traditional crafts, but knew that most of the children who lived in our villages never went to the capital as the cost of a minibus journey was unaffordable for them or many of their parents. If they were to understand local history properly, then I needed to collect together lots of visual items as museum artefacts and use them in my lessons as tools for investigation in simple historical detective work. They needed to start thinking for themselves not just to sit and memorize a lot of dates and facts in a story form to write out in an exam. They needed to understand that the history we know about comes from evidence and that is why we should preserve evidence for future generations, or one day people would say "this did not happen". I had spent a lot of time the previous term using standard humanities techniques for getting groups to handle strange historic objects of mine that they would not have seen before, in an attempt to get them to ask questions about them: what size and shape, what material made of, what possible use, what clues did it give about its owner? They had really enjoyed this kind of learning and it had helped them to think, to discuss and to write simple sentences of their own. If I could do the same thing with some artefacts from Guyana's past, it would be even better. I had also done a lot of things involving drawing and art of some sort or another. Clearly they never did anything of the like at their day school and they really enjoyed the opportunity to do it at Sapodilla. I always used scraps that cost nothing or materials from the garden, pasture and roadside or farm. I opened the library twice a week during the school holidays, so I put on a special art class once a week for those members who wanted to do it. Just as August was coming to a close, a local Indian girl who had been coming to me for help with her English brought me a surprise donation for the museum.

"This is amazing," I said, delighted. "Where on earth did you get it from?"

"Me fader find it in ze backdam by Abary river."

"Do you know what it is?" She looked at it and shook her head.

"Well, to me it looks like a very, very old axe-head. I'm not sure, but it might have been made by someone in the time before people had any metal to make axes. Look at how smooth it is. Someone had to keep rubbing it with another stone for days or even weeks, to get it smooth like that. Look at the notches on each side of the narrow end. They were probably notches to catch the twine that was used to attach the axe to a handle of wood. I must see if I can find out more about it for you, and we'll put it in the museum to show everyone who comes to the library. Thank you very much indeed!"

Later that day, I took several photos of it, planning to get someone at the Georgetown Museum to identify it. We got the photos developed eventually and then I wrote a letter explaining who I was and what I was doing to help local children learn about their history. I enclosed the photo of the stone axe that a student's father had found near the Abary River and had brought in to me and asked if they could tell me what it was, how old it was and if it was rare. We posted the letter and within a fortnight received a reply from Miss Wisheart at the Walter Roth Museum. She identified it as an Amerindian stone axe that could be anything from two hundred years old to several thousand years old. They were quite commonly found in the interior on prehistoric riverine sites. I was thrilled. This was our first tangible artefact from the indigenous inhabitants of prehistoric Guyana. It was more than I had hoped for.

Every morning at five thirty, while it was still cool and barely light, Edwin's athletes for the school sports came down to train with him in the gym and out on the street. Sometimes, Mr Nedd who had worked together with Edwin to set up the Hopetown-Sapodilla Sports Club in order to register it with the Guyana Amateur Athletics Association, came down to help coach them as well. Edwin had told his course teachers that to get the best results from athletes they needed to train every day in all weathers, so any of their best athletes who wanted to train seriously to win, should start training with him before the end of term and continue throughout the summer holiday. He insisted that athletes be punctual and reliable. No one forced them to come to his sessions, but if they wanted to stay in the group, they must turn up on time every day or be "kicked out". This happened to one or two but when the others realised Edwin meant what he said, they soon conformed. It meant that much to them to win the School's Nationals.

Although my classes had been popular before the holidays, I was worried that my new system of enrolment, which started in late August, would put people off because they had to find six hundred dollars for the term at the time of registration instead of just twenty dollars for one class. All the same, it was affordable to anyone who could buy five beers. I sent a letter home about it before the August holiday and notices went out to church and primary school for the first week of September. Word of mouth did the rest. I seemed to be spending days setting and marking entrance tests in order to have children in the right class for their literacy level. I had so many children enrol for the first week of September that all my classes were full and I had no room or seats to fit any more in. Obviously my worries were unfounded. We brought down some more stools from the snackette and got some more old tyres. For the time being, that is what we would have to use for the children to sit on. By early October, I had to start turning people away as I had no more physical space inside the room. I took their names and addresses down on a waiting list and said I would contact them if anyone dropped out of the classes. Library membership had risen to 170 and Edwin had to cancel all other appointments on Saturdays from now on. He had to stand at the gate and manage the influx and exit of library users as the queue stretched for quite a distance up the street. The Hopetown Primary School group who had visited me before the holiday wanted to come back in early October. Teacher Yvonne wanted me to start off a session on the Amerindians with them and then borrow the set of illustrated resource booklets I had made to be followed up in class. This was because I had said that I would be awarding a special history prize to whoever came top in the project they did from following the tasks set in the booklet. It was another great success, and the axe head got its first hands-on use in class. Yvonne sent up the completed work for me to mark and judge, so when I had done that, I decided to put it all out on display for the British High Commissioner to see when he visited the Primary School in November. I also set about making a display of work that my various classes had done and to fix the museum artefacts and photos on the screens that Spear and I had made.

Any hopes of educational progress that had been raised in us since his appointment as our Regional Education Officer were now dashed by the news that Mr Terry Joseph had taken an overseas post on one of the islands at the end of the summer break. Edwin found out that he had become so frustrated by the failure of the local regional administration to provide decent accommodation for himself and his family that he had been forced to accept a better alternative.

This meant that Mr Mitchell was back as acting REDO and was likely now to be confirmed in the appointment. The teachers' sports course at Sapodilla resumed in September and all over the country, Schools Sports competitions were underway. Edwin was getting a first-hand experience of how the system worked. What he found most distasteful was the exploitation of the children by adults in the community. Instead of focussing on improvement in the quality of performance and raising standards in sport, those organising it were using the occasion as a fundraiser for themselves. Loud music had to be provided to draw the crowds to the track. The community came for a day out to watch the entertainment and see what business they could catch for themselves by selling refreshments of one kind or another to the gathering spectators. No matter how hard he tried to persuade the teachers in his classes to reform these evils, it was a losing battle since he was the only one who genuinely felt making money out of poor children was wrong.

Edwin spent a lot of time talking to different teachers at the school sports and branch sports while supervising the skills he had been teaching his student-teachers. He was finding out from them what they thought of the Regional education administration. His sources revealed that Shirley Robertson had told the teachers at the primary school not to bring any more classes down to Sapodilla or their jobs would be in the balance. I was completely shocked when he told me this. How could she have done this? She had been so nice to my face and helpful when I was ill. I could not believe she could have been so two-faced. Why? I felt hurt. I had thought she was a friend that I could talk to on my own level. She claimed to share our opinions of how education needed to improve and had even appeared to encourage me. We had spent hours in her house during our first year, and since we had moved into our house, she had been our own guest on more than one occasion. Had all that been insincere?

Our paying overseas customerss who stayed at Sapodilla throughout October and November now got the chance to witness the education they were contributing towards. Harold Patterson from CARDI came back for another two nights while working on the sheep project in mid-October when Edwin was fully involved in helping the teachers with the Branch Sports at the MMA. Then CARDI sent their senior statistical analyst, Bruce Laukner to stay overnight in early November. We were expecting a whole family of Edwin's friends from England for a month at Christmas, and they would be bringing a small baby with them, so Edwin asked around for a cot for sale and when it arrived, Spear was given the task of sanding it down and painting it with fresh, safe gloss-paint.

The appointed day had arrived. Hopetown was buzzing in anticipation. The British High Commissioner was paying his first ever visit to the village and the first for any representative of the British Government since that of Governor Light in the 1840s when the village had been founded by freed slaves shortly after their Emancipation. Edwin did not care whose feathers he ruffled by arranging for this to happen. All the people we knew and dealt with felt uplifted and excited, but there were definitely some eyes who were watching that day who were not so happy with the idea of it. They were watching from the shadows, sharpening their knives.

At about ten thirty, the car with the diplomatic flag pulled up outside the snackette on the public road. We had been waiting there to meet High Commissioner Johnson as arranged. Edwin welcomed him in and he had a soft drink with us before taking us on to the school in his vehicle just before eleven. What a charming man he was, so down to earth and unpretentious. The school had been transformed from its normal drab untidy state. The teachers had really made an effort, by sticking little flags, pictures and bunting made from scraps of paper and card from the rafters and beams. After the usual formal introductions, some of the children had been rehearsed to perform recitations. A small group played a short tune on the recorders we had given them, the teachers' choir sang a couple of local songs and the Headmistress made a speech about the school, welcomed the High Commissioner, thanked him for coming and invited him to say a few words before he presented the prizes. The presentation followed a donation by the High Commission to the primary school of lots of beautiful reference books and educational posters. When it had finished, he took us back to Sapodilla. We were able to show him around the gym, the library, the museum exhibition and display of children's work I had set up. He was very impressed with it all and promised to try and help. His first gift was a pair of cricket bats and balls for the sports club. Then he came upstairs and joined us for lunch which I had already prepared for us. Edwin presented him with one of Dred's woodcarvings and a small trinket box made from purple-heart wood. Finally, he headed back to Georgetown at a quarter past three. As the car drove off down the dam, and we waved goodbye to a great man who now seemed like a friend, we both felt elated. The day went down in the annals of Folk History that Edwin Joseph had put Hopetown on the map.

Within a couple of weeks of the visit, some of the knives that had been sharpened in the shadows began to flash at us. The Ministry of Education notified us that they would be sending some inspectors from Georgetown to investigate the premises now it was registered as a private school in region five, to see if it met the necessary standards of health and safety. Edwin was suspicious. Why had they singled us out for this when they did not inspect the myriad "bottom house" schools that were run for the private profit of their unqualified teachers and had no facilities at all? It was even more ironic that we should be subjected to such scrutiny when most of the state schools were falling down from lack of maintenance. They had leaking roofs, collapsing beams and steps and no sanitary facilities at all. In spite of our private resentment, we complied willingly with their request. We put on just as good a display for the inspectors as we had for the High Commissioner and so what started out as an investigation ended with the full approval and adulation of the Georgetown bigwigs. We would not be ordered to close down after all. Our unseen enemies had lost this attempt to bring us down, but they remained dark and brooding in the shadows, plotting their next move.

Towards the end of November, Edwin was heavily involved with the regional athletes competing in the Schools National Athletics Championship at a place called Albion on the Corentyne side of the Berbice River. He complained bitterly to me about the shambolic way it was organised and the lack of care and concern for the living conditions of participating children. He was angered at the way the teachers took care of their own accommodation and food with scant regard for that of the students they were responsible for. The competition, needlessly spread out over three days, prolonged the misery and squalor of their temporary housing in dilapidated school buildings with inadequate sanitary facilities. He was horrified that they were left waiting for hours for meals. Food was cooked by travelling parties of volunteering women (usually teachers' relatives) who accompanied each school party in much the same way as bands of enterprising women had accompanied feudal armies to the battlefields of Mediaeval Europe. In this case, however, they all looked forward to the 'holiday' away from home. They took food supplies and equipment bought in their villages from the proceeds of the funds raised at their regional sports and even transported firewood from their home villages to light campfires to cook on at the venue. Regardless of the needs of competing athletes to get meals to a timetable, they bumbled on at their own stress free speed, gossiping, wandering off but eventually dishing up when they were ready. Edwin thought it was madness still carting stuff such a distance when it could all be bought a lot cheaper at Albion when they got there. He could not understand why the teachers objected to the idea of changing the set-up and organising it centrally, or better still, arrange for a local caterer near the venue to provide the food agreed on in advance at a set price and time. The reason was simple. They had learned how to derive personal economic gain while feeding themselves and their own children for free. The organisers' family members who 'owned' minibuses would profit by charging for transport not only of the athletes and teachers but also their fuel and food. The cooks would keep the cook pots and utensils and generous portions of ingredients to take home with them (or leave at home in the first place). As long as the organising teachers were fed well, no one else's complaints would be heard. All these vested interests would oppose change that would take away their income stream and put it in a stranger's hands.

I began to see a fundamental difference between the way Edwin viewed development and the way visiting overseas people viewed it. Edwin wanted to see the standards of decency and care that he was accustomed to in Britain, Europe and North America to be applied in Guyana by the Guyanese themselves at all levels. He did not take into account that local people in positions of authority would not share his standards. Their main concern was self-improvement. This was usually at the expense of those below them in the social pecking order. The majority of overseas visitors observed what was going on, compared what they saw with what they would expect for themselves, and thought the problem was just caused by poverty. They assumed that by donating money to provide better facilities, things would gradually improve. Edwin saw that this did not work because the aid money just disappeared into the pockets of the few who handled it. It did not lead to any improvement except in the wealth of those who got their hands on it. This had led to a cultural belief that the way to get on in life was to get on the committee of a community group who could access funds from aid agencies. If you could become the Treasurer, you had won a goldmine. But money was not the main reason why the conditions were so bad. It was mainly because no one except himself seemed to see the need to supervise the students in their living accommodation while they were away. There were no teachers sleeping in the classroom dormitories with the students at nights, or making sure that students themselves cleaned up the rooms and the washing areas when they had finished using them. Edwin used every opportunity he could to shame those in authority to behave differently and put the common good above their own selfish interests. He would start with the teachers he was teaching on his sports course at Sapodilla, but he was soon to find that he was up against a lot more than individual consciences.

While all this was going on, I was making sure that all the preparations were in place for the rooms to be ready for our English family staying over Christmas. They were due to arrive on the fourth of December and would be with us for a month. I must admit that I had not really designed the lounge furnishings or layout with a toddling baby in mind. In fact I had not experienced a baby in the home since I was a teenager and the last thing I ever expected to face was a small baby being subjected to all the tropical injections and risks of international travel to the tropics in order to come and stay at our resort. The first time the possibility had been put to me was when Edwin started looking around for a cot.

"How old is the youngest?" I had asked him.

"Oh, she was born about a year ago," he had said, "She told me that she would ignore the doctor's advice to leave her at home with her mother while they come out here. She said she wanted to put you off the idea of wanting a baby."

"Charming," I had said.

It was true that the main reason I had given up my career and independent life to marry Edwin when he asked me to, was because I had always wanted a family of my own. I had felt cheated of it when my first husband left me for another woman three years after our wedding. Edwin had won my interest from the outset by declaring that he would like to have another child, because although he already had a grown up family, he loved children. I knew he was a brilliant father from the way he told me he had been with his own. I never wanted to be a marriage breaker after what had happened to me, so only got involved with him once I knew he already had become estranged from his former wife. Now, fifteen years later, in a different situation, I thought we would start our own family at last and had come off the pill soon after we had moved into our house and made it comfortably habitable. I suppose I had thought that when I had a baby myself, then I would prepare properly and make the house suitable. I also knew that I would teach any child of mine to respect the furniture at home and be careful where and how a toddler was allowed the freedom to play. I believed in teaching one's own children, however small, to respect other people's property. Restraining them was what you did if they were too small to understand.

I had not really had any experience of the European childcare methods of the 1990s, which gave free reign to a toddler, encouraging free expression without intervention. Local babies in Guyana behaved perfectly whenever we encountered them. They all seemed trained from birth to be quiet, docile and unadventurous. During the daytime their mothers would carry them around in a sling and as soon as they could sit up unsupported, they were carried in arms by mother or elder sibling to see what was going on in the world around them. Safe items would be given to them to hold and explore with their mouths, but they would not be put on the ground to walk unattended, as the entire environment was filled with dangers. Exposure to such dangers would happen only when children had acquired language well enough to understand and obey warnings. Discipline was strict and corporal punishment was, sadly, usual, so witnessing this being administered to older children must have instilled the need for obedience at an early age.

The house was sparkling with its usual tropical glamour the day our new guests arrived. I had been instructed to put up the artificial Christmas tree on December 1st before I did any other preparations, as Edwin wanted all the traditional decorations. They gasped at the beautiful décor in the lounge and set the baby down on the floor. She immediately made a bee line for the tree and grabbed at its lower branches, pulling the whole thing over so the glass baubles shattered against the wooden floorboards. Jenny rescued her baby while I rescued the tree and cleared up the mess. In an effort to distract the child, someone gave her a bunch of keys to play with and then proceeded to chatter with Edwin, completely oblivious to her as she explored the sounds the keys made when slammed down on the glass topped coffee tables. I tried to substitute the keys for a soft toy from the tree but the keys were far more interesting to baby. Her parents did not seem at all concerned but I winced at every clank until I was forced to interrupt the conversation and ask if someone could get the keys off her as I was afraid she would crack the table top with them. I began to see potential disaster after disaster until they all went off to their room to bed. During the interval, I cleared the room of coffee tables, lamps and ornaments that were within baby's reach and put them all in one of the spare guest rooms along with all the small ornaments off the tree. Jenny laughed at the changes when she next entered the lounge. From now on, baby would shun her toys for the joy of opening and shutting all my kitchen drawers and cupboards in turn and pulling out all the pans onto the floor.

Our guests were Friends of the Earth. It takes all sorts to make a world. I am also a nature lover who wants to preserve the natural environment but pressure groups do not interest me. I would rather preserve the environment by my own actions and teach others, especially young people to do it by example and education. Environmental education was one of the main aspects of the geography I was teaching my students. I do not feel the need to live in a tree or a cave or to grow mushrooms in my living room in order to declare my love of the natural world. We did our best to keep the family and children occupied, safe and comfortable within our boundaries and around the village and local beach for the weeks leading up to Christmas. It was not too difficult to do this because they liked farmyards. We already had a scarlet macaw and Edwin had bought a guinea pig to keep in a pet's corner to interest the children. He also spent lots of time organising little games and sports activities for the eight year old girl to play with her father while her mother looked after the baby. They would not be able to go on an excursion to the interior with the baby, however, so the nearest we could get them to the rainforest was arranged with the help of Dr Macpherson and his CARDI four-wheel-drive. He would come and pick us all up on Boxing Day to drive us into the intermediate savannah and the Abary Water Conservancy via the green road at the back of the MMA. He thought it would be dry enough by then to get down the un-surfaced part of the cart-track.

On the appointed day, I packed up picnic lunches and plenty of drinks in our cool boxes and we all crammed into the back of Mac's four by four with Edwin in the front next to Mac. We hardly managed a couple of miles beyond the laterite section before the relatively level wheel tracks became deeply gouged pits of muddy water crisscrossed by tractor tyre marks. Mac tried to steer the vehicle's wheels on the high bits that had not yet been cut by a tractor but this soon became impossible as too many previous tyre tracks had carved up the soft mud. The vehicle began to lurch sideways violently as the wheels skidded off the ridges into the furrows. The little girl did not like the bumpy ride, so started to cry and the baby began to scream in sympathy. The way ahead was so bad that Edwin told Mac to abandon the attempt. We would just go back to firm ground, then get out and explore the environment near the five-gate sluice controlling the Abary River. In the attempt to do this, it appeared that Mac did not know how to use the four wheel drive, so we got stuck in the mud for a while but with some advice from Edwin he got it out of trouble and so managed to get back to the sluice. Four of us ventured out onto the track which ran parallel to the river bank. I had my camera on full zoom to capture some of the unusual birds and butterflies in the scrub and carrion crow bushes flanking the water. Red breasted blackbirds, locally known as robins, were quite plentiful here since people rarely visited. Crested Cara-cara, or savannah hawk, were wheeling around in the distance over the canopy. They were too far away for a decent shot, but I did manage to get a close up of a black-capped mocking thrush nestled in a waterside thicket. The muffled screaming of his children in the vehicle did not seem to bother Simon, who was content to walk across the bridge with me looking down onto the rafts of vegetation drifting slowly southwards with the current. One of them had a passenger on it: a large snake curled up asleep in the sunshine. I zoomed in on it and snapped just as it passed under me.

"All this water hyacinth looks very pretty," I explained, "But it multiplies so rapidly that it's clogging up the channels and preventing the water from flowing away from the cultivation areas and villages, so millions have to be spent on dredging the canals and removing it to reduce the flooding during the rainy season. They don't have the machinery or manpower to keep on top of it. We had a Canadian expert visiting us with CARDI who told us they were looking at biological control of it. Apparently, it's the favourite food of the native manatee, so if they could be introduced into the canals in sufficient numbers, it would soon be kept under control."

"So why don't they do it?" he asked.

"Well unfortunately, the manatee is an endangered species and because its pregnancy lasts two years, they're very slow to reproduce. They're trying to breed them at the zoo where they're protected, but won't release them back into the wild at present."

"Why not?"

"Because they provide a tasty meat supply for the local Amerindians, who would hunt them faster than they can reproduce."

Simon was interested in this and would probably have stayed longer, but Edwin was concerned that the children were well out of their comfort zone and decided we had better head back to the house for the sake of the baby. They were all unable to cope with the heat and needed to be sitting in their room under the fans.

Later that day we heard a digital alarm sounding off in the lounge. I traced it to one of the pipes under the back of the house. The baby had thrown Simon's watch down the flushing toilet in a new game. Baby's toys had been successfully fished out before they disappeared, but the watch had escaped notice. There was no way it could be rescued, but for several weeks after they left on New Year's Eve, we heard the alarm regularly sounding off as it slowly made its way along the back of the house towards the septic tank.

Chapter 14

The Wedding

The Commonwealth Games, like the Olympics, is held every four years. In every international athlete's calendar, it is a major event. In every family, a wedding is a major event. In 1994, in our family, these two major events coincided and brought a mixture of excitement, trepidation and extreme challenges to our project at Sapodilla. Edwin had received the news at Christmas that his son, Rafer, was getting married in September and that he was coming to Guyana to do so. This brought unbelievable joy to Edwin whose main preoccupation from now on would be how to prepare adequately for this family reunion and the occasion of being able to host all his children and their partners under the same roof, our holiday resort and home. It would achieve his dream of having international athletes from England coming to stay with us in Guyana in what he expected would be the first of frequent visits to grow our business from. It would be a double celebration, since both groom and bride would be aiming to compete on the England team of athletes at the Commonwealth Games in Victoria that summer. It would be a challenge for me to put on the special food for a wedding in our home and to cater for a house completely full of guests for a whole fortnight. It would be the first time that either of us had met the bride or any of her family and it was also the first time I had ever entertained any of my husband's children or their partners or indeed their mother, my husband's ex-wife. I felt a little apprehensive at being the unwanted outsider, but tried to put such thoughts aside and throw myself wholeheartedly into the task of planning the catering and household arrangements for full occupancy.

The year got off to a momentous start for the embryonic ecotourism sector of the country, with a visit by Queen Elizabeth II and Prince Philip to Guyana. Her Majesty had last visited these shores in 1966 when Guyana had been granted Independence. The Forte Crest was now the main international hotel in the country and it was taken over by the royal party for the few days of their stay. The Forte Crest river tour boat was upgraded to take them down the Demerara to the hotel's new jungle lodge known as Timberhead Resort. A special waiting room suitably furnished for a royal passenger had been fitted out at Ogle Airport in Georgetown in advance of the occasion to enable the royal couple to fly to The Kaieteur Falls. This minor airport served only interior flights but would of course now be more attractive to the eco-tourist potential that the new government was trying to tap into. We had little idea of what went on during the Queen's visit since we had no local television reception in our house as yet. We only learned about news events when they were reported in the local newspapers which we got a day or two later. Santa Mission, an Amerindian settlement near to Georgetown had also been singled out for the royal tour. It all raised the tourism profile of the country and heralded an era of British funded aid projects for the Amerindians which would enable them to make sustainable incomes for themselves by handling ecotourism in some of their more accessible villages.

At around this time, I had been sent a letter by the Caribbean Museums Association who somehow had got to know about the 'Parson Munroe Museum of Village Life' that I had set up at Sapodilla Farm. It may have been prompted by an enquiry I had previously made to the Pitt Rivers Museum in Oxford about our Amerindian stone hand axe and my subsequent correspondence with the Walter Roth Museum in Georgetown to whom Linda Mowatt at Pitt Rivers had referred me. I had ordered some copies of historic photos of Amerindians in Guyana from the Pitt Rivers Museum and from the Royal Geographic Society which I planned to add to my display for the benefit of our visitors as well as of our students. The letter asked for information about our museum to be included in a Caribbean Museums Register they were compiling. I was excited to be included in this as it could mean future business for us, so I filled it in and posted it off promptly. Although I had spent a lot of my own savings on the photographs, I thought it would come back eventually through the business takings. It seemed a good investment.

Edwin's on-going Sports Teachers course was being complemented by the work he was doing with the Amateur Athletics Association in Georgetown to put our sports club athletes into national competitions. He was spending a lot of his own pension money on the improvement of the MMA sports ground at Onverwagt so that our club athletes could qualify to take part in the C.A.C. (Central American and Caribbean) Games. He wanted to see what standard they must aim for to qualify for higher level competitions like the Commonwealth Games later in the year. He put in a concrete throwing circle for the discus and a long jump pit amongst other improvements. Not forgetting his pledge to help his alma mater, he also negotiated some funding agency help for new furniture to be made for the Hopetown Primary School. In return, the Headmistress let him have 40 old chairs and some 20 assorted desks they now no longer required. With the help of his cousin's lorry to transport them from the school down to our classroom, we now had better furniture for the teachers to work at in his classes. It meant that the children coming to my classes would also benefit from greater comfort than they had hitherto had, sitting on rickety three legged stools and car tyres. Our friend Constance from the regional resources centre, eager to include Edwin's PE course as part of her distance learning programme of the University of Guyana, introduced us to Professor Small who was in charge of the certification of its mature students. He was happy to accept Edwin's course on the programme, so Edwin put in the necessary official application forms. Now all participants on his course would receive certificates from the University of Guyana.

Our Amerindian carpenter Geoffrey Macpherson was known to locals as 'Buck-boy'. Although this is a racist term, locals thought nothing of picking out each other's race or physical appearance as distinguishing features to be continually reminded of in their 'call-name'. 'Fat boy', 'Blackie' and 'Ugly Duckling' are just a few examples of such names that people seemed to accept being known as. They did not appear to take offence at being thus renamed by their peers. Perhaps it was a way of helping each other come to terms with their physical difference from others and not be ashamed of it. I never participated, preferring to use people's proper names as a mark of respect. Geoffrey had been working for us on numerous projects since Christmas. Our water tank had burst and emptied into the back garden, so he had come in to repair and re-plaster it. In view of the forthcoming wedding, Edwin decided then to employ him to double its capacity by adding an identical second chamber onto its rear to collect its overflow. Geoffrey had subsequently concreted the area under and around the pillars supporting the house and forecourt. Then he attempted to seal up the areas of our roof that had been leaking rain and insert bat-proofing mesh around the perimeter of the roof. This was something that should have been done when the roof was first put on, but Pappa Dan had not bothered to do it because he did not see the point. Bats were in every local roof at night. You could not keep them out, so he thought we should accept them like everyone else. Geoffrey had worked on houses in Georgetown, however, so he understood that people in all the embassies wanted to bat-proof their roofs and he knew how they did it. He got the job and did it to the best of his ability, but the awkward shape of our roof made a perfect solution impossible, so we soon spotted their tiny furry bodies battling to get out of the mesh around the eaves at twilight and finding some tiny gap to re-enter later on. Geoffrey showed his artistic skills by building some decorative wooden display cabinets for my museum on the outer walls of the classroom and gym under the shelter of the house. He made them to fit some large sheets of Perspex which I had bought in town to serve as sliding doors for the front of the display cases. Finally, he made some mobile folding display boards for me to mount my recently acquired museum photographs on.

My classes were entering the final term before the summer holidays and although Bushlot Secondary School were ignoring my offers of help with resources sessions for their teachers, the recorder group I had started for a variety of my students, was making good progress. Edwin was making preparations for a special course for teachers from all over the country to attend a one week PE course at Sapodilla. The Ministry of Education Allied Arts Department in Georgetown visited us and wanted a course similar to what he had been doing for Region Five teachers. They had agreed to sponsor the cost of the teachers' accommodation at one or two of the empty houses around the MMA compound, since we did not have enough bedrooms for all their teachers. They would also cover the cost of photocopied hand-outs Edwin would need to provide for the teachers. The snackette was now being largely left to the staff to run, so large losses were being made even though it should have been in healthy profit. Lots of lunches were being provided for CARDI visitors and people sent from overseas to provide the training needed by locals who would officiate at the forthcoming local council elections. All this profit was going missing because neither of us was present continuously overseeing the staff during opening hours. Edwin was trying to get another overdraft of £2000 from his bank in England to pay the mortgage and its 32% interest from GNCB Trust in Georgetown because the snackette was not making a profit. His Bank only offered £600 so we had to make up the shortfall from somewhere and so I transferred £2000 from my offshore account to his bank to help out. We had to meet the cost of all this building work if the house was to accommodate overseas guests for a wedding in September. In June, the postman brought a telegram from Rafer about his selection for the England team at the Commonwealth Games in Canada. His points in the decathlon had increased considerably, so Edwin was really excited and proud.

In accordance with my aim to make local guided tours of the environment, history and culture for potential tourists, I used my spare time during the day to research and photograph local wildlife and heritage sites. I prepared some special illustrated leaflets about Edwin's family tree from slavery times and the history of our village, together with a birdwatchers' information leaflet on our local birds. These could be left in the guest rooms along with the menu and a sample of our postcards. At Easter, Elaine from the British High Commission brought a party of visitors down to us from the Canadian High Commission for the day, so I had to show them around and provide free refreshments for them. They all seemed impressed, so we hoped there would be future business coming our way from these diplomats and their guests. Luckily, their visits coincided with the dry season, so the mud street to get to us was not a problem for their vehicle to tackle. It was a major concern to us however, since we were at the mercy of the local government to resurface the road and that looked very unlikely to happen given their limited budgets. We were not in a position to pay for the road to be surfaced ourselves, especially when it would not be a private road and would therefore be used by the entire community. We had not hosted any tourists between Christmas and Easter, but I knew we would be busy from the summer onwards because my niece and her boyfriend were coming out for a holiday when they finished their A-levels.

In anticipation of the need to cater for extra guests for the forthcoming family wedding, we realised we would have to buy some local furniture that would suit our style and be appropriate for outdoor seating in the newly completed concreted areas under the house. This was not an easy task at that time since the only local furniture made of wood was ugly. It suited local taste and pockets but would instantly downgrade the appearance of our place. Edwin searched high and low for suppliers and even struck up a relationship with the manager of Guyana Stores who also happened to be the new president's brother-in-law. He had a factory making wooden furniture but for export only, so this did not solve our problem. Stabroek market was an unlikely place to find the solution, but we had noticed some beautiful Amerindian cotton hammocks at the stall of a trader there who also sold locally made rattan tables, chairs and basketry. They were happy to custom-make furniture to order and invited us to visit their 'factory' on the way out of town. It turned out to be a house with a backyard stacked to the ceiling of its lean-to roof with chairs, tables, settees and armchairs, chaise-longs, desks and shelving racks all made of rattan locally known as 'Nibbi-vine'. Mavis, an East Indian entrepreneur and her Negro husband, Colin, transported the stripped vine from the north-west jungle interior where it was harvested and employed local craftsmen to make the furniture in their yard. It was roughly finished and needed treating against insects, but seemed appropriate for our tropical setting, and the styles resembled the stuff I had seen in people's conservatories in Europe. We ordered a set of chairs and coffee tables and a chaise long at first, telling Mavis that we would need several more but would have to get them in instalments over the next few months, as and when we could afford to pay for them.

Collecting and transporting our first consignment of the Nibbi furniture proved to be more of a challenge than even we had imagined. We had booked Nello's minibus by private hire for the day and he had removed all the seats apart from that at the front next to the driver and the conductor's fold down flap behind it. We had other business to do in town, so when that was completed in the late afternoon we drove to Mavis and Colin's house to collect the order and load up the bus. This done, it was so crammed full at the back that we both had to sit in the front with the driver. Being slimmer than Edwin, I drew the short straw of having to sit in the middle seat with my legs wrapped round the gearbox. It was extremely uncomfortable, especially in the heat, with rough wooden furniture legs sticking into our heads. When we reached the open road far out of town, and several miles from any habitation in any direction, the bus slowed up and came to a halt. The sun was setting and mosquitoes were just beginning to bite after their diurnal twelve-hour fast. Nello got out, opened up the bonnet and scratched his head, mumbling something about electrics.

"What's the problem, Nello?" asked Edwin after Nello came back to the bus and started searching in his tool box for something.

"Meanno. Me full de tank before we leff tong. Mus' be some electrical fault," said Nello. He went back to the engine and started checking spark plugs and other things. Then he came back inside and tried to start it again. There was a spark but nothing caught on. He repeated this procedure a number of times with no success.

"Do you want us to get out and bump start you?" I said.

"Yes," he said, so we complied but with no better results.

"Are you sure it hasn't run out of petrol?" asked Edwin. "It seemed to be a fuel supply problem to me by the way the bus gradually died out before it came to a stop." Nello ignored him. After all Edwin to him was just a sportsperson who knew nothing about vehicles because he did not have one of his own.

"It would have to happen when we're miles from anywhere. How far back was the last house we passed?" I asked.

"Me know a man who live back at de last place but it far, far to walk."

"We'll have to hope another vehicle comes along soon and we can flag them down to help," said Edwin. Ages went by with no sign of another vehicle. In the end, bowing to Edwin's impatience, Nello said he would walk back to the last house we had passed. Edwin and I stayed with the bus and waited and waited and waited.

Dark fell and the ravenous mosquitos feasted on our bare legs and arms. Eventually, a dim light appeared from the direction Nello had gone off in. As it slowly got nearer, the light wobbled.

"It's only a torch light," said Edwin. He called out, "Is that you, Nello?"

"Yeah, man," came the distant familiar voice. The wobbly light approached a bit faster than walking pace and then we saw that he had come on another man's bicycle crossbar. He alighted as they pulled up behind the bus and he introduced the man to us by torchlight. They both opened the bonnet and tried starting up the bus, discussing electrics and scratching their heads. After a long period of this inconclusive investigation,

"Don't you think it might be a fuel supply problem?" Edwin suggested to the other man. "The bus slowed up and then died before it stopped just as if it was running out of petrol."

"Me full de tank," Nello insisted. "It still get some inside." He showed us the stick he had inserted into the tank and the tip of it was wet.

"All the same, there might be some blockage or leak in the fuel pipe," said Edwin. The stranger agreed that he might be right and so together the two men inspected the fuel pipe while we both got out of the vehicle to allow the front seat to be lifted to do this. All the while we had been wondering how we would get the furniture home if this could not be resolved. We had almost come to terms with the thought of spending the night on the road with it all until the mini-buses started running normally again in the morning.

"Mus' be de fuel pump get problem," the other man said at length. Edwin went round to the front of the bus with the two of them and they discussed what to do. Then he came back to where I was standing.

"They say they can rig up some sort of way to bypass the fuel pump to get us home tonight, so I told them to go ahead," he told me. "They have to connect the fuel supply directly to the engine from a reservoir that'll fill it by gravity."

That seemed to make sense to me. In short this meant that we had a choice: we would either sit in the bus all night on the road and risk being attacked by bandits in the early hours, or rig up a way of bypassing the fuel pump to get home as soon as we could. We chose the latter, but found this option was somewhat more dangerous than taking a chance with bandits. I watched as Nello syphoned petrol from the fuel tank into his plastic jerry can. Then he searched around in his toolbox for a funnel he had made from the cut off top of a plastic drink bottle. He somehow connected the bottom of this to the flexible fuel pipe that came directly from the chassis under the seat where I had been sitting. It was time to test it out. Nello turned the starting key and hey presto, the engine started up and gently ticked over, but it would cut out again as soon as all the fuel in the pipe was used up. Now we had a problem. We would not be able to move along the road unless we could feed a continuous stream of petrol into the funnel throughout the journey.

We said our goodbyes to the man on the bike and prepared ourselves for the task ahead. Edwin sat in the passenger seat holding at shoulder height the funnel attached to the end of the piece of fuel pipe that went directly to the engine, while Nello drove the bus very slowly homewards. My job was to kneel behind Edwin on the conductor flap holding at head height the plastic jerry can, while slowly and steadily pouring petrol from it into the funnel in Edwin's hand. I had chair or table legs sticking in both sides of my head as I did this and thus we endured the two hour journey home. Goodness only knows how we arrived home that night without all going up in spectacular flames, but we did. Nor did that nightmare end when the bus stopped. We arrived at the head of our street just as the neighbourhood plunged into the darkness of the nightly power cut. Thus we unloaded the bus by torchlight and had to wade through knee deep mud with the furniture on our heads to get it from the public road down to the house.

The main summer rainy season was at its height when my niece, Emma, and her school-friend Oliver arrived at the beginning of July. They had just finished A-levels and had a few months to spare before starting university, so had to visit us at the worst time of year for Guyana. During their stay, preparations were being made for local elections that were to be held on August 8th. The villages were grouped together in neighbourhood district councils and Edwin had been persuaded to put himself up as a candidate for ours. The only reason he had agreed to do this was because of the changes introduced by the Carter Centre since the 1992 General Election which had put Cheddi Jagan and his PPP party in power. These changes had made it possible for non-political development groups with no allegiance to the main political parties to stand for election. The work we had done since moving to Guyana put local people in no doubt of Edwin's leadership qualities and our good intentions. PNC opposition activists had noticed this and saw in Edwin someone who could win support from both black and Indian communities. Their plan was to use Edwin to win the election for the development group which for them would be the PNC in disguise. They knew their own party activist had been discredited as a thief and would not be elected because even the PNC supporters in the village did not want her to get her hands on local rates and tax money.

Edwin, on the other hand, wanted nothing to do with any political party, PNC included. He had no need of power either, but wanted to rid local government of corruption and allow development to happen instead of obstructing it. He wanted to see improvements in the lives of all local inhabitants, not just one race or one social class. As local residents for the past three years, we had been there long enough to see how things operated; what the true local conditions were. Edwin knew what really needed to be put right to enable businesses to thrive and grow so that real employment opportunities could flourish, instead of artificial ones propped up by overseas aid or state funding and government manipulation. He wanted family life to improve as well as living conditions, improvements in law and order, and above all, fairness. He canvassed around the villages as he went about doing business for the snackette, the church arrangements for the forthcoming wedding, sorting out the PE teachers' course and the club athletes for the Inter-Guiana Games trials. One of his strategies was to persuade the young athletes in the sports club to get their ID cards so they could vote. He wanted them to participate, since his aim was to promote education, sport and employment opportunities for them.

During this period, as with previous national elections, there was heightened ethnic tension in the country and we were careful to protect our guests from too much wandering around on their own without Edwin or a trusted chaperone. Our isolation and vulnerability had been brought home to us earlier in June when we had two strange men turning up at our gate in darkness, wanting accommodation for the night. Edwin sent them away, explaining rather gruffly that we did not accept bookings on the gate, but only in advance, from overseas customers. He had quickly deduced from their appearance that they could be Georgetown bandits who had decided to call in and case the joint or worse. They went away very disgruntled, but we quickly realised from this experience that running a resort in such a remote village location made us vulnerable in this way. It forced us to stick to our advance private booking strategy rather than an open door guest-house one. There were other places that catered for spur of the moment hospitality.

One of the activities Emma and Oliver helped me with soon after their arrival was in conducting the high-street survey I had planned for the children in my Saturday class to do. It was my way of drawing attention to the beautiful old architectural style of the buildings. I was hoping to get the community to value them and repair or restore them. Many residents on the high street who had relatives living and working in New York had recently been pulling down the old wooden houses and replacing them with modern ones made of concrete blocks. They would be more durable than wood but were uniform and ugly. I had prepared a questionnaire to ask the residents about their house, its age, building material, number of rooms, uses of the rooms, whether they had piped water supply, taps, or tank, electricity connection and septic tank and garden. Each of us had a third of the students to take on a house by house survey of a section of the street. At the same time, I took photos of the oldest ones showing 'captains' towers', 'cow-mouth' kitchens, fretwork gables, 'Demerara windows' and shingle cladding. It seemed that if I did not photograph them and record something of them, there would soon be no trace of them. I would make the results of the survey part of the heritage display in our museum. Nothing of its kind had ever been done in the village before and certainly not in the schools. It created quite a stir among the villagers, who misinterpreted it as a fact-finding survey by Edwin to get government or overseas aid agencies to improve living conditions in the village. They thought it was all part of his election campaign to win votes. As an unintended incidental consequence, he thought he would take advantage of the information we gathered to do just that as soon as he was elected.

Our young guests were eager to help us with anything we had to do, so Emma got the ice-cream machine at the snackette working and helped me to mount and label the displays in the library. Oliver fitted the new video head that I had sent for from Japan and got my video recorder functioning again. I wanted to teach the Saturday class students how to make paper from recycled materials and needed to make some paper-making frames. Emma and Oliver made them for me in an afternoon from scrap wood and mesh left over from our gym windows. This enabled me to begin a paper-making project which the children really enjoyed. Vernon and Geoffrey came round to fix up a working television aerial so we could receive broadcasts from Georgetown for the guests. After a day of faffing around on the roof and in the lounge, however, they concluded that the signal was not strong enough, so we had to continue with no TV other than the video films we had. School term ended and Emma and Oliver booked a commercial boat tour from the capital to visit the Amerindian settlement at Santa Mission. We all went together to Georgetown in their private hire minibus with a small group of our older students taking up the spare places free of charge. The children could thus visit the Walter Roth and National Museums for the first time in their lives. It was a reward for those who had come top in my history exam. Hopefully other students would work harder in future if they wanted a similar opportunity. Edwin and I chaperoned the students round the museums while awaiting the return of the boat tour, and supervised them as they filled in the activity sheets I had prepared for them. Emma and Oliver also saw some of the more spectacular scenery of the country on another commercial daytrip far into the interior by light aircraft to The Kaieteur Falls and the Orinduik Falls in the Rupununi Savannahs.

In order to put the finishing touches on my museum displays, Edwin and I stayed up until 4 a.m. on July 15th, the opening day of his one week Allied Arts sponsored course for PE teachers. Ed Caesar, the Chief Education Officer at the time would be visiting and I wanted to have all my historic photos ready along with the Amerindian craft artefacts which I had bought from Georgetown vendors. The feather headdress, tibisiri grass hammock, balata jungle animal models, warishi (basketry back-pack), matapee (woven cassava strainer) and other cooking implements added three dimensions to the museum collection and made the whole display much more interesting. I wanted Emma and Oliver to see them in context before they left and also to illustrate to the visiting teachers and education department from other parts of the country, the educational resource it could provide for both children and adults and how it could bring to life the history and culture of the country. Edwin's P.E course came to an end with the assessment of the teachers. They were tested to show their competence by taking a class on a practical session. Emma and Oliver went along as observers. They were still with us when we had an unexpected visit by four people from the Ministry of Tourism. This lent weight to us being a genuine tourist destination. The ministry officials had a long look round the premises, saw my museum displays and asked a lot of questions. Of course I provided them with free refreshments and the same service as any of our paying guests. We both explained the work we were doing free of charge to help the education of local youths and their teachers in academic subjects, recreation and sports. They promised to help us in what way they could with getting a telephone connection and a properly surfaced road, but we knew these promises were without substance. Meanwhile Emma and Oliver flew back to England and I had a few days' break before two more CARDI consultants arrived from overseas to stay with us for two days.

We now had good cause for celebration as Edwin's UK bank statement arrived, showing that after three years his early retirement pension had finally paid off the £22,000 debt we had racked up by our move to Guyana. We could now put final preparations in place for guests to come and stay in the house with us for two weeks for the wedding in September. We had written to warn Rafer and Tracy about the conditions in Guyana and that we only had three double bedrooms and a large family room, so invitations would have to be limited to the accommodation we had for only 9 people at a time. Rafer, however, wanted to negotiate a reduced block booking price with the airline and so had invited a lot more than nine to come along. We not only had all the siblings and parents of the two families, but also their spouses or boyfriends, Rafer's training partner and his girlfriend, two best men and two couples from Germany. There would be nineteen people at the final count.

We had been put in an impossible position by the absence of telephone communications and the failure of Rafer and Tracy to properly read the letters we had sent. Even a recorded message on a cassette had failed to make our warnings understood. Perhaps they dismissed them as overprotective, perhaps there was too much information or perhaps they just did not believe any of it could be true. They might have assumed that Guyana was like other Caribbean and long haul destinations, where you could find alternative bed and breakfast accommodation nearby, so they would be able to stay in that and just get a taxi or hire car to bring them to our place for the wedding feast. We knew from our experience of living in Guyana for the previous three years, that at that time, this would have been impossible. Knowing who the wedding guests were and what they were accustomed to, we knew what they would be expecting. Edwin insisted they would have to be hosted at our house. Only we would be able to provide the comfort, hygiene and food safety that was necessary. Only we would be able to guarantee their security and protection from being robbed and defrauded. We had seen with our own eyes how short term foreign visitors who had tried to do their own thing from a Georgetown hotel base had been predated upon and left with a terrible impression and memory of their stay. We had to proceed on the assumption that we would have to buy in extra furniture to cope with nineteen guests. We would have to convert the family three-bed guest room into a female dormitory with our 6 extra locally bought rattan beds and the gym into a male dormitory using numerous hammocks to accommodate them all. We collected our extra rattan 'chaise long' beds from Mavis and Colin by late July, bought some blocks of foam for mattresses and some vinyl coated cotton upholstery fabric from which I sewed wipe-clean covers for them. We thought we could put them out downstairs as sun-loungers once the wedding party left.

War broke out between Taa and Aunt Rose, her sister, on the day before Swaree at the end of July. Aunt Rose was the expert 'Black cake' baker and wedding cake icer for the village. Edwin had appointed her as the official maker of Rafer and Tracy's wedding cake, envisaging nothing more than a standard wedding cake with three tiers and the usual decoration. Aunt Rose sent a message to Edwin via Taa that she needed plenty of local fruit to set and dry ready for the cake. She needed as many bucketsful of local gooseberries and 'five finger' (star fruit or carambola) as we could pick off the trees on our farm. Taa was annoyed as she wanted to take charge of making the cakes for her grandson's wedding and doing the catering. Of course, it was the tribal custom to feast the entire extended family as well as half the village on any such occasion. They would invite themselves when they heard about it. We had witnessed the kind of thing many times in the village, but Edwin was not going to have any of it. He insisted that in the interests of the security of our overseas visitors, he had no intention of our front gate being open to complete strangers, family or not.

"I'm not inviting all your brothers, sisters, aunts, uncles and cousins to the wedding," he insisted. "None of them wrote to me to remind me of their existence in the entire forty years I lived in England, so why should I count them as family now? In any case, I've been robbed blind ever since I've been back in Guyana by people claiming to be family or friends so I've got no money left to waste on entertaining them all".

"Ya can't turn family away from ya gate," said Taa. "Jane na know to cook local food and she can't do it by she self."

"You might call them family but I certainly don't," he said, raising his voice. "My family is my wife, my children and their partners and my children's mother. They and their friends from England and Germany will not want to eat Guyanese food at the wedding. They need European style food and Jane is the best person to cook that for them. However, if you want to cook local food for your extended family and friends to eat at your house so they can share in the event, then that's up to you. Aunt Rose is making the official wedding cake, so any cake you want to make will be for the guests at your house to eat". So it was that the cake making competition began between Taa and Aunt Rose.

Election Day was due on August 8th and Edwin had his first meeting between the 'Naarstigheid-Union Development Group' that he was representing in the forthcoming council elections and Amna Ali, who was organising the election procedure. It gave him his first insight into how elections were organised in Guyana and how easy it was for cheating to happen. He had already attended village meetings to sort out the papers needed for the election and arrange proxy votes for elderly villagers who could not walk to the polling stations. He had the help of the local PNC activist who knew what to do. She made Edwin aware of all the identity fraud they could expect from PPP voters (Indo-Guyanese in the main) who would vote numerous times posing as other locals who did not bother to vote, overseas absentees and even dead people. The returning officers were usually complicit in this, so activists from the PNC would be there to try and spot such fraud but it was difficult to detect unless you knew every inhabitant of the community that you did not live in. What she omitted to point out was that she and the PNC were guilty of exactly the same fraud in the Afro-Guyanese community and the PPP activists would have the same difficult task to detect that fraud. The task for Edwin was to persuade enough people from both communities to see him as a person they could trust to represent all their interests and believe that he would not take sides with either Black or Indian.

The night before the elections, Elaine, our friend from the British High Commission, called in on us unexpectedly. She was passing back from the Corentyne to Georgetown with a young man named Mike. He had just been taken on as manager of the new Courts Furniture Store that had opened up in Main Street so she decided to call in to introduce him to us and get some free hospitality. We had just emptied the larder on the two CARDI paying guests who had checked out the day before and were unprepared for anyone who had not booked. I had made a greasy broth for the two of us out of the last scraps in our larder. I felt embarrassed to admit to Elaine and Mike that when we did not have guests to cater for, we usually scraped a frugal existence on rustic dishes hastily knocked up from any local ingredients to hand, so it would be nothing like the cuisine I prepared for guests. It must have come as an unpleasant shock to Elaine, who had told Mike I was a brilliant cook, to have to share this meagre unappetising meal for two with us. Life in a village with no fresh food shops or supermarkets was not like living in the capital, so we always had to drive to Georgetown for a big food shopping trip the day before planned booked guests were due to arrive. They would not like most local food and vegetables so we would have to buy imported stuff for them. Elaine and Mike also stayed the night free of charge, so our aim of getting a stream of custom from foreign embassies was already breaking down. They would expect free hospitality once they befriended us.

On Local Election Day, there were a few incidents at the polling station when individuals tried to interfere with officials, voters and agents. The polls were open from 6 a.m. till 6 p.m. and hardly anyone turned out to vote. Edwin's development group won control of the council by 82 votes to 68. By 20th August he had been nominated to be the Chairman (the overall head of the neighbourhood democratic council) at the preliminary meeting at 'number 29' village and by 23rd September after the swearing in of all the elected village councillors at Bushlot village office (the centre of local government of the neighbourhood), Edwin was elected Chairman by 10 votes to 8 over the rival PPP candidate. The contending PNC candidate was voted as deputy chairman. By this means, both parties felt they had won, in the sense that Edwin was a member of neither party. For PPP voters, at least the chairman was not a PNC member and although Edwin was not PPP, they felt his fairness record and popularity among many of the Bushlot Indian residents would mean that they would be protected from the excesses that they had suffered when Burnham's dictatorship had imposed PNC-appointed local officials on them. The PNC thought they had won because they wrongly believed that Edwin was just pretending not to be one of them so that Indian voters in Bushlot would support him. They also thought that the deputy chairman, a seasoned PNC activist, would easily be able to dominate and manipulate Edwin in meetings. On both counts they were completely wrong and that would soon become apparent. Edwin was very proud to have been elected and wished that his father, as well as Parson Munroe had still been alive to see him in such a role. Parson had been Edwin's role model as a child and had been village chairman under British colonial rule back in the 1940s. Edwin's father may not have been able to wallow in the pride of his son's achievement but his seventy six-year-old mother, Taa, was more than able to make up for it.

But all this was yet to come, back in the last weeks of August. Flowers had to be ordered for the wedding but there were no florists or supply of suitable flowers in the area. Dr Macpherson, who had by this time decided to enhance his waning masculinity by adopting Edwin as his free personal trainer, was happy to recommend a friend of his in Georgetown whose business was to make table decorations and arrangements from imported silk flowers. He took us to meet her that week and we selected a suitable design from her catalogue and placed an order. The same day we collected some more of the nibbi furniture from Colin and transported it home in Dr Macpherson's pickup truck. A couple of days later, he turned up early in the morning to train with Edwin in our gym and brought his young girl-friend with him. This annoyed Edwin because although he had agreed to let Mac turn up to use the gym some mornings early when Edwin was doing his own fitness regime, Mac had assumed he could bring a guest in free without first asking if he could. It was a minor irritation, however, as so much was going on at the same time now. The snackette problems loomed every day as the lack of ready cash for the forthcoming wedding expenses put even more pressure on our finances. We were overdrawn in Edwin's UK bank account by nearly £800 again.

All our attempts to scrutinise snackette staff for receipts for their expenditure and maximise profits from their sales were now confounded by requests from Aunt Rose for more and more ingredients for the infamous cake: four bottles of wine one day, then money for another four bottles which Aunt Rose herself had bought the next day, trays of dozens of eggs, several buckets of 'butter' and sacks of flour. Then Taa came across to discuss a similar flow of ingredients for her own efforts which were simultaneously underway. Firewood for the mud ovens to bake the cakes was also begged from us in unbelievable quantities. My efforts to get the house clean and ready for the family were interrupted by a constant stream of visitors at the gate. Some were parents asking to enrol children for lessons, some were staff from the snackette wanting this or that and some were the usual villagers needing to beg something off us, be it water, wood, money, references for employment or visas. Then there were the visiting extended family members, introducing themselves to Edwin for the first time in either their lives or his, in the hope of learning when the forthcoming great Joseph wedding feast was going to be so that they could invite themselves along. In the middle of all that, the fridge freezer I had brought from England failed and we had to find someone who knew how to fix it. Then there was Clifford, who had arrived with his welding kit to weld some metal hoops over the top of the wrought iron cage to add extra security to the entrance stairway into the house and provide hooks for a dozen hanging baskets full of ferns to adorn either side of it.

Clifford arrived at the front gate in the early morning of 22nd August with bare feet and his hands full of heavy welding equipment. Edwin dealt with him and showed him where he could plug his welding plant into the electricity supply using one of the sockets in the gym. I could hear Edwin's loud voice through the kitchen floorboards. He seemed to be insisting something to Clifford in the raised tone he usually used when a local tradesman tried to feed him bullshit about something they were going to do. There was a problem about the shape of the sockets so Edwin called up and asked me for a spare three-pin plug. I rooted around in a kitchen drawer and found one with a 13 amp fuse and took it down to him. I thought little more about him as he got on with the job, except that later that morning I had to go downstairs to the library to prepare some of the museum displays for the new wall cabinets under the house. From the top of the stairs I saw Clifford at work. His welding kit was at the bottom of the steps and jumbo wires were all over the place. Two great crocodile clips connecting heavy duty cables were clipped onto the steel bars that made up the decorative security cage. Clifford was seated on the steps with his back to me. Sparks were flying intermittently with the accompanying crackling sounds as he touched the nozzle of his plant onto the pieces he was joining and I could feel the vibrations through my feet. As he paused between bursts of power, I called out to him,

"Clifford, I'm sorry to disturb you, but can I please pass by you to get down the stairs and go into the library?"

"Yes, Auntie Jane," he said, removing his mask and standing up to allow me to pass, "Careful not to touch ze sides as ya com dong….i's very high voltage,"

Alarmed at the potential prospect of being fried on the way down, I gingerly made my way past him without incident and thought I had better stay down until he had finished working there. I got on with my jobs in the library. Presently, Clifford poked his head around the library door and asked me if I had any binding wire. I searched for some in the store room but couldn't find any. He cast his eyes around under the house as if seeking inspiration and then made a beeline with his wire-cutters towards the wires that had recently been tied on the fence palings at the back of the house to anchor the aerial. The newly installed TV aerial pole had been planted deep into the ground behind the building right next to the location of the mains meter. I watched curiously as he grabbed an excess piece at the end of the wire with his left hand and cut into it with his pliers in his right hand. Then he began a strange slow motion dance like some kind of tribal ritual, yelling incomprehensible utterings and bouncing up and down so that his head repeatedly hit the rafters projecting above him as he was propelled along the flowerbed flanking the fence. By the third bounce he landed on one of the old car tyres I had arranged in a row and planted flowers into. He came to a stop and looked dazed for a minute. Having realised by now that he had not been dancing but that something bad had happened, I was disturbed and worried, but had no idea what was wrong.

"Are you all right, Clifford?" I asked as I rushed towards him, "Have you been bitten by a snake?"

He muttered something I couldn't understand and gestured to me to keep away from him. Perhaps he was trying to tell me the snake's name: "car….". Carmoudie, I thought, which was the local name for anaconda. I called out to Edwin who was luckily just returning from the snackette at the time, to come quickly and find out what was wrong with Clifford and what he was trying to say.

"Corrent, live corrent in de whole back of house", Clifford said more clearly this time as he began to regain his senses.

"What? Oh my God. Jane, we have to turn off the mains to cut off the supply and send for Jimmy straight away." Edwin firmly took control of the emergency and started to attend Clifford to see if he was injured and whether he could give him any relevant first aid.

240

"Oh shit, I said, how can I turn off the mains if the house is live? To get to the mains switch, I have to go up the stairs past all those wires."

"You've got rubber soled shoes on, so you should be all right as long as you don't touch anything with your hands,"

I was not one hundred per-cent convinced, but it seemed that I would have to be brave to prevent anyone else from a worse fate than Clifford. I picked my way up the stairs more carefully and slowly than I had ever moved in my life before. The sheer terror could not have been worse if I had been asked to cross a minefield, except that I probably had a better idea in this case of where not to tread or touch. I got to the top of the steps safely and then went straight into the cupboard in the kitchen and threw the mains switch off, calling into the garden to Spear to come quickly. He rushed out of the vegetable plot, sensing the urgency in my voice.

"Please go and find Jimmy, and tell him to come at once because Clifford has had an accident and something is wrong with the wiring, so the house is surrounded by live current."

"OK, Jane," said Spear and raced off down the street into the village.

I went down without fear now, knowing that the electricity supply had been cut off, and re-joined Edwin who had been talking to Clifford to help him recover from the shock and try to piece together what had actually happened. He talked back through it all with Clifford and me. At first appearances it looked like the problem had been caused by the new television aerial. Perhaps that was bringing live current down the wires from the zinc roof. All the same, Edwin would not let Clifford touch anything until Vernon (Jimmy) had been and looked at it. Edwin told me to get the accident report book out of the gym and write down a detailed account as agreed and signed by Clifford and me, his only witness. We had a half hour or so to wait for Vernon, but in the meantime, Edwin thought Clifford should go up to the hospital at Fort Wellington and get the doctor to check him over. He said he was OK to go by himself, and walked out of the gate in his bare feet, just as he came.

"Why on earth would you do a job using high voltage electric equipment without having proper boots on?" I asked Edwin in dismay, "It's not as if he can't afford to buy them with all the money he gets from the welding work he does."

"Ignorance," said Edwin angrily, "Health and safety is non-existent here!" He was upset at what had happened to Clifford and even more upset about what worse might have happened, but at the back of his mind was that we had a potentially uninhabitable property with only two weeks to go before a house full of family and friends were due to arrive for the wedding of his son. We went into the gym to have a look at the point where the welding kit had been plugged in to our mains supply. I stared at the socket in horror.

"Look!" I said in disbelief, "he's stuck bare wires into the bottom socket holes and a screwdriver in the top one! Why didn't he use the plug I gave him this morning?"

"I bloody told him about that when I saw the bare wires as he unpacked the equipment. I asked him if he had a plug and he said he didn't need one; it'd be OK. I argued with him and said I didn't want him messing up the electrics of the house by using unsafe equipment in it and that's why I called you and asked you for the spare plug."

"So he must have waited till you left and then didn't bother with the plug."

"Don't touch it! I want Jimmy to see exactly how it was all set up when it happened, so he can work out what is live and sort it out."

Auntie Agnes now arrived with some special mangoes for us, so we went through the whole story with her while waiting for Spear to find Vernon. It took a couple of hours for him to get to us. He eventually arrived with a very worried look on his face. His reputation for being the safest electrician in the neighbourhood was at stake here and he was not happy for his work to be compromised or called into question. Hearing from me a detailed account of what I had witnessed, Vernon went around the perimeter of the house and inspected all areas including the power socket where the equipment was plugged in. At length, he came over and explained what had caused the problem. Clifford had connected his plant to the power supply without a proper earthed plug, so he had sent live current into the earth wire which was buried deep in the soil at the back of the house. This had meant that thousands of volts of current were being directed under the soil at the back of the house which was still very wet from the previous night's rain, so particularly good at conducting electricity. Clifford had stepped onto the wet soil in his bare feet and got hold of the wire on the aerial with one hand. His body was now conducting the live current, so as soon as he connected his cutters in his other hand to the wire, he had completed the circuit and was electrocuted. The only thing that had saved his life was the car tyre he accidentally landed on. I felt shaken up at the thought that I had very nearly watched a young man die in my own house in front of my eyes. He must have been saved by divine intervention. Vernon was furious. He was keen to spread his own story around the village to counter rumours that were already proliferating about his having done "cock work" at Sapodilla which were following Spear, Clifford and Auntie Agnes' progress up the High Street. He made it clear to us that he wanted to be called immediately when Clifford returned for his welder so that he could personally explain to him why his own unsafe procedures had almost killed him.

We did not see Clifford for a week or two. It was said that he had gone to see an Obeah man on the Corentyne to get treatment.

"Why didn't he go straight up to the Fort hospital like you told him to?" I asked Edwin.

"Don't ask me to explain what makes these people go to witchdoctors rather than qualified medics. The ignorance of it all! He should be paying self-employed contributions to National Insurance so he can get covered for loss of earnings when he can't work, but he doesn't do that, so he expects me to pay him compensation! Just imagine what bills would be landed on me if he had died on the job!" I knew this outward anger was concealing Edwin's own deep concern for Clifford's wellbeing. He also felt powerless to prevent this local ignorance from making victims not only of people like Clifford, but also of us who did not have the kind of bottomless pockets that international investors are perceived to have. On September 1st, with only six days left to go before our guests were scheduled to arrive, he finally turned up to complete the job at the same time as Vernon came to fix a fan in one of the guest rooms. After he had been subjected to a 'talking to' from Vernon, explaining how he had caused the accident himself and why he should always wear safety boots at work, Clifford was not allowed to resume using his plant until Vernon had safely wired on the correct plug. At last the welding work was completed.

Vernon had found someone to fix the fridge-freezer for us, but it would cost seventy thousand Guyana dollars for the new fan and compressor. Since we had no money, it would have to wait until the weekend. The repair man had it working again on Saturday which was in the nick of time, because the following day, we had two minibuses booked to collect our visitors from the airport. On

Sunday, I was busy fixing up the mosquito nets over the fifteen beds in the upstairs rooms and the four hammocks in the gym. At one o'clock, Nello came to pick up Edwin to meet them all at Timehri airport. As I waved goodbye to him from the veranda, he called out to me, "Nello brought the pork, so I put it all in the kitchen." I went into the kitchen to find the sinks and draining board overflowing with recycled supermarket plastic bags filled with raw pork meat and bones. My heart sank. This was the last thing I needed just then. What was I going to do with it all? There was eighty pounds of it. It would not all fit in the fridge-freezer. I decided the best thing to do was to roast the large leg straight away and slice it up for cold meat when it cooled down. Meanwhile, I cut up the boneless meat into cubes for making curry, packed portions to feed twenty people in separate bags and stuffed them in the freezer compartment which luckily by now had got cold enough to freeze. There was still half a pig left un-butchered, but that would have to go in the empty chest freezer down in the storeroom. It did not work and could not be repaired in time but at least it would keep the meat free from vermin until something could be done with it. It was all right for Edwin. He was accustomed to dealing with catering and supplies in massive quantities in his long career in the army and his managerial role in the sports and leisure business. He was comfortable with it all. I certainly was not. I had no experience of canteen cooking or handling huge amounts of perishable food. It put me right off the idea of eating altogether. I had envisaged being able to supply to small numbers of guests the kind of high end tourism that I had personally experienced in other tropical countries. How could I maintain such standards in an environment like this in which the capacity for quality was completely absent? Our fridge freezer was not meant to store so much. My main concern was how to prevent food poisoning. How could I keep all this food fresh and safe? It deeply disturbed me that the kind of wedding I was going to be able to deliver to the family was far short of what I wanted to be able to do. One of the guests had studied in the hotel industry in Germany. I felt I had to make a good impression. The house was just not designed to accommodate such a large number of people at one time.

The next thirteen days were something between a bad dream and a nightmare for me and probably also for the nineteen guests under our roof. The family that I had never really met, but had lived with by osmosis for the previous ten years, were now physically with us. I was glad to see Edwin so happy. I did not go to the que-que at the snackette the night before the wedding, since I needed to stay at Sapodilla to prepare the prawn curry and various salads for the wedding feast the following day. I had to rely on the reports I got later. I did not mind not going, as I could easily imagine the massive cauldron of beef broth made by Samo from the cow he had slaughtered for the purpose and the heaving crowds from the local community come to share in the traditional celebration as generations before them had always done. I could imagine the expression on Tracy's face as her head was suddenly covered with a white cloth and her chair lifted on high, above the chanting bodies that circled round and round the forecourt in their age-old ritual. I did get the chance to see the wedding of course, because I had set up everything for the reception the day before and stored all the precooked food and salads in the fridge until we returned from the church.

The wedding cakes had been delivered the day before the guests arrived. It was then that, to my horror, I realised that we had not just one three-tier 'black cake' covered in bright pink icing and decorations but also another similar one covered in blue icing and decorations. Both monstrosities were mounted on heavy plywood boards covered in re-used aluminium foil. I stared at the procession of burly boys tasked with carrying it up the stairs to the kitchen. Cakes seem to be stretching out to the horizon.

"Thank-you very much," I had said to each one as they placed them down on the kitchen table, breakfast bar and worktops. After they had gone out of earshot, I said to Edwin,

"Oh my God, where are we going to put all this cake?"

"We can't leave it here," Edwin agreed, "You need the space to be able to cook."

"More to the point, how are we going to stop mice and cockroaches from nibbling away at it overnight? You know how they scuttle out of the dark the minute they smell any food lying around. We can't put them in a tin or container because there isn't one big enough."

"We'll just have to cover it with something," he said, not really concerned with what to him was a trivial problem with a simple practical solution.

"Why so many cakes?" I asked, surveying the array that included a lot of extra iced cakes in addition to the main ones,

"Aunt Rose said that the pink one is for the bride and the blue one is for the bridegroom. Then there is one for the bride's mother and one for the groom's mother and ones for the bridesmaids and for the best man and one for the bride's grandmother. The others are for my local relatives."

"Karen and Pauline won't want to carry great heavy cakes in their suitcases back to England surely, will they?"

"That's up to them," he shrugged. I supposed he was right but I was still left with the problem of what to do with them until the wedding day.

"I can store the smaller cakes in the pantry in tins and containers that I can stack, once I wrap them in foil, but where can we put those bloody great things?" I said nodding towards the three-tiered towers.

"Put them on the dining table. We won't be using it to eat off while we have nineteen people here. It's too small to fit everyone around. We'll all have to eat under the house on those little tables we got from Colin. We can carry the cakes downstairs and put them on the buffet trestle when we all come back from the church and set out the food for the reception."

"I suppose there's nowhere else that's safe in the meantime. Well let's carry the two main cakes into the lounge now then. Once they're in there, I can cover the whole table with cling-film to keep out ants and roaches." I had done the best I could with the cling-film but the lounge was now blighted as far as I was concerned. The sickly smell of icing, sweating in the tropical heat, mingling with the rum-soaked treacle of the fruit cake, pervaded the room and made me feel nauseous whenever I passed through it. I could not wait to get rid of it.

The wedding ceremony was the Hopetown equivalent of a royal wedding. The likes had never been seen in the village before or since. It was a memorable day during which I got a better opportunity to relax and get to know the members of the two families. Edwin had been told by the mothers of bride and groom that he had to wear a suit because he could not go into the church as groom's father without one. This ludicrous insistence in temperatures of 30 degrees Celsius with no air-conditioning could only have been made by two middle-aged women with absolutely no idea of the reality of the tropical third world. We had warned them before they left England that it would be impossible to wear normal suits and that smart casual trousers with short-sleeved shirts would be more sensible and comfortable, but had been ignored. At least Rafer had got himself a beige linen summer suit which was probably just about bearable. Under pressure, Edwin had given in on the suit, sweltering in his pale grey pinstripe which was the only one he had kept in Guyana in case he ever needed to travel back to Europe or colder climes. But as a gesture of protest to show how inappropriate a suit was, he sported a pair of pale blue canvas espadrilles which made his outfit look completely ridiculous. No expense had been spared. Edwin had spent $70,000 on gold jewellery gifts for bride, groom and all the women in the two families. A local boy with a camera was paid to take the official photographs and another owning a video camera filmed the service. Reverend Pat Munroe officiated at the ceremony and in his speech at the reception, congratulated the couple on their performance for England at the just concluded Commonwealth Games in Victoria in which the bride had won a bronze medal in the sprint relay.

Just as the wedding buffet was about to begin, a group of people dressed in all their church finery arrived at the gate and called out to Edwin to let them in. It was his cousin Winnie and uncle Lambert. Edwin went up to the garden gate which he had locked to keep unwanted visitors out. He told them that they could not come in because only his close family were invited, so the rest of the family would have to go to his mother's house across the street. After they had eaten at Sapodilla, the bride and groom would go across the street and meet all the aunts, uncles and cousins at their grandmother's house. There was a heated exchange of views and then they left. Edwin had refused to open the gate to his uncle and cousin and their hangers on. He had turned them away. They were affronted at not being counted as close family. This would never be forgotten or forgiven, but Edwin could not have cared less. He had no time for Lambert, who had openly demanded money from him whenever he had previously visited, as if it were Edwin's duty to support him. Although he had a soft spot for Winnie, he could not let her in without letting in a horde of relatives that he loathed as much as Lambert.

After the wedding day, things became more relaxed. Various trips were organised for those who wanted to see the famous sights of the country as well as days on the beach and to the shops in Georgetown. We had calculated that our water supply would allow for only one flush of the toilet per person per day and had requested that laundry should not be done in the rooms as we would run out of water. We had set up a tub and buckets on a table near the washing line and water from the tank below the stairs could be taken for that purpose without affecting the upstairs supply. Two days after the wedding, one of the girls informed us that toilets upstairs were blocked and sewage was beginning to back up inside the toilet bowls threatening to spill over onto the bathroom floor. Edwin sent a messenger to get Carlton our plumber to come immediately to sort out this emergency. He eventually arrived with his assistant and spent best part of the day dismantling the sewage pipe in order to unblock it. In the searing heat of the September dry season, the sun on the pipes at the back of the house had dried the sewage-soaked toilet paper flushed from the upstairs toilets in the guest rooms before it had reached the septic tank. The gradient of the pipe being very gentle, and the proportion of paper to water being far too great, most of it had dried it into lumps as solid as concrete. It took Carlton hours to chip it out and flush through the system so it would work again. Raw sewage under the house in the area near where we would be eating in the evening had to be carted away and the repaired pipe and all the surroundings saturated with gallons of neat bleach. The limitations and poor standard of local technology and the local climatic conditions combined to illustrate that our resort was simply not up to the standard it would need to be to accommodate more than four or five guests at a time. We lived in dread of a recurrence of this problem before they all left, but fortunately we were spared that embarrassment.

The cakes continued to haunt me. I had to try to get rid of the one that had been cut into at the reception as quickly as possible, so, while Edwin took the entire company to the savannah with Samo, I spent the whole day cutting up wedding cake, wrapping it in serviettes, writing the names of aunts, uncles, cousins and family friends in the village on each portion, packing them into plastic buckets and giving the buckets to Spear and Shaun to deliver and distribute. I made sure that everyone whose name I could remember in the village got a piece. I could think of no more. There must have been several hundred pieces. At last it was all gone except the cakes destined for England. I was glad to see the back of it. I never wanted to see another 'Black Cake' again.

"Poor old Samo!" Edwin confided in me later that evening when we had gone to bed. "He'd killed a sheep and made a lovely lamb curry for them all in the savannah and no one except me and Samo wanted to eat any of it."

"I expect they were a bit squeamish. Most people's lives are so sanitised in developed countries. They're completely protected from real life unless they're brought up on a farm," I said.

Although I put up a defence for their behaviour, I really felt quite contemptuous of them for it. It was only since living away from England that I had begun to feel so estranged from the mentality of the consumer society Britain had become in my lifetime. I felt much more at home with the simple natural way of peasant life in Berbice and was prepared to put up with the inconveniences that came with it. I had made it my home and I loved what I saw as positive advantages of that environment far more than I missed the trappings of 'civilisation'. Perhaps the presence and preoccupations of some of our guests over those thirteen days helped to make me realise how glad I was to be in Guyana and not back in the rat race. It was a turning point for me.

Chapter 15

The Court Case

Ramsammy, known to locals as 'Idiot,' was a tall, gaunt Indo-Guyanese who always wore a trilby hat, so I never saw what his hair was like. His long-sleeved shirt with rolled back sleeves always had its top two buttons undone and his dark grey trousers were tied at the waist with a piece of string through the belt hooks. Scruffy trainers protected his feet from the mud he had to walk in to get from his house to the rum shop on the public road where he spent most of his day. He lived opposite our Tamarind tree. On Sundays and saints days, since he was a Catholic, he always went first to the Church and then to the rum shop. The Catholic Church for the area was on a tiny plot on the high street, two doors away from our snackette. It was visible from our veranda and seeing it every morning provided me with a sort of comfort. I had converted to Catholicism to marry my first husband but after he had left me for another woman, I had lapsed. After divorcing, I had felt I could not go back to regular church attendance, although I still regarded myself as a Christian and a Catholic at heart. Then I had married Edwin, who had been Congregational since birth and brought up in a Congregational minister's household. He did not attend church in Guyana, except on certain occasions to please his mother, Taa. I sometimes went to his church with him on such occasions as I felt it my place to support him, but I never asked him to go to the Catholic one. I had decided to keep my faith personal and not formalise it to cause complications in my life. I had explained this to Father Graham when we first arrived, when he had visited us and blessed our house after I had donated some books to his little library.

During the Burnham era, Ramsammy had risen in stature as a local figure. His sister had married a local black man who had made his fortune in the gold bush. As a result, the whole family, including their mother, himself and his siblings, had a smart new concrete block house to replace the board and mud hut they had previously lived in on that plot. The Ramsammy house was now much grander than that of all their Negro neighbours. Instead of being pitied for their extreme poverty and given spare food, the family now considered them-selves superior. They had kept apart since 'the troubles' of the sixties, when race rioting during pre-independence elections had resulted in the segregation of the races into different villages. However, their house was on the fringe of the Negro village where they had always lived. Ramsammy, now middle aged, had begun to behave like a country squire, since he now did not need to do the manual farm work he had had to do as a child. His brother-in-law was supporting his mother by a regular allowance, as was his elder brother, now an émigré in Canada. Ramsammy was in charge of their investments in Belair, which included a house for rent on the main road opposite our snackette, and a pig farm adjacent to our farm where, on behalf of his absentee relatives, he now employed young Negro boys to do the dirty work. Apart from visiting the pig-farm every day to give out orders to his worker, Ramsammy wasted away his days discussing politics and getting drunk in the rum-shop, spending his overseas relative's money on rum and high wine. Alcohol thus addled his brain. He seemed devoid of the little intelligence he was born with and as he had not attended primary school much, he was renamed 'Idiot' by locals. He behaved as if the investments were his own when everyone knew they were not. 'Idiot' himself owned nothing, as Taa and all our Negro neighbours were keen to point out to us. They now scorned his airs, particularly as he had become a staunch PPP activist once reaching adulthood.

Ever since Edwin had bought his land from Sonny Jaundoo and sent money to his mother to get it fenced off, Ramsammy had been in contention with Taa. His family had been accustomed to using the land where our farm now was. The tamarind tree opposite their house marked the boundary of Edwin's great-grandfather's farm land, which had passed into the Isaac family hands as security for a debt in colonial times. Used first as a public racecourse and later as an open pasture, it had been unfenced while in the possession of the Isaacs family. They had sold it off piecemeal to various individuals from the sixties onwards. Everyone who had bought land since the eighties had enclosed it to establish what they owned and secure the property they put on it. The Ramsammy clan had done so around their house and garden. Edwin was entitled to do the same. In spite of this, Taa had been given a lot of trouble by Ramsammy who had protested when she put the palings around our plot before we arrived in Guyana. Ramsammy had used his brother-in law's money to purchase the neighbouring lot from another member of the Isaacs family and established a pig farm on it. Then he protested that he should be given free access through our plot to reach their pig farm that he had by then fenced off completely. Soon after we settled in, Ramsammy demanded that Edwin should put a public pathway right through the middle of our farm so they could walk straight across to their pig farm from their house. Edwin was angry that his mother had been harassed and had made it clear that our fence was there to stay, so anyone wanting to cross the pasture would have to make a detour around the fenced part of our land.

I wondered why this problem had arisen, so I did some research into the local history of land ownership to find an answer. Original maps in slavery times showed that the farmland had been surveyed and subdivided into long narrow strips that ran perpendicular to the coast. This was to allow drainage canals to take water straight out to the sea by the shortest route. Originally access was only by sea, so the canals presented no obstacle and indeed formed a useful boundary between plantations. They were even used as an access route inland from the coast. The farmland between the canals was also divided into even narrower strips of the same length, because it varied in quality. Raised sandy reefs ran parallel to the coast and between these were low-lying swampy areas. In British colonial times, a public road of laterite had been built parallel to the coast on the reef nearest the sea to connect the free villages established by the emancipated slaves. Private investors had built a railway on the higher ground much further inland, connecting Georgetown to Rosignol to enable the transport of sugar, arrowroot, cattle, rice and other produce for the markets in the capital and export. After Independence, Burnham's government had dismantled the railway and sold off what it could to India. It had focused on resurfacing the public road with bitumen to make it suitable for modern motor transport. At that time, government owned land in the villages had been divided up and sold off as standard sized house-lots to those who could afford to buy them. A grid pattern of streets and ditches between each house-lot provided easy access and drainage for all of them. The former race-course in our village, however, being privately owned, was not included in this process. It had been subdivided into long thin strips by the Isaac family who still had title to the entire area by the time of independence. It therefore followed that if you bought any part of that land from them, you needed to buy the entire strip so that whether you built your property at the public roadside or on the reef further inland, you would have free access to your property from the public road. During the corrupt and lawless years of Burnham's government in the nineteen seventies and early eighties, local government had turned a blind eye to land sales and building on the former racecourse without imposing any street-plan on the subdivision. By the time we had arrived in Guyana, Peter Britton, a Georgetown lawyer, had the middle strip and had built his farmhouse on the central reef with a causeway from it across the swampy pasture to the public road. The only part he had fenced was the higher ground on the reef where he employed someone to rear chickens for him. Edwin's brother had bought another strip, but built his house at the public road end because he wanted to live near other people when he had his holidays from Brooklyn. He had plans to operate a business from that location when he retired and repatriated. However, several Indo-Guyanese families had each been sold just one house-lot at the end near the public road, so when Edwin came to buy his strip in 1984, the end of it near the public road had already been sold to an Indo-Guyanese called Albert. His house had already been built and his lot fenced off with a ten foot screen of corrugated iron. Our house therefore had to be built near the reef, but at least we could access it from any point along its longer edge because that was the outer edge of the old racecourse and the boundary line was formed by the local mud street or 'dam' and a drainage trench. Two other Indo-Guyanese families lived in their huts on the reef behind us. They had enclosed the land as individual house-lots. They had no access to these lots unless they went out by the old railway line on the back reef. It was a long walk unless they cut across other people's land. Taa had only fenced off a small part of our strip, so they could still freely walk across our land at both ends of our fence, but being neighbourly, she had allowed them a pathway level with their own fences and right through the middle of Edwin's fenced land. This alleyway had enabled the thieves of our sheep to get easy unseen access to our sheep pen during our first year in Guyana, so Edwin had blocked it off to prevent further thefts. Now Ramsammy got in league with the other Indo-Guyanese families to strengthen his own case to open the pathway. It appeared to be a concerted attempt to keep the entire pasture in Indo-Guyanese hands and frustrate a Negro from being able to effectively secure and use it. Nevertheless, Edwin was not about to let himself be intimidated out of his legitimate rights, so we just ignored it all and got on with our lives.

The recent local elections had added fuel to flare up the fire again. Ramsammy had put himself up as the PPP candidate for our village and had not been elected. He was devastated. Worse still for him was the news that Edwin had not only been elected as a village councillor but also had been successfully instated as Chairman of the 29 villages of the Naarstigheid- Union Neighbourhood Democratic Council. The salt was rubbed into Ramsammy's wounds by the local men in the rum-shop and the fact that he had to look out over our garden full of flourishing vegetables and compare that with his own neglected weed patch. His own house was now overshadowed by a massive ranch-house owned by a Negro that was right in his face every time he walked out of his gate. We were blissfully ignorant of the resentment this had unleashed but it was only a matter of time before we were shocked into awareness.

Geoffrey arrived soon after the wedding party left. His new building project for us was to make a smart permanent concrete fence on the street side of our property with some pillars at the front entrance for proper wrought iron gates. This would replace the rickety pickets that had been put up before our arrival in the country. Our aim was to improve the appearance of the front entrance, keep animals out, and make it difficult for casual thieves to gain access. At the same time, we did not want to block out our view of the community or seem to them hostile, like a prison. We had therefore decided that the bottom three feet would be a low wall of concrete blocks in a concrete foundation and the top three feet would be heavy duty wire mesh such as that used around tennis courts, fixed to a strong hardwood frame. It would cost a fortune but we would do it piece by piece as we got the money. If we started on the street side for now, then we could at a later date complete the other three sides. We were sure that the local authority would put a proper surface on the road eventually.

While plans and estimates for the work were being drawn up, my new system for classes was in full swing. One of Edwin's athletes had now left school without any qualifications and was working for us at the snackette. She was almost illiterate and had a low IQ. She needed to improve on her basic education, so I was giving her extra literacy lessons. Other students I had taught who had also finished school but needed to retake CXC exams, had come to me for help, so I had scheduled free English language and literature lessons for some of them during the daytime and social studies, history and even French for others. A group of Hopetown Primary School children were also coming to me for practical music lessons, learning to play the recorders we had given them. My time was filling up with unpaid charity work in the school but there was now a steady flow of CARDI guests whose contributions were helping Edwin to pay some of our bills. Coping with such business guests in the evenings was not a problem for me as they were at work in the daytime so did not really conflict with my teaching input. I wondered whether I would be able to cope with both if there should ever be a full house of proper tourists but this seemed highly unlikely in the foreseeable future because we still had no telephone line to deal directly with bookings. Edwin kept complaining about the impossibility of coaching sport to ignorant and illiterate athletes, and so I felt I could support him by working to change this. Most of the workforce was also completely unemployable. The only way to improve this was to teach the youngsters who came to us the skills, ethics and behaviours which would make them employable to potential developers like ourselves. This was an uphill struggle when the few existing local employers tolerated poor skills, work practices and ethics.

Edwin's sports club athletes were drawing him into deeper and deeper involvement with local schools via the Ministry of Education and the Guyana Teachers' Union who authorised and organised all school sport. It was weird that the Unions had complete control of events, finances, rules and regulations. The Ministry had almost no involvement apart from allowing teachers and pupils to have time off school. The Ministry paid teachers' travel expense claims for union work such as this and yet the union was allowed to keep all receipts from the events. There was pretence of accountability for this at PTA meetings, where sums raised from funds were always "utilised for new school furniture" but occasionally we overheard savvy parents wondering how come the money was spent on the same thing every year yet no one had ever seen any of this "new furniture". Union reps came to regard school sports as a way of enhancing their personal income while complaining that their predecessors in that post "tief out all de money". Edwin began by believing that the teachers he had been educating on his courses, who had been loudest in their criticism of past fraudsters, were free of such dishonest motives. He soon found out that their complaints were founded on a desire to win his trust in order to get their own hands on the funds. Nevertheless, each time he discovered a new "crook," it was a complete surprise to us both. Like builders, tradesmen, officials and workers, the pool of honest teachers seemed to be continually shrinking as time went by.

"School sports at the MMA was the worst sports meeting I have ever had the misfortune to be involved in." Edwin grumbled after his first officially approved direct involvement in the local school sports.

"What was so bad about it?" I asked.

"Caro as GTU rep in charge of this must take most of the blame. She didn't delegate duties sensibly to other teachers, and didn't get involved with her school team. There weren't enough officials; there was no security so there were problems with the crowd and with vendors; the PA arrived late and was so bad they'd have done better to use a home-made megaphone. The event was a complete failure, and they broke one of my javelins, so that's more expense. I'll have to charge a fee for hire of equipment in future to cover repair costs. Never again for me," he said. It sounded final but I knew by now that "Never again" for him meant "I'll make sure it's different next time" and he would move heaven and earth to find a way to change it.

Council meetings took up a lot of his time these days. Otherwise he was dealing with school sports or his own athletes' training, and their participation in national competitions run by the AAA in Georgetown. He saw corruption and incompetence at every level and everywhere he looked. He was driven on by an anger at it all and a determination to reform it by personal example and the education of everyone he worked with, especially the young. A steady flow of CARDI visitors needing accommodation with us or meals at the snackette, punctuated his community work. At the village Office, he came into contact with the Student International Health Association: a party of Canadian medical students in our neighbourhood, conducting research on health issues in developing countries. They also did health education sessions in local schools giving away tooth-care products to the children. He invited them to several meals with us to make them feel more welcome and they did a session with our sports club and students. It was great for us both to get a chance to talk to intelligent young people from the kind of world we used to live in. It gave us a bit more energy and enthusiasm to survive in an otherwise intellectually sterile environment. The contact network Edwin was building up through all this was eating into his time and mine also. I was always pulled in to give such visitors a guided tour of our home and school and rustle up some refreshments for them if I was not teaching at the time they called. There was an insatiable need for our willingly given free advice and now a new body introduced themselves to us: The Guyana Volunteer Consultancy. These new visitors were all local business people from Georgetown who wanted Edwin to join their network and contribute free advice and time to their causes around the country. He made a decision not to participate, as by now he did not have any spare hours in the day.

Geoffrey had not yet made a start on our fence building, but at the village office, public drainage works for the year were beginning before the winter rains set in. Trenches in certain streets were deepened, and the dirt piled high along the banks in order to keep the rainwater in the trench so the street itself would stay dry. The cost of the work had to be raised from rates and taxes paid by residents of the area. Edwin had come into the council and found that the village office had no money because it had "all been spent" by the previous chairman, an appointee of the Burnham government. The amount of rates that people paid had not been increased since the 1940s regardless of subsequent inflation, so it was now a derisory sum that could easily be afforded by most property owners. Indo-Guyanese residents were in the habit of paying, but many black villagers defaulted. Edwin heard that they would not pay because no work ever got done in the black villages. The office staff explained that this was because they did not pay their rates. There was a vicious circle he was determined to break. They looked to him, a black man, to redress the problem. He told them that if they paid their rates, he would get works done in their streets. As part of this deal, the engineer visited our street to assess the work needing to be done. Our street would have to wait until every other street in the village had been done. It was never part of Edwin's strategy to look after himself first and keep others waiting. However, he had been discussing the local sheep project with Mac and the CARDI consultants that visited us and Edwin had suggested that an abattoir be built to provide a market for the local sheep farmers and bring much needed employment into the village which could grow into an export business in the future. It could be located on an available site at the far end of our street on the sea side of the public road. The abattoir would need a well-drained access road, so the international agencies collaborating on funding such an abattoir could contribute to the cost of excavating that drainage trench. Edwin made a point of standing outside Ramsammy's house while discussing with the regional drainage engineer the line that the trench would eventually take. It would be straight down our side of the street, joining up the MMA trench at the back of our farm with the rest of the system at the public road. It would define our boundary and put the enormous tamarind tree firmly inside our property. Ramsammy saw this and brought some other Indians down to see what was going on. He was telling the engineer surveying and drawing up his plans that the trench could not follow that line. Edwin spotted what was going on, told Ramsammy not to interfere and sent him away.

At the village office, Edwin's vice-Chairman was now being investigated for major fraud.

"She'll have to go," he told me later that day, "she's not fit for public office and no one in Hopetown trusts her with the rates money."

"What did she do?" I asked.

"She forged council certificates so she could give land titles out to Indians for huge amounts of money which she kept for herself. That money is supposed to be in the village office account. It all came to light when they had to register them at the New Amsterdam office because the numbers on the certificates were not in the correct sequence to match the ones in the village office."

"So as long as you're the Chairman, it looks like *you're* guilty of the fraud unless you can prove that it's her and get her removed."

"In a word: yes. They all think *they're* clever and that *I'm* stupid because I haven't lived here since I was a kid but they don't know me and they seem to underestimate my intelligence. *They're* the stupid ones, not me. Take Samuel for a start. I like Samuel, but most of his ideas on development deserve to be in his pit latrine. However, I'll always listen to him just in case he says something sensible."

It was my 40th birthday that November, so Edwin took me on an excursion to Santa Mission from Georgetown as a treat. He felt a bit bad about the fact that he had taken all his family there in September, but not me because I had to stay behind and man the house for the other guests. Even though everyone in a normal place could easily have looked after themselves, it was not a normal place and the entire infrastructure that our local tradesmen had bodged together for us would have collapsed had there been a blackout. The complicated act of connecting and starting up our generator or dealing with our plumbing idiosyncrasies didn't bear thinking about in the hands of a guest who thought they knew what to do. It was just easier if I was there, since I knew exactly what to do without the property being seriously damaged. Now, with the house to ourselves again, we could lock it up and go out together for the day when we wanted to. I was glad of the chance at last to see something of the country. After 4 years of living there, I had seen nothing outside of Sapodilla except Georgetown and New Amsterdam and they were to my mind, uninteresting, nasty, dirty, run down dumps. I hated towns at the best of times but these ranked alongside the worst I had visited anywhere in the world. The tour operator had a vehicle to convey participants to the boat pick-up point on the Demerara River and once there, we were making our way into the interior by water. The riverine experience was what I had mistakenly hoped would be a regular feature of my life when I first arrived: getting into the beautiful jungle wilderness that was Guyana's hinterland. Now at last the sounds that filled our ears were those of raw nature, spoiled only by the chug of the boat engine. As we headed up a small tributary creek, I looked into the rippled black water trailing in our wake. Reflections of the towering canopies of hardwood giants shimmered and then melted away. A huge flash of vibrant royal blue the size of a small bird danced tantalisingly from one bank to the other, a few feet above the water. It was not a bird, but the spectacular Blue Morpho butterfly native to these areas. We gasped in wonder, eager for another glimpse and were not disappointed. There were several of them. I was drinking in the tonic through every pore in my body.

Santa Mission was an insight into the Amerindian villages nearest Georgetown. They had just become tinged with the negative effects of embryonic modern "eco-tourism", but any positive effects on the villagers did not seem apparent. The houses were different in character from those of the coastal plain, being picturesque thatch and pole benabs of traditional construction and the inhabitants' physical characteristics derived from their ancient Asiatic ethnic origins. In terms of their dress and Creolese language, however, they were indistinguishable from anyone in our own coastal village. The one-roomed school, which was in full session during our visit, seemed just the same as the one in our own village of Negro children: more of a meeting place and chattering house than an educational institution. The Captain, or Cacique, of the village was introduced to us by the tour-guide and a few moments of conversation with him had Edwin promising to send the school some of the books I still had back in our library at Sapodilla. Captains had the same role in Amerindian settlements as Edwin had as Chairman of our own neighbourhood district council, so there was some common ground between them that engaged the captain. We had started off in the misguided belief that somehow, Amerindians in their unspoiled seclusion were noble indigenous people untainted by the corruption and political infighting of the 'civilised' city and coastal plain. By the end of our day trip, we had begun to realise that this 'elected' captain was hated by some of his subjects who were, once out of his earshot, complaining to us that he kept for his own private use all the donations of money from visitors to the village instead of using it for improvements to the village. Nevertheless, consistent with our general goodwill and desire to help whoever we could, we arranged a way of getting two boxes of our books to the school at the mission within a week of getting back home. One thing we prided ourselves on was always keeping our promises regardless of how disillusioned we were with our beneficiaries. It must be that the village is so close to Georgetown, we thought. The native people of further flung communities must still be as we had idealised.

As Christmas approached, Sister Helen Munroe arrived from England to stay with us for two weeks. Edwin was excited to receive her as a guest because he had not seen her for years. He had gone to England in 1950 with Parson Munroe's son, Duke, and lived with him and his wife Helen for many years. She had been a home-economics teacher in Guyana and England, so she fully appreciated what I was trying to do for the students at Sapodilla. She accompanied my class and me on an educational visit I had arranged to the Guysuco sugar factory nearby and saw the children completing the investigative worksheets I had prepared for them. I had been rehearsing an end of term show with all my students since September to put on at our first prize giving ceremony while she was with us. The British High Commissioner had accepted our invitation to come to the show with his wife and three daughters. He agreed to give out the book prizes that I had bought for my top students and at the same time he brought a package of Victorian and Edwardian photographs that I had previously ordered from the Foreign and Commonwealth Office, unaware that he would be presenting them to me as a donation to our community museum. The photographs were of street scenes in Georgetown and of the different races in their traditional costumes of that period, of the sailing ships that brought the first indentured labourers from India to British Guiana, of them at work on the sugar plantations and of the foresters and pork knockers (gold miners) in the interior. They made a terrific contribution to my museum displays and most of all, were superb resources for the teaching of local history to my students. The High Commissioner and his family were very kind about the children's efforts with the show but could not stay for refreshments as they had a prior engagement across the Berbice River later that day. It was a great honour to have them as guests, however, considering we were not VIPs among the Georgetown elite. It was lucky that our street was dry enough for the High Commission vehicle to reach us without getting stuck. The winter rains had just started by the beginning of December, but the deluges that flooded us out normally came at the end of the month.

My school term ended with our show which was on a Saturday, but the Hopetown Community High School did not finish until the following Wednesday and we had been invited along to see their end-of-Christmas-term show. They had asked me to bring along my recorder group to play a couple of Christmas Carols. I was the only teacher in the region who could read music to play an instrument, so I had been teaching the recorder to students from the primary school for a couple of years by then. I knew what to expect because of school shows we had previously attended. Instead of teachers using curriculum time to teach music or drama, or extra-curricular time to rehearse their own students, they had a kind of 'rent-an act' system whereby they paid teachers and pupils from other schools to perform if they were known to have natural talent. Edwin and I always did things for free, so they would 'save' money by having us as an act. In reality this would actually enable the organiser themselves to pocket a bit more of the funds raised. Sister Helen came with us. She had never been to such a village show in the country, since her most recent Guyana experience had been in Georgetown shortly after independence in 1966. Unlike us, she had high expectations based on her memory of the colonial past. She was appalled at the standard of the children's acts, the conduct and unprofessionalism of their teachers, but most of all she was appalled at the behaviour of the audience. They had come there to gossip and chatter with their neighbours and relatives, not to watch their children perform. Their raucous laughter and banter befitted a rum shop or a market but not a school hall. The teachers made no attempt to achieve silence before the show began but announced acts in their soft spoken voices, which no one could hear. The poor children were completely drowned out and many got laughed at so they collapsed with nerves. We were seated on the front row so I could tell when my group were supposed to get up on stage. I followed them up, arranged them behind my music stand ready to conduct and then I turned to face the crowd that filled the hall. Their noise was deafening. I waited and waited and waited until some of them got the hint and stopped talking. I continued to watch and wait but still there was no complete silence. When I judged that the remaining punters would continue talking regardless, I addressed the crowd in my loudest, sternest voice,

"These children have spent a long time practising their music and I think the least you can do is to have the good manners to listen to them, so we are not going to start playing until there is complete silence in this hall." The noise dropped to almost nothing, so I turned my back to them, counted the children in, and began conducting "While Shepherds Watched". The act finished, we bowed to the applause, I chaperoned the group off the stage and folded up my music stand. Then the spectators' noise crept back up to its former levels as subsequent acts got underway. In the end Edwin could bear it no more, so we got up and walked out in disgust. The lack of discipline in local schools and the inadequacies of the untrained pupil-teachers who were staffing them was the topic of our discussion with Sister Helen all the way home and for the rest of her stay. She could not believe the state Guyana's education system had fallen into since Independence. She was the only guest we had hosted at Sapodilla free of charge thus far, because she was 'family' to Edwin. However, since she was so impressed by our own show and what she saw of the work the students were doing, she donated £45 to help towards the museum we had named after her father-in-law.

The New Year of 1995 was one of major changes in our lives and in the project we had begun. Fence building had begun at Sapodilla Health, Fitness and Organic Farm resort, but Edwin had been faced with objections to it by Ramsammy at a council meeting which had lasted four hours. This only increased his resolve to press on with the fence at a pace. Money was a problem, however. Edwin had finally closed the snackette in the face of repeated daily losses and dishonesty with receipts for expenditure made by staff. He had given them all numerous chances to reform with no improvement, so he sent them all home. Cousin Irene, the cook, had come in private to get her job reinstated. She blamed it all on her two helpers who lived next door. She begged Edwin to reconsider and reopen the snackette. He took a week to think it over and then gave in to her. He decided to allow her to continue cooking but to have his cousin Boyo in charge of the shopping and general day to day dealings.

"If one of my own family members is there every day, he'll look after my interests," Edwin explained to me. He was really reluctant to give up on the business altogether as he was still getting demand for cooked lunches for CARDI workers and other employers needing a higher standard of catering for their visiting executives than was available elsewhere. Surely this new change of personnel would start bringing in income instead of draining it.

We were still developing our tourism customer base and attractions and had been out at 4.30 a.m. with Mac to see the scarlet ibis nesting site in an in-shore lagoon at Onverwagt. We walked down to the seashore in silence by torchlight and took up our waiting places in the dark. As dawn broke, and the rising sun over the Atlantic streaked the sky with orange, the morning chorus of the colony struck up and they began to fly off in a great crimson cloud that took my breath away. There were thousands of them roosting in the mangroves around the isolated lagoon. I took photos of them and of the coastal erosion visible in action in the areas where locals had cut down the mangroves for firewood. These would form part of my educational displays in our learning centre museum. I would get my students to use the displays when we were studying environmental conservation in my lessons. I had also started up an African dance group with my students, so we could keep alive the Que-que and other traditional slave dances. It was fun and they were also learning to appreciate and preserve their own culture. At the same time it would provide some colourful cultural entertainment for our guests.

The V.S.O. had some English people in Georgetown that Edwin met up with while there on council and other business, so he got into conversation with them. They were organising a big conference for their new intake of school teachers to meet with David Green, their President, coming from England. They wanted a big enough venue for this with affordable decent accommodation. Edwin with his usual persuasive powers managed to interest them in coming to Berbice, since although we could not accommodate all the VSOs in the country at our place, we could host the President and his executives and Guyana's Chief Education Officer. The conference itself could take place at the nearby MMA compound at Onverwagt which could cheaply accommodate all the VSOs. Edwin would take care of organising it all with his contacts in the MMA management. The overall costs would be far less than at any Georgetown venue even when paying full price for our four rooms. The VSO conference went ahead as planned and was a great success. David Green, an accomplished artist, sketched in pen-and-ink the views from our veranda in the early mornings during their short stay and presented us with one of them as a gift when he left.

By the end of April, Geoffrey had made good progress with the fence. It now stretched from Aunty Lucy's house on the corner near the tamarind tree, past our front steps and ended at the extremity of the ornamental front garden we had begun to create. Things were beginning to look up. Our network of contacts was slowly beginning to generate wider interest in spite of our isolation without a telephone. The problem was that people would just turn up on the doorstep unannounced and this could cause inconvenience to me if Edwin was not around. Anna Iles was a local employee of the Canadian High Commission who had come to stay with us on a previous occasion with Mac and the CARDI people and had made friends with me. In April, she brought two people from the World Wildlife Fund, and a man working in ecclesiastical research in Switzerland, along with her from Georgetown for a day trip. Luckily, I was not teaching that day and Edwin was there, so we spent a few hours answering their questions about why we were there and what we were doing. It was all very nice, and we were always very congenial, but we never seemed to get any business out of all this use of our time and hospitality. However, I had been invited the previous week to give a talk to the Rotary Club of Georgetown about the educational work I was doing at Sapodilla Learning Centre and it may have been Anna Iles who had put my name forward for this. Later the same day, our acquaintance Desiree, the reporter from Stabroek News, turned up out of the blue with her latest boyfriend, an English VSO who had been teaching the Amerindians in the Rupununi for six years. I made another few rounds of tuna sandwiches and we sat and chatted with the couple. We then had an hour or so to get ourselves ready to drive to Georgetown, since we had recently found ourselves on the invitation list for the Queen's Official Birthday Reception at the British High Commissioner's Residence in Georgetown. It was the first time I had occasion to dress up to go anywhere in four years. It was nice to be invited, but not pleasant to make such a long journey there and back in the dark on a desolate, potholed road in a village hire-car.

The following week, we received a mysterious letter in a long envelope with a Georgetown postmark. Edwin opened it, read it and passed it to me.

"What do you make of that?" he asked. It was a lawyer's letter from Peter Britten's Office in Georgetown. It warned us that court action was being taken against Mr Edwin Joseph for 'building a solid concrete wall ten feet high and sixty two feet wide, across his land in No. 22 Belair, West Coast Berbice, preventing [Mr Ramsammy] from being able to gain access to his farm and preventing him from gaining access to water for his house and farm.'

"That's completely ridiculous!" I said, "For a start, we haven't even built the fence anywhere near his farm yet. It's only eight feet high and only three feet of that is solid concrete. The idea that it can be sixty two feet wide is nonsense. He has made it thicker than the Great Wall of China! Even the length of the wall is not that long yet. How can a serious practising lawyer like Peter Britten allow such a ridiculously impossible letter like that to leave his office?"

"It gives us a day for appearance in court," said Edwin, "Otherwise I would ignore it. Up to now, Peter Britten has been my lawyer but now I'll have to go to another lawyer to represent me in court against this because he is now acting for Ramsammy. That'll be more expense on complete unnecessary nonsense that I could well do without."

"Well he hasn't got a case," I said. "Any lawyer in court will see that this is complete nonsense and the judge will throw it out! How can he say that our fence is preventing him from gaining access to any water for his house and farm? His house has already got water. His farm hasn't but neither has ours. What water? No one has water until it rains. You have to catch it on your roof or dig a pond or a trench on your land to catch it."

Edwin believed it was a PPP plot to undermine the development of our business and discussed the letter at the village office with Samuel. At last Samuel had something sensible to say to Edwin. The best lawyer in Georgetown according to him was Rex McKay, who was the PNC lawyer that handled cases in the High Court. Next time Edwin went to Georgetown, he visited McKay's offices. Having seen the letter and heard the details from Edwin, McKay referred him to a Mr Ellis who was an English Lawyer working at the partnership at the time.

"Ellis told me he thought I was a bit naïve," said Edwin back at home later that day.

"Why?" I asked.

"Lawyers here don't have integrity just because they are lawyers; far from it."

"Didn't he see that there's no evidence for his allegations? It can't stand up in court, surely."

"In England, no," Edwin reminded me, "But we're not in England and according to Ellis, all the lawyers in the country are crooked, so if they get paid enough, they'll win the case. We have to be careful how we tread but I believe Ellis will do the best he can because he's English. I still had to pay 50,000 Guyana dollars for the fee that the McKay practice charges to take on the case, and leave the summons and the transport documents and all the details of the case with him. That's money I can ill afford at the moment. I feel at least he has integrity. He only came here under Hoyte's presidency as a government lawyer, but he's still working here even though Hoyte's no longer in power. He advised me to stop building any more of the fence until the matter's resolved, though."

"So you mean that anyone can cook up some impossible lunatic charge and as long as a lawyer somewhere is ready to take money off them to take on the case, then it goes to court and the victim of the baseless accusation has to fork out that kind of dosh for a lawyer to defend them?"

"Afraid so, and the case is likely to go on for years according to Ellis, so in the mean time we can build no more fence. He reckons that bribes are given to lawyers to encourage them to lose files and evidence regardless of whether the person with the money is guilty or innocent."

"So no justice is possible in a place like this," I said. "It doesn't seem that our on-going defence case against Sonny Lall will get anywhere either, then."

Edwin shrugged, "I don't intend to let these bastards get the better of me," he hissed.

A new sense of desolation and helplessness now descended upon me. We were completely alone in a sea of sharks that were circling around us waiting for one of us to falter. Once the weaker was devoured, the other would soon follow. How could we survive against these odds?

Chapter 16

The Ritual Sacrifice

It was the end of June. Rains were daily and torrential. We had to lend our wellington boots to our last bunch of CARDI guests so they could walk to the main road in deep squelchy mud because it was too soft for their vehicle to get down our street. Edwin's cousin, Boyo, who lived opposite, had carried their cases for them on his head, making two journeys. Since January, I had been rehearsing a children's drama I had written based on local history. It focused on the culture of the African slaves who had been brought to the colony by the European settlers in the seventeenth century when Berbice had been a Dutch Colony and Essequibo and Demerara had been French ruled. The African dance group I had set up among my Saturday class volunteered to stay behind and rehearse the drama for a show to be performed at the end of July just before Emancipation Day on August 1st. Kumfa drums had been rattling away nightly in the village. It was as if they spoke the secret messages of the African slaves to each other, plotting the overthrow of their masters. They seemed to dominate the blackness of the nights because it was so quiet then, when most people were inside their huts cooking or eating and resting. The spirits of the night were at large and candle flies flickered on and off. As I sat on the veranda in the dark, I wondered what the planter's wife, Mistress George, had felt back in 1763, on the night of the Berbice Slave Revolt I had dramatized in our play. These talking drums must have chilled her spine, knowing that she and her husband, Planter George, Mrs Shreuder (a Dutchwoman) and Parson Ramring were alone in Plantation Peerbohm far up the Berbice River, surrounded by thousands of African slaves half-starved by the famine and disease of a prolonged drought, and that only thirteen white soldiers had survived the 'raging sickness' at nearby Fort Nassau. Even greater her terror when she must have heard the musket shots out in the surrounding jungle that could only have meant that slaves had captured guns from the plantations of deceased planters and the fort must have fallen to them. When their makeshift bullets: burning balls of cotton attached to nails, had rained down on the thatched roof of the stone walled plantation house, what could she have done but throw that last precious bucket of water onto the flames to try to put them out? How she must have trembled as they waved the white flag of surrender and ventured outside to be directed down to the river at gunpoint. How traumatic it must have been to see her men-folk shot by other slaves as they descended to the boats. Yet to have been protected by the slave leader, Cuffy, because he said she had been kind to her slaves, must have been small recompense. We had come a long way since then, I thought; or had we?

Only the night before, we had been discussing the dire standard of local teachers with Harold Patterson, the portly Afro-Trinidadian CARDI consultant who had just left us. Edwin had said how the female teachers from the village primary and community high schools all travelled to Ithaca regularly for secret sessions with an Obeah man there who did group female fertility sex. He had been invited to go along with them but had declined since he regarded it all as superstitious nonsense and told them so. The people of Ithaca were held in awe by those of our village. The inaccessibility of Ithaca, far out in the savannah, cut them off from the main road. They liked it that way. Their activities were secretive because undiluted African tribal culture was kept alive there. Their location made them somehow sinister and forbidding to many villagers who saw the Ithaca people as strange. An outsider might feel threatened when venturing into their territory, so most kept away. The approach of Emancipation Day usually occasioned secret libation ceremonies in Ithaca that the Christian Churches frowned on. Taa and the elderly ladies of the Hopetown Congregational Church would never have dreamed of going there, but the teachers who did were not Congregational churchgoers. I wondered if the Ithaca people were descended from the 'Guango' tribe who had struck such fear into the hearts of gentle slaves like Cuffy during the eighteenth century revolt because they were out of his control and after driving out all the whites from the settlement, fought against the other tribes and "killed and ate the bodies" of their fellow slaves. Belladrum was another village in West Coast Berbice which shared the eccentricity of Ithaca. By contrast, however, it was on the main road to Georgetown and a few miles further up from Onverwagt. It did not look any different to me from the other villages we had to pass through in a minibus, but I had never had to get out there and mix with the adults. Edwin had organised a football league with the help of Albert Straker, which the Belladrum team had taken part in, and he told me they were very strange people. They had been playing the kumfa drums while the match was going on. To begin with, Edwin had complained to Albert about the noise which distracted from the game but Albert advised him not to say anything. Hundreds of locals had come from all directions to support their team at the match. No doubt the drums had advertised the event. I thought little of it, at that time, however.

It had been my idea to stage our show on the eve of Emancipation Day, 31st July, known locally as 'Swaree', so that local people could all come along and share in a daytime celebration of historical drama that would be educational and appropriate for children to attend. Most children were not allowed to go to the night time celebrations of Swaree that began before midnight and went on until the early hours of the morning. I wanted to show the children and local community their own history in a new way that they could develop and share with tourists coming into their midst. What better way, I thought than to invite our students' parents and siblings along to get a living history enactment showcasing the knowledge their children had gained in my lessons and also their performance skills in music, dance and drama. I wanted to demonstrate how an entire show could be around a single theme as in a Broadway musical that would make the drama accessible to every level of ability and every age group in the community. My aim was to help everyone to value their own history and keep alive tradition in the face of overwhelming influences from the Guyanese émigré in New York which drew everyone towards American pop culture. This was having a very negative effect on the country's economy and potential for development because it promoted drugs trade and the desire of everyone to follow a chain migration route out of the country. In the recent past it may well have been the only way to a better future. Corruption and racial strife had proliferated during the Burnham era and he created a police state in which his political opponents were assassinated and driven into exile. Now everyone wanted to 'backtrack' or migrate illegally to get rich quick in the USA because they saw no value in staying and developing legitimate businesses and wealth in their own society.

We had registered our property as an eco-tourism resort with the Ministry of Tourism when we first arrived in the country. This entitled us to tax-free concessions to import items we might need to provide necessary standards of facilities and service to our guests. The new Field Officer at the Ministry of Tourism in Georgetown had organised a course for hotels, resorts and tour operators using resource-people from the Caribbean islands. We were invited to attend this in July but I still had classes and drama rehearsals, so Edwin went along to see what he could learn. Instead, he became further disillusioned.

"I knew more about tourism than any of their resource people," he told me in disgust. "No-one employs any qualified people. I brought up the question of health and safety because they hadn't included it in the programme but not even the tutor had insurance cover!" Still, the course had brought him in touch with new contacts that might prove useful in future. We invited them to buy tickets for our musical drama production so they could see what we could put on for prospective tourists.

Ex-President Hoyte had come into our village in early July to speak at a big meeting there. Edwin had been asked to give a short talk about the work of the new Neighbourhood District Council. He had little respect for Hoyte after meeting him when he had been President. At the time Edwin had been directing the World Cup Football in Georgetown. On arrival at the village event, Edwin quickly realised that the meeting was really a PNC Party Political Rally and he faced vociferous hostility to some of the things he spoke about reforming. Unperturbed, he had argued his case with conviction, regardless of whether it annoyed Hoyte. He was careful to keep his distance and remain independent of any party. Nevertheless, Hoyte told the villagers to follow the advice of their new NDC Chairman, Mr Joseph, because it would lead to improvements in their lives. This must have rung true to most of them because already, new water pipes were being laid along the main public road to bring clean potable water from artesian wells further along the coast. Drainage canals in the village had been dug for the first time in decades and the mud street from the main road to the primary school had been resurfaced with red brick for the first time in its existence.

Edwin had just been discussing with Dr MacPherson the idea of tying up the Village Office abattoir and CARDI sheep project with youth education by locating the sheep project at Sapodilla Learning Centre. Mac had encouraged Edwin into thinking that he would be the manager of this project so Edwin believed it could expand the educational activities of our centre into animal husbandry and farm management. He hoped that in leasing the undeveloped farmland at the back of our vegetable garden to the sheep project, it would add to our income stream and provide vocational training for youth in the area after their schooling had finished. It would also lead to better financial and business management of such small businesses as it would engender in due course. Edwin would be happy to volunteer his own expertise in teaching the management part of such courses free of charge. While all this was going on, he suggested a marketing strategy for the produce of our local small sheep farmers, most of whom were women. Why not stage a sheep show where their animals could be on display, along with booths selling a variety of artisan food and leather craft products from the sheep? He managed to sell the idea to the CARDI consultants who stayed with us and had offered them a free venue on our land nearest the public road. It had been approved and we were now at the point where the sheep farmers were all putting up their thatched stalls and animal corrals under Edwin's direction in the manner of an English agricultural show. It was alien to the locals with their haphazard lives and enterprises to have to conform to Edwin's military neatness and organisational precision but they tried their best and things were taking shape. The sheep show had been timed for the end of July, after pay-day, when locals would have money to spend. Edwin had just met the Chairman of our Regional District Council, Geoffrey Fraser at his first Ministry of Education School Sports meeting in the Regional Board Room in June. Edwin had been put forward as the Sports Officer for the region. He had privately explained to the Regional Chairman some of the problems we had been trying to overcome and asked him if he could help us to get Sapodilla Learning Centre recognised as an educational institution working as a charity to help Ministry of Education Schools in our region. He invited Mr Fraser, an educated commercial farmer himself, to the sheep show. As my play rehearsals took shape, I had decided to run it for two nights, and put on the first performance on the last day of the sheep show. That way, the paying public from the High Commissions and tourists from Georgetown would have plenty to see and that would make their long journey more worthwhile.

The children were unable to act and had difficulty remembering their lines at first, so I had to coax it out of them. My main aim was that all of them should participate and feel included. We had mainly Afro-Guyanese children but also some Indo-Guyanese and Amerindian. I had inspiration for the musical side from a tape called "Sounds of Blackness": harmonious voices singing about the journey of slaves from the glorious African kingdoms of Ghana, Mali, and Songai into captivity. I thought its story would strike a chord with them and the beautiful melodies would help them to start singing in tune. I had been practising them since January and we were now beginning to raise the roof with harmonies they had never heard in the village schools before. Edwin had written a few extra songs to complement the cover versions we were using and provide a suitable finale. While we were in Georgetown to act as resource people for a

Ministry of Education teachers' course at Queen's College Campus, we bought a large tarpaulin to erect over our forecourt to shelter the audience watching our play.

The week before our final performances, we got word from the region that we had been formally recognised as a learning institution by Region 5 Administration. On the strength of my British teaching qualifications and experience, which I had been told no other teacher in the country possessed, I had also been given permission by the Exams Division in Georgetown to set and mark school based assessments for the Caribbean Examinations Council public examinations. This put us in a league above the myriad private 'bottom house schools' that proliferated as money-making side lines for any unqualified person who cared to set them up. Edwin, however, had not been selected as sports officer for the region after all. He was told by Mr Fraser that some of the Afro-Guyanese councillors from the district had voted against his nomination. That was a shock to him. Why had his own people on the regional committee been the ones to reject his leadership? They had been saying one thing to his face and something else behind his back. At least he now knew those councillors were not genuine.

The scenery I had made from plastic rice sacks stretched over two old clothes-drying screens and painted to look like the stone walls of an old plantation house was all set up under the house. Edwin had helped me to fix coconut branch thatch over it for a roof effect and we had wired stacks of sugar cane cut from the garden around our house pillars to disguise them. The man-powered sugar mill wheel we improvised from an old car tyre, with wooden broom handles stuck into it. We wrapped it at head height around a central pillar supporting the house. The children acting as slaves could turn it around as they sang Edwin's song evoking the slaves' daily toil. In the background behind them we placed our large palms in wooden planters. We rigged up an old heavy duty curtain on a metal pole between the stairs and the house pillars to hide Edwin sitting at his full drum console. He had been rehearsing with us for weeks under the house, so that he could know exactly when to supply atmospheric percussion to heighten the dramatic effect of certain scenes and accompany the songs. I had an amateur drama soundtrack tape including gunshots and the sound of a huge fire crackling which I would operate from behind the scenes while acting as a prompt. Our props were items from the museum and some extra new ones I got Clifford to make: a replica of a slave collar and a pair of cuffed slave chains based on pictures from history books. Everything was now ready and we had sold 37 tickets to various people from Georgetown. The price of the tickets had food factored in. I thought we should provide an appropriate post-performance meal of a calabash of 'ochro soup' with 'foo-foo' or green plantain dumplings and 'cankee' tied up in banana leaf parcels for dessert. Mauby, cane juice and water coconuts were available to drink. These were all traditional African foods that had been eaten on Emancipation Day since slavery times. The idea was for visitors to share in the traditional fare of the locals. Cousin Irene had cooked the food and was serving it dressed in one of the tie dyed African costumes we had commissioned the church sewing group to make for our dancers. After the decades of dour deprivation since the seventies, our festival was a colourful example of what tourists would now like to see. We had hoped to demonstrate this by our example to locals so they could understand what would be needed to make their embryonic eco-tourism industry begin to appeal to a wider market than just nature and wilderness lovers.

The performance was a huge success and went down particularly well with the people from Georgetown. Canadian High Commission diplomats came with their children as well as people who must have been a mixture of voluntary workers, tourists and educated Georgetown residents. We were asked lots of questions as the food was served after the show. They all gave unqualified praise. The word spread around those locals at the sheep show who had not bought tickets so we had extra sales for the show the following day. The second performance was packed with local people of all ages from Hopetown and other neighbouring villages. The children had to perform to a different type of audience this time. It was well behaved compared to the normal school shows, but we found it strange that they laughed at scenes that were meant to be tragic, so the drama was spoiled somewhat. It was all an educating process, for the children, for the local audience, and for us. At last people were beginning to understand and embrace what we were about. Edwin was stopped in the streets everywhere he went for the next few weeks by locals congratulating him on the show and what we were doing to keep Afro-Guyanese traditions alive in the community. The old folk were particularly encouraging of it. Many regretted missing it but soon got another opportunity as two weeks into August we had some more tourists staying with us and we had prepared our cast to do a repeat performance for them.

It was three days into their stay when we got news that our friend's house in number eight village had been "hit by a fireball". The house had been partially burnt but no one had been hurt, as she was visiting her son in America. It seemed that every time she went out of the country, something like this happened to her property. I already knew that the throwing of fireballs was a highland custom that could have come to Guyana with the importation of Scottish indentured workers after slavery ended. The woman at the gate was convinced that the fireball was a manifestation of supernatural power. These beliefs were very real in the credulous minds of simple villagers with little or no education. What was more disturbing was that articulate people with senior posts in the Ministry of Education held the same beliefs. They were supposedly qualified and educated but what kind of education had they received? I delved into the subject of African beliefs in the various historical pamphlets and emancipation magazines I had bought in the capital. It all seemed to be shrouded in secrecy. I supposed its appeal and thus its power over believers derived from this mystique. My own imagination could be captured by it, but superstition was not in my make-up. Supernatural portents could not scare me out of my wits. There was always a rational explanation. To my mind there was plenty of evil at large but it came from wicked people hiding in the shadows not from malevolent spiritual forces. I felt like I had been transported back to Elizabethan England and that Sir Walter Raleigh was probably still here in Eldorado after all.

Our tourists from Dubai, friends of mine from the school I used to teach at, departed at the end of August. They had visited Kaieteur Falls and Santa Mission, helped us run a sports fun-day at the snackette which drew people from Belladrum in the west to Ithaca in the east, and were the first of our guests to visit the Rupununi Savannahs via the Orinduik Falls. I had been a little surprised when they expressed horror at being offered monkey pepper-pot to eat by their host Amerindians. After all, it was traditional for indigenous people of the rainforest to eat the available meat that was around them. Clearly they would have to offer different fare to animal loving eco-tourists if they wanted them to recommend the Rupununi as an eco-tourist destination. However, it seemed to me fallacious to be so keen to see the natural environment preserved and yet not accept that indigenous humans are part of that environment and would like to preserve their customs and traditional lifestyle. Why should they have to adjust them to avoid offending the sensibilities of outsiders? Their horror at being offered for sale as souvenirs the stuffed dried heads of the endangered cock of the rock bird on sticks was perhaps a bit more justified. Taxidermy had been encouraged in Victorian times and the museum was full of specimens, so the local understanding was that white people still liked to buy stuffed wildlife curios and that was a commodity which they could supply for cash. It was a fact that Rastafarian artisans in Georgetown made a good living by selling stuffed baby alligators to American tourists. This was an extension of that trade. Not long after our friends returned to Dubai, we received a copy of a letter of complaint that they had sent to the Guyana government about these souvenirs being allowed for sale. Maybe it had the desired effect, because I never personally saw dead cock-of-the-rock souvenirs on sale, although the smuggling abroad of live wild birds remained rife. The need for improved education was thus patently obvious to our guests who went the extra mile in supporting us. After they learned from Edwin that he was going to use the money they had paid us for their board and lodging to buy enough sand to build a long jump pit in our back garden for his athletes to practice in, they pledged to raise funds when they got back to Dubai so they could send us some books and other educational materials to help us to teach more students more effectively.

As soon as they left, I prepared for the scheduled parents meeting I had sent letters home about at the final performance of our show. It was to give a statement of account of the proceeds of the ticket sales and the profits from it. We had just about covered the cost of the tie dye costumes, paint for the scenery and the food and drink we had provided, but nowhere near covered the eighteen thousand dollars for the tarpaulin. Still, we would have that for future events and ticket sales from those would eventually pay back Edwin. He used the meeting as an opportunity to announce his plans for the sports club students: two students from Sapodilla would be travelling to Trinidad next month to compete in a race. Edwin wasted no time in getting the sand pit installed. He had continued to train his athletes throughout the summer even though I closed off my classes at the same time as state schools ended their term. He was up at 5 a.m. every morning out on the street with them just before daybreak, so as to get the maximum benefit of the cool temperatures before the sun was above the rooftops. He was training them for the school sports in the Christmas term, but also he had entered his top two female athletes, a black girl from our village and an Indian girl from Cotton Tree Village, into the 'Women on the Move' 5 kilometre race in Port of Spain, Trinidad at the end of September. He had heard about it from Bruce, one of the CARDI consultants who had stayed with us, who was a keen distance runner. Bruce had offered to find free accommodation for the girls to make it possible for them to compete. Edwin could not afford to pay their fares as well as his own, but managed to get sponsorship from BWIA in Georgetown for reduced flight fares. He believed the girls could win and if they did, the prize money would cover the costs he would bear to make up the difference. He was determined to show that his methods of coaching and disciplined training would get the first wins for Guyanese schoolgirls in a women's international race. It was also a first to get any Indo-Guyanese girl in Guyana to compete in any athletics event. She had been training regularly and participating with equal treatment from Edwin, but suddenly had stopped attending. One of his younger athletes had handed him a folded note given to them by someone on a minibus.

"This is disgusting," he said, thrusting the note into my hand as he came in from training out on the street. I un-crumpled the scrap of exercise book and tried to decipher the anonymous childish scrawl on it. It was a death threat. In its illiterate language it said if Sookie came to Sapodilla again, she would die.

"No wonder she stopped turning up," I said. "What are you going to do about it?"

"I better go and see Teacher Bibi to find out more," he said. "Someone's jealous about her going on the Trinidad trip when they think it should be them-selves. I'll get to the bottom of it eventually." He had gone to Cotton Tree to investigate. Hours later, he returned but the anger was still festering.

"I spent a long time trying to persuade her parents to let her continue coming here," he said. "They're just simple fisher people, dirt poor. They live in a hovel on the waterside at Cotton Tree. They need her to help with the shrimping. She has to run miles along the beach every day, which is obviously why she has the ability to win races. They never had any interest in sport until I told them that she is the best in the country."

"Did you manage to persuade them to let her come back?" I asked.

"Well, they weren't keen, but I worked out a way with Teacher Bibi that she can be escorted in a taxi from her village to the top of this street,"

The Region Five school sports field events were hosted for the first time at our premises at the end of September. Although Edwin was disappointed that two of his javelins were broken and a tape measure got destroyed by misuse, at least the high jump bed and stands were safely monitored and since they did not need to be transported on trucks, were protected from damage in transit. For the first time the school sports were properly equipped and organised because this time he was in control of it. For the first time, long jumpers had a proper sand pit to jump into instead of a pit topped up with rice husks, which were, as he pointed out, likely to cause injury when wet. Hundreds of children and their accompanying teachers came into our garden and the surrounding areas which had been marked out for discus shot and javelin throws. Edwin wanted to prove that it was careful organisation that counted and not size of sports ground. He wanted to show them how the honest collection and banking of funds raised could be used to purchase equipment like ours, so that every school could eventually have their own instead of borrowing ours. It was an alien concept to them. They believed that any funds raised should boost their own pay packets which were miserably low. It would be difficult to get them to want to forgo this in the interest of investing in community property, because they did not trust themselves so could not trust others.

The very next day after the sports, he left with the two girls for Trinidad. It was the first time I had been left alone in the country while he went overseas. He didn't like leaving me alone but I was fine. I had my busiest days of classes on Fridays and Saturdays, so I did not have time to think about it. He returned in a blaze of glory in the early hours of Monday morning. Sookie had almost won the race and Michelle came third. They had been interviewed by press and TV in Trinidad and showered with gifts and money by well-wishers there.
"Now I'll have something good to write and tell Dave Hayes and the Poole Runners, to thank them for their letter of encouragement," he said.

He hardly had time to recover from the journey, unpack his things and tell me all the trials and tribulations of his trip, when we had unannounced visitors at the gate. This time it was two people from Emerald Towers resort on the Demerara who wanted to meet us as they had heard such a lot of good things about Sapodilla Health, Fitness and Organic Farm. We welcomed them in as usual and gave them a full guided tour of our premises. At the end of an exhausting couple of hours of our time, we realised that they had come mainly to find out what we were offering in the way of recreational activities for our guests so that they could get some ideas to copy at their place. This had become the familiar pattern of the way things were with our business. As far as Guyana was concerned, we were there to give and not to receive.

It was the start of a busy week as visitors from Germany were due to arrive for a seven day stay and we had to get the place ready for them. Then there was the excitement of getting to know these old friends of Edwin and in the middle of their stay, having to find room for one of the Munroe family children on her way to visit her father, the Reverend Pat in New Amsterdam. It was quite a culture shock for the German business people to witness a full on Saturday at Sapodilla with hundreds of children coming and going to my library, various classes and Edwin's sports activities all day. They had not been expecting the poverty and state of the country to be so bad. Coming to us from a luxury hotel in St Lucia, I think they expected it to be similar in Guyana. Unable to understand how we could bear living in such a place, they nevertheless admired our work and dedication. They left us with a promise to send funds to help us rent a photo copier so I could duplicate resources on site without having to get them done in Georgetown.

My classes for the new term were attracting a lot of interest and at registration time I had more Indo-Guyanese children than ever before. I could now teach and mark the school based assessments for CXC, so there were a lot of students who had failed in the state system and wanted to try for retakes. I signed up all the places available on registration day and yet as term progressed I had continual interruptions during my lessons by others wanting to join. The stream of new people continued unabated and it became a bit of a nuisance. I tried to deal with the problem by putting a large notice on the gate, but it did not seem to make any difference, probably because many of the applicant parents could not read. Word had got around in the Indo-Guyanese villages of Sookie's success and recent trip to Trinidad. The problem for me was that Sookie did not come to my classes, only to Edwin's sports club, but these people wanted their children to pass exams and not to do sport.

Then there came a big row between Edwin and me. He came home from a fruitless day at court in Georgetown which he had been notified by post about but when he got there, the hearing had been cancelled and Mr Ellis was no-where to be found. It was eight o'clock and I was still teaching in the classroom with all the lights on. He was furious,

"What are you doing still down here at this time of night?" he snapped and stomped off up-stairs. I was speechless. I quickly packed the children away and ushered them out of the classroom and gate and locked up behind them.

"I'm sorry, but I didn't think it mattered if I stayed down a bit longer to help them since you were in town and I knew you wouldn't get back till late," I said. I could see he was angry and I didn't like the way he was when he lost his temper because even though he would never use physical violence on a female, his voice was so loud and aggressive that it made me feel I had to apologise in order to calm him down. We had never had a row in all the years I had known him, so I did not want to start fighting back now.

"This has got to stop." He said. "When I come home at eight o'clock at night, I don't expect to find you down here teaching kids. What kind of life is this? I've been in Georgetown all day, it's been a nightmare, a complete waste of time and I haven't had anything to eat all day. Nello kept me waiting at the Berbice car-park to fill up his bus because I couldn't afford to take him as a special hire for the day, and then he farts around stopping off to pick up stuff from people all along the coast road home. At times like this I just feel like clearing off and letting them all get on with it. I've had enough of this shit-hole." He slammed the kitchen door and stormed off down to the other end of the house to get changed out of his sweaty, dusty and uncomfortable clothes. I rushed to put some food on to cook quickly so we could eat as soon as he had cooled off. It was the least I could do because I could imagine how he felt. He was still not speaking to me when we began to eat dinner, so we ate in silence. Then I thought I would try again.

"I'm really sorry," I said. "I was just trying to help them, they need so much help and I can't fit in any more pupils between half past three when they come out of school and six o'clock which is when you usually finish your training with the athletes. You're quite often out there with them still when it's starting to get dark at half past six, so I thought you wouldn't mind if I was too."

"It can't go on like this," he said. "Our lives are getting taken over by other people's children. It's not what I set out to do and it's not the way I want my life to be."

I could see that the point of no return had been reached. I was worried that he would really just clear off and leave me there running my little charity school. He sounded like he really meant it. I did not know if he had done that sort of thing in the past, but I knew I had been abandoned in the past by my previous husband. Was I revisiting that sort of experience? If he just cleared off while I was in Guyana, how would I exist? Where would I get the money to support myself from? I felt as though I had done something terribly wrong but I hadn't meant to. I fought back my tears,

"I promise I'll not do it again. I'll change the classes and tell them they'll have to come in the daytime during the same hours as the state schools. The only classes I'll have after school hours will be the French and art classes that will end at five o'clock latest." He seemed to have calmed down when he saw me crying and what I said seemed to take the sting out of his anger. We kissed and made up and I felt relieved. Then he started to unload all the annoying things that had happened that day in Georgetown and I listened with a sympathetic ear as always.

The next few days I carried out my promise and with all new students who wanted to enrol for CXC classes, I told them that classes would only be held during the school day or else I could not help them. That stopped the flow of applicants from interrupting my lessons at last. Edwin had come back with avengeance from Trinidad and wanted to be able to prepare his potential international athletes for plenty more overseas competitions. The main obstacle was their poor education in the state system. Then, there was a crisis at the local secondary school in Bushlot. Michelle, Edwin's top athlete who had been one of the students in my Saturday class since I first started the library lessons in 1993, came to training late and upset.

"Auntie Jane, me get no teacher fo' me CXC exam. Zem teacher all lef' school fo' go wo'k in Barama Company an' zey en't get no replacement teacher," We were both concerned to hear this. It appeared that there was a shortage of teachers because some had left in the summer and replacements had not been found, but the problem had been made worse by Barama, a Korean plywood company opening up a new factory in the country. They were paying wages much higher than elsewhere and the teachers from our area had left en masse to go and work there. I wrote a letter to the headmaster of Bushlot School offering a temporary solution to the problem. I was qualified to teach all the subjects that the CXC classes were missing. Although I could not leave our house during the daytime because I needed to be present at home to allow building workers to get on with their jobs while Edwin was doing his job at the neighbourhood council. I had available time during the school days, so I would be willing to teach the local CXC syllabus to his students in the exam preparation year until they found replacement teachers for those vacant positions. I would teach them free of charge if they could be allowed to leave school and visit our premises for a whole afternoon on two days a week. I would keep a register and feedback to him if any student were absent, so that legal requirements to register students would be adhered to. I had already discussed this with the students and they were excited to hear it. I also had permission from the Regional Education Officer and was an officially recognised Learning Institution in the region. I had the letter delivered to the headmaster by hand and waited for a reply. I got none. When I enquired as to why at the Regional Education Office, I was told that the Ministry had no control over what an individual head teacher wished to happen in their school. Maybe the parents were against the idea.

I called a parents' meeting to discuss the proposition with parents of all my students. It was well attended and parents declared themselves willing to sign a petition to the headmaster if I worded it. I did so and they all signed it except for one, whose mother taught at that school. All the other parents agreed to go with me to the school with the petition. I wrote to the head to ask for a meeting. Edwin visited the school in his capacity as chairman and demanded to see the headmaster. He eventually managed to find Mr Faraz and arranged an appointment with him to meet the parents who had signed the petition. Later that week, we all met at Sapodilla in the late afternoon and walked together with Edwin to Bushlot School. Mr Faraz showed us into an empty classroom and we sat down. I spoke on behalf of the parents and set out the case as to why we had felt it necessary to be there. Mr Faraz listened and when I had finished, assured me that there was no shortage of teachers and that all vacancies had been filled. At this, one of the parents challenged his assertion and others joined in vociferously. I said I did not see what his problem was, as the ministry had already sanctioned students to visit our premises for sports activities and preparation for the schools athletics championships. He said that parents of the other children in the said classes were not happy to let their children walk to Sapodilla in school time. The parents with me started to accuse the school of not getting good exam results and I said I would be able to improve their results for them. He said they did not need to be improved.

"Then can you tell us what the top CXC grades at the school were in the recent exams for History, English and Geography?" I asked.

"I do not recall," he said. The parents murmured, sucking their teeth. They knew that the results had been published in the newspapers and not one student from Bushlot School had passed in those subjects.

"Mrs Joseph," he said, "If I allow my students to come to your lessons in this manner, the other teachers at my school will be demoralised."

"Well," I said. "If I were one of these parents sitting here listening to you saying that, I would not be very happy because it seems that you are more interested in the feelings of your teachers than in the education of these people's children." I thanked him for his time and walked out with the parents following me. As soon as we were out in the street, they all started talking and voicing their discontent with his decision. One of them was Mr Baljeet, father of the little Indo-Guyanese boy who had joined my classes when he was thirteen and had been the most enthusiastic student of the lot, never missing a class and never arriving late.

"Why ya don't set up private school and then we tek de children out a Bushlot school an' send 'em to you?" he said.

"Well, it sounds like a good idea, but I can only teach a few of the subjects they need to have and it costs a lot of money to employ other people even local people, so I would have to charge fees that none of you would be able to afford. The only subjects that I could offer would be English Language, English Literature, History, Geography, Social Studies and possibly Food and Nutrition. That would be theory only, because I don't have practical facilities for a class. I couldn't teach maths as I'm not properly qualified for that."

"Dem chil'ren na get no mat' in school anyhow, so it mek no diff'rence. At lease dem could get some subjec's if you a teach 'am."

"Well if you put it like that, I can see your point. I'll have to think it over because it's a big step to take," I said, "I'll get back to you when I've had a few days to see if I can come up with a plan. They looked happy at the thought of the suggestion and said their goodbyes as we dispersed in different directions. I spent a week or so drafting up a plan for how I could proceed with an unfunded private school and tried to cost out an affordable fee. I explained it to the children and got a duplicate letter setting out how much I would have to charge, with a reply slip at the bottom for parents to sign if they thought they wanted me to go ahead with the plan and could afford the fee. As expected, only one letter came back saying that they could afford the fee as long as they could pay it in three instalments. That was from the Indian boy's parent. The other parents wanted the private school but could not afford the stated fee. I discussed it at length with Edwin.

"I think we should go ahead. The education system here is a shambles and the people running it should be ashamed of themselves. We need to show them how it should be done," he said. "I'll give you all the support you need. I'll see where we can get help and funding but just go ahead with it regardless."

"I don't want it to be an all-Indian fee-paying school but it seems highly unlikely that there'll be any black children if they have to pay fees. The whole point of it all is to help your black athletes as well as any Indian ones you have."

We both agreed that it looked like the tourism business was never going to happen because eco-tourists were mainly a British or European phenomenon and that Americans wanted their sun, sea and sand in luxury. The distance from England and Europe made the fare unaffordable for most eco-tourist types. The occasional business customer like CARDI consultants would not really be a problem. We got so few real tourist applicants that we would have to tell any other interested holiday makers that they must come during school holiday time from then on.

I decided to let the children whose parents had said they couldn't afford the fees, know that I would be going ahead but to be fair, I would not be charging any fees who-ever they were even if they had said they could afford them. All children would be treated the same. I would start it off with the students I already had who were aged 13 or above and were about to begin the first year of CXC courses in the state system. I would include all the older students who had left the state system and were currently attending my classes. I would continue my Saturday classes and I would therefore have to have one day off in the week, so full time students would have to attend on Saturdays as well but stay at home on Tuesdays, which was when we might have to go to Georgetown from time to time. I would start the full time school the following Monday for those who wanted to join it. Thus it was that on Monday November 6th 1995, my full time charity secondary school at Sapodilla Learning Centre began. It was a desperate measure to cope with a desperate situation and things did not look like getting better any time soon.

"Brooster's at the gate, Edwin," I called out when I heard the bell ring one afternoon later that week and saw the familiar face of Edwin's school-friend in his Anglican cassock standing there. I was busy preparing some 'bok-crabs' that had been brought to the gate for us that morning. They were in season and we looked forward to this annual treat of their soft pink flesh, devilled with local scotch bonnet peppers and tomatoes in a spicy sauce I concocted. It was a messy, fiddly job though and I had a bucket full of them to do because there was not much meat in each one. It usually took at least an hour. I just finished and was washing my hands when Edwin entered the kitchen with an ashen face.

"How's Brooster?" I asked, offering him a glass of water and wondering if his expression was because of a dehydration headache.

He pulled out a stool and sat down on it before answering. He looked as if he was going to be sick.

"Brooster was very shaken up," he said at length. "He just told me something very terrible." I looked hard at him, not knowing what to expect. "He told me he's just been sent down from St George's Cathedral in Georgetown to investigate the murder of the white Anglican priest at Fort Wellington Anglican church. He had just been to the scene of the crime and identified the body. He wanted me to help him to deal with it."

"Murder?" I said, shocked. "I didn't even know there was a white Anglican priest at Fort Wellington."

"Well, he was in charge of all the Anglican churches between here and Belladrum. He hasn't been in the country long and he couldn't stay at the manse in Fort Wellington because it was too run down and in need of repair, so although he did services in Hopetown, they put him in the newly built house belonging to the church at Belladrum. He did services at Belladrum church, which is opposite and then travelled to the other churches from there. Apparently he'd been a missionary here years ago when he was a young man and now he was quite elderly, he'd decided to come back because he saw a vacancy here. Brooster was shaking. He said it was a brutal murder and that the poor old man's body had been mutilated and his organs removed like a ritual sacrifice."

"It happened in the church at Fort Wellington?" I asked in disbelief.

"No, in the house he was living in at Belladrum. Apparently he was very friendly with all the community there and used to let them come in and out of his house as they pleased just like people do at Taa's house. He would sit and eat or take a drink with them and did a lot of work with the community, helping people."

"It seems all the more horrible that he should be taken advantage of for being so open and available to the people." I said and started to compare his situation with our own. Suddenly I felt all the more justified in our determination to keep our gate and our door firmly locked at nights so as not to let local adults have free access into the house upstairs.

"Brooster wanted me to go with him to Belladrum and help him to ask a few questions, but I said I didn't think it would be a good idea for me to go. Those people are really strange up there and hearing my English cockney accent will put their backs up. They see me as an outsider as it is and if I go asking questions like I'm taking over the job of the police, it'll be counter-productive. At least Brooster speaks like them and hasn't lived overseas for forty two years. He stands a chance of finding out more than I do."

"Do you think they killed him because he was white?" I asked.

"The police have no idea who it was or what their motive might have been. Brooster's been told to keep very quiet about the matter. It looks like it's going to be a cover-up by the police and the authorities, but the Anglican church in England have to have a full report because he was a British citizen. That's why they sent Brooster down. It's obvious that the crime will go unpunished."

"Maybe the way he was killed says something," I said. "Maybe they didn't want to hear him preach the Christian morality to them. They didn't want an outsider coming into their midst and telling them to change their behaviour." I kept thinking of the Kumfa rituals I had read of and the beliefs that strength would transfer to the body of the living from the spirit of the dead if their heart were consumed. I wondered what family the old man had to grieve over him in England and what details if any, they would get to know about his death. Would his body be repatriated or buried in Guyana? Once again I compared his situation with my own. I could take small comfort from the fact that I was not there as an overseas missionary, preaching unwelcome beliefs to the local adults, but as the wife of a locally born Afro-Guyanese, a descendant of a slave whose sweat and toil had earned him a right to be in this community. I was helping their children to pass examinations so they could find employment and improve their families' income, and I was not trying to change their beliefs by telling them that their own beliefs were wrong. I was leaving beliefs well alone. Preaching had never been my style. I tried to set an example of good behaviour which might inspire others to emulate. All the same, it was a bit close for comfort and I now for the first time felt a great sense of unease about our situation. Justice as I understood it was indeed non-existent here.

Chapter 17

Law, Disorder and Cocaine

A thirteen year-old boy, Robin, stood in front of me in the mud-floored classroom under our house, expectantly awaiting the start of his full time education for CXC exams in the Sapodilla Free Charity School. I can remember no occasion in my life up to that point, when I had felt more responsible for another person's life. His parents had withdrawn him from the state school up the road in an extraordinary act of faith in me. He had been in my classes since they opened four years earlier and had grasped with both hands every new opportunity I had so far offered to my students. There were seven girls and three other boys to start with. Some were already 'failed' older school leavers. I would now have to prepare timetables and work for these eleven students for the next two years on a daily basis without fail in order to take them through the public examination system in a two year course, supposed to be equivalent to the English GCSE. I would get no pay for it but would have to put in all my available time to prepare and mark their work in the same way as I had done when paid to teach in England and in Dubai. Instead of having to teach one or two subject areas to hundreds of children in a week, I would be teaching eight or nine different subjects to occupy these few students for every single lesson. Now there would be no time for me to entertain tourists in hotel style except in the school holidays, but we had already realised that Guyana was not a destination likely to take off in its tourism sector in the near future. No income was coming in apart from Edwin's British army retirement pension, and we were getting no help from any government or charitable funding agency. I set about my new responsibility with my usual professionalism. It would have helped to have money to pay for adequate resources, but the most important resource as far as I was concerned, was my brain, qualifications and experience. I knew I would be able to get these children to pass and prove that they were not genetically backward just because they lived in a remote village. I would also prove that as long as a teacher cared and carried out their duties professionally, resources were not needed. Edwin and I had already agreed that a condition of attendance at the school would be that all students would have to study all the subjects I offered, including physical education and that he would take the full timers for that every afternoon at four o'clock, at the end of the full time school day. They would join in with his sports club athletes. This would enable me to continue to teach my primary and prep classes coming to me from the other local schools at the end of their day.

Abiola had started work as a primary teacher in a village further up the coast because her mother had connections with the regional Ministry of Education. However, she had failed most of her CXC exams and for some reason wanted to take English Literature and Caribbean History, which no local school offered. She reluctantly agreed to submit herself to my full timetable because she wanted these two subjects so badly. She had been thrown out of her primary school job, owing to her indiscipline and disgusting personal habits but I was unaware of this fact until I had already signed her on as a full time pupil. During the first week of lessons, I found out for myself what she was like and she discovered what a good teacher does to get good behaviour out of badly behaved teenagers. Strict discipline did not mean lashes, but it did mean that the gate was locked and would remain so if you arrived late. It also meant you were given one warning not to misbehave again or you would be excluded from the premises and that this threat would definitely be carried out if you persisted. She soon conformed. It was also a good signal to the others as to their own fate should they slide into the lax attitudes prevalent in all areas of school and work in the wider community.

Later that week there was a night time shooting and killing in the village that involved some of a neighbour's family. I thought back to Patrick Britton, the man who had moved back to Hopetown from the USA last year. He had a huge house with a swimming pool built in a compound surrounded by high walls. He also had a gas station on the main road leading out of the village. He had a reputation for making big hand-outs among the local youth who swarmed around his premises where they could watch blue movies all night on his massive TV screen. Mr Nedd who helped Edwin with the Sapodilla Sports Club, had become friendly with this apparently wealthy and generous newcomer and had been feeding him with information about us. Nedd apparently hoped to get a sports strip and shoes for all the athletes from Britton and had put in a request. He had taken Edwin to Britton's house to meet him but Edwin did not like what he saw and had decided to avoid both the place and the man. He thought he was a drugs dealer who had plenty of cash to spend on building a property locally, while using the boys to carry packages of drugs for him. We had no proof, but he had boasted to Edwin that he had bought a vehicle for the local police. He had tried to suck up to Edwin offering him donations for the club in order to gain his friendship and some respectability from him by association. Edwin would have none of it and gave Britton a wide berth. He could not stop our athletes from visiting Britton's house or accepting sports gear from him, but he did not want to associate with someone who had a shady reputation. Patrick Britton stood for everything we despised. We were squeaky clean and wanted to remain so. We had set out to influence the local youth to avoid this easy route to an income. Mixing with narco-traffickers could only harm our respectable image. The sheer audacity of his sucking up to Edwin to gain sham respectability for him-self thereby, had made my blood boil. Besides, the fact that he was giving hand-outs to anyone who asked him for them, directly contradicted any message we had been working at delivering to local youth. How would they now believe that the only way to get on in life was the way that we had done it: by hard work at our education and hard work in the highly paid jobs we consequently got. His presence in the village now suggested that maybe we had gained the wealth to buy our property in the same way that he had: by trafficking narcotics.

By Christmas that year I had got into a good routine with the full time students and along with the part timers in the Saturday classes, was putting on a puppet show using the papier-mache rainforest animal puppet heads they had made in my art classes. Since I had sent for another portable TV to use in the classroom with the spare English system video player we had also imported a year ago, I was able to show appropriate educational programmes or clips of them in many different subject lessons every day. I had a large collection of these which I had recorded while teaching in Dubai and now they came in really useful. I was also doing lots of practical work in lessons, such as basic starch tests in food and nutrition, compass and map reading in Geography. This was fun and much more meaningful than just listening to an explanation then writing notes, yet practical work was never done in local state schools. Mac had helped us by organising a visit for our students to the Burma sheep project he was running. This enabled me to use it as a local example of a farm as a system for their geography CXC.

Edwin vowed he would try to get us help from whatever quarter he could. In his role as Chairman of the Neighbourhood District Council, he had been advised of a training scheme for unemployed school leavers which was being organised by the Social Impact Amelioration Project, a Canadian backed funding agency known as SIMAP. He immediately felt that this could help our students. The agency would pay the participants a small weekly stipend if they were engaged in a practical work training programme provided by an employer. He said that it allowed for the training of librarians and since we had a library, we would qualify. He arranged for a visit from the field worker setting up the project in our area. It went quite well except that I had to argue my case for being allowed to do a tourism work experience rather than train librarians. I had no real idea how to train a librarian properly but I had a good idea how to train tour guides and employees of an international tourism resort and was already teaching the necessary subjects to cater for this. Edwin was also teaching them sport and recreation management, which was a useful skill for any employee of a tourism resort to have on offer to a prospective employer. We were already registered with the Ministry of Tourism as an eco-tourism resort and had had plenty of tourists staying with us. Guyana needed suitably trained employees to develop its embryonic tourism industry. It all seemed to make perfect sense to me. I had prepared a detailed syllabus for our Tourism Course which we had been promised University of Guyana Certification for. We were accepted. I was not going to get any funding for the school, but at least the stipends for the students would enable them to save up for the thirty five thousand Guyana dollars they would have to pay to enter the CXC exams, since private school students were not given free examination entry like those in state schools. I added the extra elements of the tourism course into the students' timetable and began integrating it into teaching every subject lesson. There were a number of other parents who had approached me to take their children into the full time school I had already begun, but I turned them down as I had already started the courses and new students had already missed significant work. I did not want to become a mopping up operation for itinerant families or drop-outs with learning difficulties, so I made it obligatory that entry into the full time school could only be by pupils who had a minimum of three years in my part time classes and had passed my entrance exam. Most people understood when I explained this to them, and accepted that we had to adopt such rules. The main drawback of being on the SIMAP scheme was that I was now obliged to accept some additional participants selected for me by the organisers. They had not taken my standard entrance exam, so might not have been capable of the standard of work required. I had been forced to bend my rules and appeared to have double standards. That was a state of affairs I was most unhappy about. It did not take long for these girls to drop out one by one, however. They did not like having to comply with the homework I set and Edwin's physical education sessions.

One morning on a Sunday in the early part of the New Year, I was sitting on the veranda marking the students' homework when a brand new Mercedes car turned off the public road into our mud street. This was a sight never before seen in the country.

"What lunatic would try and drive a vehicle like that into a place like this? For that matter, what lunatic would even have a car like that in this country?" I asked Edwin who was coming up the steps at the time.

"Oh that's that Britton bloke," he said. "He's been driving around the village in it since he shipped it here. I heard he's brought his two teenage kids from America here and he's letting them drive it around without a licence, so I told the police, but no doubt he's bribed them to turn a blind eye."

"Letting kids without a licence drive a brand new Mercedes?" I said, horrified. "Look! Whoever's behind the wheel can't steer it properly. It's going in the trench! Oh no! I don't believe it. It's sinking in sideways!" The occupant on the higher side of the car then decided to open the door and get out, shouting and gesticulating at the driver, who then opened his door and let all the muddy water into his side as he clambered out through the waist high bisi-bisi reeds filling the trench. Normally only grazing cattle did such a thing. Both of them were kids of about ten and twelve. The Indian man from the house they were outside had been watching from his kitchen steps and came down to assist them. He started directing them to go and fetch their father. It would need a tractor to haul the vehicle out of the trench and he would have to pay for that service. An hour or so went by while the once gleaming Mercedes slowly slipped deeper into the mud. Then a tractor appeared and several men with ropes. The titanic wreck was eventually pulled out of the mire and slowly towed away.

"David Nedd told me he wants to see you about getting his kids into your full time school," Edwin said as we watched them disappear out of sight.

"Well he'll have to take them somewhere else," I said. "I'm doing this to help poor local kids who were born in this village and thus have no opportunity to get a decent education. I'm not providing a free service to Yankee drug dealers for their spoilt and badly behaved offspring. He should have left them in America with their mother, where they get educated by the state-paid teachers."

291

Later that day, a man rang the manual bell on our gate post. Edwin went down and spoke to him, then let him in and spent a while talking to him under the house. After a while, he called me down to meet the visitor.

"Jane, this is Patrick Britton. He wants to ask you to take his children into your full time school. I already explained to him that we have rules here, but he wants to speak to you himself." I looked at the man dispassionately as he tried to flatter me about my excellent local reputation as a teacher.

"I'm sorry Mr Britton, but I'm completely full up with students and have no more room. I suggest you get them in at the local state school instead."

"I can get you a new photocopier and computers for your school if you agree to take my sons on," he said.

"Mr Britton, it's very kind of you but even, if you built a new classroom for me, my answer would be the same. I have no more places in the school and will not be taking on any more full time students for another two years, once the current set have taken their exams. Besides, I have a system that entry to the full time school is only for children who've been in my part time classes for at least two years before they reach the age for exam level work. Unfortunately I have no space in any of the part time classes either. There will be no more new admissions until September."

"I told you she won't change her rules for anyone," said Edwin.

"Mrs Joseph, I'm begging you," the man whined in his Brooklyn drawl. "I need my boys to get a good education."

"Well I'm afraid you should have thought about that before you brought them here from New York," I said. "I wish you luck, but I really do have to get on with my work now." I turned and went back upstairs, leaving Edwin to carry on with some small talk and eventually get him out of the gate.

"I never want to see that man on this premises again," I said to Edwin when Britton had gone out of sight.

"Don't worry, you won't have to. I told him once you make up your mind about something, not even I can make you change it."

"Did you say anything to him about what happened to his car this morning?"

"Yes, he said it was a terrible mess and someone was cleaning it out for him."

"Well I hope that's the last we see of him anywhere near us!" I said, but although I held the pathetic little man in contempt, I feared what he could do to the youth in the local community by flashing so much money around indiscriminately. It put me in mind of the video documentary I had about the "golden triangle" in Burma, so I began working out a way to show it to my full time students and then discuss and debate the drugs issue with them. It was important for me to get the message across to them that no matter how much the offer of donations might tempt us when we really needed funds for resources, we would not accept anything from drug dealers or criminals of any sort.

One of the worries we had about operating a full time school was how we could get help from a funding agency to support what we were doing. None of the children had parents who could afford to pay any realistic fees. They had only the State education system to provide a free education and that had let them down badly. I did not want to be running a private fee-paying school only open to the children of rich professionals from Georgetown or local drug barons. It had not occurred to either of us at that time that funding-agencies can only operate in a country with the consent of its government. Getting help from one would require setting up a democratically elected constitution to govern the school. We had already gone through many of these hoops, using our parents to vote a committee based on a constitution that I had drawn up and they approved. They elected me as their president and other parents as reluctant office holders and committee members. They had nothing to do, really, except check over my records and accounts when we had meetings. We needed an auditor to sign off the annual accounts but would have to find one willing to do it free of charge, since we had no funds coming in apart from small contributions of 800 Guyana dollars a year per part time pupil (equivalent to £4 sterling) and what Edwin and I donated to make up the shortfall in covering photocopying expenses, stationary, art materials and electricity usage. My request for an auditor had been met by the Georgetown Rotary Club. A member, Mr Hing, offered his time. He kindly showed me how to set out the accounts and accompanying receipt book. Our constitution had, after much chasing around the bureaucracy in Georgetown, been officially registered as a Friendly Society with the approval of the responsible Minister of Cooperatives, Henry Jeffrey. That was the only way we could achieve official charity status.

I really wanted to be able to get a volunteer to teach maths and science to the children so they would get a more rounded timetable than what I alone could manage. I was already teaching basic practical maths but did not feel confident in taking them through CXC exams with what I knew. Why couldn't we get a VSO to help us? Edwin took me on my day off to see Rita and Helen at the VSO office in Georgetown. They had stayed with us when they had their annual teachers' conference. Helen was very frank with me. The VSO were not going to be bringing any more English teachers to Guyana to teach in the schools around the country because it was unsustainable. Their new policy was to send people to the colleges to train Guyanese teachers to teach better so they would eventually no longer need any help. It seemed to make sense but did not solve the immediate problems our students faced. We had received a surprise pre-Christmas parcel of a video camera from our friend Mitch, the former VSO printing expert back in England, who had kept in touch with us over the years. He had raised funds to get a replacement for the camera Edwin had lost in the savannah quick-sands during the jaguar photo-shoot. Mitch wanted Edwin to film Sapodilla athletes in action, send him the video, and he would use it to raise funds in his own sports club to cover the costs of shipping their own unwanted sports clothing and shoes to our club athletes. Mitch, who saw himself as a journalist, was now issuing a professional looking newsletter entitled "Sapodilla Today" to his and our friends and supporters, keeping them up to date with our progress. Maybe he could use his free newsletter to appeal for a qualified graduate teacher volunteer to come and help us by teaching maths and science in a gap-year. It was worth a try.

Mitch responded with his usual enthusiasm, although he seemed to think there would be no takers unless we were able to pay a young person not only their return fare and board, but also a monthly allowance of spending money with which they could enjoy their free time. Such a fundraising feat he did not feel equal to, given that he was working full time and had a family to consider. We fully understood and told him that it wasn't up to him to do the fundraising, but up to the individual concerned. If he could just use his newsletter to cast out a wide net appealing for potential volunteers, then that would be great. We said that since we were volunteering without any allowance from anyone, surely a young person somewhere would be willing to do the same if they could get a free return fare to exotic and tropical South America and that once they got to us, we would provide their safe luxury digs on site and feed them. It would be up to them to find their own spending money. We couldn't afford to pay out any kind of allowance, but one extra mouth to feed would be not too much of a problem from Edwin's small retirement pension. Mitch agreed to do this and soon carved out his own self-appointed mission to "run the extra marathon" on our behalf.

Christmas 2005 had brought Sapodilla Learning Centre another unexpected surprise present as well as the camera from Mitch. Edwin's longstanding German friends who had stayed with us back in October had decided to commit a regular donation to enable us to rent a Xerox photocopier from Georgetown. They would send us the money in advance in two six monthly instalments for as long as we needed it, starting with their enclosed cheque to Edwin. This was fantastic news. First thing in the New Year, we went into town and signed up the contracts for the rental agreement. Although I had used some of my own savings to buy small sets of suitable new text books for the Geography and Food and Nutrition courses in the misplaced hope that SIMAP would eventually refund them, I could not do the same for all the other courses. I needed to photocopy pages from many different books as well as my purpose-made work-sheets to cope with the needs of all my students. Now this would be no problem as I would have a copier on site. Things were looking up. I took my accounts for the year into Mr Hing to be audited and began to fulfill my promise to Mitch to teach the full time students to make a tourism video to send to him. If they could highlight the culture of the country, the history and landscape they were learning about in a brief "video guided tour" as Mitch had suggested, and if I could send him a copy of it, then he would use it to entice and prepare any prospective volunteer to fulfil our request for a maths and science teacher. Mitch also mooted the idea of an 'exchange' visit between an English youth group and Sapodilla students, with the English group visiting us first and then reciprocating when our full timers had completed their exams in two years' time. It wouldn't be a true exchange though, because we would have to house all the English students free of charge in our guest rooms for their own health and safety, whereas our students would stay in the homes of the English students free of charge when they visited England and all funds would be raised in England to cover the cost of their travel. It sounded a great idea and Edwin seized on it as a useful 'carrot' to incentivise our students to stick at their studies and attendance with us.

Edwin's Aunt Lucy lived opposite and was the local 'bush medicines' quack. I persuaded her to talk to our students about local plants used in her remedies.

She was reluctant to divulge the secrets of her craft but I explained that we would only be using the knowledge to make displays in our museum to interest possible overseas visitors. The students, armed with the notes they made, scripted and acted out their own demonstrations while they took turns at doing the filming and interviewing. Both Afro- and Indo-Guyanese students had learned to do the African dances in costume, so we put on a short dancing display while I filmed them. Then the mother of one of the Indo-Guyanese girls invited us to her home built in late Victorian times by her father, an original indentured worker, from the disbanded plantation house in Cotton Tree village. She had donated some of her heirlooms from the house to our museum before her brother who had inherited it, pulled it down to build a new concrete block house in its place. Once again the students filmed their interviews with her and their subsequent exploration of the archaeological remains of the plantation house hidden in the regrown jungle in the Cotton Tree 'back-dam.' A local Indian peasant farmer showed us the cache of original earthenware bottles and brick remains of the oven and chimney. He fired the imagination of the students with his stories of Dutch planters' ghosts surrounding the massive old 'silk-cotton' trees which had given their name to the plantation. The students were really getting an all-round educational experience. After Edwin's visit to the TV station in New Amsterdam to respond to issues raised with him on council matters, they sent reporters and camera to Sapodilla to film our students at work on their course and the facilities and gym they had access to. This media attention excited the students and the community as they were now gaining national exposure. News of this spread even though very few people in the village had access to a television to see it. Everything was going upwards and we were on a high.

The falling down to earth with a bang came in February. We had just returned from Georgetown where we had gone to collect our audited accounts from Mr Hing. We had hardly got into the house when one of the students came running over to greet us with a worried look on her face. She was clearly distressed.

"Antie Jane, a man come from Jarjetong axin' question about ze school an' what lesson' we do an' all kind a ting,"

"Oh?" I said.

"What's the problem Kelta?" Edwin asked.

"Apparently some man from Georgetown has been here while we were in town, asking about the school and interrogating the children about what they get taught in my lessons," I said. "Was it Mr Shamshudeen?" I asked her, thinking it might be the field officer who normally delivered the packets containing their stipends.

"No Antie Jane, me never see 'im before. He seh he bin inspector for SIMAP."

"What did he want to know?"

"If we does do cookin' and cleanin' an' so."

"And what did you tell him?"

"Me seh we does do readin' an' writin' an' watch video an' ting an' we writin' CXC exam." She looked anxious as if she feared some kind of punishment.

"Don't worry, Kelta, you told him the right things. See you tomorrow morning as usual."

Edwin and I discussed the matter over dinner. We had expressly told the field officer that we worked on Saturdays and took another day off in lieu so we always closed the school on Tuesdays. We could not understand why the inspector had come on the very day we were closed and instead of returning when we were present, had asked questions about us behind our backs. It was as if he had deliberately chosen to visit us when it appeared we were not doing what we were supposed to be doing and use that to gather evidence against us. Perhaps after we had been publicised recently on local television, he wanted to make sure we were not using the scheme to pay for servants to do our cooking and cleaning for us. At least Kelta had disproved that. Maybe the inspector would come back later in the week so we could explain ourselves properly. Our discussion continued with the students in class next morning, but none of them knew anything about it apart from Kelta. About half an hour into the start of the lesson, Mr Shamshudeen arrived and informed us that there would be no more payments for our students. They were bitterly disappointed at this news and asked why. He replied that we were a school and not a workplace according to the inspector. Edwin said we would be appealing against the decision and wanted the inspector to visit us by appointment when we would all be present for him to see what was really going on in our establishment instead of believing hearsay from people who did not know. I reassured the students that we would carry on as before. I was sure the inspector had misunderstood the situation.

I wrote to SIMAP asking for an appointment for another visit by the inspector, explaining why we had not been open when he called. Eventually I received a curt reply notifying us he would revisit us on March 14th. An officious little man arrived at the gate that day and introduced himself as Mr Simpson. I gave him a guided tour of the entire premises while the children were getting on with work I set them. His main argument was that we were a school and not a work-place. I wanted to show him that we were a workplace as we were a tourism business that was trying to support the charity school beneath it in order to help develop local youth. We intended to give them proper employment opportunities when they were adequately trained. The country villages had few opportunities for them other than subsistence farming and schools or the offices of the police and regional government. They tended to loiter and become thieves or drug mules if they did not move off to Georgetown or else face the dangers of the 'gold bush' to look for work. It was even worse for girls whose choices also included prostitution and teenage pregnancy.

"The student I interviewed in your absence told me that they never do any practical work, just lessons using books and they are "writing CXC exams," said Mr Simpson.

"But that's not true!" I protested, "They do practical work all the time. I mean yes, it's true that they do work from books so they understand the theory but the girl you spoke to isn't very bright. She doesn't realise that the making of a guided tour around the landscape and of our museum that I just showed you, is practical work. She forgot about the fact that only a couple of weeks ago, they all went on a field trip and made a tourism video about the local environment and history."

"She said they have never done any cooking or made any beds or cleaned the floors,"

"Well she's right!" I said. "I want them to learn better things than just doing the manual labour which they can learn very quickly in a few hours before they need to do it."

"But you cannot do cooking without practical work in the kitchen."

"Of course, I know that and we will be doing plenty of that later on but before they do any of it, I want to teach them all about the principles of the food and nutrition that they will be serving and they are doing practical experiments in the classroom to help them understand that better," I explained. I showed Mr Simpson into the classroom and introduced him to all the students. "Perhaps you would like to ask Mr Simpson some questions about the scheme and tell him why you think he should change his mind and reinstate you on it," I said.

The next half an hour they spent firing a barrage of polite intelligent questions at him and arguing away his replies with well-reasoned points. They destroyed him so he did not have a leg to stand on. I was very taken aback and impressed by their performance. Mr Simpson did not flinch. At the end of it all he said he was not going to change his mind,

"I have seen for myself that this is a school, NOT a plant." And with that he picked up his folder and turned to leave the classroom. I followed him out to open the gate, fuming with anger.

"What do you mean, not a plant? Of course we're not a plant, This is a plant!" I said sarcastically, pointing at a large palm in a pot by the gate. He ignored me, calmly waddled out and without turning back to meet my gaze, continued up the street to the main road to catch a minibus back to Georgetown.

The children were very upset about the unfairness of it all. They pointed out that other people on the scheme were just sitting around in offices at the region doing nothing all day except running out to the shop to buy drinks and lunches for the staff there. They weren't learning anything useful to make them more employable or learning to do the real jobs at the region. Others were going to a local mechanic and collecting their stipend and then going home again for the rest of the week. They weren't learning any new workplace skill either. The examples kept being cited until a clear picture of discrimination had emerged. We resumed our normal timetable of work. At the end of the day, I told them I was sorry about what had been decided, but as far as I was concerned I would continue as normal and would see them the next day. I would understand if any of them should drop out now that they were not going to get their stipend. The volume of their chatter as they all went up the street left no one in any doubt that they felt aggrieved. I was pretty sure that Abiola would not appear again after that.

The next morning all students turned up as usual. Even Abiola was there. I was pleasantly surprised and felt vindicated. They were not just there for the money. They genuinely enjoyed what we were doing. There was so much variety, so many different skills and they were learning easily because it was not dull. That evening before I turned in, I sat down and wrote a letter of complaint to the board of SIMAP and similar ones to the Minister of Labour and a top female lawyer in Georgetown, Josephine Whitehead, whose articles on discrimination against women in Guyana, I had recently read in the national newspaper. I set out in great detail our case, suggesting that we were being discriminated against. I cited all the other examples where less worthy schemes locally were still operating. Ours was the only one where trainees were genuinely learning things needed by employers, yet we had been dropped from the scheme. I had read her article about discrimination against women. Our students were mainly female and our tourism course was their only chance to better themselves enough to find work. If she could help our cause by speaking to people of influence that she knew in the country, then we would be very grateful. Before I posted it, I got the students to write their own letters of complaint to the board of the SIMAP scheme and attached copies of every one to all of mine.

Meanwhile our court case dragged on with further postponements. Edwin had to meet with a new lawyer, since Mr Ellis had decided to leave Guyana for good and return to England. His replacement, Storm Westmaas, arrived from England. He was of Guyanese parentage but new to Guyana. He would have to get used to the Guyanese legal system, so it was a set-back from our point of view. The snackette had been leased out to a couple of men, one of whom was an ex-policeman. Edwin had received a deposit of 80,000 Guyana dollars from them and had given them a contract which his lawyer had prepared for them to sign for the lease at so much per month. The men took the lease away to study before signing it but Edwin had already let them move in and start decorating. By March he was being warned that they were drug dealers so he confronted them but, of course, they denied these accusations. He believed their story that it was malicious gossip and allowed them to start running their business. Three months had gone by and they had still not signed a contract nor paid any more rent. Following his lawyer's advice, he evicted them and counted the deposit as the three months' rent they owed. It seemed that events were conspiring against us on all fronts.

I left all the worrying about our finances to Edwin. I dedicated all my time to preparing lessons and marking students work. We had long ago realised that we would never be able to leave Guyana unless we left everything we owned there and went back to England as beggars. What could I do but try to build a better future for us in Guyana. I wanted to do all I could to help the deprived youngsters around me learn how they could work to transform their own country for the better. I spent every daylight hour and much of the night working to achieve this aim and in my day to day relationship with them I could really feel that I was getting somewhere. I just wanted to be able to give them more than I could do with my skills alone. Surely someone somewhere would help us to do this. I wrote some letters to people I knew in England to try to get us a science and maths volunteer for the coming academic year and Edwin sent a letter to Bernie Grant in Tottenham to see if help could be got for the planned exchange trip. Mitch had just informed us that he had found a youth group near him at Havering in Essex. He said they were keen to get involved and would be writing to us. I worked out a way to start practical cookery in my kitchen with half of the students while Edwin began his recreation management course, certified by the University of Guyana with the other half. After lunch, the groups would change over and we would repeat the same lessons. He began to incorporate first aid and health and safety into his course to provide additional practical skills needed in any workplace.

Before we knew it, Easter had arrived. The whirring of kites filled the air in the pasture around us. Every child flew their kite. They were made of gaily coloured tissue paper stuck to palm frond frames, their tails decked with pieces of paper cut to catch the breeze so they sang out like a kazoo. Some soared higher and higher while others nose-dived ignominiously and crashed into a pile of wreckage. The devilish boys sometimes secured a razor blade on their kite's tail and deliberately flew it up close to a rival's model in an attempt to cut its string with the blade on their own. Adults all dreaded this time of year, as it would only be a matter of hours before a break-away kite collided with the overhead power lines and cut off the neighbourhood supply until the workmen located the problem and safely removed it so power could be restored. When our school resumed full session after Easter, some personnel from the Ministry of Tourism came to stay with us for two days to sample our product. This gave me the opportunity to let the students do a practical preparation of cakes and sandwiches and drinks for the guests and to serve them as waiters would do in a hotel. They also got a guided tour of our museum and grounds by the students who each had a role to play, and a performance of African dance by all the students in our tie-dyed costumes. Maureen Paul from the Ministry of Tourism returned ten days later to be taken out into the savannahs, to the beach and back-dam for bird-watching and back to Sapodilla for a fitness session. She was impressed and wrote in our visitors' book that she would definitely come back and bring others with her. We got a good write up about it in the papers. The country seemed to be moving forward a little, so there was a glimmer of hope on the horizon.

Elaine, our friend at the British High Commission had come to the end of her term and was leaving for a new posting. We had put in a bid of £3,500 for her ageing Land-rover before she left and she accepted it, even though she must have had far higher offers. She really wanted us to have the vehicle so we could take some of our students on field trips and Edwin could take athletes to competitions without having to hire a taxi or minibus. A loan from Edwin's sister Olive in England helped us to pay Elaine directly in sterling. He repaid Olive by sending her twelve post-dated cheques to be cashed at monthly intervals over the following year. It was a godsend to have a vehicle at last in our fifth year of being in Guyana and this one was suitable for our location and needs. The plan was that I would soon get a local driving licence so that we would both be able to drive the vehicle. To start with, however, Edwin drove. If we both needed to go to town on our day off, then I would be passenger. Otherwise, he would use it for council business he needed to attend to and I would stay at home working. There was always so much to do.

It was not until the end of June that I received a reply from Josephine Whitehead to my letter of complaint to SIMAP. She said that she had spoken to the Minister of Labour about our case and after careful consideration he had decided to reinstate our students on the scheme until it finished in December. They would receive backdated payments for all the weeks they had missed. However, we would not be included in any future such scheme. I had been shocked to discover, since I sent her my original letter, that the Minister of Labour was in fact her husband. Perhaps she thought I already knew this. It was a victory of sorts, but it was also a victory for Mr Simpson, who had recently told Edwin that we would be only be reinstated "over my dead body."

"The man only deserves contempt," said Edwin. "I think when I next have to go into the offices at the Ministry of Labour I will say to him, 'You're still alive then; how come?' " Edwin had a way of holding up a red rag to the small minded and officious and making it clear that they were marked enemies.

It was the end of July. We were preparing for 'Swaree' in the village and our students were expecting an influx of visitors from abroad and from other parts of Guyana to whom they could sell their tourism souvenirs made in my art classes. At the end of the school term I had closed off academic lessons for all students and concentrated on purely practical work for the full timers on the SIMAP scheme who were expected to be working throughout the year with no holiday. I had set up a mini-company project with them (on the model of the Longmans project of the same name) in order to teach them business skills. They had raised a small amount of capital by selling shares to their friends and family, and were going to use this to buy basic raw materials to make suitable craft products to sell. Now that we knew the SIMAP payments were going to stop in December, they would need to bring in an income to add to what they had saved so far, in order to pay for their examination entry fees. I thought I would test out their sales ability first by seeing how they got on with selling the local wildlife postcards I had already made and invested in. Each student had a sample set to sell at an agreed price with a ten per-cent mark-up for each salesperson. They would spend the week trying to sell the cards in the community and elsewhere and report back to the weekly company board meeting with their sales figures and money. It would all be accounted for and saved up in the mini-company bank account until time for the annual pay-out. The incentives to succeed were clear: the students who sold most cards would earn most money. Those who sold none would earn none and if any sample cards were damaged, they would have to pay for the replacement out of their earnings. I had plenty of experience of their behaviour and living conditions to know that these precautions were necessary if the losses were not to be all mine to bear. This is why I built such safeguards into our system. The first week got off to a good start with Robin and Satyanand regularly returning for more stock as they were selling well and in amicable rivalry. Others were less successful at first but shamed into greater efforts by the two Indo-Guyanese boys. There were no losses, so the system was working well.

Mr Nurse and three other gentlemen from the Board of Industry and Trade came down to visit us as an appraisal of our SIMAP project students on July 30th. Edwin was annoyed to think that we were the only establishment appraised in this way. We were definitely being discriminated against but I preferred to see it as a positive development since we would be showing them how things should be done. It might lead to improvements in the scheme for the future. We were able to show them all the practical work our students were doing on tourism, including preparation and service of food and drinks, the folk medicine video they had made, tour-guiding them around our farm and museum displays and giving demonstrations of first aid and safe, properly organised recreation and games for potential tourists' children. Every student demonstrated their proficiency at every one of these skills. They also showed their mini-company records and sales of postcards, inviting the inspectors themselves to buy some. They had been a proud proof of the worth of our Learning Centre which suitably impressed the assessors. The fact that we were a genuine tourism business was shown by the arrival the same day of Anna Iles from the Canadian High Commission along with her little son. They were staying with us to be part of the village Emancipation Celebrations over the next three days.

I had no idea that Anna, who had been a regular visitor to us over the past years with the CARDI sheep project, was assuming that now we had a full time charity school it would be a boarding school to which middle class parents from Georgetown could send their children. When she casually dropped in the suggestion that we could enrol her son for the coming academic year, I was shocked.

"I thought you knew that we were only doing this for the youth of Hopetown and its environs," I said. "I can't possibly take on the responsibility of children for their whole lives as well as teaching them all day every day." It suddenly dawned on me that this was a cultural thing. Local parents usually farmed off one or more of their children into another family for their upbringing. This was the way of life in the Caribbean. It had been Edwin's own experience when his mother, a servant of the black middle-class Congregational Church Minister, Parson Munroe and his family, had allowed him to be informally adopted from the age of about three, and eventually taken to England by them when he was ten. I had thought that all these traditions had died with the end of colonialism, but when I considered the evidence around me, it was still being practised by every local family in one way or another. The eldest child was usually sent to another family whose economic prospects and education were better. By living in the 'higher class' household, they would automatically become a member of the new family and move up the social and economic ladder. I had never seen myself as part of this archaic practice but clearly it was being expected of me. Anna looked crest-fallen.

"I'm really sorry to disappoint you Anna," I said, "but Christopher already has the option of going to good schools in Georgetown where you live, and he should be living with you, his mother, to provide the emotional security he needs. I didn't set out to make a fee-paying private school for Georgetown children. I only want to give up my day-times to help provide a free education for able children from poor families in this village and neighbourhood. They have no opportunity to travel to Georgetown to school every day and no relatives in Georgetown they can live with if they win a place at a Georgetown school in the Common Entrance." I could now see that she had been building up to this ever since she first met us and began to befriend us. I had no idea until now that 'friendship' in that part of the world was always with an ulterior motive. Such conditional friendship was a totally alien concept to me. I would have to be very much more aware from now on. It became clear as Anna's interest in us cooled off in the ensuing months, that I had been wrong to trust the apparently genuine friendship of locals towards me. If they did not succeed in their suit, then at worst, they sought revenge and at best, their friendship dissolved away. The true meaning of my Dubai headmistress's sage warning to us not to accept expensive gifts from locals as they always expected something in return now began to sink in. At the time I had thought the advice only applicable to the Middle East and for personal gifts. I had never dreamt it would apply in Guyana for aid for a charity that would benefit the recipients rather than me. I now felt like a medieval noble, unable to trust anyone at court. Anna must have expected me to take in her son as the price for her help to Edwin in securing some of the CARDI project assets for our Learning Centre.

The sheep project had finally been closed down and all its assets handed over to the Sheep Farmers' Association formed by the project's original beneficiaries. Plans for a local abattoir for them to market their produce were still in train and until they raised funds to fence off the undeveloped land we were letting them use at the back of our farm to keep an educational community sheep project going, all the assets that had formerly been located up the coast at a village named Burma, were removed and brought to Sapodilla for storage. The desks and furniture, however, were handed over to us to use in the classroom. Edwin had joined the association and was helping to advise them on their business management. Since May he had been unhappy about the way the meetings had been going. The government Ministry of Agriculture seemed to be using Edwin's document for the new educational extension of the sheep project to fund a highly paid manager whose identity remained a mystery. Edwin was concerned, because he had said he would manage it free of charge as well as allow them to use our land for free. The Ministry of Agriculture who now were handling the funding application to international donors, seemed to be ignoring Edwin and the local small farmers in their plans for the project. Were they going to appoint someone of their choice to receive this salary while Edwin was doing the work on the ground voluntarily and allowing them free use of our land and premises? He started to ask pointed questions. He was happy to do it all for free, but they should remove the manager's salary from the funding application. Things went quiet for a while.

Meanwhile, our search for a volunteer from England to help me to teach maths and Science at the school was moving forward. Mitch, with the help of Jo, an old friend of mine from University days who had links with Basingstoke College Of Technology (BCOT), had managed to find a sixth former willing to come out in their gap year before going to University. Mitch was going to arrange it all. As an ex VSO, he felt he had experience enough to prepare her for the expedition and she had already done the Duke of Edinburgh Award, so would count this as her final part of it, the service component. Mitch and his friends at Poole Runners would raise funds for her passage to come out to us, purchase the ticket and insurance for her and liaise with her and her family until she left the airport. I was not keen on accepting a teenager who had no teacher training or experience to do this work. I felt that it would be of little use to us but more of a travel experience for the youth concerned. I had been trying to obtain a VSO from early in the year and Edwin had pursued our contacts in the VSO office in Georgetown. Helen had explained to me that she could not recommend a VSO for us since we were not a government entity and she did not want to do anything to annoy the government as it would compromise the VSO position in the country so they would no longer be allowed to operate there. She did, however, pass me the address of the Principal of Froebel College of Education in London. She suggested I write to him, as he had just left Guyana in disgust having visited the University of Guyana to try to arrange an exchange programme between them and teacher training students from Froebel, but had not been impressed by what he saw at the Turkeyen Campus. I had immediately written to him, setting out our situation in great detail and he had replied, inviting us to meet with him when we were next in the United

Kingdom. This was encouraging news, but as we had no chance of leaving Guyana in the foreseeable future, it did not solve our immediate problem. Maybe we would have to accept Mitch's solution for the coming academic year, so I wrote and told him so, with all my reservations explained and asking for her to write a letter of application to me enclosing her CV and two passport sized photos. It had subsequently been arranged by Mitch. She would be joining us in September, but she was only willing to come to us until March, not for the full academic year.

"Oh, no!" I said when I read his latest letter to us. "What's the point of coming for only part of the academic year? What good will that be to us? I'll have kids left high and dry with subjects they've been learning from September to March because from April to July they'll have no teacher. The airfare is so expensive that we can't raise another fare for someone else for the last three months, and it's no good getting someone out over the summer holidays because they'll have to be occupied at a time when we want our break."

"Don't worry", said Edwin, "I'll ask Dawn Murray at BWIA if she can organise a discounted ticket to help us with the volunteer and see if it's possible to get the return journey extended for another three months once we've got the girl here.

"I'm not so sure," I said. "You can't assume she'll want to stay on and I don't want to start something we can't continue."

"It would be better to give it a go than not to try, he argued. "I'm sure once she gets here and see's why she's needed for the rest of the term, she can be persuaded to extend her stay. Maybe, being young, she's a bit afraid to commit herself for a whole year."

"I suppose you're right," I said and wrote back to Mitch with the go-ahead, adding another request to him to persuade her to do the full three terms.

"One more thing," Edwin continued, "I've decided to go to England in November for Charmaine's christening and now I know you'll have company here, I don't mind leaving you here while I am away. We can't afford the airfares for both of us, but I can manage just the one. It'll give me the opportunity to see my grandchildren for the first time and while I'm there, I can meet up with the principal of Froebel to see if we can get a qualified teacher volunteer in the future. I'll also meet the Sports Council people in London as well as Mitch to sort out the details of this school exchange he's fixed up with Havering Council."

"I don't need company to be here with me while you're away. I lived on my own for ten years before I met you, and I like my own company," I reminded him. I was annoyed by his assumption that I had to have someone with me all the time. I wasn't scared or lonely and I hated to have my companions chosen for me by someone else. However, I was in a position where I would have to remain doing the teaching, since we now had a full time school with students depending on me. In addition, I would have the responsibility of a young English volunteer to look after.

****

A lot had happened since then. Our first volunteer, Sarah, had arrived that September and astonished us both by asking if she could keep her condoms in our fridge as Mitch had advised her that if kept at tropical room temperature, they would not work. We had expected someone to help us teach maths and science. Had she come to Guyana in order to get casual sexual experience? We spent quite a lot of time with her trying to explain the differences in culture between England and Guyana and the appropriate respectable behaviour that would be expected of a teacher living and working in our small village community. We could not fault Mitch for bending over backwards to help us find, fund and prepare Sarah, but this shone a glaring light on the fact that he was not a trained teacher and had no idea what qualities any teacher needed to have as a role model for youngsters in their care. He was a printing expert working as an adult male in the newspaper industry when he was a VSO. His own behaviour could be quite different from that expected of a teacher. We had to make our eighteen year old girl realise that whatever she had been told was not appropriate to her or to this situation. She was far too busy to think of anything outside the work she had to prepare for the first few weeks in any case, so seemed happy to stay in and rely on us to take her to places she needed to go to shop or to change money, and to chat with us or the students in her free time. She had also brought with her some valuable donations from her college in Basingstoke, namely a small microscope with slides, some dissection equipment and several boxes of test tubes and flasks. This was fantastic. Now the full time students could for the first time in their lives start to learn some basic science from the biology syllabus with real practical experiments.

Edwin had taken Sookie and Michelle, his best female athletes, to Trinidad again to take part in the Women-on-the-Move 5 kilometre road race in October in Port of Spain. They had nearly won but Michelle, in a superhuman effort to be first, had collapsed from overheating and Edwin had to pull her out of the race within metres of the finishing line in the stadium and administer emergency medical aid. He had gone to England for a month in mid-October. Back at the ranch, I had established some sort of a routine on my own with Sarah and had taken her with me on a long trip to the Kaieteur Falls and those at Orinduik in the Rupununi Savannahs by light aircraft one Sunday in November. At last I was getting to see some of the spectacular landscape, wildlife and geology of my adopted country. I had no idea when I had married Edwin that it was going to take me into a five year imprisonment in an uninspiring and intellectually baron environment with no funds to escape it and a husband who had no desire to see any of the marvels of the interior of his own country. I had stoically accepted all this, believing that he had not expected it to be like this either. We just had to make the best of what we now had. At least now I had the opportunity to make this trip in his absence as a concession for not going back to England with him.

The tiny waiting room at Ogle airport which had been refurbished for the Queen's visit to Guyana in 1994 was far better than that of the International airport at Timehri when I had passed through it in 1991. I began to understand why undeveloped countries like Guyana were keen to get royal visits even though they were independent and hated their colonial connection. The Commonwealth was just a great big funding agency and the Queen was the head of it. Now I knew why countries that had never been part of the British Empire wanted to join the Commonwealth. The World Wildlife Fund was another such organisation. The airport at Ogle was the only way to reach Iwokrama, the world's leading biodiversity centre in a huge National Park of virgin rainforest, visited only by scientists and VIPs. Hardly any Guyanese Nationals ever got to go there. We could only read about it or see it in videos or printed leaflets. The Kaieteur National Park was a little easier to get to, but the cost of a light aircraft journey there was more than an International flight to the Caribbean islands, so Guyanese nationals rarely got to see Kaieteur either. Margaret Chan-a-Sue marched into the waiting room with a bundle of rolled up maps under her arm and greeted us warmly in her Scottish accent. I knew a bit about her already from Edwin who had been on the tourism course with her. She had met and married Malcolm, a Guyanese pilot, years before when they were both working for British Airways. They had set up their own civil aviation business flying diplomats, business people, officials and any others who could afford to charter their tiny light aircraft into the interior. They had been the only ones doing it for years but recently faced competition from other operators. Their experience and safety record made them the only choice for me. Margaret got down to business straight away as she unrolled the maps on the coffee table and talked us through the itinerary pointing out on the map features we would be flying over. Malcolm was waiting out on the runway for us to board the tiny plane. As we took off, Margaret's airhostess training came into effect as she gabbled away to take our minds off any turbulence or nerves, continually plying us with plastic cups full of neat rum. These she topped up from her seat behind us as she pointed out features below us that she had identified earlier on her map. She spilled more on her blue apron than she got into the cups as the plane was buffeted by sudden up-draughts. The gold-mining dredges in the Essequibo River, the Mazaruni granite company quarries and logging activity were all clearly visible, but they hardly made any impression on the vast sea of green that rolled out in all directions beyond the horizon. This forest was part of the lungs of the world that we were all so keen to preserve. Malcolm flew the plane straight up the mighty Kaieteur gorge towards its head as if he were intending to crash into the rock face in front of us. At the last possible moment, he pulled back and lifted the nose of the plane above the rim of the falls so giving us a spectacular view of the scale of it all. He touched down safely on the tiny landing strip in a clearing beyond the trees. Margaret led us silently through the forested area so as not to scare off the wildlife and in the distance we caught a glimpse of scarlet; a solitary male cock-of-the-rock perching in the understory. It flew into the shadows where the cacophony of songs of all the other creatures came from. Malcolm was keen to find a golden frog for us. There was one, swimming in the cup of rainwater collected in a bromeliad plant conveniently at shoulder height near the edge of the path. He enjoyed being the expert, giving us a potted geography lesson about continental drift and tectonic plates to explain the uplift of the Guiana Shield and how it had caused the Potaro River to incise the gorge into it. The highest single drop waterfall in the world was tumbling over the cliff in front of us now. After the months of drought the river had shrivelled up so the falls were not even half their normal width, but the awesome power of the water as it plunged down the eight hundred feet or more of sandstone was breath-taking. I stepped right out over the dry rocks that had been worn flat and smooth as a pavement by the raging torrent that normally thundered over them. What was it about vertigo that made me feel an almost overwhelming premonition of tumbling over the edge to my watery grave? I drew back and moved to a safer spot from where I could revel in the spirituality of natural wilderness.

We took our picnic lunch at a grassy spot beside the falls with a full view of them to our right and the vista down the gorge to our left. Then we flew on to the Rupununi as Margaret had to make a delivery to the Amerindian settlement at Orinduik. Children bounded across the savannah, dodging the massive termite mounds in order to get to the plane and collect any parcels they had been sent to collect. Their thatched huts in the distance were not part of our itinerary as Malcolm was keen to get all his female passengers to strip down to their bathing costumes and get into the water at the beautiful but gentle waterfalls of Orinduik. Our time was limited because he had to get back to Ogle airport in daylight. Some of the children hung around talking to us. They looked forward to this occasional contact with the world outside their isolated community. I wondered how far their village had moved on from the customs of their prehistoric ancestors, how long it would be before a road reached them with services and commerce that would transform their lives. I wanted my romantic idealisation of their community to be true, but experience had by now taught me otherwise.

In England Edwin had spent time reconnecting with his family there and as well as meeting Mitch Mason, Dave Hayes and the Poole Runners and all the other contacts he had planned to see, he succeeded in securing support in our quest for a volunteer from Froebel College. Edwin had talked with a number of teacher training students coming up to their finals at a reception organised for the purpose by the college. The Principal, Dr Weston, had suggested that final year students might like to do a gap year at Sapodilla before starting their first teaching post. The college would sponsor their air fare if we could raise funds for their upkeep during the year.

I had found it quite a strain during Edwin's absence trying to keep Sarah on the right track with her lesson preparation and making sure she had someone to talk to when she needed it while still fitting in all my own preparation, marking, housework and cooking. I split the full-time students into two mathematical ability groups and gave her two half days to teach maths at the two different levels so that I could do food and nutrition practical with each alternate group. She had another half day to do science with the whole group, which allowed me to give tuition to those students who were capable of passing the international GCE O-levels in English language, Literature and West Indian History. Sarah also had an hour after school for the younger primary and secondary Saturday class students. The rest of the time was for her to prepare lessons, worksheets and mark or do her own letter writing and personal chores. It had been a drought and the two of us nearly used up the entire rain water supply from all our tanks but were saved at the eleventh hour by three days of deluge that refilled the main tank just before Edwin got back. After Edwin's return, it was a little easier for me, as he could entertain her while I was teaching and take her to see a few local places so she could get her bearings. By Christmas, she had begun to find her own way round on minibuses and to make friends with youths in villages further up the coast. This was rather alarming to Edwin as he had no way of knowing who she was mixing with and was concerned that they might be trying to take advantage of her or worse still, that they might be potential bandits with whom she could come to harm. Then we received warnings from the elderly ladies in the village that she should not be wandering around the village late at night. The marks on her neck were being whispered about by the children and this shocked us both. We could warn her again about the folly of this but we could not keep her captive. By December, Edwin had introduced her to a couple of older American Peace Corps boys we knew quite well who were volunteering in the area. We felt more at ease with her spending time with them as they had graduated from college, had already been in the country for a year and were sensible.

The President, Cheddi Jagan, had suffered a heart attack during February and been flown out of the country for treatment. Rumours were rife that he had died, but this was being kept a secret so as to prevent unrest. The Vice President, Sam Hinds, took over the day to day running of the country but there was tension and Sarah perhaps understood why we wanted her to stay in more and concentrate on her work. I felt I had learned some of the pitfalls about taking on the responsibility of a volunteer without the backing of an inter-national charity overseeing it. All credit to Sarah's parents for allowing her to do this. Edwin had visited them while in England to reassure them who was taking care of their daughter. He had also been to her college to thank them personally for their donation of science equipment. After Christmas, we had asked her again if she could reconsider staying on the extra three months to complete the syllabus with the maths students. They had paid their exam entrance fees back in October and would need her help most of all in the lead up to the exams. She had promised to think about it and write home to ask her dad. She had planned a summer holiday expedition to Pakistan with friends, so did not want to miss the chance of a few months of working to pay for that. No decision was made, but it took over six weeks for the reply to arrive with the go-ahead. By the time she could tell us "Yes" she could stay, it was too late to extend the return date of her air-ticket. Sadly, we had to explain to the students and say goodbye to her in March. I then had to pick up the pieces with the students for their last exam term. The whole experience had made me more determined than ever not to repeat the same mistakes. The VSO had long ago ditched the practice of sending sixth formers as volunteers. Back in the seventies when I was at school myself, I had applied just after they made this change. I had been told that sixth form leavers were no longer going to be considered because the recipient countries had specifically requested experienced people with degrees or professional qualifications. I now fully understood why this was a vital policy change. There were so many reasons why school leavers were not suitable and we had found all of them out by our own experience.

Cheddi Jagan's death had eventually been announced. Edwin was with Sarah at the airport just as the President's body was being returned to Guyana for the funeral. Troops were swarming everywhere. Sam Hinds was officially sworn in as President until the next General Election could be held later in the year. While all this was going on, we had received news from Mitch that he had met up with Froebel students. He had enclosed their letters of application and CVs. Quite a few wanted to come to us, but most had studied subjects like my own. One of them was ideal: a science and maths student who had already done 'Operation Raleigh' in Belize during a college vacation. I wrote to all the applicants explaining that we could only take one person and we only needed a maths and science teacher. Our funding was limited. I could cover all other subject areas myself without the need for other volunteers. I had referred our successful candidate, Louise, to Mitch for preparation and fundraising, with the proviso from Edwin that the student herself should play a part in raising their own funds for their stint. It might make the volunteer appreciate the experience more if they were not just having a trip at other people's expense. It surprised me therefore, when I received a second letter from one of the unsuccessful applicants, a Primary school English teacher, begging me to reconsider and to allow her to come along as well. Against my better judgement, Edwin persuaded me to agree if she could herself raise all the funds for both her airfare and full board for the year. I informed her and quoted the exact amount required, which had to be paid in full to Mitch before he bought the tickets. In response, she wrote promising to do so, saying that she had been working as an office temp to put herself through college, so she would be using this money to pay her own way. I agreed and informed Mitch of all the details of these developments.

Although the students had been upset at losing their maths support just before their CXC exams, I had used the time to give them extra lessons in their other examination subjects. The first Food and Nutrition practical exams had gone smoothly as had the art and the school based assessments for the other exam subjects. All we had to worry about after that was revision and the final exams. I was now teaching twelve different exam subjects and doing all the associated examination administration for them. This included Caribbean Examination Certificates and our first three international GCE O level subjects. After the exams had finished and I had sent home detailed school leaving reports to parents of all students, I had called a parents' meeting to pass on information about the two new qualified teacher volunteers that would be joining us in September. I discussed with parents who wanted their children to become full time students at Sapodilla Learning Centre what the opportunities for them would be. There would now be a sixth form for full time students to continue at the school after passing CXCs to do GCE "O" levels. They needed to commit to joining as early as possible because I would need time to draw up their timetables and have the right number of resources in place before we began the new school year in September. Most of the parents signed up their children straight away without further thought. Others came back within a few days and were keen to get us to adopt a proper school uniform. I had not realised how important this was to poverty stricken parents. It appeared that it was a status symbol and a means of student identification in the local community. They were proud. I bowed to the reasons they gave for their demands.

By now the efforts of the sheep farmers had fizzled away once massive funding from CARDI had dried up. The wooden boards from the dismantled pens which had been piled up between our water tanks and the garden had begun to be eaten away by termites. Their trails had spread unnoticed into our back fence and all the way along it to our house. We first discovered the damage they could do when we noticed these long brown ridges going up the white plaster of the gym walls into the wood cladding behind our study and thence inside some of the many personal books we had in our own library upstairs. The terrorist within had completely eaten out the inside of a large tome on the Mau-Mau rebellion in Kenya and yet the cover of the book was completely intact to outward appearances. A fumigation exercise with insecticide began. It became a daily night-mare, a race against unstoppable nature which taught us that we could never get a night's sleep without checking next morning what these insect hordes had devoured while we slumbered. There was no point in providing them with free food and cover, so we gave away all the sheep pen wood to our neighbours for firewood. The last time Mac brought funding agency representatives to see us, I had asked them why the project documents mentioned Sapodilla Learning Centre yet so carefully avoided any mention of Edwin's name or mine. The usual procedure was to do this, they said.

"What guarantees do we have that someone isn't just using our name to apply for funding which they intend keeping entirely for themselves?" I had asked one of the consultants from the USA.

"Absolutely none!" was his reply.

"Then I do not want Sapodilla Learning Centre to be any part of that project document," I said. It would be some time before we saw Mac again.

It was July. Our sixth wedding anniversary had arrived and we had the house to ourselves again for a while. It was bliss, apart from the daily assault on termites and sweeping up of dried bat dung from the floors. At the end of the month, Maggie's O-level results arrived. There was a great stir in the community. She had passed all four and got Grade A in English Language. Never before had someone at a school in the village passed at O level in English Language or Literature. In fact there had been no O level passes in any subject for many decades. I was inundated with people wanting to enrol their children in all my part time classes after that and it increased when the CXC results came in later in the summer. The students who wanted to stay on to the sixth form came in to help preparations for the school makeover. Edwin had inherited two large calor-gas canisters from the Reverend Pat Munroe following his death earlier in the year. Once it was clear that we had a qualified Froebel science teacher joining us, Edwin had decided to convert the room adjacent to our library cum classroom, which up to now had been a massive store-room, into a proper laboratory for the school. We would dedicate it to Pat. After all, Pat had qualified in medicine in England and had worked for the World Health Organisation before he had become a Congregational minister. He had served as

315

a government Minister under Burnham after Independence and had been responsible for the clean-up operation after the terrible mass suicide in the Jonestown scandal that had shocked the world in the seventies. We did not need to let ourselves get used by others in their massive projects and funding agency applications in a futile attempt to get a laboratory for our students. We could use the canisters bequeathed by Pat Munroe and the copper pipes we still had not installed upstairs to make a hot water system in our home. We could get Albert to find us someone who could safely fit up gas pipes and install a lab for us that way.

We wasted no time in getting plans in place for the work to be done. Edwin informed Pat's older sisters living in North America about the idea and they were delighted. They not only donated some funds themselves but sent out appeals to scores of Pat's friends in the Yankee diaspora and collected a large sum which could pay for some of the work required. We would install the gas taps for Bunsen burners, fit out the laboratory with two new sash windows with security locks and grills and build a new storeroom onto the back of the house for the garden tools which would be made homeless by the new lab. I had decided to use some of my savings to put in a proper damp course and tile the floors in both lab and classroom now that a new source of supply of sturdy ceramic floor tiles had opened up in Georgetown. It would be much easier to keep clean. I wanted to improve the conditions from the dirty, rising damp of the existing bare concrete. I could do the same in the gym but Edwin wanted a softer surface for the Physical exercise so we decided on some rolls of local vinyl floor covering. The changing room could be lined with all the tiles we had originally expected to use on our upstairs bathroom walls.

The full time students who were still awaiting results for their exams had agreed to come in and help with some of the work. Their wages would go into their savings accounts. Michelle, Maggie and Kelta cleaned and painted all the legs of the chairs and desks, while a local builder did the floors and windows. As he finished each room, the boys helped me paint the walls and ceilings and put back the furniture. We had sent Kelta on a short librarian's course in Georgetown after her exams, so on her return, she and Maggie helped me to catalogue all the library books. It was gradually taking shape with our own efforts and a little help from friends. It was disappointing that my recent application for funding for the school from the Canadian agency CIDA had been turned down, but we carried on regardless. We now had our jeep and were able to use it to collect the windows, tiles and other materials from Georgetown, which cut the cost of paying a haulage contractor to do so.

Edwin had been trying to arrange my driving licence at the local police station so that I too could drive the jeep. While he was there, the inspector told him that they wanted to question Michelle's older brother for drug offences. Instead of allowing them to go ahead and arrest him, when Edwin got back, he told Michelle that the police were looking for her brother. She went home for her lunch and we did not see her again for the rest of the day. I was annoyed. She not only missed my afternoon lessons but also missed her training session with him and the other athletes that afternoon and he was disappointed not to see her there.

"Why are you surprised?" I had said. "It's obvious that if you tell her, she is going to go off and warn him to do a runner. If he's in trouble, let him answer for it. How can there ever be any justice in a community where people all help their friends and relatives to escape the law?"

We had now been in Guyana for six years. The commerce in the capital had developed quite a bit since our arrival and we had slightly better electricity supply now, but services and infrastructure were still pitiful, especially in rural areas like ours. In late July, we were both invited to take part in a national radio discussion programme in Georgetown coming up to Emancipation Day. Edwin had accepted even though it would mean travelling late at night back from the studios. I felt a little odd at being the only white person on the panel of scowling Afro-Guyanese political activists visiting from New York for the purpose of promulgating their political agenda about the marginalisation of blacks under the PPP government in Guyana. I was invited by the local presenter to explain what we were doing to help the education of poor black children in rural Berbice and reconnect with their history and culture from slavery times. I did my best to explain this and it was received well by the elderly local members of the panel but the American activists patronised my "well-meaning efforts" at reviving African dance. Their hostile comments about education in colonial times by white missionaries being an attempt to brainwash colonial children with history, literature and geography that was pro-empire and pro-colonialism may have meant to imply that I must be doing the same thing. I mistakenly thought, however that I was participating in a democratic and genuinely open discussion of history and educational issues, so I attempted to open another angle in the debate. I simply suggested that methods of education had been pretty backward in English schools at the time also, and I did not think it was deliberate brainwashing of blacks to accept their role as an underclass as much as the unfortunate effect of a universal system of rote learning and recall that was not changed until the education reforms of the nineteen seventies. English children had accepted rather than questioned information until then as well. I was immediately set upon by a hostile onslaught. They put me in my place. What right did I, a white woman, have to speak on a radio show about black people and black history? What could I possibly know about these things? One elderly local academic made a kind attempt to defend what I had said but the damage was done. I had been publicly humiliated as these black racists clearly felt all whites deserved to be. Maybe it was payback for the Ku Klux Clan or the treatment blacks had suffered in the racist and segregated USA as well as for any colonial exploitation and cruelty by the British in the West Indies. I must suffer for the sins of others of my colour. Such is the injustice of racism. I would not put myself up for this kind of treatment again, however. I was cowed into silence because I did not belong on black turf. The three-hour journey home in the early hours on the desolate coast road overshadowed by grotesque silhouettes of its silk cotton and mango trees seemed more threatening and ugly than it had ever done before that night.

I felt more comfortable within the confines of Sapodilla Learning Centre. At least the community of Hopetown had made me feel welcome and Edwin's elderly aunts in particular. August was upon us and Samo came to visit us. He had come out of the Savannah for a few days. I showed him the jaguar skin that I had just mounted on some wire mesh and displayed as a specimen in the lab. He was excited by the idea of the lab being an extension of our museum into local wildlife, so he went away and came back in a day or two with a massive anaconda skin for us to mount and add to the display. I had written to Louise telling her that we hoped she would be able to help us add to our collection of museum specimens while she was with us. We visited the National Curriculum Research Development Centre in Georgetown and negotiated the free loan of small supplies of basic chemicals, some Bunsen burners and some more equipment for our new intake of students to do the full integrated science syllabus. A fax had arrived by post from Georgetown telling me of the arrival of a box of books from Dubai, so we went back to town fairly quickly to process the documents. It turned out to be not one box but twenty two and there was no need for us to organise or pay for their transport. It had all been done from Dubai and they would be delivered as soon as the processing had been completed in a few weeks' time. I couldn't believe it. I was overwhelmed by emotion at the extent of support I had received from my friends in Dubai, especially Alison who had organised it all.

I had to get a new multi-system television for the house. Thanks to the damage done to the others by voltage fluctuations, it would be the third one we had bought since 1991. The new furniture chain-store Courts which had taken over and refurbished a semi-derelict retail space on Main Street a couple of years before had a choice of goods and displays which outshone any other store in the country. After years of being devoid of any retail temptation, we now had a range of things we might actually want to buy, so we browsed. We would drive round to their warehouse later on and collect the TV to take home with us. I saw a large tropicalized fridge freezer like the one we had bought from them before the wedding. I decided to spend a bit more of my savings on one now that we would have to cater for two extra people living in our house. As we were making our way from there to Stabroek market to buy a few fruit and vegetables, a strange man I had never seen before approached us and greeted us as if we were his close friends. He was a political activist who wanted our support for his cause. It felt spooky. He had been tailing us around town and decided to approach us in the open market place. Who really was he? Why was he following us? What were his intentions? Edwin made some polite conversation with him and took one of his hand bills so we could get away from him. It didn't feel nice being followed. I had never noticed it happening before, so why now?

Preparations for the new term and new intake were coming together. Then we got another letter from Mitch about the funding of our volunteers. He was complaining that Louise, our science teacher wasn't playing ball with his fundraising. He was organising a sponsored bike ride from London to Brighton and Louise was refusing to do it but Nova, the other girl was taking part. He was pushing the case for giving all the funding he had raised to support Nova, the superfluous English teacher, and none to Louise, the necessary maths and science teacher.

"What's the matter with him, he's lost the plot!" I cried as I skimmed over the contents of the letter. "I can't believe it." I read it again, carefully and realised I had to act fast as it was the second week in August and they were supposed to be with us at the start of the term next month. "Things would be so much easier if we had a phone. I'll have to write an urgent letter back to him and explain that he has to use the funds for Louise because it is a science and maths teacher we need not a primary English teacher. It will be a disaster if Louise does not come out to us because she is not funded for her board and lodgings. I know that I originally told him we wanted the volunteer to do their own fundraising so they weren't getting a free trip at someone else's expense, but there is a principal involved here that is more important: I asked for fundraising to go to the science and maths teacher because that's who we need. Only if there is extra funds raised should any of it go to Nova even if she is doing Mitch's bike ride, because she agreed to my conditions that she would fund the entire cost of board and lodgings herself. It's up to Froebel if they want to sponsor Nova's flight as well as Louise's but if there is only one ticket, then it must go to Louise. " I dropped what I was doing and wrote a carefully worded reply which I sealed up, went straight up to the local post office and posted it express post. I could do nothing more but hope for the best.

Now we were ready at the school for our forthcoming term. There were a few days left in August for us to take a break ourselves.

"I've never been to Linden where the Bauxite mines are that your dad went away to work in," I said to Edwin. "While we have a few days with no school going on and a vehicle of our own, why don't we drive to Linden for a day?"

"It should be just possible to get there and back in a day," he said, "but we would have to leave very early in the morning and get back very late at night." So we planned our journey. At training that afternoon, Edwin told his athletes not to come to the gym the next day because we would be going to Linden. We set off before dawn, pulled in at the first petrol station we came to, and filled up the jeep for the long journey ahead. It was about seven o'clock and the sun in the eastern sky had not yet appeared above the tops of the coconuts on the coastal reefs but it was now broad daylight. Just outside Belladrum, on a deserted spot on the road near Foulis, a battered blue vehicle which had been following us suddenly overtook and swerved in front of us, forcing Edwin to slam on the brakes to avoid crashing into it. He thumped the horn and yelled out in anger at the unseen driver, who got out of the passenger door of the car and looked towards us. Edwin jumped out of his door, slammed it behind him, marched up the road to the car, which had stopped a fair distance away from us, and proceeded to speak to the man. They were out of earshot so I sat and waited, thinking Edwin must have given him a piece of his mind about driving safely. After a while, I saw them both walking towards me. The man was armed with what looked like a revolver on a belt at his waist, but he was dishevelled and looked as if he had slept rough. Edwin got back in the car and the man returned to his. As we drove off again, the car waited for us to pass it and then pulled away after us.

"Those guys say they are from BASS, the new drugs unit of the police," he said, "The one I spoke to said his name is Colin James. I think he must be Julian James's relative. I saw him before, once, at Patrick Britton's house. He said he wanted a loan of $40,000 to buy diesel in Georgetown for a boat which will be used to help the BASS undercover agents to carry out their work against smugglers. I said I couldn't help him because we were using what little funds we had to run the charity school. He showed me his ID and some customs papers for electrical items such as computers which he said he'd seized off Indians who'd smuggled them. He said the items had to be dumped, but I could have them for the school if I would let him have this money. I said I didn't have that kind of money on me. I said I didn't want the computers as people would want to know where we got them from. I couldn't give him the money, but I would lend him it to him when I next got some. He said he could come with me now to my bank and I could give him the money there."

"You didn't agree to that, surely," I said.

"It'll be OK. He said he would come by our place tonight after 6.30 and pay it back," he said. I looked behind and saw the car following us. We were the only two cars on the road.

"In any case," I went on, "what kind of a police anti-drugs outfit is it if they have to beg for money for basic stuff like diesel for a boat to do their work? I thought they were getting funding for this from America."

"Well guys doing that kind of work sometimes have to stay under cover for days on end and they can't get to a bank or base before they need supplies."

"Oh, I see," I said. "I still don't think it's a good way to go about getting essential supplies by trying to bargain stuff you seize from smugglers that's supposed to be dumped in exchange for cash. It seems he doesn't really want to pay us back the money."

I tried to change the subject but there was nothing to say really. I kept looking round in the vain hope that they would no longer be there. The car followed us all the way to Georgetown close on our tail. We parked outside the bank and joined the queue. The man followed us into the bank. He now had a jacket on, concealing his weapon. I did not like the look of him. I did not believe that he was BASS and resented giving him this large sum of money that we were unlikely to see again. Edwin drew out $50,000, his pension from England, and gave the man his forty thousand, keeping ten for us. The man thanked him and at last disappeared. I was relieved but scared.

"I did not like him at all. Following us all the way here like that. Why did you give him the money?" I asked. "You never normally do."

"What could I do? They were both armed to the teeth and were a bit desperate," he said. "They've been on a stake-out without any sleep for days. It'll be all right. He'll give us the money back. I trust him. Those guys have a tough job." I was not convinced, and still a bit shaken up by the desperadoes, but they had gone now, so we should put it behind us and make the best of the rest of the day.

After the tension had eased, we found the road leading to the Linden Highway, filled up with more petrol and headed for the Emerald Tower resort which we had wanted to see since it had opened as the interior eco-tourist resort belonging to the Tower Hotel in Georgetown. A large notice was posted at the end of the drive saying that it was closed.

"Seems as if they only staff it when they have a booking there, otherwise it's closed up," I said. Edwin was not impressed. We drove on and had reached Linden itself when the Landrover broke down. That was all we needed. Three nice local men helped us to fix it enough to get us home but said we would need to get certain spare parts which they did not have at their garage. We paid them three thousand of the ten we had and then had lunch at a little hotel café and bar owned by Dunstan Barrow, the chief executive of the Bauxite mines. That took four thousand dollars and left us with three until Edwin's next pension was paid in. We used it to fill up the tank and drove home after our meal as we did not want to leave it too late. Linden seemed even more run down than the rest of the country. It was not a place to get excited about so why stay, especially when the car had a problem.

It was already dark when we reached Georgetown and I think Edwin's mind was on getting home before there was another "high-jacking" from men like those who had ambushed us in the morning, so he did not stop again for petrol, but forged ahead down the east coast road of Demerara towards Berbice. In any case we had no money left. I never gave petrol a thought, until we passed Mahaica and started losing power. We gradually fizzled out of momentum outside the one house for miles around. It was pitch black. There was nothing for it but to go and knock on the isolated farmhouse door and beg for some petrol to get us home. Edwin left me in the car and went sheepishly up the long drive to request help. A lone security light shone out at the front and dogs began to bark menacingly. It took some time. Then a very frail and elderly Indian farmer came out, led Edwin to the barn at the back and after a while they appeared with a small jerry can. The farmer came down the drive to the car with Edwin and waited for him to tip the petrol into our tank. Edwin got a stern lecture from him about being so irresponsible as not to carry enough fuel for such a long journey. He hardly needed it, but ate humble pie in view of the situation.

"It is just enough to get you down the road to the regional chairman's house and you will need to ask him for some more so you can get all the way home," the old man had said as he waved us on our way. After waking Geoffrey Fraser, the Regional Chairman, from his slumbers in his roadside farmhouse at Half Way Tree and getting him to lend us a jerry can of petrol which we promised to return refilled the next day, we could breathe a sigh of relief. As we made our way back down the coast road to Hopetown, I couldn't help wondering what would have happened to us that night if Edwin had not been the Neighbourhood District Chairman and thereby won the trust of Geoffrey Fraser.

Chapter 18

The Road to El Dorado

There is a legend in Guyana dating back to the sixteenth century, when Sir Walter Raleigh, hot on the tail of Columbus, mounted an exploratory expedition to the mainland coast of South America. He had been lured by the Amerindian tales of El Dorado, a "Golden One" who inhabited the deep jungle interior of the Guianas and was attired completely in gold. Guiana means "land of many rivers" and so it is. Raleigh's explorations took him up the two largest estuaries facing the southernmost Caribbean island of Trinidad that by then had been colonized by the Spanish. These rivers: the Orinoco and the Essequibo are in Venezuela and Guyana respectively. They are indeed the source of deposits of gold from the Guiana shield, although Raleigh himself never found "The Golden One" personified. The native Arawaks and Caribs in those regions would certainly have melted away into the forest to watch their visitors from a safe distance and protect anything of real value they had. It was far easier for them to do this in the vast interior of a continent than it had been for their unfortunate 'cousins' trapped in the confines of tiny Caribbean islands. However, settlers from Europe soon made inroads into the continent named after Amerigo Vespucci but discovered by Columbus, and began to find placer deposits of gold in these rivers. These first settlers in the Guianas were mainly Dutch seafarers bringing slaves to the Caribbean plantations to sell to the Spanish and Portuguese. I wanted to make all this history relevant to my students and bring it alive for them. As yet, no visible evidence of developed ancient civilisations had been uncovered by archaeologists in Guyana. There were no great Mayan, Aztec or Inca temples to visit, but I could seek illustrations of artefacts found in Guyana from the days when Raleigh met the Arawaks, and that way, with my help, my students could find a connection between their own country's present and its distant documented past. If I could take them into the interior with me to experience the environment these encounters took place in, then it would be even better. I would find my own road to ElDorado.

Princess Diana had died in a horrific car crash and England was mourning. The world was mourning. Even in Guyana, the television news was full of it. Everyone was very sad. The very same day, Sapodilla Learning Centre had the best news it could have hoped for: the CXC results had arrived and all our full time students had passed all their examinations. Robin, Trevor, Maggie, Michelle and Abiola in particular had top grades in all academic subjects I had put them in for. They were excellent results. The children were jubilant. Sapodilla Learning Centre had got better CXC exam results per capita than any other school in the region. Word spread like wildfire. I was inundated with enquiries for classes that day and for several days after. I had twenty two students who by July had reached the correct age and ability level in my part time classes to become full time students. They had all enrolled and were due to start in September. I could now take on another twenty three part-time secondary and the same number of primary prep students. This gave me enough funds to pay for photocopier paper for the year with a little bit spare for art materials.

The local Congregational Minister, Reverend Paul was on a church course in England but in his absence, his wife, who was a teacher in New Amsterdam, brought her sixteen year old son to me to join the full time school. Once again I was being asked to bend my rules. He had failed his CXC exams in New Amsterdam. I was expected to transform failure into success and furthermore, to include agriculture on my curriculum because that was his best subject. I liked Reverend Paul. He seemed a kind and genuine person. He was a close friend of Edwin's mother and thus relied a lot on Edwin for advice on how to manage his diocesan affairs. I found it difficult to turn down their request. However, the boy had never been to any of my part time classes. I said he could spend most of the week doing practical work on the farm with Spear as his supervisor and could join in with the full time classes for the theory and a few of the other subjects that he was capable of doing. He would not be a full time student as such and would not wear their uniform. Mrs Paul reluctantly accepted this compromise because the alternative would have been to pay thousands of Guyana dollars a week for him to have private lessons with a local teacher in New Amsterdam.

I had not considered agriculture up to now in my curriculum but tried to work out a way to do so in order to help him out. I had no knowledge of animal husbandry, but the crop science and botany involved was a hobby and interest of mine that I could teach myself more about. I could teach the theory to the full time students on Saturdays while the junior secondary part time students were being taught maths by the volunteer. I decided that agriculture would be a useful thing for all our students to take as a compulsory subject, since even though the sheep project had died off, I felt a need to justify our acquisition of all the furniture from them. In any case, agriculture was the main realistic employment opportunity for young people in Guyana. If done scientifically, young people could develop their own business on their idle family land. Small farmers could make profit and expand. They could become commercial farmers and develop the natural resource that Guyana had in abundance: good fertile arable and pastoral land. There was no shortage of local and export markets for the potential products it could produce. The main obstacle to this happening was the perception that land work was slavery and condemned one to poverty. I would show by example, as I had always done that there was no shame in cultivating the soil and it could turn a tidy profit. I enjoyed growing crops myself and was happy to get out my fork and spade and get my hands dirty. I would enlist help from local ministry of agriculture specialists to do the practical animal husbandry stuff that I knew nothing about.

We never heard from or saw Colin James again after our recent dawn high-jacking, nor got our money back, but that was no surprise to me. It was a case of Robin Hood in reverse: a redistribution of wealth, robbing the good to give to the bad. Edwin didn't see it that way. He believed they were genuinely fighting against drugs, so he felt his money was doing some good. I would have agreed if I had thought that fighting against the narco-traffickers was genuinely what our money was being used for, but using the tactics of a bandit to force contributions from law-abiding citizens was not my idea of the right way to get support from willing donors. The idea of me taking off for a solo drive in the jeep suddenly became less appealing. How would I ever get time for it now, anyway?

The political backdrop to all this was that Sam Hinds, the Prime Minister and therefore deputy leader, was now President. However, he had nominated Janet Jagan, Cheddi's wife, a white American by birth and ethnicity, to be Prime Minister. This would mean she would be the PPP candidate for President in the forthcoming general election. The Afro-Guyanese people in their villages saw this as both Cheddi's dynastic and Janet Jagan's suppressed personal political ambitions now being unleashed. Sam Hinds was PPP but at least he was black instead of Indian, so in their eyes was on their side. They were also justifiably feeling that black communities were being marginalised. Tensions were rising as the year wore on and many Indo-Guyanese made no secret locally of using their current political power to get revenge on the blacks for all the years they had suffered marginalisation at the hands of the blacks under Burnham's dictatorship. As part of the election reforms put in motion by the Carter Centre, more political parties were beginning to form. Earlier in the year, Bernie Grant's office sent a researcher from Tottenham to stay with Rupert Roopnarine who was leader of one of these. The young London based Asian girl brought us a donation of a pack of exercise books and a pack of biro pens from Bernie Grant. She had presumably come to find out about us following our letter to Bernie to arrange a school exchange. The unexpected visit was a bit of an embarrassment, as it looked like we were taking on a political alignment with Roopnarine's party. One thing I had learned about life in Guyana by now was that everyone in the country, however young or old, was highly political. They were as aware of the political affiliations of people you mixed with as they were aware of termites inside the wood of your house, long before you were aware of them yourself.

The exchange project between us and Havering youth group had died in July, when we had received a letter from them saying they could not do it after all. I was disappointed on behalf of our full time students who had been promised a place on the exchange as a reward for their all-round efforts. Edwin was disappointed because he had always gone the extra mile when organising such things in his working life in England. He had always made sure things happened, galvanising sponsors and participants to fulfil his plans. He concluded that the youth leaders he and Mitch had arranged it all with the previous November were a "bunch of useless wets that just talk big and can't deliver." He would put the idea on hold for now, but not for ever. For the moment, we had volunteers to prepare for and another weekend trip to Trinidad for the Women on the Move race in October. Edwin had already selected Keisa, a much younger girl in the sports club who was now winning the local female and some of the national races. She was a part time, not a full time student, but would become full time when she was old enough. I asked if we could take the sixth formers to Trinidad with us for the long weekend at the same time. They could do coastal and urban field work for their Geography O-level. I could do some proper map-reading with them using ordnance survey maps, which really did not work for the purpose in Guyana. This would make up for their disappointment over the exchange not happening. The new intake would be able to do the same the following year if they worked hard. Edwin thought it was a great idea. He went to BWIA and negotiated sponsored reduced fares for the seven of us. The volunteer teachers, Keisa and I would all be running in the 5k race to represent the school and Guyana. We would have to take the teachers with us, since we could not safely leave them alone in the house while we both went away.

I had received notification from Mitch that he was not able to get flights to Guyana for the volunteers until the end of September. I realised that I would have to start term without them. That could have been a nuisance but I had learned to be exceptionally resourceful in the last six years. I saw it instead as an opportunity to build team spirit between the sixth form, who had been in our full time system for the past two years and the new ones switching from part to full time. For me to teach them all at the same time, it would mean vertical mixed ability grouping. I could introduce them to several new subjects that they would all find useful and relevant. The topics would have to be teacher-led but follow up activities could be done at each student's own ability level. Although I had already drawn up separate timetables for our two volunteers and myself, and separate timetables for sixth form and the new intake, I would delay the operation of these until the volunteers arrived.

I decided to use the three weeks of solo teaching to introduce the new students to the mini-company project which our first participants had named "Summersplash". To that end, the sixth formers would be useful assets, as they had already been doing it for the last two years and understood how it worked. Indeed, we had built it up together. It was a reality role-play exercise in work ethic, discipline, business and financial management. The agriculture exam syllabus had a strong element of this in it. Business is a fundamental part of farming so Summersplash would reinforce the agriculture syllabus by practical business management work. We could simultaneously have some interesting and appropriate careers education. I would put each of them through a job application process for a post in the mini-company. First, I would teach them how to write a letter of application and prepare their curriculum vitae. Then each student would choose a post advertised on the school noticeboard, and apply for it by letter with C.V. Later, they would have to be interviewed by Edwin and me while the other students observed. I would start with the strongest and leave the weakest till last so they had the chance to gain confidence and learn from watching those who went before them. Afterwards, we would sensitively appraise each interview to the group as a whole and do the same when we later announced the appointments, so they all understood why they had succeeded or been offered an alternative post more suited to them. I had to make sure that all students felt important and that no one would be just a lackey to be bossed about by another who did no manual work. I would achieve this by making every student either a manager or a deputy of some aspect of the company and that every single student would have to be a worker doing the manual labour. Every student would also have to buy a share in the company and become a shareholder. I had been the general manager up to now, but the best sixth former to apply for the post would take over this role from now on and I would just be their technical adviser.

The mini-company would now not only sell its hand craft products and postcards but would be producing food on the farm and selling it in the local community. Each student would have a small plot in our farm on which to grow the vegetables they learned about in agriculture. We could jointly begin the production of live chickens for meat. They would set their own wages which would be based on hourly time sheets and sales of crops and chickens. Their wages would be paid into the mini-company bank account of which I was one of the signatories. They could withdraw their wages when needed for examination entry or field trips. Those who worked would end up with more than those who were lazy. The company profit would be paid out annually in dividends to the shareholders after some had been retained for re-investment in tools and assets. The farm labouring would be the practical work that they needed to do for the agriculture syllabus. The full time students would get on with this practical work every afternoon before sports training started while I was teaching the primary students. They would also do it all day Saturday after their theory class ended until Edwin was ready to do sports training with them. I would not need to be there to supervise them because the sixth form managers would now do that and report back to me if they had any problems. We would have a weekly board meeting of the whole school at which each manager would have to read out his or her written report on his or her area of responsibility for the past week. That way I could monitor what was going on without actually being there. I would timetable the board meeting in assembly time on Wednesdays before academic lessons began. On the other four weekday assemblies, Edwin and I would take turns to introduce a topic of moral education to the whole school and discuss it with the students.

329

Democracy and elections were an important part of the social studies syllabus, so I thought with the upcoming government general elections, these first three weeks of term would also be an ideal opportunity to run our own election campaign role-play. The sixth form students, who now would all be styled 'prefects' could form imaginary political parties to improve and develop the school. They would have to devise their own manifestos and make speeches to the others. We could then have a secret ballot election to vote for a school Head Boy and Head Girl.

Since our PTA would have extra new members and would be held concurrent with the next AGM of the remnants of the original sheep farmers' association, we called a joint meeting. We asked all parents to join the sheep farmer's association so that office holders of both associations could also be elected by a larger number of people than had hitherto happened. The existing active members of the sheep farmers association had also enrolled a family member into the school. Members agreed to change the name of the group from sheep farmers to "Small Farmers' Association" as every parent kept a few sheep or goats or had a cow, a pig or some poultry. It was an ideal way to bring divers members of the community together, to foster their interest in farming as well as education. It would also give Edwin an opportunity to promote among the wider adult community his ideas about public health, community development and realistic solutions to local youth unemployment. It would be non-political and not divisive on ethnic grounds. In this way it would be more effective than the local authority but would help achieve the aims of his efforts with the neighbourhood district council. I drafted in Edwin to teach careers and sports management to the sixth form as well as first aid to the new students as he was highly qualified in these subjects and it would help to fill gaps in their timetables with useful and important educational activities. He was also starting a new CCPR course in Sports Leadership for the region's teachers who had missed out on his last one.

Just as school was about to open at the start of September, we got a visit from Mr Leit Scamar, the headmaster of the Amerindian school in Moraikobai village in the interior of our region. He had been told at the regional office to come and see our museum because we had displays of Amerindian artefacts, photos of Amerindians in long Victorian dresses and others in native attire performing long forgotten war games. We showed him the exhibits and he was interested, no doubt spotting in us a potential customer for the craft products of his villagers. He invited us to visit his own school for the Amerindian Heritage Month Festival in the last few days of September. We accepted and made arrangements for the whole school, including our two volunteer teachers, to make another field trip into Moraikobai. It would be a fantastic way to start their time in Guyana, could be squeezed into the few days between their arrival and the Trinidad trip, and would remove the awkward problem of interrupting a new timetable we had barely started. Geography, social studies and history field work could all be integrated on the Amerindian theme. The first segment of the Caribbean History exam course was about the Arawaks who were the tribe living at Moraikobai. The students could also do some art work, and keep a diary. At the same time they could interact with the children of the village and learn their customs first hand. Edwin would take in some sports equipment and organise some physical education together with the local children and even a friendly match or two.

None of our students had ever been into the interior to see how the Amerindians lived, so the thought of it was very exciting for them. We had explained it all to parents at the joint PTA meeting, answered their questions and addressed any concerns. One parent, who operated a minibus, offered to drive us to the pickup point on the river if students paid the petrol money. It would be a challenge taking twenty-six people on a boat trip up the Mahaicony creek to the settlement. Bibi, the Indian parent from Cotton Tree who registered voters in Moraikobai for the elections commission, took us to meet Buddy Deo, an old man with a slow launch that normally transported supplies in and lumber out of the settlement. He agreed to take us on the six-hour river journey and told us how much diesel we would need to bring for the return trip on his launch. Then we had to calculate what other supplies and provisions we would need since although there would be catering facilities in the visitors' lodge at the settlement, we would have to take our own food. Edwin and I had our own personal life-jackets but he raced around getting officials at the region to agree to lend us their life jackets so we had one for each of our charges. All was set for the occasion and for term to start. I got on with photo-copying the homework diaries that I had drawn templates for. Every student would have one from now on. I would monitor the homework and see that they did what they were set by the volunteers as well as me. They would have a homework timetable for every subject included on their class timetable. Students would no longer have a day off on Tuesdays. It would be a six day week for all of us except the volunteers, who would get at least one completely free weekday as well as Sundays and some other free periods during the week for their marking and preparation.

Term had started by now. The drought had set in worse than any we had seen in our time in the country. The national news broadcasts said it was due to the El Nino phenomenon. Water was running very short already. We would have to ration the volunteers as soon as they arrived. It was September 11th. A young man with a very middle class English accent came to see Edwin. He said his name was David Lammy. He had been studying law at Harvard University. Someone had advised him to see Edwin about a business venture he wanted to undertake in Guyana. Edwin spent some time with him upstairs in our house. They arranged to meet again at the Tower hotel in Georgetown on the day Edwin had to collect our Trinidad tickets. It turned out that David's mother was Guyanese and was born in our village but she had gone as an adult to England where David had been born and educated. David's older brother lived at the end of our road in his mother's house but David was staying in the Tower Hotel in Georgetown where the living conditions were better. Now he had graduated from Harvard, he had brought two English college friends with him to Guyana hoping to set up a joint business, shipping high end furniture from Guyana to Heals in Tottenham Court Road. Edwin had taken them to see the 'factory' in Guyana making the nibbi rattan pieces we had bought from Colin and Mavis. Two days later, David brought his friends to Sapodilla and the sixth formers had to take them on a guided tour of our farm and museum while I was teaching the younger students. I made lunch for us all while the students had their break. The visitors were very young and green and did not seem to me as if they had much idea about the realities of business. They wanted to look at my furniture. Their questions soon made me realise that David, who had already seen my high quality bamboo furniture from the Philippines and had assumed we bought it in Guyana, had told the others about it. They had not been impressed by the poor quality of the locally made nibbi Edwin had taken them to see in Georgetown and wanted to know where they could get the bamboo stuff. I had to tell them that Guyana as yet did not produce anything of quality. It would take a very brave investor with a very large investment to initiate the production of anything that good and so far it had not been done. They went away a little wiser and we wished them good luck with their careers in law.

The next day, Edwin picked up the loaned lifejackets from the region. At the eleventh hour, he collected our vehicle from the local mechanic who had fitted the spare parts needed after our breakdown in Linden. A van later arrived at the house bringing the twenty two boxes of books from Dubai. They were beautiful brand new books covering all sorts of subjects. Alison's letter explained that she and other members of staff had helped her students in Dubai to raise two thousand pounds to ship the books to us. It was fantastic. I was busy unpacking them once classes finished for the day and Edwin helped by the sport club athletes, was preparing the snackette premises on the main road for the local Lions Club. He had agreed for them to use it free of charge for their annual fundraising barbecue the following evening. They had presented his young top athlete Julian James with a new pair of spikes recently. After a full teaching day for both of us, with the Lions about to set up their equipment for their invitees' entertainment, Edwin had to set off on the three and a half hour journey to the airport to collect our volunteers whose flight was due to arrive at 9.30 p.m. I got on with preparing their rooms. The amplifiers from the Lions Barbecue carried on the sea breeze across the pasture to Sapodilla until late in the night as I sat on the veranda in the dark, awaiting Edwin's return. Finally at 2.a.m. his headlights turned into our street, which fortunately was dust dry from El Nino. The girls both seemed very nice. I let them settle into their rooms so we could get straight to bed as we had a busy day ahead of us in less than a few hours.

I had scheduled a PTA meeting for that very evening at four p.m. so we could explain the final details of our field trip to Moraikobai the next day and the subsequent one to Trinidad for the sixth form. It would be the ideal opportunity to introduce the faces of our two new temporary teachers to the parents and children. I had given everyone the day off school to pack and prepare. First I had to give the volunteers a preparatory talk about local conditions, customs and the environment as well as the do's and don'ts of the house and the school rules. Then I explained our itinerary over the next week and what would be expected of them on the field trips. We had time to chat and get to know each other a little as well as to pack our things ready for the Moraikobai trip. We took our own hammocks and lent two of ours to the girls.

It took us an hour and a half to drive to Vick Persaud's house on the creek at Governor Light village where we boarded Buddy Deo's boat and put on our orange life vests. The excitement of the students was equalled by that of the volunteers who used the opportunity to chat and get to know each other and us. We had six hours ahead of us as the boat quietly chugged slowly through the remaining remote riverine villages with rice fields grazed not by the usual zebu cattle but by Chinese water buffalo and entered the more mysterious uninhabited reaches of the Mahaicony River. Here the dense moca-moca bushes cloaked the banks in an impenetrable screen between daylight and darkness; between the benign worldly environment and the sinister underworld of forest spirits. They cast their heart-shaped reflections onto the face of the black water, masking the other underworld beneath our boat. What pirhana fish lurked there, I wondered, with that curiosity-that-killed-the-cat desire to put in my finger and see if it came back out fully fleshed. Among the branches of the Moca-moca, safe from predators, Hoatzin birds with their majestic crests roosted in numbers.

"Look everyone," I called out, "The Canje Pheasants are up in these bushes. Who can tell me what is their other name?"

"Hoatzin, Miss," called out Robin, "They're the national bird of Guyana,"

"Stinkin' Hannah" said Satyanand.

"You're both right," I said, "It's also called the fossil bird because it is unlike any other bird. The young ones have a claw on each wing, visible before the feathers develop, to help it climb among the branches. Does anyone know why the locals call it Stinking Hannah?"

"It smell stink," said Delon, one of the younger students.

"Yes, but why does it smell?" I looked around at a sea of blank faces. "Well they think that because it eats mainly the leaves of these moca-moca trees that the smell comes from the fermenting vegetation in their stomachs." It was true. As we passed their habitat, the feint aroma of fresh cow dung wafted over the water.

"Look Miss! Water dog," said Colin Watts, pointing ahead of us to where the creek narrowed. Sure enough, in the distance, the sleek wet fur of a giant otter's whiskered nose pointed up out of the water, then dived downwards, arching its back and disappearing under as another one surfaced with a fish in its mouth. The splashing water echoed strangely, mingling with their distinctive yelps. We all watched their antics, spellbound as we approached. As the boat slid by them, they retreated to a safe distance. How many English teachers have such iconic endangered species virtually in their own back yard? I thought. This thrilling rare glimpse was not repeated as our journey progressed but the fact that we had been privileged to witness it on our first school field trip was a priceless bonus.

It was a long day and the sun was setting as we finally reached the transit point which was a lumber camp in a small clearing. The old man Buddy drew the boat slowly up to the jetty and told Edwin that we must disembark there and wait for the pick-up truck to come from Moraikobai. The children picked up their packs, clambered off the long, narrow boat onto the small jetty and through the overhanging trees. We all piled on to the platform of planks that the Indo-Guyanese lumberjacks had constructed with a makeshift framework of poles for their hammocks to attach to. They were a friendly crew of men who had just finished their working day and were happy to accept our intrusion into their camp while we awaited our pick-up. After an hour of good-humoured banter between us and our hosts, there was still no sign of our contact. Edwin began to grow anxious. We had no means of communication with the Amerindian settlement and our boat had pulled away and left us an hour ago, promising to collect us at 9 a.m. the day after tomorrow. The men on the platform invited the children to tie up their hammocks and rest for a while as it was getting late. They had a bright gas lamp which cast a good light around the platform area. It was a measure of protection from the many lethal predators that lurked in the surrounding rainforest. I could read Edwin's mind. He was beginning to think that no one from Moraikobai knew we were there. The lumber workers had no vehicle or truck in the camp, otherwise we could have asked them to take us out instead of waiting. Edwin told me he didn't much like the idea of being stuck in the lumber camp with these children for two days until the boat came back for us. He spoke with one of the men and asked how far it was to the village. Walking was out of the question in a terrain of lethal wildlife. Meanwhile the children, who were very tired, tried to get some sleep in their hammocks. There was very little shelter, only a flimsy tarpaulin tied over the platform, but it was dry weather so it did not seem to matter. Another hour went by. Edwin told us that one of the men had kindly agreed to travel to the settlement on his ancient but rugged BSA motorbike and tell the captain that we were all waiting at the lumber camp for their truck to come and pick us up. He normally used the bike to deliver any mail brought down river to the village. Off he went and in an hour or so he returned, saying that the captain was sending a driver with a truck to pick us all up. At least the uncertainty had been removed, knowing that someone was on their way.

It was past 4 a.m. when the truck finally arrived. The driver, one of the Amerindian villagers, was completely drunk. The truck was an old army one with a canvas tarpaulin stretched over a hooped metal framework. It was standing room only as there were lots of us and no seats. Kitbags were thrown in around the edges and after all the others were safely in, Edwin and I climbed aboard. I found that holding on to the overhead framework was the only way to keep balance as the truck jolted over the bumpy forest trail and the children laughed and squealed as they were unexpectedly thrown against each other. The truck lurched from side to side, hitting overhead branches at every turn in the seven mile trail. Huge parasol ants dislodged from these branches found their way through holes in the tarpaulin and dropped onto us like rain. Edwin must have been on overdrive, as he had not slept for twenty four hours by now. Dawn was almost breaking by the time we got our hammocks up in the rest house at Moraikobai. We slept for a couple of hours and then it was time for breakfast.

I was no stranger to the charm, from the point of view of visitors, of life in a jungle clearing with the indigenous people who live there. I had visited remote longhouses in Borneo back in the eighties, before it became the tropical equivalent of Benidorm for the boomerang fliers between Australasia and England or the expat paradise of the Asian Giants. I enjoyed playing at being David Attenborough. Now that I lived permanently in the Amerindians' front garden, I was more attuned to the realities of their lives. They were, by choice, out of reach of 'civilised' Guyana, but wanting to gain the benefits of its goods and services without it changing their culture or self-determination. We in the west want to carry on viewing their 'picturesque' thatch and pole huts and hand crafted clothing and utensils made from traditional forest materials, but instead we see poverty-stricken subsistence dwellers racked with disease and alcoholism using recycled imported synthetic clothing and plastic and metal goods. Academics and colonial apologists teach us to blame ourselves for this, for exploiting them by taking away their riches and giving them drug dependency in return. While I am no defender of imperialism or subjugation of one people by another, I am an advocate of speaking the truth about what I observe even when it appears to contradict what I have been taught.

By now, I had decided it was a western myth that 'the white man' had corrupted indigenous people by giving them alcohol in return for their gold or beautiful craft work instead of trade goods that would 'improve their lives'. In reality, the culture of the Amerindians revolved around the harvesting of natural forest products and communicating with the spirits of the forest that they believed controlled their lives. The production of home-made alcohol, 'Paiwari', from cassava, was traditionally central to this since prehistoric times. They now not only made it from cassava but also from sugar cane. The men wanted to become drunk and since they ruled their community, then accepting ready-made alcohol was often more attractive to them than money because it was more useful to them than money. Whatever money they were given would be spent on things they wanted, which was often more alcohol. I was sure that the modern day Amerindian men got drunk because it was a tradition and what men were expected to do. In this, they were very much the same as Negro or Indian men in Guyanese coastal villages, but the tradition of getting drunk was rooted in their ancient animist religion because of the need to induce visions and communion with the spirits of the environment and of the dead. It was an educational experience for us all over the next two days.

The fair we had been invited to was scheduled for that afternoon and we were told that traditional cooked dishes would be on sale then. We made tea for breakfast in the rest house kitchen and shared out the bread, butter, jam, bananas and mangoes that we had brought with us. We let the children make up their own sandwiches. They had all brought packed lunches with them the day before, which to Guyanese children means a container filled with cook-up rice and peas or roti and curry with a few chopped vegetables and small bits of meat bones, skin, gristle and fat mixed in. We knew they had eaten well, as they consumed most of it on the boat journey and anything left, when we were waiting in the lumber camp. Now we just needed an energy boost to last until lunchtime when we would buy cooked food at the fair.

It was a tradition for Amerindian settlements to have rest houses. They were places where itinerant visitors from other settlements could stay for a few nights when trading, hunting, socialising or visiting relatives who had married someone from another settlement. For a small fee they could sling up their hammock in this communal dormitory. This rest house was a new modern concrete structure with a corrugated iron roof. The government, using funding agency money for the purpose, had built it fairly recently for regional education or other government officials to overnight in on those rare occasions when they visited to carry out their jobs. For this reason, it had two flushing toilets that worked with an overhead rainwater supply tank and a septic tank, a few showers and wash basins. Our students were staying in accommodation that was far more luxurious in this respect than their own homes. The back of the rest house was divided into small dormitories with wooden beds and mattresses. We had put the girls on one side and the boys on another with ourselves in between them in the main and much larger front room. Any of the students who had brought their own hammocks like we had, slung them up between us and the back wall. Edwin's hammock was the one nearest the front door where the villagers, or any other guests visiting the village, could come in and out. He said he wanted to make sure we were all protected and later on that evening, I realised why. For now, though, it was time for the children to get to know their counterparts and to explore the village.

The Moraikobai children were very friendly and immediately flocked around us as we emerged from the rest house. We had not been able to see anything in the dark when we arrived, but now it was daylight, we could see that we were in a large circular clearing in the rainforest and the rest house was facing a central plaza of white sandy soil around which the other buildings of the village were arranged. There was a large wooden building with corrugated roof similar to those in the coastal villages, which they said was their school and another that was the cacique's (captain's) house. The villagers' homes were thatched wooden huts arranged randomly on the opposite side of the plaza from the rest house. I told everyone that we must wait until we had seen the captain and the headmaster before we moved away from the rest-house, so we chatted with the village children meanwhile. The effects of inbreeding were obvious from the start as many children had slight physical deformities. One little boy was clearly a dwarf. Our children wanted to know why his name was 'Moon Man'. He said it was because he was born at full moon and that is why he looked different from other children.

Mr Scamar eventually came and greeted us. The captain was still sleeping having been up all night. He would meet us later in the day but Mr Scamar told us to feel free to walk around the village and speak to the people. The fair would start at midday and the people would set up their stalls with craft and food so we could buy whatever we liked from them. Edwin could organise some sports activities for the children on the plaza after we had visited the fair. He also wondered whether we would be so kind as to judge their Miss Washiji Pageant that afternoon in the school hall. He said it would prevent disputes between the villagers who would accept our choice because we would not be biased. Of course we agreed to do that.

After he left us on our own, I told the children that I wanted them to find out as much as they could about the Amerindian customs and beliefs, about their farming, fishing and hunting and about the bush medicines they used as well as any plants and other natural materials that they used in their craft work and for dyes. I wanted them to take their rough-books and make notes and sketches of what they saw and found interesting. The jungle around the clearing was full of dangerous snakes and animals but the plaza had been stripped of any vegetation so it was safe. They must not go outside the village circle or wander off out of sight of one of us teachers, so we knew where they were at all times. They would have to meet back with us at the rest house at midday. The children were all very good about that sort of thing. By now, when they were with us, they behaved as if they were our own children. I liked that about them. Other Guyanese people who visited us always remarked on how different the Sapodilla children were from children in other local schools. They were so well behaved. It was meant, and taken, as a compliment.

One of the Amerindian boys was called Pijari. Our boys asked him about any war games or similar customs they still played in the village. He said they had a ceremonial game nine nights after anyone in the village died. All the people would gather at the dead person's house. The women would sit on one side and the men on the other side. They would give commands to someone on the opposite team as if they were speaking as the dead man's spirit. It involved removing items of clothing until they were all completely naked. If anyone refused to do so, points would be knocked off their team's score. This game always lasted for the whole night. They believed that a spirit called Jacoo haunted you. If you were out walking in the night alone, it might attack you by entering your shadow, making you feel uncomfortable. If this happened, they believed that they must throw themselves down on the ground or run and hide in their house where it was dark and no shadow could be cast. This would prevent Jacoo entering your shadow. Although this response to the evil spirit was peculiar to the Amerindians, the spirit itself was very similar to the evil spirit known in the coastal villages as 'Bacoo', so I guessed that there had been some mingling of beliefs over time. Negroes and Indians all tended to have 'Nine nights' ceremonies for their dead too, but they did not play any game during these.

Pijari told the students, to their disappointment, that the Amerindians do not use a bow and arrow to hunt any more. Instead, they go out into the savannahs in a group, burn some bushes and camp for the night in the area. During the night deer and labba come and sleep in the ashes left by the fire. Then the men close in around the animals and fire their guns at them. We were not able to see this in action of course. There were hardly any men in the village that morning. I assumed it was because they were all away working in the lumber camps to get money from the local timber trade, which was controlled by black or Indian entrepreneurs, many of them ministers, living in Georgetown. Forestry was the main occupation of Amerindian men living in the interior.

As we wandered around the village, women were making their large flat cassava breads and setting them to dry in the sun on their roofs. One house had a matapee set up outside for the cassava to be grated into and squeezed dry. The juice collected in a bowl underneath was saved to be fermented to make the casareep that the children all knew so well as the chief ingredient of the pepperpot their mothers and grandmothers all made at home. By now, the village captain, Mr Winston Jacobs, had joined us. He escorted Edwin to another area of the village and I followed. At the time I did not think about it, but maybe he just wanted Edwin on his own. When Edwin asked where all the men were, he said they were sleeping.

In the far corner away from the other houses, a man was boiling up cane juice to ferment into an alcoholic drink they called Pirimofri. He explained what he was doing while we watched. He offered some to Edwin, who declined, saying it was too early in the day for him to drink alcohol. Other children were bringing wild plants to our students and explaining their medicinal or craft uses to them. The midday sun was high in the sky by now and we needed to get refreshments as the children were hungry. The captain pointed us over to where the fair was taking place and said it was ready for us to visit now.

We gathered our group all together and wandered over to the other side of their school, where women had set up their tables on a flat area facing the river. The children had all brought a little spending money for this purpose, so could choose whatever they wanted that was on offer on the stalls. There were two kinds of pepperpot for sale: one of Powis, a rainforest bird they called 'bush chicken' and another of a river fish known as Houri. I tried both types. The pepperpot was served as expected with their wafer thin cassava bread. It looked and tasted completely different from the dark coloured beef version of pepperpot we were all familiar with at home. It had a lot of sweet pepper in as well as hot pepper and the paler coloured sauce was more delicate, but of course it was full of tiny bones like most local wild meat. To all Guyanese, sucking the bones in one's food is a joy, not a nuisance. I observed the reaction of the two volunteers while I tucked in to mine. Nova took one look at the cracked enamel bowl it was served up in and declined to eat any at all. Louise tried some, but unenthusiastically.

The craft work that the women had spread out for sale was mostly table mats of various shapes and sizes, woven from dried tibisiri grass. One item was unique. It was a little trinket basket with a lid woven into the shape of a woman's body. Her features were embroidered onto it using grasses coloured with the pinks, purple and blue dyes of local plants. I already had lots of these table mats but I bought the doll-lidded basket. I had expected to see beautiful wood carving or balata animal models and traditional hunting implements or hand-woven cotton hammocks such as those I had bought in the shop in Georgetown, but none of these items were on display. I could see they no longer needed them for their daily lives. Their own hammocks were made out of jute rice bags. They were rugged and more practical in these living conditions. In any case these women did not appear to grow cotton as a crop, and so would have to buy the soft cotton hammocks imported from Brazil to Georgetown. They had no personal incomes large enough to afford such luxury and the men appeared to spend all theirs on alcohol. Obviously, delicately crafted items were seen to have no value in the coastal economy because there was no demand for them from local people. The international tourist trade was virtually non-existent and consisted mainly of expat Afro- or Indo-Guyanese who came back to stay with relatives in the city or coastal villages. Most of these were not really interested in buying such items either, so with no demand for them, no-one bothered to produce any.

I put in a request for a carved wooden stool but with little hope of it ever being made. It was unlikely, with such a geographical distance between us, that they would believe we would come back to visit them again. They hardly ever got visits from outsiders, even when they were official ones. It was down to them to come out to the coast and they did not usually bother. Why should they? They liked their isolation. They liked being able to live free and unregulated by timetables and routines. Anna Iles had once told me that many Georgetown entrepreneurs had tried to get them to export craftwork like hammocks and nibbi furniture, but Amerindians did not like having to produce a certain number in a certain time, sweatshop fashion. I knew the export trade depended on regularity, on being able to fill shipping containers with items going to the same destination on a regular basis. The end value would have to justify the massive transport costs. No development was going to happen unless they wanted to change their way of life totally, and welcome outsiders into their midst and they did not really want to.

It was time for our sports activities, so we met up on the plaza with the Amerindian school children. Edwin sent one of our children to fetch the equipment from the rest-house. We had brought a football, volleyball and basketball for them, some hockey sticks, some cricket bats, some tennis rackets and their respective balls. None of it was new, because it had been donated to us to fill our original shipping containers. A couple of extra crates had been shipped out to us since, so we were sharing it. Edwin wanted to help the Amerindian community in our region to participate in the sport just as much as the coastal villages. He wanted to include all sections of the community in whatever he did and so did I.

He organised the children into a group, explained what he was there for, showed them the equipment and asked them some questions to see what they already knew and did. Then he began with a simple catching game using the volleyball. He divided them up into two teams, mixing our students with theirs and invented some simple rules to get them into the idea of volleyball. It was a bit wild as little else could be done in a single session. He had hoped that one of their teachers would participate in his sports leader course so could teach the game properly from then on, but the distance and logistical difficulties of anyone getting to us once a week was plainly obvious to him now we had done the trip ourselves. The youngsters had a lot of fun and then Edwin let them have a go at some football, hockey and circle tennis (a local game similar to rounders with a tennis racket and a wicket instead of a net). After that, he presented the equipment to Mr Scamar who thanked us and went away to store it all.

The children ran across to the river to swim, inviting ours to join them. It was a very shallow pool in the small tributary stream that the villagers all bathed in daily and did their laundry in. It had no weed except on the far side and was sandy with a pebble beach on the village side. It had probably been widened out by the villagers to make it suit their needs. At the deepest part it was waist height. Our children were accustomed to bathing in field trenches and could all swim so I had no safety concerns. Nevertheless we watched them play together in the water until they all came out.

The pageant had to start soon as it would all have to finish before darkness fell. Once dried and changed, those who had been swimming joined us and we went over to the school hall and took up our places. I dished out to Edwin, Louise and Nova three of the four score-sheets we had been given. Once the hall had filled with our party, the village boys and various adults (including some of the men we had not seen during the day) Mr Scamar mounted the stage. They had set up a temporary P.A system, so he used it to welcome us officially to the village. He said we had come to judge the pageant which he then introduced. It was Amerindian Heritage Month, so the students of the school would be modelling traditional costumes which represented the traditional activities of the Amerindian community. There followed a delightful series of presentations depicting cassava farming, fishing, hunting, cassava making, basketry, weaving and pottery. One student performed a verse about each activity while another mimed the activity dressed in costume made entirely of local grasses with the appropriate implements crafted from local materials.

There was a brief interlude. Modern popular music on a cassette struck up for the second half and a series of the same slender girls, aged eleven or twelve, came on wearing body-hugging long evening dresses of variously coloured shiny and glittery materials. Each girl was introduced by name as she paraded around the stage, gyrating provocatively to the music. The men were looking on. This was a beauty pageant, a bit like the Miss World competition. Although these competitions were normal in state schools along the coast, where even the youngest black girls revelled in the exercise, it was not what we had expected to see here. We conferred on our scores and then handed them to Mr Scamar to announce the winner. I began to see why he had pressed us to be the judges to prevent a fight breaking out among the audience. The men, who had been watching on, had selected which of the girls they would bed that night. It was a meat market. Our results, based on an appraisal of the artistic beauty of the traditional costume rather than on the beauty and sexuality of the girl wearing it, may not have met with their approval but they did not show it. There was a fitting round of applause as the winner and runner up was announced. We shook hands with Mr Scamar and made our way over to the rest-house as it was getting dark and we all had to bathe and get into our hammocks or beds for the night.

After giving out bread, cheese and fruit to the students and seeing that they were in their separate billets behind us, Edwin and I sat in our hammocks and chatted with Louise and Nova about the activities of the day before we were ready to sleep. Edwin made no secret of his views on the pageant. He was fiercely protective of these under-age girls. It was easy for us to be judgemental, I thought, but by local law they were not under age. The age of consent was twelve in Guyana. It suited many ministers of any ethnicity to have it that way, and it was acceptable to the male dominated Amerindian culture. In principal I agreed with Edwin, but knew that it would not change unless the women themselves saw a need for change and broke away from their family security by moving out of Amerindian communities and abandoning their culture. It wasn't for outsiders to come in and start upsetting the communities by preaching different values.

It was getting dark. One of the village men came in to light a large modern hurricane lamp that hung near the entrance door. There was a bit of a flurry and some other men brought in a long handled brush while another held a torch to the rafters to illuminate a very large spider lurking in the shadows. They stabbed at it with the brush until it fell to the ground where they finished it off. It must have been a poisonous one. We were all tired from the heat and activities of the day so decided to settle into our hammocks but Edwin remained standing in front of his. He had noticed that men were coming in and out at the far end of the hall where a bar had been set up by the door. They were drinking cane spirit and paiwari (an alcohol made from fermented cassava) and their laughter was becoming more boisterous. The music from the PA was still playing in the distance. Captain Winston came in and invited Edwin to drink with them. Edwin accepted out of politeness and spent some time chatting with the men by the bar. He was master of the art of talking continuously so as to make one drink last hours. After a while, he came over and sat on his hammock facing outwards to them but turned towards me first.

"I'm staying here to keep guard," he whispered. "Some of those men have been eyeing up our girls and I want to make sure they don't get at them." His eyes were sunken through lack of sleep. He must have been running on pure adrenalin.

"Really?" I whispered back. "Which girls? Do you mean Nova and Louise?"

"Yes," he said "But more particularly Melina, Jessica and Devi." That possibility had not occurred to me but after he pointed it out I could see why he was worried.

"In that case I'll keep you company" I said. He spent the rest of the night talking to the men by the door while pretending to drink from the bottle he was clutching. I dozed in my hammock. Eventually the music died away and the village men drifted out of the rest-house but Edwin stayed awake, whispering to me, in case any of them came back later. He wasn't going to take any chances.

In the morning, we all got up at five and packed. Edwin paid the captain the four and a half thousand dollars he had asked for and at five thirty, still in darkness, we left in the truck for the transit camp with "Uncle Dean", after his late night carousing, at the wheel again. It took an hour to get to the river jetty but the journey seemed amazingly quick in reverse. Dawn had broken and Buddy Deo was there waiting with his boat as promised, so our six hour return journey went smoothly. At Vick's house at Governor Light at twelve thirty, Satynand's dad was already there with his minibus to take us home by two o'clock. That meant we had until midnight to wash, unload and repack for our Trinidad trip. Edwin caught a few hours much needed sleep and we were off again without any time to think.

Trinidad was quite a contrast to our last three days. It was a brief entry into a civilised world that our students had never seen before and which I had forgotten existed. It had changed completely since my last visit in 1991 and now had a sparkling modern airport. We spent our first full day touring the northern range mountains, swimming in the sea and doing geography fieldwork on Manama beach while Edwin trained Keisa for the race. The second day was the race, which we all took part in except Edwin and the boys, who cheered us on. The final day we managed to fit in a tour to see the location of the oil refinery, cement and sand quarries and to visit a cocoa plantation before our check-in at the airport for departure at quarter to six in the evening. We managed to get back to Sapodilla by ten so we could prepare for school to start the next morning. We had been travelling in a whirlwind for a week. Now we could resume some kind of normality.

I had by now established a good relationship with Louise and Nova. We had had plenty of opportunity to get to know each other socially as well as professionally. I thought we were going to have a good year in front of us. The first day of the new timetable went well. It was that evening when Nova dropped the bombshell. After our evening meal, Edwin asked the girls for their share of the field trip expenses and for their cheques for the year's board and lodging. Louise, with no hesitation, paid for her share of the field trips in local cash and pulled out a cheque from Mitch for part of her keep. We looked at

Nova for her full contribution. She said she could not pay it as she had no money. Edwin was stunned.

"What do you mean you've got no money?"

"I'm sorry but I haven't got any money. I spent what I had in Trinidad."

"How can you come away for a year to the other side of the world without any spending money?" he said, sensing that she was trying to avoid paying it to him because she wanted to keep it for herself. "You must have got some."

"Well I'm afraid I haven't; only a hundred and thirty pounds," she said "Mitch was supposed to be sending on some money to you."

"But you wrote to me and agreed to pay your own way when I said we could only fund one volunteer. You said you were earning money as a temp," I reminded her.

She looked askance at me as if I had invented the idea and she knew nothing about it. With that I got up from the table, went into the study and found the correspondence between me and her. I read it out aloud to her in front of Edwin and Louise and then pointed out the paragraphs where she had written it. It was clear that she was embarrassed because she had not expected me to keep her letters and copies of mine to be able to quote as evidence. What did she have to say to that? I was angry now to think she had tricked us. She had allowed us to think she would pay, conned us into getting her a free sponsored return ticket to Guyana, conned Mitch into letting her get on the plane without giving him the money she was supposed to have raised herself, and assumed that once she had arrived in our care, we would have to support her anyway until the date of her return ticket.

"We can't afford to feed an extra mouth that we do not really need to be here," I said, "especially as you were clearly told not to come unless you could pay your own way."

"Well I'm sorry but I don't have any money."

"Well I'll take what you've got for now and you better write home and get some more soon," said Edwin, taking charge of the situation, "because if I don't get the full amount by the end of the month, I'll have to take you back to the airport and send you home again." Nova's face reddened as she realised she was not going to pull off her ploy. She went and got her cheque book and wrote out a cheque for three hundred pounds. Louise looked uncomfortable at witnessing all this. I took her aside.

"I'm sorry that this has happened, but you mustn't feel bad. It's not your problem. *You've* done nothing wrong. The money was raised for your benefit because you were the only one we really wanted and needed. We didn't need Nova and only gave in to pressure from her because she said she was working and would raise all her own funds. Then Mitch complained about you not wanting to do his bike ride."

"Yes," she said, "I did refuse to do it because I had a job in a bar and I was earning good money that I needed to support myself while I'm here and when I go on around the rest of South America after I leave here in July. I didn't want to lose wages by going on a London to Brighton bike ride and finding sponsors. It seemed a waste of time when I can be earning money in a bar."

"I quite agree," I said, "I think Mitch got the wrong end of the stick when we said students should fund themselves. Funding doesn't just mean having to get other people to pay for your trip by sponsoring some leisure activity or stunt you do. In fact it is preferable to my mind if someone works and earns the money in a legitimate job like you've done. If I were going to sponsor a young person's gap year in a foreign country, I would rather back someone who had done it your way, than someone who's basically begging friends and relatives to sponsor a parachute drop or a sausage eating contest! For a start, it shows you have the experience of hard work and application which we need in a volunteer, and also it adds to the skills and life experience you can apply to your role as a volunteer."

There was a bit of an atmosphere for the rest of that evening, but Louise had a good attitude and from the start threw herself into the work of preparing and delivering a first class introduction to science and maths for all the students on her timetable. It was uplifting to Edwin and I to see our plans come to fruition and to see proper science experiments being conducted in our purpose built if somewhat makeshift laboratory. Louise had a sunny personality. She beamed from ear to ear whenever we exchanged glances in the course of a day. She enthusiastically subjected herself to Edwin's training regime after school and earned herself the affectionate nickname "Little Legs" on account of her diminutive size. I got a buzz from working with Louise as she was a high achiever and had the same commitment and dedication as I had. It was professionally exhilarating working as a team with someone I felt to be an equal.

I helped Nova to feel that the situation had been resolved once she had given Edwin the cheque for three hundred pounds. We both assumed she would be obtaining extra funds in due course. I knew I would never be able to trust her fully after what had happened. It had diminished our respect for her as a person, but I did not let that show. They were both young women away from home and I showed equal warmth to them in welcoming them into our home and as team members, serving the educational needs of the school children. Nova for her part got into the work of primary English. She had no need to prepare resources as we now had lots of sets of English books at different literacy levels. She spent most of her time reading through them, selecting what to do, and planning lessons. I noticed that she had a good relationship with the children and liked to read stories to them and let them talk about imaginary situations. All this was good and an extra dimension to what they had been getting from me alone. She had a very light timetable compared to Louise because she had only one subject area to offer and not really been needed for that. She therefore spent quite a lot of time sitting in the sun in the garden or writing her personal letters and Edwin was able to sit and chat with her or answer her various questions about the country and people. Edwin was never short of conversation. In fact if he got on a roll about his pet theme, it might be hard not to lose track of time.

Ten days went by and Edwin had posted Nova's cheque to his bank account in England. The post girl delivered a letter to us that Friday from Mitch. Inside, his brief note explained that he was enclosing a cheque for a hundred pounds that Nova had given to him before leaving England. He had given her that amount of cash from his own pocket at the airport, as she said she had forgotten to bring any for the journey and had no time at the airport to draw it out of her bank account. When he had paid the cheque into his bank, it had bounced and left him with an undeserved hole in his finances. Could she please send him another cheque? Edwin was furious. We now doubted everything she had said to us, including her claim to have been training with the Olympic rowing team with whom she had claimed to have shared her London student digs.

"That cheque she gave me is obviously worthless," he said angrily. "I'm not going to be fooled into supporting her for weeks and weeks while waiting for my bank to return another bounced cheque to me. I'll go straight to Dawn

Murray and get her flight changed so she can go back to England next Thursday. I'm not having a con-trickster staying under my own roof. How could she do that to poor Mitch after all the help he gave her? The poor bloke doesn't deserve that. It makes me even madder to think she could do that to Mitch than the idea that she's trying to con us."

Edwin confronted Nova that evening and told her he was going to send her back the following week. She was stunned.

"You can't do that," she said. "How are you going to explain it to the children?"

"That's for us to worry about, not you," he said, sharply. Having lost any ounce of respect he still had for her, he was no longer of a mind to be civil. "Please go and get your travel ticket and papers so I can get your return date changed. You have four days to do your washing and pack up your stuff and I'll take you to the airport at the end of the week and put you on a plane to the UK."

She stormed off to her room to get the airline tickets and papers she had travelled with. Edwin took them, thanked her in a cool, business-like fashion and disappeared with them into the study. Nova went back into her room and soon began to seek solace with Louise for the rest of the evening. Edwin was still seething.

"She got here under false pretences," he snarled. "I'm not going to let her con Froebel into sponsoring a free holiday so she can spend a year dossing round the Caribbean or South America when she leaves us. She'll go straight home to England with no stop offs on the way. I still think she's lying about not having any money."

"I can't believe that someone with a university degree can be so callous as to deliberately set out to get a personal joyride at the expense of a tiny charity," I said. "It's bad enough to think that anyone would set out to do that to a multinational corporation or an organisation like a university, but to do it to a tiny little outfit like ours that so obviously is being run on a shoestring is disgraceful. She must have some hard neck to come and expect to live with us in our house for a year knowing that we would find out that she had deceived us as soon as Mitch's cheque had bounced."

"Maybe she wasn't planning on staying for the year," suggested Edwin. "Maybe she was going to cut and run when it got to Christmas, thinking we could do nothing about it."

"Perhaps you're right, and in any case I agree that she should be put on a direct flight to return with no stopover time," I said. Changing her flight would have to wait until after the weekend, when the airline offices would be open. The following Tuesday, Edwin duly took her papers into Georgetown and explained to Dawn Murray at BWIA why the ticket needed changing. She gave her full support in achieving this.

The next day I announced to the children in assembly under the house that, sadly, teacher Nova would have to return to England suddenly as she had an unexpected death in the family. Mr Joseph would be taking her to the airport the next day and as she was now packing her stuff, she would not be seeing them again before she left. The children were naturally sad for her "loss" but as they were not scheduled for lessons with her that day, they soon forgot as they were swept on by their normal daily tide of activities with Louise and me. Edwin insisted that she write out another £100 cheque for us to send to Mitch to make up for the bounced one. She did this. By the time their weekly lesson with her was due, she was already on her way to the airport with Edwin and I had added her timetable to mine without much difficulty. Edwin returned from Georgetown that evening after seeing that her plane had taken off with her aboard.

He brought back with him a large box of extra science equipment and chemicals for Louise which he had obtained from the government education and curriculum development offices in the capital. Louise was now in her element with what she had asked for and needed to do the science practical work. We did clear the air with her that evening, now that she felt she could talk freely about what had passed. She said Mitch had told them that he would raise the funds for both her and Nova and send them on to Edwin as he got them. She said she really did not know Nova at all before they boarded the plane to Guyana, so had no idea what her true character was or whether she had a paid job while studying.

While we were both teaching the next day, Edwin cleared out Nova's room in his usual methodical way when guests left us. When I came up for lunch, he told me he had found incriminating evidence in Nova's room. When emptying her rubbish basket, he had found a torn up letter which he had pieced together. It was to her brother, saying amongst other things, that she would meet him in Barbados and that first she needed him to put some money he owed her in her new account (quoting the number), because she had closed her old bank account in August. The new bank account number was not the number on the cheque she had given Edwin which he had posted to his English bank the week before, nor that on the returned cheque from Mitch which Edwin still had. She had deliberately written out cheques to both Edwin and Mitch from a bank account which she knew she had already closed two months before. The fragments of the old account cheque book cover and last few cheques were also lurking in amongst the scrap paper.

"You must have been right about her planning to meet up with someone in Barbados on the way home," I said. That evening, I wrote a letter of thanks to Dr Weston at Froebel, for the computer they had donated that Mitch had shipped out to us with Louise. I was full of praise for everything Louise had done for us so far and could see that she was going to be an excellent help to us and the students that year, I also thanked him and the governors for funding the tickets of their two volunteers that they had sent us, but that regretfully we had just sent Nova home because she had been dishonest with us as well as with Mitch and I outlined how. I enclosed copies of the correspondence between Nova and me as evidence of what I had explained. I was very sorry it had come to this and also shocked at how a student had shown such feckless disregard for the good name of a college like Froebel. However, I hoped that we could count on their support to get another science and maths student to follow on from Louise the next year. I also wrote a similar letter to Mitch, explaining what had happened. I was sorry but even though she had given Edwin another cheque for Mitch that we had already forwarded to him, it would be no good as it was from a bank account she had closed in August.

The Nova experience had left us all with a bad taste in the mouth. However, we had so much going on that there really wasn't any point in dwelling on it. Louise was happy to play around in the lab connecting up the second-hand computer and getting it working. She would soon be able to teach the students how to use it and let them try it out themselves. She also said she would write and ask Dr Weston if there was any possibility of sending some more to us when they upgraded their own. Meanwhile, she enthusiastically set about organising pond dipping exercises and setting insect collecting traps around the farm as well as scouring the neighbourhood for corpses of animals to rot down and strip to the skeleton. She was taking her promise to add to our museum display collection very seriously and wasting no time in involving the students to bring in samples of a wide variety of local fauna dead or alive. Every day there was a new excitement and they loved her. She occupied herself in all her free time after preparation and marking, in creating an organised and beautifully displayed laboratory. Louise could see how hard I worked at bringing the history, geography and other subjects to life and she worked equally hard at doing the same in her areas of responsibility.

Summersplash mini-company was now functioning smoothly. The lesson that the older students had learned from their experience with their mini-business thus far was that they had not made many sales from their craft production. They could not come up with a reason why. I suggested that it was because we had very few tourists and the local market did not want to buy crafts because they wanted to use the little money they had on basic food, rent and electricity. Any money for luxury would go on new tools or equipment to make their lives easier. If they wanted to make more money, they would have to take up items that local people would regularly need to buy, because the main market Summersplash had was the home market, the one around them.

The students therefore decided to use some of their capital to set up a tuck-shop so they could buy snacks at break and lunchtime. Their soft drinks could be kept cold in the fridge in the lab. I said that was a good idea, so we gave the position of tuck shop manager to Delon, as he was the assistant finance manager. They made suggestions of what items they would regularly like to buy and Delon made his first shopping list. I reminded them that the best way to get guaranteed sales was to set their prices a little bit lower than the same items in the local shops. They would be able to make a profit if they ran the tuck-shop well, bought their stock at a low enough price and decided to be a bit less greedy for profit than the local shops were. In the long run they would make more money as people would buy more of their stuff. I had never understood why local people had not already thought of this strategy. Instead, when one shop raised its prices, all the others followed suit because they thought they would lose money if they did not. I wanted to show them how the laws of supply and demand worked, but how they could manipulate demand a bit even for items where it was fairly fixed.

I was concerned that Summersplash might reinforce in the students the local view that setting up a shop to resell stuff other people produced was the only way for a business to make money. I wanted them to be involved in the actual production of goods. Guyana had plenty of idle land and producing something economic on it was the only way for the country to develop. From the natural resources that the land produced, its people should start manufacturing for themselves. We had seen how craft production had not really succeeded, so I suggested that we needed to produce some food that people would definitely want to buy. That would be crops and meat. We were all learning agriculture, and they needed to do practical work for that. What we should do was to grow vegetable crops on our farm plots and keep some chickens for meat because there was always a local demand for chicken, especially if you could undercut the price of other producers in the area or of imported chicken from the USA. The students all agreed that it was something they could do, but before we could produce chickens we would have to build a pen and we did not have enough capital in the company for that. Edwin said he would donate some scrap wood we had and the corrugated iron sheets that were left from the sheep project. Robin and Satynand, who were now sixth formers, volunteered with some of the other boys to build a small pen in their free time on Sundays. They followed guidelines given to us by a field officer from the ministry of Agriculture. With some of their capital they bought wire mesh to ventilate the sides of the pen. They also bought feeders, waterers, a batch of forty day-old chicks and the recommended amount of commercial feed.

I oversaw everything that they did. I advised them to buy two cash boxes: a general one for the farm and one for the tuck-shop. This they did. I monitored and audited all their financial transactions. Any takings were counted out in front of me before the tuck-shop box was emptied and all money transferred into the general cash box, which I locked and kept in my desk drawer until expenditure was needed. I would take out the requested cash from the box and put in the receipts and change when they had done their shopping. They knew that I checked everything so there could be no disappearing funds. Everything was double-checked and accountable. Mr Hing had shown me how to set out a balance sheet, so I passed on that knowledge to Delon and Robin, who was now their finance manager. They were forced to keep accurate records, which I checked at the end of each day with an eagle eye. Their weekly finance report was read out to the whole school at the board meeting and anyone present could raise questions or complaints or make suggestions. It was completely democratic.

The aim was for the chickens to be reared and sold to raise a profit that eventually would pay for a better, more hygienic concrete based rat-proof pen to be built. This would enable better productivity because a more scientific approach to their care could be followed in a deep litter system. Chickens were live animals that needed to be fed and watered on Sundays as well as school days. We would have to have a system to ensure that students took the care of chickens seriously and did not neglect them. I said that to begin with, Robin and Satynand would raise a batch of forty chickens from start to finish and they would get the profits of that batch. They would have to see to the chickens every morning before school started, check on them every break and lunchtime and top up their containers before going home after school. They would even have to come in on Sundays to do this. Other students would each take their turn in raising a batch and keeping the profits as the year went on. There were a few teething problems, but I sorted them out and the agriculture course progressed hand in hand with the mini-company.

They also began copra production from the dry coconuts that fell from our trees around their plots. Copra is made by shelling the coconuts and spreading out the chipped flesh in a clean dry place in the sun for a few days, turning it regularly until the oil begins to concentrate enough for it to be pressed out in a mill. Our students began to do this work on Saturdays after tending their vegetable plots. The drying process was a daily activity before and after school until the copra was ready for bagging. Then Edwin helped by taking the sun-dried copra they had weighed and bagged up to the copra factory at Cove and John village on his way to Georgetown. Here he would sell it for coconut oil production and bring back the money for the children's cash box.

The old sheep and cow enclosure, which was now a large patch of fertile rich soil, was lying idle because it tended to flood in the rainy season. Bananas and plantains like to be in wet places as they use a lot of water. I suggested that planting some in the former cow pen would help absorb any flood water as the plants all grew bigger. In a year's time, they would have another staple crop to sell. Robin's father kindly donated some banana and plantain suckers and the students planted up an orchard. Soon, we had a working productive farm that was a small business run by the students for the students. It generated small amounts of money. Not enough to sustain a family, but it was an example of good business practice that I hoped students could take into their daily working lives when they left school. I had no doubt that it could only succeed at our school because I was prepared to devote unlimited amounts of my own time to supervise and monitor every single activity they did. It was an example of a co-operative in practice that would put the adults in the community to shame because they could not make a success of farming co-operatives. None of them could sustain an economic co-operative without stealing off each other.

That term, I got my first identity card for voting. I had still not been granted Guyana citizenship or a Guyanese passport, so I remained technically an illegal immigrant, but I could now vote. Election campaigning had begun and all parties were stepping up their attempts to appeal to voters in the lead up to it. On his way back from Georgetown, Edwin had been flagged down by Albert. He had just seen Edwin's name on the list of PNC candidates for Member of Parliament. There were rumours that his name had been put forward to be Regional Chairman. Edwin was shocked. He had no idea, but realised that this had been done without his permission or knowledge in order to fool those floating voters who respected and trusted Edwin into voting PNC, thinking he would be their Regional Chairman and MP. The election would be on December 13th.

Edwin had more than enough on his plate than to worry about that. He was still trying to complete the will Pat Munroe had named him executor for. He was helping the late Pat's daughter to sell her inherited property and deal with all the estate agents and prospective buyers. Her lawyer in Georgetown was sending him from one place to another to get officials to stamp various papers. It was difficult enough to do this if he had lived in Georgetown, but he had a three hour drive each way to get there and if someone was not in the office the day he went in, it was a frustrating inconvenience and a complete waste of time and money to us.

As the effect of El Nino began to turn our farm into a dust-bowl, water was becoming a real problem. We had rationed it since Louise and Nova had arrived, but I was now worried that we would soon run out of clean water to cook and clean dishes with. The trenches were dry and crops and cattle were dying around us. In the savannah, Samo had lost cattle and so had we. In the midst of all this, Reverend Pat's daughter and her mother arrived in Guyana expecting to stay with us. I had to send a letter to them with Edwin apologising about the fact that we could not possibly entertain them at the house as we had no clean water supply. It was best if they stayed in a hotel in Georgetown. This news must have cut short their stay as, not wishing to pay the hotel prices, they departed within a week. On the day they left, Queen's College, one of the top Georgetown High Schools, was burned down in an arson attack. It was the usual kind of happening around election time. Those who felt marginalised by the government in power showed their protest against them by surreptitious attacks on government buildings.

Edwin had become really ill with all the racing around he had been doing to get Pat's probate passed and had to stay in bed unable to eat anything all day. He said he felt as if he had high blood pressure. I suggested easing off his salt consumption and drinking more water. He was also worried by a letter he had just received from the bank in England demanding the return of his cheque book and card. Nova's bouncing cheque had not helped the cause. Fortunately, a day's rest in bed had helped him to recover so he had been able to go into Georgetown the next day and hand in our application to CIDA for funding to help the school. He was told that we would not get it because we were too small, and did not reach the whole community.

"Sorry we can't help you, but keep up the good work. You are doing a wonderful job," the Guyanese lady had told him. However, earlier in the month, we had put in an application to them on behalf of Summersplash mini-company for some garden tools, a water pump, hose, watering cans and wheelbarrows to help them produce food to sell so they could fund their exam fees and help with family finances. That application had been successful. We were notified that Summersplash would be given a fifty-fifty grant for the cost of these items. So it was nothing to do with being too small. Summersplash had even fewer members than Sapodilla Learning Centre. It had just been an excuse. The real problem was that the teacher at the school was white and English. It would have been different if my skin colour had been black or brown.

Matthew from the VSO had visited us in late November to try to persuade us to visit him in the Rupununi at Easter. I had explained that we could not afford that. Internal flights were dearer than international ones. When I said that we were already using Edwin's pension to support not only myself but also the science volunteer and all our attempts to get any funding for the school itself from any source had been turned down, he had told us that the only way for us to get funding for the school would be to set up a market stall and fill it with all the produce we could find.

"Go and buy it in a shop," he had said, "take photographs of it with all the students and parents and send the photos in with the application and say these are the crops you are producing." I had been appalled at the idea of doing such a dishonest thing. I would not countenance it and neither would Edwin. It may have been how Matthew had succeeded in getting funding for projects for the Amerindians in the Rupununi, but I was not going to go down that route. I just could not understand why international aid agencies using donors' money from countries like England and Canada did not fund a small educational project like ours that was so clearly helping to improve the education of poverty stricken rural children. Every penny of our money spent and earned was recorded and accountable. We even had it independently audited every year. We both wanted to have proof that we were not liable for any personal income tax on an imagined income that we did not have. It did not seem fair when all around us we could see projects being started and managed by locals with status and political influence being given vast sums of aid money which they put in their own bank accounts and did not deliver any of their promised benefits to the local poor. They were the ones employing the kind of dishonest tactics Matthew had recommended. None of them kept truthful records or any records at all for the most part. Did donors care that their hard-earned money was subject to such corruption? In a way we would rather not apply for aid if it put us in the same class as all the corrupt applicants around us. We would have to keep struggling on as we were. People would soon start asking why our school was so successful when it did not get any support from funding agencies. We would be able to say to them "Just that. We don't get any help from funding agencies. They are the ones who mess it all up. They institutionalise dependence and corruption."

We had planned our usual annual prize giving and show for the end of term in December. While we had been in Trinidad, Edwin had invited the veteran Olympian MacDonald Bailey to come and stay with us for a few days in December to present our prizes. The elderly and rather frail athlete was almost blind but he had agreed to come and be our guest accompanied by his secretary and carer, Luana. Edwin got BWIA to sponsor their flights. He hoped that MacDonald would inspire our students and athletes to strive to achieve international status by giving them some of the secrets of his success. After all, he had been born of poor black parents in British Guiana and become a world famous celebrity in his time, winning a Bronze medal in the 1952 Helsinki Olympics and yet he had trained in bare feet with no fancy stadium; just sweat, discipline and determination. The British High Commissioner, David Johnson, had also accepted our invitation to attend, as had Professor Small from the University of Guyana. He had to present the UG Distance Learning Tourism

Certificates and Sports Leader Certificates to our students who had completed their two year courses the previous July.

Somehow, I had managed to find time to write a historical drama based on the Angel Gabriel race riots in Georgetown in 1856 and on Edwin's family history, which I had been researching. I had imagined the scenario, which was all based on recorded detail and the folk memory of the elders. The year was 1856. Hopetown had just been founded by a group of ex-slaves on the former cotton plantations where they worked. Edwin's great, great, grandfather, Pompey Joseph, and forty nine other newly freed slaves, saved up their wages until they had two thousand dollars which in 1840 they took as coins in a wheelbarrow to buy the land off Mr Blair, the plantation owner. Until then, Pompey had driven horse-drawn cart-loads of cotton to Georgetown for Mr Blair. It was a three-day journey before the railway was built. Then there had been a slump. Cheaper, better quality cotton from the USA had put Mr Blair out of business and he had decided to sell off those small cotton plantations to the slaves he had freed. Many of them still worked for wages on Mr Blair's sugar plantations further up the coast.

By 1856, Pompey and the others had built "neat little cottages" for themselves, according to the report of a local magistrate who visited their newly founded village. He had said it gave hope for a better future to see this, so the village became known as "Hopetown". With the coming of the railway in the 1840s, some of the villagers had been lured away from the poorly paid sugar plantations to work on railway construction, or in gold prospecting and lumber felling as the country began to open up to colonial investors. A number of Chinese, Portuguese and East Indian immigrants had moved in to replace the blacks as indentured workers on the plantations. By 1856, some of these newcomers had finished their indenture-ships and had saved up to buy or rent land off some of the ex-slaves in the new village. They set up shops selling dry goods and cloth to villagers. Some had intermarried with the Negroes and moved into their family homes. Pompey's eldest son, Charles, had meanwhile caused a village scandal by developing a relationship with a white girl from Fort Wellington named Hannah Gibbs. She was the overseer's daughter. He had "taken her" to live with him "in the back-dam" where Sapodilla Farm now was. No doubt her family did not give their consent, so he was accused of "kidnapping" her. They had stayed together in spite of this and went on to have numerous children of whom Edwin's grand-father, Charles, was one.

I imagined a torrid teenage love affair leading to pregnancy and elopement. I could identify with Hannah's situation, although mine was very different. There had been an outbreak of racial violence in Georgetown at Christmas in 1856, against Portuguese shop owners there. It had been led by Daniel Sayers Orr, whose nickname was "Angel Gabriel." He hated the Portuguese because they were Catholic and seemed to monopolise the shop trade. He thought they got privileges before the law because of their white skin and this had seemed to be borne out when he and two Portuguese were arrested for being in a drunken fight. They got released on bail but he did not. This had sparked a riot of two thousand Negroes smashing up Portuguese shops in Georgetown. The same year, two Portuguese-owned shops in Hopetown had also been attacked.

It was all the stuff of a stage drama and set against the race problems of the time it would strike a chord with the locals, given the racial tensions brewing nationally over the upcoming elections. I would use it as a vehicle to promote a message of peaceful reconciliation and racial harmony in the local community from the mouths of all our ancestors. I wrote a short play based on these facts, using the names of the real villagers for characters. I imagined the racial tension in the village being settled by the good leadership of Pompey Joseph, Edwin's ancestor. He would bring the discord to an end by invoking the Christmas spirit of the 'Real' Angel Gabriel and bring the community together to prepare for the Christmas celebrations and a mixed marriage between his son and Hannah Gibbs. I decided to use Louise to act the part of Hannah Gibbs the white girl, whose elopement with Pompey's son, Charles, and their respective families' reaction to it, would be central to the drama. I wrote a part for every student commensurate with each one's ability to act and memorise information. If they all had a part, then they would all feel involved. It was for a local audience who would understand creolese, so with the help of my sixth form students, we translated all the lines into creolese so it would more accurately reflect the dialogue of the real villagers of the time. We used traditional African dances and songs for the wedding Que-que and carols for the Christmas celebrations as well as a traditional Indian dance that a new student, Melina, already knew. Edwin composed some appropriate songs to start and finish the show. Christmas time was traditionally a time for flouncing in masquerade costumes, so I decided to incorporate that into the final scenes as well. We already had some of the costumes, and in my art class, we made some more that we needed, such as stilts and a papier-mache horse's head for the flouncers. The rehearsals were going well by the first week of December, against a backdrop of PNC political meetings and rallies in the village.

The election went off as planned on the 13th December. Edwin and I were both able to vote this time. We went to the polling station at half past ten that morning while Louise was teaching junior maths. We had to queue for a long time, as large numbers of villagers had turned out to vote. They were all black at this polling station, so were nearly all PNC voters. Edwin had to supervise the sealing of ballot boxes and see them taken by the returning officers for security to the village office where the boxes for all the neighbourhood polling stations would later be collected by election commission vehicles. He was disappointed at the poor showing of PNC voters. We had both believed that a change in government to PNC would be good by now, since there were some very good people lined up as potential ministers if that had happened. Already by the following morning, there were rumours of ballot boxes being fished out of trenches. The results were not announced first thing and there was a delay in counting that lasted all that day. The PNC had been accusing the PPP of vote rigging and that was said to explain the delay.

Edwin went to the airport early to collect MacDonald Bailey and Luana. After they had returned, settled into their rooms and had lunch, he took them down to the beach and showed them around the local area. They came back for his afternoon sports club session, where he had fifty seven athletes assembled to hear MacDonald Bailey's talk on how to be successful at sport. It was well received and the athletes fired many questions at him. By the end of the day, there had been riots in Georgetown and eleven people had been shot. The results had still not been announced. A week later, Janet Jagan was sworn in as President and yet still no election results had been announced. Tension was mounting. We were getting at least two power cuts per day. The primary school at nearby number eight village was burned down in an arson attack. Edwin was called out to see it.

Our show went ahead regardless, with 108 people present. The students performed brilliantly. The local television station sent a reporter and photographer, and Professor Small came from the University of Guyana. In his presentation speech, he complimented us on the play, which he said sent very important messages in the current climate as well as bringing the country's history to life on the stage. This was the kind of thing that all local schools should be doing. Not surprisingly, the British High Commissioner did not show up after all. With a crisis brewing, he had more important things to attend to. The next day Edwin took MacDonald Bailey and Luana back to the airport without incident. It was four days before Christmas. The PNC leader, Corbyn, was leading street demonstrations and effigies of Janet Jagan were being burned in the streets, but she did not budge. We still had not been given the election results.

The unrest continued after Christmas and on the 29th December, the PNC launched a court case against Janet Jagan being appointed as President when no election results had been announced. It was against the constitution. That day our show and prize giving appeared on local television. The election results were finally announced the next day. The PPP had won 29 seats and the PNC gained 22, with just a seat each for the TUF and Alliance parties. Edwin was convinced it was a sham but at least we now had a result. By the second week in January, when he went into Georgetown, he was held up by a mass demonstration of over 20,000 PNC protestors. The country was at a standstill. A bomb had exploded close to the diplomatic residences of the British and Canadian High Commisioners and the American ambassador. It served to speed a Caribbean peace initiative culminating in the signing of the Hurdmanston Accord. Marches and demonstrations would be suspended while an independent audit of the election results was carried out. A commission would be set up to advise the two sides on Constitutional reform. The Jagan government was to remain in power but only for three years instead of five, so there would have to be another election in early 2001. Things settled down a bit after that.

Louise had busied herself over the Christmas holiday in getting ahead with her lesson preparation for the coming term. This had included clearing out and sweeping the lab and arranging it how she wanted. Her specimen displays were all beautifully set out with carefully stencilled labels and other teaching aids hanging from the ceiling and stuck to the walls. There was hardly a space between them. When she wasn't doing that, she was scouring the trenches, pastures and hedgerows for more specimens. Edwin started to make jokes about the garden becoming "Boot Hill" as skulls and bones she had set out to bleach dry in the sun greeted our view from the bedroom when we got up in the mornings. What a joy it was to have someone who did not need to be taught how to teach properly to work alongside me. Since Dubai, I had forgotten what that was like.

In the interests of helping the children to have a better education regardless of having no purpose-built facilities, we had overlooked the dangers of having a laboratory complete with carcinogenic and flammable chemicals right under our bedroom. While we were in bed one Saturday night, an almighty crash and the sound of breaking glass below alarmed us. Edwin thought we had a burglar. We rushed down, unlocked the lab door and found that a neighbourhood cat had sneaked in by the open lab door and got accidentally locked inside overnight. Whether attracted by the smell of a fish carcass in the displays or following a mouse or frog, its nocturnal explorations around the displays led to disaster. Broken glass mixed with some of the chemicals from bottles of acids and alkali substances which had formed part of the displays were all over the lab floor. It took some careful cleaning up. We made sure that did not happen again. Edwin began to refer to the lab as "The morgue". Then Louise's enthusiasm for specimens turned from the dead to the living and she got the students to help her set up a small aquarium in one corner of the room. This was fine until she put into it a baby alligator that Quacy had caught for her. Edwin drew the line under that.

"You can't keep those things in the house," he said, "They're dangerous predators. It'll climb out of the tank and escape into the house somewhere. We won't know about it until it attacks someone."

"But it's only a little one," she protested.

"Those things quickly grow into great big monsters," he insisted.

"But creatures stay small if they're kept in an environment of a restricted size," she argued, reluctant to set her captive free a long distance from the farm.

"It might be true of terrapins and bonsai trees," I said, "but it won't apply to a monster with his genes, because if you don't feed him enough, he'll just go exploring for more! I'm with Edwin on this one. You really can't keep him on the premises. Stick to patois fish and caddis fly larvae." Reluctantly, she had gone with Quacy and the others to release it safely where it had been found. A live iguana brought into the lab soon after this event did actually escape, to her surprise. She had not realised how fast they move or she would not have untied it from the children's stick. Fortunately, the children caught the iguana before it could wreck the lab like the cat had done. This was an occasion where she found out the hard way that what we had been telling her should be listened to and was the last time she ignored our advice. There was never a dull moment at Sapodilla Learning Centre.

Although Louise had spent Christmas with us and been treated like another daughter, she had also by now made friends with some local environmentalists at Georgetown Zoo and spent occasional weekends in town with them, bringing back specimens of feathers, small stuffed birds and even a dead horse's head to strip of flesh for her skeletal displays. Edwin, always willing to put himself out to help us achieve resources that were freely available, agreed to drive past the zoo to collect the horse's head on our way back from a shopping trip in town. He had not expected it to be a massive sack-full, weighing almost more than he could lift, and taking up the whole back of the jeep.

As term progressed, Louise taught Robin and Michelle how to dissect and skin a small dead alligator that some younger students had found. They pinned its hide on a stretcher to dry and later displayed it next to the anaconda. It was Delon, however, who won her star prize. Delon was Vernon, our electrician's only son. Since his parents lived separately, Delon had been brought up by his mother and grandmother who were very protective and treated him like a girl. He was Vernon's pride and joy. He spoiled him and proudly nurtured his intelligence and interest in his own electrical work. Delon had been enrolled at Sapodilla since he was at primary school. He stood out among his classmates because he was very good at arithmetic. He had shown his attention to detail in his role as tuck shop manager and assistant finance manager of Summersplash. Now, with encouragement from Louise, and being spurred on by all the different science investigations she had been conducting with them, he had taken on the ambition of becoming an inventor of machines. He was not short of wire scraps from Vernon's workshop, but cardboard boxes were his favourite raw material. Having impressed us all with his version of a simple 'computer' he made out of a cardboard box, Louise nonchalantly challenged him to make an electric shock machine to use on two of the girls whenever they day dreamed in class. Delon was eager to show that he was capable and the next day brought in a small contraption of battery, wires and cardboard. He volunteered Quacy, a disbeliever, as a test guinea-pig in front of Louise and applied part of his device to Quacy's mouth. He then activated the switch. Within a flash, Quacy shot up in the air and landed a couple of paces back from his starting place. "Miss, it works" he had said when the squeals of laughter of the onlookers had subsided. It was only a small battery, but it must have been a little painful as well as startling, so Louise thanked Delon but said she had not really wanted him to take her seriously. She did not want to hurt anyone, daydreaming or not. Delon's inquiring mind continued to get him into safety scrapes, however. One morning, when he had come into school before all the others had arrived, I looked over the veranda to see him at the bottom of the house gutter, half submerged head first into one of our rainwater barrels. He was grasping the sides of the barrel with his hands, and his feet were kicking out in the air behind him.

"What on earth are you doing, Delon?" I called out, alarmed. He swung backwards and let himself back onto his feet, shook the water off his short frizzy hair and wiped it out of his eyes before staring up at me and catching his breath.

"Seein' how lang me can hol' me breath under water, miss," he said. It had been a question raised in science by Louise when teaching respiration in mammals. I realised that, unlike his fellow students who could all swim in the local canals and safely duck under holding their noses, Delon was not allowed by his grandmother to go in the trenches to play with other village children. He had thought to do his own investigation in our clean rainwater instead. I commended his initiative, but pointed out the danger of drowning if he had overbalanced and fallen in with no one around to see it happen. My assembly that morning was dominated by a serious talk about safety rules on the school premises, using the example of Delon's experiment to explain why and prevent a repetition.

A couple of months into the new year, some post arrived that had been delayed by the Christmas overload. It included a letter addressed to Nova. As, for obvious reasons, Nova had not given us any forwarding address, I had to open it to find out who had sent it so I could return it to them. Inside was a letter from a lady in Lancashire who reminded Nova that she had responded to Nova's appeal in the newspapers the previous summer, for financial support for her year's volunteering at Sapodilla Learning Centre in Guyana. She thanked Nova for writing to her on her arrival in October and sympathised with the terrible conditions she was living in. She hoped that her work with the children was going well and did she need any more money?

"So she obtained money for herself from complete strangers, using our name, and even had the cheek to make out that she was living in terrible conditions here, as if she's in a mud hut," I said to Edwin after reading the letter out to

364

him. "I've a good mind to write and tell the lady that she's no longer here and why."

"Do it!" he said.

"I suppose you're right. Otherwise the lady might wonder why she doesn't hear any more from her. At least I can thank her for attempting to help the education of our children at the school, even if her donation never reached us." I duly wrote to the lady at the address on her letterhead and fully explained why I had opened the letter she had sent to Nova and why we had sent Nova back to England months ago.

I also had received bad news from Froebel that they did not have any final year maths or science specialist teacher who wanted to do a gap year to follow on from Louise in September. This meant that I would have to try placing an advert in the Times Educational Supplement to see if nationwide I could find someone suitable. I posted the advertisement with a cheque to pay for it. I had already decided that it was too much to ask Mitch to handle all this fundraising as well as dealing with the volunteer selection work. It wasn't working well enough because teacher volunteers needed to have a sense of moral responsibility and professionalism that he did not seem aware of. He was a wonderfully helpful person with a great sense of humour but his lack of efficiency and inappropriate use of sexual innuendo had certainly not impressed Louise.

"He's not professional," she had complained.

"It's just his way," I had said in his defence. "I can't really demand that he changes his approach when he's doing all this out of the goodness of his heart. We really appreciate all the time and effort he has put into getting our volunteers up to now. I wouldn't want to offend him."

"Well you should think about how he offends female volunteers by the lewd comments he makes to them," she said. I knew she was right, but I had to think of a solution that would not cause Mitch to be upset. He had become a good friend by now. In the end I wrote and told him that we had decided to separate the volunteer selection from the work he was doing because he was already doing too much. He was spending a lot of time helping to publicise our charity by producing his "Sapodilla Today" professionally printed news bulletin and posting it to over a hundred of our friends and contacts worldwide who had supported us in some way or another since 1993. We did not have the equipment at that time to do any such thing, so that alone was an enormous help to us. He had already helped raise funds to ship out sports clothing and books and a video camera for us. That kind of thing had also been enormously helpful and we knew how much time and effort that took, so from now on that was enough. The volunteer interview and selection would now be done by Edwin's daughter, Kirstin, who was at the time at home on maternity leave and had agreed to do that for us.

Louise and I spent the two terms of 1998, including most of the Easter vacation, running a first class educational establishment that would have equalled any state funded school in England at that time in terms of results, methodology, pastoral care and extra-curricular activities, except for its lack of space and resources. The seventeen full time students were getting a good all-round education and were learning by practical experiences and investigations in every subject. They also did P.E. and sport, first aid and careers with Edwin and business through the mini-company project. The forty nine part time junior and primary students were getting a good grounding in essential maths and science skills as well as English, humanities and sport. Music, art, drama and French were now optional extras for them as well as the full timers. We had a professionally run institution and it was receiving none of the pay or support that the local state or private fee-paying schools in the country were receiving. Even before Louise had joined us, our examination results had shamed all the other schools in the region, so we had confidence that two more subjects, which Louise was teaching, would reap similar results at the end of two years. She had also put the sixth form through the CXC and GCE O-level biology and maths exams that Sarah had started them on the previous year. Parents realised that they were getting far better outcomes by sending their children to us even if they had to pay the examination entry fees in full. My main concern now was to find a successor to Louise to complete the work she had started. I was anxious for news that my advertisement in the Times Educational Supplement had been taken up, so we went to town to book a phone-call to Kirstin to find out. The news that several enquiries had been made, she had interviewed them all in London and selected the one she considered best fitted our needs, was a great relief to me. She had told him to write to us with full CV and accepted his deposit for the cost of the flight. As soon as she heard that we were happy with his CV and references, she would collect the rest of his payment, arrange his flight and pay his fee for his food bill for the year into Edwin's UK bank account. By the time we took Louise to Georgetown for her summer tour of

South America to begin, Sapodilla Learning Centre had taken on a new significance in the local community and could not be ignored by the powers now in Government.

I did not have to wait long to get the letter from Neil, a science graduate of Hull University, who had just achieved qualified teacher status. He had come into some inheritance money from his grandfather who had recently died, and had decided to spend it on a gap year adventure in South America, starting with us. God was definitely giving us a helping hand, I felt. Although term had ended and Louise had left, I still had the marking of internal school exams in my many different subjects and all the reports to finish writing for all sixty or so students. It took me until the middle of August to complete these. Then we got the exciting news that Rafer was setting off to Kuala Lumpur to compete in the decathlon with the Great Britain team at the Commonwealth Games, twenty eight years after his father, Edwin, had represented Guyana in the same event at those Games in Edinburgh. Meanwhile Edwin had been conducting his Red Cross First Aid Course with the help of Canadian medical students from the Student International Health Association, one of whom was based at the Red Cross Headquarters in Georgetown. After this, he had been involved in a summer sports and recreation activity 'camp' for the youth of the Region. It was an initiative for which the newly elected government had provided funds and which the Ministry of Culture Youth and Sport had organised. It was widely recognised that drugs and crime were a huge problem because of a lack of provision of worthwhile recreational activities for the youth. Edwin had been identified as the best sports resource person in our region, so he was invited to take some sessions. The 'camp' was at the MMA facilities he had helped to restore for his teachers' course and their school sports competitions. Jennifer Wishart from the Walter Roth Museum in Georgetown had been earmarked as one of the other resource persons. She was supposed to do some archaeology with the participants, but this did not involve any work on local sites, just a basic introductory talk on the subject and some drawing. Edwin managed to get her to pay a visit to our small museum after she had done her session. At last she had seen it and was taken by surprise at how good it was.

The summer holidays were drawing to a close. I had been giving the lab a clean-up in readiness for the new term, and was checking round the garden to pull out weeds and trim back overgrown plants. The rubber tree we had planted as a small cutting back in 1993 had by now become a massive specimen flanked by a splendid fan palm and a flamboyant tree smothered in scarlet flowers. I marvelled at the maturity everything had reached so quickly with paw-paw trees, bananas and a small guava tree bearing fruit. A giant prickly pear, yuccas, bitter aloes and crown of thorns high on the rockery behind the pond had all survived the drought and floods. The borders were packed with cannas, heliconia, crotons and variegated tropical shrubs for colour. It was a wonderful home to the large yellow-footed land tortoise, Geochelone denticulata, which Samo had brought from the savannah as a live specimen for our collection. It had come out of hiding in search of water and he had found it. Now it had a domestic paradise to roam, safe from predators I thought, as I watched it munching away at some fallen guavas in the shade. A voice called out from the other side of the picket fence and I looked up. A figure the other side of the palings was too short for me to make out without getting closer to see if it was a parent wanting to enrol a child in the part time classes. I did not recognise her. She was an elderly Amerindian with long grey hair and a wizened, sallow, complexion. I asked if I could help her.

"Me see ya get big turtle," she said.

"Yes," I answered.

"Turtle taste good," she said.

"So they say, but I don't want to eat it; it's part of the little zoo we keep for the children who come to this school," I explained.

"Oh, ya get school here? You English?"

"Yes," I said, "but I live here all the time. This is my home. I haven't seen you here before. Do you live in the village?"

"We jus' move in to Mr Britten farm over so," she said, nodding her head in the direction of the Georgetown lawyer's farm on the reef behind the pasture. "Me husban' lookin after cow an' fowl for 'am."

"Oh, so you are our new neighbours, then. Welcome to the area."

"OK Mistress," she said, giving me a sly look, and carried on her way down the street past Taa's house and eventually out of sight.

A few days later, the tortoise disappeared from the garden and we never saw it again.

Edwin had been in contact with the new government quite a lot since the beginning of the year. He had been to see the Minister of Finance, Bharrat Jagdeo, to get help for the drainage and irrigation works he had identified as urgent in our neighbourhood since bad flooding had swamped local villages in early January. Bharrat had been trapped in his office all day by Edwin, who sat outside, refusing to leave until he had a personal interview with the young minister. Eventually the imprisonment proved too much and Mr Jagdeo had to emerge for a call of nature, which enabled Edwin to tackle him and extract a commitment from him. He had also met the Chief of Staff of the armed forces, Brigadier Joe Singh, and discussed with him the idea of bringing the International Duke of Edinburgh Award to Guyana. Edwin had been in the very first group to take the Gold Duke of Edinburgh Award in the British Army Junior Leaders Regiment in 1957 and had also been a unit leader in Milton Keynes in the 1980s. He was therefore in a good position to advise the government how to set up the scheme in Guyana. It had been put forward and a training camp for Unit Leaders had been organised to start at Madewini on September 11th with Edwin as the Training Officer. The Ministry of Culture Youth and Sport had attempted to co-ordinate the disparate sports provisions for youth in all the various regions under one umbrella. This was mainly to make sure the youth were not being diverted through sports clubs into subversive political groups that could undermine the government. Few Indo-Guyanese participated in sport apart from cricket and none were interested in football, boxing or athletics which were almost completely the preserve of Afro-Guyanese. The post-election riots had stoked fears in the Indo-Guyanese communities that football clubs were being used by the Opposition to build up private 'armies' of black resistance that could be used to overthrow the government. They wanted to centralise sports clubs and associations to keep an eye on them and promote other youth activities that would draw in all sections of Guyanese youth. That way they could nurture youth support for the PPP government by directing propaganda to them, offering funding for trips and other rewards for participants in these activities.

Summer 'camps' like the one Edwin had just helped out with at the MMA were a part of this policy. They were not a camp as we understood the word. No tents or overnight accommodation were usually involved. Free transport was provided for the participants who lived beyond walking distance from the venue. The participants met at a designated public building where free snacks and meals were provided for them every day that talks, and occasionally activities, were organised by paid resource people. Edwin agreed to be a resource person at the first of these regional youth camps but did not get any payment for his contribution. He always volunteered his services free of charge in the same way that he refused to take any stipend for his work as Chairman of the neighbourhood council. He believed in setting an example and showing that he was above corruption. He did not want to be beholden to anyone in government. It was at this camp that he first met Colonel Keith Booker, the Permanent Secretary of the Ministry of Culture Youth and Sport and struck up a friendship with him that would take us both on a new voyage of discovery to many unintended destinations.

The first week of September 1998 we started the school term with our volunteer already in place. Now we controlled the selection of the volunteer, we could also control his date of arrival. It felt like we were well on the way to institutional stability. The International GCE O-level results had just come in for the sixth form and we had a full set of passes, with Robin achieving the top grades. They had also passed their maths and biology CXC that Louise had taken them through. This news was a great boost to the younger full timers who had another full year of study before they would enter their CXC exams. We had another Moraikobai trip planned for the end of October and expected to take the students on a field trip to Trinidad too, but this time we would go in May. They had exam entries to pay for in October, so could not afford a field trip at the same time. May was the Hampton Games, and Edwin wanted to see how Keisa would perform in the Haseley Crawford stadium in her track events. It was also just before the CXC exams, so we would have completed the syllabus and it would be a kind of reward for the students' hard study up to that point and before they would be doing practical exams or in full revision. It gave their families time to accumulate the funds to go.

Neil would now be teaching the animal husbandry and economics half of the agriculture course as well as maths and integrated science for the final year students. The sixth form would do maths, biology and chemistry GCE O-level with him and continue the rest of their subjects with me and Edwin. I now had enough time to start Robin on his A-level History and Geography courses and was looking forward to getting back to this level of my own academic subjects. I knew the geography A-level syllabus had changed a lot since I studied it myself in 1973, so I got an excellent textbook sent to me by the Geography department of Hull University and updated myself with this, my National

Geographic subscription by post and relevant videos I had ordered from Channel 4 Educational. It was stimulating my brain at last. My daily contact with Louise and now Neil, the visitations of SIHA students and our occasional other guests, removed any feelings of isolation or mental stagnation that I might have experienced if the school had never happened and the village had remained as undeveloped as it had been in our first few years in the country.

The new government was now giving us some hope that things would continue to improve. Water pipes were being laid in the villages to connect up to new deeper wells with more powerful pumps so that the supply would reach more outlying homes. This was part of a British government funded project with Nottingham Trent Water Company supplying the technicians. It had been in the planning for years and now we were seeing the fruits of it. Edwin, with his village office hat on, was pulling his hair out when he discovered that local residents had been digging up the pipes as fast as they were being laid.

After coming back from the training camp in Madewini with the Duke of Edinburgh Award unit leaders, Edwin was promoted to the Board of what was now to be known as "The President's Youth Award Republic of Guyana," just to make sure that no one could think the British Queen or her government still ruled their former colony in spite of funding the scheme. He had to visit State House the next day for the launching of the PYARG. Two days later he was back in Georgetown at the Culture Centre for the Investiture ceremony. He had not realised that this was the Investiture of President, Janet Jagan, and was a purely political gathering, where he had to mix with all the MPs and local celebrities. He was taken by Brigadier Joe Singh to be personally introduced to the President.

"She asked me what I thought the country needed to help it develop properly," he told me when he got home.

"What did you say to her?" I asked.

"I told her that the only way to get this country to develop was to get a whole load of white people here long term to educate the people like my wife is doing!"

"Oh, you didn't say that,"

"I *did.*" He insisted.

"What was her response?"

"She just said that people are free to come and go from the country but there is more to development than just education. I said that the education is rock bottom here and any improvements made in other ways are soon destroyed by the people because of their ignorance. Then Joe Singh took me aside and said he agreed with what I had said about the education but it was not a very good thing to have said to the President. I said 'It's the truth and I say the truth to anyone who asks me, President or not.'"

"Have you changed your opinion about her now you've actually spoken to her?" I asked.

"Yes, she seems just like a normal old lady who wants the best for the country. I think she quite likes me because Joe Singh said I should pop in and see her whenever I come to Georgetown. I didn't say it, but I have no intention of doing that. The PNC spies will think I've joined the PPP so I'm keeping well away. I'm not letting myself get used as a political tool."

Edwin wanted the best for his country too, and so he was balancing metaphorical plates on sticks as usual, organising this new youth award at the same time as planning a visit by an American medical team to visit our area the following year to perform eye cataract surgery free of charge to the villagers who needed it. Then he had to show a German Professor and his wife around the area in Bushlot that he and the council had identified for an internationally funded dumpsite to be located for the improvement of public health. He was on the West Berbice Cricket Board, as well as training the students and athletes daily and doing the teaching I had scheduled him for at Sapodilla. As if that was not enough, he was also supervising the erection of street name signs sent by an association of Hopetown expats living in Brooklyn.

"You would think they would learn something after living in the USA for decades," he said angrily. "I told them they should put their money into education in the local schools, but no, they aren't interested in education. They say they don't want their aid money to make the PPP government look good. They wanted to put up a bus shed so people don't get wet when waiting on the road for a bus in the rain, but all they really want is a monument to themselves, or something for their own convenience when they visit. Local people don't care about a bus shed. If the association put one up, it'll just get taken over by vendors selling stuff and it'll become an obstruction or cause a fight and more problems for me to deal with. At least with street signs they can have their monument without causing the trouble. People will get their letters faster when the post girl knows where the streets are."

I understood why Edwin said these things but I did not agree with the way he often dealt with people when they resisted supporting his priorities. I could see why health, hygiene and education were important but could also see why locals did not share his enthusiasm for dumpsites or flushing toilets. He could be very aggressive with a brutal tongue when faced with bigoted ignorance. He held such people in contempt and was not afraid of letting them know it. Sometimes I worried that they saw me as the origin of Edwin's views and ideas and hated me all the more for being white. He wanted instant results and steam came out of his ears when he did not get them. Sometimes the frustration building up inside him was tangible and seeped into me by osmosis. I did not like the feeling. I was a very patient, calm person; a necessary quality to be able to teach effectively. I was now being driven by an external engine; one that was an international gold medal winner. Everything was a race. We had to be the best. I always did the best that was humanly possible, but was happy to do it in whatever time it took. We would get to the same goal in the end.

Our trip to Moraikobai was set up for October 20th. We got to Governor Light with all our supplies and waited with Vic Persaud as before, but this time the launch did not show up. Buddy Deo had died since the previous year and his son was not a reliable replacement. It was a bitter disappointment for the children, and Neil. Vic kindly helped us to make something educationally worthwhile out of the day by giving us a guided tour of his rice farm. I asked questions that would be relevant to the agriculture syllabus and the students asked others. We all took notes and drew diagrams of his machinery and a sketch-map of the farm layout so something was salvaged. We ate our packed lunches and then went home early. Edwin was silent all the way home. I could sense that he was angry with embarrassment at the failure of his countryman to deliver a simple basic service as promised. He wanted to impress Neil with the same experiences as we had been able to give Louise and Nova. So did I. Our disappointment was multiplied a hundred times by the disappointment of letting down the children after we had built them up to this for a whole year. All the weeks of planning, the expense we had all gone to in order to get there, the wasted time and effort in getting lifejackets and boxes of supplies that were staring at us all the way home, were reminding us of this failure that we had been powerless to prevent. Once back at the school gates, we shared out the supplies for the children to take home to their families and arranged for school to be open as normal the next day after all.

"Well," said Edwin, after the last students had walked off out of sight, "That's that dead! It's the last time I waste any energy trying to get into Moraikobai for more than one reason." I knew what he meant and I understood. It was such a shame, but the extra responsibility of taking children with all the uncertainties it involved made such explorations into their own country unthinkable. It was easier to take them to Trinidad than to Moraikobai.

I was writing a script for a new drama to put on at our Christmas prize-giving. It was about the Bush Negro revolt in Demerara during the French Revolutionary period and based on the letters of an army doctor travelling through the country in the 1790s. I called it "Liberty, Equality, Fraternity." Neil had the part of Governor Van Hoogenheim. Every full time student had a part specially written for them. Rehearsals got underway during November and early December. The GUM medics came to the area at this time and Edwin took our students during his management and careers sessions to help with reception duties, filling in the paperwork of each patient the doctors and dentist screened. Edwin, as the chairman of the local council, was in charge of queue management for the hundreds of aged citizens who turned up to be seen. He had been asked by the GUM doctors to publicise the visit through his council meetings and there had been a massive response. The Hopetown Association had supported this mission and some of their members had come to see what they could help with on the ground. This caused a problem with ugly scenes of racism in the waiting room. The overseas blacks were trying to prevent Indo-Guyanese from getting access to the medics. They seemed to feel that they had raised money only to support their own kind. If the 'Coolie' wanted help, they would have to get their own people to raise funds to bring a team of doctors in. Edwin was disgusted with them and had to step in to keep them out of the way. The doctors were there for everybody, regardless of skin colour. He had intended everyone to come inside the waiting room, but found that many had been forced to stand outside. One elderly lady collapsed from standing for so long out in the hot sun and although they brought her inside and the doctors did what they could for her, she died.

"I can't work with these ignorant blacks from Brooklyn," Edwin said. "They're not my kind of people. All they're interested in is money and tax relief. They used this mission to get their own stuff shipped in for relatives among the medical supplies the doctors brought. I had to get the ministry of Finance to waver the duties on it because it's medical supplies but when it's delivered, I find boxes of stuff hidden in the middle with people's names on. I'm the one who's made to look bad if the customs inspectors had found it. I'm going to resign from the Association. I don't want anything more to do with them."

Louise returned from her adventures around South America on the second weekend in December. She had promised to return to help Neil with the marking of the integrated science school based assessments. She brought her travelling companion, an Austrian girl she had befriended at University and arranged to meet in Cayenne after she left us. We invited them both to stay for the weekend. They were in time to watch our final rehearsals for "Liberty, Equality and Fraternity" and Louise was keen to tell the students and us about all the strange animals and places she had seen from Brazil to Chile, Peru to Bolivia. She even brought some porcupine quills for the lab collection and a hand woven Bolivian rug for us. Edwin set them off at Rosignol on the final leg of their journey to Cayenne whence they would fly back home via Paris. Then Eddy Johnson, a retired Guyanese soldier who had served with Edwin in the British army, and had recently moved back to Georgetown to care for his aged parents, came down for a few days. He helped Edwin to set up the scenery under the house for the day of the show. We needed a small thatched mud hut frontage with a doorway to pass through and lots of natural branches to create a rainforest backdrop. They strapped some suitable vegetation around the pillars supporting the house to disguise them as trees in the fore and middle ground. Eddy agreed to film us using the video camera we had from Mitch.

We had invited people from Georgetown to see the show, including the press and the Ministry of Culture Youth and Sport. Now that the students were all entered for the first ever Bronze Award of the Presidents Youth Award Republic of Guyana, and Edwin was our unit leader while I was a skills teacher, we had made drama the skill that our students would offer. I had written out a drama syllabus for the purpose. Keith Booker, the Permanent Secretary of the Ministry of Culture Youth and Sport who was in the area visiting the MMA Sports ground and wanted to see Edwin, came to our dress rehearsal and was so impressed with it that he made the instant decision that we should repeat the show in Georgetown on Republic Day in February at the National Culture Centre. I was reluctant to agree because of the sheer size of the effort of putting on a production in our own premises. The children were in their final exam year and the idea of disrupting lessons to put on a tiny production like ours on the massive stage at a national venue without it looking ridiculous did not appeal to me.

Keith understood these concerns but suggested that if we needed a more intimate venue he could arrange for it to be put on at the Umana Yana Exhibition Centre next to the Forte Crest International Hotel in Main Street. It was a huge Amerindian thatched round house, so definitely would have the right feel for our drama. I still could not be persuaded. How could we rehearse it properly in a new setting at such distance? How could we get all our props and scenery there? How could we afford to get us all there? I did not want it all changed in a way I could not control. He was not a man who could be put off easily, so he pledged that he would provide transport to get all of us and all of our props there and back on the day of the performance and that he would get his team to do the scenery as we wanted it. Edwin agreed to go down the day before, to manage and oversee the stage set-up to get exactly the same effect with natural trees and branches that we wanted. I had no more obstacles to put up apart from obstinacy, so I agreed on condition that all those promises were fulfilled.

I put the thought of it aside and got on with our own final production the next day. In addition to our friend Anna Iles from the Canadian High Commission and Danny Da Costa from the LRTV Station in New Amsterdam, a bus full of personnel from the Ministry arrived in time for the 'curtain' to go up. Mrs Lowe was in charge of Culture in Education and Mrs Dewar, her sister, in charge of all music exams in the country, including the United Kingdom ABRSM theory and practical exams. I already had dealings with Mrs Dewar from entering my own students for recorder and keyboard practical exams. The ladies came with their own children and said they enjoyed the show. It was the first time I had met Danny from the TV station and he was also very impressed. It would be on the TV news in the next few days. Unfortunately Eddy's video camera technique did not leave us with a watchable film. He had forgotten to tell me that he had never used a video camera before, so the sound track accompanied pictures of everyone's feet. We were glad to see some footage on the TV news however. Sapodilla Learning Centre was now getting major national exposure. After Christmas, when we took Neil to Georgetown to introduce him to the VSO volunteers there and so he could arrange for a trip to Kaietuer Falls, Keith Booker told us that everything was set for our show at Umana Yana on

Republic Day (23rd February) and that he would take care of the publicity. It would be for a select audience of invitees such as overseas diplomats, government ministers and the education establishment hierarchy. His intention was to show them what he wanted them all to be doing in the schools in the country to improve the standard of culture as a whole. I was very flattered, but knew it put me under a lot of extra pressure to deliver something worthwhile with children who were only a step above illiterate because I had put them there. They were not full time professional actors. Keith let me have an electric keyboard on permanent loan from the Ministry as a sweetener and as encouragement to help my music teaching. I was very grateful for that.

On New Years' Day we had an unexpected visitor at the gate. He was a tall, thin, mixed blood stranger whose long grey hair, tied in a ponytail hanging down his back suggested some kind of ageing hippy. He said his name was Errol Brewster and he had just been made director of the Burrowes School of Art in Georgetown. He was a Guyanese expat who had been brought back from Barbados by his old college friend Keith Booker and had heard we had a wonderful school with highly qualified English teachers that would be ideal for his children if he brought them back to join him once he had settled into his new post. He was certainly not afraid of asking for outright favours and had the cheek to expect affirmative answers. We explained, while showing him around, that it was only me and Edwin and one self-financing volunteer and that we were not a fee paying school but a free charity for poor rural children in our area. We would not be able to take any more students than we already had because there was neither enough space nor staff.

"Funding agencies must be falling over themselves to help you with what you are doing," he said arrogantly.

"You must be joking," I said, "We don't get any help from any of them. Everything we do is out of Edwin's pension. None of us get paid nor even a food allowance." He seemed disbelieving but we continued in genial conversation. After our usual courtesy of giving uninvited visitors from Georgetown free lunch with us, we spent a lot of time telling him about the state of education in the country. When Edwin mentioned the show we were doing for the Ministry, that I had written based on original historical sources that Errol said he had never heard of, he wanted to see it. I told him I had no spare copies so he would have to come down again to see a rehearsal, which he later did. His verdict on the dramatic production was that it needed this and that to improve it.

I was not minded to have someone who had not written it make changes to it at this late stage. I thanked him for his helpful suggestions but reminded him that I was dealing with children who had few acting skills and even less ability to remember.

"They're not professional actors who can rehearse all day. They're doing exams soon and I found it hard enough to get them to be able to remember what they're doing as it is, without changing it all around again," I said. "You're perfectly right and I bow to your superior artistic appreciation but it'll have to stay as it is."

Neil was now finding his feet. As well as taking our students for football on Saturdays, he had joined a local men's team and went off to play every Sunday afternoon. He had been to Kaieteur Falls in the Christmas holidays and although he had spent Christmas day with us, he had gone to a village dance in the evening. He had made friends with Lindy, who lived in a watch hut on the reef on Edwin's brother's land at the back of us and seemed also to have made friends with the neighbouring Amerindian man, John, whose wife had admired my tortoise so much that it had disappeared. I was sure by now that she had taken it. Amerindians regarded turtle as a delicacy. It must have been too much of a temptation to see ours on display in the garden as in a butcher's shop window.

Neil liked his drink, so it became a regular leisure pursuit of his, to go out on a Saturday night, just as he had started to do in the holidays and come back in the early hours with a skin full. Edwin did not mind being woken up to let Neil in if he rang the bell on our gate. He understood as a man that he could look after himself and needed freedom to enjoy his own chosen recreation pursuits. It was preferable to stay up late or be awoken than to let Neil have his own front gate keys. We both knew that locals would love to get hold of them and were not above stealing them off Neil, especially if he were too drunk to know what was going on. Neil had also made friends with Edwin's nieces Althea and April. They lived with Taa but were now in their late teens, unskilled, unemployed and looking for a good time. Neil said he had been "to church" for the annual youth club party with them on "Old Year's Night" (New Year's Eve). He also went into the village to see Lindy's sister who had "baked a cake" for him. It all seemed quite innocent at the time, although Taa had been complaining about Althea, who had been acting very strangely that day. Althea claimed to have been sent £100 by her father and gave it to Edwin with her bank book for safekeeping. This in itself was questionable, since Althea's father was a drugs dealer who had no contact with her since she was born. Lindy, known to be a dope smoker, had been holding illicit social gatherings with Althea and April and others in the privacy of Edwin's brother's empty house on the main road for which he had a set of keys. Taa had complained to Edwin so he had taken the keys away from Lindy. Edwin had also been to try to get his firearms licence and got into a long discussion with the CID about the local police force. They advised him to warn Neil to keep away from certain houses in the village which were known drugs bars and likely to be raided by the drugs unit. It would bring the school into disrepute if one of our teachers were present when such a raid took place. Lorraine, who used to work for us at the snackette, died of AIDS early in the New Year and the shock of that news enabled us to discuss with Neil over dinner, the widespread problem of AIDS and HIV among the local community. We also took the conversation in the direction of Althea and her character since we wanted him to be under no illusions about the company he was mixing with. He seemed a nice young man and we knew how easy it was to get conned into the pretences of innocent martyrdom that locals, especially girls, used as a hook to get foreigners onside. We had been caught up with it ourselves many times over. We told Neil in a delicate way without appearing to suggest that he had any connection with the girls.

Edwin had been trying to help both Althea and April since they had begun attending my lessons at Sapodilla in the early days, but had dropped out fairly soon because of the discipline needed with attendance and homework. They had gone on to fail at their state schools. April had passed woodwork because her teacher did the school based assessment for her. Otherwise she had no qualifications and neither did Althea although Althea had intelligence and potential. In an attempt to give them another chance, after they received the jolt of their results, Edwin sponsored them to enrol at the technical institute in New Amsterdam and got his brothers to promise to help them too. The problem had arisen before Christmas that when he went to their 'graduation' ceremony at the end of the first year of the course, which they had not expected him to actually do, he met personally with the principal and found that they had not been attending their classes. They had taken the travel money Edwin had given them, and spent it on travelling to the ferry stelling where they picked up with young men with whom they spent their time. It had come to a head. Edwin had confronted them. He would no longer give them the travelling money but arranged for a local minibus driver to take them at a regular time every day and he would pay the driver weekly. He really struggled to find an incentive for them to take their study seriously, but all they wanted was an easy route to Brooklyn or failing that, they just wanted money to get the immediate pleasures they sought locally.

It was the first week of February. We had just allowed our neighbours to dig a trench through our garden to bury the pipes carrying mains water to their house. Once they had done that, the whole village would have been connected and we would be able to lay a connection to get mains water for ourselves at last. Edwin always put us last on the list for getting amenities. Once again, rightly, he wanted to set an example. Any other local chairman would have seen to getting himself connected up before anyone else did. Neil had just given us his leaving date in June for his South American holiday tour to begin and Edwin was about to go off to Madewini for another training camp. The Minister of Sport, Gail Texiera, had recently offered him a job as her personal advisor for sport, but he had declined the post, feeling unable to commit the time to do it. He was happy to help her where he could, without a salary, however. An elderly mulatto lady, Mrs Sybil Paterson, paid us a surprise visit from Georgetown. She had heard such good things about Sapodilla Learning Centre. We were the ideal place for her to focus her pilot group to help young women in skills training in our area. There was a funding agency that was promoting this specific target group to make women employable, since they formed the majority of potential workforce in the country. Edwin gave her the usual guided tour around the house and school then introduced her to me during the students' lunch break. She looked around her in wonder as if she had never seen so many resources. This was the usual response of local visitors. We had learned by now that it was not because other schools received no resources, but that whatever they were given soon disappeared because it was not valued or looked after, or was stolen by staff and pupils. The reason we still had ours was because Edwin and I had an eagle eye on every resource we possessed.

"Who funds you?" she asked, seeing all the books and equipment we had by now amassed.

"No one," said Edwin. "Jane's school where she used to teach in Dubai gave us nearly all the books we have and we shipped it here when we first arrived in the country. Otherwise we've bought stuff ourselves out of my pension over the years and with the money Jane had from selling her house in England to come here."

"I see, but someone pays the voluntary staff."

"No, my wife does all the teaching for no pay. We tried to get a VSO but they stopped sending them to teach in schools and the young man you saw in the other classroom funded himself entirely for the year."

"No pay at all?" she said, looking at me in total disbelief.

"No," I said. "It's not that I don't want pay, but the local education ministry said I was too qualified to teach in the state schools. Local people are poor. I believe they should be getting a free education paid for by the state. It's just that I can't live in a place where children are getting such a poor standard of education when I have the ability, qualifications and experience to make a difference. That's why I do what I do."

"My dear, the Victorian Age of the great philanthropists is dead! You should both be getting properly paid for what you do. If you fill in these forms I leave you with, make sure to put down a realistic amount of pay for the teachers. I suggest $40,000 a month for it to be in line with the normal teacher's pay in the country."

She thrust two wads of printed forms into our hands with a smile.

"Remember, they are looking for practical skills, not academic ones," she continued.

"Well I'm doing first aid and sports leaders courses, so they are mainly practical," said Edwin.

"They will not accept those because they are not realistic careers in the local environment," she said.

"They could be in the future, if the people in government had the understanding that sport can be a major employer for people like it is in most other countries these days. A government has to take the lead in this by paying properly qualified people to teach the sports in schools and then we can get a decent standard to be able to perform for a paying audience. That's what I'm trying to do with this course," he argued.

"All the same, they mean skills that you can use your hands to make something local people will buy or perform a service that people will pay for and which will provide permanent employment to give these girls a sustainable future."

"I get that", he said "but I don't do that kind of teaching as I don't have the skills for that sort of stuff. Jane's the one who does all that and it's her school. *She's* the qualified teacher."

"Is there anything you *can't* do?" she said casting me an up and down look as if it was a crime. I felt a bit embarrassed.

"Well I currently do dressmaking classes as an option for some of my students. There's always a local living to be made out of that, and all students do cookery as part of the food and nutrition CXC. I also do a tourism course which is certified by the University of Guyana, and together this would provide qualifications for girls to work in hotels and as tour guides."

"No not really. The funding agencies want girls to be doing things boys normally do like carpentry and sheet metal work. That's the thing you can get money for now. It's all about gender equality."

"Well, although I can do the carpentry myself as you saw from the kitchen I built upstairs, I can't take on teaching it when I'm already doing all these other subjects."

"No matter," she said, "You can get someone else from the local community to do the teaching of it." I glanced at Edwin as I was about to say something but he could read my mind and before I got it out of my mouth, he said.

"Ok Jane, I think I know what we can do here. I have premises up on the road that is vacant at the moment and I know the ideal teacher we can get to teach these subjects." I immediately assumed he meant Eddie Johnson, whom I hadn't thought of, so I relaxed until after Mrs Paterson had gone. Later on that evening, I mentioned it to Edwin and he did his usual trick of smiling knowingly at me to make me think that he too was thinking of Eddie when in fact he probably wasn't. He gave me one of the booklets.

"I should still fill in one of these with your tourism course and other skills. Never mind what she says. The overseas agencies may have a different idea about it when they see your application," he said. We spent hours filling in the ten page forms she left with us.

"This gender equality stuff is all very well in western countries," I said, "but I can't see girls here wanting to do things like sheet metal work and carpentry, even if there's money from doing it. You have enough problem getting them to

382

believe they can do sport once they reach school leaving age because they think it's only for men. Although I don't want to reinforce their prejudices, it's a sad fact that they just want to get pregnant and have babies. Look what happened to Maggie when we tried to get her to stay on and do A-levels, and Terraine as soon as she got the job I gave her the reference for at the Post Office."

"Well, I'm going to put it to the test," he said. "I'm going to have a serious talk with April and Althea and tell them what we're applying for. It might be just the incentive they need to pass the business course they're on at New Amsterdam Technical College this term. If they do, then they can take a further course in sheet metal work and plumbing and start operating as teachers themselves up at the snackette."

"I hadn't thought of that, but I'll be very surprised if the idea of hammering out sheets of galvanised steel into buckets and cake tins or making gutters and climbing up ladders to fix them will appeal to them," I said sceptically.

"We'll see," he said. "Althea is brighter and better at writing than April. The first test I'll give her is to go to people who do the subject at the TA and find out what equipment she would need to run a course on sheet metal. She can make an itemised list, find out what each bit of equipment will cost and bring it to me. That shouldn't be too much trouble for her to do. The business course she's doing is supposed to include doing stuff like that."

"Well I hope she does it, because that would be a major breakthrough in changing the face of Guyana! I still don't understand why gender equality has to mean forcing females to start doing things that men traditionally do."

Termites were steadily attacking our property all the time now, especially after the rains came, forcing them out of the ground under the pasture and up any convenient tree trunk, power pole or house pillar in search of a dry nesting place and source of food. Edwin decided to look up in the attic on a hunt for new trails. The access to the loft was in Neil's bedroom, so he told Neil he would have to go in there with a ladder one day while he was teaching. He did what he had to do and then complained to me about the state of untidiness in Neil's room. He called me to show me as he was bringing out the ladder. The mosquito net was all torn and the rattan chair behind his bed looked like a rugby scrum had landed on it.

"He's a right scruffy so and so. What on earth has he been doing on this chair to get it like that?" he said. I made an excuse for the untidiness but couldn't explain the chair or the net. When I asked Neil what had happened to tear the mosquito net, he said he had been having terribly frightening dreams because of the larium he was taking to prevent malaria. I accepted that explanation because I knew from friends in Dubai that mild hallucinatory dreams were supposed to be a side effect of larium which is why I had opted for daily chloroquine and weekly paludrine. I had stopped taking any prophyllactic long term in Guyana because I discovered that along the coast where we were, malaria carrying mosquitos could not live.

The next day was Valentine's Day. After school, Neil went out, but this time he went alone with Althea, who came to meet him at the gate all dressed up. It was henceforth, no secret that they were dating. We thought nothing of it. He was an intelligent, sensible graduate who was neither handsome nor ugly. We knew he already had a girlfriend back in England. He knew Althea was Edwin's niece and what kind of character she had, but we had also warned him about the AIDS problem and local girls, so he could look after himself and was probably just taking Althea out to fend off the advances of other local girls.

Three days later, Edwin was in Georgetown preparing the stage for our drama performance at Umana Yana. He came back shattered and very late. It had been sorted in the end. He said he had some problems with the workers getting the right kind of greenery he wanted to dress the backdrop and basic hut structures with, so he had gone out with them to get it and when they used it all up, found they had to go out again to get some more. He had left it incomplete but they knew what they were supposed to do and would finish it off before the next day when we were performing. The show had been brought forward to the 18th February because Republic Day was reserved for the Mashramanie Carnival Parades.

The following morning we were all ready and packed up at school at 6 a.m. with the costume rail and the boxes of props. A small truck arrived first, loaded up our costumes and props and Edwin's drum console into the back, and left. We waited for the minibus to collect us. It was late. When it arrived, the driver was complaining about having to come all the way from Georgetown to fetch us and then having to do the same two way trip late at night to bring us back. It was a bad start to the day to get there at nearly eleven o'clock and find that we would have to wait even longer as the scenery was still under construction. It was so incomplete that I was afraid we would not have time for a rehearsal before the performance. At least the ministry provided sandwiches and drinks for us all and by the time we finished them, the set was ready for us to do a blocking run-through so the children knew the slightly new moves they would have to make in this new, larger, setting.

We did a complete rehearsal after the blocking, but I was not satisfied, so I pointed out where we needed to improve and we did another, much better rehearsal straight away. I had wanted the sound effects tape played over the sound system and the technicians only got the idea of their cues at the last minute. Edwin had set up an apparatus for a flaming torch to be lit to 'ignite' the pyre to 'burn' the bush-negro martyr named Amsterdam at the stake. As soon as the flaming torch was lowered and extinguished in a bucket of wet sand concealed within the 'pyre', a flickering light would start up from the area of the stake accompanied by the sounds of a huge fire crackling. It all worked smoothly in the final rehearsal. The only thing I was concerned about was the sound of a single gunshot at the right moment. I had one on tape, but Keith Booker had promised to get one of the security guards to fire a blank shot from a pistol at the crucial moment and that could not be rehearsed. The actual show was due to start at six thirty. We were provided with a packed meal to eat at about five o'clock. Then I did the student's make-up and got them into their costumes. Make-up consisted of turning a few of the black faces white so they could play the parts of the colonial soldiers. The audience began to arrive and take up their seats. As they did so the entire exhibition centre was surrounded by armed security guards in uniform. The Prime Minister and Minister of Culture were due to arrive at any minute and then the show could begin. The performance went like clockwork as did all the special effects including the deafening shot that rang out when I gave the cue backstage. The show was well received by the Ministers and the various dignitaries, who all came up in turn and congratulated us before leaving. We received a very nice congratulatory letter from the newly promoted Major General Joe Singh a few days later.

Republic Day was a national holiday, so I always closed the school on such days. I had school based assessments to mark and mock exams to set for the month before Easter. Edwin took a party of our students down to Georgetown to participate in the Mashramanie parades. The President's Youth Award had its own carnival band and Edwin as Unit leader, spent the day tramping the streets following the procession of bands. It was a more colourful occasion than had been seen in the town since we had been in the country. While he was waiting at the Ministry of Culture before the parade started, he met Wendy, a VSO from England who had just arrived to become the Minister's adviser in sport. This was the very post which Edwin had been recently offered and turned down. Wendy said she had just graduated in sport at University. She seemed to know the Head of the Commonwealth Youth Programme in Guyana who had recommended her. Edwin promised to help her do the job. She in turn introduced him to Phil Carey at the VSO who had come to Guyana to work at the physical education curriculum in the primary schools. He was trying to get his father's United Kingdom Rotary Club to fund a basic bag full of sports kit to be distributed to primary schools throughout the country and he would go out to the regions to show the sports teachers how to use it with their pupils. Edwin gave him some advice and invited him down to stay with us and see our school.

Neil was now going out with Althea every night and coming back in the early hours. A young man was murdered in Hopetown that week. Edwin was concerned about Neil's safety and indirectly warned him about the young girls in the community and how they operated. This was particularly poignant as Lilian Douglas, one of Edwin's former top athletes who was still in her teens, had been told she had AIDS-related cancer in her arm and would have to have it amputated. Lilian had been extremely promiscuous ever since puberty as with most, if not all, local youths. Some of her boyfriends had already died of AIDS and Lilian would soon follow them. Althea's course at the TI had finished in March and Edwin went to the graduation. She was not there and had not passed. He visited the principal and found out the truth. She had not been going there at all. Nor had she done anything about his sheet metal instruction centre equipment list. Clearly she had no interest in it as I had suspected. Edwin had now washed his hands of any further attempt to help her. He did not bother to pursue the document with Mrs Patterson, who had already rejected my own application. I had the school internal mock examinations in full swing and was invigilating them, so Neil had the day off. He told us he was going to Georgetown and left early, but Edwin thought he saw him at two o'clock walking across the rough pasture to Peter Britten's farm at the back of us. That was where the new Amerindian family lived. He returned to us for dinner when dark fell. Edwin asked if he had a good day in Georgetown and he had said "yes" with no further comment. Why would he lie to us about going to Georgetown? Edwin must have been mistaken.

Edwin had received a card at Christmas from a former work colleague whose son, James Hildreth, was at Millfield School and in the West of England under-15 cricket team. It said they were doing a tour of the West Indies at Easter. Edwin had sponsored James for the tour, found out the dates they would be in Trinidad and planned to meet up with the team there. He already had set his sights on meeting the tour coach and convincing them to add Guyana to their next tour of the West Indies, given that he was now on the West Berbice Cricket Board. He was also on the Board of the PYARG with a good relationship with the Ministry of Sport to facilitate any such tour. He booked up for us both to get away for a few days' break together in the Easter holidays. It would be my first holiday alone with him in eight years. I was looking forward to that and to get the chance to properly set up our field trip for the students in May. Just before we were due to go at the end of March, David Lammy paid us another visit. He stayed with us for dinner and got to know Neil at that point. Neil told David he was going overland by truck from Georgetown to Lethem on the Brazil border and so David asked if he could travel with him. The next day they set off on the journey from Georgetown together.

We left for Trinidad the following day and did not return till six days later. It had been a wonderful refresher and we had gone to every cricket match to see James play. Edwin and I had managed to spend enough time with the parents and coaches to spark an interest in bringing the team to tour Guyana and an interest in our educational project at Sapodilla. He returned to pursue those aims while I returned to practical exams and revision classes. Having received the official examination timetables, we could now finalise our planned field trip to Trinidad for the Hampton Games in May. The day after we returned to Sapodilla, Neil got back from Lethem and David Lammy flew home to England. We had a few days of holiday left to prepare for the start of exams.

Froebel College had written telling us that they wanted to send us some more computers. I therefore had to write to Mitch to see if he could help to ship them. Mitch had begun the Sapodilla Appeal through the newsletter he had been producing and distributing. He now had the support of the Princes Trust, The Poole Runners, a Guyanese lady who worked for Luton University, various businesses in Romford where he lived and himself. He was using any funds that he got this way to finance the cost of printing his leaflet and posting it out to people. Any extra he got went towards the shipping costs of the computer and sports equipment we had so far received. However, it was beginning to become a drain on our time and income having second hand clothing and shoes shipped out to us in Georgetown. When it arrived, we had to make many return journeys to Georgetown to deal with customs paperwork that bureaucracy ensured could never be done in one day. Then we would have to pay various duties that were mandatory even for charities, and finally, hire a truck to deliver the crate or barrels to Berbice. This was all a very costly business and meant that basically we were being forced into using large chunks of Edwin's modest pension to hand out free clothing. This had to stop. Any appeal money would now go to ship out the computers from Froebel that Dr Weston had promised us. Once that had been done, we just wanted any donations in cash, so we could buy educational supplies of our choice and hopefully eventually pay for some more teachers.

We managed to pack into our final term Phil Carey's course with Edwin's region five primary school sports teachers, my remaining coverage of syllabuses and school based assessments, Edwin's reconnaissance trip in Bartica for the PYARG Gold award expedition in July and August, a successful five day fieldwork tour of Trinidad, and full on revision for the students every day when they had no exams. Term ended and Neil departed on 18th June. He was headed for Peru for the summer, but we allowed him to leave most of his possessions in safekeeping with us until he returned for his flight home to England in September. We had booked to fly to England on 20th June ourselves. It was essential to visit Froebel in person to try to get a replacement for Neil in September. I was not looking forward to the shock in temperature of being back in England after living on the Equator for so many years, but at least I would be able to visit mum and dad whom I had not seen or spoken to for nine years. I had written long letters regularly with pages of news from us, but got fewer and fewer lines in response. My sister had stopped writing completely, so I had no idea what was going on with my family. Our sixth form students Louis and Robin had been paid to stay as sleep-in watch men while we were away in Trinidad in May and were now prepared to do the long haul of six weeks at Sapodilla while we were in England. On no account were they to leave the premises unless there was an emergency and even then, only one could leave while the other stayed on guard. Robin's father or sister would deliver their food to the gate every day until we got back. It was a test of their trust in us to return and of their reliability as workers.

It was strange going home after living for eleven years as a guest in other people's countries. I had no idea how Edwin felt, but I certainly felt like a social misfit from the past. I had been propelled into the future for three and a half years in Dubai and then travelled back in time to live in an eighteenth century village on the Equator for eight more years. England in 1999 was a complete culture shock for me, it had changed so much. In the high street banks, people in queues were all talking loudly to themselves about what they were going to buy in the supermarket, or so it seemed, until I realised they had tiny mobile phones pressed to one ear. Children's toys behaved like gremlins, jumping into action like living monsters, making weird robotic noises when you opened cupboard doors. Daytime television was an endless stream of exotic holiday reviews, home handyman demonstrations, instant garden makeovers or cookery using gimmicky ingredients. Did people ever really eat that stuff? Supermarkets had become cities of wall-to-wall shelves stacked with a bewildering range of choice. How could you feel that this was progress? How could twenty five different types of everything from cornflakes to shoe polish be necessary? Did cats really mind which of the fifteen different packs of cat litter their owner provided for them? Women were grabbing products indiscriminately and loading them into mountainous trolleys in their race to the checkouts. It gave me a headache trying to decide which product to buy. I longed for a smaller supermarket with a more restricted range. Too much choice must create waste. People seemed to be consumed with self-interest and self-promotion. Everyone was chasing money to get more and more things, more and more properties. No one seemed the least bit interested in the lives of those eking an existence on the other side of the world.

It was lovely to see Edwin's children after so long and the new grandchildren for the first time. Rafer's wife was expecting their first baby in July and so we might well be there for the birth. I was pleased for Edwin, as he clearly missed them so much by being in Guyana. He had expected that they would be frequent visitors since he had built Sapodilla for them to stay in, but they had only been once, for Rafer's wedding and never since. I knew it was a great disappointment to him. He had given everything to them as children and had a very close relationship with them. He believed the strength of their relationship with him would draw each of them in turn to visit us every few years for a holiday in the sun. There may have been many reasons why they did not. The distance, the cost of airfares, the busy lives they led, the fact that Sapodilla did not have a swimming pool, tennis courts and air-conditioning, the muddy beaches and the mosquitos, the lack of classy shops, restaurants and supermarkets and the absence of reliable electricity or a multi-channel twenty four hour satellite television service could all have influenced their choice. The plain truth was that they did not feel Guyanese and were more comfortable in the society they had grown up in and now lived in.

Edwin, for his part, had left England not because he felt more Guyanese than English, but because as an impressionable child of ten, he had made a promise to his mentor, Parson Munroe, that he would return to Guyana when he could afford to do so, in order to help develop the country of his birth. He believed in keeping promises and he had done so, at great personal cost. He had tried to put in place in our home the things that were lacking in the local infrastructure, but he had not calculated for the lasting damage caused by the post-colonial brain drain and chain migration that still followed it. He had not expected local people to be so resistant to changes in their way of life, so reluctant to work to improve their conditions, so ready to bite the hand that feeds them. He was caught between two worlds and seemed unhappy because of that.

Although it was midsummer's day, we had been shivering with cold since we arrived in Ascot, where we were staying with Carmen, his elder daughter, and her family. Edwin had gone down with flu and spent the first day or two in bed trying to keep warm. Carmen and Tony were out at work all day and three year-old Charmaine was with a child-minder. We were told that if we were to look after her instead, she would lose her place with the child-minder. Someone came round to do the garden, a Bosnian girl came in to do the cleaning and someone else collected ironing once a week. We were there for six weeks so there was plenty of time to see the family in the evening and at weekends but we were dependent on them for transport and so were marooned. I wanted to hire a car but Edwin flatly refused because we could not afford it. Being trapped in someone else's home in suburbia with nothing to do except read or watch television nearly drove me mad. I couldn't wait to get back to Guyana with all its poverty and crime. It was the simplicity of life there that I missed; the warmth and sunshine, the beauty of nature free of traffic pollution and the feeling that whatever we were doing was worthwhile even though an uphill struggle all the time. However unhappy Edwin was about living in Guyana, we could never have afforded to live in England anyway, as things were so expensive, he was retired, I might not be able to get a job back in teaching and we would have to come back penniless. There were plenty of people who would have loved to have our home and its contents in Guyana, but none of them would have given us a cent for any of it.

I rang Dr Weston to find out if they had another volunteer for us and was told that they did not. It seemed that neither Kirstin nor Mitch had visited the college on our behalf so there had been no response. Dr Weston had twenty computers lined up for us as they would be replacing that many in the college. The 'millennium bug' was expected to interfere with their function on something called the internet which was apparently coming into use. He was very irritated that no one had contacted him and wondered whether we were going to get them off his hands or not because if we didn't collect them soon he would give them to a school in Poland. I apologised and explained that Mitch Mason was doing the shipping on our behalf as an act of kindness so we had to depend on when he could fit it into his busy life. Dr Weston had little sympathy and suggested that we get someone else to deal with these things for us in a more efficient and professional way. I apologised profusely and asked if we could arrange to meet with the students while we were in the country. This he agreed to but it was really the wrong time as it was the end of term and students were going on vacation. It would be difficult to get contact with many of them. We would be able to go to Froebel in a week's time to meet with the tutors and put our cause to them in the hope that they would pass on our message enthusiastically enough to their students at the start of the new term.

As soon as I put down the phone, Mitch called. I explained about the computers and tactfully asked him if he would be able to get in touch with Roehampton immediately to arrange for the shipping. It seemed no problem to Mitch. Nothing ever did. Perhaps Dr Weston's office had not made the urgency clear to him but now I had done so. I immediately posted off an advertisement to the Times Educational Supplement with our phone number at Carmen's so as to cast the net over all the other universities and colleges training maths and science teachers.

Roehampton Institute and Froebel College laid on a splendid reception for Edwin and me and the education tutorial staff. My talk about Sapodilla Learning Centre, our aims, modus operandi and need for a qualified maths and science teacher were well received by the tutors and principal. I was full of praise for Louise, their last sponsored volunteer and answered lots of questions. We both spoke to the tutors informally as we tucked into the enormous spread of food and wine. One student, also named Louise, said she was considering whether to come out to us, so we did our best to encourage her. The Vice Principal told me that not only would student fees be off-putting to volunteers but the new requirement that they must work in a school for a year immediately after training in order to ratify their qualified teacher status would make it even less attractive. They would be another year older and even more in need of a job to pay off their student loan. By the time they had ratified their qualification, they might be offered a permanent job and thinking of settling down and buying a house. It seemed as if circumstances had conspired against us. The age of the useful qualified teacher volunteer was more or less dead.

Everything had seemed fine when I first called mum at home to say we had arrived and where we were. I had explained that we did not know when we would get to see her. Having no transport of our own, we would have to wait till someone could take us to the nearest station so we could get to her by train. She seemed a bit disappointed but understood and took the phone numbers of all Edwin's children in case she wanted to call for a chat. By the day after our visit to Froebel, My brother, Guy, called me at Carmen's to say that mum had gone into hospital and dad was temporarily in a nursing home. My sister had deteriorated so badly with multiple sclerosis that she was also in a nursing home while her partner was in the USA on a respite holiday. I had a long conversation with Guy who said he was in the process of splitting up with his wife because of her anger management problems and substance abuse. I could not take in this catalogue of catastrophes, so I said I would try to get there as soon as possible. Kirstin agreed to take us down for the day, but she felt unwell the morning we were to go, so we ended up taking the train.

It took all day to get there and we had to hitch a ride from the station with a commercial van because there were no buses or taxis. We found mum out of hospital and dad back home by then. Dad was eighty and had put on a lot of weight but looked as well as could be expected. We stayed over for two nights so my brother could bring his two young children to see us. I was shocked to find mum unable to walk properly because the arthritis in her knee had contorted it outwards at a right angle. The house was in a terrible mess because she could not stand long enough to use the vacuum, so I spent the day doing her housework for her. I felt I should stay longer to help but she said she could manage now she was feeling better. She was worried about my brother and his children, though. I listened to his story at length when he arrived. I had no idea all this had been happening to my family while I had been in Guyana out of contact with everyone except by letter. Mum's one page air-letter forms had given no indication of any of it. No one else had bothered to write at all. I felt helpless and unable to do what I felt I ought to. We had to leave on the third day because of an appointment Edwin had made in London to see the Central Council of Physical Recreation, so Guy took us to the station on his way to drop his children home. I promised mum and dad we would make another visit before we left the country but I did not know when that would be.

The next two weeks were filled with meetings and get-togethers with Edwin's family members and a few friends. Carmen had arranged a barbecue with some of Edwin's former colleagues from the army and Tony's athletes including Roger Black, his Martinique fiancée and future in-laws. Then it was arranged for us to attend their wedding nearby and meet up with Daley Thompson, Mark Richardson, Sally Gunnel and other celebrity athletes that knew Edwin from his days as the England multi-events coach. Louise, Mitch and Sarah and my university friend Jo all travelled to see us in Ascot. We went down to Poole for a couple of days to give a talk to the Poole Runners and thank them for their fundraising, while staying with Dave Hayes and his family. We also had a good meeting with Ron Tulley at the CCPR in Victoria about Edwin's Sports Leaders' course and I received two calls from prospective volunteers seeking further information which I sent to them. I spoke to mum on the phone but because of all these arrangements, would not be able to visit till 22nd July, four days before our flight back to Guyana.

When we finally got to my parents' home, for another two night stay, we faced a traumatic visit to the nearby Sue Ryder Home where my fifty three year old sister was in care. It was a terrible shock to see the once attractive, slim person I had left nine years before now unrecognisable, obese and completely immobile in a sanatorium bed. The only muscles she could move were her eyes and lips. My nephew, who had taken us to visit her, was feeding her with a straw and spoon like a baby and the only word she could utter was "yes". It was tragic. I learned that she had a crane fitted at home, like the one in this private ward, to get her from bed to toilet and back. Otherwise she was completely helpless with a television to watch whatever was put on for her. No wonder she had stopped writing letters to me. I returned to Ascot haunted by these memories and feeling unable to do a thing to help anyone.

Edwin vowed he would do everything he could to get us a mobile phone when we returned to Guyana. They were just being introduced at tremendous cost but we would be able to speak at least once a month to our families when we had one. Rafer's wife gave birth to their first child, Caios, two days before we left, so we managed to see him on our last day in England. By eight thirty the following evening, we were back in Guyana, jet lagged but relieved and warm at last.

During our absence, there had been mass murders in Buxton, a large black enclave between Georgetown and Berbice, and a major strike had been organised. There had been petrol and food shortages before we left for England and a lot of discontent had built up. President Janet Jagan had suffered a heart attack, so the opposition were taking full advantage of the situation. We drove through Buxton in the dark without incident. At least Eddie Johnson had serviced our jeep while we were away and filled up the tank for us, so we had no breakdown. The boys were asleep inside the gym with all the shutters locked so we had to wake them up. The only bad news about the property was that thieves had broken in at the back of the farm one night and stolen the zinc sheets belonging to the Small Farmers' Association. It was a relief to find nothing worse than that had happened. The boys had done a good job and reared a batch of forty chickens that were all still alive and ready for market. Now we were back, we called the students in for a meeting following which they went out in the community to collect orders and organise the slaughter and sale accordingly. It was coming up to Emancipation Day so everyone was preparing for a feast involving chicken. Once the chickens were all sold, Robin and Louis could go off on their own holiday, a planned cycle ride to Surinam together, using the money we had paid them for their six week guard duty.

Another murder occurred in the village in August. It was in Paris Street at the end of our own road. Edwin had to drop off Jaxine, a local CID policeman, at the house where it happened to investigate the crime. They went through the motions, but no murderer was ever caught or brought to justice in our area in Guyana. It just got forgotten about after a time, like the English priest who had been victim of a sacrificial ritual in Belladrum.

Edwin was told he had to attend the Annual General Meeting of the PYARG in Georgetown and a CASC meeting, which was opened by Major General Joe Singh. The media was there in full force as were lots of VIPs including Phil Brown the England Sprinter who had come to represent the Duke of Edinburgh Award and to make links between Guyana and his school in Nottingham. The new British High Commissioner, Mr Glover, had arrived from his last posting in

Berlin. He was a very introverted man whom neither Edwin nor I took to. He did not seem right for the job. However, Edwin extended a gesture of friendship to him by offering to get help for his son Rupert through Edwin's high level cricket contacts in England. Soon after this, Edwin met Dave Clarke, the Regional Head of the Duke of Edinburgh Award, who was visiting the country at the education campus of the University of Guyana. Dave informed Edwin that the training camp for Unit leaders would be at Madewini in September and Prince Edward would be coming to Guyana in order to meet the unit leaders and welcome Guyana to the scheme as it was a new country joining and at the end of its unit leaders' first year.

Edwin had already started to have misgivings about the way the PYARG was being organised in Guyana.

"It's not the Duke of Edinburgh Award," he told me. "It's nothing like it. They've watered it all down. It's bad enough that even in England they've made it all soft compared to the way that it was when I did it myself, but the unit leaders here are a bunch of jokers. They don't like my way of doing things."

"Perhaps you should have a bit more patience with them," I said.

"None of the female unit leaders have done any sport, and even the men are useless. The men try their best, but I don't think they understand what they're supposed to do, because they've never done the award themselves. The problem is that when I criticise the way we're doing things and make suggestions for improvement, they don't like it. The Minister herself doesn't understand and wants to leave it how it is because it's the way locals do things. Everything's a one week course. How can you train anyone properly to do any worthwhile sport when you have only a week to learn it? They wouldn't let me do the survival stuff for the expedition properly. They're letting people go off and do the skills with people that aren't vetted and they don't bother to check and see whether the skill is being done properly or even if the participants have turned up on a weekly basis to do it. No one keeps any records; it's just done on hearsay."

"You make it sound like we're the only unit doing the award properly."

"We are," he said. "Even the expedition's not a proper one with camping in tents and survival techniques. They just want all the units in the country to come together in one great gathering at the Madewini hostel where they get meals cooked for them by paid caterers. That's their idea of a camp. The government have selected people to be unit leaders on the basis that they're party supporters who've signed up to do it so they can get sent on trips at the government's expense. The whole thing is about party politics just like the People's Militia was for the PNC under Burnham. It's just a way of rewarding the youth of the Party with perks provided by international organisations. They don't really want to do proper sport or expeditions that are a physical challenge."

"That's a shame," I said. "It also makes a mockery of the whole thing if our students are being put through the year of learning in a proper rigorous way and yet they end up with the same award at the end as all the other people who hardly did anything to get it."

"Exactly. They just want me to be involved so I can help them to get funding from the UK. They don't really want to take any notice of what I say we need to do. The whole thing is supposed to be voluntary and sponsored by local business to develop the youth and make them more employable. The government is paying salaries to people in the department of Sport to do all the organising when it's supposed to be completely independent of government. Here, it's just something to make the government look good. I don't feel I want to be associated with a scheme like that just to make the country look good in front of Prince Edward."

"I can see your point, but give them a bit more chance to make it work. Maybe things will improve as they start to get the hang of it. Perhaps our students can become unit leaders and make a better job of it since they will have done it properly with us."

"Yes, well I've already decided to send Robin on the next unit leaders' course in Madewini in September when he comes back from his holiday, since he already did the Bronze expedition," he said.

The Sapodilla Learning Centre sign that Kenson had painted for me on the large noticeboard attached to our front fence stated that enrolment for new students at the school would begin on 31st August every year. I had already indicated to existing Saturday students that if they wanted to move up to the full time school, they would have to do so before we left for our holiday in England and that they needed to bring their token enrolment fees of $2000 Guyana dollars for the year (£10) on 28th August to confirm this. I now had twenty three students beginning their two year CXC courses and seven sixth formers wanting to do GCE O-levels including Robin who alone was doing A-levels. We would have our first set of true athletes as full time students. They were the product of the daily training they had had to do since starting Saturday lessons at least two years ago. Some of them had been coming to my lessons since primary school for five or six years.

I was concerned about having no volunteer to help me this time and had posted another advert to the Times Education Supplement on our way out of England but had heard nothing from any of the people I sent further information to back in June. Edwin and I went to the VSO Office in Georgetown again thinking that we would have more success in getting one now that we were established and approved as an educational institution by the government, although not funded by them in any way, and because Edwin was helping them with the PYARG. The person in charge of the VSO office was now a Guyanese lady. She was very helpful and co-operative but made it clear to us that we would have to pay the person $50,000 per month as the standard living allowance because the government would only pay that for VSOs working in government schools and offices. Any private organisations or NGOs who had VSO help would have to pay that money from their own funds. This was something we had not realised. It was a blow. We would never be able to have a VSO because we did not even have a cent to pay ourselves let alone a VSO. It made sense for a commercial business to do that because they had an income from their product but we were a tiny charity with no income at all from our highly valuable product. Peace Corps did not work like that. The U.S. government paid for everything. Maybe we should try them.

Neil returned from his tour of Peru and called in to collect his stuff before flying home to England. We had a meal together, chatted about his adventures and he stayed overnight. He was much changed. He had matured a lot since we first met him and seemed a good person. We wished him luck in his future career as a teacher in England and he left. Edwin and I had a serious discussion about how we would cope with all the new students and no volunteer. We had decided to share the teaching for the year as we had done for a short while before Louise had arrived. This time Edwin would have the fourth years when I had the sixth form and vice versa. I would not only teach my subjects and all the agriculture, but I would also take on the maths teaching using the store of answer papers prepared by all the previous volunteers to check my own answers. It would be good for me to relearn and improve on my maths now everything else was more or less automatic. At least I could do the easy topics first until we got another volunteer to do it. Edwin would teach the fourth year First Aid and careers and do some extra sport with them for the CCPR course. The sixth form would do the same subjects with him but at a more advanced level and also management. We would each do one assembly a week, the sixth form would take it in turns to do one and the new full timers would also do an assembly, summarising a book they had read recently from our library.

We received a letter from Mitch saying that he had shipped the twenty computers, so we decided to get Brian, our carpenter, to partition off the end of the lab to make a separate small computer room. I had been working hard to redecorate and relocate Louise's specimen displays. Vernon had been installing extra lights and the correct cables and power points to serve all the computers and printers. We adapted the long tables formerly at the snackette to fit along the entire length of the lab wall that would now be inside the computer room. Stools from the snackette could just squeeze into the narrow room at each station. Edwin footed the bill for all this out of his pension. It was a struggle but possible thanks to the low cost of basic local raw materials and labour. We just had to wait for the computers to arrive. The exam results came in at this time and once again we got the top results in the region. Out of a total of eighty subjects entered, seventy two were in the top three grades with one student gaining grade ones in several academic subjects. Two of the parents came personally to thank me for my contribution to the community with these results.

Term started. There was just the two of us again. I was still enrolling students for the junior classes and had decided to use Robin to help me with the primary maths group. The water supply had almost run out and we had to carry buckets up into the house from the spare tank across the yard. A swarm of African bees decided to invade the veranda at the back of the kitchen so we had to send for a man called Rajkumar, who was a trained beekeeper, to get rid of it. We evacuated that area of the house and waited hours for his arrival. When he finally came with his assistant, he seemed more interested in collecting the honey and the swarm of bees for his business than ridding our house of a problem. He prised open the woodwork with his crowbar and pulled out the honeycomb, leaving a trail of damage. Neither he nor his assistant had on any protective clothing. Apparently the bees were all out during the day collecting nectar. They would return from foraging at about four in the afternoon and go into the box that he left balanced on the veranda sill. He said he had put the queen inside the box and the bees would come back to find her in there. He would return in a few days to collect the box. The bees came back in the late afternoon and swarmed in fury around the wreckage on the veranda. Dying bees had been crawling through the channels of the wood panelled walls onto the floor inside the house all day and I could not pass those swarming around their old nest and the box he had left. It was dark before I could safely get into the kitchen. The next morning I got up at dawn and saw the great angry cloud take off and head out towards the tamarind tree at the back of the garden. They did not return that afternoon. They had gone. We had paid him to damage the house in order to collect his product. Edwin was not going to be caught like that again.

Eight of our students had been to do the Bronze Award PYARG expedition and camp at Madewini while we had been in England and the remaining nine went off to do it in September. The first year of the Award in Guyana had come to an end. Three days later, Robin came back from the Unit Leaders' camp in Madewini and said only eighteen people had taken part in it. Edwin had not gone this time because he had to stay at Sapodilla and teach. Sixteen Sapodilla students were to be given the Bronze Award, but the presentation was going to be midweek because that was when Prince Edward was scheduled to visit. He would be handing out the certificates to the awardees. I told Edwin that royalty or not, I was not going to close down the school to spend a day sitting around in a hall for hours with gum chewing ill-disciplined teenagers from other units who had not done the award properly. These occasions were always badly organised. I had exam curriculum to cover in a limited period. Time on weekdays was too precious to waste sitting around in halls while inept people made a mess of a presentation. It would have been different if it was at the weekend. I did not go, and the children did not go. Edwin decided not to go either. We sent our apologies and explanation. We would collect their certificates at another time. The people at the Ministry were upset. They could not understand such behaviour. To them attendance at formal functions took priority over everything else. They had also wanted us and our students to make their version of the scheme look good, when it was not.

The computers arrived in Georgetown and on his one day off a week, over several weeks, Edwin dealt with their processing through the customs and transported them back to Sapodilla. While visiting Phil Carey at the National Centre for Educational Research and Development about the sports teachers' course Phil was due to deliver at Sapodilla for Region five teachers, Edwin met a VSO computer technician called Camillus. With his usual persuasiveness, Edwin managed to get him to agree to visit us and help set up all our computers. Camillus came down for a weekend in December and worked for two days at making good the computers and printers. He took the best ones and used others for spare parts to get thirteen of them working, of which eight were working very well. Even though he wasn't supposed to do anything other than what he had been told to do by the VSO, he agreed to come down to us on his free weekends once a month to teach our students how to use the computers. In return he got free board and meals with us.

During the term, a letter came from David Hildreth asking if the West of England Under-15 cricket team could come to play two matches in Guyana at Easter 2000 and could Edwin arrange everything with the government? We were both by now doing a seven day week. The teaching contact time for me was six days and Sunday was left for me to mark and prepare lessons or do other administrative jobs. Housework would have to wait until the holidays. Edwin was busy making arrangements with the Ministry of Culture Youth and Sport for the English schools cricket team tour in the time he had between teaching and doing village office work, as he was still Chairman of the NDC. Sea defences were being discussed at a coastal zone seminar in the rural district council board room and Edwin took his management class along. His idea was to involve them in local government development work and teach them the correct way to go about efficient project management. In the same way, he took them with him to check out the dumpsite at Bushlot and after showing them the size and extent of the district and the places where indiscriminate waste tipping was occurring, he discussed the problems and possible solutions with them and got them to come up with a plan for rubbish collection in the NDC which he then tried to implement in practice.

We received an unexpected cheque for a thousand pounds from the Charities Aid Foundation via Mitch at the end of October. I had no idea who this was or why we had got it at that point but by Christmas, got a card from two dear friends of University days who were running that Foundation and had decided to respond to our appeal in Mitch's newsletter. It was a fantastic boost. It meant we could buy our own new heavy duty photocopier machine and voltage stabiliser from Xerox suppliers in Georgetown instead of having to rent one from them. They would guarantee it for the first three years and come out and service it every three months. We would get it organised in the Christmas vacation when we could both travel together to town.

The millennium had arrived. It was the year 2000. Elton John's recent song release was ringing out from the local loudspeakers and seemed somehow to have been written for us. "The Road to Eldorado" had been a long and hard one but we had almost got there. Our love affair, which began when we sang music together in Milton Keynes in 1984, had lasted in spite of all the odds stacked against us. We sang the words of the song together as we drove along in the sunshine to sort out the photo-copier. We were in tune. We were in love more than ever. We were soul mates who had found our own El Dorado. We had been a real force in helping this community to develop and it looked like the pace of development would now speed up. We had just been connected up to the mains water supply from the street. The international agencies were funding a brand new well nearby with a six hundred feet deep borehole into the underlying water table. A private company had taken over the running of electricity provision in the country and had put an enormous amount of investment into it, so it looked as if we would be able to expect a steadier more reliable supply of power from now on. Edwin had bought one of the first mobile phones available in the country at great expense, and had given it to me on Christmas Day so I could call mum and he could call his children. I had bought an automatic washing machine from the new Courts store with the money mum had sent me for Christmas. Now it was plumbed in, we had better power and a mains water supply I would no longer have to trample the sheets and towels in a plastic tub in the garden. We had a brand new photocopier to print resources and a set of thirteen working computers and printers. The West of England cricket tour would be coming to Guyana at Easter and our students had just completed the first Bronze Award of the International Duke of Edinburgh Award known locally as the PYARG. We had led the way in that and were being held up as a shining example by the government Ministry of Culture Youth and Sport. We had just received a letter from a Froebel student interested in coming to Guyana and requesting details which I was about to post. Eldorado was almost in sight and we were going to live out our lives happily there. What could go wrong now?

All That Glitters is Rust

Chapter 19

Eldorado and The Midas Touch

During the three years since the millennium, life at Sapodilla Organic Farm and work at Sapodilla Learning Centre downstairs had become increasingly manic. So much happened in the space of a week that it felt like a year had gone by between weekends. We didn't really have a weekend as such. I only knew it was Sunday because it was the day after the Saturday classes and I had to do laundry, housework and marking that I had not had time to do in the week. Edwin was usually taking athletes, cricketers or footballers to competitions, or organising sports events or extra courses for teachers on our premises.

The words of my last employer and headmaster in England came back to haunt me sometimes. "You'll always work hard," he had told me when I had announced I was resigning to take up a humanities teaching job in a government school in Dubai. "I'm fed up with being undervalued for all the hard work I put in and I'll be paid more money in the new job without having to take on ever more duties to qualify for it," I had said. He had laughed as he added, "You're one of those people who will work hard wherever you are employed!" "Well at least there, I won't be taken for granted!" I had retorted. He had been right, though. I had worked even harder in Dubai for a smaller number of children, but I had wanted to do so. It had been a joy to me to work hard for employers and children who were grateful for the hard work and showed their gratitude without being prompted to do so. Somehow the hard work had been more enjoyable because it was quality work instead of mass production in a sweatshop of poor achievement. I had received a generous pay rise every year without even asking for it. It had been given as a reward for what I had already done. It made me feel like working harder to repay them for their kindness and I did so. I had cried the day I left my school in Dubai because I had been so happy there. It was only my marriage to Edwin and our mission to be development pioneers in his native country that had made me leave, or I might probably still have been there.

I had felt miserable in my new homeland at first because the mountain we had to climb in order to have a decent home and life was so daunting. Nevertheless, I had always looked forwards with optimism and encouraged Edwin to do likewise, because we had invested too much to walk away from it with nothing. In his darkest days of despair and depression I had encouraged him to "think positive" along with me, citing the speed of development that the people of Dubai had witnessed in only twenty years since the late sixties.

"You've got more patience than me," he had said. "I don't intend waiting twenty years for it to happen here."

"Nothing will happen here without improvements in education, and I'm going to do something about it right now," I had said. He had agreed, but concentrated on continually nagging the local teachers, sports clubs and organisations and local adults in his ever widening sphere of influence to improve their standards. I had started off with a library and a few after-school lessons which had gradually evolved into a full time school of my own design. My school had flourished because I had put in the same hard work for no monetary reward as I had done when being paid to teach in my previous life. In fact I had used up my savings in the process of doing so and any donations from a handful of well-wishers had been poured into resources for the school to make it better. Edwin had done exactly the same for the sports club and the two were now merged into one educational academy, affectionately known by some of our Afro-Guyanese villagers as "Hopetown University" on account of our exam successes and sports achievements. We could do this without charging fees because the cost of living in Guyana was low enough for both of us to survive on Edwin's tiny retirement pension. Surrounded as we were by a community where average wages were below subsistence, no one could have paid realistic fees for a private school. Most locals had few material possessions. We had no need for consumer goods other than what we had shipped out with us. We were free from the pressures of advertisements that continually drive consumer spending and waste in the developed world.

A lot had happened in 2000, much of which became an annual feature of our lives in the following three years. Since our new phone number had gone out in Mitch's millennium newsletter, we had received a call from David Johnson, the former British High Commissioner to ask if we would have his daughter, Pippa and her school friend, Caroline Byron, Lord Byron's daughter, to stay with us for three months to do the service component of their gold Duke of Edinburgh Award at Sapodilla Learning Centre in September that year. We had also been visited by the local Director of Peace Corps, an affable, portly African-American called Hardy, who promised us help with a Peace Corps Volunteer from the next batch due to arrive in August.

Kurt Barling from BBC London had brought a team to film us at Sapodilla for a programme about the death of Tottenham MP Bernie Grant. Apparently Bernie Grant had helped Mitch to help us in some way. We never knew exactly how and had to assume it was to do with the Princes Trust and getting the computers shipped out to us from Roehampton Institute. Mitch's subsequent newsletter had said Bernie Grant had donated equipment to us, but the only equipment we knew had come from Bernie Grant's office to us had been a packet of exercise books and twenty ball point pens which his assistant brought out to us in 1997. Maybe Mitch had made a mistake, or was being tactful.

Edwin had been re-elected as President of the West Berbice Cricket Association and had arranged for the Guyana Government to host the first tour of Guyana by the Millfield English school-boys cricket academy from the West of England. Their party organiser, Malcolm Broad, had visited Sapodilla Learning Centre after their game at Blairmont. Shortly after their return to England, he had called us up and arranged for four of his sixth form students at Treviglas Community College to do work experience with us for two weeks at the end of June. These two connections with English schools had recurred annually ever since.

The Permanent Secretary of the Ministry of Culture Youth and Sport had been pleased that Edwin had brought Malcolm Broad and the England Schoolboys Cricket Team to Guyana because the links that had been forged had led to several more tours bringing the boys and their families to Guyana. This had brought welcome business for tourism enterprises in the capital. Malcolm Broad had also obtained British government funding to help send the Guyana National Under-15 Cricket Team on a summer tour he had organised for them in England. Edwin had been offered the chance to go as a chaperone, but he had declined, so that a member of the Guyana Ministry could get the chance to see how sports events and coaching was organised in England.

Edwin's teaching of First Aid to our students had led him to forge links with the Guyana Red Cross and medical students from Canada's Student International Health Association. This had enabled him to get successive generations of our students trained as Red Cross first-aid instructors. A team of American doctors and dentists in an organisation known as G.U.M. came and stayed with us while screening for, and at a later date performing at Fort-Wellington Hospital, free cataract operations, minor plastic surgery and dentistry for hundreds of poor villagers in our region. Our students had all acted as volunteer receptionists and administrators for them, under Edwin's guidance, and also got to see a cataract operation being performed.

Neil, our last volunteer science teacher had reappeared in Georgetown as a VSO, based at the National Centre for Educational Research and Development (N.C.E.R.D) after only one year teaching back in England. We had soon been shocked to discover that the rumours received from Taa that he had come back to marry Althea were true when Edwin had received an invitation to attend their wedding and give Althea away in place of her father. It seemed unbelievable that a graduate with his intellect could seriously have considered spending the rest of his life with a girl who had no meaningful conversation, absolutely no interest in learning and who was so devious. He must have taken leave of his senses. However, just before Christmas in the year 2000, Edwin had travelled to the Botanic Gardens in Georgetown (where Neil and Althea were married) in order to perform his duties in "giving away" his niece, while I was in full swing teaching Saturday classes at Sapodilla with the help of eighteen year old Caroline Byron and our Peace Corps Volunteer, Lori. Caroline had accompanied Edwin to the wedding reception in Hopetown village that evening in order to get a taste of our local village social life.

Neil had continued to visit us and help Lori with the science coursework assessments at the school on some weekends. During his two year stint with VSO since then, sadly, he was the subject of an on-going scandal in the village. Althea was "carrying on" with village boys in Hopetown while Neil was at work. Then she became pregnant, the baby was born and, to the delight of the village gossips who cruelly named it "Tar-baby," it was a dark black colour and so obviously not the pale skinned Mulatto that would have been clearly Neil's child. This seemed further proof of the personal strain Althea's behaviour was putting on Neil's marriage. Although Neil was delighted to have a daughter and saw no reason to suppose she was not his own, a few months later he was clearly unhappy with Althea's continued wayward behaviour. From time to time we would hear that he had been seen arguing and shouting at Althea in the village. He had got involved in fights with local boys. Then we heard the rumour that they were getting divorced but even before that had happened, Althea had moved in with the child's real father in the village. Eventually Neil had returned to England and we heard no more about him. It was a sad business. We wondered whether he had learned anything from the experience.

Since Edwin had been working with the local police to try to help them with their training, we had been informed that Neil's Amerindian friend, who had been living in the farmhouse on the reef behind us, had been involved with drugs distribution locally and had now vanished from the area. Peter Britten, who owned the farmhouse, had found it awash with empty rum bottles. The local police were in dire need of help. An ambitious and reforming new Inspector recently promoted and sent from Georgetown to take charge of our region's police, had visited our school and given the students a careers talk about working in the police service. It was an effort to attract a better quality of recruit. He was a breath of fresh air in our region, so Edwin agreed to help him by giving some free adult education to the existing officers. Their standard up to this point had been dismal as most of the officers were functionally illiterate. Many of them were women. None of them had any kind of physical fitness. They had a reputation for failure to respond to matters reported to them and finding reliable officers always on duty at the station was difficult if not impossible. Arrests were seldom, if ever, made because the police were always relatives of the accused and so warnings would get out to the criminals allowing escape before the police could catch them. It went without saying that bribes were commonplace. Edwin had begun to train the local police in adult literacy and better work practices as well as fitness and shooting practice. This had given him better intelligence of what crime was going on in our community and how completely inadequate the police force was to deal with it.

I had refurbished our museum displays in the summer of 2001 in order to open to the public on Emancipation Day in August. My sixth form students had volunteered to come in after they had finished their public exams in June and help me make replicas, models and dioramas to illustrate scenes from Guyana's history. Every full time student had a role as a tour guide in character from an era of Guyana's past so they could bring to life the displays of historic photographs and artefacts. They each learned a speech they had written about their section of the display and delivered it as if they really had come back from the past to tell present day visitors about their life and times as well as answer questions. All the students were wearing appropriate period costume we had made. One student was demonstrating the olden method of threshing rice by driving a small bullock around a post it was tied to, while another was baking cassava bread and yet another was making brooms from palm fronds. All these traditional crafts had almost died out by this time. The Minister, Gail Texiera, had come in person to be guided around the museum by each student-actor in turn. The local television station cameras followed. Students repeated their acts to members of the public in small groups as they arrived, with a short interval between each group, until the very last visitor had been escorted through the displays. It had all been broadcast on television the next day, really showing the students to their advantage. We had repeated this living museum open day many times since then with successive groups of students on various occasions for overseas visitors and local dignitaries alike. One such visitor was Major General Joe Singh who had been very impressed by it all.

Following the success of my first children's drama production at Umana Yana, I had gone on to write another one: "Down in Demerara," based on the life of the Missionary John Smith who had died in prison in Georgetown and had gone down as a martyr in the fight against slavery during the Demerara Slave Revolt of the 1820's. This also had been taken to Umana Yana by the Ministry of Culture Youth and Sport and had been even more acclaimed. I had subsequently written and produced "Berbician Thunder" about the Berbice Slave Rebellion against Dutch rule in 1763 which had not only been staged at the National Culture Centre and broadcast in its entirety on national television, but which I had been asked to repeat later for all the schools in Georgetown and Berbice in two extra matinee performances during term time. I had reluctantly agreed to do it after gentle pressure from Colonel Booker but had been horrified by the unruly behaviour of the Georgetown school children in the audience as their teachers exercised no control over them. I had felt compelled to march onto the stage mid-scene, stop the performance and yell at the audience in my loudest schoolmarm disciplinarian voice last used in an English Comprehensive. The show would NOT continue until there was COMPLETE silence in the auditorium, the students should remain in their seats and have the good manners to be quiet so that those who wanted to hear the actors would be able to do so, and if anyone felt that they could not do that, they should leave the building at once so that those who wanted to see and hear the show could do so in peace. Some had got up and walked out. When the movement and noise had stopped, then I had allowed the show to start again. I had to repeat the whole scenario for the second showing when the equally unruly audience had been all the secondary schools of West Berbice, bussed in by coaches paid for by the government.

After that experience, I had been subjected to hate mail on the letters page of "The Stabroek News" by a Georgetown teacher who had slated me for producing a play about slavery when I was a white person who must therefore know nothing about it. He falsely alleged that I had called the children in the audience animals when I had yelled at them to be quiet. He also assumed that we had been given a lot of money by the government for producing the play, which to him was unfair because local people would not get that kind of money when they wrote plays. I had replied to the editor refuting all these false claims. It had all been done voluntarily. I had written the play myself and created a part for each of the students in the class so that no child was left out. The children did the rehearsals in English lessons and in their free time. They were not professional actors. We had made our own costumes and props in our art lessons from scraps and "papier-mache" which cost nothing. The children were re-enacting episodes of their history which helped them to understand it better. They were learning to sing and dance in choreographed moves. The whole thing was a model example of learning through integrated studies. There was nothing to stop other schools from doing the same thing and getting the government to stage them at the Culture Centre too. My letter appeared to silence the critics in the papers. However, I had decided I would not take another production to Georgetown. I did not need to be subjected to public abuse by Georgetown racists.

Robin and Lance, two of our sixth formers studying A-levels and O-levels respectively, who had the highest all round academic and physical achievements of any of our students, were selected by us to go on an educational tour of England and Germany for two weeks with Malcolm Broad and Treviglas Community College in Newquay. It had been paid for by sponsors and fundraising organised by Malcolm Broad. The two boys had the trip of a lifetime and were good ambassadors for Sapodilla Learning Centre. The following year, having passed both A-levels with good grades, Robin stayed on at Sapodilla for another term in which Edwin physically prepared him for entry into officer cadet school with the Guyana Defence Force. Lance did the same, having passed all his O-levels but not wishing to take A-levels. Edwin had loaned the two boys the funds to buy all their uniform and equipment and we had proudly watched them both at their passing off parade eighteen months later.

World Welterweight boxing Champion Andrew "Six-head" Lewis had been sent to us by the Ministry of Culture Youth and Sport while he was on a victory tour of the country. This had been televised, showing our students in the gym doing boxing training, so it was soon followed by the appearance on our doorstep of down-and-out former world boxing title holder Terence Ali, looking for help from an overseas patron. The best Edwin could do was to offer him the chance to come to our sports club once or twice a week to train our student boxers in return for being personally allowed to use our gym and equipment at certain times. Edwin also provided him with some furniture and food and sought help from local sponsors to get him some groceries. A young boxing coach from Poole, Neil Partridge, came from England and stayed with us for two weeks to help further the boxing so the entire school including girls were given a taster of the sport. One of our younger students, Tegana, had emerged as having the talent and interest to become a good boxer. We were grooming him for a future trip to Poole to be helped by the boxing club there.

There had been elections in March 2001 and we had hosted the team of international observers from the OAS in our guest rooms. I had voted again in these elections, but by now had decided to vote for the PPP to keep them in government because I felt that the ministers were trying to make improvements and had made a lot of headway since they had been in power, whereas the PNC seemed capable of nothing but negative obstruction. We had been living in Guyana under the government of first PNC and now the PPP and we both felt that the latter had at least made many visible improvements whereas under the PNC we had seen none. The PPP had been returned by a huge majority of 40,000 votes, which could not be disputed, as impartial observers had verified the count. There had been rioting along the East Coast after the results were announced and this further blackened the PNC in our eyes as their supporters set fire to tyres in the newly surfaced roads and burned bridges disrupting traffic for several weeks.

Rob, the son of my close friend since university, had taken a gap year to come and help us in September 2001 and had hardly arrived on our doorstep when the announcement had been made on world news channels of a dreadful terrorist attack blowing up the twin towers in New York. Things changed the world over after that year. Guyana was soon experiencing a surge in new Islamic educational establishments with funding from the Islamic world. There had always been a mosque in Bushlot, but now it seemed to assume a higher profile in the local community and stepped up its educational expansion programme.

While Rob was with us, Mitch Mason had decided to turn up out of the blue one day. He had called up to me from the gate as students were milling around under the house finishing their packed lunches and getting on with their lunch-time activities and duties. I was getting ready for the afternoon lessons and I had nearly died from shock as I realised who it was. People did not normally travel thousands of miles from the other side of the Atlantic on the off-chance that we might be at home when they made a surprise visit. Mitch had been equally shocked to see for himself exactly what progress we had made since he had shared a campfire lunch with us under our unfinished shack in 1992. All these years he had been helping us through his newsletter, he had no idea of the true scale, scope or quality of what we had been doing. He had stayed with us for a week before returning and not only saw Rob, Edwin and I in action with the students, but also got taken by Edwin to the Ministry of Culture Youth and Sport, to do television interviews, and to see Edwin in action in the local neighbourhood district council.

A month or two later, our friend Anna, the Guyanese official in charge of Agriculture and fishery projects at the Canadian High Commission, had turned up completely unannounced one evening. She had been in distress following an argument with her mother who had accused her of being an addict. She had asked us if she could stay the night and we of course agreed. She had behaved very strangely at dinner, however, and in front of Rob had begun accusing Edwin of being an operative with the British military intelligence. He had been decidedly embarrassed and had tried to steer the conversation in another direction, but she had turned quite venomous in her tone of voice. Her mother had telephoned Edwin to find out if she was with us, explaining that she had discharged herself from hospital in Georgetown and could he bring her back the next day. Next morning when we got up, he had found her standing on top of the water tank which she had climbed over the balcony balustrade to reach. Rob, who slept in the room next to the one she occupied, had been kept awake by the sound of Anna sweeping out her room with a brush in the early hours. Edwin had taken her back to the hospital as he had promised her mother, but when he had gone back later in the week to see how she was, they had no record of her as a patient. We had found pages of unintelligible scribble all over the room where she had stayed. After that encounter we never saw nor heard from Anna again.

We had taken the students on two Geography field trips to map two different river cross sections at Madewini Red Water Creek in the interior and another location off the Linden Highway. Mitch was still with us when we did the first expedition. I had succeeded in getting a grant from the Geographical Association for this to buy us a water flow meter and some ranging poles, compasses and clipboards. Preparing the illustrated report for them to show we had done the proposed field work was quite a task. It had taken up a good few weeks of my vacation time. I got a tiny taste of what expedition leaders face when embarking on more important scientific field projects. It certainly is not easy money.

The student mini-company project had gone from strength to strength. They had taken our advice and ploughed back their profits to build a concrete-floored, zinc-roofed and mesh-walled chicken pen to house two overlapping batches of sixty chickens. The increased productivity had quickly repaid their investment and enabled further improvements to be made, including concrete feed bins, slaughter cones and a concrete based plucking table with an easy clean stainless steel surface and a roof to shelter students from rain while plucking and dressing the meat birds for sale. The orchard of bananas and plantains had grown into a leafy plantation, regularly yielding a crop with little or no work apart from harvesting the ripe bunches, dividing and weighing them. The students had also become proficient at harvesting the dry coconuts from the farm and making copra which they bagged and sold to the copra factory on the East coast for oil production.

Some of our students had moved on to local agricultural college after leaving us and one of these went into the forestry commission. Two others had completed their agriculture college courses and won scholarships to study veterinary medicine for four years at the University of Havanna in Cuba.

In an attempt to improve our sports facilities so our students had somewhere flat and dry enough to play all sports, even in the rainy season, Edwin had decided to fence off our land beyond the front garden and fill up the enclosed area to raise it above flood level. The cost of doing this properly was beyond our pocket, but we could do it piecemeal, fifty feet at a time. The students did the foundations and bricklaying as a work experience project on Sundays and during the holidays. It was also part of their service for the Presidents' Youth Award Republic of Guyana. Eventually, they had built a concrete block wall three feet high with eight foot pillars cast in reinforced concrete at intervals around three sides of the designated field plot. Then we had ordered the greenheart wood to make the framework to nail the mesh on to and they had cut, nailed and bolted this framework onto the pillars to top the sections of wall.

Finally they had nailed on the mesh and treated all the wood with tar to preserve it.

We had won the Pan Commonwealth Youth Award for 2001 for our small-a-side sports area and by December 2002, had been handed a cheque for £3000 by the local Head of the Commonwealth Youth Programme in the presence of the British High Commissioner, Canadian High Commissioner and the Permanent Secretary of the Ministry of Culture Youth and Sport. This money, plus two thousand pounds from an anonymous donor in England whom we had never met but who had read our newsletter, helped us to finish off the sports area by completing the mesh, bringing in sixty lorry loads of sand to fill up the surface area within the walls and getting wrought iron gates made at the end nearest the house.

I had been presented with an award from the "Georgetown Rotaract Club" for the work we had done in education at Sapodilla Learning Centre and a cheque which was also put towards the sports area.

The street to our door from the main road had finally been surfaced with red brick and topped with bitumen, so vehicles could drive down to us from the main road without getting stuck in mud. More importantly, the athletes could now use the street as a running track and a place to set up the hurdles. With any kind of progress there is usually a drawback and in this case, vehicles started driving down our street far too fast. Edwin had to install speed bumps to deter this before a child got killed on the way to us. I found myself going out one Sunday and painting the words SLOW DOWN in large white letters on either side of the bumps.

After a long wrangle with the Guyana Telephone and Telecommunications Company and with President Jagdeo, Edwin had ensured that our village had been included in the expansion of land line connections that had originally only been planned to extend to Bushlot, where large numbers of PPP voters resided. Edwin as NDC Chairman had refused to sign the document for the work to start in Bushlot until Hopetown had also been included in the plans. We had been the last applicant in the village to be connected to a land line on 30th December 2001.

There were now internet café's in small village shops as well as in the capital, where anyone could pay for use of the computer by the hour and 'surf the net'. There was one in Rosignol, so Rob and subsequent volunteers had been able to send home and receive back email messages. Rob's father even ordered music CDs for him from a company called Amazon and they were posted direct to our address. Anna Iles on her last visit had told us how the Amerindian settlements in the Rupununi now had their own internet connection by satellite so they could sell their hammocks worldwide direct to customers. Things seemed to be changing fast but our own lack of finance had excluded us from keeping up with this technology as yet.

Although our water supply had been fairly reliable since we had been connected to the mains, there were times when we went for days on end without any supply at all from the mains, so we would have to revert back to what we had stored in our rain tanks. The mains water supply depended on electric pumps which failed whenever there was a power cut. Now all our once beautiful ceramic sinks, toilets and acrylic baths were coated with unsightly deposits of rust that could not be removed. It appeared that the new deeper wells drew water from underlying rocks that were rich in iron and this iron oxidised on contact with air at the surface. I discovered this too late to prevent all our laundry from getting rust stains on it while soaking. It was particularly annoying when the power cut off while the washing machine was in mid-cycle. It meant that from now on any clothing, towels or bedding would soon be ruined in appearance. To add insult to injury, we had just received notification from the new water company, GUYWA, that they would now be charging us $119,000 a year because we were a farm and a school. Prior to this we had been paying the normal fee for a private residence which was $5,000 a year. It was impossible. I had spent two days negotiating with the new company boss over the telephone to get this decision reversed. I had explained that we were a charity but had been told that private schools must pay more than state schools. I had explained that none of our students paid fees and no income was earned by the school so we could not pay teachers. We received no funds from the government as we did what we did out of charity in the true sense of the word. I explained that students of the school did not use any of the water that was on tap as they had a pit latrine in the back yard and used rainwater collected in barrels for washing their hands and for their chickens to drink. They did not use piped water to irrigate crops on the farm, but dipped water from the trenches with their watering cans. We only used small amounts of piped water in our domestic residence and so we should be billed as before, as a domestic residence. If not, we would be forced to shut down the school and stop the good work we were doing because by continuing to open our house to students as an act of goodwill, we were being unfairly punished by the water company. I had been advised to write a letter setting out all these details which I had done and was now awaiting a decision.

Easter was coming up. We had just ended term with a kite making and flying competition for the new batch of full-time students. I now taught all their examination subjects single handed, including maths and science. The previous term's nerve-racking experience had pushed me into the decision never to have any more volunteers to help me. It had been about two weeks since we had seen off our last volunteer at the airport and breathed a huge sigh of relief. It had been a three month nightmare for both of us. "Never again," we had both vowed on our way back to Berbice.

Neither of us had seen it coming when towards the end of 2002, Malcolm Broad had called us from England on the landline which had been installed in the house since the last day of December, 2001. One of his colleagues at his community college in Cornwall had a daughter who had been a top student in science A-levels and had taken a gap-year from studying for her degree in medicine. She had seen our newsletter and school hand book which Malcolm had received for distribution to the students from his college who had been coming to us for a two week work experience placement in June every year since 2000. He was calling to ask if we would have her to act as volunteer for three months after Christmas, as we were already into the first term of the academic year. I had said, regrettably, "no", as it would be too much of a disruption and I had already taken the decision to teach the science myself from now on. The failure of our American Peace Corps volunteer to meet the standards required of teaching science exams in the British education system or to embrace our school philosophy had already put us off. Malcolm was very persuasive. He was not going to give up easily. Fay was of the highest academic and personal calibre. She could help me do the science experiments that I was not yet confident with. Her mother was the college science technician. Would I at least let her call me to discuss why she wanted to come? Then I could tell her myself if I still did not want her. I had allowed him to talk me into agreeing.

When Fay had telephoned, she had wanted a friend to accompany her. I had flatly refused this outright, explaining that I really was far too busy to have unwanted extra visitors in the house during term time as school leavers tended to distract each other. They were too young and inexperienced and needed too much of my time to help them cope with being away from home in a strange

417

environment. I only wanted someone who was already trained to teach so I would not have to teach them how to do so but could just expect them to get on with it and do so to a high standard because we had a reputation for good results. I did not want someone who was too afraid to come on their own and stand on their own two feet. I did everything I could to put her off, but she insisted that she would be fine on her own and she had been helping her mum at the college doing all the experiments for the GCSE science courses, so already knew what she would have to do. I caved in under the pressure, saying that I would have her if she could not only act as a science technician for me, but she could also be a school secretary to type up on one of our word-processors the minutes from weekly student meetings and any resource material that I needed to prepare for the students. At that time, the sixth form student who had been doing the job for me while studying for her CXC in French had just got herself pregnant and been pulled out of the school by her father, so I had no one else yet capable of doing that work. Fay had agreed and sent off her application letter in writing to me along with her C.V. I had replied with a clear statement of what I expected her duties to be and how much she would have to pay for her full board and lodgings with us for the three months. I had left it to Malcolm to organise her travel, medical and insurance arrangements, which he did with the help of the sponsorship of Torquay Lions Club.

It had come as a complete shock when Fay announced to me in the bank on the day of her arrival that by the way, she was epileptic. I had been taken aback to think that neither she nor Malcolm had mentioned this fact until she was already with us. I had put aside my private indignation.

"Oh, don't worry," I had said, "We recently had Lord Byron's daughter, here for a three month stint and she is epileptic, but it was absolutely no problem," I had reassured her. "She was a lovely girl and was a great help to us. She had come with Pippa, her school- friend, in case she had needed help in the night, but she never did, and when Pippa had to leave suddenly because her father, former British High Commissioner, was rushed into hospital with a terminal brain tumour, Caroline stayed on with us alone to the end of term with no trouble at all. We are quite used to that sort of thing. Anyway, Edwin is a trained paramedic so he would know what to do if it was needed." All the same I could not help feeling annoyed that we had not been informed of her condition by Malcolm in the beginning, in the same way that David Johnson had told us about Caroline Byron, asking if we minded having her with such an infirmity.

Fay must have known that we were unaware she was epileptic or why would she bother to make the announcement to me in the bank?

That evening as we had sat at the dinner table talking after our evening meal, Fay's eyes had glazed over and she had slumped in her chair. Edwin sprang up and rushed round to her chair and I had helped him carry her over to the sofa where he lay her down in a safe position under the fan. He propped her head on a cushion and sat there watching to make sure she did not choke and waiting for her to come round so he could give her reassurance. He spent a couple of hours with her until he was sure she was fully recovered and then took her to sit out on the veranda in the fresh air and chatted away the rest of the evening till he thought it was safe to let her go to bed. It must have been the jet-lag, we thought. She was most apologetic but we said it was not her fault and not to worry about it. I had been able to get on with the work I had to do because Edwin was taking care of the situation. I thought nothing more about it till the same thing happened at exactly the same time of the evening a couple of days later. Edwin's response was the same and all was well again. The next day, Fay had not slumped in the chair but had collapsed head long onto the hard wooden floor of the kitchen while helping me do the dishes. It had been a miracle that she had not crashed her head on a hard piece of furniture on her way down. Luckily Edwin was there to deal with her again.

Then school had opened, and on her first day while I was teaching I had asked her to prepare the equipment in the lab that we would need for the experiment we had planned to do the following day. I had heard smashing glass from next door in the course of the lesson and had rushed round to see what had happened. She had had a mild seizure while doing the job I had set for her and dropped the conical flask. I comforted her as best I could and told her to leave the mess and go upstairs to rest till she felt better. I would clear up the glass later. I felt it would be unsafe to leave her alone in the lab after all, so from now on assigned her to typing on the computer alone and any work with equipment would have to be done when I could be there with her, after school. Even so, I was nervous about letting her be alone in the computer room since the floor was ceramic tiled and there was hardly any space between the crude home-made hardwood stools. I was afraid she would sustain a serious injury to the head if she fell down in there. "I want to give her a sense of independence by letting her do this work but I can't help feeling permanently on edge," I said to Edwin.

"It's the same for me," he said. "She collapsed in the sports field when we were doing simple exercises so I had to let her go and sit in the shade of the trees by the fence," he said. "I'm petrified that something will happen to her and we have absolutely no medical back-up here. I'm not happy with the way things are here. It's affecting our private life." By the end of Fay's second week, she had been having a full on seizure every night after meals and I felt I would have to phone Malcolm about the matter. She needed to be sent home.

Malcolm was not happy that my call awoke him at five o'clock on a Monday morning but I had not been able to sleep for worrying about the situation so at one o'clock in the morning, calculating for the five hour time difference, I had decided to catch him before he left for work. He sounded concerned when I explained the problem. I asked him why he had not told me about Fay's problem and he said he had known about a medical problem she had had in the past but as far as he knew, she had got over it. He said he would ask her mother to telephone me later in the day after he had discussed what to do about it with her. Eventually Fay's mother called and told me she had discussed the problem with Fay's specialist, who had concluded that the heat must be affecting her medication and she would need to double the dose. "Could you let me speak to Fay to explain this to her?" she asked. I of course did so. Malcolm called shortly after and explained that he would be coming out to the Caribbean at half term with a party of colleagues and the president of the Newquay Lions. If there had been no improvement by then, he would take her back to England with him.

After this intervention, it seemed that Fay's extra dosage of medication had been effective as she had no further seizures for the next three weeks before Malcolm and his colleagues came out for half term. Our nervous dyspepsia had not left us however, as every night we were expecting her to keel over and were unable to relax until she was safely in bed. The Lions had come out to see how she was benefitting from the placement, since they had funded her trip. She basked in all the attention and the excitement of the day of activities we put on especially for them. They left and the very same evening that they had all flown out of the country, Fay had another seizure. It was too late to send her back now. It was unbelievable that from then on, she had three to four seizures per week at almost exactly the same time in the evening, until she departed at the end of her three months. It was almost as if she had fought against the seizures and controlled them long enough to prevent her stay from being curtailed but as soon as the threat of being taken home early had gone away, she could relax and give up trying.

That was all behind us now. We could enjoy Easter and look forward to the summer. I had just booked up a fortnight in St Lucia for us at the end of July from the latest BWIA package holiday brochure. We had been away to the islands every year since the millennium once Edwin's loan to his sister for the jeep had been paid off and his pension had increased a little. We looked back through the photo albums at the snaps we had taken in Antigua with Kirstin and Harry and the children in their condo at Dickenson Bay in August 2000.

"That was the first proper holiday we ever had together," I reminisced.

"Well we'll take a break every year now we can afford to do it," Edwin promised.

"Grenada was nice in 2001, wasn't it?" I said. "Look at you there, posing on the rocks like some movie star." He leaned over my shoulder to see the pictures, nestling the side of his head tenderly against my ear.

"You're not so bad yourself," he teased.

"I'm glad you told me to book up early this year. I never want to end up like we did last year in Tobago, having to take what seemed like the worst hotel on the island because we left it to the last minute to book and all the decent tourist hotels were already full. I never want to go there again. Why do they play those music systems so loud that the whole street vibrates, let alone the rooms in the hotel above it?"

"Yes, I thought it was just a Guyanese problem, but it seems that the American boom box disease has infected people everywhere in the Caribbean."

"Whoever invented those things should be shot," I said. "Those ignorant young men who get their Brooklyn relatives to send them powerful sound systems so they can put on discos, have no consideration for the poor old folk in the village like Taa and Auntie Agnes, who live right next door and have no-where to escape to. All they think of is themselves and an easy way to make a living. Those things are designed for use inside great sound-proofed halls in closed concrete buildings, not for open air concerts in tiny villages where people live in flimsy wooden huts with open windows because it's too hot to have them closed. The noise goes right through them and out the other side."

"It's what they call progress," said Edwin in a sarcastic tone of voice.

"It's a matter of debate as to how much change is for the better and how much for the worse," I said "but when you think about it, quite a lot has changed here in the last few years, hasn't it? I can hardly believe we have a German company coming to take over the MMA compound with all that massive engineering equipment they've installed and that they're going to build modern new bridges over the Mahaicony and Mahaica rivers."

"Yes. Peter, their English site manager came round to see me this afternoon and I've set up a meeting with Major General Joe Singh to arrange a check of the area for four phone lines for Germans coming to live in the compound. They want to have satellite television and internet connection with the rest of the world, so they have to set up a special exchange from our village office in Bushlot."

"Satellite television won't be much use to them with all the power cuts we get," I said.

"Oh they've taken care of that, they've got their own massive generator to power the whole compound."

"I can't blame them for wanting to have something better than the local TV stations here, with a daily diet of death announcements and televised church services, the news is the only thing worth watching. It's a sobering thought that the live Iraq war coverage by CNN is being broadcast nightly on the local network as if it was some sort of American war movie and so we're actually seeing it as entertainment. It's perverse," I said. "Changing the subject somewhat, I wonder if Malcolm Broad will phone tonight as it's Friday and it's getting dangerously close to the date that the England boy cricketers are due to come out for their annual tour."

"Yes, I've been expecting him to call since the beginning of the week. He's leaving it a bit late this year. Luckily I've got everything in place as normal."

"Well he's a very busy man now he's been promoted to deputy head of the college so I expect his life is a lot more manic even than ours is and he knows he can rely on you to get everything right this end," I said. "He has the permanent secretary's direct number so he'll be in direct contact with him about the airport pickup this end." As I was speaking, the phone began to ring in the kitchen. "Oh, maybe that's him now," I said as I went to pick up the receiver.

"Hello, Sapodilla Learning Centre," I said, expecting to hear a local accent or that of Malcolm Broad. Instead, I heard my brother.

"Hello Jane, It's me, Guy. I'm afraid I've got some bad news. Mum and dad have both died today."

I was, for a brief moment, stunned.

"Both?" I asked in disbelief.

"Yes"

"How come?" I sat down at the kitchen table, shocked. "I was half expecting a call about dad one of these days, but mum too?"

I listened to his explanation but while he was talking, my brain was operating on two simultaneous channels. Memories of my last telephone conversation with her came flooding back. She had not been talking much sense and it seemed as if she did not know she was talking to me, her daughter. Instead she kept telling me what a lovely girl Emma, my niece in Australia, was. This had hurt me badly. Not because she should not love her granddaughter as much as she loved me, but because she seemed to have replaced me, her daughter, with images of Emma. Maybe she now thought Emma was her daughter and I had ceased to exist for her. I had been troubled by these ramblings ever since she had come out of hospital from a knee operation last September. It had been a sudden change from the loving mum I had always known, with whom I had been chatting on the phone before she went in for the operation. I had felt helpless. I had lost my mum and yet she was still there talking to me. I had cried and got upset with Edwin over it. It was all very well him saying that I should go and visit her. How the hell could I when I was running a school with no staff except me and I had no money now? Over the years I had used all my personal savings up on refurbishing the classroom and buying a few things for myself and the house. How could I pay for the flight? What good would it do now anyway? It was too late now. She did not know who I was. I had done all my crying in my sleep since then and now there were no tears to shed because I felt numb. Now there was a funeral to go to and it was the Easter vacation. We would have to make arrangements to fly to England in the next few days.

Chapter 20

Don't Mention Ze War!

I didn't know how to deal with the prospect of travelling back to England for a funeral. It had not been expected of me when mum had called me to tell me my sister had died from multiple sclerosis in November 2000. It had been lucky that we had obtained mobile phones in Guyana at the millennium or I would not have known about it until weeks or even months after her funeral anyway because that's how long a letter posted so close to Christmas would have taken to get to me. My family understood. They knew that I was running a school in which I was the only teacher and that I did not even have a volunteer helping me that year.

"We'll all be there on your behalf," mum had said to me. Penny had been in a slow and sad decline since I had seen her in the nursing home the previous year, so her death had not come as a real shock. My students, however, had all been shocked when I told them that I would not be attending my sister's funeral because it was happening in the middle of term. Their exams were all coming up that summer and they all needed me there for their education to continue. It had been inconceivable for them that I did not just up and go to the funeral regardless. My professionalism as a teacher had prevented me from doing so. I saw it as my duty to keep running their educational ship. They would always have put their personal and tribal interests first and so would any local teacher.

This time, however, I would have to go. How could anyone not go to their parents' funeral, however strong their sense of professional duty? At least it was vacation time, so term would not be disrupted. I would call up the airline office, a luxury we now could enjoy since we had a landline in the house, and book the first available return flights to England for us. I would use my credit card to pay for the flights and the last bit of money I had left in my personal offshore account. Then it was a matter of sending out messages to all the children letting them know that we would have an extended Easter vacation and term would resume on May 12th, two weeks later than expected, because we had to return to England for the funeral of both my parents. I would add an extra two weeks to make up the time at the end of the next term. This was possible because the group of students I then had at the school were all new to the exam courses and had no public exams until 2005. We also had to call on our only sixth former,

Jelani, and a younger student, Tegana, who was our boxing star, to come in at short notice with their parents' permission and look after the premises for us while we were away. They were happy to give up their vacation in order to earn themselves some money. We would pay them when we got back. Jelani had already had experience doing the same thing while we were on holiday in Tobago the previous summer. He wanted to do the Officer Cadet training for the army to follow Robin's example. Edwin rushed around during the remaining three days before our flight, setting up arrangements for the English schoolboys' cricket tour which we would now miss and the German company's dealings with the village office.

I was inundated with sympathy cards from all over the community in the next few days. It was very touching and kind of the children and their parents. If there is one thing Guyanese people understand it is a death and a funeral. Everyone follows the daily death announcements on radio and television without fail. It was still the main method of contacting family members scattered in remote villages on the coast or interior without any telephone service. It would have been a disgrace to any Guyanese family if all its disparate members did not attend a family wake and funeral, so young and old alike listened eagerly every night to make sure that none of their many aunts, uncles, cousins, or other kin, however distant, had not passed away since the previous day. If there were any funerals in the community, even those who were not related would all go and pay their respects.

The journey to England and our time there was strained in some ways. We depended on the children to ferry us around because we could not afford to hire a car or take public transport. Kirstin met us at the airport and dropped us off at Rafer's house in Basingstoke where he was entertaining his wife's family for the Easter celebrations. I called Guy from Rafer's phone to let him know when Rafer would be bringing us down to my parents' house. We would have to wait a day or two until Rafer had time off work to do that. It was April. We were both frozen to death even though Rafer's heating was on. Rafer was brilliant about it all, but when we were alone together with him that first night, his words struck an unforgettable and chilling chord in my heart.

"I don't like you being there, dad," he said. "We've all been talking about this since we got the news about Jane's parents and it's made all of us here in the family think a bit. What will happen if something happens to you, dad, when you're out there? I think you should move back to England near to us all and I won't feel happy until you do. I know Carmen and Kirstin feel the same way. Quite frankly, I don't want to be the one who has to come to Guyana to pick Jane down off a tree if something happens to you."

It startled me to hear him say this. His words seared an image in my brain that kept returning to me over the days and weeks that followed. The tune of Billie Holiday's song, a favourite of mine, haunted me. A white woman's body dangling from our tamarind tree would be a "strange fruit" indeed. Rafer had been insensitive towards my feelings, given my bereavement at the time. I felt his consideration for me was less important to him than the potential for inconvenience that his dad's future death would cause him. However, I also realised that the sudden death of my parents had suddenly brought him up short about how he would feel if the same thing happened to him. I understood this feeling. We all tend to think our parents are immortal until they are taken from us. They are usually such a big part of our lives and make-up that we take them for granted. Living apart from them in a distant country even if you have telephone contact, makes you imagine that they are still the same as they were when you last saw them, decades ago. You don't see how the ageing process eats into their actions and minds even if you get photographs of them from time to time. I had not even had the benefit of photographic updates because my mother did not have a camera and my brother was too preoccupied with his own domestic problems and caring for our geriatric parents and aunt.

"It's not as simple as that, Rafe," said Edwin. "Our home and lives are all tied up in the country. Everything we both worked for all our lives is there and we would never be able to get anything for it because no one would buy the place if we tried to sell it. We would have to come back to England penniless leaving all our property in Guyana like Brother Sonny did. I'm not prepared to do that. In any case, I'm looking after my mother there who's now in her eighties."

"It's true Rafer,"I added, "We would never be able to survive on your dad's pension if we moved back to England now. We would never be able to afford to buy a house here with the way property has gone through the roof since the eighties and I would have to find a job."

"Yes," he said, staring at me in disbelief, as if I were living the life of a lady of leisure who was upset at the thought of no longer being on a permanent holiday. Blimey, I was working harder there than I had ever had to work anywhere else and getting no pay! I was hardly a skiver or a passenger.

"I don't mean that I don't want to work," I said, "I just can't face the thought of coming back into this freezing cold and to a life of misery teaching in an English comprehensive when the way they were going in the late eighties was the reason I left to go and work in Dubai." The real difficulties of needing to retrain for curriculum changes at the age of forty nine with no money to do so had not yet even crossed my mind.

"Well I've said my bit," he said waspishly, bringing the discussion to an abrupt end and Edwin changed the subject onto sport and the grandchildren, as he was so adept at doing.

Once delivered back in my parental home, Edwin and I found ourselves in yet another completely different world for a few days. The formerly warm and homely Victorian red-brick farmworkers' cottage of my tidy and house-proud parents had by now declined into a dreadful state. The front room was filled with dad's empty invalid bed and redundant medical equipment. Clutter filled every chair, table and cupboard. The kitchen was littered with unwashed utensils, medicine and pill bottles and bric-a-brac stuffed with receipts, bills and various envelopes and bits of paper. It had become as gaunt and drab as a badly run old people's home, except on a smaller scale. I could only imagine the degradation for them both to find themselves slowly slipping into this "lace curtain poverty" with my brother Guy trying his best to move between them and the farmhouse at the other end of the village where he lived and cared for our aged aunt. A bevy of state carers had been visiting all of them several times a day and Guy had been doing their meals in shifts in between.

"I had no idea it had got as bad as this," I told Guy as we sat up till midnight that first night, talking about his struggle to cope with caring for all three of them as mum's arthritis gradually crippled her and prevented her from caring for dad as she had always done.

"She had the second knee operation to try to restore her mobility but the full anaesthetic they used for it caused her rapid slide into dementia," he explained. "I have to drive over to Milton Keynes to pick up the children and bring them over here at weekends when it's my turn to have them and then drive them back again on Sunday nights so they can go to school the next day." There were so many factors that had conspired against him in his personal life and career that it was not surprising that he looked haggard and aged and seemed to lead a depressing existence. I wanted to help him bounce back. He still had auntie to look after but at least that was easier than having all three of them bedridden. It was almost as if mum, knowing that dad had just been taken into hospital for the last time, had wished herself dead to release Guy from some of his burden. He left us at midnight to go back to his bed at Auntie's farm. We would be sleeping in the now empty house. I did what I could to clean up the kitchen and living room and the bedroom we would be sleeping in. At least the central heating was on and I could control it, so we were warm enough at last.

Dad's cremation was the next day and mum's church funeral two days later. I volunteered to speak at the church service because Guy did not want to do it. I was so used to getting up and addressing audiences that I never got nervous or needed to prepare speeches. I started off bravely without even thinking it would affect me, but as I searched for what needed to be said, I found myself overwhelmed by the emotion of it all. I felt the tears rolling down my cheeks and heard myself not making sense for a while before I could regain control. It was over. We could move on. The one happy thing about a funeral is that it reunites family members who may not have seen each other for decades. It was great for me to spend a few hours catching up with my late sister's children, Emma and Jason. I now had to get to know Guy's two adolescents, whom I hardly knew. It was difficult getting any conversation going with all the text messaging they seemed to be engrossed in. I put it down to the effects of their parents' broken marriage. I was totally unaware that this disease was universal among the teenage generation of the new age.

Guy was understandably anxious that he needed to have his future secured. Mum and dad were now both dead and there was a will and a property to deal with. Knowing that I was one of the three beneficiaries (along with our dead sister's two children) and was just about to return to my home on the other side of the world, he suggested that we all go to the solicitor and that I give power of attorney to Guy to process the will on my behalf. I did this but was cautious about giving in to pressure from him to sign away all claims I had to the house. It was all a bit too soon to make such decisions. The will would take a couple of years to process, he said. We had already booked an inexpensive local flight from Guyana to St Lucia for our summer holiday this year, but we would come back and visit for a longer time next summer when Edwin had been able to save up the fares for us from his pension. Guy, for his part, promised to get the house into a better state of repair and decoration by that time as he felt he would like to have somewhere pleasant to retreat to at weekends when he had his children to visit. If we came over next summer, we would also be able to stay there.

One thing I wanted Guy to understand was that we were not living in an expat paradise of wealth, sunshine and glamour in Guyana. I was sure he and mum had assumed we were. I had not sent home tales of misery and despair because I hadn't wanted to worry mum. He had already made the assumption that I would never come back to England.

"I'm under no illusion," I said, when I was alone with him at Auntie Lorna's on our last day in the village, "That if Edwin dies and I'm living alone there that no matter what good I've done to help the people there, they could turn against me if I don't have him there to protect me. His own family would want to turn me out of his house if they could, regardless of the fact that the laws of inheritance there safeguard the rights of a wife to inherit her husbands' property. They don't see me as one of them and they never will. If there's political turmoil like in Zimbabwe, I might one day be driven out of the country to save my life and if that happens, I want to have a safety net. I might have to escape back to England."

Kirstin came to collect us two days after the funeral. While we were staying with her and Harry in Wokingham awaiting our return flight, Dave and Hilary Hayes came to visit us and bring us a laptop donated to Sapodilla by a Poole Runner who had just upgraded hers. It had internet capability, so Harry's colleague, a computer expert, set it up and showed us how to use the internet. At least we would now be able to meet one of Rafer's gripes: namely that he could not keep in touch with us easily because we had no email. As soon as we got back to Guyana I would find out how to get us a connection. The other gripe: moving back to England would not be so easy to address. We went into a financial adviser in a branch of my bank in Wokingham to seek investment advice on my expected inheritance, estimated to be likely to be fifty thousand pounds. We also went to seek mortgage advice at Edwin's bank. It was conclusive that no way would we be able to get a mortgage sufficient to buy a house on Edwin's pension, even with a fifty thousand pound deposit. What we had said to Rafer was true. In fact we would not even be able to buy a house to use as a holiday home ourselves and rent out for the rest of the year. I was not distressed by this problem, as the idea of living in England again still did not appeal to me. I had learned to cope with life in Guyana by now and at least it was beginning to be a bit more comfortable than it had been at first. The thought of throwing ourselves into another melting pot of poverty and struggle in England seemed crazy.

We gained five hours in time zones on our return flight and so arrived back in Guyana late at night on the Saturday before school was due to reopen. That gave me Sunday to sort out the laundry and clean the house before the students consumed all my time. The rainy season was full on by the end of the week and such torrential rain fell on Thursday night that we woke up on Friday to find the water tank at the back leaking and the gutters overflowing violently onto the generator control unit cables entering the kitchen. Carlton and his son responded to our emergency phone call but he refused to address the leak because he said the whole of the roof of the house was alive with current so we had to fetch Vernon from the village to sort it out before we could switch on the mains to restore power. We certainly knew we were back on the wild frontier.

The following Sunday Malcolm Broad called to give me the dates of the two students from Treviglas who were coming for work experience at the end of June. "I'm so sorry to hear about your parents," he said "The Permanent Secretary told me about it when we arrived with the cricketers."

"Oh thanks," I said. "I'm sorry we weren't there for you all as usual and we couldn't let you know because it was all a bit sudden. Did it go all right?"

"Yes, thanks."

"We had been expecting to hear from you the week before we left to know if Fay got back safely, but since you didn't call, I presume she got back OK." I added. "We were worried because as soon as you left with the Lyons, she started having seizures again almost every night until her return flight date and it was a terrible strain on us. Since it was then too late to send her back, we just had to deal with the problem as best we could till the end of her three months."

"Well actually, her mother thinks she might have caught malaria while she was in Guyana."

"Malaria," I said. "That's nonsense. She didn't go anywhere where she could have caught malaria. She stayed in the house here with us all the time she was in the country and the mosquitoes that carry malaria don't live in the environment along the coast here. We've both lived here for years without taking any malaria tablets. The only reason we recommend our visitors to take them is because they usually want to go off on journeys into the deep interior jungle where they'll be sleeping in thatch and pole camps in malaria areas, but Fay didn't do any of that. Dengue fever is possible, but unlikely, since we provided her with a mosquito net. There certainly is something seriously wrong with her, though, but she had it before she came to us, not as a result of her being here."

"Her mother told me she was upset that you didn't telephone her when you were in England so she could offer her sympathy to you."

"I'm afraid that I had too many upsetting things on my mind in the last three weeks," I said, wondering if any of them had any consideration for my feelings. "In any case I didn't carry her phone number with me." We concluded our conversation with the details of the two boys we were to expect at the end of June and beginning of July. I put the phone down not knowing what we would find for them to do in their work experience because they would be coming to us in exam week and staying for a week after our school term ended. However, Edwin decided to have an end-of-year school summer activities camp on our premises and that the boys could help him with that. I was relieved to have that pressure lifted from my shoulders. I could get on and mark all the exam papers and write the reports while the children were occupied in the recreational camp. I could give back their papers and announce the results at the end of each day. When the camp finished at the end of the week, I would have their reports ready to hand out.

It was always a small financial help having Treviglas work experience students to stay, since they paid for their board and lodgings for the two weeks and that allowed for a little bit of profit after the cost of their food, transport and electricity usage had been deducted. The drive for Edwin to save money on costs that the school was burdening us with was greater than ever now that the local bank we had mortgaged the house with had changed hands and kept sending us demands for changes in our interest rate. Edwin had gone into town on more than one occasion and queried it with the bank clerks and demanded to see the chief executive, who never seemed to be available. What was puzzling me was that our fifteen year repayment mortgage, which we had taken out in 1992, never seemed to get any smaller. We still owed three million Guyana Dollars and it was now 2003. We had known that the massive monthly repayments we made at the very beginning consisted almost entirely of interest. That was the way in our experience mortgages worked. After twelve years, however, you would expect the repayment mortgage to start making an impact on the amount of capital you had initially borrowed. Our annual statements showed the outstanding capital as the same every year, in spite of us never missing any of the massive monthly instalments in cash which Edwin carried from the main Scotiabank branch where he withdrew his pension direct from England every month throughout the whole of that time. Indeed, whenever we went out of the country on holiday, before we left the country, he pre-paid all the mortgage payments scheduled in advance of them being due so that no one could claim repossession of our house while we were away. He never seemed to be able to get an adequate explanation from the counter clerks as to why the capital sum remained the same. He was particularly irritated when he was charged extra interest for late payments when we came back from our Easter trip.

"We *didn't* make any late payment. I paid it all before it was due as the payment book dates show you, here, so why am I paying extra interest?" he had argued with the clerk. But she had insisted that he had only paid the payments, not the interest that was due for those months. It was one of those arguments that defy logic but you are powerless to do anything about.

"I want to get some money to pay off this bloody mortgage once and for all," he grumbled. "They're all bloody crooks and I don't trust any of them. I'm going to write to the army pension people to see if I can commute my pension for a lump sum to get rid of this never ending debt round my neck. It's bad enough that the cheque we got presented with for the Commonwealth Youth Project Award had to be handed back to the Permanent Secretary after all the show of the presentation. We still haven't had any of that three thousand quid for all that concrete work we did on the sports field. I keep calling in at the Commonwealth Youth Programme office every time I go to town. It's been months now and they haven't passed on any money to us. I got told that it's protocol that the cheque has to be cashed through the government. They're supposed to pay it into their account and then issue their own cheque to us. They seem to be just sitting on it so they can gain the interest, but I owe the supplier for all those materials. He keeps coming to me for the money but I can't give it to him because I haven't received it yet. It looks like I'm lying to him because the cheque was handed to me at the presentation and the photo is in all the local papers."

"Well I guess your mistake was doing all the work before you got the money for it," I said. "You try so hard to show that you're not like everyone else here and they look at you having finished the project and think 'He must be loaded if he can do all that work' so they keep the money because they don't think you need it." True as this may have been, the fact was that our charity institution was not sustainable and we still did not seem to own the home we were living in. Edwin would be sixty four at the end of the year. He searched for a way to earn some extra money to pay off the mortgage completely.

By the end of that term, we had struck up a friendship with one of the German engineers whose wife had just joined him in his chalet in the compound at Onverwagt. Edwin had been to visit the Dywidag Company boss about their telephone connection and he had introduced him to Heinz, their chief engineer. Heinz had been impressed by Edwin's fluency in conversational German and amazed to find in a Guyanese village distant from the capital, a locally born Afro-Guyanese man who had formerly lived for the best part of twenty years in Germany serving in the British Army of the Rhine. He could not believe that Edwin had an encyclopaedic knowledge of all things German, especially German football, German food and German classical music. Heinz was an enthusiast of classical music and Helga liked art, craft and cooking. She could not speak any English so my rusty German was dragged out of the depths of my memory as I listened to Edwin talking to them fluently. I could understand some of what they were saying and chip in now and again in German. Otherwise Heinz and Edwin acted as translators. Edwin invited them for dinner some weekends and they reciprocated. It was a pleasant change for us to have some social life and conversation with mature educated people who lived nearby so we could visit regularly. Heinz was learning to play a German hunting horn he had brought out with him. Edwin gave him some help with this, while also practising the bugle he had been given by his old army buddy in England at Easter. Edwin's aim was to use it to blow "The Last Post" at the Regional Remembrance Day service in November, since no one in the area had a bugle or could play it. He hoped to teach some of our students to be able to do it too, so he could hand over the job to them in the future.

Through visiting Heinz, Edwin got to see the Onverwagt compound regularly and meet with other members of their German and international staff. He heard how the overseas staff had been held up at gunpoint in their Georgetown office and robbed of large sums of cash. He also found out that they were losing a lot of valuable equipment to petty theft. Edwin felt embarrassed about the dishonesty of so many of his fellow countrymen and wanted to protect the

Germans from harm and predation. If all overseas visitors kept getting treated like we had been treated, they would go away with a bad impression of the country and no developer or decent person would want to come there. If Guyana were to develop, then it needed to welcome foreigners who were executing development projects, not fleece them. Edwin could see how the Germans were being exploited by officials in the Ministry of Labour and locals to whom the company had been referred to help them set up in the capital.

He soon began to see flaws in their security system and made sure to point them out to the Dywidag boss. He was disgusted to see that the security company in Georgetown was charging them two million Guyana dollars a month for providing security, yet only paying the locally recruited guards a paltry seven thousand dollars a month to wander round the compound. Workers might feel they were being exploited by the foreigners, but it was the local middlemen who were doing the exploiting. The majority of the money was going to a Georgetown entrepreneur who never even bothered to check if his staff of thirty two guards ever turned up. As a consequence Dywidag often had no guards at the Onverwagt compound and valuable plant kept disappearing. Edwin suggested that he could do a better job with only fifteen guards at a fraction of the cost of the Georgetown security company. For a start, Dywidag did not need an expensive office in Georgetown with its high rent and expensive reception staff sitting around with little to do but handle cash. It was just inviting armed attack. All of their business was being carried out in Berbice and along the coast. It would make more sense having the main office and accounts together in the Onverwagt compound with all the security in one place where it could be properly monitored by him. There was now a bank nearby at Rosignol with internet connections, where cash could be easily accessed for wages and other purposes. Edwin said he could do it all for six hundred thousand Guyana dollars a month. He did not want huge pay himself, but insisted that the fifteen guards he recruited would be paid thirty thousand dollars a month (more than three times what the Georgetown security firm had been paying them). He thus believed he could ensure their loyalty and could demand high standards from them. By October, he had succeeded in winning the security contract from Dywidag.

That Christmas, Edwin received two months' salary that he was able to use to pay extra mortgage payments to reduce our capital sum quicker, he thought. He bought a new, more powerful generator for the house, since the one we had originally brought from England had finally expired. He determined to use his salary for mortgage and expenses in Guyana from now on so he could leave his pension to accumulate in his bank account in England in order to pay for two flights there the following year. He also received a letter from the army pension service advising him not to commute his pension, so the Dywidag work had come at the right time, but it would only last for the three years they would be in Guyana.

We had spent a relaxing couple of weeks in a lovely resort, near Souffriere in St Lucia that summer. Life was feeling good for us both by the time we returned to prepare for the new academic year. I did not have many new part time students to enrol because I already had a full complement of examination students staying on to complete their education. They were the best academic students I had so far had and many of them had been with me since they had been six or seven. Now they were in their final exam year, I had high hopes for the best set of results we had yet had at the school. The top achievers were girls so that would also be a first for us. The new laptop I had been given by Gill Welmsley and her company VWR, from Poole, was a godsend. I could now prepare all my worksheets upstairs in the mosquito-free comfort of our study at nights. I could also update and prepare the school handbook that I gave out to new parents. A lot had changed since the first one I had produced back in 2000. During the summer holidays I had found a service provider in Georgetown and signed up with them, so we could now send and receive emails from our house or the classroom. I had spoken directly to the chief executive of the telephone company in Georgetown who had sent a directive to our local office in New Amsterdam to come out and fit an extension for us in the classroom. I could now answer parents' calls in the classroom as well as in the house. It made it easier if calls came to us from England at times when I was teaching and Edwin was out. In time, I would be able to use the internet in the classroom as well.

I soon learned that having the internet connection did not lead to better communications with any member of either Edwin's family or mine. I would send out emails and be waiting for replies from Guy or Edwin's children for weeks. Our previous lack of internet connection had apparently just been a convenient excuse for their failure to contact us by letter. We had made time to write even though we were working every available hour. We sat up into the early hours of the morning to find this time. I had kept my side of the bargain but it had made absolutely no difference, except to our cost of living. We now had an extra monthly expense to find funds for. It did help the school however, as my articles for Mitch Mason's newsletters could now be sent instantly to him on a Word document. He could just copy and paste it into his newsletter instead of retyping it from the printed version I had posted to him in the past. I now had a way of preventing typing errors or misinformation from going to print in my own articles at least. I was also able to get up to date information off the internet that could help us understand and deal with some of the problems we were encountering. A young boy with sickle cell anaemia had recently joined the school so finding out about his condition and its implications for what physical exercise he could do and what to watch for, helped us to be more sensitive to his needs. Luckily, the English company Mitch had persuaded to sponsor the wages for Sharon, the school secretary that we now no longer had, was equally happy for us to use the funds to pay for our internet subscription instead.

I was teaching every subject on the curriculum once again and now had all the science practical work and school based assessments to do myself with the added pressure of exams looming, but I had the confidence now. I really enjoyed being in the lab with the students. It was improving my own understanding of a subject I personally had never understood properly at school, because in the sixties, it had been taught so badly. The wonderful key stage primary science books I had been given by a teacher on a previous England cricket tour and the GCSE science books from Treviglas which Fay had brought out for us, together with those sent to us that year by Dr Weston and the Froebel science faculty, had really made clear the principles behind the subject. I had sent for some excellent Channel Four educational videos on all the key topics and had been using them in the junior science lessons for the past couple of years. For the first time in my life, I understood the states of matter and how they impacted on life in all its forms. Suddenly, everything from cooking in the kitchen to growing plants on the farm seemed to make more sense. No wonder Integrated Science had been made part of the compulsory common core curriculum when I had been teaching in Milton Keynes. As I taught the maths to a group of students who had the ability to understand equations and the trigonometry of the harder parts of the CXC syllabus, I also found new enjoyment in another subject I had always hated and lacked confidence in at school. I couldn't have attempted it, however, without all the answers in the teachers' copy of the CXC text book as well as clear working examples at the start of each new chapter to remind me of the principles of working each topic.

The Newquay Lions had sent us a donation of £520 to buy some electronic scales to measure weights of less than a gram in the science lab. The surplus was to be put towards fencing off the fish pond for the students to begin a fish-farm project. I had ordered the scales and Edwin had begun fencing the pond area at the back of the farm which he had recently had mechanically excavated by a local contractor. I was grateful to the Lions for their help. When they had visited us in February to see Fay, they had already given us $310 US to buy the new English Literature set texts for the coming exams.

It was around this time that the new British High Commissioner in the country, Stephen Hiscock, first met Edwin, who was liaising with the High Commission in connection with the Presidents' Youth Award and the England youth cricket team tour. That November, Dave Clark, the Director of the Americas for the International Duke of Edinburgh Award, visited us at Sapodilla to present Edwin with a special Award from U.N.I.C.E.F. The award was in recognition of the five years of voluntary service Edwin had so far contributed to the Duke of Edinburgh Award scheme. Dave was also concerned to find out why we had not gone to the event earlier in the year when Prince Edward had come from England and had recently seemed to distance ourselves from the rest of the country's Award scheme. We had done our own expedition, with tents, in the savannahs that September instead of joining in with all the other groups in the country in their nationally organised 'camp'.

Edwin explained to Dave that from the start he had tried to get the government scheme organised in the same way that the Duke of Edinburgh Award was done in England. The expedition was supposed to test the participants' ability to survive in the natural environment using survival skills that they had been taught by the leaders of the scheme. The government had resisted his suggestion that camping was supposed to be in tents, with the students doing their own cooking and carrying their own supply packs during the specified hike. They should, he argued, be finding their route by reading maps and using compasses. The government had a different mind-set about the whole thing. The reason for their interest in this national scheme hinged on the political influence which they could exercise over the youth of the country if they could offer a 'trip' as a reward to youngsters who towed their party line. Maybe they could even win over some of the opposition youth if they provided such rewards. Since the majority lived in abject poverty at home, then the idea of a holiday camp in a distant part of the country where all the transport, food and accommodation were paid for and provided by the government, would appeal to them more than battling with nature in a survival test. The PYARG expedition was a primitive 'Butlins' style holiday camp and many participants cheated on the walk by hitching a ride on the army truck that accompanied them along the designated trail. Edwin felt that the whole thing had become a mockery of what he had originally tried to set up. It was part of the International Duke of Edinburgh Award Scheme under false pretences. At first, Edwin had gone along with their argument that they must do it this way because local people would only want to do what they were accustomed to do in the past. He thought that once the scheme had been in operation for a couple of years, he would try and gradually reform it. These reform attempts had been resisted by the ministry and the PYARG secretariat it had set up to administer the scheme.

I had done all the documentation for our group at Sapodilla using exercise books that the children kept as daily diaries of their activities. I checked and marked them all weekly. No other group did this and our students told us that when they met participants from other units, the others had not even done any of the skills or service but just went on the expedition and got the same award as ours who had done everything by the book. When Edwin had questioned the lack of record keeping by other unit leaders and documentation of participants to check that they had actually done the skills and services they had claimed to do before they were given their awards, he was told that there were no funds for such documentation. The British High Commission had stepped in and provided the official pass-books of the scheme. Henceforth, we all had official passbooks to sign and stamp, for what it was worth. It did not make any difference to whether other units ever did the activities that they claimed to do, since signatures in passbooks with a couple of sentences written on the relevant pages could easily be cobbled together a day or two before they had to be handed in.

In National Advisory Council meetings, Edwin had pointed out that it was wrong to present any award to participants if they had not been fit enough to complete the walk but had been picked up by the truck. It brought the scheme into disrepute. It was a disincentive to those who had made the full effort, to see that they need not have done so because the same award also went out to people who hadn't walked the whole way. He also had argued again for the camp to be done properly in tents. He had been told that there were no funds to buy tents. Once again, the British High Commission had stepped in and offered to buy appropriate tents for the units to use. Since these tents had arrived, they had remained locked up in the store cupboard at the secretariat office in Georgetown and mass camps had continued just as before in the designated government buildings.

The only way to achieve change, as far as Edwin was concerned, was for Sapodilla to set an example by doing it the correct way as a separate group. At least that would get use of the tents that were gathering dust in a cupboard. The government field officers in charge of the scheme, who were paid a salary by the government for doing it, turned the tables on Edwin by saying that they wanted to bring the youth of Guyana together through this scheme, not to have one of the units going off and doing its own thing. The field officers did not like the idea of having to travel to various sites at different times to verify that the camps were being conducted properly. He had not been put off by this. Why should it be any different from checking up on the service or the skills of each unit, which were also done in different places and times? Clearly the field officers had not been doing that but did not want to admit it. In the end he had got his way and that September, we had taken our Bronze Award students into Samo's ranch in the savannahs on our own proper camp which had been approved by the National Advisory Council. We had walked through the cane-fields of the Blairmont Estate to get there. Each group had pitched their tents, which we had on loan from the Ministry. Each group carried their own supplies, lit a campfire and cooked their own food on it. Edwin stayed up all night keeping watch but I slung my hammock under Samo's hut until the mosquitoes attacking my face got unbearable, then I moved into the back of our jeep which Edwin had used to transport the tents. We had a programme of educational activities which tied in with our school curriculum. Samo demonstrated the cowboy's work roping and branding the steers and answered their questions on all aspects of caring for the cattle. This was relevant to both their agriculture and geography courses. I had also fitted in a geography fieldwork study on the beach on our way there. The Field Officer had visited us on our second day and we had all had a good time together in the true spirit of the Award. Surely that would be enough to tempt the National Council to start implementing the same change with the other participating units. It did not happen.

On the day Dave Clarke visited, a Sunday in November, Edwin had invited all the parents to an open-day he had organised. It was a display of extra-curricular sports activities for the children to participate in and for Dave and the parents to watch before the presentation of their Awards. Dave made a speech in which he praised everything he had seen about Sapodilla during this and his previous visit when Mitch Mason and Rob had been with us. He said it was a model school and that we set an example that all schools everywhere in the Caribbean ought to follow. He had a long discussion with Edwin after the parents and students had left. He understood Edwin's desire to dissociate himself from what was going on with the other units and the political interference in the scheme by the government. It was a problem also experienced by other Caribbean countries, although to a lesser extent. However, he urged us to continue with the Award and doing it the way we were doing it. It didn't solve the problem of injustice, though. Awards were still being given out to young Guyanese people that had done nothing to merit such distinction, yet our students had the same awards for doing so much more. It devalued their achievements and they had been quick to point that out to us.

That month I was busier than ever and Edwin was out and about more and more. He would go back to check his security guards at the Dywidag compound after dark sometimes and not come back till late. Some of the time he had been going out in the early hours of the morning to check that his guards were actually doing their duty as planned. The best thing was to make surprise checks to keep them on their toes, he said. That way, they would always turn up for fear that if they didn't and he came to check on them and found them absent, he would sack them. He had already done that with one such defaulter in the first week of his contract. Another, a female had been given a warning for lateness. The wages were too good for the rest of his guards to want to risk losing their employment. He was getting a good system in place and the Germans were pleased with their new effective security. At the same time, Edwin was working closely with the local police detectives to try and trace the thieves who had been removing expensive plant from the Dywidag compound. A massive generator had gone missing. He had to work out a better way to monitor the vehicles leaving the compound, otherwise his guards would be responsible for the losses and he couldn't be there all the time looking over their shoulders. One problem he noticed was that there were several entrances and exits at various points on the perimeter. He could only monitor security effectively if there were no other gates except the front one where the guard huts were. He got the German boss to agree to him sealing off all other entrances and allowing his guards to climb up on the trucks to search all vehicles leaving the compound, even those of the German workers themselves, so as to set an example. That way no equipment could be taken out of the compound without a record being made of what it was and who took it.

One of the German engineers (aptly named Rommel since he reminded me of someone who ought to have been in the Gestapo) lived in a chalet near the back of the compound. He was furious with Edwin for closing off the back entrance next to his house. He claimed it was inconvenient for his maid to come through the main entrance, as the back one was nearer her house. Edwin suspected that Rommel was more angry that his maid could no longer slip in and out of his house unnoticed at nights and was probably using the back entrance as a way for his suppliers to reach him. Another German manager had privately tipped Edwin off that Rommel was a cocaine user who kept his stash in yoghurt pots and chocolate bars in his fridge. Edwin ignored Rommel's protests and managed to keep the support of the management so he could improve the security of the compound. After all, he argued, if he was to keep the engineers and their wives safe, how could he do so if unknown people could enter and leave the compound unnoticed under cover of darkness?

One night, late in the month, Edwin unintentionally awoke me in the early hours of the morning. He was shivering and crying and was soaked in a pool of sweat. It was something that happened quite a lot since we had lived together. He never usually wanted to talk about it and I understood. I knew he had done some difficult work in his army years and that such traumas stay with a soldier for life. I couldn't possibly understand how he felt because I had never been through that sort of thing, but I knew he needed comforting and have never been the sort of person that keeps pressing to know what someone is thinking about or pestering them. If he wanted to tell me then he would do so when it suited him. However, this time, he decided to tell me what had been troubling him. He said that earlier in the day he had read in his weekly English newspaper about his Fijiian friend helping the British Army in Iraq. This must have triggered memories of his personal ordeal in Borneo during the communist insurgency period in the sixties. He started to talk about when he had been shot up on the ferry at Bau.

"I was laying there on the ferry in a pool of blood from my mates who had been shot up and killed. It had soaked into me as I lay there," he said, choking back the tears, "but I kept still as if I was dead because I could hear the communist soldiers coming up and rejoicing at killing the British soldiers. When they'd all gone, then the locals came in and it was only then that I knew I was safe, so I got up. They all screamed when I did. They thought one of the dead was rising up, but when they realised I was alive, they calmed down. They washed me and my clothes. I was all on my own. All the others had been wiped out. I had to speak with my commander on the radio and tell him what had happened and that I was the only survivor. He needed to get out the dead bodies. They couldn't get in by helicopter or any other means and I had to ask the locals to keep the bodies for them rather than bury them, so they put them in water and then wrapped them in leaves. When the officer finally came to get me out, he was cross with me because I hadn't washed the blood off the deck of the boat for the ferry to be decent to take away the bodies."

"Oh my God," I said, "Didn't he understand that you were probably still in shock?"

"Well I explained to him that I hadn't gone near the boat for the three days since the shooting happened because they were my mates and I didn't know why I hadn't been killed like they had. I couldn't bear to see the place where it had all just happened. He apologised to me later for being so insensitive. I went back afterwards to look for my stuff where I'd holed it up. I found it hadn't been touched because I'd mined all around it. I'd told the locals I'd mined all along the stretch of river I'd been guarding in order to keep people away from my 'safe' area."

"God, you must have felt terrible," I said.

"I did. All I wanted to do was to get revenge for them killing all my mates, so later, when I went to the border area at Tebidu, I mowed down a whole area of trees on the Indonesian border which were hiding communists. This was an effective deterrent and it kept them away. Then I went to Miri. The Sultan praised me because I'd lured communist insurgents into the area I'd holed myself up in and dug in, and so I successfully wiped out wave after wave of communists who had come into the vicinity looking for the ones who had gone before them. In this way, he said the oilfields were successfully defended."

"So that's how you got mentioned in dispatches," I said. I had always wondered. Edwin never went about telling people he had been mentioned in dispatches. It wasn't something he wanted to talk about or even remember.

"Yes," he said, "But you're the only person I've ever told about it. I don't want my children to know the stuff I've been through."

442

"Why ever not? I'm sure it would make them feel very proud of you."

"No one should feel proud of stuff like that. You just do it. My kids don't need to know any of that. And that's why I don't want to have anything to do with the military here in Guyana. They all strut around full of self-importance, with medals all over their uniforms; medals they got for attending courses. They're a joke! They expect me to go and tell them war stories to entertain them in their officer's mess. I don't want anything to do with any of them. They all make me sick. If they want to know what it's like on active service in a combat zone then they should go and do a bit of it themselves!"

I fully understood and respected his feelings so I never brought the subject up again. It helped me to make more sense of why he had no time for the local military chiefs. The only exception was Major General Singh, who had asked Edwin to advise the military on safe storage of explosives after a terrible accident had occurred at Camp Brumes. A massive explosion had occurred in a store of ammunition given to Guyana by the Chinese government and terrible injuries had been inflicted on some of the soldiers on duty in the Camp on that day. Edwin had made recommendations such as building reinforced underground concrete storerooms but never knew if any of them had been followed. He blamed it all on ignorance and false economies.

It was Christmas and I took stock of what we had been trying to do that year with final examinations coming up in the summer of 2004. It had been a real struggle trying to teach the food and nutrition practical to twelve students in our kitchen upstairs in the house. I had been rotating the groups through one practical per group of four every three weeks while Edwin took the rest of the students for extra sport. It worked but meant that we would not have time to cover enough practical skills before the final practical exams started in May. I had taken the decision in September to drop four of the students from the subject so I could give intensive practical sessions in the remaining terms to the eight students most likely to pass. It was not what I wanted to do, but it was the only thing I could do given our restrictions. We really needed a proper school kitchen where I could teach all the students at one time in a single session. That way I wouldn't need Edwin to occupy the other students twice a week, which was going to prove a problem for him if he now had to work with the Germans as well as with the Neighbourhood Council.

We discussed the possibility of erecting a purpose built kitchen on the plot of land we still had at the end of our sports field. If we could do that, perhaps it could be big enough to include a hall for our dramas that could also house a permanent indoor display of the community museum I had set up. It could double up for indoor sport when the rainy season set in. Edwin said he would look into how much it would cost. He had his doubts though, because he could see it would be a massive expense and the possibility of getting any funding help for it was remote given our past experience. His interest in the idea was slight, but I put out an appeal for donations for it in the newsletter I wrote and sent by email to Mitch for the Christmas edition.

In the first week of the New Year, the Food and Nutrition practical was still going on at six when Edwin got home from his day of meetings in the neighbourhood. The children were like snails at practical work and even worse when it came to cleaning away their stuff to vacate my kitchen so I could prepare our own meal. He came upstairs, took one look at the mayhem in the kitchen and stormed off down the other end of the house. I did my best to get them out quickly and saw them off down the steps and off the premises. I then had to get our own dinner on the go but was dreading the rest of the evening because I knew he would be in a foul mood at me. It was my fault. I should have got them out at the right time. Instead, I had let them finish their cooking properly so that they got a reasonable product out of the ingredients they had brought along. Didn't he understand? No he didn't. He didn't care either.

"I'm pissed off! I want out," he would say, in his loud, threatening voice. Why did I always feel so intimidated when he behaved this way that I spent the next few hours grovelling around to try and get him in a better mood so that I didn't feel all churned up inside. I always allowed him to make me feel that it was my fault for even suggesting that our kitchen could be a practical home economics facility for our school. I was only trying to help these children in whatever way I could, just like he did with the sport. Now my personal life was suffering because my doing so was making him angry. Yet a few hours later, he would have forgotten all about it and would be as nice as pie. I realised he had a short fuse and didn't really mean to be like it but he just couldn't change. It didn't make it any easier for me to take however, as I never could predict what would set him off. He could safely take it out on me when other people had frustrated his efforts all day.

An incident in the CXC practical examination in April that year spurred me on to get a cookery practical classroom separate from the house. In the presence of the examiner from New Amsterdam, one of the students, Sharonda, got so nervous when lighting my gas oven to preheat it for her cakes, that she forgot the safety procedure I had taught her. When she struck the match and opened the oven to light it, it exploded with an enormous bang, lifting the top of the cooker clean off and scaring the living daylights out of all of us. The whole kitchen was covered in particles of soot and smuts. She had turned on the gas bottle and filled the closed oven with gas before opening it to put in the lighted match. We were all badly shaken up. Thankfully, the examiner allowed us all some extra time to recover from the shock and for me to check that the cooker was safe and the kitchen cleaned so that the students could resume their practical exam. She said she would take it into account when assessing the marks. Miraculously the students all went on to produce excellent end products. As I went over the incident with Edwin that evening, we both marvelled that nothing worse had happened. At least no one was injured. Insurances did not exist in the country to adequately cover anyone in such an instance, so it was a timely reminder that we needed some other way to protect ourselves and our personal property from the charity work we were doing. The house could have burned down and no agency would feel sorry for us and help us. There wasn't even a fire service where we were. That was part and parcel of our life in the developing world.

The Germans were very much a feature of the local landscape now, and would be for the next three years. The knowledge of this gave everyone a lift in many ways. Heinz and Helga were our social friends and so was Holger, the young commercial manager whom Edwin and I particularly liked. He was in his thirties and impressively talented, speaking fluent Chinese as well as English and other languages. We liked young people and their ideas and vivacity. A new boss who had been sent out from Germany that year had decided to save the company money by bringing out German civil engineering students for practical experience before their finals. These youngsters were also frequent guests at our dinner table. They helped me to understand how to use the internet and my new digital camera. I could now illustrate documents with photographs as well as save and organise master-copies in digital storage folders. It made us feel that Guyana was on an upward trajectory and we had a positive future there. I was distracted from the elephant in the room that was growing bigger all the time, but signs of its presence were right under my nose and I didn't even notice.

Chapter 21

Aid or A.I.D.S?

The May-June rains were setting in and everywhere was already flooded. The garden was under water as usual and it was impossible to walk anywhere downstairs without getting wet, muddy feet. As usual, I kept a bucket of fresh rainwater by the bottom of the steps so we could rinse off our feet and flip-flops before going upstairs. I had an old towel hanging over the wrought iron caging at the side of the steps so I could dry my feet and change into a pair of dry flip-flops that I kept at the top of the steps. It had always been impossible to dry the washing for days in this sort of weather and it would soon start to smell sour on the line and need to be washed in soap powder a second time before it could be dried, otherwise newly laundered clothes would smell offensive as soon as they were put on. A year or so after I got our new washing machine, I had bought a tumble drier from Courts for use in such weather. It used a lot of electricity but it was a godsend for towels, tee-shirts and bedding in these prolonged rainy spells. I had put the spun-dried laundry into the tumble-drier, set it going and gone upstairs to check that the buckets and bowls I had put down in various parts of the lounge and our bedroom to catch the water dripping through the holes in the corrugated zinc were actually still doing their job. If a new leak had sprung, I usually had to move one of the containers to the new position or find another bowl. Edwin was always walking round the veranda checking that the gutter was coping with the volume of rain running into it. He would be rattling the downpipes to dislodge any blockages and checking that they were actually going into the barrels or tanks under them. Sometimes the sheer force of the rain dislodged them or the school children had removed them to get their water cans in at the top and then failed to put them back when they finished watering their plants. If these small details were overlooked, the entire ground floor of the building would soon be under two or three inches of water.

"We really will have to try and do something about this roof," I said to Edwin. "I noticed that there are some houses on the Georgetown seafront near the American Ambassador's residence which have got what looks like proper roof tiles on them. They look beautiful. Surely they must be better at keeping out the rain than overlapping zinc sheets full of nail-holes."

"I was talking to one of the German students the other day and he said the best material to use for a roof is concrete now," he replied.

"Concrete? But surely our wooden structure wouldn't support the sheer weight of that," I said.

"Well he seems to think it's the thing to use now. Anyway, I've invited him round this evening for dinner and to have a look at our roof to see what needs to be done. His name is Manuel."

"I hope his last job wasn't at Fawlty Towers," I joked.

Manuel was, however, a charming and bright young German engineering student who was a delight to entertain and who seemed very confident of his own ability. He showed us digital photos on his camera of a house he had built in Germany with his friend Philip the previous summer which certainly looked very impressive. After going up in the loft and taking dozens of photographs of our roof from all angles inside and out, he said he would contact his friend and give us a quote for the work. He was confident that he and Philip would come over and together put a new concrete roof on our house. A couple of days later he dropped off the estimate of seven thousand pounds for the job to do it in eighteen months' time when he had finished his stint at Dywidag and also his university course. It struck me at the time that this well-meaning offer by an enthusiastic youth dependant on the agreement of an older friend, living thousands of miles away, whom we had never met and who probably had a lot more sense than his protégée, would never materialise even if we could have conjured up seven thousand pounds out of the air so quickly. However, it set us both thinking of how we could ever achieve any plan to improve the state of the roof over our heads.

For now, Edwin's immediate goal was to earn the money to get us both back to England at the end of that month and mine was to complete all the revision classes and practical exams for the brightest batch of students I had yet processed through Sapodilla Learning Centre. I was still on a high. Only the week before, I had been invited to attend an evening reception at the National Culture Centre by the Guyana Theatre Arts Guild. I had been nominated for four local 'Oscars', for my musical drama "Berbician Thunder" which I had put on in 2001 and which had caused such controversy. I had done no more productions since then, mainly because I lacked the time since I now was teaching all the science and maths as well as the rest of the curriculum. I wanted to succeed at getting passes in both of these new subjects in the forthcoming public exams. I had so much to do that I had to work through the entire night of April 5th in order to complete all the school based assessment marking and sample packing by the deadline the following day. It might be possible in future to do another drama but only when I had developed a routine of successful experience with these two exams. In any case we had distanced ourselves a bit from the ministry over the PYARG awards and I had vowed never again to expose myself to the racism and vitriol of some Georgetown teachers. However, Edwin had persuaded me to go with him to this special occasion because the elderly ladies who instigated the awards wanted to see more of the kind of thing I had produced on the national stage. He said they wanted to encourage me and hoped I would do another play. They wanted to encourage other teachers to follow my example, so I agreed to go.

The ceremony, attended by the local glitterati and literary elite all eager to win one of the coveted awards, was nothing to do with the government. I thought I had been brought to town for another humiliation but had been shocked to be called up as the winner of "Best Children's Play." There had been other nominees, but apparently I was the only one who had written my own script on a local historical theme, whereas the other contenders hadn't written anything original. They had just produced a performance using commercially available scripts written by known authors of other countries. I had made a short speech trying to use the occasion to encourage other teachers to have a go. I was no expert, but I just wrote, directed and produced a play to provide my students with an experience they would enjoy and learn many things through. I wanted to help bring their local history alive and make it more meaningful for them. I did not know I had the ability to do it till I tried. Anyone else could do the same thing in their schools and I thought they should do so. I sat down with my wooden trophy, donated for the occasion by the University of Guyana and watched the remaining award presentations but soon found myself being called up a second time, this time as winner of "Best Play." It was quite a relief to me to hear my name in the lists of nominations for the other two awards of Best Director and Best Producer but not to be announced as winner in those categories as well. I could almost feel the heat of jealousy and resentment welling up in the ranks of those who had come expecting to win all the top accolades. Despite this, I had left the occasion with a warm glow inside which was still making me sparkle.

Since it was late when we finished our meal with Manuel, Edwin took him back to the Dywidag compound in our jeep. I thought nothing of it that he did not come home for several hours. I expected that he had to make his checks on the security guards at the compound and make sure they were doing their jobs properly. He always went out with the front gate keys and padlocked the house as if we were inside it, so I just went to bed when I had got too tired to do any more report writing. He would be able to let himself in at whatever time he got back. I went to sleep with the light on as security because I would have to leave our bedroom door unlocked. It was the kind of lock that did not open with a key from the outside if you had pushed up the sliding lock from the inside. He would have to wake me up when he came into the room. He came back in the early hours and once in, locked up, put out the light and got into bed beside me. I was half asleep but I did sense he was a bit agitated. If I needed to know why, he would eventually tell me, so I slipped back into unconsciousness.

Edwin had become edgy about our telephone since we had the new extensions installed on our landline. He had been told by one of the mature students from New Amsterdam who had done his Sports Leaders' Course recently that the PNC had activists working in the Guyana Telephone and Telegraph Company in Georgetown and that they had bugged our phone so they could get intelligence about Edwin's relationship with the government and what he was planning to do with the village council. This had probably been going on ever since we had a phone, but we had not really taken much notice. We had joked about the house being bugged ever since we had lived in it, because we seemed to discuss ideas for improvements in the country over dinner at nights and within a few days we were hearing announcements that the government was introducing this or that measure almost as if they had been listening to our conversation. Now, it was more disturbing. Anti-government ears were apparently listening in and we did not know what evil intent they had but it could well be connected with the fact that Edwin had by now successfully prosecuted his vice chairman for fraud and had her jailed for three years. The fact that she was the key activist for the local PNC party was a coincidence. Edwin did not do it for a political motive. He just hated dishonesty and corruption and wanted to root it out wherever he could. He was now trying to expose a fraud involving the regional chairman's wife who had been handing out school uniform vouchers under her house to her family and friends who were supporters of the ruling PPP party. The vouchers had been provided by an international aid agency for children of families too poor to buy uniform. The aim of this was to attempt to get those children to attend school. Clearly a whole section of the poorest in our area were not getting any of these vouchers because they were of the wrong race and voted for the wrong party in the election. Edwin had been drawn into the controversy and was trying to sort out a fair distribution of these vouchers.

Since December, he had also decided to help with a regional AIDS fair at Blairmont scheduled for 29 January in spite of his previous misgivings. He had yielded to pressure from some ladies from UNICEF in Georgetown who really wanted him to keep an eye on the spending on their project to prevent low level corruption creeping in. Since then it had been put off several times and was now scheduled for May.

"It's amazing," Edwin had said as he broke the news to me, "That after decades of denial that anyone in the country had AIDS, when we've had people of all ages dropping off suddenly like flies around us from a mystery 'sick', how we've suddenly become so honest about the number of AIDS cases that there are in the country! It's a remarkable coincidence that now the international community have decided to make millions of dollars available to the developing world in the fight against AIDS, almost everyone in Guyana is reckoned to have the disease according to the official government estimates now published in the papers."

"I know," I said, sniggering at his sarcastic tone, "It is predictable, really, when you think that the fashion for aid projects a couple of years ago was all about gender equity and skills training for women in traditional male occupations, and then it was all about the war on drugs, These politicians sitting in their ivory towers in Geneva and Brussels are well-meaning but they're completely out of touch with what's really going on in countries like this. Locals will just invent projects around the latest fashionable 'cause' the aid agencies are supporting, so they can suck the available aid in their own direction, but the way they decide to spend the money locally ensures it has absolutely no effect on the problem it's meant to address. I suppose you could argue that regardless of who gets the money, it helps anyway because it boosts the local economy by swelling the income streams of all those selected to administer the project. It's just sickening that they're all the usual corrupt government or opposition party supporters, not the really deserving powerless poor. I take issue with that, because it reinforces the idea that the only way to get help is to be corrupt like everyone else."

"What pisses me off is those Foster brothers at the Rose Hall Youth Club on the Corentyne,"

"You mean the ones that came here a few months back to look round our gym and sports field so they can get more funding for them-selves to try and copy what we're doing?"

"That's them. They keep trying to stop the AIDS fair at Blairmont from happening. They seem to want to control it themselves because they want us to come under the umbrella of their Rose Hall outfit so they can claim they serve the entire population along the coast of Berbice. They see us as small fry since we only cater for a hundred or so children. They were bragging to me that they serve thousands in the local community. But what they offer isn't quality education like us."

"What did you see when you went there with Danny DaCosta?" I asked, "He only did that news report on them because the Canadian Catholic priest whose Church building they use for all their activities was trying to expose them for all the fraud and corruption he alleged they were guilty of."

"That's right," said Edwin. "Well they just have a big hall which they've got a load of computers and other equipment in, but it's more like a drop-in centre where people just come and go when they feel like it. They don't have any proper instruction or safety procedures for sport, so they'll never get any sports person to reach any standard when they operate that way."

"I suppose they prefer to have huge numbers and a loose kind of open door modus operandi so they can claim to cater for the masses and that way the international funding agencies will give them huge amounts of money that the Fosters can then hive off to pay themselves massive salaries and fund their trips to Canada to do courses and see the world."

"Exactly," he agreed. "Overseas governments are only interested in funding projects that appear to reach thousands of poor people, so the more people the Fosters can claim to serve, the more funding they get their hands on. That's why they want us to come under their umbrella. They want to get access to any funding we might help them get because they can claim they have all these excellent standards in education and sport that we achieve simply because we would nominally be a part of their outfit, but they wouldn't pass any of that funding onto the kids this side of the river. It would just go into their grubby little pockets to improve their own lifestyles while they actually do nothing to improve the education or sport in the region. That's what Danny was trying to warn me about when he said we shouldn't get involved with them."

"I expect it'll just be another march with people wearing free tee-shirts printed with 'Say No to Aids' which ends up in a rally with a few pompous speakers reading prepared speeches about aids and abstinence. Boxes of food are handed out and then everyone goes off into the rum-shops or the back-dam in order to spread the disease to a few more victims," I said, sceptically.

"Well *I'm* trying to get away from all that. If I can get Mrs Mackintosh to involve all the region's schools in this, then we're targeting the young people who have chance of a future if we can only get them to understand how to protect themselves. They seem to be the main casualties at the moment."

"That's true," I said "and yet it didn't help Sharon, even after all the proper teaching about it that she got from us here for free!"

Sharon had only recently been diagnosed as HIV positive. A couple of years before, when she had passed her French, Needlework and Textiles exams with me while working as voluntary school secretary in the sixth form, she suddenly left. Her father had kicked her out of his house for entertaining boys there while he was at work. He had been unaware of this until she was pregnant and as soon as he discovered that fact, he had pulled her out of Sapodilla. She couldn't take up the job of paid secretary that I had been trying to find a way to fund a salary for.

"All that effort for nothing," I had said, exasperated, when Edwin relayed to me what he had heard on the village grapevine. "Now I've got the embarrassing task of writing to tell the sponsor. Why is it that they learn stuff, get top grades when they write exam essays about it, but never seem to think that they need to apply it to their own lives?"

I was now even more disturbed at the thought of this teenager, whom I had taken under my wing and spent ten years giving one-to-one tuition to, would end up just like Shell, an uneducated middle-aged member of her kin, who had lived in the shack twenty five yards away from our house until two years before, in 2002.

Shell had lived with a succession of different women over the years we had been neighbours. That year, we had observed him sickening and wasting away over a period of months and it was quietly whispered around the street that he had 'the sick'. One day that July, we had been sitting on our veranda, talking over a cup of tea and as we looked out over the neighbouring yards, we saw the emaciated skeletal figure of Shell, too weak to stand, crouching in the shade of his steps. He did not move at first. Then he coughed, a spurt of blood came out of his mouth and he keeled over, dead. Edwin and I both jumped up out of our seats.

"Give me the keys, Jane, I'd better go across and help," Edwin had said. He had taken charge of the situation, told Shell's teenage daughter what to do to clean up the body, burn the cloths she had used and wrap his body in a clean sheet. Then with the help of her older brother, they lifted his remains into the back of our Jeep and Edwin drove them to the mortuary at Fort Wellington hospital and helped them get some ice from Rosignol since the mortuary had no working refrigeration. For weeks after that, locals had been strangely reluctant to accept lifts in our jeep. At first we did not know why, but eventually Edwin heard from Taa that Shell's son had been praising Edwin for carrying his dead father to the mortuary because no one else would do that. Taa had explained that people would be afraid the spirit of the dead would still be in the vehicle. The normal way for dead to be transported was on an open dray pulled by horse or donkey.

So many teenagers and young people in the village were dying suddenly that it seemed the Cumfa drums were ringing out every night. Whatever the planned AIDS fair came up with, it would be a hopeless waste of money because its message would fall on deaf ears. What hope was there for the message delivered in a day's publicity to have any effect if we had not managed to get through to one of our students the same message continually reinforced in different ways over a period of ten years or more? The local culture of promiscuity was stronger than any understanding of the cause and effect of the disease was likely to be. Did anyone really believe that Shell's death was anything to do with his casual sex with numerous women who all had multiple partners? It was like trying to convince a smoker that they should give up cigarettes because it causes cancers and strokes. Some believe it and stop smoking, some believe it but carry on because they say they can't give it up and others neither want to give it up nor believe it no matter what evidence you show them. They even put about contradictory evidence to justify their habit and seek to influence others around them to carry on smoking like they do. The problem is that such denial by smokers or AIDS sufferers destroys society by inflicting the disease on unsuspecting and unwilling third parties. Effective education can only be achieved if it is continuous, universal and sustained over generations. That was unlikely to happen in Guyana when the people delivering the educational messages did not seem to believe them enough to follow them in their own personal lives. It wasn't even a case of 'Do what I say and not what I do' but rather: 'Learn to say this to each other and to overseas people, so they understand we already know about this disease, but it has nothing to do with the way I live my life.'

Sharon had come to Edwin for advice on getting medical help when she knew something was wrong and she had been suffering from diarrhoea for several months. She must have remembered something about the symptoms from the hand-outs we had passed on to them from the World Health Organisation. We had sent two of our students, on their peer-educators course about HIV and AIDS. They had then taken a session teaching Sharon amongst all our other students and showed them-selves to be excellent communicators of all they had learned. It was always our policy to make the course participants pass on their knowledge to our students as soon as they came back from any course we sent them on. Otherwise a course just became an expenses-paid weekend trip to Georgetown, with participants staying in a fancy hotel with fancy food, funded by overseas agencies. There was an added bonus of an attendance certificate at the end which they could use as an extra qualification when getting a job somewhere. The female student we sent on this course had been Sharon's best friend at the time.

I shivered as I remembered her face, since I had none of the compassionate feelings towards her that I had for Sharon. Sharon had been a disappointment to me, but her behaviour had only affected herself and her family. She had not set out to affect me adversely in any way. Her friend, however, was more intelligent and slyly manipulative. I remembered the day in June 2001 when, blissfully ignorant, I had woken early one morning and found no sign of Edwin in bed or in the bedroom. I went out along the veranda but saw the gate was all locked up and the chain looped round the gate at the bottom of the steps as if we were both still upstairs. I knew he trained his athletes early, but the gym door was firmly shut, all the shutters were bolted and everywhere was in complete silence as if they had all gone home. It seemed strange that the chain was not padlocked but looped over itself as if intended to warn us of anyone opening the gate to go upstairs. It would make a clanking noise if I just pulled it loose. I became suspicious and decided to silently remove the chain. When I got to the gym door I could still hear no noises from inside. I twisted the clumsy door handle, opened the door and went into the darkness to put on the light. As it flickered on, I saw one of my sixteen year old female students lying in her gym clothes on a mat in the centre of the floor. There was no sign of Edwin, just a pile of his clothes beside her. She made no attempt to move or speak but I grabbed up Edwin's kit and walked into the changing room calling out his name. Eventually he responded from behind a closed toilet door. He opened it when I suggested that I was holding his clothes and he might need them. He had by then realised I had caught him red handed so there was no point in pretending that he had anything on. He pushed the door ajar just enough to take his vest and shorts, revealing his naked body crouched in a comical attempt at modesty in front of me, his wife, who was used to seeing him wandering around nude in bath and bedroom all the time.

"Thanks" he said rather sheepishly as he took them. I said nothing but turned and walked out. I may have prevented something from happening but whatever it was, it was not innocent. I glared at the girl still brazenly lying there.

"You can get out of here right now and never set your foot in this premises again!" I said with all the dignity I could muster in order to control my rage and humiliation. I followed her out of the gate, locked it behind her and watched her disappear up the street. It was Sharon's friend, whom we had sent on the AIDS course. Then I turned and walked back up the steps to our bedroom. Edwin followed me now he was dressed again.

Once safely in the privacy of our room we had to confront the situation.

"I take full responsibility" he said. I felt sick in the pit of my stomach. The thought of catching AIDS, my sex life and happiness being instantly cut off, and a chaotic future deflated any feelings of vitality I had awoken with.

"What were you thinking of? She's a student here. I'm her teacher…….. It's just as well that they only have one more exam to do and these are just revision classes so she can do the revision at home, because I'm not having her set foot inside this gate again."

"We didn't do anything, and I had no intention of doing anything," he said.

"Then why were you naked in front of a female student and alone together in our gym?" I asked.

"She was taunting me, to get me to have sex with her, saying that they all say I'm anti-man because I don't have local girlfriends like all the other men. I just got sick of being accused of being anti-man. I was stupid. I stripped off to show her that I was a man. I don't know what I thought it would prove to do that."

There were a hundred other questions I could have asked to get to the real truth, because his explanation did not make much sense to me but I could feel the ground dissolving beneath my feet and before I fell into a whirlpool of uncertainty, I grasped at anything solid I could still see.

"But we are their teachers. We're supposed to set a good example and they're supposed to respect us. How can I carry on in that role now if the other students get to hear of this?"

"I was completely wrong, I apologise. I'll move out and you can have the house," he said rashly.

"I came here because of you. How can you expect me to want to stay and live here in this community on my own after you've made a laughing stock of me in this way? I won't be able to exist here on my own because I'll have no income here and if you leave, you'll need your pension to survive on. What use is a property to me that I can't sell, because we both know that no one in the country would give us a cent for this place even if you put it up for sale, never mind if I, the white woman do. They all want it, but for free." I was sobbing by now. "You promised my mum that you wouldn't treat me the way Paul did!" I remonstrated.

He did not know what to do. He never expected me to wake up, go downstairs and find him like that. I had always slept in and trusted that he was training a crowd of athletes as I had no reason to think otherwise. I had no idea why I had got up early that day and stumbled on a scene so totally unexpected.

"You'll stay here and so will I," I said. "We'll get over this. If as you say there's nothing in it and you weren't going to do anything apart from show her your naked body, it shouldn't matter to you that she'll never set foot inside this gate again, either as a student or as an athlete."

He sat and thought about it. He felt bad.

"It's my fault not hers," he said. "I don't think she should be punished for it."

"I'm not going to let that little madam ruin my life and take away everything I have just like that. I'm certainly not going to allow myself to be humiliated on a daily basis by having to face her in my own home after this has happened. After all the help I've given her, if that's how little she thinks of me for all the years of dedication I've given to help her get all her examination passes , then I think nothing of kicking her out. In any case I've taught her all she needs to know to pass the exams. We're just doing revision classes for the last one and she can do that herself at home and just turn up at the exam centre to do the exam as usual. It won't affect her."

"How will you explain it to her mother?" he asked.

"She can explain it to her mother herself," I said. "If her mother calls to find out why she's been kicked out, I shall tell her it's a personal matter in which she has caused me great offence. She knows what she did and it's up to her to tell her mother what happened because I have no intention of doing so." I knew perfectly well that the girl would say nothing. She would probably lie and say she did nothing or that she did not know why I had just turned her out. She knew what had happened and that she was in the wrong but would not want to admit it to her mother. She would rather make me look harsh for kicking her out without good cause. Edwin was more upset that his best female athlete was prevented from being in the club any more now I had banished her, but he would have to be the loser on that one because I was not going to accept her presence under my battlements under any circumstances. She had invaded my relationship with my husband under my own roof, and if she were to continue to train as an athlete, she would always be looking at me with that private triumph in her head, mocking me.

Somehow, in the two hours left before the students arrived for the day's revision lessons, we managed to collect our relationship back together again in a spirit of contrition and forgiveness. It was a measure of the true strength of our feelings for one another and the fact that he had none for the girl other than as a star athlete. I knew that her interest in athletics was a shallow means to an end. She wanted to use it to win Edwin's attention and favour and she was prepared to use her body to secure any further advantage for herself. I had subsequently been proved right in this. She had no real interest in becoming an international athlete, or she would have continued doing it by joining a club in New Amsterdam or Georgetown. After leaving us she had gone on to do a course at the University of Guyana and dropped athletics completely. Recently, she had showed up at the Dywidag compound as the girlfriend of the young commercial manager, aiming to get overseas connections by a different route.

Since then, I had not thought of her once until now and it was only because of the AIDS menace all around me. I felt secure from it because I was not promiscuous and I believed Edwin wasn't either. I trusted him. He was always at home before dark. The fact that he had always wanted to tell me about it when local women tried to proposition him, somehow reinforced my trust. He told me he had no interest in them because he was happy with what he had. He had been eager to make public on many occasions the fact that he had volunteered for an AIDS test in England when they were first available because of worry about his promiscuity in the past and since he had tested negative, he had only had one partner, me. I believed him but my confidence had been momentarily shaken by the fear that he might not have told me the truth about that day in the gym. I would have to put that out of my mind. I was good at burying the past in the deepest recesses of my memory. It was how I had got over my first marriage and moved on with my life.

The rainy season had started and I got flu. That was nothing unusual, but what was weird this time, was that my ankles swelled up like balloons. I started to worry that I might have got 'big-foot' as the locals called filariasis. It was a condition caused by a microscopic worm that multiplied in the mud all around us in the rainy season. It could be transmitted to humans by mosquitoes. Supplements were put into some of the local brands of cooking salt to help protect people against filariasis. I wasn't sure if we had been using that salt and as my ankles seemed puffy and full of water which would not go away, I wanted medical attention. It would be best to visit a doctor when we went to England at the end of the month. Meanwhile, I would have to keep elevating my feet when seated whenever I could. I had marking to do and reports to write so I was working late into the night every night. Edwin was visiting the Dywidag compound regularly at nights. His brother Victor had recently moved back from New York to the new home he had built on the main road and married a local woman to share it with. It was mid-June and Edwin had been invited to go up to Victor's house for a whisky that evening. He said he would eat when he got back. I had therefore cooked food a bit later than usual but since he had not returned when it was ready, I had eaten mine and left the rest in the covered pan for him to have when he came in. He returned very late and seemed to be a bit drunk. I sat and let him tell me about his evening with Victor while he started to eat. After a while he said he could not finish the food as he did not feel well. He needed to go and sit on the veranda in the fresh air. I went out with him. He had barely sat down on the rattan sofa out on the veranda when he rose suddenly, launched himself towards the flower planters that rested on the sill and projectile vomited everything he had just eaten, and a good deal more, out over the balcony and down onto the lawn below. He continued to throw up several more times and then to retch violently. As he did so, he started sobbing,

"I'm so sorry, I really am, but you don't really know me and if you knew some of the bad things I've done in the past you wouldn't want anything to do with me, Jane."

"Don't be silly," I said softly, conscious that our conversation would otherwise be heard by Sago who lived only fifty feet away across the road, and would probably be most interested in listening to this public confession. "I understand that whatever you had to do when you were a soldier was part of your duty and I would never judge you for it. In fact if I had been in a war, I'm sure I would do the same thing myself."

"I've done some really bad things in my life," he continued, beginning to get a bit more control but still remorseful. "I met up with some of my old army mates on the road. They're in the country doing special work. We went to have more drinks together after I left Victor's".

"No wonder you're ill if you had all that drink on an empty stomach," I said. "You better drink this water." He sipped at the bottle I put into his hand and seemed to have settled down a bit. Then he started vomiting all over again.

"They want me to do bad things but I can't do it to my own people," he blubbered. "I just can't." I could only guess at what he was suggesting.

"They wouldn't ask you to do anything bad to a good person," I said. "They must be dealing with very bad people who are drug-traffickers, so you shouldn't feel bad about that. They're just bad people, not your people at all. I certainly won't think you're bad if you help them catch these bad people." He had stopped vomiting by now and just lolled weakly back on the uncomfortable sofa. I suggested we move back inside because I didn't want the conversation to be overheard and now there was nothing more inside him to come out. I helped him along the veranda to our bedroom where the breeze from the sea and the fan over the bed could help sober him up while he was resting more comfortably.

"Is it anything to do with that little Scottish bloke we bumped into in Fogarty's cafeteria the other summer?" I asked, remembering a pint sized white man looking like a scruffy ancient rocker in jeans and sneakers with long grey hair trailing down his back, who had approached us as we were about to join the queue for drinks and said in a broad Scottish accent, "Mr Joe Joseph, I presume," and held his hand out to Edwin, adding, "I'm James Gordon, formerly of the Highland Black Watch regiment. I've heard a lot about you and your good work down in Berbice," Edwin had seemed surprised and a bit embarrassed but carried on as if he were a complete stranger, explaining that I was his wife and we ran our own charity school in Berbice. I remembered asking the man if he was on holiday in Guyana, or working on a contract. He had told me that he had inherited family lands in Mahaica creek and he had come back to have a look at them and see what he could do with them. I had found it surprising but not unbelievable that a white Scottish person should still have family lands in such a place, so I accepted his story and we wished him luck and went off to take our refreshments. Many months later, Edwin had told me he bumped into him again in Georgetown and he had spent some time chatting with him in a local bar. It was then that he had admitted to me that although he had acted in front of me as if the man was a complete stranger, he had known him from the army and worked with him before. He called him "Jock." He had told me that Jock was really helping the drugs squad track down cocaine smugglers in the country. He had tried to get Edwin involved in helping them. "I don't want to get involved with guys like that," he had said, "because I can't leave you alone here while I disappear off into the hulu for weeks on end with them. Those guys are tough and they live really rough, you wouldn't believe it. " Since then I had heard no more mention of him, but I now wondered if he had resurfaced.

"Oh, you mean Jock," said Edwin, "No it wasn't him. It was someone else that I was in the army with back in the fifties. But those guys are all in the same mould. They're tough bastards. I don't know why they want to be doing work like that when they're my age. They seem to have nothing else in their lives. I couldn't be like them."

"So you all got drunk together," I said.

"Well I'd already downed a bottle of whisky at Victor's but when a load of local tarts came in I decided to make an exit and I went up to Dywidag and bumped into these guys on the road so we went and had a few beers at number 28. It was good talking over old times, but I can't do what they asked me to do, I can't spy on my own people."

"Well I think you should, if it'll help to catch criminals who are ruining people's lives. I won't think badly if you tell them what you see. Why would you happily do the same thing in England or Germany or Malaya and not in your own country? Surely a criminal is a criminal and worth catching where ever they are."

I looked down at Edwin on the bed and saw that he had finally passed out, so I left him snoring while I went to clear up the other end of the house and lock up for the night. We did not revisit the subject of that night's discussion for a very long time. As far as I was concerned, it was history.

In a week's time we would be flying out of the country and back to England for a holiday with the family and grandchildren. I did not feel like a grandmother, but as I had been cheated of a family of my own by the cruel twists of my personal life, I was looking forward to being able to look after Edwin's small grandchildren as if they were our own children for a while. I still had plenty of marking and reports to write for the students whose last day of term was in two days' time. I sat up all through the night finishing them so I could give them out before we left, along with the term dates for the new academic year. Edwin was rushing around sorting out last minute business for the Dywidag security team and the village office. We were both quite exhausted and showing signs of it. Tegana, our boxer, would have to be in charge of the security while we were away and Kerdell would stay with him this time. We were a bit nervous about leaving them in charge, as they were less intelligent and less mature than any previous students we had entrusted with the job, but they were the only boys we had who could be asked to do it this time. Our most responsible students were all female and Edwin did not think girls could be asked to do the same job. Their parents would not want them to be sleeping on their own away from home. In view of the local culture, it was a sensible decision. They would not have been physically able to fend off any male intruder. Luckily, Robin had just returned from his first defence force posting in the New River Triangle on the Surinam border, where he had been on exercise with the Wai-wai Amerindian tribe. He had some leave and agreed to come down and check in on the two boys in our absence. Thank goodness for Robin, we both thought. It gave us some peace of mind.

Chapter 22
Roots and Spies.

*"The incessant rhythm of Af*rican drums which began yesterday morning has been going all night. It is the wake of our 95 year old neighbour who died this week. The drums are to help send her spirit safely to join the ancestors. As I sit here typing this article, I marvel at the juxtaposition of 21st century technology with such ancient tribal culture. The extended family next door are all sitting in a makeshift shelter in the yard of their little two-roomed wooden house, singing hymns and popular tunes to the drums. The men become slowly intoxicated on the rum and get up in turn to trance-dance in the centre of their gathering. The intrusion of the past into the present is comforting for a historian like myself, as we seek to help local youths to become more self-sufficient in the competitive *material world we are trying to catch up with here in Guyana…….."*

I broke off writing the introductory paragraph of my article for the January 2005 issue of Mitch's newsletter "Sapodilla Today" to listen to Sherwyn's powerful fingers pounding the taught goatskin of his comfa drum. I was aware that we all lived out our lives in public in this little rural community. Just as I was able to see and hear their wake from my veranda and Sago's frequent violent rows with his elderly mother in his search for the money he accused her of stealing from his room, they too could watch every move and hear most of what was said in our home, especially if we were out on the veranda. Windows were all open. Sounds carried on the breeze in the silence of the night. Privacy was impossible.

Death, funerals and wakes were now a weekly and sometimes a daily feature of our lives in the village. They had also become a recent feature of my own family. While we had been in England during the summer, my elderly aunt, in the care of my brother, had died while we were staying there. It was almost as if she had waited to do so when she knew I would be there to see her for a last time. She had died in hospital from the stroke that she had been rushed in with two days after my last chat with her. My sister Penny, who had died three years before, had remained with her in spirit. All Auntie Lorna kept saying to me was "Poor Penny, poor Penny." It had been a cold impersonal ward where I was able to visit and see her before they took her to the mortuary. Her wizened face was contorted horribly and frozen into the scream-like grimace of an Eduard Munch painting. It haunted me as if she had died in horrible pain. Which was better? Lorna's death in a bleak impersonal clinical ward filled with strangers or that of old Nancy, opposite us now? Somehow the setting of sunshine, warmth and tropical trees with friendly familiar faces all around seemed preferable. Death in an English hospital seemed final, scientific. Death here seemed different, somehow organic, physical but transient. Something of the person was still there: in the soil, in the trees, in the community. Death did not scare me here.

We had both been so glad to get back to Guyana in August after our six week stay in England. It had been lovely to see the family again and to have the grandchildren staying with us for a week at my old family home where we could have some quality time with them, but our stay had been marred by funerals and hospital visits including seven of my own. Having consulted my own family doctor about my puffy ankles in the hope of a blood-test to see if I had filariasis, I was rushed off to hospital for ECG tests and a seven day course of warfarin injections in the abdomen as a precaution against DVT. It had not helped solve the puffy ankle problem however. Although my ankles went down considerably while we were in the cooler temperatures of an English summer, the condition returned as soon as we were back in Guyana. Edwin had failed to get anywhere with a medical assessment in England, so once back in Guyana, we had both booked up for tests to be done in a new private hospital in Georgetown in November. These tests had all proved negative for me apart from being told I had signs of osteo-arthritis in my ankles, but Edwin was alerted to his high sugar level which indicated diabetes. He was told to go on a sugar free diet and take a baby aspirin every day. He had been complaining of tiredness all the time and numbness in his feet. The aspirins did not make any difference to those symptoms. I had no real idea what diabetes was or that it was as serious as the doctors seemed to think it was, so I did not really understand how Edwin was feeling. I just thought he should not eat or drink sugar or sweet things and cut down on salt and that would lead to improvement. A simple cure rid me of my own problem: I changed my thick-soled sandals to thin flip-flops that allowed me full range of movement through the feet and ankles. With the improved circulation that this enabled, the swelling disappeared and did not return.

I now had a new intake of full time students who had moved up from my part time classes in September and become full time students at Sapodilla. They were drawn from villages as far away as Belladrum in the west and New

Amsterdam in the east. It was a healthy ethnic mix of Negro, Indian and Amerindian children. Kesha, who had just come out as one of my top students in the recent CXC exams, had decided to stay on to our sixth form to do GCE 'O-level' exams while waiting to be accepted onto the Guyana Defence Force Officer Cadet Training Course. Kesha had the experience of running our Summersplash student mini-company project and so became the manager to initiate all the new students into their roles in running the company. The agricultural work on the farm and in rearing the chickens for meat soon got smoothly underway as did the weekly meetings which I presided over.

One morning at a mini-company meeting near to the end of their first term, O'Neil, one of the new students, used the time in our Any Other Business slot to complain about his garden plot.

"Miss," he said, clearly aggrieved, "This morning when I came into school and went down to my plot to wet up my plants, I noticed that the big pumpkin that I was going to reap this afternoon has disappeared and there is a big boot print next to it." There were some giggles from the other children and I found it hard not to join in with them because O'Neill had such a cheeky, mischievous little face and was usually the instigator of some joke, so it was hard to take him seriously.

"Oh dear," I said. "That's never happened before. I think we'd better all check round the fence to see that it's secure. Keep an eye out for any other missing crops and let me know straight away."

O'Neill's pumpkin wasn't the only thing going missing over the next few months. I always kept my giant tub of washing powder downstairs in the changing room because that was where the washing machine was plumbed in. These days I usually did the weekly wash on Sunday mornings when there were no students around and I could hang it all out to dry on the line across the back lawn. One Sunday, I noticed that the brand new tub that I had only opened the week before seemed more empty than I remembered leaving it after the previous week's wash. I thought I must be imagining things as no one was allowed in the changing room without Edwin present. I though no more of it till the following week when the level of powder was so low it was nearly half empty. I decided to find out if Edwin had been letting the students use it for something.

"No," he said, "Why?"

"I've noticed that the new tub we bought the other week seems to be disappearing and it's not me that's using it. I'm going to keep it upstairs from now on."

"Good idea," he said. All the same, I couldn't help finding it a bit strange that he didn't say more, as normally if something went missing and he thought the children were responsible, he would make a big issue of it with the students and a long lecture about honesty and trust would follow. This time there was no further mention of it.

We had received an invitation by the British High Commissioner to attend an evening reception at his residence for the famous cricketer, Clive Lloyd. Edwin hired a car to take us there and back on the Monday evening so that he would not have to drive the jeep late at night through the villages. He made the excuse that he wanted to be able to take a drink at the reception, but I knew that he wanted to avoid the possibility that we would be high-jacked on the roads leading through Buxton. There had been a lot of violent attacks in those areas. Ever since five prisoners had escaped from Georgetown prison during the February Mashramanie celebrations of 2002 and remained at large, armed and dangerous, until the police laid siege on the lodge where they were holed up, Buxton had been a refuge for criminals on the run. Police had shot dead a man called Shaka Blair in his home in Buxton.

Everybody knew our jeep and we were a target in it. If we were in the local hire car of a trusted family friend from the village, it would not stand out and so would not be likely to be stopped. The evening was an interesting one. We were introduced to Clive and spent quite a long time talking to him about our educational establishment. He seemed genuinely interested. I suppose it must have been a change for him to be asking the questions instead of being grilled about cricket by reporters or fans. There were others there who were involved in West Indies cricket, so I circulated a bit and met a few wives of Guyanese magnates, who seemed intrigued to learn of what I was doing because they spent their days pursuing hobbies such as silk painting. I went through the motions of polite intelligent conversation, interrupted from time to time by staff bearing platters of the usual cheese straws, vol-au-vents and various canapés. Such social encounters always seemed meaningless and false to me. I could never see the point of small talk with people I was never likely to meet again. The new High Commissioner, Stephen Hiscock, and his wife Dee, however, were somehow on my wave-length and I felt an instant affinity with them.

Stephen said he had invited us because he thought Edwin was a personal friend of Clive Lloyd. This, he now realised, was not the case. However, he could be forgiven for making that assumption. Edwin indeed personally knew many sporting celebrities, not just cricketers, but tended also to talk about those he had a brief encounter with as if he knew them personally too. Most of the people I met that evening were local ladies. I had no idea I was under surveillance at this time by a British person unknown to me in the crowd of diplomats and other invitees circulating in the High Commissioner's garden.

As we left to find our car in the close leading to the residence, Lance Carberry, a senior Afro-Guyanese intellectual, approached and introduced himself to us. He said he had heard of all the wonderful work we were both doing in our Learning Centre in Hopetown, Berbice and was delighted now to have met us. We chatted briefly but as Edwin was eager to start on our journey home before it got very late, he gave Lance an open invitation to call in on us any time he was passing through Hopetown on his way to New Amsterdam.

A lot was going on as usual. Edwin had organised a volleyball officials' course for the region five P.E. teachers, so we were hosting some of the Volleyball Association Officials from Georgetown who were the instructors. It had all been part of his attempt to develop volleyball in Berbice as a pilot project for Lenny Shuffler, the Georgetown President of the National Volleyball Association, who had recently approached Edwin for help. He also had begun to practice "the last post" on the bugle he had been given when we were in England. He needed to get it right for the Remembrance Day service in November. I thought he was doing it to impress Heinz who was a beginner learning to play his hunting horn. I just could not understand why he always left it till about ten o'clock at night to do this. Another thing about his changed behaviour was the interest he started to show in the cars that now passed by our house late at night as soon as headlights could be spotted turning into our street from the public road. I did not really think it strange at the time, because before the road was surfaced, cars were never able to come down to us from the public road in the dark. They would easily have stuck in the mud or gone into the trench that they could not see. Now the road was surfaced with bitumen, cars frequently came by and at any time of night or day. I assumed his inquisitive need to go to the window and watch any late night passing cars was to watch where the car went, in case it posed any security threat to us.

Smoking is anathema to me. Edwin knew when he first met me that I hated it and would not have anyone smoking in my house, car or garden. He said he had smoked in the army but never inhaled it because as a sportsperson, he needed to protect his lungs. In all the years we had been together in Guyana, he had never smoked, but now, for some reason he started to take a single cigarette at night on the veranda when I was not around. No matter how much he tried to hide it from me, I could always smell it and would take him to task for it. He said he needed it to calm his nerves. It seemed a phony excuse to me. It was not as if he had a stressful job any more. One evening at dusk when I was in the middle of cooking our evening meal as usual, I had to go to the other end of the house to our bedroom to fetch a mug I had left there. It was blackout as usual. I got halfway along the veranda in the dark when I met Edwin coming from the other end towards me in a hurry. He was hyped up. He grabbed hold of my arms and swept me back the way I had just come, towards the seating area outside our lounge.

"Blimey Jane, I just got a terrible scare when I went round the corner of the veranda to go to our room just now. That great big owl came screeching towards me as if it was after some bats. It scared the living daylights out of me. I'll have to sit down and take a cigarette to calm my nerves." I could almost feel the fear thumping through his veins. Adrenalin seemed to be transmitted across from his chest to mine on the airwaves. I had never seen him like it before. How could a battle-hardened soldier like him be so scared of a bird of prey, I thought?

"Well let's sit down here for a minute till it goes away but I don't want you smoking while I'm sitting here next to you. If you must have one, when you've given it time to fly away, go and hang over the veranda away from the open bedroom window and let the breeze blow the smoke away," I said. We sat and chatted for a while about the owl and all the bats in the roof, and then I went back to the cooking and he went off down the other end and had his cigarette. Over dinner, we discussed how we would ever find a capable and trustworthy builder locally to replace the roof of our house to make it watertight and bat-proof for once but there seemed to be no obvious solution. We would just have to put up with the bats and the owls.

A few days later, we were taking breakfast on the veranda outside our bedroom overlooking the front garden. It was now full of mature tropical trees that screened the ugly view of the distant shanty between us and the public road. A local Indian haulage contractor nicknamed 'Jumbo-Jet,' since that name was painted on his lorry, had bought one of the houses and turned it into a noisy pool hall, disco-bar and gambling den full of Amerindian prostitutes. Our house would have had a view of its junk-filled back yard, but for the brilliant scarlet-flowered Flamboyant and massive Rubber trees we had planted. We also had some graceful twenty foot high Casuarina pines, one of which was right near our veranda and obstructed the ugly vista now presented by a ten foot high concrete compound wall that Jumbo Jet had built around the entire perimeter of his newly acquired strip of land parallel to us on the far side of the pasture. He had bought it from 'Brown Rat', the umbrella repairer, whose hovel was on the land on the other side of the public road, enabling the vendor to migrate to Canada. The compound seemed to be a dumping ground for all Jumbo-Jet's scrap, heavy machinery and vehicles that were off the road.

"I'm going to get Trevor to come this afternoon after he finishes at the village office and cut this tree down," said Edwin suddenly, pointing at the Casuarina that flanked that side of the veranda.

"Oh no," I said, "It's such a beautiful tree and it screens off that eyesore over there."

"It's too near the house," he insisted. "Look, the branches are touching the house so termites can climb up it into the roof."

"Well that's true, I can see a trail of them right now, but surely if I just cut off the branches that touch the house then it'll be enough."

"I got advised to take it completely down," he said in his stern, final comment voice. "It's a security risk. Anyone can get over the fence and climb up onto the veranda by it."

"Oh I see, well of course, I hadn't thought of that. Yes it must go," I said sadly. I didn't think to ask him who it was that advised him.

Later that day, he had to collect items of nearly new furniture and a television from the Dywidag compound. Their bridge building contract was coming to an end and Rommel was leaving that Christmas, so Edwin had asked him if he could buy his glass topped coffee tables, three piece suite and other items when he left. I had just had my fiftieth birthday and Edwin his sixty fifth. He would be getting his old age pension this month as well as his retirement and army pension, so we would be able to afford to get these things to make our life a bit more comfortable. Helga and Heinz were staying on until February but they were going to drive to Surinam over Christmas with Otto and his wife, so we dined with them a couple of nights before they left. Holger whose mother was visiting him over Christmas, was going to bring her to eat with us on Christmas Day. I was busy cleaning up the house in preparation for the visit and the festive season. I never went into the three guest rooms unless we had visitors staying and no one had been in the little room that volunteers had usually occupied for several years now. I just checked around in it for signs of termite trails on the wood. I didn't see any but one thing I noticed, which was like a glacial erratic in our house: an old chipped enamel mug was hanging from a nail just inside the shower cubicle.

"Who put this here?" I asked Edwin, who was passing by outside the door.

"I did," he said. "I brought it upstairs when I wanted to have a shower in that room after sport and the water wasn't running so I used water from one of the fire buckets on the veranda." There was always an explanation for everything and it was always a good one. The only mystery that remained unexplained was the pair of dark green overalls that I had never seen before which appeared on a hook by the washing machine in the changing room. Edwin just took them from my out-stretched hand, looked at them, shrugged his shoulders, folded them up and put them on a shelf in the changing room, which by now had been turned into a sick-bay and first aid room with one of the beds from upstairs set out in the centre of the room.

"I suppose one of the kids must have left them here," I said. He went off to the village office to make arrangements for his staff Christmas meal.

This year, now he was feeling he could afford it, Edwin had decided to take them to the "New Thriving," a luxurious Chinese restaurant which had opened up in Georgetown since the millennium. It was to save me having to do all the cooking, and I could come along too. It was also how he could avoid having to hold a party for all the village councillors in the village office, as by now he was feeling distinctly uncomfortable with many of them and did not want to have to socialise with people he could not stand the sight of. I had not had any opportunity to get him a Christmas present yet and so I decided to lock up the house and garden while no one was there, and walk into Bushlot to see if there was anything worth buying for him in Phagoo's shop. I had to pass by Brown Rat's old hovel on my way there and I saw Jumbo Jet's massive compound walls on my left. Lorries were even parked higgledy-piggledy on the roadside verge outside the compound and I could not see into the yard as the walls were so high. The steel gates at the corner of the plot were padlocked and immediately behind them were diggers and other heavy machinery parked in a disorganised way right behind the gates, obscuring the view further into the yard. I walked on to the shop and stood behind the crowds of customers waiting my turn. Phagoo saw me and wanted to deal personally with me as a special favour so I would not have to wait. I couldn't think of anything he might have, so I asked him if he had any cases for mobile phones. He was happy to show me that he did have three to choose from, so I made my purchase and walked back home. This time I passed over to the opposite side of the road and was surprised to see an obsolete orange submersible craft parked in front of Brown Rat's house just inside his garden fence. It was the same submersible I had seen abandoned in the creek by the lagoon at Onverwagt years before when Dr Mac had taken us both there to see the red ibis nesting sites. What on earth is it doing there, I wondered?

Later, when Edwin came home, I asked him if he had noticed it.

"That's been there for quite a while", he said, "A few months."

"I never noticed it before, but then I haven't been anywhere since August when we came back from England. I wonder why they want that stuck in their front garden."

"That's all since Jumbo Jet took over. He's involved with drugs. They probably used that to bring it into the creek at Onverwagt. He's going into the furniture trade now and he's got a whole load of furniture in the upstairs rooms of the Poole Hall. I bumped into one of my world cup footballers the other day who's involved with the Black Clothes Police. He said they've got their eyes on him and raided the premises recently."

I was interested in the connection between the furniture trade and the drugs trafficking because I had noticed there was a lot of beautifully carved wooden Chinese style furniture in the upstairs rooms of the New Thriving restaurant when we had visited a year or so before and I had asked the girl behind the counter if they were selling it. She had referred me to the manager, John. I asked him the price of a piece I particularly liked, but he said he did not yet have the price for any of it. I left our contact number with him in the expectation that he would soon call me, eager for a sale. I had heard nothing more so had telephoned to speak to him some weeks later and got the same response. When we visited the place for the staff Christmas treat, I noticed that all the same furniture was still there, over a year later with no prices on it and my queries met with the same lack of response.

"Why have all that furniture there and make no attempt to sell it?" I had asked Edwin.

"Why indeed?" he had answered, "Unless you want to use it to ship cocaine out concealed in the hollowed legs." I nodded sagely at his suggestion. It all seemed to make sense now. While we had been in England in the summer, a massive shipment of cocaine had been found hidden in a frozen fish export shipment. The low value commodities being exported in containers were hardly worth the cost of shipping them, but it was worth it if something with a much higher street value were stashed inside the legitimate cargo.

The New Year of 2005 brought the worst floods we had ever witnessed in Guyana. Georgetown and the East Coast were submerged under three feet of water and the threat of an epidemic of leptospirosis was publicised. The government announced a warning that people should not walk through this water and advised them to stay in their houses above flood level. Our own garden was flooded. The water had not entered our classrooms or gym, because after previous flood experience, we had constructed concrete barriers fifteen centimetres high across the doorways to prevent it or we would have had three inches of filthy water throughout all the ground floor rooms. Even so, I was forced to send the children home at ten o'clock on the first day of term, the day of maximum flood, because parents in outlying villages were calling me on their newly installed telephones asking me to do so. They wanted their children home before the rain flooded their streets and homes so much that they would not be able to walk through the water in wellington boots without it going over the top of them. I delayed the start of term till the following week. We were able to function as a full time school after that by doing all the sport inside in the gym. However, even after two weeks the water level in the grounds had not dropped enough to make them usable so I had to send home all the Saturday students at ten o'clock because heavy rain was set to continue all day. We simply had no room for the sixty of them indoors at the same time.

We had put our own measures in place but the rest of the country had not. The East Coast of Demerara was by now so badly affected that people were marooned on the roofs of their shacks and the army had to take food aid out in boats to reach people who could not get to shops and markets. Needless to say crops were ruined and the after effects of these exceptionally heavy rains of "La Nina" lasted long after the water disappeared.

The floods underlined for us the importance of trying to find a way to extend our indoor space. I had already put out an appeal in Mitch's newsletter before Christmas for help to buy a damaged port-a-kabin office from the German company that was leaving in the coming year. Edwin had told me months before, that thieves near Georgetown had used a backhoe to open up the roof of a Dywidag mobile office left in a roadside compound there one night in order to steal a generator and other equipment from it. I had asked him to find out how much they wanted for it, as we could try and convert it into a kitchen fitted out for all our students to cook at the same time. He had said it wouldn't be big enough but he explained to Holger what it was for and at our Christmas dinner, Holger had offered us one of the undamaged port-a-kabins, worth U.S. $7000, for half price. If we could find the U.S. $3,500 for that, we could also have the damaged one free. I had hoped to get some response from the newsletter which went out in January but meanwhile, had organised a raffle of some items we had been given from Rommel's household effects. The idea was to make a great effort at fundraising ourselves for something that would become a community asset. I never expected to achieve the target because it was such a huge amount of money, but it was worth a try. At Easter, the west of England schoolboy cricket team and their families came over as usual and our students managed to sell large numbers of our postcards to them to add to our fundraising total.

On May 7th, we had an unexpected phone call from our mutual friend Dave Hayes to tell us the tragic news that Mitch had suddenly died from an aneurysm while out on a routine jog. We were stunned and shocked. He was only in his forties, a sportsman all his life and had only recently got married. Poor Julie, she must be in a terrible state. His two young children by his first marriage still had a very close relationship with him. They must be traumatised, especially the little girl who was with him in the park when he collapsed. How could we pay tribute to him as mark of thanks for his years of support apart from sending the usual wreath? We would dedicate our new Home Economics Centre to him when we had raised enough funds for the port-a-kabin. Edwin decided to dedicate the Media Trophy which Mitch had donated to us a few years before, to a new ten kilometre race in Mitch's honour and get the students to find sponsors, raising money from their friends and families for the fund. I composed an obituary news bulletin and emailed it to all our supporters telling them that we intended to do this. The students were saddened by the news. Some of them remembered Mitch from when he had paid us a surprise visit a few years before. They all made a tremendous effort with the sponsored run, including Conroy, the boy with sickle cell anaemia, who was not supposed to do excessive exercise because it made him ill. He insisted on completing the whole race because he did not want to let the school down, so even though he did not win, we decided to present the trophy to him.

We had managed to collect over five thousand pounds by July, mainly from our overseas supporters (including The Poole Runners and Mitch's family and friends, who dedicated a funeral collection in his honour). This enabled me not only to pay for the container package, but also to purchase from Dywidag two more twenty foot long containers, three up to date internet ready computers and a colour printer for the classroom, extra filing cabinets, bookshelves and storage cupboards for the laboratory, two fridges and five calor-gas cookers for the kitchen, teacher's desks and chairs, comfortable upholstered chairs for the computer room, a boardroom table and three large refectory tables with benches. Holger and his boss, Falk Trempel, provided the concrete piles for the foundations and sent their workforce with the cabins on a low-bed with crane to move them and set them in place. This all happened on the 27th June after we had brought in many lorry loads of sand to build up the site and had it all levelled ready to receive this instant building complex. The whole community came out to watch as the crane moved the massive concrete piles into place. Then the low-bed with the cabins arrived. One by one, the crane lifted them into the air with a man on top of the cabin giving directions to the crane operator. I had to be there with Holger to make sure that each cabin was aligned correctly, with the doors facing the way I wanted them. Then the two containers were put in place so as to create a horse-shoe around a quadrangle. The whole operation was by then a local spectacle of gigantic proportions.

The funds we had raised also covered a secure fence and gates, repair charges for the broken container and the cost of fitting it out with four sinks, built in worktops and cupboards, plumbing, a water connection to the mains, sink waste pipes and a septic tank for the flushing toilet that was already inside the undamaged container. An electricity connection was installed to the undamaged cabin so as to power the two fridges we had bought from Dywidag. The connections for the gas bottles for the five gas stoves and eight identical sets of utensils and cooking equipment used up the remaining funds. Local workmen did all this work for us over the next few months. We had a granite plaque engraved for the door of the front cabin to dedicate it to Mitch's memory and a special sign board with

"THE MITCH MASON CENTRE" painted in large capital letters.

The Treviglas work-experience students, two lovely girls, were with us at the end of term to witness the hand-over of funds sent to us by the Newquay Lions which went towards the cookers and fridges. We put on an activities week for the children so the girls had something to help us with. This concluded with a living museum day for the girls with Holger as special invitee, to be guided around the displays by our students in historic character roles, wearing their appropriate costumes.

During July also, a local contractor named Reasat, who had been doing road building works for the local neighbourhood district council, excavated our fishponds at the back of the farm free of charge so the students could take on a fish farming project for tilapia. We had used some of the donated funds from the Newquay Lions to fence off this area securely with wire and mesh. I had already taken the students on a field visit to study another local fish farm project which was failing due to visibly obvious shortcomings and we felt we could do a better job than that farmer provided we dug the ponds deep enough in the first place. We arranged for a ministry of agriculture specialist to come and give us the necessary instruction for setting up the fish production later in the new academic year.

All this help and massive development of our tiny charity attracted a good deal of media attention, which in turn attracted unwanted interest from prospective predators and political enemies. Such was the potential threat that Edwin was checking the underside of our vehicle every morning for possible explosive devices having been planted on it. I was aware that he was worried more than usual, but I put that down to the fact that he was making himself unpopular with some local political activists. They made no bones about accusing him of being in cahoots with the government simply because we were getting a lot done at Sapodilla and people wrongly assumed politicians were helping us to do this. In his village office meetings he was sharp tongued towards those who put up ignorant reasons for obstructing his policies.

Heinz and Helga had left at the end of January. We had a farewell dinner with them the night before. We bought quite a lot of their stuff, as well as over five hundred pounds worth of items from Otto and Janis. This included his "Sky" dish, receiver and television set. The Sky equipment Edwin gave to his brother Victor in the hope of being paid for it when Victor had the money. Rommel had already given his 'Sky' dish to Edwin because he did not want the dealer in Georgetown to get it back. He felt he had been ripped off. Edwin had it installed and paid the same dealer only the basic rental package. By the end of February, we had it working. It worked for two days and then cut off. There followed months of run-around and frustration as we discovered that the dealer, the only one in the country, was yet another shark who collected money for six months up front and then delivered no service. He could never be contacted as his telephone number always rang out or else his wife gave the excuse that he had gone to Brazil to get some more receivers. Telephone calls to Sky HQ in England informed us that it was not in any way connected to the Sky Company in Brazil. A call to the HQ in Brazil revealed that the card number for our set was not registered with them as they could only supply service to addresses in Brazil. Finally I telephoned the Brazilian Embassy in Georgetown, only to discover that the export of Sky TV service from Brazil to Guyana was illegal as yet and that the operator was collecting receivers and cards registered to a house in Boa Vista on the Brazil-Guyana border. The illegal operator had three months' free service on the card in the receiver, which he shared between six subscribers, each of whom were under the impression that they were the sole recipient of the card and each of whom received the service for a week or two before it was cut off, while another customer got the service for a short period and so on.

It took several months before Edwin got his contacts in the black clothes police in Georgetown to track down Barrington, the dealer and apply some pressure on him which he was too afraid to ignore, so eventually he appeared with a new card and set the equipment working again so we could finally get some of the service we had already paid for months before. Along with the good international channels such as National Geographic, HBO movies, CNN news channel and the like, we found we also had access to some unbelievably explicit Brazilian sex channels which brought hard porn directly into our living room. I found it a turn-off to be honest and somewhat comical, but one night, after surfing the channels and watching it for a few minutes before changing channels to an action film, Edwin caught hold of me, pulled me over to the sofa and started getting passionate. We spent most of the film having rabid sex on the living room floor completely oblivious to the storyline. It wasn't anything we didn't normally do every now and again, but somehow he seemed to be acting a bit strange that evening, with a sort of crazed look in his eyes that I had never seen before. It had made me feel a bit uncomfortable at first, but it passed off and I thought nothing more about it.

The last day of Edwin's security contract with Dywidag was July 30th. I had paid Holger the 400,000 dollars I owed him two days before at a farewell dinner we had invited him to and Edwin now collected the filing cabinets, storage cupboards, computer and other stuff we had bought as well as a lot of stationary, another computer, plants and other things Holger had donated to the school. Then Edwin organised the collection of furniture from the Dywidag staff houses which he had negotiated as end of contract bonuses for all his loyal and hardworking security staff. He was elated. It had all gone so well and now he was released from it all. The most important part of it was that he had proved a point by the way he had managed his security staff. They were all thrilled to receive bonuses in the form of luxurious almost new furniture that they could never have hoped to afford in their homes on the kind of wages unqualified labourers normally earned. Edwin had proved a point to all those guards he had sacked along the way because of their repeated poor attendance, unreliability, poor work ethic, drunkenness or dishonesty. They would all now see what they could have had if they had done their job properly. There was indeed a lot of talk in the local community following all this. Edwin's name was being talked a lot in the street and in the church, in the back-dam and in dark corners. The drums of Emancipation Day were now singing out in celebration of good times in Hopetown.

Chapter 23

The Invisible Man

It would be difficult for me to pinpoint a happier time in my relationship with Edwin than that August in 2005 when we finally escaped away from Sapodilla to a beautiful self-catering apartment on the coast of St Vincent for two weeks. It was almost an out of world experience. We were at last having the kind of holiday together that I had dreamed of, paddling barefoot in the gentle surf along the paradise white beaches to a different open air beach restaurant every day. Some afternoons we toured the island to the forts and plantations or to the atmospheric beach location of the film-set for "Pirates of the Caribbean". It was a time for feeling free from prying eyes of the neighbourhood in Hopetown. We at last had privacy and could explore each other in complete liberated intimacy. It was also time for a revelation that I had not been expecting.

The first day as we walked out to reach the rocky cove our apartment overlooked, Edwin started unloading some of the experiences he had been having in our last few months in Guyana.

"I'm really glad to get away," he said. "It disgusts me that even at the highest level, I mean government ministers, are involved in narco-trafficking."

I looked at him without speaking. I was trying to guess which government ministers he might be referring to. He had been working closely with Minister of Culture Youth and Sport, Gail Texiera, for a few years now. Surely he couldn't mean her. She seemed to be one of the few decent government Ministers who was genuinely trying to make improvements in the country. He wasn't likely to state a name and I wasn't going to ask him to. He must be referring to Minister Gajraj whose name had hit the news in the last few months in connection with death squad killings. A man called Bacchus whose brother had been killed in a drive-by shooting, had alleged that Gajraj sanctioned the death squad's activities, supported by senior policemen and prominent businessmen. I let Edwin carry on talking.

"The drugs problem is getting worse and worse," he continued. "I'm getting deeper and deeper into this business since I got asked to help the local police, but they're all involved in it. There's not one of them you can trust."

"I'm sure you're right. I felt that was the case ever since we arrived in Guyana, especially after you told me that Patrick Britton gave a brand new vehicle to the local police. It was clearly a bribe so they would turn a blind eye to his trafficking activities in Hopetown."

"Don't worry Jane, that's why he got put in jail in New York. You saw how much the community respected him for all the stuff he gave them by what they did to his house and gas station once news was out that he was in prison in America."

"Yes, they stole everything he had inside the house and then broke down the place brick by brick so it's a ruin now," I said. "Worse still is what that horrid man Colin James did to us by hijacking us on the road to get funds."

"Well he was working with BASS in the drugs squad," Edwin reminded me. "I can't work with people I don't trust. I feel happier working with people I feel I can trust."

"Who's that then?" I asked.

"Army people; the Brits," he said.

"You mean the guys you met up with that night you got paralytic and threw up all over the veranda?"

"Yes."

"Are they still in the country?" I asked.

"Yes….. It's really dangerous work they're doing. They're up against guys with illegal pump guns. They have to move round in the dark and they have to live out rough in terrible conditions in all the heavy rains and mud being bitten by mossies while they're doing these stake-outs, waiting and watching suspects. Some of them are blokes my age that are still doing all this shit. They've all had broken marriages, some of them three or four times, and now they've given up on a home life and retirement and they've gone back to this kind of work with the army. What are blokes my age doing playing Rambo? I feel sorry for them. For the last few weeks before we came away, I let some of them stay in the gym under the house so they could get a shower and a kip on the mats in there."

"Really? Is that why you kept listening out for noises downstairs late at night?"

"Yes," he said with a chuckle. We walked down the steep, deserted road to the sun-drenched beach as he continued his train of thought. "They've got the most amazing equipment now for the work they have to do. I've never seen anything like it. They've got cameras on tiny telescopic antennae that they can push through the floorboards of a house from the ground below and swivel round to see what's going on in the room above and you wouldn't have a clue you were being watched. I didn't believe they could do what they said, so they told me to put the porn channel on the sky TV and they would be able to watch it from downstairs by using this antennae camera."

"So is that why you put the porn channel on that night the other week? I thought you were behaving strangely, especially since you've never shown any interest in putting it on before."

"They got a bit more than they were expecting though," he went on, "because they filmed you and me making love on the sofa in front of the television and then played back the tape of it to me when I met up with them the next time."

"What?" I said, horrified. I flushed with embarrassment. He saw my reaction and felt some need to exonerate himself from the plot.

"I didn't know they would be able to do that. They were all laughing. That's what army blokes get up to. They play pranks on each other. They started playing back the tape to me and I was expecting to see the Brazilian porn channel we watched and I saw this bald head and then I realised it was me and then the camera panned around and I saw you and me in action."

"I don't know what to say," I said, flushing. I was burning with a mixture of mortification at unknowingly having my intimate moments invaded and humiliation at the thought that the most private parts of my body had been exposed in public in a very unflattering way. "I'm really glad that you let them stay in the house and get some decent facilities to make their work a bit safer, but I feel terrible that you let them do that to me."

"I didn't know they were going to do that," he protested. "I hadn't got a clue they could position the antennae to look at the telly and then turn it round in the opposite direction to see what we were doing on the settee."

"But you knew they were going to watch the porn that night so you could have waited till we got in the bedroom before you started having sex. I wondered why you were behaving so strangely. I know we often get in the mood and do it in the lounge some nights when we're watching a film, but that night you had a sort of crazed look in your eyes that I've never seen before, like some sort of dirty old man in a mac about to expose himself."

"They gave me some of these tablets they get given to help them get an erection," he explained. "I took one that night to see if they worked. You know; that Viagra stuff."

"Well I suppose it did work, not that you needed it, so that's some small compensation," I laughed, trying to diffuse the feelings of shame I still had.

"I've got some more of the tablets here with me."

"Good! I'm in for a second honeymoon then. Or come to think of it, this will be the first because we didn't have one when we got married!"

We had by now walked down to the water's edge. I took off my flip-flops and began to let the waves lap over my toes as we continued along the shoreline.

"I feel really sorry for those guys all in their sixties, some of them past retirement age, yet they still have to do work for the army. One of 'em's wife died. The rest are divorced," he said.

"I suppose it gives them something to do and a purpose in life now they're here working in a warm country with a bunch of guys in similar situations. It's better than turning into a vegetable in a freezing cold house in an English winter, feeling self-pity."

"They're all envious of me having someone like you, half my age, looking fantastic and sexy like you do, and so much younger than you really are."

"Well I may look sexy when I'm fully dressed, but I'm not so sure about it when I'm completely naked, with white stripes and excess fat on all the bits normally covered up." I said, still feeling self-conscious and somehow robbed of something.

"One of them really fancies you. He actually carries a photo of you around in his wallet," he said, as if it would be of some consolation to me. I swung round, flushed with suppressed rage.

"How did he get a photo of me to put there? Did you give it to him?" I demanded.

"He took the picture himself," Edwin said. He was now attempting to bring all the charm and persuasion in his intelligence-training repertoire to bear on me so as to win me round as he usually did when he had annoyed me. This time, however, I felt it had gone far too far.

I always believed him on these kinds of topics because ever since I first met him, he had always been truthful with me in everything else that could easily have been a load of bullshit and never was. I had lived with him long enough to know that, so I took everything he said at face value. He wasn't the sort to spin a yarn like this just to tease me. Over the years he had confided so much in me about his special work in the army, because he found it easier talking to me than to the post-combat trauma shrinks the army had repeatedly put on his case years before he met me and whom he had refused to communicate with because they were

'Bloody civvies who don't understand what it's like. They've never had to go through what I went through and I'm not having them trying to get inside my head.' I had always made a case for them:

"They were only trying to help you cope mentally with what makes you have all those bad dreams you get." But he always snarled and spoke aggressively about the subject, so I always dropped it. Days, sometimes months later, he would unload his experiences on me because he now trusted me completely. He knew I would never pass on what he said, either to his family or mine or to people I knew. He knew I was not someone to go and gossip with neighbours or even a close friend. I certainly had hardly any friends that I still kept in touch with. It was difficult to keep contact with people when they lived on the other side of the Atlantic Ocean and hardly ever replied to letters because they didn't have time to write. He knew I would make no close adult friends in Guyana as I locked myself inside our little island in our village every day of the week teaching students who came to my little "bottom house" charity school. I was too busy and I hardly went out alone for my own safety and because I had little in common with the local adults. I was just a target for scams or favours. I knew this from our first years in the country. I was willing, in this context, to allow myself to be so isolated. He wanted to keep me where he knew where I was, so he could protect me from harm. At the same time it gave him the knowledge that he could confide some of his innermost secrets in me without fear that they would go any further.

"Oh, so I've been spied on and photographed by some sort of voyeur, have I?" I asked, indignantly. I now felt a mixture of protest and resignation over what seemed to be a matter of spilt milk. I might as well come to terms with it.

"It's only a tiny little picture," he said, as if that would make it any better. "He took it from a long distance when you were out on the veranda. They use this equipment they've got to blow up the size of the face from almost a pinprick in a landscape."

"So where was he when he was taking this picture?"

"He must have been in Jumbo-Jet's compound using a kind of periscope device to take pictures of things going on outside without being seen doing so," he said.

"He must be weird like some kind of stalker, taking a picture of a complete stranger like me and then carrying it around in his wallet as if I'm his girlfriend," I said, bemused.

"Oh don't be like that! He's a great guy. He was my best mate at boy's school when we were there together in the fifties. We used to share girlfriends sometimes. There was this girl Sylvia in Swanage that we shared. She didn't mind. When one of us was on duty the other one went out with her and vice versa."

"So she had the best of both worlds."

"She was a nice girl"

"It sounds like it!" I said with all the sarcasm I could muster. "So he thinks he can do that with your wife as well?"

"I would do it for him," he said. "I feel really sorry for him he's had five broken marriages. How can you be that unlucky? I wouldn't bother if the second marriage didn't work. I'd just go it alone. But five times. How can you marry five times? I feel so sorry for him. He told me he came back from an overseas intelligence job expecting one of his wives to meet him at the airport in a brand new car he had bought her with the money he'd earned on the job and 'd had delivered to their house, but when he got off his flight she wasn't there. He took a taxi home and found the house empty and she'd cleared off with the car and everything. "

"Oh dear that wasn't a very nice thing to do."

"No. He said another wife didn't like being away from mummy and had tantrums, like when he wouldn't drop everything to go to Switzerland to buy some special handbag she wanted. She said I want to go NOW and he couldn't because of his job, so in the end, he ditched her. Another one was a lot younger than him. He took her on a holiday to Venice and other parts of Italy. When they were in a hotel looking out of the window at a mountain peak he suggested climbing it and she wanted to go with him but part of the way up, she started to get panicky and hysterical so he had to pay for a helicopter to come and fetch her off the mountain because she couldn't cope with it."

"Sounds like he didn't know how to pick the right women," I said. Finding myself feeling sympathetic towards someone I had never met and whom only minutes before I had utter contempt for.

"He thinks I've been really lucky to find someone like you. He can't understand why a woman like you would be living in a place like Guyana doing what you're doing. He says any other English woman would have lasted five minutes there." Now I felt flattered and complimented. This stranger, this invisible man had become a friendly figure that must be every bit as honourable as my husband. Not some dirty old man wanking over a picture of some bit of stuff he had been staking out while he was whiling away the boring hours of a surveillance operation. This was the true art of chivalry at work. They had both learned it in their time in the cavalry. I was the damsel, the Rapunzel.

As we walked along the half empty beach I learned more and more about the invisible man. Edwin spoke in soft sexy tones about his friend of old and what he knew about him. I was building up a picture of him that completely dispelled any misgivings I initially had about being spied on and filmed. I felt aroused by the conversation. The sound of gently crashing waves and the setting of a tropical beach contributed to this feeling as warm sand oozed through the toes on my bare feet. We stopped for lunch in one of the beach side restaurants just as it was opening. We were the only customers. I was getting more and more curious about the invisible man as our chef-prepared seafood lunch came and Edwin's revelations expanded into the invisible man's food preferences. He liked prawn sandwiches with brown bread and had turned up his nose at the Kentucky fried chicken which Edwin had brought for them all as a treat from Georgetown. Clearly, he was a man of refined taste, I thought. I had learned that

Edwin had been getting food supplies for them while they were in our area and doing so in a way that concealed the presence of a sizeable group of men needing a month's rations to last them on covert stake-outs in the area at the back of us and along the coast where drug dealers were suspected of moving narcotics. The dealers brought the shipments into Guyana from Columbia and were moving them out across the Atlantic to Europe via Africa or to the USA via the Caribbean.

I gradually began to make sense of all the strange happenings I had noticed at home over recent months. The boot print in the pumpkin patch and the missing pumpkin; the disappearing washing powder; the submersible wreck at Brown Rat's hut; the green boiler-suit hanging in the changing room; the tin cup in the upstairs guest room shower; Edwin's state of anxiety when an "owl" supposedly flew at him on the veranda that night.

"It wasn't an owl at all was it?" I said.

"What do you mean?"

"That night when you met me on the veranda and told me you had just been scared by a low-flying owl going to get bats on the roof. It wasn't an owl was it? It was someone waiting on our veranda or under it and you just said it was an owl so I wouldn't suspect anything."

"Yes," he said, now it was safe for him to admit it because they had just gone away.

"I knew something strange was happening. For a start why would you suddenly start smoking the one cigarette a day after all these years of never smoking a puff? You never let people scare you, let alone the owl that's lived in the roof for years and regularly swoops for bats after dark when we're passing along the veranda. Its near misses never made you show such nervous shakes before. I can see how a human being that you are trying to hide in the house and who might just about be going to be spotted by me might make you react that way though," I said. I was remembering the time when I first met him and he had been like this just after being away on 'special work' that he had only admitted to years later when we were well established in Guyana. I had sent for an S.A.S. video which we began watching and saw some footage on it of a job he had taken part in. He was horrified to think this job was now showing him in masked form carrying out work which he had, up to that point, understood to be

485

secret and never to be revealed in public during his lifetime. He refused to watch it further because he said it gave him nightmares, so I put it back in the box and never looked at it again in his presence. I remembered at the time he actually did the job in the 1980s thinking that he must have been involved in news events I was watching on television, because of a sixth sense I felt about him based on his body language and the little he had already told me about his former military life. He had denied it when I had asked him so I had let it drop but hadn't believed his denial. An admission of sorts had occurred now he knew I would not tell anyone about it.

"And that's why you cut the tree down that enabled whoever it was to get up on the veranda," I continued, "You wanted to stop it happening again in case I actually caught them in the act the next time they might try to do it." He smiled without answering. It was the next best thing to saying 'Yes'.

"I wondered why you suddenly wanted to smoke a cigarette every night after I started making dinner. You knew once I was getting on with cooking, that I wouldn't be coming down that end of the house until after we'd eaten."

"The cigarette smoking was a signal to him that the coast was clear for him to get an update from me," he revealed. "I could then go downstairs in the dark and do what I had to do to communicate with him."

I had no further need of information from him to make sense of the riddles which had puzzled me. Now every strange happening would be due to the presence of covert operations in our house. It was little wonder that we had been branded as English spies when we had first arrived, even though the irony was that we had not been involved in any such thing back then. ...or had we? I would never know and did not really want to at this point. I was just happy that in some way, my presence in Guyana was helping to prevent the drugs trade from ruining so many lives. If I could have done anything myself to help them, I was willing to do so and told Edwin as much.

"I'm really fed up with being in Guyana," he said. "I can't stand the lies and the deceit. I can't stand the backwardness of everyone even the politicians. The house is falling down around our ears. I've had enough. I don't feel safe there. I don't want to spend the rest of my life doing this."

"I understand," I said, "but how can we leave? All we own in the world is here. Your pension will never support us both in England if we have to pay a mortgage or rent and I won't be able to get work easily after all these years of being out of the system. How will we ever be able to afford to buy a decent house with the way property prices in England are going through the roof, even if I do get any money from mum and dad's will? Not only that, we'll never get a cent for our house and land here in Guyana. Look at the trouble you had selling Reverend Pat's house and that was in the capital city. Who's going to want to buy a house the size of ours right out in the sticks where no proper business can survive? No one who wants to live or retire there will have the money to pay us what it is worth. "

"I know," he sighed. "There are plenty of people who will say they want to buy it but they'll never come up with the money. You sign an agreement and they pay a legal deposit and then you never get the rest of the money from them. Look at the trouble I've had so far trying to sell the snackette and that's only a tiny little place that ought to be affordable to at least some locals. It's been over fifteen years so far and all I'm doing is wasting money on lawyers whose only interest is to keep the case going as long as possible so they can squeeze a regular income out of a mug like me or an unwitting overseas expat."

"The only likely buyers would be some overseas person in England who wants to come back here and retire just like you did." I said. "It's a minefield of uncertainties, only this time we would be doing it in reverse. No one like that would be very encouraged to buy from us if they know we're going back. They would suspect that we were finding the place inhospitable and so that would make them wary. It's only because we've been here and are still here after all these years that people like that actually buy other small properties on the main road and install local family members in them to look after them for when they come back for a holiday, just like your brothers in Brooklyn have done. Who has actually come back to live here apart from Carl and Doreen? People like that don't have the kind of money we would need for our place even if they were honest enough to pay in full up front. At least here we own our own house and your pension can support us comfortably because the cost of living here is much lower than England. It just seems completely impossible."

The days went by and Edwin told me a little more each day about what was going on with the illicit drugs trade in our area and how he had helped the undercover forces to get information. He had been told that our house phone was bugged and he felt it was getting more and more dangerous in the country with death squads in the capital and first-world trained criminals now being repatriated back to Guyana from the USA who knew all the first world methods of criminal activity which were beyond the capacity of local police to deal with. He also fed me more titbits about the Invisible Man and his personality, his likes and dislikes. He was a mountaineering expert. I pictured a Ranulph Fiennes type of person. He was a loner, an adventurer, a very ambitious man. He owned a vineyard in the South of France with a large house which was currently being used as a rest and recuperation centre for military personnel coming back from war zones. There was a sunken bath and underfloor heating and a large number of bedrooms. He had shared it with his last wife before she had left him and "gone back to mummy".

When we got back to Guyana and went through customs as usual. There was a handsome, uniformed young English man working in the customs searching area who greeted Edwin with a knowing smile "Mr Joseph, Sir" as he waved us through. Our eyes locked in a gaze for an instant and he began to smirk as I passed him. I felt at that instant that somehow he must have seen the video of me naked, in intercourse. Why would he have smirked at me in that way otherwise? It gave me the creeps. I felt like a prostitute. Why? I was married and had been in the privacy of my own home. How dare he look at me like that?

In the next few weeks everything at home was extremely busy. I was taking enrolments for the new academic year all day long for the first few days and then when all the places had been filled up I had preparation to do and the classroom and lab to clean out. I had to organise all the teaching materials for the many subjects I had to teach to the various age-groups in my charge. I had a reputation to maintain and very high standards. Luckily there were no external syllabus changes that would have made all this impossible for one person to cope with, so the only changes that occurred over the years were ones I imposed on myself in order to modernise and improve my teaching. I did so along the same lines as seemed to be happening back in England with the help of the Channel Four videos I had been buying by mail order and the books we were being sent by my teacher friends in England, our Treviglas connection and past volunteers who kept in contact with us. Now everyone was using DVDs and we had some of that equipment from the Germans who had just left the area. If friends sent us useful DVDs I could show them to students on the new computer in the classroom that we had received from Dywidag.

Edwin was spending a lot of time out and about on local council business now Dywidag had left. The neighbourhood district stretched miles along the coast to include many villages and he wanted to visit all the areas regularly to oversee works and visit contractors who were doing it. Overseas development agencies were involved in projects which he also had to liaise with. A massive development work to reinforce the sea defences was underway and a new bridge was about to be built spanning the Berbice River which would open up the coast road between Guyana and neighbouring Surinam and remove the dependence of motorists on the old ferry service between Rosignol and New Amsterdam. Personnel from the World Bank and the European Union were often seen passing through the neighbourhood, so white faces were no longer the rarity they had been in the nineteen nineties.

The state of our roof had become a great worry to us by now. Over recent years, various forms of wildlife had taken up residence in it. First the colony of bats with Hoodwink, our owl, as their main predator; then the Africanised bees building their honeycombs between the double wood panelled walls in the lounge and study; termites whose trails had wreaked havoc in our library books in the study on their way up from the pasture via the picket fence and the softer pieces of outer wall panelling into the veranda roof; maribuntas, a kind of hornet, whose papery nests suspended from the backs of outdoor chairs and the veranda roof put their grubs in prime position to feast off the termites present in our timbers and lately we also had possums nesting in the attic. They had entered through rotten wood around the fascia boards and added a dimension of terror to our lives as they would urinate and defecate up there. Sticky orange coloured diarrhoea after their mango feasting would drip down on us through the joints between the planks of wood that made up our ceiling. It would never be in the same place so you couldn't predict where they would strike next. One night I had been at the table eating and it poured down onto the floor right next to my seat. "What if mess landed in our dinner another time?" I said as I mopped it up. I had already narrowly escaped getting it all over the bedding when one had decided to empty its load in a spot right over my side of the bed. It was the last straw. If I waited until Edwin found a local contractor capable of doing the job properly, it would never get done. There just weren't any that either of us had any confidence in. I decided to act myself, using the telephone and the yellow pages.

I managed to source a reputable building contractor from Georgetown to visit us and give us an estimate for replacing our old roof with a brand new bat-proof and leak-proof one. Desmond Correia impressed Edwin with a credible plan that would cost us six million Guyana dollars (over seventeen thousand pounds).

Now where would we get the money from? We discussed it after he left. We would transfer the five thousand pounds we had saved up in the joint account in England. I would let him have the six thousand pounds I had received as an initial payment from my parents' will. The final six thousand he would get as a loan on the premier card and pay it off as his future pensions came into his account. He signed up the contract with Desmond and workers and materials all arrived in October and November. There were a few hiccups in transferring such large sums of money from England to Guyana. We were afraid the local branch of Scotia Bank were holding onto it and making out it hadn't arrived, but apparently it was due to new money laundering regulations which we understood. Eventually the money arrived and the new roof was completed by the end of November. It was just in time as we had overseas visitors due to arrive on 4th December. It made a massive difference to our lives now the wildlife had all been banished out of our home and back to the trees where they belonged. It was the talk of the village because Desmond's supervisor employed quite a few of our neighbouring young men as labourers. There was also some resentment by village contractors that they had missed an opportunity to defraud us of more money just as they had done in the original build.

Edwin soon let on to me that he was still helping the Invisible Man and his anti-narcotics force by getting food supplies for them, but only now and again when they needed them to be dropped off at positions in their secret interior locations. They were no longer staying in our house but had moved far out into "the backdam". One evening, he was looking very down and preoccupied and I pressed him to tell me what was troubling him so much. Eventually he let on that one of the old soldiers he had been helping had been shot while he was doing surveillance in the Abary Creek. Edwin had helped organise his evacuation out of the country for medical treatment and had been worried about the poor man's fate. "I told them not to trust those Amerindian girls, but they think they know better than me," he said. "They got him while he was asleep in one of the Amerindian houses."

"Why was he sleeping there?" I asked.

"He got friendly with one of the Amerindian girls and her family turned on him. He shouldn't have been fooled by their friendliness. Not only that but they stole a lot of his equipment off him including his weapon. It's really serious. Once you get gunpowder in a wound it takes a long time to heal and causes all kinds of complications whoever you are, but to get that sort of wound when you're his age is much more serious because healing takes even longer and it may never heal properly."

I understood his mood and asked no more. After a few days he came back from a trip to Georgetown and said he had word that the old boy had made a recovery and was going to be all right. That evening, I asked him if he had seen the Invisible Man lately. He smiled, so I knew he had. Then while we were lying in bed in the dark with the ocean breeze blowing over us, he began to tell me what they had been talking about that day. I was the topic of their conversation. He really liked me and had promised Edwin that the video of us had been wiped.

"It's not that I'm trying to get rid of you or anything. I just think I'm not able to satisfy your needs like I used to, so with two of us, it would be better for you. That way he could have you as well." I was disturbed at the idea of the last bit.

"How could I do that when I don't even know what he looks like? I don't even know his name," I said. "At the very least I have to find someone physically attractive."

"Oh you'll like him. His name is 'Rick'. He's a very good looking man."

"It's for me to decide that," I said. "How old is he?"

"He would be about a year or two older than me."

"So he's some balding geriatric with bad breath,"

"No not at all. He's very tall and strong and has a full head of hair."

"If he looks anything like Jock, you can forget it. There's no way I could find him attractive enough to want sex with him."

"No, he's nothing like Jock."

"Even if he were better looking and sexier than you are, I don't want to get AIDS or any other STD," I said.

"There's no risk of that with Rick," he said.

"How can I be sure of that when you've already told me that one of his men was shot while he was sleeping with some Amerindian girl in the creek?"

"Rick wouldn't expose himself to anything of the sort. His own health and career are very important to him. I just feel so sorry for him that he can't enjoy what I'm enjoying because none of his five wives were as understanding of him as you are of me, so he has no-one in his life to come back to. The man is risking his life for his country. He has the kind of job that means he has to go where he's told to go. People can come and take him away in the middle of the night and he might be away for weeks or months without being able to communicate with home. I just think that it would be nice for him to have you to come back to. It's not that I'm pushing you away from me or that I don't want you. You would have me all the rest of the time but I'd be sharing you with him when he needed you."

At this point I found myself feeling sorry for Rick, whom I had never met or even seen. I began to wonder what he looked like. I pictured the tall powerfully built white man I had seen staring at me searchingly in Fogarty's the previous Christmas. He had a large scar down one cheek and his haunting blue eyes had caught me like a searchlight and followed me across the store. It had been unsettling because I had wondered why he had singled me out. I supposed I had stood out, being the only white woman in the store and with my long blonde hair in contrast with everyone else's short black frizzy cornrows, it would catch anybody's eye. He had looked like a military man in civilian clothes. I recalled that I had found him attractive but a little frightening. It was the scar I suppose. Was this Rick, I wondered?

"Does he have a scar on his cheek?" I asked Edwin.

"Why do you ask?" he said. I told him about the scar-faced man resembling the film actor Tom Berenger I had seen in Fogarty's.

"Don't call him scar-face," he said. "It's not nice. It's not his fault if his job left him disfigured."

"I'm sorry I didn't mean it like that. It's just that it was noticeable and it made him look a bit fierce and aggressive." I never got an answer to my question, but from the response I got, I assumed the scarred man must have been "Rick".

"He can't understand why someone like me is still in a place like Guyana," continued Edwin. "He likes all those cultures of the Far East, Nepal and the Himalayas. He thinks the Himalayan landscape and the Sherpa culture is far more interesting than here. He says the Sherpa women have more than one husband, because there aren't enough women to go round."

"Sounds like the kind of culture that would suit me," I joked. I kept thinking about what he had said over the next few weeks and every time I did, I pictured the man I had seen in Fogartys. Here was my husband feeding me information about a man he knew who admired me, and I was building up a montage in my mind of a character who was beginning to turn me on. I was beginning to be seduced by the Invisible Man. I couldn't get him out of my head. Like the Flying Tiger, he came to me in the night and opened every sense in my body to let the passion pour out in uncontrolled torrents. I would be there for him, as long as Edwin wanted me to. I would have two husbands who both loved me and loved each other like brothers. That's what SAS blokes did for each other. I was the kind of wife who had understanding for the undercover military man. I even felt I could do that work myself, but knew I did not have the physique or skills needed. If I was realistic, I could not be of any use because I had not undergone the training and most likely wouldn't even have been selected. At least I could help in this little way if it would help a close friend of my husband to have some happiness to return to and to live for. I told Edwin that I agreed to the idea in principle, but I would need to see what he looked like, and meet him so I could get an idea if he was a person I could get to like.

"That will be difficult," he said. "These guys are working undercover so they won't allow themselves to be exposed to people who know the kind of work they're doing. He'd have to come here in the dark at night when no one else knew except me and you." The next day, he pulled an old photo out of one of his albums and showed me a tall young man in his twenties taken with a bunch of friends back in the 1960s. He was good looking then, but what would he look like now? He didn't look anything like the scar-faced man I had seen, though. For the moment I would be in suspense, wondering whether a silent figure would one night creep from the fields at the back into our farm and break into our home in pitch darkness in order to meet me.

The work we had to do for the smooth running of the school took over our lives as usual, and my main preoccupation was Edwin's role in the students' curriculum as far as sport and first aid was concerned. He also continued to monitor his sports teachers who had recently completed his sports leaders' award. This meant he had to help them organise school leagues and sporting fixtures in all the sports he had taught them. He had begun arranging a 'Volleyball Extravaganza' in our region for all primary and secondary schools to participate in, so he was liaising with the Regional Education Officer and the head of the Guyana Volleyball Federation to bring this about. We were expecting two women, Roz and Suzanna, from the British Sports Trust to stay with us in December to validate our school as the official centre in the country, indeed of the entire Caribbean at that time, for the delivery of their courses. They would witness the work of the teachers and youth leaders he had trained at Sapodilla. The British High Commissioner had obtained funding for their air fares from England and while the visitors were still with us, he was going to bring his wife down to an open day at our school to present the Sports Leaders Award certificates to Edwin's trainees.

Edwin's volleyball extravaganza in May had been a great success in publicising the game through the schools of the region at all levels from nursery through to secondary. It had been one of the fixtures Edwin had organised to get his sports leaders to put their learning into practice. He expected the teachers to be able to stand on their own feet and continue to organise events like this in the way he had shown them. Edwin also thought that Lenny Shuffler, the Federation president, would see how he did it and do the same thing in the other regions. Lenny was invited to our December presentation with the teachers and overseas guests and while he was there, took the opportunity to tap up the High Commissioner for funding to enable the roll out of the volleyball extravaganza to schools on the other side of the Berbice River. Edwin made clear that he would have no involvement with that programme, however. He believed in showing the way and letting others follow his example without needing him to be there doing everything himself. That was the underlying principle on which he had undertaken the sports leaders' course in the first place. He knew that qualifications from England were held in high esteem by locals. His aim was to get authorised centre verification for Sapodilla Learning Centre to put on these courses for all local teachers so that once he was satisfied that they had been properly trained and tested, they would replicate what they had been taught and it would roll out through the schools to clubs and sporting bodies so as to eventually lift the standard of sport in the country. It was ambitious but he was prepared to expend enormous personal energy and resources to make it happen.

The presentation day came and was another great occasion for the local community to enjoy with their village as a media focus and important dignitaries present. British High Commissioner Stephen Hiscock and his wife Dee not only met the two sports leaders that the British Government had funded to get to us, but also presented the awards to all the participants and declared open our new "Mitch Mason Centre" for home economics which we had completed in August and started using with the current full time students when school reopened in October. Dee was speaking to Edwin and the overseas visitors while Stephen Hiscock chatted with me about the porta-kabins.

"Ideally, we needed a much bigger, purpose-built room but that would have cost thousands of pounds more than we could ever hope to raise from supporters," I told him. "These cabins were a compromise and even they were far more costly than our own resources could stretch to. If it hadn't been for the generosity of the Poole Runners and the extended family of Mitch Mason as a funeral tribute to him, we would not even have what we now have."

"Isn't it a bit hot inside them while you're trying to cook with all those ovens?" he asked me.

"Well, yes," I explained, "That's why I arranged it so that all the cookers and the fridges are in the best cabin with its toilet compartment, but the worktops, sinks and equipment storage are all in the cabin we had to repair. It had more room in it, because the toilet was ripped out by the thieves that broke into it. The extra space allowed us to fit it out to accommodate all the students simultaneously while they're doing preparation. That one has its windows and doors open all the time, so it gets the cooling breeze flowing through it. When they have to use the cookers, they go round to the other cabin and so they don't have to stand inside it with all the heat for any longer than it takes to put something in an oven or take it out and set food to cool. The windows are all open when it's in use but can be closed and locked for security once the class has finished for the day."

"Edwin has been telling me that there's possible room for expansion into the pasture behind your house," he casually added.

"Oh well, yes, technically, I suppose there is," I said, "but it's unlikely that we'll ever be in a position to afford to do that. In any case, the existing owners are locked in an inheritance dispute that could go on unsettled for years." I added. I wondered why Edwin had mentioned expansion. I began to feel that I had supplied the High Commissioner with information that contradicted what Edwin had told him.

That night, when we were basking in the feel-good factor that the day's activities had left us with, I told Edwin about my conversation with Stephen

Hiscock. "Why did you tell the High Commissioner that we were considering expansion into the pasture behind us?" I asked him, "I told him about the Isaac family dispute over it. I don't know why he was interested enough to ask me such a question. I hope I didn't talk out of turn."

"I've been trying to find out whether they can buy our property for the use of aid workers to live in when they're working in this rural community. That way they would have a safe local base to operate from instead of renting lodgings from locals who then turn on them," he said.

"So what happens to us then?" I asked. "This is our home, where will we go? What happens to the school?"

"I don't feel safe here," he sighed. "I don't want to stay here any longer. I've outstayed my welcome long ago."

"What do you mean?"

"I mean that I don't fit into this culture and I can't get through to these people. They're all backward. It's all right for you. Everyone can see the effect of all your hard work with the school and the exam results. I haven't achieved anything that I set out to do and I'm not accustomed to failing."

"You haven't failed," I counselled. "Your problem is that you expect things to happen too quickly. It takes years for the kind of change you want to see to actually happen."

"It's not just that. It's too dangerous here now the way things are going and I don't like being asked to spy on my own people. It puts us both at risk because we're so exposed here." I knew he was right.

"How could we leave, though? Our whole lives have been dedicated to this country for the past fifteen years and I don't think I could fit back into England now. It's changed so much with all the new technology and the way people live their lives. It's the opposite of everything I stand for. I hate the cold. Even the summer's freezing when everyone else thinks it's hot! After talking to Roz and Suzanna from the Sports Trust it sounds as if standards in English schools have gone right down. You can now be a teacher without even having a degree! That's how schools were before the reforms of the 1970s!"

"We wouldn't have to live in England. We could go to one of the islands or somewhere else hot. Anywhere's better than here," he said with a finality to end the conversation. Then he rolled over in bed and turned his back on me. I lay in the dark in turmoil. It was some time before I could get to sleep.

Christmas came and went. School reopened amid heavy rains. I was getting on with marking and lesson preparation. Edwin was training Kesha who was now in the sixth form, waiting for her officer cadet course with the GDF to commence and Edwin was beasting her in training. She was up for it and was one of the first girls we had ever had who was prepared to turn up in the pouring rain to train in it. In fact she was beating all the boys we had ever had. In connection with getting her entry organised, Edwin was making lots of trips to Ayangana, the military HQ in Georgetown, and also running from one end of the region to the other to visit nursery schools to set up arrangements for his sports teachers to put on a nursery school potted sports competition in February.

One night in January, he had a terrible nightmare in his sleep. I woke up because he was kicking me as if he was dreaming about being in a fight with someone but unfortunately it was me who got the kicking. I shouted in pain as I awoke and realised what was happening. Reflexes had saved me from a worse injury than just bruising, making me jump out of bed. Then I shook him and called his name in order to wake him up. When he had regained his senses I told him what he had done and he was mortified. We spent some time talking him down from the shock and the trauma. He had obviously been spooked by something he had been involved in during the recent weeks. All he kept talking about was getting away from Guyana and the kind of people he was working with now that Rick and his men had apparently left our area after Christmas and gone elsewhere in South America. They would not be coming back. Apparently he had been at our house at Christmas and Edwin had taken him into our lounge for a Christmas drink before they hugged and said their goodbyes. I had been in bed asleep and all this had happened in the early hours of the morning.

"He asked me to go with him but I said I couldn't leave you here alone. He understood and said it was a pity because they needed me back on the team," Edwin told me. "It was very sad. He sat right there on your rocking chair on the corner of the veranda. I went to Mahaica the other day and I had to check over the place where they'd been to see that they hadn't left any tell-tale clues behind. I had to walk miles out into the middle of nowhere. It was late at night when I was on the way back from Georgetown. I got into a bit of a situation and

I don't really want to talk about it but I'm getting more and more to dislike this place. It wasn't a problem when I was working with the Boss and his team because I know I can trust them. We would do anything for each other. We've both been trained to be the best and we don't make mistakes in that sort of thing. I can't work with people I don't know and I can't trust any of them. They haven't had the same training and they don't work to the same standards. I don't want my life to be put at risk by some idiot who makes mistakes. I never have liked Yanks and now the Boss has gone, I'm told I have to work with them and the Canadians as well as people from the European Union. I gave my word that I would help them as they took over from the Brits who left, but no one understands how exposed we are here. Everyone in the country knows my jeep and I can't go anywhere without being spotted and followed. Our phone line's being tapped and strange people on motorbikes keep coming down this street looking in here as they go past us to visit Ramsammy on some pretext."

"Well, if it's making you feel like this what do you suggest doing about it?"

"Rick's got his own vineyard in France with a large house. He'll be going back there after he finishes the assignment in South America. We could go and live there with him, as a threesome. He says it's a luxurious place with a sunken bath and underfloor heating, so you needn't worry about the cold weather. He's got three more years to do before he finally retires, so he wouldn't be there much to start with."

"He might not like me when he gets to know me. I can't believe a grown mature man who's had five failed marriages would seriously consider living with someone he hasn't even met even if he has seen me and finds me physically attractive. What if we get on each other's nerves?" I said. "You can't just jump into something like that. Does he smoke? I couldn't live in a house with someone who did."

"No he doesn't smoke, He's like you, into healthy food and all that. He goes off climbing a lot because he's into mountaineering in a big way, so that and his work would mean he would be away a lot of the time."

"So what would you do if we went there?"

"They would have work for me to do. When I was away doing it, he could be there and take you out. He says there are some nice shops in the area near his house. He's into theatre and opera and all that stuff you like. At the moment

498

he's reading "Paradise Lost". He quite likes the idea of being able to take you out to functions when he needs a female companion to be with him." I felt a bit alarmed at the thought of my husband going off indefinitely to unknown places to do work, leaving me to be entertained by someone I had never met. It sounded unreal, but I could never be sure with Edwin. He claimed to have done outrageous things in the past so I believed anything was possible with him.

"I'm not sure I would like that if I didn't know where you were," I said.

I began to wonder whether Edwin was at last trying to find a way of ditching me. I began to feel a little insecure. Ever since I had been married to him I had noticed times when he seemed to be restless and struggling to break free from whatever environment he had put himself in. His feelings of frustration vented on me put me into a state of anxiety which I would never be in if it were not for having him in my life. I would be in this state on and off for days until he was distracted by another project he had initiated and decided to throw himself into. All I could do was to try and talk him round to some sense of reason.

"I just want you to be happy," he said.

"I am happy.... doing what we are doing here, with you," I said, "but if *you're* not happy then I can't be happy. What really would make you happy?"

"I want to be out of here in a place where I can relate to the people I'm mixing with. Nothing happens here. It's all so backward. There'll never be any progress."

"So if I agreed, what would happen to the school, our house and all our stuff?"

"I don't really care. We could get whatever we wanted. We would be looked after for the rest of our lives. Rick's got plenty of money and I would be able to earn plenty as well."

"You've made him sound like someone with a privileged background. Surely he wouldn't want to give up his bachelor lifestyle to have people like us cluttering up his life."

"What do you mean, people like us?" he snapped, defensively. "We go back a long way, Rick and me. He was my best friend."

"Maybe he was but you're not eighteen year old boys any more. He hasn't seen you for over thirty years. Perhaps he's forgotten what you're really like."

"It's something you wouldn't understand. We were buddies. We went through a lot together. He saved my life. That's how close we are. He'll do anything for me and I'll do anything for him."

"Well if you feel like that about him, he must be a very special person," I said, "and if that's what you really want, then I'll do it if it will make you happy."

I was troubled a bit by Edwin's nightmare that night, and what he had repeatedly said to me in private ever since he had first suggested that he could share me with Rick, who for me was the Invisible Man. His words "I'm not trying to get rid of you, I just want you to be happy" far from reassuring me, made me begin to wonder if he was going to murder me in his sleep. Maybe I was an encumbrance that he could not find any other way to rid himself of. Was Rick going to lure me away to a place where an unfortunate accident would happen to me just in case I really knew too much? It was an idea that kept haunting me, but I kept pushing it to the back of my mind.

A few days later, Edwin had to go up to a place far up the coast to where overseas contractors were working on the sea defences. He said, as NDC Chairman, he had to see overseas diplomats about the funding of the sea defence works in our region. When he got back at dusk, he was excited about something he wanted to tell me.

"I made contact with the Boss today and told him you had agreed to the plan. I got told to tell you to have an overnight case ready with a change of clothes so we can leave at a moment's notice if someone comes to pick us up. They'll take us out through Cayenne to the airport and to France and a car will pick us up and take us to Rick's house where we'll be safe. Then you'll get to meet him."

I was shocked. "What about all my jewellery? I said. I can't leave that here if we do a moonlight flit."

"There'll only be room for minimal luggage in the vehicle. We mustn't draw attention to ourselves. You can only take hand luggage with you; just one piece. You won't have to worry about clothes. Rick has loads of money. You'll be able to go out and buy a whole set of new clothes when you get to his place."

The next evening after school had finished and we had eaten, we both sorted out our overnight cases and packed them ready to go. I put my jewellery into a soft fabric roll that would fit into the case at the last minute. We put them in a corner of our bedroom and there they sat, staring back at us, reminding me of the dramatic change our lives could take at any minute. Meanwhile, I would carry on with my daily work as if I were going to run the school at full pelt for the next two decades at least.

Sisters Cherie and Tookie, the last surviving siblings of the Munroe Family, were due to arrive to stay with us in February in order to visit the graves of their loved ones as they did every couple of years. Edwin had organised the teachers to put on their regional nursery school potted sports day during their visit so the two old ladies could go along and watch it. He had made further contact with Rick and been told that he was coming back from his latest tour of countries and would be visiting us at Sapodilla on 14th of February to discuss the final arrangements about our plans.

"Oh no," I reminded Edwin, "Sisters Cherie and Tookie will be with us then. Surely he won't want to be meeting them. He'll want to be alone with us in the house."

"You're right," said Edwin, "It had slipped my mind about them being here. It'll be all right, though. We can meet him in our bedroom. He'll come late at night and will know where we are. He'll be able to get in for himself."

Valentine's Day arrived and so did Sisters Cherie and Tookie. Luckily, at eighty five, Cherie wanted to go to bed early and so did we. I had placed them in the two spare rooms farthest away from ours. If Rick came, he would have to climb in for himself. He would have to get up on the water tank near the rocking chair where he had sat when he was last in our house. We would leave the security lights off when we went to bed so that it would be too dark for anyone to spot him doing this. He would know where we were and would tap on the glass when he arrived and wanted to come in. Edwin had got a bottle of Champagne from Georgetown to celebrate when he got there. We had it waiting in the room with three glasses but we wouldn't open it until he arrived. Midnight came and went. We lay in bed in the darkness, with a Bill Withers album playing quietly in the background, whispering about Rick and our plans and what we would do when he arrived. The hours ticked on and it was past three o'clock. We lost count of the number of times we made love while listening out for the tap on the sliding glass doors. Eventually we fell asleep and woke up at daybreak. He hadn't showed up. Perhaps he was held up and would come tonight instead. Perhaps he had second thoughts about getting involved with us after all. He had never met me and I only had Edwin's word for it that he was in favour of the plan. Maybe Edwin had misunderstood what had been going on. Maybe it had been a ploy to recruit him and leave me to get on with it.

Once again no one came in the night. By dawn, Edwin was sulking. He never let anyone down when he made a promise, why did other people let him down? He had to go off later in the day while I was keeping the elderly ladies entertained. Thank God it was half term and I had no classes to teach until the following week. I felt half dead after our two sleepless nights but summoned up the necessary energy to entertain the guests. I had also been arranging the return flights for us both to go to Sydney, Australia during the Easter vacation where my niece Emma was getting married. We would have to go via London and change flights there. I had done this on the internet, now we had this facility. I booked up a hotel in London and tickets to a musical show while we were there. I also booked our hotel rooms at the stopover hotel in Kuala Lumpur and in Sydney for the two weeks as well as tickets for a Mozart concert at the Sydney Opera House. It would be the trip of a lifetime paid for by my recent inheritance.

When Edwin came back, he managed to get a private moment with me to tell me that he had called up his contact at the British High Commission to find out what had happened. There had been terrible storms overnight in North America and all flights had been grounded so Rick had been stuck in Barbados unable to get a flight to Guyana. He was very apologetic. We would not get to see him now. He was headed off for his next mission somewhere in the Pacific. However, Edwin had passed on all the details of our Easter trip, travel and hotel arrangements to the contact. It could happen that we would be met and picked up for our rendezvous with Rick at any point in this itinerary.

Chapter 24

A Bad Dream

There are times in everyone's life when things don't go according to plan. The two months leading up to our great adventure across the world were fraught with unexpected and life-changing challenges. Edwin's teachers failed him in their potted sports competition at the Guysuco Estate in Blairmont, because they left all the preparation to him. He allowed himself to become dehydrated in order to ensure the event was a resounding success but ended up with a severe urinary tract infection which only antibiotics could cure. Although he had appeared to recover while he resumed his council duties with funding agencies, he was unaware of underlying health problems that this infection had triggered. At the time, he was helping the local police force and the local Special Forces to tackle rising crime, now that convicted first world criminals with all their skills and equipment were being repatriated to Guyana by the US government. Edwin was travelling up to the sea wall at Foulis and elsewhere to meet overseas contacts who could communicate with Rick, now promoted to colonel. The offer of France was still open to us, but we would have to travel there and be met by people Edwin did not know. He refused to do that. He would only go there if Rick were there to meet us and show us around. Was it going to happen while we were in transit to or from Australia?

Back at the school, one Sunday in March we got news that Tanza, one of our full time girls, had drunk poison and killed herself. The shock and horror of this was ameliorated to some extent by learning later that she had recovered in hospital and so the process of welcoming her back to school with sensitive understanding began. She had quarrelled with her parents over a boyfriend she was seeing that they did not approve of. Amid this crisis we learned that Tegana, whom we had trained up for a boxing scholarship in England with the Poole Boxing Club, had been pulled out of our school before he could take his exams because his mother had got her papers through to migrate to the USA. This kind of thing was a problem I had to live with just as the Guyana Government had to live with it. It becomes soul destroying if you keep training people in skills to benefit their home country, when in the end they migrate, taking their skills with them to a far wealthier country so their homeland can never develop. It was particularly annoying to me in that I had been unpaid for doing the training, and only did so in order to help the poverty-stricken country

I was living in to develop. If I had known I was providing free education for the future population of the USA, I would have expected to be paid the same as a US state teacher!

By mid-March, all Edwin's travelling around day and night to help achieve improvements in the standards of local government, public health, education, sport, law and order, pulled his health back down. He became weak, developed flu-like symptoms and vomited up any food he ate. He lost his appetite and could not get out of bed. Hiccups started and remained with him for weeks, only subsiding while he was asleep. I would have to get him to England to a doctor or he would starve himself to death. He pulled himself together enough by the beginning of April to put in place the systems needed to cover our absence over the Easter vacation. We closed up the school on April 8th and set off for England three days later. By this time he was skin and bones. He willed himself enough strength to endure the twenty four hour non-stop travelling via Trinidad to Heathrow. As soon as we were at Carmen's house and she had gone to work, he collapsed and became bedridden again.

Rafer's doctor in Basingstoke diagnosed Edwin with diabetic hyper-glycaemia and told me I should cancel the Australia trip. Edwin was immediately admitted into hospital, put on rehydration fluid and an insulin drip and kept there for eight days. Sitting in the chair beside his hospital bed, I read just about every book available on diabetes and how to care for diabetics. I learned things I had never understood about the disease and diet. I was shown how to inject him with insulin and test his blood sugar and told this would have to happen for the rest of his life. This was because his pancreas no longer produced any insulin. I would now have to be his eyes and ears. In fact I was his twenty-four-seven carer. A nurse was the last thing I had ever wanted to be, but I had been selected for the role by a power greater than either of us and I alone was responsible for keeping him alive. Privately, I cried my heart out. It was eight days that changed both of our lives for ever.

Our return flight had to go ahead before Edwin had fully recovered. A blister on the sole of his foot had not healed and had not been treated at the hospital. Neither of us knew how to dress it properly. It was steadily getting worse. Travelling and walking on it did not help matters. The transatlantic flight was worrying as the time difference led to complications about when he should take his insulin injections. We had a huge insulated bag of medications and special equipment with no knowledge of how we would obtain a supply in Guyana, apart from an assurance from the manufacturers in Denmark that they would be able to sell us six months' in advance through their agent in the Caribbean who in turn supplied a company in Guyana. Anyone who has ever had to negotiate Heathrow Airport with a passenger in a borrowed wheelchair will know what a nightmare that is. The ancillary staff there spoke no English and had come from Bosnia or some other Eastern European country with little concern for efficiently responding to disabled air passenger needs. Borrowing a wheelchair to disembark in Barbados proved much easier than it had done in London. Even Guyana had no trouble quickly whisking one out to us when it was requested. Edwin suffered badly on the ten hour flight to get home. His sugar levels rocketed to double figures while in mid-flight and he was shivering uncontrollably for quite a long time until his blood sugar dropped down again.

Jolly was shocked to meet us at the airport and see Edwin in a wheelchair. In April, when Jolly had waved goodbye to us, Edwin appeared to be his normal fit and healthy self. Now it was May, the dismay on Jolly's face was plain.

"Ya look like cripple," he said in disbelief. After explaining what had befallen him, and how grateful he felt to be alive, Edwin asked Jolly what had been happening in the country while we were away.

"Oh, big shoot out in tong', Joe," he said. "Minister of Fisheries and he entire family gunned down in zey own house,"

"What? That's Sahadeo Sawh! You remember Jane? He used to be Minister of Tourism."

"Oh my God, yes," I said. "How terrible! He's the little man who came to see our place when it first opened and told us we would have to have a second staircase for safety regulations. I'm very sorry to hear he's been killed. Do they know why?"

"Zem say drugs, Auntie Jane," Jolly said, leaving the rest to my imagination. The media were full of the tragedy and since all our papers had been delivered to the house in our absence, Edwin was able to read all about it when we got home.

"Remember how Sahadeo Sawh visited us when he was Minister of Tourism in the PNC government under Desmond Hoyte?" I said to him. "He had to come down from Georgetown in a minibus as I remember, and walked down to see us from where it dropped him off on the main road."

"Yes," he said, "and you have to ask yourself: how is it that he got himself so advanced in such a few years? He went to Canada and was off the scene for a while. Since he came back, the PPP appointed him Minister of Fisheries. He never went anywhere without being in a convoy of four or five black SUVs with blacked out windows..... I'm glad we were in England when all this happened."

"Why? Were your people involved in this?" I asked. He looked knowingly at me but said nothing.

The May-June rainy season had already started and Sapodilla was wet and muddy everywhere when we arrived. We spent a day unpacking, cleaning up the house and getting in food. I made some calls to the insulin supplier I had been referred to by Novomix in Denmark and then got Jolly to take us back to Georgetown to sort out a supply of sugar test strips, needles to fit the injection pen Edwin had been started on in England and order the same insulin cartridges that he had been prescribed. Edwin stayed upstairs in the house most of the time trying to rest his blistered foot, so had to conduct his village office duties from the house. A stream of visitors came daily to get his signature or instructions. I was teaching the students downstairs in the classroom, lab or in the porta-kabin kitchens, then going up to see if he needed anything when there was a break in lessons.

We had been back two weeks and Edwin's blister was still not healing. He told me to boil some water, add salt and let it cool down, which I did. I trusted him to know what to do to clean it himself. After all he was a trained army paramedic who knew more about these things than I did. However, neither of us realised that due to diabetic neuropathy he had lost all feeling in his feet, so had immersed them in water that was far too hot. Three of his toes came up with massive blisters all over them. Now the problem was a good deal worse. I had to call the doctor out to the house. Thank God we had a telephone now. He was not able to come until the following day. When he arrived and examined the foot, he said the blister was a diabetic ulcer. He explained that the dead skin on the scalded toes would have to be pared away and dry dressings applied and replaced every day. He did this job and showed me how to do the dressing so I could change it every day. I did not tell Edwin, but I was feeling scared as hell. I could see him ending up with an amputated foot. The thought of dealing with such a disability in the environment we were living in was terrifying. I couldn't let this happen to him. In any case, he had to return to North Hants Hospital for a three month check-up, so I booked return flights for us to England as soon as I could. We would be going back on July 20th and Royden and Eldio, our two students who had been looking after the property while we were away at Easter, were happy to come back again and do the summer holiday as well. They wanted to earn the money. By the time we were due to leave, the foot had improved a lot but was still not completely right.

It was a relief to be back in England where we could get the hospital to treat the problem with the correct dressings that would promote quicker healing. Although we had arranged to stay with the children for the first few weeks, I had booked a cottage in a farm near my parental home where my brother was now living. My brother had sold our aunt's farmhouse in order to pay the inheritance tax and share out the proceeds between us, but we still jointly owned mum and dad's house and most of Aunty Lorna's farmland. We would have to have a family meeting to decide how to proceed. Guy needed a home and had no job to buy us out, but I did not want to give up my share of any potential income from the future sale of it. I had no pension to look forward to any more than he did. Could Edwin and I build on the farmland my siblings and I had kept?

We both wondered if Rick would visit us while we were at the cottage. All our travel details had been communicated to him before we left Guyana. We were kept in suspense after a mutual friend telephoned us while we were staying at one of the children's. Rick was now on a three year diplomatic mission in Asia so would not retire till he had fulfilled it. Edwin would do nothing until Rick had retired and was free to meet us. We had three years to work out how to transition the school so it could continue in someone else's hands. Uncertainty hung over us both but we were excited by the prospect of a mystery visitor while we were in England, so we could formulate plans for the future.

I bought a new laptop and began to learn how to use it. Since I would be travelling back and forth across the Atlantic or elsewhere regularly now, I needed to be able to communicate on the move. By the time we were ready to fly back to Guyana on the 4th September, Edwin was well on the way to full recovery. His ulcer had completely healed, his sugar control was excellent; he had regained his lost weight and a lot of his lost muscle strength and was getting back his lost confidence. He would have to have a cataract operated on in one eye the following summer, so we needed to save up for a return flight next year and another stay at the rented cottage. Since he had not appeared this time round, maybe then Rick would show up.

Chapter 25

The Real Pirates of the Caribbean.

The antelope grass around the fishpond at the back of the farm had grown six feet high during July and August and could be harbouring dangerous wildlife such as alligators. Royden and Eldio were supposed to have kept it trimmed and generally maintained the grounds while we were away but they had neglected it. They may have assumed that we would not return, having seen how the diabetes affected Edwin in the final term before the summer holiday. Edwin was not pleased. He got the boys to come in and cutlass the grass down. There was always such a lot of cleaning for me to do in the house and classrooms whenever we returned from a long trip away. Lizards continued to leave their droppings all over the skirting boards and flooring, although since the new roof had been installed, there were no longer buckets full of bat dung to sweep up in the rooms. Once we had been to town to collect Edwin's six month supply of insulin, pay the mortgage and buy essential supplies, I was able to reopen school two weeks after our return.

Edwin by now felt well enough to start teaching his new Sports Leaders Course and to set in motion his new employment projects at the Village Office. He was trying to organise the manual cleaning of the drainage channels by the unemployed in each village for an agreed wage. Prior to this, the job had been done mechanically by contractors with backhoes. This was fine for the contractors, who charged huge rates for the work. It was not as good for the inhabitants of many coastal villages as it meant very few canals could be tackled each year because of the cost. The clogged waterways resulted in flooding of villagers' homes. It seemed common sense to Edwin to get them done manually because it would be cheaper, so more trenches could be cleaned. If unemployed villagers got paid for doing the work in their own villages, it would provide them with an income to feed their families and their money would circulate back into the local economy. In all the local villages, there were unemployed young men who were willing to do such work when Edwin explained to them what his terms were.

Carol retired from the village Office that December. She had only been doing the job for a year or two. Her predecessor as CEO, Berta, had been in the post for her entire working life, having 'inherited' the role from her Aunt, head teacher of a local primary school. Berta had applied for an extension to continue in employment after retirement, but Edwin had refused.

"It's only fair that Carol should have a turn at the senior post since she'll be retiring herself in a couple of years' time and if she doesn't do it now she'll never get the chance," he argued. He had been glad to see the back of Berta who had opposed almost every change he had wanted to make. It was time to take stock of what had been happening in local politics since Edwin had been Chairman of the local Neighbourhood Democratic Council. At last he had got permission from the Minister of Local Government to open a village office bank account at the new local branch in Rosignol.

"I can't understand why Berta tried to block me every time I suggested opening our own bank account for rates money so we have the cash to pay contractors immediately, instead of having to wait for the region to give it to us. She used to take a whole day out of the office once a month and charge expenses for a taxi to carry her and the rates money to Georgetown."

"Quite simple, I said. "You're not seeing it how she would see it. She wanted to get a free trip to town to do her shopping. I dare say she also paid in to the government a considerably smaller sum than the amount of rates collected. That gave her a bigger income than she would have if she just depended on her salary. That's also why she was against you raising the wages of the staff at the village office. She said she was happy with the wages that they already had even though they were a pittance. She knew she would make up her wages out of the rates with no accountability for it. The more rates the girls in the office collected, the more that was available to her to take her cut from. She wouldn't like the idea that the rest of the staff got more pay out of it because it would mean proportionately less for her. By going to town with all the money she would be in control and free from your scrutiny over how much got paid in and to whom."

"You're right," he added. "It's exactly what I found was happening to Dywidag. My security guards told me that the Ministry of Labour representative that the company was forced to employ, was taking a cut out of every guard's wages before paying them. He threatened them with the sack if they refused to sign for the correct amount on the wage sheet even when they knew they did not get that much. No doubt Berta used rates money to make donations to the PNC for party funds over the years as well. She would still have plenty of money at her own disposal. You have to wonder how someone on such a tiny salary as hers could afford to have such a smart well-built house and so much rice land in the area."

"Position means power to manipulate people," I said.

"And power to make sure you keep your position by paying off the political party that keeps you in it," he concluded.

It was a busy term. The Ministry of Agriculture was organising courses for young farmers to learn about hydroponic horticulture techniques as a means of promoting food supply in underdeveloped countries like ours where peasants had little or no land and large families to feed. It was being funded by the United Nations FAO. Our school was included in the programme as we were teaching agriculture to village children. We were still the only school in the region that had a functioning school farm that the students themselves worked and ran as a real business and were getting adequately supervised daily practical experience of the husbandry techniques that matched the theory they were learning. Other schools were pretending to have school farms, but in reality it was a sham.

The resource person who came to teach us hydroponics was an Indo-Guyanese ministry employee who had recently learned about it from an overseas expert teaching the course in Georgetown. He showed us a film on our own video equipment which had been made by US horticulturists working in Mexico, Peru and other Latin American countries. I took extensive notes as I watched. The process was very technical and depended on precise measurements of apparatus and special chemicals used. The man then personally demonstrated how we could adapt what the film had taught us by improvising equipment from recycled household plastic and polystyrene packaging. It was here that the whole process began to fail through a combination of his own dilution of what the film had shown and complete misinformation because of his own lack of attention to the crucial details. Using materials which we provided for him, he constructed demonstration pieces which broke all the rules so precisely insisted on by the film. Then he proceeded to mix up his mystery chemicals by estimation and guesswork instead of using a measuring jug. We were given a small starter pack of the same chemicals to proceed with and told that when we needed more, he would supply them. The chemicals could only be obtained from him and no one else in the country. They were extremely expensive and were beyond our reach as a school. This was even before factoring in the return transport cost for us to reach him in Georgetown. I had no doubt that villagers would not have had such money nor been convinced to part with it for such a project even if they had. I calculated how much it would have cost against the projected output supposed to be achieved and even the optimum yield made it uneconomic for anyone to attempt. Either he was expecting us to be taken in by his own personal moneymaking scheme or the whole project was flawed from its point of origin from the FAO. In any case, why would anyone need to grow crops hydroponically in Guyana when everyone had plenty of soil on their garden land that was idle and uncultivated?

I supervised our students to continue with the hydroponic cultivation project over the following six weeks. Just as I had expected, within a couple of days, the very problems that the film had warned against began to happen. The vegetable seedlings and equipment were soon engulfed in a mass of slimy algae. The plants grew weak and spindly and were overrun with ants and insects. It was hardly an incentive for us to buy any more chemicals or to get any local converted to believe that hydroponic agriculture could ever work. I discussed all these shortcomings with the students. They understood why the accurate measurements would have prevented the problems but also how uneconomic such culture would be for us. I was not surprised that no further mention was made of hydroponics in the country. It was a bright idea from the FAO made by people who had no real understanding of what happens at ground level when you try to roll out these programmes in countries with educational levels far below what is prevalent in the developed world.

Drama in some of our students' home lives continued to unfold as term progressed. We had two East Indian students from Cotton Tree Village among our full-time students that year: Sharana and her cousin, Riad. Sharana's father, Coco, was a fisherman from Cotton Tree village. He was Bibi Ishak's brother, who had inherited the house their grandfather had built as an original East Indian indentured worker on the plantation. It was the same old house that our first full-time students had visited and filmed for history and tourism field work years before. Tragically, during October, the old house burned down to the ground. The family escaped unharmed but poor Sharana lost all her files of notes for the forthcoming CXC examinations in May. She would have to copy up the notes from another student but it must only be done on our school premises to safeguard that student's work. She had to do it at lunch time and come in to school on Sundays and holidays until she had a personal copy of the notes of all her different subjects. Coco complained that he had hundreds of thousands of dollars in cash stored in the house and he lost the lot in the fire.

"Why on earth didn't you put it in a bank account?" Edwin asked him when he came to drop Sharana off at the school. He did not seem to have an answer other than,

"Me na believe in dem ting,"

"Well maybe from now on you should." Edwin advised. "If you'd put it in the bank, you would still have it all." He knew that Coco did not want it in the bank because he did not want the government to know he was getting such large sums of money. They would want him to pay tax on it. The begged question, however, was whether he was involved in any other activities that would bring large quantities of cash into his hands, especially as he was selling fish to the new fish freezer factory.

We all donated clothes and stationary items to help Sharana in the immediate aftermath of the fire. Coco had to find somewhere for his family to live while he rebuilt the house. He came often to visit Edwin as I am sure Edwin lent him money to get back on his feet. Coco would be one of the few locals who would pay it back as soon as he got his boat out to catch fish. He brought us our favourite jumbo prawns or large fish now and again and these were always welcome. He was now selling most of his catch to the new frozen fish processing factory in Rosignol for export overseas, but he would always keep some back for us. Edwin was very adept at getting information out of people without them even realising he was doing so. He had a lot of avuncular chats with Sharana during the course of school days when she was awaiting her team's turn at whichever sport they were playing that day. Otherwise there would be the opportunity when she arrived early or at the end of the day before she left, when he would call her back to hand over some clothes or stationary to help her replace items lost in the fire.

Riad, her cousin, was not as bright as Sharana. He struggled with written work and found concentration in lessons difficult. He had been coming to my lessons since he was a toddler but had stopped when his abusive alcoholic father took him away. In his early teens, he returned to my Saturday classes and eventually earned his place in the full time school, but was struggling with the examination level work. He was not going to pass easily like Sharana was. He was now causing problems for his mother, Bibi, who came in to see Edwin about it. She wouldn't want to admit such things in front of me, but in a private chat with Edwin, she revealed Riad was getting hold of drugs "from bigger boys in Rosignol" and she wanted Edwin to have a word with him and put him on the right track. Always willing to oblige in such matters, Edwin also managed to find out other things from Riad. He built up a good picture of what was going on and who was involved with it.

It was remarkable how quickly Coco rebuilt his house on the same lot as his original that had burned down. He was a good Muslim who cared for his family, especially his daughter. He cared so much about her, in fact, that he had arranged a marriage for her to a business contact of his, a middle aged Indian based in Canada. He would be taking Sharana to Canada after the wedding. For now, she was allowed to complete her examination courses and since she was promised, she would have to be closely watched to protect her from developing any relationship with local boys. Coco was almost keeping her a prisoner and making it very difficult for her to participate in our extra- curricular activities.

BBC World News recently broadcast that customs officials in Southampton had discovered a big haul of cocaine shipped in between frozen fish in a cargo exported from Guyana. The source of it was now being traced. I remarked on the coincidence that the Minister of Fisheries and his family had not long been massacred. Perhaps they had dealings with the operator of the fish factory. All the Indian Ministers had family connections in our region as well as in Canada. Some also had links with Britain. I began to wonder if there were connections between the fish factory owners and the Rosignol residents we knew who had relatives working in Kuwait and nearby Gulf countries. There was now a failed state in Somalia; piracy and high-jacking of shipping between the Gulf States and East Africa; and Al Quaeda was getting financed by narco-trafficking from, amongst other places, South America. It was a new cocaine trail, across the Atlantic, through West Africa and across the desert to Somalia. The criminal underworld was undergoing its own globalisation, targeting tiny little countries like Guyana where local security forces were weak and easily compliant. The country was awash with guns and heightened political tensions. Unknown persons had broken into the munitions store at Camp Ayangana and stolen thirty AK47 rifles which the army was still searching for. It was around this time that I too noticed strange Indo-Guyanese people on motorbikes who kept passing by our property to visit the Ramsammys opposite. They always looked in at us as they passed, to see what was going on in Sapodilla grounds.

Uncharacteristically for locals, they wore crash helmets, thus concealing their identity.

One day later in the term, Sharana came into school covered in bruises with her face swollen, black and blue. She had been badly beaten and was shaking. One of the girls called me downstairs as soon as she arrived in this state and I spent some time privately trying to get her to tell me who had done this to her. Eventually I discovered that it was her father, Coco. He had set about her and punched and kicked her because he had found out that she had been seeing a boy on her way home from school. Since she was promised, Coco inflicted this punishment on her to teach her a lesson. She did not want to go home, understandably, but I felt the incident should be reported to the police who recently had appointed a dedicated female officer to deal with domestic abuse issues. We treated her injuries and let the female officer take a report so she could caution Coco. Sharana would stay with her aunt until Edwin had spoken to Coco and tried to reason with him and calm him down. It was an uphill struggle trying to change his attitude. He had a viciously violent streak. As far as he was concerned he had given her everything and she had betrayed him. He was unforgiving. I wondered if there was more to the incident than what we had been told. Perhaps she had been suspected of giving information to Edwin about what was going on with the fishing trips, deliveries and shipments. I felt bad for Sharana. She was a powerless victim of male-dominated Indian culture, unable to control her own destiny.

Now there was a new CEO at the village office: Alexis, appointed by Edwin who remained in his position as Chairman because the local elections kept getting postponed by the government. He decided to revamp the office by giving it a fresh coat of paint and putting down some new vinyl on the floor. It was with a mixture of shock and disbelief that in the process of taking up the old, damaged lino, he and Trevor discovered that there were some loose floorboards and that underneath them were concealed hundreds of ledgers and documents that had "gone missing" during the "reign" of Berta. Edwin was furious. Many residents had been prevented from developing their land or gaining title deeds over the years because their records could not be found in the village office. Our own deeds and plan were among those that had mysteriously disappeared. It prevented us from being assessed for payment of rates, so we were not able to pay any for years until Edwin had circumvented Berta's obstruction by inviting a valuation officer from Georgetown to come and reassess all the properties in the region that had not yet been assessed for rates.

"Why would those women deliberately hide these documents?" he asked, unable to understand their purpose or motivation. "You would think they would want people to pay rates, especially us."

"I can only suggest that by making it impossible for you to pay your own rates, Berta would prevent you from getting the councillors to vote for a rates increase because it would look bad if you made everyone else pay more taxes when you weren't paying any yourself," I said.

"Well if that was her plan, she failed," he said. "I'm struggling to find anything good about that woman."

It was almost Christmas and we got a visit from the German student engineer, Christophe, who had worked with Dywidag. He had come to do a final year project on the Berbice River Bridge that was due to be constructed in the coming year. It was always great fun to entertain Christophe. He was a welcome voice of truth in what was a deepening sea of corruption. After he left us, as we moved into the New Year of 2007, Edwin and I reassessed our personal situation. He resolved to sell Sapodilla if he could find a buyer. I did not believe it would ever happen, and by now Edwin's medical condition convinced me that we would hear no more from Rick, whether or not he had ever existed outside Edwin's imagination.

The New Year's Resolution was no bluff as far as Edwin was concerned. He redoubled his efforts to try to sell the snackette to Carwyn's relatives in the USA, but kept being strung along by them as Carwyn was a sitting tenant and they had no intention of paying for the property he was already running a business from. Edwin had now lost patience with them and wanted to get Carwyn to buy the property himself. He worked for the local power company after all and had recently been promoted with a good salary. He encouraged Carwyn to arrange a mortgage from his bank, but I was sure Carwyn never even tried to do this. He just told Edwin he had done so in order to get him to proceed with legal documentation to transfer the title of the property to Carwyn. His main objective was to keep us thinking he wanted to buy, so that Edwin would allow him to stay there and eventually, if Edwin's health failed, Carwyn would take it over by default as he was already in it. Lots of money had changed hands throughout this process and most of it went out of Edwin's hands into those of the dubious lawyer at Rosignol. This was the time of year that business was slack after Christmas festivities had left everyone broke. Carwyn defaulted on his rental payments as usual, but it seemed his business was declining also. There was always an excuse to justify cash-flow problems.

The school was gearing up for the final examinations for the current batch of full time students but Donalta did not come back after Christmas. We soon discovered from Taa that she was pregnant and her mother had kept her home out of shame. I was disappointed that in spite of my well balanced sex education tied in with social studies work targeted at preventing teenage pregnancy, she had not applied it to her own personal conduct. Her illegitimate child could not be said to result from lack of appropriate or accurate sex education, nor from lack of understanding of the social issues surrounding teenage pregnancy. It could not be blamed on lack of condoms or other contraceptives as these were now freely available to anyone in the local community. We even left out a help yourself box of them in our gym for students to privately take a supply from if they wanted. She had deliberately had unprotected sex so she could become a mother. It was very irresponsible of her, but it was done and there was no use in making her feel ashamed about it. It seemed a tragedy that all her education would now go to waste and she would miss the chance to get qualifications that could help her to get a job and support herself as well as the baby she would now have. I therefore took the unprecedented step of allowing her to continue to attend school up to the exams as her belly grew bigger by the day. I had not given thought as to how it would look to locals to see a heavily pregnant girl in our school uniform walking down the street past them every day. I was more concerned with setting an example to the local community that girls should not be shunned and shamed out of an education when they made such mistakes. I had not foreseen what unintended messages her continued attendance at school would send to younger girls in the community who also came to our school. To them it seemed that I was advocating unmarried motherhood. I had not even considered the risks I was taking of a potential miscarriage or premature contractions in the classroom as her pregnancy advanced. Thankfully I did not have to deal with any of that. After Easter, she stayed at home while I was doing revision classes and made her own way to the exam centre. Her healthy baby was delivered soon after the exams finished.

The new International Cricket Stadium, financed largely by aid to Guyana from the Indian government, was completed in the nick of time. World Cup Cricket was in the Caribbean for the first time. Edwin had advised the government in the early stages of its planning but had been ridiculed in meetings by ignorant members of the Board who disregarded the need for parking or adequate sanitary facilities to be discussed. He had dropped out of the process in despair and felt vindicated when the ICC pulled Guyana up on all these shortcomings as the stadium building progressed. The security arrangements in the Caribbean were beefed up ahead of the opening. Everywhere was on high alert for potential terrorist threats at the event. Large numbers of British security forces were involved and some of them had already been in Guyana for quite a time. Edwin had been meeting up with them now and again. He had sent messages to Rick through them. The tournament started on March 10th in the Islands and was coming to Guyana soon. Duke Munroe Junior was coming from England to see two of the matches and arrived to stay with us on 18th March while awaiting the Guyana match. Two days before he left us, the shocking news broke that Bob Woolmer had been found dead in his hotel room in Jamaica, believed to have been murdered. Was it a terrorist attack? There was plenty of speculation but it was clear that the local police were not adequate detectives, so a team from Scotland Yard was drafted in to work on the case. After a few weeks no more was heard about it in the media. It must have been hushed up for security reasons.

Our cow pasture at the back of the farm had been loaned to Edwin's brother Malcolm as a place to keep his small herd of cows and he had fenced the area at his own expense. He lived in Brooklyn but paid a young local man to look after them for him. Malcolm was expecting to retire soon and repatriate to Guyana to look after the cows himself. Edwin began to make arrangements with the lawyer to transfer this portion of our land to Malcolm as a deed of gift. At least Malcolm would be paying the lawyer's fees for this.

All the full time students were away by now doing their public examinations at the government's local examination centre. I was in the middle of my own end of year school examinations with my part time students when David Lammy turned up at the gate with his new wife, Nicola. He had brought her to Guyana to meet us and see how I had coped with living in the country for the past sixteen years. They were buying a new house on the coast nearer Georgetown as a holiday home in the sun. David was on his way to Venezuela on British government business. He was going to see a successful school orchestra initiative for slum children in action there. He hoped to do something similar for disadvantaged youth in England in his new role as Minister of Culture under Tony Blair. Edwin talked with them for quite a while until I was able to come out of the invigilation. In our gym, David gave a speech to the children gathered round the table tennis table as if he were canvassing for support in a Tottenham youth group. He told them he came from our village (which wasn't quite true) and put himself across as a role model for them. I went upstairs made some tuna sandwiches and drinks and then they came up for lunch. We sat and ate them together while they asked me about how we were getting on with the school and what problems there were in the local community. As usual we spent a lot of time giving information and insight to our visitors but never seemed to see any benefits returning to the school or community. We felt we were just being used.

We had completed our first batch of CXC Food and Nutrition practical exams in the Mitch Mason Centre complex. The visiting Examiner, Leslyn Edwards, complimented us on the standard of their work and said we had ideal conditions for the practical examinations. It was praise indeed but said more about the low expectations of even the examiner, with her years of experience of such exams in the far from ideal conditions of other schools, than it said about the actual standards of our own improvised facilities. Soon this group of full time students would be leaving us for the world of work. I had low expectations of their results however as they were a far less able group of students than any that I had hitherto taken through the exams. There must be a reason for this. I puzzled over it.

I had noticed over recent years that parents had taken to enrolling their children in the school at a later age than they had done in the past. They were waiting until their children had finished primary school and done their first year at secondary school before bringing them to register in my school. They seemed to be playing the system so they could meet the minimum entry requirement I set rather than try to register at the earliest possible age so I could properly prepare them for the courses I would be teaching at CXC. As a result, few of them had done the foundation work they would have done with me in my junior classes. They were waiting until the child performed badly in their local secondary school and then expecting me to do an instant repair job. Part of the problem was that parents from villages far from Hopetown were hearing about our results on television so the children would have to travel by minibus. They could do this more easily when they were older than when they were still at primary school. Their ability was still so low by the age of ten or eleven that they would have to go into my prep or primary literacy and numeracy groups together with the bright six year olds who were doing that work. We were a victim of our own success.

I would have to find a way to reverse this trend. The current batch of Saturday students did not look to me to be capable or ready to start CXC work in September. I told them and their parents at a PTA meeting, about my concern and warned that if none of them reached the required standard in their basic literacy and numeracy in my end of year exams, then the full time school would be on hold for a year until they did.

By the time I had finished marking all their test papers in mid-June, I realised that I would have to carry out the changes I had warned of. There would be a new regime in the coming academic year and that would mean all the Saturday students would remain at their normal day school but would come to me every day after school to do an hour each of extra maths and English, after which they would stay for physical education with Edwin. On Saturdays they would do their normal classes covering science, maths and humanities skills and topics to prepare them for full time school the following September. They were disappointed, but all enrolled for the coming year before we set off for the UK at the end of June.

We had grave concerns about either Royden or Eldio staying in our property during our absence again. Since we had returned after last summer's trip to England, Edwin had noticed many things from the gym had disappeared. It was not easy to spot at first, but only as the weeks went by that he went to use certain equipment and found it missing. Realising they could not be trusted, he called on Robin to act as our security guard instead. Robin had kindly agreed to do this by taking his own leave while we were away and using his presence in the village as an opportunity to shape up the local unit of the GDF. He was well known and liked among the black people as well as the Indian community where he had lived all his life. Robin, being an army officer, was now armed with a gun, so no sensible opportunist would attempt a break-in.

In England once again, we witnessed on television the terrible scenes of the London July bombings. David Lammy was now on our television screens lamenting the death of a close friend who had been a victim of the bombed bus. The world was descending into madness. Were we safe anywhere? Edwin had his cataract operation and had to spend a couple of weeks being very careful not to damage what had been done. While he was recuperating at our rented farm cottage, I had my family meeting to decide what would happen with the remains of our inheritance. I had to face the fact that one day return to England would have to be on the cards. We explored the possibility of getting a mortgage to make a self- build. It all seemed impossible given that I had no paid employment or income and Edwin was now drawing his old age pension. I did have my share of capital from my inheritance to put down as a deposit, but that together with the maximum mortgage Edwin could raise would not get us a ready built house anywhere in the country. We still had a mortgage to pay back in Guyana. The only way forward was to build a kit house on some of the family land we still had. I would pay for a survey to be done to assess the likelihood of plans being passed for this. The surveyor would assess the situation after we returned to Guyana but would communicate with me by email. It all seemed hopeless and yet again Rick had not made contact. He must be involved in all these security operations in Pakistan. All military leave had been cancelled.

Although the sun was shining as usual back in Guyana, a gloom was hanging over our future like a great threatening thundercloud. I collected the exam results of our recent school leavers from Georgetown but was pleasantly surprised to see that once again, we had the top results in the region. Odessia had the top grades. I was pleased for the students but felt that the overall standards must be declining if these students had obtained such high grades. They were not up to the standard of previous groups I had taught. However, I got stuck into preparing the classrooms for the school to reopen and we kicked off the new term with a great feeling of enthusiasm from the students that they would make a success of the coming academic year.

Nicola Lammy paid us another visit in November, bringing her parents with her to meet us and have lunch. David had not come this time as he was now the Skills Minister in the Department of Education and was busy in his new role. Nicola's parents had come to investigate the property potential of repairing David's mother's house for a holiday home in the sun. They were very down to earth people acting as councillors in London. We discussed local conditions and problems. I expressed concern at the increasing influence we had noticed in the last couple of years of Islamic schools in Guyana. It seemed to be a worrying trend. Increasing numbers of young girls from Afro-Guyanese Christian families were becoming Moslem and had taken to wearing hijabs and black robes. Some were being promised scholarships in Iran and were indeed going there. I got the impression that my comments did not go down well with my audience. Coming from multicultural London, such cultural changes would go unnoticed and probably seem unimportant to them. To us it had sinister undertones that mirrored problems in Africa and Asia. It seemed to be a cover for unethical activities rather than genuine religious conversion.

I was glad to have the daytimes free under our new arrangements. It meant I could mark and prepare for the students before they arrived at three thirty and had enough time to set up practical work and experiments as well as keep on top of the laundry and housework. I also found time to do some proper keep fit daily. I could feel myself getting into better shape at fifty three than I had been at earlier times in my life. It was like a drug to me. I needed to do it every day or I got withdrawal symptoms. As I ran round the circuit in the garden while Edwin had the students out in the sports field, I day-dreamed of tending the lavender in Rick's garden in the South of France. It would be sunny and warm there but without the harsh excesses of climate that killed off most of the flowers I had tried to cultivate here. I would miss my bananas and papaya trees but I would gain such a great variety of colourful beauty. These months I used to reflect and prepare myself mentally for the task ahead. I would have to convince myself that life in England would be better than life in Guyana. I did not know how I would do it but I would have to focus on positive things about moving home so that I would not regret leaving all this behind. Then I got the report from my surveyor back in England that made it clear that we would never get planning permission to build any home on our family land as it was just outside the village envelope and the farm acreage was too small to sustain a livelihood as a working farm. It was hopeless to even think of moving back without an act of God happening.

One day in November, I was preparing a science lesson for the children due to arrive that afternoon when the sound of a huge heavy vehicle like a tank came rolling down the street past the house. It made the earth shake under my feet. I ran out to see whatever it was but there was no sign of any vehicle. Then a shout came from the back of the house and water pouring out of the burst pipes made me realise we had just had an earthquake. Edwin rushed to the water tank to see if he could stop the pipes up somehow and I called all the children to stand away from the building in case there were after-shocks or falling concrete. It seemed we had escaped without too much damage but a house at the end of the road had completely collapsed onto its side. After the classes finished and we went upstairs, I noticed that the veranda was parting company from the house so we would have to call in a builder to strengthen the supports below. It would need large amounts of money spending on it but we had no alternative. Insurance policies provided no cover worth having on a property of this size. If it collapsed completely we would lose everything.

Just as Robin returned from his first overseas military course in Beijing, Benazir Bhutto was assassinated in Pakistan. We were worried about our invisible friend, Rick, again. He must be in the thick of all that. We could see from the CNN World News that Pakistan was becoming an extremely dangerous place with a failed state on its doorstep and porous borders. The fact that it had recently become a nuclear power did not send out reassuring messages for world peace. Weapons of mass destruction potentially falling into the hands of terrorists left those of us with an understanding of current affairs in a state of fear akin to that of The Cold War years. The difference was that now it was far more terrifying. At least back then, there were heads of governments that could be engaged in diplomacy. Now there seemed to be no clear enemy to defeat and no government with which to deal or negotiate.

Terror struck in Guyana at the beginning of 2008 with a massacre in Lusignan, further up the coast. Eleven people were shot dead and three children injured amongst others by unknown criminals. By the end of that week, the country had all but shut down. No one was travelling along the coast road. Children were not going to school and bandits were on the loose. The local security forces were not up to dealing with it. "Poor education, Poor training and Poor Leadership," was all Edwin could say. He was now meeting up with people from the European Union that were visiting the country. Since the Berbice Bridge had opened, there was a lot of movement along the new coast road that had been completed after Dywidag left Guyana. It was fantastic for farmers and traders to have such easy access across the Berbice Estuary to New Amsterdam and the Corentyne coast to Surinam, but it also made it easier for drug and people-trafficking across the border. These problems could well become worse as a result.

Edwin travelled to Cotton Tree to see Coco and order some prawns and nice fish for us. He asked Coco if he could arrange a field trip for our students to visit the fish factory to do some humanities field work. Coco took Edwin straight there. Unusually, he made Edwin wait outside the high compound gates while he went in to enquire. After a time, Coco emerged and told him they didn't do visits. It seemed suspicious behaviour for any bona fide company. There was a strong likelihood that they were involved in the shipments overseas of illegal drugs coming up the Berbice River from the interior. The factory was in an ideal location for that. There were countless numbers of illegal landing sites in the rainforest where light aircraft could drop cocaine from Columbia and Venezuela unnoticed by the government even if they had wanted to intercept it. As it was, many if not most of the government agencies were actually part of the illegal process, accepting bribes and profiting from turning a blind eye. Even government ministers had been involved and it would have made no difference whichever party was in power. Edwin couldn't demand entry as chairman of the local authority, because Rosignol was outside the jurisdiction of Edwin's NDC. This fish factory's owners had no interest in educating local youth.

On February 18th, another fifteen people were gunned down by bandits in Bartica. This was the time of year when all the Mashramanie celebrations took place and the Guyanese diaspora from the USA usually came back for their vacations. The government toned down the Mash parades in Georgetown to try to avert further incidents. With all these security problems, it seemed unlikely that Robin would get released from his job to look after Sapodilla for us again in the coming summer. It was now exactly two years since Rick and his team had left Guyana. His current mission would end in a year's time. Would we hear from him in the summer and meet up to set things in place? I had by now assumed he would never retire and that our little menage a trois was just a dream that Edwin had sold to me to interest me in leaving Guyana. I didn't buy a dream like that. Was he testing me out to see if I was fickle and willing to be unfaithful? I would not do anything he didn't want me to. Was he trying to find a way to rid himself of me? I couldn't believe that a career soldier like Rick, who had signed on for dangerous extra time at retirement age, would seriously settle for domestic life in his dotage with an old army friend and his unknown wife whom he had never even met. Still, I have often been known to be wrong.

Chapter 26
A Tricky Escape

I had been running the school for too long. I now found myself teaching three of the six year-old children of my very first full time female students. All of them had been unmarried mothers, but at least one of them, Maggie, now had a full time job as a teacher. Bonny and Quacy had both returned with degrees from their veterinary scholarships at Havana University and had been given responsible jobs in the Ministry of Agriculture, Leroy was working for the Forestry Commission in the interior, Robin and Kesha had senior jobs in the Guyana Defence Force. Delon managed the finance department at the Onverwagt office of the Guyana Power and Light Company while Alistair had a managerial role with the local National Insurance Office. Several of the girls and two of the boys had become teachers like Maggie whereas Joy had just joined the broadcasting team at the local Television station in New Amsterdam. Many others had gone overseas, however. I realised that the brain drain would always be a main factor in impoverishing poor countries of their skilled workforce. Unless the attractions of overseas wealth and loose border controls disappeared, it would continue to be a problem.

It had been our policy ever since starting the school to help our students and any other jobless villagers to find employment locally. Edwin, with government permission, had recently set up a scheme to train local people to act as valuation officers for the neighbourhood district council. They would assess properties that had not been valued yet so that the owners could start paying rates. It could be done fairly now that Edwin had discovered all the missing documents and ledgers under the village office floorboards. It also helped us to pay up all our backlog of rates and enable our lawyer to complete the deed of gift of our rear farm pasture to Edwin's brother, Malcolm.

Sharana, who had left school with a good set of exam passes the previous June, telephoned us in the middle of March to complain that she was being held captive at home by her parents. Fearing she was being abused again, Edwin went to see Coco and got a lot of information from him in the process, but also learned that Sharana was 'grounded' because of her behaviour with local boys. He tried to smooth things over and to persuade Coco to give her more freedom. By May, Coco's wife had drunk poison and died. Edwin learned that it was because of Sharana's behaviour. She had run away from home to live with some young Indian men and this had brought such shame on the family that her mother chose to take her own life rather than live with that shame. Coco was dismayed at what he saw as ingratitude from an only daughter that he had "give ev'ryting to" and who would now be rejected by any "good husband." He had "lost" his daughter and also his wife. It was a sad story that reflected the plight of so many Indo-Guyanese females.

Sapodilla Learning Centre was taking its new aim of educating youngsters for a career in the Guyana Defence force seriously. Robin, who had achieved promotion to Captain, was a role model respected by good people in our area. Kesha had so far set a fine example for the girls. Edwin was concerned by the poor working conditions of the Guyana Defence Force, however. The fact that as a profession, it attracted recruits of a very low educational standard, made it weak and unable to carry out effectively the tasks required of it. He could see the urgent need for this to improve to cope with the recent upsurge in crime, narco-trafficking and associated violence. Training and the quality of leadership needed to be improved and we would try to contribute towards this. The career might attract a better quality of recruit if it took more care of its soldiers, especially when they had suffered illness or injury while on active service. He had realised what little help was available to those poor victims of the Camp Brumes ammunition store explosion when Major General Joe Singh had called on him for advice on dealing with the incident. There was the Guyana Legion, of course, attempting to fulfil a similar role to that of the Royal British Legion. However, the personnel of the local organisation left a lot to be desired.

Nick, one of Edwin's friends from army days, had just become a Chelsea Pensioner and had accepted our invitation to come and stay with us for a couple of weeks in November. He would bring eighty-year old Fred with him; another Chelsea inmate who had served in Guyana with his regiment in the sixties and wanted to revisit the country he had fond memories of. If they came in uniform and lay a wreath on the Commonwealth Forces Memorial in the special graveyard in Georgetown, the Royal Hospital would contribute to their fares. The British High Commissioner would help and also organise a suitable ceremony for their act of Remembrance. We paid the Guyana Legion a visit at their head office in Georgetown in order to arrange for a poppy wreath which Nick and Fred could lay on the memorial. They also agreed that the pensioners could take part in the official Remembrance Day parade down Main Street when the president and overseas diplomats lay wreaths on the cenotaph in the centre of the capital. The Guyana Legion clearly thought that they would be getting access to some overseas donations for their cause, but Edwin's main purpose was to shame the Guyana Government and various high profile and relatively wealthy local individuals to donate to the Legion themselves. That way they would better provide help for soldiers wounded in the course of their duty and a dignified old age for retired soldiers unable to care for themselves. Edwin was consistent in his belief that self-help was the way towards sustainable development, not beggary. It was all set up by May.

We had engaged Cleveland our builder to do extensive work strengthening the foundations of the house to support the veranda and make good the damage done by the recent earthquake. Obama was gaining ground in the primaries and an American millionaire business man called Stanford had been flashing money around in the Caribbean, setting up a sensational 20-20 cricket tournament in the islands. Our potential full-time students were shaping up with their sport, but by the end of year exams, I had to call their parents to a meeting to break the disappointing news that their academic standard was still not good enough to graduate to the full time school in September, and since Edwin was going to have another cataract operation in the summer, I did not feel that it was fair to keep them back another year if all their peers in the state schools were entering their exams at the end of the year. I advised them to enter their children for the CXC exams through their state school and I would make provision to give them special help with exam level work if they continued to attend my classes on weekdays after school and on Saturdays, while I continued to teach the younger students at the same time. Edwin's health might deteriorate unexpectedly and need special treatment which would mean we would have to travel to England at short notice at any time. They understood and notwithstanding, re-registered for the coming year's classes at the end of June before we left for England.

Health wise, things looked optimistic for Edwin once we were in Blighty. His medical was encouraging and he was told his sugar control had been so good that he did not yet need an operation on the other eye. He was motivated to get back into training with vengeance after Usein Bolt stunned the world by winning the Olympic gold with an unbelievable time of 9.69 seconds. We were doing two or three-mile walks a day in the beautiful Chiltern Village we were staying in. Edwin now determined to make them "power walks" because he never did any exercise gently, so he carried all the heavy shopping in his backpack and I almost had to run to keep up with him. It wasn't until two days later that our grandchildren visiting us for the day, noticed blood on Edwin's foot. That was it. By the end of the week he had blisters on the ball of his foot that became infected and looked like they were turning into ulcers again. I had to take him to the local surgery, where the nurse dressed his ulcers with special dressings thrice a week. She ultimately referred us to the podiatrists in the diabetic clinic at Luton hospital. After that I had to drive him twice a week in our hired car to Luton for more suitable dressings to be applied. It soon became clear that we would need to postpone our flight back to Guyana for a month so they could have time to heal properly before we left England.

September was a miserable month, as we languished in the tiny rented apartment with Edwin not able to walk anywhere for fear of delaying the healing process. All I could do was look out of the window at the rain or go for solitary walks while he slept on the sofa. I emailed Robin, who these days had his own laptop, and explained why we would not be back for another month. I hoped he could still monitor the security of our house. I also telephoned Joly in Guyana to let him know our new arrival date and time so he would be there to pick us up in his hire car. He promised to make sure Taa knew that we were delayed and to let the children know that term would not now start until November 1st.

This all happened against the backdrop of an impending collapse of the world's financial institutions. Every day the warnings of doom and gloom in the news became greater. The US government had rescued Fannie May and Freddie Mac from bankrupty in one of the biggest bailout in US history. Major financial institutions around the world began to go down like dominoes. Property prices in England began to fall rapidly and we could suddenly see a slim chance that we would be able to buy a small house in England to move back to. If only we could sell Sapodilla to someone and get enough out of it to buy a house in England outright with cash, since we would now no longer be able to get a mortgage. Looking at property websites in my laptop, I worked out that we would need to get £200, 000 from the sale in order to buy anything in the cheapest part of England. I had to have a garden. It was the only thing that kept me sane in times of adversity. Sapodilla and its eleven acres of farmland had been valued at four times that amount. No one with that kind of money would want to put themselves in our particular location, but if they could get it as a bargain for a quarter of that price, then we might tempt someone who was thinking of retiring back to Guyana in comfort from London or the USA. We made a decision to make the move. It was now or never. If we hung on any longer waiting for Rick we would be trapped in Guyana to live out the rest of our lives with dwindling income, failing health and no medical care.

Our return flight was due in a couple of days and Edwin's foot had still not properly healed. We took the month's supply of dressings that the hospital allowed us and headed back home to Sapodilla so I could fulfil my promise to see out the academic year for the students we had signed on in June. We also had the upcoming Remembrance service to arrange and our Chelsea Pensioners to visit us. There was a huge amount of cleaning and shopping to do before we could get back to normal, not least to collect from our supplier in Georgetown the medication and insulin we had ordered in June to last Edwin for the next six months. Then we had to prepare the classrooms and grounds ready for the children's classes.

Edwin's youngest brother from Brooklyn was staying at Taa's house when we returned. That Sunday, while Edwin was resting with his feet up in the bedroom and I was preparing breakfast at the other end of the house, I looked out of the window to see shadowy figures moving about among the coconut trees at the back of the farm. They were cutting them down. I went out and shouted from the veranda to them,

"Hey what do you think you are doing in our garden?"

"Brian tell we to chop de trees dem," said one of the boys nearest to me. I was about to order him off our property because it was no business of Brian to tell them to do anything, when Brian came out from behind them with a cutlass in his hand.

"They all have disease, Jane. They need to come down," and with that he turned round and went back to his work as if my presence counted for nothing. I was exasperated. They were perfectly healthy trees that were bearing a good crop. He must take me for an idiot. How dare he? I went straight down to our bedroom and told Edwin what was going on. He did not respond in the way he normally would have, with anger and speed. He was obviously feeling ill and weak, so he slowly got up and pulled on some shorts and socks. He hobbled along the veranda and down the steps and I waited for him to return. He had got there too late. By the time he came back the trees had all gone. Edwin was annoyed but resigned to the fait accompli. He remained very silent about the matter for the next few days but I knew he was drawing his own conclusions about what his brother had done. Eventually he spoke about it to me.

"My brother thinks I'll be giving him that part of the land to build himself a house on. He thinks he has a right to it because Malcolm has the pasture by deed of gift. What he doesn't know is that Malcolm paid me a healthy sum of money for the pasture and he's paid his half of all the lawyer's costs but Brian thinks he's going to get a house lot on the reef as a free gift from me. He hasn't offered me money for it, so he'll get nothing,"

The undergrowth at the back of the farm had grown six feet tall through neglect since the June rains. Malcolm was concerned that his cows would be attacked by a jaguar that was nesting in the area behind our pond. Edwin could not do any of this himself because of needing to keep off his feet most of the time. We paid a local man aptly nicknamed Tiger to come and cut the grass down at the back. Early in the morning, there was a hullaballoo as I was walking towards the classroom door. I looked across to the street to see what was happening. A flash of spotted yellow sped past the garden gate towards the high street, hotly pursued by Boyo brandishing his cutlass over his head. He did not have the animal's speed, but the creature was not taking any chances. Unknowingly, it headed further into celebrity and danger as it raced towards the village huts at the far end of the street to get away from Boyo. Squeals of fear and terror arose as children on their steps or in their yards realised what was racing towards them. At last the poor creature seized its chance to escape and rounded the end of our front fence so it could make a dash for the wilderness in the back-dam by means of the open pasture and deserted coconut reefs.

"It's moments like these that I shall miss most," I thought, as I went back to trimming our overgrown ornamental shrubs. I was looking forward to seeing all the children again, but I knew I would have to break the bad news about closing the school once Edwin had put out the advertisement for the sale of Sapodilla to his mother and siblings in Brooklyn. I would rather tell them personally before they found out by gossip.

On the first day of term, I sent home a letter calling a PTA meeting that Sunday, so I could make my important announcement. I explained to the parents and children with regret, our reasons for having to sell up and return to England. Uncle Edwin needed better medical care than he could get in Guyana. We were looking for an organisation to buy the house, land and school as one entity so that the school, sports club and museum could be continued for the future. We did not want to split it all up into smaller lots and sell it to different people. We could not donate it to an organisation because we had to get some money from it or we would have no home to live in when we got to England. I would continue to teach the children until Easter when the older ones would be starting to take their CXC exams at their daytime schools. Uncle Edwin would continue training them in our sports club. After that date if we had managed to sell the house, Edwin and I would be busy packing and preparing to move out. Hopefully we would find a buyer who would reopen the school the following September so the younger students would get their chance to resume studies at Sapodilla.

I saw many sad and disappointed faces that afternoon and it tugged at my heartstrings. What could I do? I had spent eighteen years of my life trying to help the education system of Guyana get on its feet but I was only one person. Like Edwin, my efforts were not helping to change Guyana; they were helping to get people a ticket to Brooklyn. I was swimming against a tide that was threatening to wash me out to sea if I did not swim for the life raft I could see in the distance while I still had strength to do it. I would swim for all I was worth, but the faces I left behind would continue to haunt me.

Obama was in the Whitehouse the day Nick and Fred arrived. It was a momentous day in world history. The leader of the world was a black man, a role model for all of us in many ways. Edwin's foot had still not healed and we still had no buyer for Sapodilla. None of that seemed to matter as we all celebrated in the good news. There was hope after all if the electorate of the world's most powerful democracy had overcome the attitudes and inequality that hitherto had prevented the highest office from being held by an American citizen of any other race than white Caucasian. We welcomed our visitors who were certainly happy to see Edwin and Jolly at the airport. Nick was travelling with a recently installed pacemaker and both he and Fred caused quite a stir when they passed through the arrivals gate wearing their distinctive red coats that were hardly designed for the equatorial temperatures they now found themselves in. Showing all the British bulldog spirit characteristic of their generation, they dutifully took part in the Remembrance Day march and ceremonies in sweltering heat wearing their heavy red coats and black trousers and hats. I suppose to some onlookers it may have seemed reminiscent of the colonial redcoats back in town, but other locals just loved a brightly coloured uniform which meant nothing to them more than "style".

A special reception in their honour was held by the Guyana Legion at the Guyana Defence Force Officers' Club. All Guyana's top military brass and leading dignitaries were invited including the new British High Commissioner and his wife whom we hardly knew as yet. Many speeches full of empty words were made and generous donations promised as those present seemed to try to outdo the pledges that preceded their own.

"It's all for show," Edwin explained to Nick and Fred as we made the long journey back to Sapodilla afterwards. I felt a sense of disappointment that he was probably right in his assessment and that the occasion was typical of its kind in its falseness.

"I had a few moments of conversation with the new High Commissioner's wife about our intention to sell up and make the move back," I said, "but she seemed to fundamentally misunderstand everything we stand for, since she suggested that we approach the Georgetown "Children's drop-in Centre" as they might be interested in taking over Sapodilla to use as an extension of their services into Berbice."

"Oh, wonderful," said Edwin. "As if that load of Georgetown crooks would ever part with any money for it. I'm sure they'd love to get their hands on the property and send us to the land of never ending excuses as to why the money they were supposed to pay us hadn't yet come through. Do we look that green after having been here all these years?"

"Even if they weren't crooks and if they waved the money in banknotes in front of us, I wouldn't want to sell it to people who would make it into a drop-in-centre," I said. "Where is the educational benefit in that? It would just be another feeding station. It wouldn't help the country to develop properly. Everything we've worked for and built up over nearly two decades would be wasted."

Our two visitors had a good couple of weeks' holiday enjoying the hot sunshine, my healthy cooking, several crates of the local Banks Beer and participation in our programme of sport and other activities with the children. While I was teaching, they and Edwin put the world to right as they chatted on the veranda about old times and new. There had been many changes for the worse in the

British military and society since Edwin had been in Guyana. He was well out of touch.

The day Nick and Fred departed, there was a terrible hotel bombing in Mumbai. Edwin and I wondered if the incident had given Rick any more white hairs. We still hoped to hear from him, but we would work at selling the house nevertheless. If he contacted us, then we would be free to join him and if we heard nothing by the time we got out of Guyana, then at least we would have some money to buy a place to live in till he was able to get in touch. Edwin had been speaking to the pastor of the Congregational Church in Hopetown. Edwin knew the church possessed some money in overseas investments. He suggested that they could use some of it to buy Sapodilla for the Church and that way continue the school in the village. If Iran could fund and set up Islamic madrassas all over Guyana, and the Reverend was complaining about declining Congregational Church membership among the youth in the village, why couldn't the Church do the same thing and set up its own school to counter these new trends? If attractive educational opportunities were available within their own faith then village children would not need to convert to Islam in order to get a good education. By 5th December he had obtained an agreed deal with the Congregational Church of Guyana. It would be a nail-biting month of negotiation and prevarication before we had a cheque for the contents and the majority of the agreed sale price handed over to us in the lawyer's office which we could pay into our personal bank account. After that were the few days of uncertainty as to whether it would be honoured.

I inventoried all the fixtures and furniture content that the church wanted to be included in the purchase deal. They would also be getting the school and sports club resources in their entirety as a free gift on the conditional understanding that they would run some sort of school for local children with it after our departure. We had set aside a few personal belongings to pack up in a few barrels and a wooden crate in the hope of finding a company that would ship them back to England for us. I discovered a new company in the local 'yellow pages' phone book who were the only ones willing to ship barrels door to door to England. The problem would be the cost. It would be the local equivalent of £770 sterling per barrel. This was ten times more than the cost of shipping an individual barrel from England to Guyana. I was told that the high charge was because barrels had to be unloaded in Miami and transferred to a transatlantic ship at the docks there as containerships from Guyana only went to the USA. It was the lading and storage per barrel that escalated the cost, but if we crated them all up in one group, we could probably reduce these costs a bit.

We would need to buy new furniture and household goods when we had found a house to put them in and to pay for shipping the few barrels containing heirlooms and irreplaceable personal belongings that we would keep for sentimental reasons. If we kept that to a minimum, we could keep the costs down or it would eat away the available cash for buying a house. We would have to sell off the rest of our stuff to pay for the shipment of the few barrels we had limited ourselves to. I organised all the belongings we could sell into different categories such as kitchen equipment, garden tools, potted plants, electrical items, small items of furniture and such like. Then I priced them up according to their condition, making them a bargain compared to those on sale in local shops. Notices went home with the children and at the village church as to which day during the first week of December that I would be selling each category. I also posted a timetable of sales on our gate so all passers-by could see. I had anticipated that we would need some crowd control but had no idea quite what the response would be. We were astonished. Each morning by the ten o'clock start, an enormous crowd had built up in the street and were crushing each other up against the gate in order to be allowed in first. When I opened the gate, locals behaved as if we were an aid relief truck handing out water bottles in a desert refugee camp. I did not believe that people would almost kill each other to get hold of a bed sheet a plate or a saucepan that had come from England rather than a local shop. Edwin supervised the stall where the items were set out and separated fights over who could have any disputed item. I sat by the gate with my cash box to take the money before people could leave with their purchases. We were cleared out of items by the end of the week and could then concentrate on our own packing.

On Christmas Eve, Robin, Quacy and Bonny accepted our invitation to eat with us. At that point, we presented the latter two with our personal lifejackets to enable them to safely travel into the hinterland in their new jobs as vets. Robin already had been given items from Edwin's book and video collection that would help him in his military work. He would be setting up a library in his office to help young recruits with sport and fitness. After the seasonal festivities, we had important business to conclude to see that the sale was properly completed so we could get the rest of the money from the church. It was the sixteenth of January when we had to travel to New Amsterdam to pay our taxes to the government officials there and collect the tax compliance document that the Church would need before the sale could procede. Edwin and Robin had made many prior visits to the tax office and finally spoke to the top man who would have the authority to issue the document. He had said that the tax would be eight million Guyana Dollars and it must be paid in cash to him in person. I can only surmise that this request would enable the official to keep a huge bribe for himself. We had no way of knowing the amount of tax the government required on a property such as ours. It seemed to be an arbitrary amount that the official decided on a whim. We were at his mercy or we would get no document to prove we had paid.

It was an extremely dangerous thing to carry huge amounts of cash anywhere in the country. It only needed the whisper to get around that cash was going to move and we could have been attacked by bandits and stripped of it before we got to the tax office. It would be no good withdrawing it all in Georgetown and driving back to Berbice with it. We would be able to get it from the branch of Scotiabank nearest to the tax office in New Amsterdam. That would minimise the risk. It must have been the scariest day of my life up to that point. On the appointed day in mid- January, Robin drove us across the new Berbice Bridge and we went into the bank. I was alarmed to see one of our female ex-students, who I had never really felt to be genuine, as a new employee of the bank. Had she already heard of our expected arrival and was she going to pass on intelligence of our departure to a local crook? We were shepherded by the manager into a tiny cubicle in the bank vault. I was puzzled when Edwin pushed me forward to make the withdrawal and sign the papers. The manager wanted to know why I wanted to withdraw such a large sum in cash. Were we using it to buy a car? I did not know what to say, so I said "yes" in case we were unwittingly breaking the law if I told the truth. I just wanted the sale to go through without a hitch and here I was, being made to feel like a money launderer or a drugs mule. We watched nervously as the clerk counted out every note of the eight million Guyana dollars on a counting machine and packed it up with elastic bands. Our ex-student was hovering around in the background with her back to us. I could see the bones in the back of her ears rotating like radar to try to pick up the details of our transaction and my palms began to sweat.

We packed up the wads of cash into an old sports holdall Edwin had brought along. Then we made our way out of the bank and into Robin's car. Edwin had given him half a million dollars from our house sale in cash to enable him to put down the deposit and buy his new vehicle so he could drive us around safely before we left. It had been an advance payment of money he would be entitled to for acting as our power of attorney. He might have to complete the sale if we had to leave before it had all gone through. It was small comfort to me to know that Robin was covertly armed with his military weapon should we have been attacked. We drove slowly to the tax office car park and sat there. Apparently we were waiting for Robin to get a call on his mobile phone to say the tax official had arrived. We made nervous conversation while we waited in the car for about half an hour. It had all the semblance of a set-up. Could I even trust Robin at this point? Was he going to stitch us both up and show a side of his character we had not even dreamed of? Anything was possible in the light of recent events in the country. If we could trust anyone in the country it would only be him, so it was a chance we had to take. Then Robin got a call.

"They're coming," he said. We waited a few worrying minutes more until a silver grey car with tinted windows pulled up alongside ours. The doors opened and four burly Indo-Guyanese men with mean looking faces got out of the car in the manner of Al Capone and his gang. The hairs on the back of my neck bristled. I was wondering whether these were bandits who were about to roll us over. Robin got out and spoke to one of them, Then he said "Let's go" to Edwin. The two of them followed the men across the car park towards the tax office with Edwin carrying the sports bag full of cash. I waited in the car. They were gone for quite a long time. I remained nervous. It might still all go wrong. At length they both reappeared and Edwin put the empty sports bag in the boot of the car. They got in.

"Did you get through with the document?" I asked.

"Yes, we got it," was the reply. We breathed a sigh of relief and set off for home.

Three days later, we had another hurdle to jump. We had to pay off the mortgage we still had on the Sapodilla farm house building, so that when we handed the property over to the church there would be no outstanding debts still secured on it. It wasn't such a scary exercise as the tax operation since instead of cash, we could take a managers' cheque from Scotiabank to GNCB Trust, the bank that had loaned us the mortgage. It just meant making two trips: one to find out how much we needed to pay to clear the debt so we could go to Scotiabank and get the manager's cheque for the right amount payable to

GNCB Trust; the second trip was to actually take the cheque to GNCB Trust to pay off the 1.8 million Guyana dollars we still owed. At last we owed no one any money.

"They must have changed our mortgage from a repayment mortgage to an interest only one without our knowledge," I said. If we hadn't sold the house now, we would still have been paying the mortgage when we were in our nineties and goodness knows how much the bank would have made out of us."

"The bastards," said Edwin. "No wonder Nelson wanted to lend me another six million dollars for the roof repairs. Thank God I didn't take him up on it." From then on we were able to transfer the money in instalments from Guyana to England. It was too large a sum to be done all at once since the bank had to wait until it had enough foreign currency deposited in it before it could make a transfer.

Now we technically still owned Sapodilla but had all but sold it to the church. We had agreed on a leaving date of March 18th, but made it clear that if they failed to hand over the rest of the agreed cash before that date we would cancel our flight and remain in the house until they paid up. They still owed us twenty two million Guyana dollars. Their desire to get us out of the property secured the deal and speeded up their processing of the paperwork. Reverend Paul collected the keys to our land-rover from us in February. Shortly after this, an English lady called Gillian from the World Council of Churches paid us a visit to assess the new property that the Congregational Church had acquired from us and what it was currently doing for the community. Throughout the two terms while all this had been going on, we still kept up our teaching of the classes and sports activities every afternoon from three thirty. Gillian was able to see all the resources that we were giving the church, how we were currently using the resources and how we were managing the small student farm business to produce profit to plough back into the charity. She could see that very little was needed for the church to continue with all that and develop it further to produce an income for its own upkeep.

"Stanford has just been arrested on fraud charges in America. All his workers in Antigua are shocked," said Edwin looking up from reading the local papers. "I always knew there was something wrong with that man. He didn't seem genuine to me."

"I wonder how many others are going to come crashing down following that revelation. The US economy seems to be in meltdown, capitalism gone mad. I just want to be away from here and safely back in England before all that happens," I said.

During the daytime we packed our things into barrels or dealt with lawyers. Most of our clothes we gave away. Edwin took them across to Taa to hand out at Church for the needy. The barrels and crates were all filled. There were supposed to be seven but in the end, Edwin had filled another six as he was determined not to leave his vinyl collection and treasured sports trophies. When the Williams Shipping Company came to assess the cost of our cargo, they told us it would be cheaper to pay for a twenty foot container than send these barrels individually. If only we had known this at the start, we might not have given away so much of our stuff. They gave us a collection date five days before we were due to leave. Robin had sent us a message that Colonel Booker wanted to know what we were doing with the museum. The next day, Jenny Daley from the African Heritage Museum in Georgetown made a special journey down to us expecting to be given our artefacts. I explained that they had already been donated to the church, but that we had eighteen woodcarvings for sale which we had purchased off the late Berbician sculptor, Arthur Tudor. We would prefer to leave them in their country of origin. She had expected to be given them as a donation, but Edwin was not going to lose out on items he had over the years paid the artist more than five hundred thousand Guyana dollars for. Now we had a container, we had room to take them all back to England with us. She left without them and we wrapped them carefully in newspaper and packed them up in a few more cardboard barrels awaiting the removals van.

I had my final lesson with the children on March 6th and the following day was the last of Sapodilla Learning Centre's existence. Edwin organised some fun games and sports activities and we enjoyed our last end of term meal together. He had ordered chicken with vegetable rice in food boxes with local ice cream desserts and soft drinks for all twenty three children. It was his last act of generosity after eighteen years of unconditional giving. They collected their reports from me and their marked art work, exercise books, folders and prizes. The oldest girl presented us with a gift, a photo frame which we could remember them by. It meant a lot to us. They all left with letters inviting their parents to a meeting with ourselves and the new owners in five days' time. We would be handing over the school and all its assets to the church at that meeting.

Parents would be able to put their questions to the church at that time. Next day Robin took us to the little bank at Rosignol where the Learning Centre and Summersplash Mini-company had its account. We drew out the small amount of money in it and closed the account.

"I'm going to Foulis with Robin today," Edwin said as he got ready next morning. I knew what that meant. He would be contacting Rick and seeing if he could get any news. I spent the day as I had done most of the last two weeks, preparing the museum for the hand-over to the church. I had put all the most treasured items in the glass-fronted cabinets upstairs in the main lounge of the house and carefully labelled and catalogued them. I had also arranged all the paintings inherited from the late Reverend Pat Munroe on the purple-heart panelled walls. His carvings were set on his coffee tables and some of ours around the edges of the room. I now brought up all the other artefacts which had hitherto been stored in the classroom along with all the historic photographs of life in Guyana in the past. I set them out on the glass topped table so that the new owners' attention would be drawn to them and they would be valued and understood. I had trained up Jelissa and she had come for two weeks voluntarily to catalogue everything with me. Most of it had been completed. Reverend Paul had promised that she would be employed by the church part time to act as curator of it and that the museum would remain a tourist attraction to visitors staying in the guest rooms when the church used the building to host paying guests.

Edwin returned and Robin drove off. He had spoken to his contacts on the sea defence works while Robin had chatted to some other local workers. Edwin had learned a lot of new things about the Guyana Defence Force and about the Special Forces now working in the country.

"They took one look at Robin and said he wasn't the kind of material that they could consider taking on," he told me. I wasn't surprised, but surely he hadn't seriously suggested that they should. Why did Edwin always hang these carrots in front of youngsters in order to motivate them? It sent the wrong messages and got people to do things for the wrong reasons. It gave them false hope and unrealistic aspirations. They would end up disappointed having tried their hardest to take a bite from a prize that would always be beyond their reach. Then I remembered the fact that we were more vulnerable than ever right now. Maybe he had done this to keep Robin's loyalty until we were safely out of harm's way. It was a chance worth taking. Perhaps I had too much faith in

Robin's good nature. I reflected on all the times when I had previously had issues with Edwin's way of treating people in Guyana. It worked in Guyana. He was Guyanese and understood how Guyanese people ticked. It had stood us in good stead up to this point.

"Any news of Rick?" I asked, nonchalantly.

"No," he said. "The guy I met doesn't know him personally, but he sent my message through, telling him we would be leaving on the eighteenth and how to get a message to us after that." I wondered if all this had just been a ploy to motivate me. Had I been another unwitting donkey trying to get a taste of the carrot while running along, willingly pulling my cart?

The Williams lorry arrived early next morning and the two men loaded all our barrels and crate into the back of it. We both clambered into the cab next to them and accompanied them all the way to the docks. The routine paperwork took ages as expected. Then we had to wait a while for a customs officer to come and inspect our contents before the container could be sealed. I was quite impressed at how efficient these things had become since our first months in Guyana. It had certainly come a long way since then. We would not even have got our personal possessions safely to town in those days never mind be able to get a container to ship them back to England, although plenty of people would have taken our money in the pretence of doing so.

Our meeting with the church and parents was due to take place the following afternoon. We welcomed the parents and students who had all come along to witness the hand-over. The representatives of the Church had travelled down from Georgetown. They sat and listened to my final speech and statement of account for the resources of the mini-company which we handed over in their entirety to their organisation. All the documents and records were in meticulous detail and neatly stored in a large set of folders for all to inspect and scrutinise. Edwin and I set out our hopes for how these assets would be managed by the new owners for the good and benefit of the community we had served during our eighteen years of living there. We officially handed it over to the representatives and suggested that they answer any questions the local community might have. This was perhaps a shock to the rather dour and inarticulate female financial administrator who had been deputed to us for the occasion. She was unable to provide the parents with any satisfactory answers to their questions about the expected reopening date for the school or who would be able to attend it. In fact I soon concluded that she had volunteered for the mission in the misguided belief that she would be carrying back a cashbox full of banknotes to Georgetown rather than a list of equipment, books and museum artefacts that had all been neatly laid out upstairs. She went back empty handed. Our evening was an unexpected pleasure, however, as Bonny and Robin had secretly arranged a farewell party for us at the newest restaurant in the village. All our mature past students had been invited and many of the village teachers known to be our friends. It was a very touching occasion. Perhaps it was the nicest thing that had happened to us in all our time in the country. It was the community saying 'thank you' to us as well as 'goodbye'. I had never expected to leave Hopetown in this way and had no experience of anyone else having done so. Normally people just disappeared without warning and left bad feeling in their wake. To me it showed that if you always do things the decent way, then people will respect you for it. "The evil that men do lives after them. The good is oft interred with their bones." It was, in our case, comforting to know that we had not left our community on a sour note.

We handed over the keys of Sapodilla to Reverend Paul in the late afternoon of March 18th and Robin drove us away from the house for the last time. I looked back at its familiar silhouette framed by the coconut trees on the far reef and the red tinge of sunset. We would never see it again. It was a wrench, like abandoning a baby we had given birth to, and leaving it to shrivel in the parching heat. We had little faith that the people who had control of it now would honour their promises to us and the community. I looked back wistfully knowing that a part of my heart was still vested there with the ancestral spirits who had long ago claimed it. I would no longer be lulled to sleep by chirping frogs nor awakened by the throbbing sun as it rose above our rubber tree, illuminating the wooden spire of Father Graham's Catholic Church that nestled in the crux between our fan palm and casuarina pine. The car headed up the road past the neighbouring village of Eldorado, named thus by its colonial planter. We had found another Eldorado but our affair with it had fizzled out like all the others before us. The jungle would reclaim it and it would disappear without trace.

IV. The Final Epistle

Chapter 27

A Letter from France

Southern France

31st August 2009

Dear Nick,

I have received the e-mail from Robin which you forwarded to me from the account I set up in England. We were very disappointed to read it and to see the pictures he sent. In less than six months, the church has managed to destroy the school, the museum and the sports facilities we left for them. They didn't keep their promise to continue all these things for the benefit of the local community. As Robin says, the people of the villages know what Sapodilla was and they now realise what they have lost.

Please don't worry about us, we are both fine. We couldn't wish for a happier life now. We have the things we need for a modest and comfortable life. I am working on my writing now. It's a kind of therapy to get all our bad experiences in Guyana out of my head and help me to focus on the good ones.

I don't know if I'll ever be able to meet up with you again. We have to protect our identity and keep our whereabouts a secret. You can't be too careful with all this computer-hacking going on.

I like the Mediterranean climate here in France. I have a beautiful garden to keep me sane. It's where I spend all my days, managing the herbaceous borders. Apart from Edwin and Rick, my friends are the bees and insects buzzing around the lavender bushes. Sometimes when I look into the borrowed landscape beyond the trees of the far perimeter, I think back to those times when Sapodilla was at its height and wonder was it all worth it, but I know if I had to make the same choices again, I wouldn't change a thing.

Love as always,

Jane